THE OXFORD

RELIGION AND EMOTION

THE OXFORD HANDBOOK OF

RELIGION AND EMOTION

Edited by

JOHN CORRIGAN

UNIVERSITY PRESS

Oxford University Press is a department of the University of Oxford.
It furthers the University's objective of excellence in research, scholarship,
and education by publishing worldwide.

Oxford   New York
Auckland   Cape Town   Dar es Salaam   Hong Kong   Karachi
Kuala Lumpur   Madrid   Melbourne   Mexico City   Nairobi
New Delhi   Shanghai   Taipei   Toronto

With offices in
Argentina   Austria   Brazil   Chile   Czech Republic   France   Greece
Guatemala   Hungary   Italy   Japan   Poland   Portugal   Singapore
South Korea   Switzerland   Thailand   Turkey   Ukraine   Vietnam

Oxford is a registered trade mark of Oxford University Press
in the UK and certain other countries.

Published in the United States of America by
Oxford University Press
198 Madison Avenue, New York, NY 10016

© Oxford University Press 2008

First issued as an Oxford University Press paperback, 2016

All rights reserved. No part of this publication may be reproduced, stored in a
retrieval system, or transmitted, in any form or by any means, without the prior
permission in writing of Oxford University Press, or as expressly permitted by law,
by license, or under terms agreed with the appropriate reproduction rights organization.
Inquiries concerning reproduction outside the scope of the above should be sent to the Rights
Department, Oxford University Press, at the address above.

You must not circulate this work in any other form
and you must impose this same condition on any acquirer.

Library of Congress Cataloging-in-Publication Data
The Oxford handbook of religion and emotion / John Corrigan, ed.
p. cm.
Includes bibliographical references and index.
ISBN 978-0-19-517021-4 (hardcover); 978-0-19-060858-3 (paperback)
1. Religions—Handbooks, manuals, etc. 2. Emotions—Religious aspects—
Handbooks, manuals, etc. 3. Theologians—Handbooks, manuals, etc.
4. Philosophers—Handbooks, manuals, etc. I. Corrigan, John, 1952–
BL41.O94 2007
204'.2—dc22   2007007041

Contents

Contributors, ix

Introduction: The Study of Religion and Emotion, 3
John Corrigan

Part I Religious Traditions

1. Buddhism, 17
Maria Heim

2. Islam, 35
Anna M. Gade

3. Hinduism, 51
June McDaniel

4. Japanese Religions, 73
Gary L. Ebersole

5. Judaism, 95
Joel Gereboff

6. Christianity, 111
Andrew Tallon

7. New Religious Movements, 125
Douglas E. Cowan

Part II Religious Life

8. Ritual, 143
Pamela E. Klassen

9. Sexuality and the Erotic, 162
Jeffrey J. Kripal

10. Gender, 181
Melissa Raphael

11. Music, 200
Frank Burch Brown

12. Material Culture, 223
John Kieschnick

Part III Emotional States

13. Ecstasy, 241
Angelika Malinar and Helene Basu

14. Terror, 259
Harvey Whitehouse

15. Hope, 276
W. Watts Miller

16. Melancholy, 290
Julius Rubin

17. Love, 310
Nancy M. Martin and Joseph Runzo

18. Religious Hatred, 333
John Corrigan

Part IV Historical and Theoretical Perspectives

19. Augustine, 349
James Wetzel

20. Medieval Mysticism, 364
Niklaus Largier

21. Kierkegaard, 380
David Kangas

22. Jonathan Edwards, 404
Michael McClymond

23. William James, 419
    Jeremy Carrette

24. Emile Durkheim, 438
    W. S. F. Pickering

25. Friedrich Schleiermacher and Rudolf Otto, 457
    Jacqueline Mariña

26. Constructionism and Its Critics, 474
    John Kloos

27. Emotions Research and Religious Experience, 490
    Robert C. Roberts

Index, 507

Contributors

HELENE BASU is Full Professor at Westfaelische Wilhelms-Universitaet Muenster. She has been an Associate Professor at the Free University of Berlin, and in 2003 she was Visiting Associate Professor at the University of Iowa in their Crossing Borders Program. The recipient of numerous grants, she has coedited *Embodying Charisma: Modernity, Locality, and Performance of Emotion in Sufi Cults* (1998) with Pnina Werbner.

FRANK BURCH Brown is the Frederick Doyle Kershner Professor of Religion and the Arts and Director of the Master of Arts in Church Music Program at Christian Theological Seminary. A composer with nearly two dozen commissioned works, he has also recently been named Alexander Campbell Visiting Professor of Religion and the Arts at the University of Chicago Divinity School. His most recent book, *Good Taste, Bad Taste, and Christian Taste: Aesthetics in Religious Life* (2000) received an Honorable Mention from the Association of American Publishers. He is currently editing the *Oxford Handbook of Religion and the Arts* (forthcoming).

JEREMY CARRETTE is Senior Lecturer in Theology and Religious Studies at the University of Kent, UK, and was previously Head of the Department of Religious Studies at the University of Stirling, Scotland, until 2004. He is the author and editor of numerous books; his most recent publication is *Religion and Critical Psychology: Religious Experience in the Knowledge Economy* (2007).

JOHN CORRIGAN is the Edwin Scott Gaustad Professor of Religion, Professor of History, and Chair of the Religion Department at Florida State University. His recent books include *Business of the Heart: Religion and Emotion in the Nineteenth Century* and, with Lynn Neal, *Religious Intolerance in America: A Documentary History* (forthcoming).

DOUGLAS E. COWAN is Associate Professor of Religious Studies at Renison College/ University of Waterloo and has previously taught at the University of Missouri–Kansas City. He is coeditor, with Rebecca Moore and Catherine E. Wessinger, of *Nova Religio: The Journal of Alternative and Emergent Religions*. His has written *Cyberhenge: Modern Pagans on the Internet* (2004) and, most recently, *Cults and New Religions: A Brief History*, with David G. Bromley (2007).

GARY L. EBERSOLE is Professor of History and Religious Studies and Director of the Center for Religious Studies at the University of Missouri–Kansas City. He has taught at the University of Chicago and the Ohio State University. Author of *Ritual Poetry and the Politics of Death in Early Japan* (1989) and *Captured by the Texts:*

Puritan to Postmodern Images of Indian Captivity (1995), he is in the process of completing *Telling Tears: A Comparative Study of Ritualized Weeping*.

ANNA M. GADE is Senior Lecturer in Religious Studies at Victoria University, Wellington, New Zealand. She has written *Perfection Makes Practice: Learning, Emotion, and the Recited Qu'ran in Indonesia* (2004) and has most recently concluded fieldwork on a new project on Muslim communities in Cambodia.

JOEL GEREBOFF is Associate Professor and Department Chair of Religious Studies at Arizona State University. A medical advisor on bioethics, he has also taught at York University and the University of California at San Diego. Author of several recent articles on Judaism, he has written *Rabbi Tarfon: The Tradition, the Man, and Early Rabbinic Judaism* (1979).

MARIA HEIM is Assistant Professor of Religion at Amherst College. Author of several journal articles, she has written *Theories of the Gift in South Asia* (2004), the ninth volume in the Routledge series Religion in History, Society and Culture.

DAVID KANGAS is Adjunct Professor of Philosophy and Religion at the Graduate Theological Union and Lecturer in the Department of Philosophy at the University of California–Berkeley. He is the author of *Kierkegaard's Instant: On Beginnings* (2007). He serves on the editorial board for the new critical edition of Kierkegaard's Journals and Notebooks (Princeton University Press).

JOHN KIESCHNICK is Reader in Buddhist Studies at the University of Bristol. He is the author of *The Impact of Buddhism on Chinese Material Culture* (2003) and *The Eminent Monk: Buddhist Ideals in Medieval Chinese Hagiography* (2001).

PAMELA E. KLASSEN is Associate Professor, Department and Centre for the Study of Religion at the University of Toronto. She has written *Blessed Events: Religion and Home Birth in America* (2001) and *Going by the Moon and the Stars: Stories of Two Mennonite Russian Women* (1994), in addition to many journal articles. Her latest project is a book to be entitled *Healing Christians: Religion, Medicine, and Anxieties of Difference* (forthcoming).

JOHN KLOOS is Professor of Religious Studies at Benedictine University. He has written *A Sense of Deity: The Republican Spirituality of Dr. Benjamin Rush* (1991) and coauthored, with John Corrigan and Eric Crump, *Emotion and Religion: A Critical Assessment and Annotated Bibliography* (2000).

JEFFREY J. KRIPAL is J. Newton Rayzor Professor and Chair of Religious Studies at Rice University. He is the author of *The Serpent's Gift: Gnostic Reflections on the Study of Religion* (2006), *Roads of Excess, Palaces of Wisdom: Eroticism and Reflexivity in the Study of Mysticism* (2001), and *Kali's Child: The Mystical and the Erotic in the Life and Teachings of Ramakrishna* (1995). He has also coedited several collections, including, most recently, *On the Edge of the Future: Esalen and the Evolution of American Culture* (2005), with Glenn W. Shuck.

NIKLAUS LARGIER is Professor and Chair of the Department of German at the University of California–Berkeley. He has written numerous books and articles on mysticism in German and English. His book *Lob der Peitsche* (2001) has been translated and published in 2007 as *In Praise of the Whip: A Cultural History of Arousal*.

ANGELIKA MALINAR is Senior Lecturer in Hinduism in the School of Oriental and Asian Studies at the University of London. She is the editor of *Time in India: Concepts and Practices* (2007).

JACQUELINE MARIÑA is Associate Professor of Philosophy and Chair of Religious Studies at Purdue University. She is the author of numerous journal articles and editor of the *Cambridge Companion to Schleiermacher* and of the forthcoming book *Transformation of the Self in the Thought of Friedrich Schleiermacher*.

NANCY M. MARTIN is Associate Professor of Religious Studies at Chapman University. A Life Member of Clare Hall, Cambridge University, she is the Cofounder and Associate Director of the Global Ethics and Religion Forum. She is the coeditor, with Joseph Runzo, of the Library of Global Ethics and Religion.

MICHAEL MCCLYMOND is Associate Professor of Theological Studies at Saint Louis University. He has most recently edited the two-volume *Encyclopedia of Religious Revivals in America* (2007). His book *Encounters with God: An Approach to the Theology of Jonathan Edwards* (1998) received the Frank S. and Elizabeth D. Brewer Prize from the American Society of Church History.

JUNE MCDANIEL is Professor of Religious Studies at the College of Charleston. She is the recipient of a Fulbright Senior Scholar grant, as well as a grant from the American Institute of Indian Studies. She is the author of *The Madness of the Saints: Ecstatic Religion in West Bengal* (1989); *Making Virtuous Daughters and Wives: An Introduction to Women's Brata Rituals in Bengali Folk Religion* (2003); and *Offering Flowers, Feeding Skulls: Popular Goddess Worship in West Bengal* (2004). Her current research is on religious ecstasy in the modern West.

W. WATTS MILLER is recently retired from the University of Bristol, where he was lecturer in sociology and philosophy. He is the author of *Durkheim, Morals, and Modernity* (1996) in the McGill-Queen's Studies in the History of Ideas series and is editor of the journal *Durkheimian Studies*. He has contributed to *Debating Durkheim* (1994) and, more recently, *Virtue Ethics and Sociology: Issues of Modernity and Religion* (2001).

W. S. F. PICKERING is General Secretary of the British Centre for Durkheimian Studies, which he helped to found and is located in the Institute of Social and Cultural Anthropology, Oxford University. Author and editor of numerous books, he has recently edited *Durkheim Today* (2002), *Marcel Mauss on Prayer* (2003) and, with David Martin and John Orme Mills, coedited *Sociology and Theology: Alliance and Conflict* (reprinted 2003).

MELISSA RAPHAEL is Professor of Jewish Theology at the University of Gloucestershire. An Honorary Research Scholar at the University of Wales, Lampeter, she is a delegate of the British Government on the International Task Force for Cooperation on Holocaust Education, Remembrance and Research. Her book *The*

Female Face of God in Auschwitz: A Jewish Feminist Theology of the Holocaust (2003) was shortlisted for the Koret Jewish Book Award in 2004. Her latest study is *Judaism and the Visual Image: A Post-Holocaust Theology of Jewish Art* (forthcoming).

ROBERT C. ROBERTS is Distinguished Professor of Ethics at Baylor University and has previously taught at Western Kentucky University and Wheaton College. His most recent books are *Spiritual Emotions: A Psychology of Christian Virtues* (forthcoming) and, with Jay Wood, *Intellectual Virtues: An Essay in Regulative Epistemology* (forthcoming).

JULIUS RUBIN is Professor of Sociology at Saint Joseph College. He is author of *Religious Melancholy and Protestant Experience in America* (1994) and, most recently, *The Other Side of Joy: Religious Melancholy among the Bruderhof* (2000).

JOSEPH RUNZO is Professor of Philosophy, Religious Studies and Honors at Chapman University and Life Member of Clare Hall, Cambridge University. Founding Executive Director of the Global Ethics and Religion Forum, he is co-editor, with Nancy M. Martin, of the Library of Global Ethics and Religion, and has published widely on religious pluralism, the comparative religious ethics of human rights and war, and the comparative religious ethics of love and sexuality.

ANDREW TALLON is Professor of Philosophy at Marquette University and Director of Marquette University Press. His editorial work currently includes *The Collected Philosophical Works of Pierre Rousselot*, Marquette Studies in Philosophy, and Marquette Studies in Theology. He is the author of *Head and Heart: Affection, Cognition, Volition as Triune Consciousness* (1997) and *Love: Philosophical, Theological and Scientific Perspectives* (forthcoming).

JAMES WETZEL is Augustinian Chair in the Thought of St. Augustine at Villanova University. In addition to journal articles on the thought of St. Augustine, he has contributed to *The Cambridge Companion to Augustine* (2001) and written *Augustine and the Limits of Virtue* (1992).

HARVEY WHITEHOUSE is Professor of Social Anthropology and Head of the School of Anthropology at Oxford University. He is the author of, among other works, *Inside the Cult: Religious Innovation and Transmission in Papua New Guinea* (1995), *Arguments and Icons: Divergent Modes of Religiosity* (2000), and *Modes of Religiosity: A Cognitive Theory of Religious Transmission* (2004). He has edited many volumes, including most recently *Ritual and Memory* (2004) with James Laidlaw, *Theorizing Religions Past* (2004), with Luther H. Martin, and *Mind and Religion* (2005), with Robert N. McCauley.

THE OXFORD HANDBOOK OF

RELIGION AND EMOTION

INTRODUCTION: THE STUDY OF RELIGION AND EMOTION

JOHN CORRIGAN

THE study of emotion has a long history in the West, and almost from its beginning that study has been wrapped in religious phrasings of questions about meaning, contingency, ultimacy, and intention. It also has been to a certain extent characterized by attempts to understand whether and how cognition and emotion are related one to the other. Adopting the physicalist language of his predecessors Empedocles and Hippocrates, Socrates steered theory freighted with heart, blood, and brain imagery into consideration of the moral and good, without losing the corporeal inflection or the specific emphasis on pleasure and pain. Plato added the claim that emotions associated with the immortal soul affected the experience of the body, and Aristotle, who elaborated on the role of blood, heart, and breath, likewise offered a theory of emotion that rested on a philosophical explanation of emotional response, pleasure, and pain, at the same time it linked emotion to cognition. The latter claim has proven to be fundamental to subsequent theorizing, and particularly to interpretation concerned with the roles of emotion and reason in determination of judgments of right and wrong. The Stoics pronounced even more emphatically the intellectual aspect of feeling, making emotion out as a judgment, and adding as well a warning against what they referred to as "passions," or sudden, ill-founded, or unreasonably formed opinions. Plotinus, in the early Common Era, developed thinking about emotion more decidedly in the direction of ethics and metaphysics.

For Augustine of Hippo, whose thinking about emotion has profoundly shaped the development of Christian theology, feeling was best understood in connection with volition. Writing within the context of his theologizing about human sinfulness and virtue, Augustine argued that emotions, at bottom, were expressions of will. But differentiating his thinking from that of the Stoics, Augustine imagined emotion at its best in connection with a soul joined to God, and as shaped by that relationship in such a way as to incline it toward the good. At the same time, Augustine, keenly attentive to the likelihood of mixed feelings in people, the conflict of desires, questioned the premise that persons can rely on feeling as a guide of any sort. Accordingly, his thinking about emotion encouraged a searching, empirical psychology of feeling undertaken alongside a rather tenuous reliance on cognition, all framed by a certainty of the need for the directing power of redeeming grace.

As Christian discourses about emotion came to hold sway in the Middle Ages, ideas about the strengths and weaknesses of emotion found their way, in differing emphases, into religious practice as well as intellectual life. The Stoic preference for *apatheia*, or lack of affect, which could be read in Gregory of Nyssa as well as Augustine, and in various early medieval writers, was never a simple matter of deciding for passionlessness. An emergent Christian rhetoric joined erotic sensibility—writers frequently explored the language of the biblical Songs of Songs in constructing theories of emotion—to an ideal of willful action untainted by passion under the cognitive canopy of "love of God." As the Middle Ages established knowledge and love of God as two pillars of the religious life, so also did it foster an approach to spiritual rectification through the cultivation of the affections, and through mysticism that offered in many instances a concept of self constructed as the fullness of both feeling and knowing.

Renaissance writers who theorized about religion and emotion echoed Aristotle. They were interested in Thomas Aquinas's processing of Aristotelian ideas generally, and specifically his proposal that passions such as love and hate should be understood in connection with the body, with sensible appetites. They also explored the idea, rooted in Aristotelian thinking and developed by Aquinas, of the "passivity" of the passions in contrast to the "activity" of the soul. In some quarters, thinking about emotion remained until the nineteenth century within the framework proposed by Aquinas, but the debate about emotion shifted ground in the seventeenth century with the publication of works by René Descartes and Benedict Spinoza. Descartes proposed a metaphysics that distinguished physical substance from mental substance, or more specifically will and cognition from human bodies that are limited by the laws of physics. Cartesianism as such profoundly shaped the course of Western philosophical investigation. But Descartes's location of the emotions in that scheme proved problematic. He asserted that emotions were a matter of heart, blood, and brain—that is, physical phenomena—and that the experience of emotion was a matter of sensation of stimulus or activity in the body. At the same time he described emotion in connection with mental phenomena such as belief and conceptualization, leaving it to appear as independent of the body, a part of mind or soul. He eventually concluded that the pineal gland in the brain brought the activated sensations of the body together with mental processing, so that bodily agitation, conveyed through tubes to the pineal gland, was rendered there as fear, surprise, hope, or other emotions. Spinoza, who pursued the topic of emotion as part of his ethical writing, challenged Descartes's theory, rejecting its dualistic metaphysics, and, in a manner similar to the Stoics, arguing instead that emotions were to be resisted as imperfect or defective thoughts about the world. When critically considered, all emotions—and Spinoza defined forty-one of them—in fact were species of pain, pleasure, or desire. There was no free will to massage sensation into emotional forms experienced as beneficial to the person. The soul did not have potential mastery over emotion in that Cartesian sense. Like Spinoza, David Hume sought to construct a theory about emotion in connection with ethics, arguing that "direct" emotions were simple sensations having to do with pain or pleasure, but indirect passions arose in the mind in connection with ideas.[1]

Charles Darwin built a case for the similarity of emotions in humans and in other animals, and proposed that emotions develop for their adaptive value, the edge that they provide for survival, preeminently in the collective. The Darwinian notion of the biological and evolutionary basis for emotional life was pursued by various scholars in the twentieth century—notably Paul Ekman and Nico Frijda—but by then other, alternative approaches also were well established, including that of William James, whose theory of emotion, worked out in collaboration with C. G. Lange, echoes Descartes in its claim that emotion is a matter of physical sensations, and Darwin in its references to instinct. James's own thinking about emotion, however, developed in complex ways that the James-Lange theory did not predict. James eventually conceived of an embodied emotional consciousness that could be understood with reference to cognition and to cultural setting as well as to neurological patterns and physical sensation. That complexity is especially in evidence in his writing about "religious emotion" in *The Varieties of Religious Experience* (1902).[2]

Much subsequent writing on emotion, including that focused on religion and emotion, has attempted to define more precisely relationships between cognition and emotion. Robert C. Solomon and Martha Nussbaum, among others, have written about emotions as cognitive judgments, Nussbaum exploring value and ethics in connection to emotion. Robert N. McCauley, Harvey Whitehouse, and Ilkka Pyysiäinen, for example, have applied the insights of cognitive science—a composite of perspectives drawn from the social and behavioral sciences, neuroscience, philosophy, and, increasingly, artificial intelligence modeling—to the study of religion. Cognitive science theories, which generally view emotion as inherently joined to cognition, have been deployed to explore a range of issues, including the manner in which ritual impresses belief through emotional intensity, how "emotional cognition," derived from brain structures, makes persons susceptible to religion, and how reasoning becomes integrated with feeling in religion.[3]

The investigation of religion and emotion has been an important part of theological writing, and Christian-inflected in its tone, through centuries of Western history.[4] It likewise has been advanced significantly through utilization of the perspectives of philosophy, psychology, and emergent "cognitive science." But those approaches are not the only ones Westerners have taken in the study of emotion in religion. That is, the central questions about emotion and religion are not exclusively located within the context of the thinking outlined above. Historians, for example, have surveyed the diverse ways emotion and religion are related in various geographical and chronological settings.[5] By extending and complicating the study of historical *mentalité*, and by drawing on a range of scholarship in the social sciences, historians have charted the ways emotionality has changed over time, and from place to place, and how its role in religious life has varied accordingly. Fear of God meant something different to seventeenth-century Puritans than it did to twentieth-century evangelicals, and hatred of sin, an ideal of medieval Christianity, was less valuable an emotional performance to later Unitarians. Historians of religion who research emotion have found it possible to explore profitably in many parts of the world and outside of discourses shaped largely by Christian traditions of understanding religion and emotion. Such research has helped to shape a panorama of variability in the relation of religion and emotion, to foster understanding, for example, about how key emotions having to do with family relationships in Korea changed from the fourteenth to twentieth centuries, as Buddhist ideas took root in Korea and challenged the moral order of the Confucian universe; about how feeling is interwoven with recital of scripture among Indonesian Muslims; and about how sixteenth-century Jewish mystics constructed emotion itself as seeing, weeping, semen, and death.[6]

One of the virtues of investigating religion and emotion through the exercise of historical or social scientific approaches is that such approaches make possible observation of how emotion is performed by persons in religious contexts. As a part of religious practice, the expression and concealment of emotion can take many different forms. Certain emotions take precedence in religious life in some cultural settings, while elsewhere other emotions are prominent. Likewise, emotions that play central roles in ritual in one community occasionally impress as being unlike emotional states found in rituals in other communities. The emotion called *nuga* by the Newar of Nepal denotes a complex of cognitive judgment, moral knowing, consciousness of the divine, and physical sensation: *nuga*, the physical heart and at the same time a sacred emotion, is actually felt as it flutters and sinks, is pained or leaps.[7] Similarly, in devotional activity surrounding a cult of saints in India, worshipers conceive emotional life and enact it in dramas that challenge Western distinctions between conscious and unconscious, individual feeling and collective emotion, rational cognitions and irrational feelings, and embodied emotion/spiritualized emotion.[8] The religio-emotional culture of a seventh-century Frankish woman differs from that of a sixteenth-century Spaniard and from a nineteenth-century American businessman.[9] Such insight is conditioned, in recent decades, by scholarly inclination toward a view of cultural difference rather than universalism. Investigators have focused on how emotional life appears to unfold in different ways depending on what cultural group one observes, and with regard to gender, age, class, and other factors within communities. Scholarship has focused in many instances on demonstrating that the components of emotionality—the way a group conceives emotion in relation to thinking and doing, its understanding of particular emotions, its strategies for conveying emotion and for obscuring it, its networking to language—vary from context to context. Nevertheless, most researchers continue to embrace, in some measure, the notion that certain aspects of emotional life are consistent across cultural boundaries.[10] Such a position should not be confused with an orthodox universalism but appreciated rather as an openness to discovering what aspects of emotionality are shared, and especially as those might be identified by psychology, neuroscience, and philosophy.

Studying Religion and Emotion

Emotion plays a fundamental role in religion. In the nineteenth and early twentieth centuries, theorists ranging from Friedrich Schleiermacher and Rudolf Otto to Emile Durkheim, Sigmund Freud, and William James attempted to define that role. Whether the emphasis was on the power of emotion to bind social collectives or on emotion in religion as "oceanic feeling" or "feeling of absolute dependence," most writing about religion proceeded on the assumption that human emotionality was a constituent element of religious life. In the latter part of the twentieth century, theories of religion that emerged especially from the social sciences reiterated the claim that emotion was central to religion. In the work of Robert Bellah, Clifford Geertz, and, eventually, Rodney Stark, "feeling" of one sort or another was integral to religion.[11] But in these theories, and others of the time, emotion itself remained largely undefined. Was it the processing of pleasure and pain? Was it evidence of the movement of the soul? Was it learned, all or in part, from culture? Were there specifically religious emotions? What emotions were more important than others when it came to religion? Was emotion all nerves and chemicals? To what extent was language a guide to emotionality? Was there a bodily language of emotion? Theorists' reluctance to venture theory that would follow from serious attention to such questions is partly understandable in view of the fact that it is only in recent years that research has begun to press those questions systematically. That is, the formation of a scholarly consensus that emotion was as susceptible to analysis as any other aspect of human experience was slow in arriving. In addition, as is sometimes the case in moments of rapidly developing scholarly research in a certain area, studies of emotion did not always line up with each other in a manner that pointed the way to the most fruitful areas of study. There was until recently insufficient intellectual ballast to the field of emotions studies—at least in terms of its place as a subject that easily crossed disciplinary bounds—to steady research on the more promising courses of investigation. Moreover, discussion of emotion, which calls onto the playing field an assortment of often deeply held beliefs about self and culture, has been prone to polarization. Looking across the chasm from one side to another can discourage writers from undertaking works of synthesis that can serve as acknowledged markers of the state of the field and as theoretical platforms for progressively extending the study of emotion into new areas.

As research on emotion has advanced at accelerated rate in recent years, and as that research has crossed from one field into another and gained coherence in so doing, the new study of religion and emotion has been able to articulate its agenda more clearly. Most important, the potential rewards of approaching religion through a focus on emotion have become more visible. By looking at religion as a human undertaking in which emotion plays a key role, and by recognizing that there are many different ways to legitimately define emotion and describe its place in culture, researchers greatly enlarge the territory that might be surveyed for its religious aspects. More specifically, by focusing on emotion, those who study religion position themselves so as to be able to include in their investigations data drawn from sources that often are neglected. The study of religion and emotion provides a way to discuss religion as a human activity that is embedded in everyday life in the felt relations individuals experience with other persons, nature, and the holy personages to whom they are devoted.

The study of religion and emotion, in one instance, can pursue understanding of the religious lives of persons by exploring the linguistic expression of emotion. That is, one way to enhance understanding of, for example, an act of prayer, is to approach the act linguistically, centering investigation on the ways emotion is expressed in the spoken words of participants. When persons tearfully pledge their "heart" to a deity, are they referring to a composite thinking/feeling self, as did, for example, the Shakers? Does a reference to the heart, when viewed against the background of cultural meanings about emotion, cognition, and the body, identify a physical state, a physical feeling? Is heart metaphor or substance? Does it signify a form of attachment that is to be distinguished from the kinds of attachments individuals form with other persons or things? Are there practiced, culturally grounded performances of emotion that frame the offering of the heart as a possibility only in religious contexts? What are the interlocking vocabularies of feeling that are religiously drawn together in reference to the heart? Is a woman's heart different from a man's, and if so, is her religious offering meaningful in a different way? Do children have the same hearts as adults? The short answer to questions such as these is that the way to making sense of what is happening when a person pledges the heart is through the investigation of social relations, family dynamics, physical states, conceptions of self, local epistemologies, and other factors. Emotion taken for granted as something that "everybody knows," or universally experiences or conceives in the same way, discourages exploration into the personal and cultural bits and pieces that lie behind the scene of an emotional event. Emotional life is to a certain extent culturally constructed, and it is through the examination of elements of culture that we can uncover the meanings of enacted emotion.[12]

The study of religion and emotion also opens opportunities to draw into analysis, in a pointed way, local ideas about the body and about cultural practice that dramatizes the body, including eating and sexual behaviors and exercising, grooming, and dressing the body. A central aspect of the current renaissance in the academic study of emotion is the focus on the display of emotion in facial expression and in other bodily postures, and the place of such physical exercises in broader ideologies of the body. Building on research that relates emotional expression to the body, religion scholars can fashion more richly textured interpretations of religion. Tracking emotional expression backward, as it were, into culturally specific notions of the body and its activities enables investigators to link that expression of emotion more confidently into interlocking ideologies, such as those having to do with gender, age, race, disease, and healing. So, for example, as Paul M. Toomey has shown, we learn much about religious ritual when we attend to the ways emotional expression is accomplished through the preparation and presentation of food in worship. Analyzing emotional display among Indian pilgrims, Toomey explains how different kinds of emotions—maternal emotion, amorous emotions, and others—are represented as different kinds of food and styles of eating in various groups of pilgrims. Observing a strong correlation between certain emotional states and certain styles of eating food, Toomey concludes that food in fact is a metaphor and metonym for emotion. Such analysis opens a pathway into engaging underexplored aspects of the pilgrim's devotion, including how ritual performance is framed by emotional relationships within the family who prepare and eat the food, and between members of the collective who share assumptions about the social meaning of eating.[13]

Another example of how a focus on emotion can enrich scholarly interpretation of religious life is through examination of religious cultures with respect to specific emotions. Jean Delumeau, in *Sin and Fear: The Emergence of a Western Guilt Culture, 13th–18th Centuries*, narrates a cultural history of sin by demonstrating the centrality of a specific emotion to that culture. Delumeau is able to incorporate a remarkably broad range of data into his interpretation, weaving together multiple themes by invoking the human experience of fear as connective tissue between them. In his account, identity, memory, self, consciousness, art, family, political revolution, anorexia, the topics of Catholic sermons in France, the preaching style of Gilbert Tennent at Princeton, and the *danse macabre*, among many other things, acquire meaning inasmuch as they are positioned as cultural artifacts in a Western society preoccupied by fear and guilt. Similarly, Charlotte Hardman, in *Other Worlds: Notions of Self and Emotion among the Lohorung Rai*, is able to assemble a richly diverse body of evidence for her exploration of the religious ritual and metaphysics of a Nepalese community through focusing on what the Lohorung Rai call *saya*—a complex emotion experienced in connection with one's relationships to an animated community of deceased ancestors and living family members and neighbors. Hardman is able to demonstrate how a community metaphysics is constructed around an emotional center. Her recognition of the embeddedness of everyday life in emotionality leads her to realizations of the profound interdependencies in Lohorung Rai thinking about such things as dress, food, property, space, death, marriage, illness, consciousness, loss, and more familiar emotions, such as anger. In short, Hardman's strategy of exploring religion in Lohorung Rai culture through emotion furnishes her with opportunities to illustrate the relevance of a great many cultural artifacts, interconnected through an ideology of feeling, to the fashioning of a religious life.[14]

The study of religion and emotion in current scholarship is particularly important for its interdisciplinary quality. The work of historians, social and behavioral scientists, philosophers, psychologists, literary critics, and neuroscientists, as well as writing that incorporates a theological perspective, has been important in defining the area of study. The way work in these various areas has overlapped, the way insights have been pursued across disciplinary lines, is especially impressive. As is often the case when scholars prospect a new area (or rediscover it), the study of emotion generally, and the study of religion and emotion particularly, has been shaped by intellectual exchange between groups of persons who approach the topic from different directions. Academic curiosity no doubt accounts for some such cross-pollination, but it is also likely consequent to the fact that the literature of emotions studies is not yet firmly cast into discipline-specific languages that frustrate thinking across academically established boundaries. Accordingly, the new study of religion and emotion is an academic undertaking that holds potential, at least at this relatively early stage in its development, for underwriting a conceptualization of religion as something more complicated than has been traditionally supposed. Whereas in the past emotion was often considered to be an explanation in itself, something irreducible, there currently is a critical mass of research in the sciences and the humanities sufficient to overcome that chauvinism. As interdisciplinary endeavor continues, it can provide opportunities for clarifying the ways emotions are involved in religion by stretching theory to new applications, in the way that groundbreaking work by Peter N. Stearns and Carol Z. Stearns on "emotionology" joined psychological insight to historical investigation.[15]

The Essays on Religion and Emotion

This volume is organized in four parts. The first, "Religious Traditions," includes essays that explore the emotional component in religion within the framework of a certain tradition. It includes as well an essay on emotion in new religious movements. These essays, on Judaism, Christianity, Hinduism, Japanese religions, Buddhism, and Islam do not attempt comprehensive overviews of emotion as it is conceptualized or practiced throughout the tradition but, rather, explore emotion in the tradition with respect to a certain cluster of ideas or practices. The authors of these chapters likewise remark on ways emotion has been overlooked in the study of religious traditions, and how a focus on the emotional can lead to fresh understandings about how persons create, through religion, relationships with nature, deities, and each other.

In part II, several essays address the emotion component in various areas of religious life, including ritual, gender, sexuality, music, and material culture. Emotion, whether as part of specifically devotional activities that are undertaken at sacred sites or in connection with the everyday behavior of persons, can be seen as integral to the practice of religion. The analyses of religious life in these chapters make it clear that emotional life is profoundly shaped by religion, and that religion, in turn, directs and reinforces the construction of emotional ideologies having to do with a wide array of behaviors. Of particular importance is the place of emotion in the creative and imaginative aspects of religious life—how music, for example, or sexuality, or the production of material culture are shaped through appeal to feeling, and how feeling leads to innovation and experimentation in form.

The essays in part III address specific emotions: ecstasy, love, terror, hate, melancholy, and hope. In different ways, each of these essays explores the way a religious emotion is conceptualized and expressed, and how it is woven deeply into the fabric of religious life. Again, the aim has been to illustrate each emotion with reference to a limited number of settings in which it appears, rather than to comprehensively survey it, although each of the essays in this section offers an interpretation of the role of an emotion in religion generally.

Part IV includes essays that analyze the thinking of persons whose theories about emotion and religion historically have been influential, as well as essays that address leading themes in recent research. Augustine and William James, already mentioned, are of particular importance. So also are the perspectives of the French sociologist Emile Durkheim and the German intellectuals Friedrich Schleiermacher and Rudolf Otto. In this part of the book, the contributions of brain science and cultural anthropology to the study of religion and emotion also are described and positioned *vis à vis* older schools of thought.

Taken together, all the essays provide a preliminary base on which to rest the new study of religion and emotion. They are meant as contributions toward defining this area of investigation, and they are likewise meant to provoke new approaches and interpretations. Taken together, they identify the study of religion and emotion as an enterprise that has deep historical roots in philosophy and theology on the one hand, and on the other, as an undertaking that has only recently begun to cohere as a scholarly project, as work in a wide range of disciplines has converged. One of the most important consequences for the turn to emotion in the study of religion is that research will be better positioned to incorporate emotion more substantially into interpretation of all religious belief and practice. Emotion no longer can be set aside as an unknown, as a hopelessly complex area of human life unsusceptible to analysis. Emotion is a fundamental part of human experience. To study religion without reference to it is to strip religion of one of its central components, and in so doing to render it motionless, inert, and monotonous.

NOTES

1. René Descartes, *The Passions of the Soul*, translated and annotated by Stephen Voss (Indianapolis: Hackett, 1989); Benedict Spinoza, *Ethics*, translated by G. H. R. Parkinson (Oxford: Oxford University Press, 2000); David Hume, *A Treatise of Human Nature*, edited by David Fate Norton and Mary J. Norton (Oxford: Oxford University Press, 2000).

2. Charles Darwin, *The Expression of Emotion in Men and Animals* (New York: Oxford University Press, 2002); Paul Ekman, *The Face of Man: Expressions of Universal Emotions in a New Guinea Village* (New York: Garland STPM Press, 1980) and "Biological and Cultural Contributions to Body and Facial Movement," in *Anthropology of the Body*, edited by John Blacking (London: Academic Press, 1977); Nico H. Fridja, *The Emotions* (New York: Cambridge University Press, 1986).

3. Robert N. McCauley and E. T. Lawson, *Bringing Ritual to Mind: Psychological Foundations of Cultural Forms* (Cambridge: Cambridge University Press, 2002); Harvey Whitehouse, *Modes of Religiosity: A Cognitive Theory of Religious Transmission* (Walnut Creek, Calif.: AltaMira Press, 2004); Ilkka Pyysiainen, *Belief and Beyond: Religious Categorization of Reality* (Åbo: Åbo Akademi, 1996), and "Cognition, Emotion, and Religious Experience," in *Religion in Mind: Cognitive Perspectives on Religious Belief, Ritual, and Experience*, edited by Jensine Andresen (Cambridge: Cambridge University Press, 2001), 70–93.

4. See John Corrigan, Eric Crump, and John Kloos, *Emotion and Religion: A Critical Assessment and Annotated Bibliography* (Westport, Conn.: Greenwood Press, 2000), especially 121–74, "Theological Studies."

5. John Corrigan, "History, Religion, and Emotion: An Historiographical Survey," in Corrigan, *Business of the Heart: Religion and Emotion in the Nineteenth Century* (Berkeley: University of California Press, 2002), 269–280.

6. JaHyun Kim Haboush, "Filial Emotions and Filial Values: Changing Patterns in the Discourse of Filiality in Late Chosŏn Korea," in John Corrigan, *Religion and Emotion: Approaches and Interpretation* (New York: Oxford University Press, 2004), 75–113; Eliot R. Wolfson, "Weeping, Death, and Spiritual Ascent in Sixteenth-Century Jewish Mysticism," in Corrigan, *Religion and Emotion*, 271–303; Anna M. Gade, *Perfection Makes Practice: Learning, Emotion, and the Recited Quran in Indonesia* (Honolulu: University of Hawai'i Press, 2004); Joel Marks and Roger T. Ames, eds., *Emotions in Asian Thought: A Dialogue in Comparative Philosophy* (Albany: State University of New York Press, 1995).

7. Steven M. Parish, "The Sacred Mind: Newar Representations of Mental Life and the Production of Moral Consciousness," in Corrigan, *Religion and Emotion*, 149–83.

8. Paul M. Toomey, "Krishna's Consuming Passions: Food as Metaphor and Metonym for Emotion at Mount Govardhan," in Corrigan, *Religion and Emotion*, 223–47.

9. Catherine Peyroux, "Gertrude's *Furor*: Reading Anger in an Early Medieval Saint's Life," in Corrigan, *Religion and Emotion*, 305–25; William A. Christian, Jr., "Provoked

Religious Weeping in Early Modern Spain," in Corrigan, *Religion and Emotion*, 33–49; John Corrigan, *Business of the Heart*.

10. A criticism of universalism is in Catherine A. Lutz, *Unnatural Emotions: Everyday Sentiments on a Micronesian Atoll and Their Challenge to Western Theory* (Chicago: University of Chicago Press, 1988). A criticism of the antiuniversalist position and a proposal for a theoretical middle ground is in William M. Reddy, *The Navigation of Feeling: A Framework for the History of Emotions* (New York: Cambridge University Press, 2001). See also Gary L. Ebersole, "The Function of Ritual Weeping Revisited: Affective Expression and Moral Discourse," in Corrigan, *Religion and Emotion*, 185–221.

11. Robert Bellah, *Beyond Belief: Essays on Religion in a Post-traditional World* (New York: Harper and Row, 1970); Clifford Geertz, "Religion as a Cultural System," in *Anthropological Approaches to the Study of Religion*, edited by Michael Banton (London: Tavistock, 1969), 8–12, and *Local Knowledge* (New York: Basic Books, 1983), for a more refined view; Rodney Stark, "Micro Foundations of Religion: A Revised Theory," *Sociological Theory* 17 (1999):264–89.

12. Sally M. Promey, *Spiritual Spectacles: Vision and Image in Mid-nineteenth-century Shakerism* (Bloomington: Indiana University Press, 1993); June McDaniel, "Emotion in Bengali Religious Thought: Substance and Metaphor," in Corrigan, *Religion and Emotion*, 249–69; Helene Basu, "Hierarchy and Emotion: Love, Joy and Sorrow in a Cult of Black Saints in Gujarat, India," in Corrigan, *Religion and Emotion*, 51–73.

13. Toomey, "Krishna's Consuming Passions."

14. Jean Delumeau, *Sin and Fear: The Emergence of a Western Guilt Culture: Thirteenth–Eighteenth Centuries*, translated by Eric Nicholson (New York: St. Martin's Press, 1990); Charlotte Hardman, *Other Worlds: Notions of Self and Emotion among the Lohorung Rai* (Oxford: Berg, 2000).

15. Peter N. Stearns with Carol Z. Stearns, "Emotionology: Clarifying the History of Emotions and Emotional Standards," *American Historical Review* 90 (October 1985): 813–36.

PART I
RELIGIOUS TRADITIONS

CHAPTER 1

BUDDHISM

MARIA HEIM

BUDDHISM deals directly with the emotions as a chief concern of its doctrine and practice, in ways perhaps more central than some of the other traditions considered in this volume. The Buddha's core teaching of the Four Noble Truths begins with an emotional truth, that is, that life inevitably involves sorrow, suffering, and grief (*duḥkha*). This foundational truth is shared across the diverse range of Buddhist schools and traditions that developed across Asia, and now globally, in Buddhism's twenty-five-hundred-year history. The Buddha grounded his teachings on recognizing the fragility and uncertainty of the human condition: none of us will elude the frustrations, disappointments, grief, and fear of living in a world that is inherently unstable and impermanent. We will all experience the loss of those we love, observe the decline of our youth and health, and ultimately face our own deaths.

This painful reality is met directly as the first of the Buddha's teachings, but it is followed by three further truths that offer a means of escaping this plight. In what is sometimes seen to be modeled on a medical diagnosis, the Four Noble Truths follow a physician's analysis: the symptom (life entails suffering), has a cause (craving), a cure ("awakening"), and a "prescription" that leads to the cure (the "Noble Eightfold Path"). The First Noble Truth involves the intuition that we can know the nature of the world directly through our emotions—we know affectively of our fragility and vulnerability in a world that is constantly changing. The cause of our suffering is a bottomless craving or desire that takes many forms, but is chiefly the desire for pleasure and permanence and an aversion to pain and change: we want health, stability, the enduring presence of the people we love, and lasting life. The answer to our suffering is to cease this desire, and the name for this ceasing is *nirvāṇa*, in which we extinguish desire and ignorance and awaken to the true nature of the world. This experience is sometimes interpreted as the opposite of suffering and thus a kind of bliss, although it is a reality that is beyond the conditioned nature of ordinary experience and understanding. Finally, the means to this awakening are enjoined in the Eightfold Path, that is, eight "right" practices: holding right views and practicing right resolve, speech, action, livelihood, effort, mindfulness, and concentration. These practices comprise the Buddhist path of morality and insight.

Given their foundational concern with human vulnerability to suffering, it is not surprising that Buddhist traditions developed various systems of knowledge that explore human feeling with great subtlety, and advanced certain technologies to redress the pain in our emotional experience. But we should note at the outset that in the various languages used by Buddhists there is no term that corresponds exactly to the generic category "emotion," and thus emotion as such is not theorized in Buddhist thought. This observation reminds us that emotion is not a natural category or kind but is but one way that modern English speakers demarcate human experience.[1] We should also recognize the historical particularity in which the contemporary use of the word *emotion* holds sway. During previous periods in Western thought, people used the language of the "passions" or the "affections" where we use the term *emotions*, emphasizing in the case of the passions turbulent impulses either beneficial or harmful to the soul, and, in the case of affections, our reactions to how things and mental states move or affect us. While there are important areas of overlap with the earlier concepts, the term "emotion" is of more recent vintage, stemming from the early seventeenth century, in which an emotion was a physical perturbation or disturbance. In time, the term took on the sense of a disturbance or agitation of the mind, and came to be defined, according to the *Oxford English Dictionary*, as "a mental 'feeling' or 'affection' (*e.g.* of pleasure or pain, desire or aversion, surprise, hope or fear, etc.), as distinguished from cognitive or volitional states of consciousness."

Here emotion is defined in contrast to thought and will, and it is mental rather than physical. We might also notice in this definition a sense that an emotion is a discrete experience with one particular valence: pleasure *or* pain, desire *or* aversion, surprise, hope *or* fear. The possibility that emotions might be related to more enduring moods or dispositions is not raised, nor is the prospect that they might be complex states of mind inhabiting thoughts, beliefs, and various other feelings in one and the same episode. The category emotion is often defined, as it is here, by reference to that which it includes and classifies, enumerating various lists of emotions, such as pleasure, pain, desire, and so on.[2]

Whether in the context of the passions, the affections, or the emotions, the partitioning of the mind into three faculties—affective, cognitive, and volitional—runs deep in Western philosophical discourse.[3] Reason is often depicted as being at war with the passions, and which of them prompts the will is a matter of considerable philosophical dispute. In other discussions, emotions or passions are seen to be cognitions or motivations of a certain sort, and efforts are marshaled to determine where and how the affective, cognitive, and conative overlap.[4] This tripartite division of the mind may be particular to the West, for we find no analogue of it in Buddhist systems of thought. This is not to say that we cannot identify experiences in Buddhist psychology that correspond (often very roughly) to these different functions, or to deny that this framework might yield insights when applied to Buddhist thought, but only to suggest that what we isolate out as emotions are in Buddhist thinking so interwoven with cognitive and conative value that the framework itself can seem artificial.[5]

Consider, for example, compassion, an experience dear to Buddhists that is also currently receiving attention from cognitive scientists. To feel compassion involves a cognition that someone is suffering. This is not as obvious or straightforward as it may seem. To discern suffering in the world entails vital modes of attention, sensitivity, and awareness. Compassion also entails a feeling of sympathy or concern and a motivation to alleviate the suffering. It can involve a behavior in the form of an altruistic act. Cognitive scientists, some of whom are working with and learning from Buddhists, are discovering that compassion may be expressed on the face, and it may have a bodily component.[6] We might also see compassion as a disposition, an inclination or virtue of a person that characterizes a trait as well as an episode. Compassion's contexts and applications also form a large part of its meaning and significance, as we will explore in several places in this essay. Like compassion, other "emotions" can be seen to be multifaceted phenomena, which suggests a complexity that may not best be served by a traditional Western division of faculties.

Buddhist descriptions of mental processes invite us to think differently about how human experience might be described. The discussions treated here, drawn from diverse genres from South Asia, also invite us to reflect on how Buddhist thinkers have shaped human experience in distinctive ways through their analysis of affective life. We turn first to the Abhidhamma texts as the most systematic rendering of early Buddhist treatments of psychology, and a body of knowledge that continues to occupy an important place in certain Theravāda and Tibetan communities. We will then consider meditation techniques and their work with mental processes, as another entry into the territory of the emotions. Finally, we will look at how certain literary traditions invoke and explore affect and how the meaning and significance of emotions are located in narrative context. Our approach aspires to be neither systematic nor exhaustive in describing these various kinds of reflection on emotions, nor will we attempt to survey all that might be labeled an "emotion" in Buddhist thought. Rather, our aim is to begin to consider how Buddhists in different contexts have thought formally about affective experience and what it entails for human life.

Classification and Metaphor in the Abhidhamma

The Abhidhamma literature offers terminology that is both narrower and much wider than the English "emotion," but no single term coincides exactly with it.[7] The term "feeling" (*vedanā*), which designates painful, pleasurable, or neutral impressions the perceived world makes on us when we experience an object, is a narrower conception than emotion. It would not include, for example, emotions like pity, anger, surprise, and so on but is rather the bare reaction to a stimulus. Feeling is one of five formations that constitute a human being; the others are the material body, perception, dispositional and intentional activity, and consciousness. Feeling is also said to be present in every moment of consciousness. In our conscious experience in the world, we are constantly feeling and reacting to stimuli.

A much broader designation than both this sense of feeling and the English word *emotion*, on the other hand, is the list of all phenomena or states described in the Abhidhamma. The method of the Abhidhamma is analytical, abstract, and scholastic; its lists attempt to break down human experience into its most irreducible elements and their interrelations. On the face of it, this would seem to be an essentialist move, but the literature's many listings and classifications of the irreducible happenings of experience show them to be multifaceted events that resist a static or absolutist interpretation of a human being. In its listings, the Abhidhamma offers intricate and precise terminology for a wide canvas of experiences ranging from bare sensory contact with the world to experiences achieved through advanced meditation. Among these states or events we can locate what we would call emotions,[8] but they are mixed in with other experiences—dispositions, inclinations, habits, and ways of knowing—that might have emotional force but would not always be considered emotions in Western psychology or philosophy. Many of these states have both mental and physical attributes, demonstrating a mutual dependency of body and mind or even a lack of duality between them. In addition, many of these states have at once cognitive, conative, and affective qualities. One and the same state can involve emotional salience, thoughts and judgments, and motivations and volitions.

While we are unable in the space provided to present a full overview of early Buddhist psychology,[9] the Abhidhamma typologies are worth considering at some length because they describe a distinctively Buddhist attempt at ordering and analyzing the complexity of human experience. While the tradition itself does not make this distinction, implicit in the Abhidhamma project is the assumption that it is describing innate experiences that, in their barest forms, are not the product of culture or social life. The states the Abhidhamma lists depict a generic template of human experience. For example, the operations of shame and self-assessment, which are often taken by other scholars and traditions to be learned or social emotions (see Ebersole, chapter 4 in this volume, for example), are listed in the

Abhidhamma as natural occurrences built into human psychology. Two factors do the affective work of self-evaluation: shame itself (*hiri*) and an experience of apprehension or fear of one's evil action (*ottappa*). These potentialities may be weaker or greater in an individual and are much subject to development in moral training and meditation techniques, but they are listed in Abhidhamma texts as "powers" or resources of our natural endowment. In addition to being listed as powers, they are also called "guardians of the world." They are affective factors humans possess that make us wary of our own potential for evil and thus can protect the world from our damaging incursions on it.

The Abhidhamma tradition offers two main strategies in its treatment of psychology—classification and metaphor—that are often encountered in other treatments of the emotions as well. In its canonical texts, the Abhidhamma consists primarily of lists, definitions, and classifications that can be challenging for the modern interpreter coming to them without the aid of a commentary. Yet lists and taxonomies are crucial for our efforts to understand Buddhist approaches to emotions, since much of the theory itself is embedded in its choices of classifications. We know the particular nature of shame and apprehension, for example, according to how they are classified—as powers and as guardians of the world. But the tradition also offers commentaries that expand on these classifications and provide further definitions of essential psychological terminology. Such definitions often proceed through simile and metaphor. They offer rich and vivid explorations of human psychology finely tuned to the nuances of experience.

It is noteworthy that the Abhidhamma texts classify states in moral and religious terms; all states can be designated good, bad, or neutral. The term I am translating as "good" or moral (*kusala*) is defined in Abhidhamma as that which is salutary, blameless, and skillful.[10] States that are good are wholesome, free from faults or stains, and make one proficient at promoting happy results. "Bad" (*akusala*) is the reverse—bad mental states lead to unhappy results, blemishes on one's disposition and character, and illness and decay in one's body and mind. Mental states such as hatred or anger that lead to violence, destruction, or pain, for example, are considered unhealthy and immoral.[11] The moral shadings implicit here may recall the moral sentiment tradition in Western philosophy in which emotions carry with them a sense of their own approval or disapproval. Like the moral sense theorists and those influenced by them in the Western tradition (Shaftesbury, Hutcheson, Hume, and Smith, for example), the study of affect is for the Abhidhamma theorists a kind of philosophical anthropology in interpreting how our natural inclinations have moral valence.

Further classification of states in the Abhidhamma marks out categories and divisions of mental life that have no analogues in English or modern Western thought. Rather than attempt to describe all of these, I will offer several examples of different kinds of description that will provide glimpses of how this system works. A basic principle of Abhidhamma analysis is to search for the roots and underlying causes of experience. We can understand our experiences only through determining their causes and relations with other events. For example, six motivational "roots" with strong emotional salience are seen to drive much of human action and experience and exhibit Buddhist concerns with causality and interdependence that guide Abhidhamma interpretations of experience. There are three bad roots: greed, hatred, and delusion; and three good roots that are the opposite of these: nongreed, nonhatred, and nondelusion. Though these roots are deeply planted in the human psyche from actions (karma) in this and previous lives and prompt much of what we do and think, they are also *felt* experiences.

The term for greed, which can also be translated as "passion" or "lust," is a disordered desire or inclination, a grasping and clinging to things in the world. One commentary describes greed as adhering fast to its object like meat thrown on a hot pan, or the stain of lampblack sticking to fabric.[12] Hatred, a close ally to anger, is hostility and ill will described in quite graphic terms, with the commentary piling on similes to bring out the quality of the experience: hatred is like the ferocity of a snake that has been beaten, it spreads like swallowed poison, it burns like a forest fire, and it gives offense like an enemy seizing an opportunity.[13] Delusion, which we might normally think of as merely cognitive error, has affective qualities. Delusion in the Buddhist view is not mere ignorance but rather is described as an intransigent fidelity to wrong views, stubborn persistence in holding false doctrines, and a perverse and stupid rejection of right views; clinging to wrong views can also be drifting in a bewildered state of confusion in which one is suspicious and fearful like a person lost in a wilderness thick with thieves, wild beasts, and evil spirits.[14] The good roots are the opposite of these, and can be interpreted in terms of positive states—being generous, loving, and wise—but are also often described simply as the absence of the bad states. To be free of hatred, greed, and delusion is to enjoy a quiet, happy, and clear mind.

Another important classification refers to certain "latent tendencies" that underlie conscious experience (also as the result of past karma), and are manifested under certain conditions. They are seven: sensuous desire, aversion (or anger), conceit, wrong views, doubt, craving for existence, and ignorance. These factors are part of one's disposition in ways that one may not even be aware of yet govern one's ways of being in the world. For example, anger is here seen as a subterranean current lying dormant until it erupts.[15] A related classification defines four of the latent tendencies—sensuous desire, craving for existence, wrong views, and ignorance—as *āsavas*, a term with no ready English equivalent but that can be translated as taints or "oozings" such as those that seep from a wound. These psychological factors are also largely subconscious yet inform the quality of one's experience and interactions with the world. Full manifestations of the latent tendencies and taints do not appear out of nowhere. Emotions in this sense do not spring on us from external causes or seize us unbidden; rather they spring from deeply seated sources that generate our experience and interpretation of the world.

Lest these categories seem to emphasize only a negative or problematic psychology, we might also consider some of the more positive categories or good mental events. We encounter, for example, a rich psychology of happiness in this literature. One variety of happiness (*somanassa*) is considered in a listing of eight good or moral faculties, which also includes faith, energy, mindfulness, concentration, wisdom, consciousness, and vitality. As a "faculty," this kind of happiness governs and rules over other mental states and habits of the mind, making one agreeable and optimistic. It colors and frames the rest of one's experience. Two other varieties of happiness are described as well: joy (*pīti*) and pleasure (*sukha*). These are listed as "factors of absorption," a term that gets at their quality of focusing and intensifying one's experience of other mental states and their objects.[16] Joy is described as gladdening the mind and body and is manifested by a sense of elation. Moreover, according to the *Atthasālinī*, there are five kinds of joy: lesser joy, momentary joy, recurrent joy, transporting joy, and pervading joy.

> Lesser joy is able to raise the hairs of the body. Momentary joy is like a flash of lightning moment by moment. Recurrent joy is like a wave on the ocean shore, falling and falling on the body as it breaks. Transporting joy is strong, it makes the body sit straight up and even lifts it into the air.... When pervading joy arises the entire body is saturated like a full bladder, and it gushes forth like a great flood of water springing from the womb of a mountain.[17]

Notice what these kinds of joy do to the body and the very visceral, physical descriptions of them, suggesting how essential bodily experience is to them. Elsewhere, joy is also classified as an element of human intentions or dispositions (*saṅkhārakkhanda*),[18] emphasizing its constructed nature, perhaps the enthusiasm we bring to certain experiences. Pleasure, on the other hand is a feeling, a reaction to pleasing stimuli. The *Atthasālinī* says that "joy is when one weary from the desert wilderness sees or hears of water at the outskirts of the forest, while pleasure is when one enjoys the water in the shade of the forest."[19] Joy is anticipation, excitement, and enthusiasm; pleasure is the relishing of an enjoyable experience.

This brief example suggests something of the subtlety Abhidhamma analysis brings to human experience and how classificatory choices cast light the different shades and qualities of happiness. We might also be struck by the earthy and evocative language of these descriptions and their reliance on metaphor. These experiences come to life when joy is described in quite bodily terms as crashing upon us like an ocean wave or hatred is felt like a beaten snake lashing out. The use of simile and metaphor in describing emotions is ubiquitous in this literature. This may be in part because many emotions are so tied to vivid bodily experience that they can arise perhaps only through physical sensations, images, and representations. This is most clearly observed in cases in which the very terminology for an experience is a metaphor—the oozings or taints, for example.

At the same time, the use of metaphor in the commentaries adds philosophical substance to its conceptions. Abhidhamma taxonomies can go only so far to elucidate concepts. Much of the rest of the work is done through exegesis in which metaphor is perhaps the most useful of the commentator's tools. Iris Murdoch is correct to argue that "metaphors are not merely peripheral decorations or even useful models, they are fundamental forms of our awareness of our condition," and that it is "impossible to discuss certain kinds of concepts without resort to metaphor, since the concepts are themselves deeply metaphorical and cannot be analyzed into non-metaphorical components without a loss of substance."[20] There may be something inherently elusive about affective phenomena that requires us to know them only in terms of more concrete and tangible experiences. Coaxing the intangible into graspable realities is critical philosophical work.

Murdoch is also right to recognize that metaphors often carry a "moral charge," though she does not explicitly connect this moral charge to metaphor's aesthetic impact.[21] Even as they do essential conceptual work, metaphors operate on our sensibilities to move us in certain directions. Our emotional reactions to these descriptions are themselves morally shaded. When we recoil in disgust from experiences described as the oozings that seep from a wound and when we are drawn irresistibly toward the delight that lifts us into the air, the text is deliberately shaping moral sensibilities. Buddhist traditions are keenly aware of the power of the aesthetic use of language to stimulate moral sentiments, an issue to which we will return in our examination of meditation techniques and literary treatments of the emotions.

Cultivating the Affective Life

While Abhidhamma has sometimes been called a descriptive philosophy in its attempt to reveal human experience in its most irreducible and subtle events, it should also be understood as part of a larger program shared by other Buddhist texts to learn to manage one's psychological life through meditative contemplation. Part of figuring out what emotions are is learning to see how they can be altered or changed. While newcomers to Buddhism sometimes assume that meditation involves a stoic retreat from the emotions, in fact, meditative techniques in various Buddhist traditions are much more complex than this portrait suggests and depict a range of different relationships one develops with one's own mind. In early Buddhism, the chief word that we translate as "meditation" is "cultivation" (*bhāvanā*). To cultivate one's mind is to take an active role in uprooting harmful thoughts and emotions, planting beneficial ones, and providing the right conditions for the nurturing of a peaceful, harmonious mind. Assumed here is that the mind is pliable; while we may struggle with deeply rooted tendencies and dispositions leading us to anger or hatred, for example, these can be slowly dug out, eliminated, and replaced with positive dispositions and experiences. The Buddha once asserted: "I do not see any single thing that, if developed and cultivated, is as pliant and workable as the mind."[22] Buddhist meditation techniques are practical guidelines for eradicating dispositions and motivational roots that cause us and others suffering.

Meditation in all Buddhist traditions involves reflexivity, in which one learns to observe one's mental processes. Learning to watch the rising and falling of emotions is to begin to stand clear of them. For example, in anger—a particularly powerful and consuming passion that threatens to overwhelm one entirely—a part of the mind can learn to stand back and observe the rage arise, noting its conditions, its arc, and its dissipation. To see something as conditioned is to help dispel its force, for what is conditioned will end. To observe mental episodes and habits in this way does much of the work of liberating us from them; one is no longer swallowed whole by the anger. Some traditions of meditation are not unlike modern cognitive therapy where one sorts through one's habits of thinking and consciously alters them. Śāntideva, a key thinker in the early Mahāyāna traditions and an important authority for Tibetan Buddhists, describes an intriguing repertoire of strategies for surmounting anger by intensive scrutiny of one's inner life. One first becomes aware of anger's horrors and destructiveness and how it leads to harm for oneself and others. Convinced of its addictive and malevolent nature, one actively seeks to diffuse and contain it by observing what causes it and how one might respond differently. The virtue of patience or forbearance is a key weapon in one's arsenal against anger. In strength and fortitude, one becomes unflappable even in the face of wrongs and violence committed against one; as one develops, one comes to revere all beings, even hostile enemies, enjoying a mental state that "drives away the sorrows of the world."[23]

Not only can meditation techniques ameliorate and eliminate negative emotional experience and dispositional traits but they can also be deployed to enrich one's experience of positive mental experience in ways conducive to mental health and morality. One schema of moral sentiments involves four "immeasurables" or "sublime states" that describe four varieties of love: loving-kindness, compassion, sympathetic joy, and equanimity. Each of these emotions is regarded both as other-regarding and as bringing about happiness in one experiencing it. Loving-kindness refers to a feeling of friendliness toward all beings, wishing that they could all be happy. Compassion is a strong desire that beings not suffer; it is, notably, a positive experience that the texts insist is not a condition of sadness: in it, one is not consumed with pity or dismayed by suffering but rather is concerned and involved with the fate of others. Sympathetic joy is taking real pleasure in the happiness of others, being delighted by their successes. Finally, equanimity is the experience of impartiality and evenness in one's regard for all beings—it is a feeling, not an absence of feeling or dispassion, as it is sometimes mistaken to be. These states are said to be "immeasurable," in that one cannot get to the bottom of them: properly cultivated, they go on and on, in every direction.

The immeasurables are encountered in meditation traditions across the Buddhist world, where they are approached in the context of practice. One meditation technique from the Theravāda tradition suggests a strategy for developing these feelings of love by first directing them toward those close at hand. By experiencing the particular qualities of these feelings toward those one already loves, one comes to "inhabit" them in ways that are immediately accessible. Once one knows these feelings well and can call them up readily, one can begin to expand them to include others, directing them to neutrals and even enemies, and eventually to all beings.

The following text explores the love parents have for their children in its varieties and subtleties, to illustrate the nature of these different kinds of love, which would then be expanded toward others.

> When a baby is in the womb, the parents think with *loving-kindness*, "when will we see our child healthy and endowed with all his major and minor limbs?" Then when this tender creature lies on his back and cries and wails because of being bitten by lice or fleas or because of being bothered by troubled sleep, the parents hear this noise and feel *compassion*. Furthermore, when the parents observe the youth in his most desirable years, either at the time of play when he runs and races or at the time he sleeps, their minds become tender, like a hundred fluffy balls of cotton soaked in the finest clarified butter. The parents' minds are satisfied and joyous. They have *sympathetic joy* at that time. Then, when the son is able to provide adornments for his wife and settle in his own house, the parents become even-minded and think, "Now our son can live on his own." In this way they have *equanimity* at that time.[24]

These kinds of love are rich with content and value. They are happy experiences where pleasure is being taken in the other in these very concrete ways. Starting with the immediate and concrete love toward one's intimates, the meditator learns to expand gradually the narrow spheres of emotional reach, and the love becomes unlimited.

The Impact of Emotions in Literature

Buddhist literature is fertile ground for exploring the content of emotions and their power in human life, and the very artfulness of literature can prompt sensitivity and compassion in its audience. Many stories from the Buddhist world are expressly invoked to create analogical ties with others through stimulating emotional experience. Two narratives from an early tradition of autobiographical poems grapple with grief in ways that are deeply sensitive to our human vulnerability to loss. The vivid and profound feelings of love, especially in the form of parental love that we have just seen, may be matched only by the sorrow of the loss of those we love, illustrating a key Buddhist truth that "from love comes sorrow."[25] At the same time, these stories suggest that grief can lead to truth and is a particularly affective route to awakening itself. Both stories we will consider explore the depths of the sorrows of mothers who lose their children.

The story of Paṭācārā is one of the most moving of all tales in Buddhist literature.[26] As a young woman from a well-born family, Paṭācārā disobeyed her parents and eloped with a household servant. When she was about to deliver her first child, she, in the tradition of Indian women, wanted to return to her natal home and give birth in the presence of her family. On the way, however, she gave birth on the side of the road, and then decided not to return to her family after all. When she was pregnant with her second child, she and her husband and first child set out again, but she again went into labor before reaching her parents' house. Unfortunately, the young family was caught in a terrible storm, and when her husband went in search of some kind of shelter for Paṭācārā while she delivered, he was bitten by a snake and died immediately. Paṭācārā spent the night in labor exposed to the storm; she crouched with her body to try to protect her babies from the lashing rain and wind. When morning arrived, she went in search of her husband, only to find him dead. Taking the two little ones, she continued to her parents' home but found she had to cross a river swollen from the rains. In her weakened state she was unable to carry both children across the river and so left the older child at the river bank and carried the newborn across, setting him down on the far bank. While she forged the river to reach the other child, a hawk swooped down and carried off the baby. As she thrashed about in the water trying to ward off the hawk, the older child thought she was beckoning him in, and he entered the river and drowned. By now the wretched woman was nearly insane with grief and shock and sought only to reach her parents' home. As she was going, she met a traveler coming from the direction of her home town, and she asked him for news of her parents' household. He begged her to ask her about any other house but that one. At her insistence, he revealed that in the storm her parents' house had collapsed, and everyone in it had perished.

At this Paṭācārā did go insane and in her horror and grief tore her clothes. She wandered naked—a most vivid physical image of her vulnerability and loss—and was abused and reviled by people who encountered her, which may indicate a certain hardness in human beings that leads us to shun and despise the unfortunate. Eventually she encountered the Buddha, who did not reject her but instead drew her near and pierced through her grief. She regained her senses, became a nun, and was eventually awakened. She came to her awakening by one day gazing sadly at water from her water pot trickling in streams on the ground. A little water flowed only so far, a second spilling of water flowed further, and a third flowed yet further. This image she took to indicate the larger and universal truth that some die in youth, others in midlife, and yet others in old age, and that her experience is part of the universal flow of life in *saṃsāra* in which karmic destinies prevail over life and death for all beings. She was thus led out of the particularities of her own sorrow.

A second story also involves a mother's grief. Kisāgotamī was a young woman from a poor family who married a kind and well-born young man.[27] Despite his fondness for her, her in-laws were quite derisive of her until she finally bore a son. In traditional Indian values concerning women, bearing a son enhances a woman's status considerably, and Kisāgotamī came to be very happy. Unfortunately, the child died as a toddler, and she was left bereft and confused, never having encountered death before. Taking the child's body on her hip, she roamed about seeking some sort of medicine that could help him, but was met only with scorn.

Finally a kindhearted and wise man sent her to the Buddha. The Buddha offered to help, but required her first to bring him a mustard seed from a household in which no one had ever died. She readily agreed to go in search of it, but discovered before long that such a thing is impossible, for no one lives in such a family. In her awareness of the universality of death and loss, her own sorrow was assuaged, and she, like Paṭācārā, joined the monastic order.

Like Paṭācārā's, Kisāgotamī's grief, gently guided by the Buddha, led her outside of herself into an awareness of others' pain—no one can escape death and the loss of those they love, and no one is unique in their claims of suffering. This knowledge is not only crucial for providing the wisdom of the First Noble Truth that life for all of us entails unavoidable pain, but it also has affective resonance. The loneliness and isolation of grief is here diffused by her knowing that others have shared it. In fact, Kisāgotamī's poems invoke Paṭācārā as she ponders Paṭācārā's grief in the context of her own. Her poem brings her into dialogue with Paṭācārā, whose tale of loss is even greater than hers, and in some verses she even takes Paṭācārā's story as her own, using the first person: "Going along, about to bring forth, I saw my husband dead. Having given birth on the path, [I had] not yet arrived at my own house. / Two sons dead and a husband dead on the path for miserable [me]. [My] mother and father were burning upon one [funeral] pyre." Then Kisāgotamī shifts to the second person, addressing Paṭācārā: "Miserable woman, with family annihilated, you have suffered immeasurable pain, and you have shed tears for many thousands of births."[28] In this intriguing instance of intertextuality, Kisāgotamī gains some distance from her own sorrow by her compassion and empathy for Paṭācārā, telling Paṭācārā's story as her own. She is able to reach outside of herself and form an empathetic bond with someone else, which allows her some detachment from her own consuming grief. As she seeks to comprehend the bottomless, unfathomable sorrow of the loss of even one child, she considers Paṭācārā's loss of her entire family, and ultimately the loss of all one's loved ones throughout all previous lives, which we have all experienced in our migrations through *saṃsāra*.

A modern example of the power of others' stories to help us interpret and manage our own emotions can be seen in Anne Hansen's work with Cambodian refugees from the Khmer Rouge. When asked about their experiences of the Khmer Rouge genocide, her informants responded by invoking Buddhist stories, and often, like Kisāgotamī, told the story of Paṭācārā. Her story with its harrowing losses and helplessness and ultimate triumph stood in for their own, in which they, too, had suffered the deaths of their families, homelessness, nakedness, and social rejection. Charles Hallisey and Anne Hansen suggest that configuring their own trauma through telling Paṭācārā's story simultaneously created "empathetic involvement" with the particularity of her condition and gave them distance from their own condition to achieve some degree of detachment and thus relief from it. If this is so, then the power of literature not only provides the ability to access, interpret, and articulate aspects of our own experience that are still inchoate, raw, and unspeakable but it also can pull us out of ourselves in ways that keep us from being entirely consumed by our emotions. Telling Paṭācārā's story allows those suffering grief an "accessible means of regaining possession" of themselves.[29]

The Sensibilities of Friendship

In considering meditative and literary techniques aimed at prompting and cultivating certain emotions, we find that we have traveled considerable distance from the Abhidhamma's bare description of the natural template of human experience. We have come to consider the social aspects of emotions—that is, how they originate in and through our interactions with others and with modes of social life. Although in Abhidhamma lists the person is represented quite unproblematically abstracted from social context and the narratives that constitute human life, in many other Buddhist reflections we find a deep sensitivity to how others condition our affective life, especially in ways deemed ethically and soteriologically significant. Buddhist thinkers have had much to say particularly on the affective aspects of faith, gratitude, generosity, and friendship. The emotions associated with these values are often key clues to discerning what Buddhists regard as important and significant in human life. For example, in literary, ritual, and doctrinal contexts, the Buddha is sometimes referred to as the ultimate "Good Friend." Buddhists seek friendship with him and express it with acts of gratitude and devotion. He offered friendship to both Paṭācārā and Kisāgotamī during their darkest moments and provided refuge and solace, and it is his friendship that they recall as enabling the turning point in their sorrow.

Close attention to context is necessary to appreciate fully the nuances of friendship and the social nature of other emotions. The relationship between the Buddha and Ānanda, his closest disciple, attendant, and friend, evinces a quite complex relationship of care and friendship that can serve as one example in which the full meaning and significance of a set of emotions can be glimpsed only through consideration of the contexts that give rise to it. A small detail in one account of the Buddha's death signals an intriguing linking of grief and love. At the time when the Buddha's death grew near, Ānanda, who was not yet spiritually awakened, began to weep. The Theravāda texts depict the Buddha's body in his final hours and days as getting old and frail, falling apart like an old cart held together by straps. Ānanda, foreseeing the loss he was about to face when the Buddha would no longer be present in the world, could not refrain from weeping. The Buddha comforted him by recalling to mind Ānanda's careful and loving attendance on him. "Ānanda, you have attended me for a long time with loving physical activities, with loving verbal activities, and with loving mental activities, in ways that were beneficial, happy, consistent, and measureless."[30] Indeed, Ānanda had been his personal attendant for over forty years. The Buddha wanted Ānanda to remember him in the context of these quite concrete activities of care and service. Grief is here conquered by love; by recalling the tenderness of his own love toward the Buddha, Ānanda's grief is ameliorated. The commentary on this passage explains with some detail what is meant by the "loving physical activities":

> This means that Ānanda, with a loving mind, gave [the Buddha] gifts and performed physical acts of care such as washing his face and so forth. And this was *beneficial*, meaning increasing his welfare. And they were done with pleasure and happiness, not with pain or small-mindedness. *Consistent* means that this was done with two sides, that is, some people do such acts of care only in one's presence but not when others are around; others do them only in the presence of others, but not when they are absent. But he was not divided in this way. *Measureless* means without limits. This means that his loving physical activities were so great that the world is too narrow and the heavens are too small to contain them.[31]

The text is trying get at the experiential content and value of these feelings associated with love, care, and generosity through an exploration of the friendship between these two men. The text's insistence that the memory of their friendship linger on these loving physical activities suggests that the friendship does not exist separately from the actions and habits that constitute it. We are also struck with how the infinite or the measureless resides in these concrete, mundane actions of care and love—washing the Buddha's face has so much love that it cannot be contained in this world.[32]

We might also notice that it is difficult to talk about friendship with this degree of nuance and feeling without attending to the narratives and contexts in which it occurs and noticing its small moments of tenderness, its slight gestures of intimacy, and the ways it is known in the body. This seems to be an important feature of emotions that we must recognize as we learn how to describe them—we need to know what contexts and circumstances give rise to the emotions, how they are held, expressed, or generated in gestures of the body, and how it is that intricate relationships with others, with all of their actions, habits, and rituals, themselves constitute emotional sensibilities. A related set of inquires, which unfortunately we lack the space to pursue, involves the social mores and cultural aesthetics that make emotions possible. Once we acknowledge the importance of their situatedness in interpreting the very meaning of emotions, we must then be attuned to cultural forms that give rise to and constrain emotions and their modes of expression.[33]

Conclusions

From this cursory and somewhat selective treatment of Buddhist approaches to emotions, we have discerned contrasting approaches to them. The Abhidhamma lists attempt to depict the barest descriptions of human affect, while its commentaries show how particular emotions are known through simile and metaphor. Meditation practices and narratives stimulate and develop certain emotions, encouraging a greater awareness of the human condition through explorations of grief, love, and other affective experiences. They are particularly attentive to the moral and soteriological dimensions of affective experience, and how our human emotions can be managed to make us more compassionate, loving, and generous, and less angry, greedy, and hateful. One feature revealed in all of these discussions is that Buddhist traditions are interested in increasing our awareness of our emotional life—what one modern interpreter has described as becoming "sensitive to our own sensitivity."[34] A better understanding of our condition entails a deepest sensitivity to how we are intricately connected with the world and others. Depictions of Buddhism that portray its aims solely in cool and dispassionate terms should be revised in light of considerable evidence from the tradition that demonstrates close attentiveness to and work with affective experience.

Robert Solomon argues that emotions "lie at the very heart of ethics, determining our values, focusing our vision, influencing our every judgment, giving meaning to our lives."[35] Scholars of religion and ethics do well then to investigate emotions, because through them we can detect the things religious traditions care most about. In Buddhist traditions, emotions are important clues to our own fragility and vulnerability that can, when properly guided by the Buddha or his teaching, lead to insight about the contingency of human existence. At the same time, many of the experiences described in this essay contain the seeds of the infinite—the "immeasurable" experiences of love, the endless tears we have shed from losing our loved ones, the gesture of love and devotion to the Buddha that is so great that the world cannot contain it. Emotions betray our vulnerability and exposure to the world, even while they contain the potential to allow us to transcend it altogether.

NOTES

1. Even within the context of the modern West, the category of emotion is not settled, and there is no clear and universally agreed upon criterion of what counts as an emotion. See Amélie Oksenberg Rorty, "Aristotle on the Metaphysical Status of *Pathe*," *Review of Metaphysics* 38 (1984): 521–46, for a useful overview of Western philosophical treatments of emotion and why contemporary discussions of them are beset with "conflicting intuitions" about what they are.

2. Paul Ekman in *Emotions Revealed* (New York: Times Books, 2003), for example, defines the category emotion according to what it includes. By examining facial expressions across diverse cultures, he argues for a class of universal human emotions deeply embedded in the species: anger, sadness, fear, surprise, disgust, contempt, and happiness.

3. The Greeks were content with a bipartite psychology dividing the mind into rational and passionate faculties (though they were certainly aware of various volitional forces). It was Augustine who gave us a fully articulated tripartite psychology that has been with us in different forms ever since.

4. Martha Nussbaum, for example, drawing on the Stoics, sees emotions as particular types of cognition (*Upheavals of Thought* [Cambridge: Cambridge University Press, 2001]), as does Robert Solomon, *Not Passion's Slave* (Oxford: Oxford University Press, 2003). While these attempts to define emotions as cognitions or judgments begin to question the dichotomy between reason and the passions, they are still operating within these terms. A certain freedom comes in when we can think about experience without these terms at all, which is one of the many refreshing benefits of exploring Buddhist material.

5. See Georges Dreyfus, "Is Compassion an Emotion? A Cross-cultural Exploration of Mental Typologies," in *Visions of Compassion*, edited by Richard Davidson and Anne Harrington (Oxford: Oxford University Press, 2002), 31–45, and Daniel Goleman, *Destructive Emotions* (New York: Bantam Books, 2003), 158–59, on the incommensurability of Western and Buddhist typologies of mental experience.

6. See Davidson and Harrington, *Visions of Compassion*, 100–101. Recent collaborative work between Buddhists and cognitive scientists on compassion and other emotions is also described in Goleman, *Destructive Emotions*.

7. Abhidhamma is the Pali version of the Sanskrit term Abhidharma. This essay draws on the Pali sources.

8. The Abhidhamma describes an event ontology rather than a substance ontology, and the term "state" for *dhamma* should not be taken to indicate anything stable or enduring. In fact, these events are extremely fleeting, with millions of them occurring every second.

9. Consult Padmasiri de Silva, *An Introduction to Buddhist Psychology* (Lanham, Md.: Rowman and Littlefield, 2000), for an admirable overview and study of Buddhist psychology.

10. Atthasālinī 62–63, hereafter abbreviated as Asl. All references to Pali editions use standard abbreviations from the Pali Text Society and are from the Chaṭṭha Saṅgāyana compact disk, published by the Vipassana Research Institute (Nashik, India, 1999).

11. Unlike certain Western ideas about anger in which a righteous or virtuous anger is possible (such as that which might fuel the battle for social justice), Buddhist thinkers see anger as always afflictive and harmful (see Goleman, *Destructive Emotions*, 103–5).

12. Asl. 249.

13. Asl. 257.

14. Asl. 252.

15. De Silva, *An Introduction to Buddhist Psychology*, 53.

16. Nyanaponika Thera, *Abhidhamma Studies* (Somerville, Mass.: Wisdom, 1998), 53–54.

17. Asl. 116–17.

18. Caroline Rhys Davids, trans., *A Buddhist Manual of Psychological Ethics* (New Delhi: Oriental Books Reprint Corp., 1975), 11 n. 4.

19. Asl. 117.

20. Iris Murdoch, *The Sovereignty of Good* (London: Routledge, 2003), 75; Robert Solomon, "The Cross-cultural Comparison of Emotion," in *Emotions in Asian Thought: A Dialogue in Comparative Philosophy*, edited by Joel Marks and Roger T. Ames (Albany: State University of New York Press, 1995), 282, also recognizes the importance of metaphor in describing the emotions.

21. Murdoch, *The Sovereignty of Good*, 76.

22. A.i.10; see note 10 here.

23. Śāntideva, chap. 6, v. 127, *Śāntideva, The Bodhicaryāvatāra*, translated by Kate Crosby and Andrew Skilton (Oxford: Oxford University Press, 1995); also see the Dalai Lama's commentary on Śāntideva in Dalai Lama, *A Flash of Lightening in the Dark of Night*

(Boston: Shambala, 1994), 73, and Robert Thurman, *Anger* (Oxford: Oxford University Press, 2005), for close readings of Śāntideva's treatment of anger.

24. AA.ii.204. Translated by Harvey Aronson, in *Love and Sympathy in Theravāda Buddhism* (Delhi: Motilal Banarsidass, 1999), 70.

25. Dhammapada, 213; see note 10 here.

26. Paṭācārā's story can be found in *The Commentary on the Verses of the Therīs by Ācariya Dhammapāla*, translated by William Pruitt (Oxford: Pali Text Society, 1999), 143–54.

27. Kisāgotamī's story can be found in ibid., 222–32.

28. *Theragāthā-aṭṭhakathā* 218–20, translated in ibid., 225.

29. Charles Hallisey and Anne Hansen, "Narrative, Sub-ethics, and the Moral Life: Some Evidence from Theravāda Buddhism," *Journal of Religious Ethics* 24, 2 (1996): 321–23.

30. D.ii.144, my translation; see also Aronson, *Love and Sympathy in Theravāda Buddhism*, 31.

31. DA.ii.584–85, my translation; see also Aronson, *Love and Sympathy in Theravāda Buddhism*, 31.

32. The frequency in which emotions are said to be measureless in this literature suggests that this idea is more than literary hyperbole and is in fact philosophically important, though no study that I am aware of deals with it. I suspect that the assertion that certain emotions are measureless involves the sense that certain experiences can be so rich that nothing, including reflection and language, can contain them.

33. Emerging work in anthropology directs us toward the embodied and socially contextual meanings of the emotions, and moves us beyond mind/body, cognitive/emotional, and subject/object dichotomies that limit our interpretation of them. In his work on sorcery in Sri Lanka, Bruce Kapferer shows how emotions are the "irreducible expressions" of the unity between human beings and their worlds. The emotions can be understood "only by the way an individual human being is embroiled in the processes of the life world and involved in the activities with others" (*The Feast of the Sorcerer* [Chicago: University of Chicago Press, 1997], 223–24). See also Robert Desjarlais's study among the Yolmo wa (a Tibetan Buddhist community in Nepal) on emotions, sensibilities, and bodily experiences as they are intertwined with cultural forms. He calls for a "less cognate, more sensate" anthropology that is concerned with how the "imaginative structures" in a culture "relate to the basic filaments of a given cultural tradition, derive from the way in which social interactions occur, and give form to the most visceral of bodily experience"; *Body and Emotion: The Aesthetics of Illness and Healing in the Nepal Himalayas* (Philadelphia: University of Pennsylvania Press, 1992), 29, 37.

34. Thanissaro Bhikkhu, *The Wings to Awakening* (Barre, Mass.: Dhamma Dana, 1996), 26.

35. Solomon, "The Cross-cultural Comparison of Emotion," 257.

BIBLIOGRAPHY

Aronson, Harvey. *Love and Sympathy in Theravāda Buddhism*. Delhi: Motilal Banarsidass, 1999.

Śāntideva, *The Bodhicaryāvatāra*. Translated by Kate Crosby and Andrew Skilton. Oxford: Oxford University Press, 1995.

Bhikkhu, Thanissaro. *The Wings to Awakening.* Barre, Mass.: Dhamma Dana, 1996.
The Commentary on the Verses of the Therīs by Ācariya Dhammapāla. Translated by William Pruitt. Oxford: Pali Text Society, 1999.
Dalai Lama. *A Flash of Lightening in the Dark of Night.* Boston: Shambala, 1994.
Davidson, Richard, and Anne Harrington, eds. *Visions of Compassion: Western Scientists and Tibetan Buddhists Examine Human Nature.* New York: Oxford University Press, 2002.
Desjarlais, Robert. *Body and Emotion: The Aesthetics of Illness and Healing in the Nepal Himalayas.* Philadelphia: University of Pennsylvania Press, 1992.
de Silva, Padmasiri. *An Introduction to Buddhist Psychology.* Lanham, Md.: Rowman and Littlefield, 2000.
———. "Theoretical Perspectives on Emotions in Early Buddhism." In *Emotions in Asian Thought: A Dialogue in Comparative Philosophy,* edited by Joel Marks and Roger T. Ames. Albany: State University of New York Press, 1995, 109–20.
Dreyfus, Georges. "Is Compassion an Emotion? A Cross-cultural Exploration of Mental Typologies." In *Visions of Compassion,* edited by Richard Davidson and Anne Harrington. Oxford: Oxford University Press, 2002, 31–45.
Ekman, Paul. *Emotions Revealed: Recognizing Faces and Feelings to Improve Communication and Emotional Life.* New York: Times Books, 2003.
Goleman, Daniel. *Destructive Emotions.* New York: Bantam Books, 2003.
Hallisey, Charles, and Anne Hansen. "Narrative, Sub-ethics, and the Moral Life: Some Evidence from Theravāda Buddhism," *Journal of Religious Ethics* 24, 2 (1996): 305–27.
Kapferer, Bruce. *The Feast of the Sorcerer.* Chicago: University of Chicago Press, 1997.
Marks, Joel, and Roger T. Ames, eds. *Emotions in Asian Thought: A Dialogue in Comparative Philosophy.* Albany: State University of New York Press, 1995.
Murdoch, Iris. *The Sovereignty of Good.* London: Routledge, 2003.
Nussbaum, Martha. *Upheavals of Thought.* Cambridge: Cambridge University Press, 2001.
Rhys Davids, Caroline, trans. *A Buddhist Manual of Psychological Ethics.* New Delhi: Oriental Books Reprint Corp., 1975.
Rorty, Amélie Oksenberg. "Aristotle on the Metaphysical Status of *Pathe,*" *Review of Metaphysics* 38 (1984): 521–46.
Solomon, Robert. "The Cross-cultural Comparison of Emotion." In *Emotions in Asian Thought: A Dialogue in Comparative Philosophy,* edited by Joel Marks and Roger T. Ames. Albany: State University of New York Press, 1995, 253–94.
———. *Not Passion's Slave.* Oxford: Oxford University Press, 2003.
Thera, Nyanaponika. *Abhidhamma Studies.* Somerville, Mass.: Wisdom, 1998.
Thurman, Robert. *Anger.* Oxford: Oxford University Press, 2005.

CHAPTER 2

ISLAM

ANNA M. GADE

In many Islamic religious traditions, emotions and affect may be considered to be an access to or an expression of a moralized and aestheticized ideal. This theme contributes to emotion theory in diverse Islamic systems, the heritage of 1.3 billion people worldwide, as informed by sources such as the meanings of the Qur'an, histories of the early Muslim communities, the flexible guidelines of jurisprudence, and patterns of esoteric piety. Such ethical, expressive, and aesthetic dimensions of emotion are available for elaboration within specific communities, where they are also often seen potentially to mediate between lived experience and universal Islamic ideals. The latter tension has led Muslims to theorize affective expression and performance within varied global religious contexts.

Sources of tradition, such as the Qur'an and Sunni jurisprudence, highlight emotions as an access to and an expression of a moral order. Early traditions of piety preserve and transmit exemplary models of moral and affective comportment into Muslim traditions worldwide. Issues of emotions as ethical conduct and experience are further intellectualized in influential systems of thought and practice. Related global patterns of aesthetics and ritual, such as the recitation of the Qur'an, poetic expression, and veneration of the Prophet Muhammad, highlight the relation of these ideals to the realities of social and religious practice. Finally, world systems of religious revitalization show how moralized aesthetics may be fundamental to contemporary mainstream movements of Muslim reform. Throughout these domains, Muslims of many perspectives have imagined emotions to be linkages from personal and social experience to more encompassing religious dimensions.

Emotion and Qur'an, Sunnah, and the Law

In the Islamic sciences, the most authoritative sources for Muslim thought and practice are the text of the Qur'an, the normative model of the Prophet Muhammad, and interrelated frameworks of jurisprudence and ethics. These have been applied, studied, and adopted by Muslims since the earliest development of the religious sciences in Islam. Each of these types of sources highlights emotions as a means of access to an ethical ideal. In the Qur'an, for example, emotions are presented as transformative and expressive; this also includes the practice of reading and hearing the Qur'an. The model of the Prophet is called *sunnah*, known through the early oral transmission of *hadith* reports, which are accounts of the Prophet's sayings, actions, and attitudes. Through this information, the expression of emotions in Muslim religious systems is moralized and also given a legal status. Islamic ethics provides emotional comportment with added normative characteristics.

The Qur'an is the Speech of God, according to Muslims, as it was revealed to the Prophet Muhammad. The Qur'an is highly self-reflexive and self-referencing, in both content and experience. For example, the Qur'an gives information about the emotional reaction to its recitation, even as it is being recited. The text of the Qur'an also links emotion to expression thematically. In the Qur'an, the description of emotion often conveys the recognition of the Message and a transformation of state. Qur'anic narratives emphasize the emotional comportment of prophets and others. These model the appropriate emotional conduct for Muslims in this life. Finally, the Qur'an portrays consequences of action in the next life in vividly emotional terms as well; through the dynamic and dramatic expressive rhetoric of these scenarios, the Qur'an may further impact the lived present with affective dimensions of soteriology and piety.

The Qur'an claims an immediate, embodied encounter with its Message to be transformative of the enduring moral, ethical, and social characteristics of a person. The Qur'an makes numerous such claims about its capacity to affect human experience in the present, to remake a person, reorienting him or her to moral sensitivity, social responsibility, and an appropriate relationship to the Creator. The Qur'an continually asserts itself to be a "guide and a mercy" to humankind, and this claim is a key to understanding the representation of its transformative effect. These ideas are inseparable from the event of revelation, an occurrence associated with the experience of peace, blessing, and earth-shattering power, as well as the alternative human responses of acceptance or denial. The Qur'an's self-presentation also suggests that it progressively and cumulatively works on the hearts of beings capable of recognizing and accepting its Message. For those people, the Qur'an describes (and thus prescribes and even proscribes) affective states.

The Qur'an prescribes both immediate and enduring feeling as the appropriate response to creation and revelation, just as it construes feeling as an essential component of religious life and social conduct more generally. Feeling forms the basis of a receptivity to the Message, a message recognized "by heart." The Qur'an teaches, for example, that God gave emotions to the beings he created. This could be seen as analogous to the Qur'an's many statements about God having provided the faculty of reason to people, another mode by which beings recognize, validate, and accept the Qur'an. By explicitly including feeling as an aspect of creation, the Qur'an renders the emotional capacities and thus responsibilities of persons in moral, ethical, and cosmological terms. The Qur'an instructs that created beings are in an emotional relationship to their Creator, obliged to him to feel emotions such as thankfulness and adoration, with hearts "turning in repentance" and patiently anticipating God's impending judgment.

The natural world God created also evokes feeling; the Qur'an associates the experiences that nature inspires with a moral-affective response to creation and to revelation. God made "hearts," bodies, and also emotions for beings so that they could—and would and should—glorify Him when beholding His Signs (*ayat*) in nature. The Qur'an often moves from the theme of the emotive power of nature to the didactic power of the Message of the Qur'an, which, like God's Signs in the natural world, makes beings react and behave in appropriate praise and sensitivity. Feeling is a mode of orientation to God; it is both motivation and means for attaining peace, righteousness, and reward.

The Qur'an employs language about feeling to assert the immediate, transformative power of its revelation. An example is the ending of 7 al-A'raf 143, a verse that describes the event of the revelation to the Prophet Musa (Moses) at Tur (Sinai):

> When his Lord manifested His Glory on the Mount, He made it as dust, and Moses fell down in a swoon. When he recovered to his senses he said: "Glory be to You! I turn to You in repentance, and I am the first to believe."

The Qur'an provides numerous descriptions of embodied, emotive responses to itself which lead to a permanent change of state. Its ongoing recitation causes the senses of the faithful to react with "shivering" skin and "trembling" heart (19 Maryam 58, 39 al-Zumar 23). Description of such embodied responses to the Qur'an's Message is often immediately followed in the Qur'an with a statement about a corresponding long-term or permanent change in moral state (examples are 17 al-Isra' 107–9 and 5 al-Ma'idah 83).

The Qur'an provides paradigms of appropriate feelings (such as those of prophets and other exemplars, whether humans, angels, or *jinn*) for believers to follow. The Qur'an prescribes ethical conduct and provides examples of moral transformation through nuanced descriptions of the emotions of exemplary groups and authoritative individuals, particularly prophets. The Qur'an often states that God eases the emotional troubles of prophets, especially the burdens of the Prophet Muhammad.

The Qur'an highlights the Prophet Muhammad's own emotions, and entire chapters (*surahs*) are built around his experiences. The Qur'an explicitly identifies the comportment of prophets to be *uswat*, examples or models, for Muslims. The actions of righteous believers are also models and influences for others. Through reading the Qur'an, ordinary Muslims may gradually affect others' religiosity, and potentially transform them through emotional modes, as indicated in the following verse: "The believers are only they whose hearts tremble when God is mentioned; and, when His signs [or "verses," the Qur'an] are recited to them, they multiply in faith and put their trust in their Lord" (8 al-Anfal 2).

Following the methodological "roots" of classical Sunni jurisprudence, as formulated by a thinker such as al-Shafi'i (d. 820), the procedure for deriving the norms of Islamic law is to seek rulings first in the Qur'an, then in the *sunnah*, and then through rule-guided types of legal reasoning. In the law, "actions are known by their intentions," whether or not they are subject to an explicit ruling. Intention is called *niyya*, which may be a ritual act in itself. It is one of the requirements that validates obligatory acts of worship ('*ibadat*), which are, beyond the first "pillar" of the testimony of faith (*shahadah*), as follows: canonical worship five times daily (*salat*), fasting daily during the month of Ramadan (*sawm*), legal almsgiving (*zakat*), and pilgrimage to Mecca at least once in a lifetime (Hajj). *Niyya* for these acts can be an affective orientation, and is often rendered as a means of attention. Of the required "pillars" of Islamic worship (above), intention for Hajj is possibly the most affectively textured. Not only does the act require undertaking an initial intention for valid completion, as do other acts, but also the relation of sacred history to intentional religious action throughout the Hajj determines an emotional itinerary. The believer undergoes the affectively charged experiences of past figures at the stations of the Hajj, such as the "running" between two hills like Hagar searching for water for her child, the "standing" on the plane of 'Arafat like Ibrahim (Abraham), and the stoning of the three pillars that represent the devil, as Isma'il (Ishmael) cast stones at Satan when he was being carried to near-sacrifice. Throughout the Hajj, the believer is continually aware that he or she is following the Prophet Muhammad and the first Islamic pilgrimage, as he or she strives affectively to imitate his pious conduct.

In both the ritual and social-transactional "branches" of Islamic law, the *sunnah* is the most authoritative guide for normative conduct after the Qur'an. This is the model of the Prophet Muhammad, and it is a legal as well as a pious category. It is known through *hadith* reports, which relate the expressive behavior of the Prophet in the form of his sayings, actions, and tacit approval or disapproval. The material in *hadith* reports covers examples of the Prophet's affective comportment, such as his weeping reaction to hearing the Qur'an, his display of other emotions, and preserved statements by him about emotional conduct overall. There are in fact many *hadith* that specify prophetic injunctions related to emotional states, such as traditions that promote kindness and gentleness toward others, traditions that discourage acting in anger, and accounts that warn against the dangers of another's envy. The category of *sunnah* shows how systems of Islamic law and Islamic ethics may overlap.

In the classical system of Islamic law, actions are assessed along a range of acceptability, according to that which is required, recommended (called *sunnah*), permitted, tolerated, and, finally, forbidden (*haram*). Particular actions at each end of the spectrum tend to have clear rulings: examples of required acts are the "five pillars" of Islam, and a prohibited action would be, for example, any unlawful killing. All human actions are "recorded," the Qur'an states, and are subject to the *shari'a*, or the will of God, even if there is not a specific jurisprudential ruling for them. In the absence of actual rulings or prophetic stipulation, which often occurs for actions that are not required, classified as *sunnah*, or clearly forbidden, there is a large gray area in between. Jurisprudence (*fiqh*) does not cover much of this comportment with positive law; instead, the assessments provided by an ethical concept known as *adab* often address this area.

Texts on *adab* compile material from a number of authoritative sources, detailing the model of pious figures of the past along with those in the Prophet's community. The term *adab* has a wide range of meanings, but all express some conception of a quality conduct that is cultivated or learned. Material included under the heading *adab* was collected and systematized with respect to early institutions of formal education, especially legal colleges. The world of learning that scholars depict for the "classical" period (about the ninth to thirteenth centuries) was shaped by *hadith* collection, transmission, and study, especially in relation to the field of jurisprudence (*fiqh*). By the time treatises on *adab* were written, vocations such as judges and Qur'an memorizers had articulated particular codes of *adab*. *Adab* treats the comportment for particular situations, how to behave like a cultivated or educated person, including how to "manage" emotion and affective behavior. Alongside legal colleges and related vocations, much *adab* material developed simultaneously within institutions and systems of esoteric piety called *tasawwuf*, or Sufism. These were in the mainstream of Islamic religion for almost a millenium. Scriptural, legal, and mystical traditions in Islam have thus all combined to yield a robust theory of emotions as moral and affective comportment, emphasizing emotions as a means of expressing and experiencing universal norms and ideals within lived experience.

THE CULTIVATION AND EXPRESSION OF SENTIMENT

Adab, as a set of normative standards for cultivated and ethical Muslim comportment, developed within influential communities of religious learning, including institutions devoted to esoteric and internalized piety. These communities were part of a revolution in Islamic thought and practice that took place in about the fourth

Islamic century (the eleventh century in the West), called Sufism, that approaches knowledge as a mode of experience. Within the Sufi lodges that proliferated in the Muslim world in that century and after, an *adab* developed for the hierarchies of spiritual authority within lineages (*tariqahs*) and for cultivating the "spiritual chivalry" (*futuwwa*) of adherents, as well as other qualities. These systems for the cultivation and expression of sentiment provided methods for the internalization of fields of Islamic knowledge, such as Qur'an and *sunnah*, and other ideals.

Sufism began as a rather elite movement in about the tenth century. Centuries later, with the spread of the renown of holy figures and related practices, Sufism became associated with global Muslim piety. Aspects of elite and popular "Sufism" have also been very controversial since the earliest period. Some patterns of Muslim piety influenced by Sufism extend to "non-Sufi" systems, such as dimensions of Qur'anic engagement; these areas of overlap are not always contested in contemporary systems. In general, the "Sufi/anti-Sufi" tension that marks colonial and postcolonial Muslim polemics is an inaccurate anachronism when used in reference to the early and middle periods, since Sufism was at the mainstream of Islamic thought and practice. Even Sufism's well-known critics, such as Ibn Taimiyyah (d. 1328), often worked within the framework of Sufi initiation, and many Sufi orders were themselves committed to Islamic renewal and reform.

In any period, Islamic Sufism is grounded in Qur'an, *hadith*, and the institutional systems outlined above. It is a radical attempt to personalize and internalize Islamic norms, scriptural and otherwise, and it thus represents, in a sense, a unique Islamic "fundamentalism." Shared sources for Sufi systems include the models of early figures, as well as understandings of the "path." Elite traditions have continued Sufi patterns in intellectualized modes, while their expressions in poetry, ritual, and other forms have produced some of the most beautiful and widespread aspects of Muslim piety. It is, in fact, a characteristic moralization of aesthetics that may lead to the debated stances of Sufis toward affective experience and expression of universal messages.

"Chains" (*silsilahs*) of the transmission of doctrine and tradition did not become established in Sufi orders until the twelfth century or so. Early figures were incorporated into these lineages, which were imagined to extend back to the time of the Prophet. Early ascetics who lived even before the label of *tasawwuf* was first applied serve as models into the present, exemplifying pious affective comportment. One such figure is Hasan of Basra (d. 728), who was part of a larger phenomenon known as the "weepers" in the early period of Islam. Qur'anic weeping is documented as a practice of the Prophet, thus considered praiseworthy in tradition, and Hasan of Basra is remembered especially for his copious tears. He is also a model for the world-rejecting and ascetic strains in Sufism and other modes of piety. In Sufism, a paradigm of weeping and hardship would come over time to express the suffering of separation from the "beloved," however understood. Hasan of Basra is also known in multiple Islamic systems for his persuasive preaching, Qur'anic piety, and theological position on issues such as free will in the formative Umayyad era.

The emotional hagiography of Hasan of Basra is matched by a figure, Rabi'a al-'Adawiyyah (d. 801), whose name is often linked with that of Hasan, even though they may never in fact have met one other. Traditional sources, however, place Hasan and Rabi'a in dialogue, gendering their parrying exchange. In hagiographical accounts, Rabi'a, a woman, even refuses a marriage proposal from Hasan, at the same time that her own world-rejecting and emotional orientation is said to be superior to Hasan's weepy piety. Rabi'a is known for "love" mysticism, which would later become theorized as a key mode of access to knowledge and experience. Radical love came to be associated with the goal of ecstatic union or recognition of divine unity. The paradigmatic emotional possibilities represented in hagiographies of Hasan and Rabi'a, affliction and love, are thus at the core of key expressive and poetic themes of global Muslim religious traditions.

One of the key controversies in Sufism that is imagined to have first begun in the earliest period is the question of the communication of affective experience and the limits of that expression. Like Hasan of Basra and Rabi'a, two other figures from the early period who have come to be emblematic of emotional themes are Abu Yazid al-Bistami (d. 874) and al-Hallaj (d. 922). They were known for their antinomian behavior ("drunken" Sufis), counterpoints to the "sober Sufism" of contemporaneous figures like al-Junayd (d. 910) and others in his "circle" in Baghdad. The names al-Hallaj and al-Bistami have been linked to the issue of *shath*, or "ecstatic utterance." "Ecstatic utterances" are exclamations Sufis claim can only be understood from the standpoint of the speaker's experiential awareness; in an ordinary context and to most others, they seem ridiculous or heterodox. Al-Bistami is said to have exclaimed "Subhani!" ("Glory be to Me!"), which alters a common pious expression, "Glory be to God" ("Subhan Allah"), and al-Hallaj is known to have pronounced "I am the Divine Reality" ("Ana al-Haqq," this being one of the Names of God). For centuries, Muslim intellectuals have weighed in on the acceptability of the behavior of al-Bistami and al-Hallaj, usually coming to the conclusion that their expression is to be understood and excused as an effect of an extraordinary experiential state.

Although the hagiography of these figures emphasizes transgressing the acceptable limits of expression (al-Hallaj, also in precarious political circumstances, was put to death), Sufi systems in Islam could rarely be accurately described as antiestablishment. They are in fact among the most structured and hierarchical Muslim institutions; the adept is always supposed to require a "guide" along the path, and Sufi orders represent great, transregional networks overall. The enduring controversy and discussion over accounts of *shath* and other material, such as treatments of Muslim ritual and religious poetry, reveal an ongoing thematic tension between emotional experience on the one hand and the limits of expression on the other, all within structured religious and social systems that tend to moralize and aestheticize emotions.

Early expression of the intellectual doctrines of Sufism came in Sufi manuals introducing the new science of *tasawwuf*. Al-Kalabadhi (tenth century), al-Qushayri (d. 1072), al-Hujwiri (d. ca. 1072), al-Jilani (d. 1166), and others offer influential systematizations of the "path" in their handbooks. The word for "path," *tariqah*, is the same as a named Sufi order (such as Chishtis, Qadiris, Naqshbandis, and others), linked insofar as both usages express the "way" of the lineage or a *shaikh*. The idea of the "path" was established before the institutionalization of named orders and particular practices, however. Among other things, the earliest works develop a formal vocabulary for the progressive stages toward an ultimate access to the goal. The writings of a thinker such as al-Muhasibi (d. 857), focusing on the assessment of emotional experience, demonstrate the sophistication of early Sufi moral psychology. The ultimate goal of the path came to be understood as the "extinction" of the self (*fana'*), which is expressed in a range of ways. This annihilation is understood to be a complete transformation of spiritual attributes of the subject or his or her perceptive state of unity (*tawhid*), and not an actual merging of created and Creator; the latter would be categorically unacceptable from an Islamic standpoint. In Sufi theory, beyond *fana'* there may be a further goal; this is a permanent, not transient, "residing" (*baqa'*) within the awareness of divine unity.

Classical Sufi manuals emphasize the "states" (*hal/ahwal*) and "stations" (*maqam/maqamat*) of the path toward ultimate "extinction and residing." States and stations are named qualities of experience and in fact represent named "emotions" or emotional orientations. A "state" is an impermanent condition, said to be bestowed by God, whereas a "station" is a more lasting dimension that the Sufi passes through more gradually along the way to the final goal. Thus, a Sufi may experience many "states" as aspects of a single "station." The early manuals list states and stations, sometimes in reference to metaphors of self-cultivation such as layers of the "heart" (*qalb*). Although each manual offers a unique listing, similar terms are commonly used by authors overall. Within lists, some states (such as *tawakkul*, or reliance on God) also tend to appear at the beginning, while some, like "love," usually appear more toward the end of an ordering. Sometimes, what is a "state" in one list is named as a "station" in another list. This is consistent with Sufi theory, since the states are said to appear first as "flashes," which may then be more permanent as they are cultivated.

States and stations are sentiments, which sometimes come in contrasting pairs, such as "fear and hope" or "constriction and expansion." These merge affect and experience with moral qualities; an example is the key Sufi category of "sincerity" (*ikhlas*), which is a felt sense as well as an abstract ethical quality. These sentiments may be "microcosmic" or "macrocosmic" in the theory, as when they are imagined as the prophetic "realities" or modes of consciousness characteristic of prophets such as Adam, Musa (Moses), Ibrahim (Abraham), and so on, culminating in a prophetic reality illuminated by the light of Muhammad.

Although Sufism provides much emotion theory in Islam, to generalize about such intellectual traditions is notoriously difficult. The presentation in even the earliest and most systematic Sufi treatises, featuring definitions and lists, is not straightforward; much Sufi language belongs to what Michael Sells has termed languages of "unsaying." In addition, sources of experiential knowledge include dreams, insights, and other modes of access that are nonverbal; they are indicated semantically in a language of "illumination," "unveiling," "finding," or "discovery." Some intellectually oriented Sufis have rendered the faculty of imagination as a mode of felt experience, for example, the famous figure Ibn 'Arabi (d. 1240); his voluminous and difficult works have been highly controversial because of his emanationist and seemingly monist expression of divine unity.

One powerfully influential Islamic thinker who synthesized multiple Islamic intellectual traditions is Abu Hamid al-Ghazzali (d. 1111). Not so much a Sufi—as was his brother—he appreciated the Sufis' affective piety and experiential approach to knowledge. His own autobiography highlights psychological and emotional struggles with the academic world, while he also lived during a time of great political turbulence. He criticized Aristotelian philosophy, which saw a relatively decreasing significance in the mainstream of Islamic thought after the ninth century, and he also challenged the theosophical (*batini*) doctrines of the Isma'ili Shi'a, whose direct influence also declined after the end of the Fatimid era. His compendium of religious knowledge, the *Revivification of the Religious Sciences* (*Ihya' 'Ulum Al-Din*) treats aspects of Islamic knowledge and religious life comprehensively, emphasizing personalization and internalization of transcendental norms and ideals. It can be read as a handbook—and is to this day—for a pious, experiential, and affective understanding of the moral order.

AESTHETICS: THEORY, PRACTICE, AND FEELING

A key Islamic idea (*hasanah*) equates the qualities of the "good" and the "beautiful." A paradigm of the good and the beautiful for Muslims is the model of the Prophet Muhammad, the "beautiful model." Through an affective focus and devotion to the Prophet, as developed in the "middle period" (1250–1700) of Islam, Muslims may in effect achieve a radical internalization of the idea of *sunnah*. Veneration of the Prophet is expressed through poetry, calligraphy, and the recitation of texts in a cycle commemorating the birth of the Prophet and events in his life (the Mawlid/Mulud tradition of chanted praise). Such prophetic piety is symbolically and emotively multivalent. For example, a doctrine from the middle period articulates the possibility of the "complete human being" (*al-insan al-kamil*); the idea of the "perfect man" is most appropriately applied to the Prophet but has also been understood in terms of a particular *shaikh*, guide, or even political authority. Poetic expression praising the "beloved," characteristic of the veneration of the Prophet, may also be understood to have a range of referents, supporting a richly multivalent system of affective piety in Islam.

In Muslim religious aesthetics and expression, as in traditions of prophetic piety, theory about affective expression often arises with respect to thought and practice that attempt to render universal models into actual experience. One example of this is Qur'an recitation, in which Qur'anic aesthetics reference the Speech of God. *Hadith* reports emphasize that the Qur'an should be recited "beautifully"; to follow this injunction requires the resolution of tensions over expression and its limits with respect to revelation. A second example is poetry, which is recited in some musicalized performances of audition (*sama'*). Poetry also carries distinctive Islamic emotion theory through its themes and content. Although Sufism greatly enhanced affective patterns of moralized aesthetics for the Qur'an, audition, and poetry, it did not determine them. They have their roots in the earliest community of the Prophet, and they have been preserved in diverse modes of piety throughout the Islamic world since that time.

The word *qur'an* is usually said to mean "reading" or "recitation." In voice and improvised pitch variation, the accomplished Qur'an reciter is understood to embellish the expressive rhetoric of the Qur'an in voice; he or she thereby enhances the moods of its meanings for listeners. In classical treatises on Qur'an recitation, some emotion theory centers on the agency of the performer to feel, as well as his or her potential to affect others when voicing God's Speech. A metapractical theory identifies the affecting presence of the recited Qur'an with the Qur'an itself, effectively erasing the recognition of human technical artistry from an encounter with revelation. In practice, the reciter is actually to strive to diminish felt aspects of performance that are not experienced as amplifying an idealized presence. Al-Ghazzali outlines such techniques in the eighth book of his *Revivification*, a treatise on recitation and audition.[1] Expert performers may apply well-defined techniques of feeling and embodiment in order to manipulate feeling and experience in the service of emotional norms. An example of al-Ghazzali's resolution to a potential "sincerity problem" is to recognize that performative techniques like "choking up" and weeping, which may at first be merely technical or affected, become emotionally "sincere" (*ikhlas*) for the reciter and audience within an authentic Qur'anic encounter framed by the correct pious intentions.[2]

Qur'an recitation is not music, and to say so in an Islamic system would be a mistaken confusion of the Speech of God with a human product. This is one reason why pitch variation is said always to be improvised for the recited Qur'an. The recitation of the Qur'an always does have musical qualities, however, determined by norms of rhythm and pitch change. Since the early period, the modes and melody types of art music have also been applied to the recited Qur'an. Outside of the context of the recited Qur'an, the debate among *'ulama'* (religious scholars) about expression, reception, and musicalization of performance has been concerned with the contexts, intentions, and affective experiences associated with musical arts rather than the permissibility of "music" as a general category. Much of this theory comes out of discussion of the idea and practice of *sama'*, or "spiritual audition." *Sama'* is a basis for the appreciation of much classical poetry, which may also be sung in many Muslim systems. It a key idea and practice for

Sufis, and has been controversial because of a concern that states of appreciation could be expressed and pursued for their own sake, rather than being subordinate to an encompassing religious intention or goal.

Poetry naturally deploys an emotional and expressive language. The themes of Sufi poetry, in global and local traditions, tend often to focus on the very idea of emotion as well. Despite the enormous diversity of Muslim linguistic and cultural systems, poetry in Islamic systems is linked to poetry in the Arabic tradition dating back to the pre-Islamic period, insofar as that is what the Prophet encountered. These poetic sources were studied rigorously in the early Islamic sciences to aid in the development of the formal fields of Arabic grammar and Qur'anic rhetoric. In addition, there are direct thematic continuities between the Arab tradition and other poetic traditions, especially religious ones. For example, pre-Islamic odes that feature the movement of the poet from one campsite ("station") to the next, weeping and searching for his lost lover, are later reflected in poetic traditions that embellish the theme of longing and separation from a beloved (which may be allegorized as the Prophet or even as the recognition of Divine Unity itself). Similarly, the tradition of wine verse in pre-Islamic poetry came to express the theme of spiritual intoxication in later expressive genres.

Transregional and cosmopolitan systems of culture and language, such as Turkish, Swahili, and Malay, as well as imperial and court languages of Arabic and Persian, have led to expansive traditions of poetic expression in Islam. Classical poets in the Arabic tradition include 'Umar Ibn al-Farid, composer of a famous "Wine Ode" who was known from Spain to Syria;[3] Ibn al-Farid was not exactly a Sufi but became venerated as one at his tombsite over time. Persian was the language of the Ottoman, Safavid, and Mughal empires, which spanned the African and Eurasian continents in the early modern period (1500–1800). The Persianate tradition is known especially for aestheticized religious themes. For example, the *ghazals* of Hafiz al-Shirazi (d. 1391) feature love lyric and wine poetry, both seen to be allegorical of experiences of the Divine.[4] The Persianate tradition also includes the work of Jalal al-Din Rumi (d. 1273), who relocated from present-day Afghanistan to Anatolia (Turkey) during the period of the "Mongol disruption" of the thirteenth century. His compositions are known for their kinesthetically affective dynamics and expressions addressed to his beloved. Another work in Persian, the great epic poem *Layla and Majnun* (by Nizami, d. 1202), genders modes of expression within the theme of love and separation: the mad (*majnun*) poet, Majnun, expresses his suffering profusely, balanced by the experience of the beloved, Layla, who suffers their separation no less intensely in her secrecy and silence."[5]

Global systems of Muslim poetry represent worldwide diversity; even within one system, poetic practice may embrace a wide range of social functions and sentiments. Lila Abu-Lughod, for example, writes on the gendered expression of emotion in Bedouin poetry.[6] In many locations of the Muslim world, poetry and musicalized or aestheticized affective expression are the basis for cultivation of emotion and affective states. Some of these religious modes have now come to be promoted as projects within larger contemporary systems of global Islamic religious revitalization.

Affect and Performance in Global Systems

Aestheticized performances such as poetry and recitation show how Muslim religious expression, while connected to global religious themes of Islam, always occurs within particular social and religious contexts and cultural settings. Normative sources, like the Qur'an, law, ethics, and systems of self-cultivation and expression in Sufi systems (*adab, sama'*), convey patterns on which diverse Islamic ritual systems then build. Performed aspects of these systems often reveal the doubly local and global embeddedness of these traditions. Even the required observances common to all Muslims are always socially specific. For example, the Hajj is inscribed in a particular time and place, and Muslims who participate in this enactment of a shared sacred past later return as *hajjis* to specific locations situated the world over.

Shi'i Ashura observances are commemorations of the martyrdom of Imam Husayn, the son of Ali and grandson of the Prophet Muhammad. These rituals suggest how a narrative of the Islamic past may be specifically and affectively inflected in Muslim communities of faith. For observances held at the time of Ashura, the tenth of the month of Muharram, Shi'a participants may reenact the narrative of the events at Karbala' in *ta'ziyah* plays, which includes the bloody massacre of Husayn's forces by the Umayyads. Other observances of Shi'i Ashura are highly emotionalized, known for public displays of mass mourning. These rituals express affectively charged root symbolism for a range of global communities of Shi'a. They also suggest how Islam may embrace overall ideological and emotional diversity within what are in fact shared intellectual, historical, or performative frameworks.

A global Muslim ritual of the cultivation of affective states, known as *dhikr*, also highlights particularized expressions of core religious themes. Along with a spectrum of practices associated with *sama'*, *dhikr* is sometimes definitive of Sufi "orders" or "ways" (*tariqahs*). A *dhikr* is usually participatory, is often chanted or sung, and is most often communal, led by a *shaikh*. Controversies over *dhikr*, common among Sufis themselves, evidence tensions similar to those about *sama'* (discussed above), as well as other controversies over of the acceptable limits of affective display. Across the Muslim world, *dhikr* has been observed differently, in part because it is closely tied to local traditions of Sufi leadership and saint veneration; this diversity is reflected from *qawwali* performances in South Asia to popular performances in Egypt and North Africa and beyond. *Dhikr* has become the basis of a contemporary Islamic movement in the world's most populous Muslim-majority nation, Indonesia, since the end of the twentieth century. Given global anti-Sufi polemics of the colonial and postcolonial period, this is somewhat surprising. Given, on the other hand, the close linkage of the cultivation of emotion, moral states, and social or political action in Sufism and other mainstream Islamic traditions, it is perhaps not so surprising after all.

Patterns of "Islamic awakening" are socially specific, while participants also increasingly link them self-consciously to the idea of the global *ummah*, or Islamic community. In contemporary systems, emotion is a strategy for involvement that is being adopted and applied energetically within a range of mainstream activities of Islamic revitalization. This may be seen in many types of religious performance, such as the preaching of the Friday sermon (*khutbah*) and in other modes of ritual speech and popular and musical performance. In addition, movements in Muslim global systems cultivate emotion self-consciously among individuals and groups as an aspect of long-term religious programs. For example, affect and aesthetics are key to a widespread movement of Qur'anic revitalization in Indonesia. The worldwide dynamics of such *da'wah* ("Islamic outreach," almost always directed toward other Muslims) leads Muslims to develop new Islamic emotion theory in order to inspire others affectively to become involved in personal and social religious change.

From the norms of global Islam (Qur'an, *sunnah*) to socially specific manifestations like Shi'i Ashura observances, Sufi *dhikr*, and contemporary movements of the "Islamic awakening," some emotional themes, such as moralized affect, are shared across diverse Muslim religious systems. Classical Islamic systems formulate emotion theory and practice with the same characteristic flexibility, robustness, and rigorous understanding of the categories of "general and specific" that typifies the formal disciplines of Qur'anic study, the law, and *tasawwuf*. Normative emotion theory within such global frameworks, starting with the reading of the Qur'an, tends to be moralizing and aestheticizing. Emotional states are well-defined vehicles for religious cultivation in diverse Muslim contexts, in which they are seen to draw on shared ethical norms such as the *sunnah* of the Prophet. Since affect often mediates between ideals and actual experience in Islamic theory and practice, as in Sufi systems, Muslims have often questioned the limits of affective expression and participation. This may perhaps be the case especially because Muslims recognize that the proper expression of emotion is a personal responsibility in religious settings; emotional experience and affective display may not only alter one's own moral state but also palpably affect the shared ethical order for others in this world and in the next.

NOTES

1. Al-Ghazzali, *The Recitation and Interpretation of the Qur'an, Al-Ghazali's Theory* (*Ihya' 'Ulum al-Din*, bk. 8), translated by Muhammad Abul Quasem (Boston: Kegan Paul International, 1983).

2. For more discussion, see Kristina Nelson, *The Art of Reciting the Qur'an* (Austin: University of Texas Press, 1985).

3. 'Umar Ibn al-Farid, *'Umar Ibn al-Farid: Sufi Verse, Saintly Life*, edited and translated by Th. Emil Homerin (New York: Paulist Press, 2001).

4. Hafiz, *The Green Sea of Heaven: Fifty Ghazals from the Diwan of Hafiz*, translated by Elizabeth T. Gray (Ashland, Ore.: White Cloud Press), 1995.

5. Nizami, *The Story of Layla and Majnun*, translated by Rudolf Gelpke, G. Hill, Zia Inayat Khan, E. Mattin, and Omid Safi (New Lebanon, N.Y.: Omega, 1997).

6. Lila Abu-Lughod, *Veiled Sentiments: Honor and Poetry in a Bedouin Society* (Berkeley: University of California Press, 1986).

BIBLIOGRAPHY

Abdel Haleem, Muhammad. "Dynamic Style." In *Understanding the Qur'an: Themes and Style*. London: Tauris, 1999, 184–210.

Abdel-Kader, Ali Hassan. *The Life, Personality and Writings of al-Junayd: A Study of a Third/Ninth-Century Mystic*. London: Luzac, 1962.

Abu-Lughod, Lila. *Veiled Sentiments: Honor and Poetry in a Bedouin Society*. Berkeley: University of California Press, 1986.

Boulatta, Issa J. *Literary Structures of Religious Meaning in the Qur'an*. London: Curzon, 2000.

De Jong, Frederick, and Bernard Radtke, eds. *Islamic Mysticism Contested: Thirteen Centuries of Controversies and Polemics*. Leiden: Brill, 1999.

Denffer, Ahmad von. *'Ulum al-Qur'an: An Introduction to the Sciences of the Qur'an*. London: Islamic Foundation, 1983.

Denny, Frederick M. "Exegesis and Recitation, Their Development as Classical Forms of Qur'anic Piety." In *Transitions and Transformations in the History of Religions: Essays in Honor of Joseph M. Kitagawa*, edited by Frank E. Reynolds and Theodore M. Ludwig. Leiden: Brill, 1980, 91–123.

———. "Islamic Ritual: Perspectives and Theories." In *Approaches to Islam in Religious Studies*, edited by Richard Martin, 63–77. Tucson: University of Arizona Press, 1985.

———. "Qur'an Recitation: A Tradition of Oral Performance and Transmission." *Oral Tradition* 4, 1–2 (1989): 5–26.

Eickelman, Dale F., and James Piscatori. *Muslim Politics*. Princeton, N.J.: Princeton University Press, 1996.

Ernst, Carl W. *The Shambhala Guide to Sufism*. Boston: Shambhala, 1997.

Ernst, Carl W., and Bruce Lawrence. *Sufi Martyrs of Love: The Chishti Order in South Asia and Beyond*. New York: Palgrave Macmillan, 2002.

Ewing, Katherine Pratt. *Arguing Sainthood: Modernity, Psychoanalysis, and Islam*. Durham, N.C.: Duke University Press, 1997.

Fakhry, Majid. *A History of Islamic Philosophy*. New York: Columbia University Press, 1970.

al-Faruqi, Lois Ibsen. "The Cantillation of the Qur'an." *Asian Music* 19, 1 (1987): 2–25.

———. "The *Mawlid*." *World of Music* 3 (1986): 79–89.

———. "Music, Musicians, and Muslim Law." *Asian Music* 17, 1 (1985): 13–36.

Gade, Anna M. *Perfection Makes Practice: Learning, Emotion and the Recited Qur'an in Indonesia*. Honolulu: University of Hawai'i Press, 2004.

Gaffney, Patrick D. *The Prophet's Pulpit: Islamic Preaching in Contemporary Egypt*. Berkeley: University of California Press, 1994.

al-Ghazzali, Abu Hamid Muhammad Ibn Muhammad al-Tusi. *The Faith and Practice of al-Ghazzali*. Translated by W. Montgomery Watt. London: Allen and Unwin, 1953.

———. *The Recitation and Interpretation of the Qur'an, Al-Ghazali's Theory (Ihya' 'Ulum al-Din,* bk. 8). Translated by Muhammad Abul Quasem. Boston: Kegan Paul International, 1983.

Graham, William A. *Beyond the Written Word: Oral Aspects of Scripture in the History of Religion.* New York: Cambridge University Press, 1987.

Halm, Heinz. *Shi'a Islam: From Religion to Revolution.* Princeton, N.J.: Markus Wiener, 1997.

Hallaq, Wael B. *A History of Islamic Legal Theories: An Introduction to Sunni Usul al-Fiqh.* Cambridge: Cambridge University Press, 1997.

Hirtenstein, Stephen. *The Unlimited Mercifier: The Spiritual Life and Thought of Ibn 'Arabi.* Ashland, Ore.: White Cloud Press, 1999.

Hoffman, Valerie J. *Celebrating the Prophet in the Remembrance of God: Sufi Dhikr in Egypt.* Video recording. University of Illinois at Urbana-Champaign, Office of Instructional Resources, Division of Educational Technologies, 1997.

———. *Sufism, Mystics, and Saints in Modern Egypt.* Columbia: University of South Carolina Press, 1995.

Homerin, Th. Emil. *From Arab Poet to Muslim Saint: Ibn al-Farid, His Verse, and His Shrine.* Columbia: University of South Carolina Press, 1994.

Ibn al-Farid, 'Umar. *'Umar Ibn al-Farid: Sufi Verse, Saintly Life.* Edited and translated with commentary by Th. Emil Homerin. New York: Paulist Press, 2001.

Ibn Naqib al-Misri, Ahmad. *Reliance of the Traveller: A Classic Manual of Islamic Sacred Law ('Umdat al-Salik).* Translated with commentary and appendices by Nuh Ha Mim Keller. Beltsville, Md.: Amana, 1994.

Kassis, Hanna E. *A Concordance of the Qur'an.* Berkeley: University of California Press, 1983.

Keshavarz, Fatemeh. *Reading Mystical Lyric: The Case of Jalal al-Din Rumi.* Columbia: University of South Carolina Press, 1998.

Knysh, Alexander. *Islamic Mysticism: A Short History.* Leiden: Brill, 2000.

Lapidus, Ira. "Knowledge, Virtue, and Action: The Classical Muslim Conception of *Adab* and the Nature of Religious Fulfillment in Islam." In *Moral Conduct and Authority: The Place of Adab in South Asian Islam,* edited by Barbara Metcalf. Berkeley: University of California Press, 1984, 38–61.

Lewis, Franklin. *Rumi, Past and Present, East and West: The Life, Teaching and Poetry of Jalal al-Din Rumi.* Oxford: Oneworld, 2000.

Nasr, Sayyed Hosein. "Islam and Music: The Legal and Spiritual Dimensions." In *Enchanting Powers: Music in the World's Religions,* edited by Lawrence E. Sullivan. Cambridge, Mass.: Harvard University Press, 1997, 219–36.

Nelson, Kristina. *The Art of Reciting the Qur'an.* Austin: University of Texas Press, 1985.

Netton, Ian Richard. *Sufi Ritual: The Parallel Universe.* London: Curzon, 2000.

Nizami. *The Story of Layla and Majnun.* Translated by Rudolf Gelpke, G. Hill, Zia Inayat Khan, E. Mattin, and Omid Safi. New Lebanon, N.Y.: Omega, 1997.

Powers, Paul Richard. "Intentionality in Medieval Islamic Law." Ph.D. diss., University of Chicago Divinity School, 2001.

Qureshi, Regula Burckhardt. *Sufi Music of India and Pakistan: Sound, Context, and Meaning in Qawwali.* Chicago: University of Chicago Press, 1995.

Rahman, Fazlur. *Major Themes of the Qur'an.* Minneapolis: Bibliotheca Islamica, 1989.

Reinhart, A. Kevin. "Islamic Law as Islamic Ethics." *Journal of Religious Ethics* 11, 2 (1983): 186–203.

Renard, John. *Islam and the Heroic Image: Themes in Literature and the Visual Arts.* Columbia: University of South Carolina Press, 1993.

Rosenthal, Franz. *Knowledge Triumphant: The Concept of Knowledge in Medieval Islam.* Leiden: Brill, 1970.

Said, Edward. *Orientalism.* New York: Vintage Books, 1979.

Schimmel, Annemarie. *And Muhammad Is His Messenger: The Veneration of the Prophet in Islamic Piety.* Chapel Hill: University of North Carolina Press, 1985.

———. *As through a Veil: Mystical Poetry in Islam.* Oxford: Oneworld, 2001.

Schubel, Vernon James. *Religious Performance in Contemporary Islam: Shi'i Devotional Rituals in South Asia.* Columbia: University of South Carolina Press, 1993.

Sells, Michael. *Approaching the Qur'an: The Early Revelations.* Ashland, Ore.: White Cloud Press, 1999.

———, ed. and trans. *Desert Tracings: Six Classic Arabian Odes.* Middletown, Conn.: Wesleyan University Press, 1989.

Shiloah, Amnon. *Music in the World of Islam: A Socio-Cultural Study.* Detroit: Wayne State University Press, 1996.

al-Shirazi, Hafiz. *The Green Sea of Heaven: Fifty Ghazals from the Diwan of Hafiz.* Translated by Elizabeth T. Gray. Ashland, Ore.: White Cloud Press, 1995.

Sirriyeh, Elizabeth. *Sufis and Anti-Sufis: The Defense, Rethinking and Rejection of Sufism in the Modern World.* London: Curzon Press, 1999.

Waugh, Earle H. *The Munshidin of Egypt: Their World and Their Song.* Columbia: University of South Carolina Press, 1989.

Wensinck, A. J. *A Handbook of Early Muhammadan Tradition.* Leiden: Brill, 1927.

CHAPTER 3

HINDUISM

JUNE McDANIEL

Types of Hinduism

Emotion is viewed in both positive and negative ways in the Hindu religious and philosophical traditions. In those traditions that are more ascetic and emphasize mental control, emotions are distractions which need to be stilled. In those traditions that emphasize love of a deity, emotions are valuable—but they must be directed and transformed.

However, in order to study emotion in the Hindu tradition, we must first look at the meaning of the term "Hinduism." There are many different kinds of Hinduism—it is not a monolithic tradition. The word "Hindu" derives from a British description of the people living along the Indus river—it was not initially intended to refer to a specific religious tradition. Over time, the term came to be accepted as an umbrella term that covers a multitude of different belief systems.

There are at least six major types of Hinduism, and numerous minor ones—it is said that no two villages have the same deities on their altars, as there are different ancestors and regional gods and goddesses in every area. Of the major types, the oldest is Hindu folk religion—the worship of local deities and sanctified natural places, and the propitiation of spirits and ghosts. This is for the most part a non-literate system, handed down by oral tradition, with a reverence for nature and an appreciation for song and story. It is primarily studied by anthropologists and religionists doing fieldwork, as the rituals and stories are usually not told to outsiders.

Emotion is valued in the folk tradition, with religious joy and sorrow shown frequently during possession rituals. People often live in extended families, and marry according to clan rules (or caste rules, if they are members of a group accepted as part of the caste system). There is no elaborate study of self or emotion in folk Hinduism, though there is often a distinction between body and soul, or between levels of soul.

Vedic religion is based on the ancient Vedic texts, written by the sages or *rishis* approximately 1500 B.C.E. Vedic Hinduism is the oldest form of Hinduism for which we have written texts. The four Vedas and their commentaries emphasize ritual worship of the gods. The most important is the Rig Veda, a compendium of hymns to such gods as Indra, Agni, and Surya. While there is ecstasy from such rituals as the *soma* sacrifice (in which Vedic priests would ingest a drug called *soma* in order to have visions of the gods and communicate with them), there is no general discussion of emotion per se. There is an appreciation of the physical world, full of women and cows and other good things, and people should appreciate it and become wealthy and have many children.

Analysis of emotion really begins in texts that come after the Vedas, such as the Upanishads, and this brings the third type of Hinduism: Vedantic Hinduism. Vedanta is the philosophy of the Vedic and Upanishadic texts. According to the Advaita or monistic form of Vedanta, the ultimate state is an infinite and tranquil ocean of consciousness. It is disturbed by illusion (*maya*)—the world of names and forms, which creates ignorance. Emotion is a part of that world of becoming, that changing universe that does not allow the person to perceive things as they really are, merged in Brahman, or infinite reality, knowledge, and bliss. The Vedantin seeks wisdom (*jnana*) to the exclusion of emotion, and renounces attachment to the illusory world. Emotion muddies the waters, disrupting awareness and distracting the sage. According to Advaita Vedanta, emotion is one of the bonds that attaches people to the illusory world, and both love and hatred are illusions that must be overcome.

There is another approach to Vedanta that is dualistic, Dvaita Vedanta. According to this view, the ultimate reality is understood as a personal god, the creator of the universe and the Inner Controller. In this approach, love and obedience are important qualities, and in this understanding of Vedanta we see the roots of the later devotional or *bhakti* traditions.

A fourth type of Hindu tradition is yogic Hinduism, following the classical *raja yoga* of Patanjali. In *sutra* 1.2 of his *Yogasutra*, Patanjali gives the definition of yoga: "Yogas citta-vrtti-nirodhah": yoga is the control or dissolution of the fluctuations of the mind.[1] The mind is understood as a field or ocean of consciousness (*citta*), which is ideally peaceful and still. However, in most human beings, it is full of activity, with waves and eddies of passion and desire. In the yoga tradition, emotion is for the most part a distraction to clear awareness.

Both the Vedanta and yogic traditions are basically dualistic and ascetic, with an emphasis on the radiant spiritual world over the dark and illusory physical world. This means that the world is not to be enjoyed but rather overcome, and emotions that bind people to the physical world are to be avoided.

This is different from the fifth type of Hindu tradition, that of dharmic Hinduism, or daily morality. This tradition gives instruction on whom to marry and with whom to eat, how to live and work, and how to attain good karma. Dharmic Hinduism guides people through the joys and sorrows of daily life, giving rules for what is allowed and what is forbidden. Some books stereotype this as the only form of Hindu religion, along with the belief in karma, cows, and the caste system. While dharmic Hinduism is widespread today, it basically says little about the religious side of life—except for encouraging good rebirth. We should also note that while cows are good, they are not gods, and that prejudice on the basis of the caste system has been illegal in India since Indian independence in 1949.

The aspect of Hinduism that is most important for the study of emotion is the sixth type of Hinduism, *bhakti* or devotional Hinduism. This form of Hinduism has some of the most elaborate analyses of emotion to be found in world religions. It emphasizes the love of a god or goddess, and describes stages, types, roles, and triggers of emotion. This is the form of religion that is most intense in modern India, and probably most widespread. The major deities of the *bhakti* tradition are Shiva, Vishnu, and Shakti, and they are worshiped though the ritual of *puja*, which usually involves offerings of flowers, fruit, and incense.

There is also a more controversial sort of Hinduism, the tantric tradition. In this practice, people deliberately disobey the rules of dharma, which emphasizes a slow and gradual growth in spirituality. Instead we have the fast path, where the passions are deliberately generated and overcome—in the death rituals (where people go out at midnight to the burning ground to meditate on a corpse, and the transitory nature of life) and in the sexual rituals (where the participants chant mantras and identify with the god and goddess, experiencing and overcoming sexual desire). Intense emotions (fear of death and lust) are part of the rituals, which are understood to lead eventually to detachment.

All of these involve emotion in various ways, but two traditions—those of Bengali Vaishnavism and *raja* yoga—have written about emotion in greatest depth. We shall examine what the term "emotion" means in India, and then describe the beliefs about emotion in Vaishnavism and Yoga in greater detail.

What Is Emotion?

In the Sanskrit and Bengali languages, there is no exact term for emotion. The term used most frequently for emotion is *bhava* or *anubhava* (the physical expression of the state of *bhava*). Sometimes the terms *raga* or *abeg* are used, which refer to intense emotions or passions. In the yogic literature, we see the term *vedana*, of Pali origin. It refers to a feeling, usually of a negative kind, such as pain and sorrow.

The term *bhava* has many referents—the Monier-Williams Sanskrit dictionary has four large columns of definitions for *bhava*, and the *Bangala Bhasar Abhidhan* dictionary has two columns. Definitions in the *Samsad Bengali-English Dictionary* include mental state, mood, emotion, condition, love, friendship, ecstasy, rapture, passion, inner significance, essence, and existence—thus covering a wide range of phenomena.

Bhava is an emotional complex, a form of experience, with connotations of associated perception, thought, movement, and expression. It is a way of being, a sense of identity that may be individual or shared. It is believed in many of the Bengali devotional traditions that religious ecstatics can create waves of *bhava* (*bhava-taranga*) that can spread through crowds of people, causing them all to share in the ecstatic's intense emotions.[2] The person who is *bhavavesh* is possessed by *bhava*, that is, he or she is either intensely emotional or is taking on the *bhava* (the emotion and identity) of a deity or other being. The person may be *bhava laga* (affected by an emotion or idea), *bhava praban* (emotional, sentimental, maudlin), or *bhava bihbul* (overwhelmed with emotion or ecstasy). As a term derived from *bhava*, *bhavana* is thought, meditation, creation, and visualization; but it can also refer to worry and anxiety (the term is used in the Indian medical tradition for the repeated maceration, pulverization, and purification of herbal medicine—an interesting metaphor for analytic thought).

In the Bengali and Sanskrit languages, terms for emotion and thought, mind and heart, are not opposed. Indeed, most frequently the same terms are used for both. A term often heard, *mana*, means both mind and heart, as well as mood, feeling, mental state, memory, desire, attachment, interest, attention, devotion, and decision. These terms do not have a single referent in English, and must be understood through clusters of explicit and implicit meanings.[3] Verbs based on *mana* include *mana kara*, to make up one's mind, to resolve or agree; *mana kara*, to captivate the mind or win one's heart; and *mana khola*, to speak one's mind or open one's heart.

A term used less frequently by informants, *hridaya*, means the heart as both organ and inner seat of feeling. The heart may be melted (when a play is *hridayadravakara*, touching or evoking pathos), may be broken (the heart is pierced, *hridayabhedi*), and may overflow with an outburst of emotion (*hridayochvasa*). A person unaffected by emotion may be called unfeeling or heartless (*hridayahin*). The heart is also understood as a space or locale, in which persons or deities may dwell. Thus we see the heart called a canvas for painting (*hridayapata*), a shrine or temple (*hridayamandir*), a seat for a loved one or deity (*hridayasana*), or a space as broad as the sky (*hridayakasa*). As one informant described it, his heart was an empty box that needed to be filled. In poetry, the loved one may live in the heart as in a garden, and in worship, an aspect of the god may live there enthroned, surrounded by the devotee's love like an aura of light. In a poem quoted later in this chapter, the poet Ramprasad Sen speaks of the "burning ground of the heart" and had visions of the goddess Kali dancing there.[4] In *kundalini* yoga, the heart is a doorway to the worlds of the spirit, as the *anahata chakra* or heart center.[5]

There are several other terms often used in discussing emotion. *Raga*, a term better known in the West as a mode of Indian classical music, also means passion, ranging from love and attachment to anger and rage. It has the meaning of dye or color (especially red)—the soul is understood to be "dyed" by passion, which permeates it the way a dye permeates cloth.[6] *Kama* is desire, lust, and pleasure, while *prema* is selfless or spiritual love. *Abeg* means tremendous force, passionate outburst, intense feeling, uneasiness, and suspense, while *anubhava* refers to both power and physical expression of emotional states (such as tears and sighs). Yet emotion is *suksmata*, subtlety, delicacy, invisible to the senses, as well as *komlata*, gentleness, tenderness, softness. As *anubhuti*, it is both perception and intuition, realization and feeling.

The terms for thought, or cognition, often imply emotion. We have the word *cinta*, meaning thought, idea, and cogitation, with associated meanings of anxiety, worry, and fear. *Dharana* means idea, conception, memory, belief, impression, as well as feeling, and is associated with the act of holding, catching, wearing, carrying (thought is "borne" in the mind). *Anubhava* means knowledge, perception, and realization but also feeling, and *kalpana* refers to thought and imagination.

We see in these terms and definitions that emotion is a powerful force that is at the same time subtle and delicate, invisible to the senses yet capable of generating physical expressions, associated with perception, intuition, and realization. There is no sharp distinction between emotion and cognition. Thought is associated with knowledge and discrimination, and the mind grasps and holds memories and ideas. Yet thought is also associated with feelings, especially anxiety,[7] as well as imagination.

Bhava in itself is a complex term with a range of meanings, from a broad understanding of experience and identity (*bhava* as a way of being) to a specific *bhava*, an emotion or thought that is clearly defined. Using the same term for these events shows that the range of experience—emotion, mood, identity, mental state—is understood as a continuum rather than a collection of distinct and opposed categories. Both emotion and thought are part of the wider category of *bhava*.

The Nature of Emotion: Bhava and Rasa

The most extensive analyses of aesthetic and dramatic emotion in Indian philosophy have probably come from the writers of the Alankarashastra, the Sanskrit literary tradition that focuses on aesthetic experience. For this tradition, aesthetic emotion is *rasa*, which is experienced by the person of taste (*rasika*) during identification with a dramatic character or situation. According to the Alankara, the spectator is totally involved in the dramatic event, and feels an emotion that is powerful and extraordinary (*alaukika*) yet impersonal and generic. It is joyful, rather than pleasant or painful, and brings a sense of wonder. In some ways, it is similar to the religious goal of realization of Brahman. Visvanatha writes that aesthetic enjoyment requires subconscious impressions (*vasanas*) that support an emotional disposition.[8] Aesthetic emotions have a variety of effects on consciousness.[9]

The writers of the Alankara describe both permanent and temporary emotions. They base their organization of emotions on the list of the writer Bharata in his famous book *Natyashastra*: love, mirth, grief, anger, energy (zeal), fear, disgust, and wonder[10]. These permanent emotions (*sthayibhava*) are dominant, and cannot be suppressed by other emotions. According to Singa Bhupala's *Rasarnavasudhakar*, "they are permanent emotions, which transform other emotions into themselves, even as the ocean transforms the waves into itself."[11]

The temporary or transitory emotions (*vyabhicharibhava*) are easily influenced. According to Saradatanaya's *Bhavaprakashana*, they appear and disappear within the permanent emotions as waves appear and disappear in the ocean, contributing to its excellence.[12] They are like bubbles in the ocean, or beads or flowers of a garland, and they help, promote, and strengthen the permanent emotions that they ornament. Some of the transitory emotions include shame, exhilaration, dejection, eagerness, apathy, ferocity, and anxiety.[13] In the first chapter of his *Natyashastra*, Bharata compared the aesthetic experience to eating—as spices add flavor (*rasa*) to the main dish, which is enjoyed by the gourmet, so the permanent emotion in drama is spiced with transitory emotions and literary ornaments, to be enjoyed by the connoisseur (*rasika*).

The sentiment of *rasa* is a transformation of the basic, more "concrete" emotion of *bhava*. The term *rasa* means sap, juice, liquid essence, and taste, and is often translated as flavor, relish, mood, and sentiment. Emotional *rasa* can be tasted and appreciated.[14] When emotions became *rasa*s, they may be viewed as art objects, and combined in aesthetic fashion. They may blend harmoniously with each other (*sandhi*), arise and disappear, or conflict with and inhibit one another.

When two moods clash with each other, this conflict is called *rasabhasa*. It is understood to result in an inferior emotional experience. It is a damaged or incomplete sort of emotion, tainted by pride or power, or generated by some inappropriate source. The conflicts that might generate such a damaged emotion could include the clash between parental and erotic love toward the same object, or the emotions of disgust and fury combined with the attitude of loving service.

The associated emotions or *bhavas* may be simple or complex. They are called compound emotions when several transitory emotions arise in quick succession, especially when some are inhibited by others.

From this perspective, the *bhava* is a "raw" emotion, not "cooked" or transformed into an aesthetic emotion. In order to transform the emotion, an internal distancing is needed from the emotion, so that the experiencer also becomes an observer, in some ways like the "witness-self" described in Vedantic philosophy.

The eight basic *bhavas* and *rasas* relate as follows.

Bhava	*Rasa*
love	erotic
humor	comic
grief	tragic

anger	furious
energy	heroic
fear	fearful
disgust	terrible
astonishment	marvelous

The *bhava* is the basic emotion, the *rasa* is the mood that results from it. *Rasa* is characterized by impersonality or generalizing (*sadharanikarana*), the distancing of the person from both the object and from his or her own emotions. In *bhava*, the person experiences emotions directly, while in *rasa*, he or she empathizes and observes the emotion and situation, feeling *as if* he or she felt the emotion but not actually being involved enough to feel it directly. It is impersonal, generic, the experience of a type. As De states, "Generality is thus a state of self-identification with the imagined situation, devoid of any practical interest and, from this point of view, of any relation whatsoever with the limited self, and as it were impersonal."[15]

The feelings of the poet or actor are also excluded from the aesthetic experience. The elements of particular consciousness are expunged to create generalized emotion, valuing universals more than particular acts. The *rasika* or aesthete is both observer and participant.

Bhava is a personal emotion; *rasa* is an impersonal or depersonalized emotion or mood, in which the participant is also an observer. In the Alankara aesthetic theory, *rasa* is superior to *bhava*, and a more desirable state. Why is a depersonalized emotion considered to be superior to a personal one? Because the aesthete can experience a wide range of emotions yet be protected from their painful aspects. Emotion is appreciated as if through a glass barrier that keeps out unpleasantness. Though the glass is clear, which allows a union of sorts with the observed object, the window is always present, which maintains the dualism. This becomes important for the religious dimensions of *rasa*, where the duality between the worshiper and the god (an important concept in *bhakti* devotion) must always be maintained.

The Alankara tradition strongly influenced the development of Bengali or Gaudiya Vaishnavism, which developed a complex theory of spiritual and emotional development based on the love of the god Krishna.

Emotion in Bengali Vaishnavism

Vaishnavism is the worship of various forms of the god Vishnu or Krishna, and in West Bengal a tradition developed that emphasized emotion as extremely important to spiritual growth. It came to be called Gaudiya Vaishnavism or Bengali

Vaishnavism, and it emphasized the worship of the god Krishna (who is understood as the one true god, though he has emanations and manifestations) and Krishna's later form on earth, Caitanya Mahaprabhu of Navadvipa (who was believed to be a joint incarnation of both Krishna and his consort Radha).

Like the philosophers of the Alanakarashastra, the Bengali Vaishnavas also value *rasa*, but they emphasize its religious aspects. In the Vaishnava understanding of emotion, secular aesthetic *rasa* becomes *bhakti rasa*, or devotional sentiment. The religious goal is not liberation but rather love, and the devotee must go beyond dramatic emotion to become filled with religious emotion. The connoisseur (the *rasika* or *sahridaya*, the person with heart) who can truly appreciate the fine points of the arts becomes the devotee or *bhakta*, tasting the forms of joy brought by the god Krishna. He or she is both observer of divine play (*lila*) and participant in the divine drama (which occurs in human history and in Krishna's paradise, not merely on a stage). The aesthetic experience is universal, *bhedabheda*, simultaneously individual and eternal, material and spiritual.

In *bhakti* yoga, emotion becomes discipline—the emotions are generated and transformed consciously, especially in that form of practice known as *raganuga bhakti sadhana*.[16] There is a sort of "ladder of emotion" one must climb to the highest emotional states, and it is described in two important texts, the *Bhakti-rasamritasindhu* and *Ujjvala-Nilamani* of Rupa Gosvamin. While the former (the Ocean of the Nectar of Devotional Love) looks at the earlier stages of religious emotion and its transformation, the latter (the Blazing Sapphire—describing the god Krishna) focuses on the more advanced states of mystical love.

The *Bhakti-rasamritasindhu* has the devotee begin with ritual action (*vaidhi bhakti*) and progress to ritual emotion (*raganuga bhakti*). Through physical action and imaginative visualization, the devotee builds a soul, a spiritual body composed of love, which can experience emotion more intensely than can the ordinary personality. The *bhava* becomes deepened, and the heart is softened. Emotion becomes intense selfless love (*prema*), and there is continual focus of attention on Radha and Krishna, the divine couple. In the highest state, called the greatest emotion (*mahabhava*), the person experiences all possible emotions simultaneously, including the opposite emotions of separation and union, in passionate delirium (*madana*). As O. B. L. Kapoor states,

> *madana* has the unique capacity of directly experiencing a thousand different kinds of enjoyment of union with Krsna.... It presents these multifarious experiences of union simultaneously with multifarious experiences of separation (*viyoga*) involving craving (*utkantha*) for union.[17]

The "ladder of emotion" includes *sneha*, a thickening of spiritual love (when the emotion gains a consistency and taste like clarified butter or honey); *mana*, or sulking and hiding emotion; *pranaya,* or deep sharing and confidence; *raga,* or intense passion (also defined as the person being totally concentrated on the desired object); *anuraga*, in which the beloved appears eternally new; and *mahabhava*, the experience of emotion so intense and complex that all extremes of emotion are felt at once.

In the orthodox Bengali Vaishnava tradition, only Radha may experience the state of *mahabhava*, though her companions and their handmaidens may share in her emotional states. Indeed, these handmaidens or *manjaris* are said to feel Radha's emotions one hundred times more intensely than she does, for they are not as personally involved (selflessness is understood to increase sensitivity to the divine).[18] The devotee may also share in these states by visualizing the mythical situations and characters in which they occur.[19]

These states of intense emotion are expressed by ecstatic bodily changes (the *sattvika bhavas* or *sattvika vikaras*). There are eight of these: trembling, shedding tears, paralysis, sweating, fainting, changing skin color, faltering voice, and hair standing on end. Like the transitory emotions, these symptoms are understood to develop and intensify the permanent emotions, and they are an extreme form of emotional expression (*anubhava*).[20]

In the Bengali Vaishnava tradition, emotion may be used to build spiritual bodies. Disciplined emotion and concentration can generate nonphysical selves, which are highly valued. The person may not be able to determine his or her secular personality, based as it is on past events, but he or she can build a soul, a spiritual body that is sculpted out of emotion. This alternative personality, or "subtle body," is composed of selfless love (*prema*) and represents the person's ideal self. It is understood that this body will live forever in Krishna's paradise, after the person's physical body has died.

The idea of alternative selves has often been dismissed as "split personality" or multiple personality disorder by Western observers. However, it is interesting to note that, in the West, the focus on alternate selves has been on multiple personality disorder generated by trauma—by abuse or events too painful for the person to bear (and earlier on by demonic personalities that possess the person against his or her will).[21] Nonetheless, the description given by the American Psychiatric Association's *Diagnostic and Statistical Manual of Mental Disorders* fits the Indian case in many ways:

> A. The existence within an individual of two or more distinct personalities, each of which is dominant at a particular time. B. The personality that is dominant at any particular time determines the individual's behavior. C. Each individual personality is complex and integrated with its own unique behavior patterns and social relationships.[22]

Western alternate personalities are considered to be involuntarily created and pathological, a result of trauma. It is assumed that emotion cannot be deliberately used and controlled to create a new personality—such generation is an unconscious event.

From the Indian devotional perspective, developing an alternate self based on emotion is a conscious and creative act, building a spiritual body made out of overflowing love. This *siddha deha* (perfected body) or *prema deha* (body of love) becomes the true self of the person, and is believed to continue after the death of the physical body. The alternative self is generated by will and love rather than pain, and emotion is utilized rather than repressed or endured. In this understanding, emotion is the foundation of identity, the substance from which it is constructed. Selfless love, or *prema*, is also the substance of the Krishna's paradise itself—heaven is literally made of love.

The term *bhava* is also used for the five basic roles or emotional relationships through which the devotee may relate to the deity: through friendship, parental love, service, peace, and erotic love. Thus, the devotee and the god may be close friends who confide in each other; the devotee may be the loving mother or father of the baby god; the devotee may be the servant of his or her divine master; the devotee and god may be understood to be equally divine or ultimately the same; and the devotee and god may be passionate lover and beloved. Among these roles, the relationship of lover and beloved in considered to be the ideal one, full of sweetness and joy. The relationship of equal and equal, as one might see in the Advaita Vedanta understanding of all selves being equally Brahman, is least desirable, as there is no passion and sweetness involved.

Among the Bengali Vaishnavas, *bhava* is the emotional ground for subtler and more complex emotional states. Emotion is desirable, as the way to get closest to the god, and the way to best understand the universe as it really is—full of joy, happiness, and creativity.

Emotion in Raja Yoga

The yogic approach to emotion is quite different from the *bhakti* or devotional approach. According to yoga philosophy, the ideal state is one totally without emotional extremes, a state of perfect peace and tranquility. Emotion distracts the person from that state of pure awareness and clear insight, binding him or her to the physical world. The mind is a field of consciousness full of areas of tension and anxiety that attract the person's mind, and make perception distorted and thinking erratic.

These changes or fluctuations are the *citta-vrittis*, the whirlpools of consciousness that disturb the clarity of the mind. Some of these disturbances are of external origin, originating in the surrounding physical world, and some are internal, arising from memory and impression.

According to Patanjali's yoga, these memory impressions may become inclinations or propensities of the personality (*vasanas*), which are accompanied by repeated habits of thought. The associated mental fluctuations become laden with emotion and are called *kleshas*, impurities or afflictions. There are five *kleshas*: ignorance, desire, hatred, fear (especially fear of death), and pride (the sense of the self as an important individual entity).[23] These should be avoided: the yogi should control his emotions, withdrawing his perceptions and concerns into himself as a turtle pulls his legs inside of his shell.

These *kleshas* or painful aspects of consciousness arise from misunderstanding, especially from thinking that the individual, egotistical self is identical to the universal, ultimate Self. They also arise from attachment to ephemeral material things and the desire to possess them, and from hatred and aversion to material things and to people. The fear of death and the desperate craving for life also crate bondage and attachment to the world.

In Western psychology, we divide the mind into conscious and unconscious aspects. In yoga psychology, there is an area of conscious awareness (mediated through *manas* or mind, and *ahamkara* or ego). There is also an unconscious area of the mind, and that is where we have the whirlpools of emotion, the *citta-vrittis*. These originate from traumatic or passionate memories, which fill the unconscious with anxiety and desire. In meditation, the person may perceive these traumas and be caught in them. These centers of repeating emotions, ideas, and tendencies are called *vasanas*. These whirlpools must be "stilled" so that they no longer have power over the person.

Whether conscious or unconscious, most of these emotional attachments are understood to have their origin in past events. Thus, current emotion has a basis in karma—not only from events in this life but also from past lives. As Eliade notes, the whirlpools of traumatic emotion may be transmitted "impersonally" over the generations (through culture and its values, thus ethnic and historical transmission) or directly (through reincarnation and the person's development in each life).[24]

Western psychology allows for conscious and unconscious aspects of mind, but no superconscious aspect. In yoga psychology, there is also a superconscious area of the mind, reached through the intellect or *buddhi*. This part of the mind determines what is ultimate reality for the person, and allows the awareness of more and more subtle aspects of the mind. In meditation, the immediate passions and desires are stilled, and then the unconscious complexes or *vasanas* from the past are perceived and calmed. It is only when the murky waters of awareness have been calmed and clarified that the yogi can see clearly.

The mind is often compared to a river or ocean. According to the commentary of Vyasa on Patanjali's *Yogasutra*, "The river called mind flows in two directions"[25]— toward the world of desire (*samsara*) and the world of peace (called *kaivalya* or isolation from the turbulence of daily life). The mind-stream or river of consciousness (*citta-nadi*) needs to be directed and "one-pointed" toward peace and freedom, and one way to direct the river is to dam it through dispassion (*vairagya*).[26] This is a major goal of yoga practice.

It may be noted that there is a positive approach to one type of emotion in *raja yoga*. This is the ecstatic emotion of *ananda*, or bliss. In the state of *samadhi*, the state of perfect peace and contemplation that precedes total liberation or *kaivalya*, the person enters a state of great delight. It is traditionally described as having the qualities of ultimate truth, infinite awareness, and overwhelming bliss (or *sat*, *chit*, and *ananda*). To be in the state of *ananda* is to have great joy and love, which comes from the experience of the unity of all things.

Hinduism's Wide Variety

There is no single system or understanding of emotion in Hinduism. Ideas range from emotion as a distraction to emotion as concentration, as pain, as pleasure, as the substance of spiritual bodies and paradises, as a pathway to the god. Emotion has been explored in great detail in both philosophical and religious systems. This chapter can only give a few examples—there are many more. There are many variants of devotional love or *bhakti*, with different formulations of emotion and appropriate roles for god and devotee. In Shakta *bhakti*, for instance, the goddess is the mother, and the devotee is the child, and the most important type of emotion is the love of a child for its divine mother.[27]

Emotion can act as a distraction or as an aid to concentration, helping to focus the mind. Passion can direct the mind and fasten it on its object. In the stories of Krishna and the *gopis* or milkmaids who loved him, their fascination for him is often described as meditative, and Radha's passion for Krishna is often compared to yogic concentration. The love object is the focus of the mind, for there is no split between thought and feeling. The spiritual practice of remembrance (*smarana*) involves *mana*, which is both mind and heart, and is directed to a single end, so that even thinking of anything else becomes difficult. Depending on how it is used, the same emotion can distract from concentration or be a means of mental control, and can limit or increase knowledge.

Emotions can be controlled and combined to become something analogous to art objects. Rather than passions or disturbances, emotions may be aesthetic objects, which are arranged as dominant and transitory, central and peripheral, clashing and ornamental, as an artist might arrange different color relationships on a canvas. Emotions are in a sense colors (*raga*), which define and structure experience as art. During the dramatic performance, the emotions represented by the actor are experienced in the observer, who is simultaneously a participant. As the trained observer is aware of the subtlety and interplay of emotion, he or she becomes involved in what might be called performance art. It is a conscious awareness of his own shared dramatic experience, which is paradoxical because it is both close and distanced. Raw, "concrete" emotions can be transformed into aesthetic and religious ones.

Emotion is often a means to an end in the Bengali aesthetic and devotional traditions, and that end is the good life. Emotion is not a passive response but an active *eros*, involving meaning, beauty, and creativity, which structures both self and world.

The Literary Tradition

One good place for examining emotion in Hindu tradition is in literature, especially in religious poetry. Some of the clearest and most intense examples of love, for instance, are shown in the poetic interactions of the gods, and in the relationship between the gods and humankind.

In the Vaishnava *bhakti* tradition, there is an emphasis on *madhurya-bhava*, the mood of Krishna as divine lover. The major forms of love described in such poetry are love in separation (*vipralambha*) and love in union (*sambhoga*). These are considered to be situations of *prema* or selfless love, though there are often elements of *kama* or lust. Here is an example of love in separation, of Radha longing for the god Krishna, by the medieval poet Vidayapati:

> Harder than diamonds,
> Richer than gold,
> Deeper than the sea
> Was our love.
> The sea still washes the shores
> But our love went dry.
> I wish my lover
> Who is dark as the clouds,
> Would come in torrents...
> How I remember
> Those hours of passion
> when he would swear to me
> that day was night...[28]

Here is another example of Radha's sadness and bitterness over Krishna's desertion, by the Bengali poet Chandidasa:

> I brought honey and drank it mixed with milk—
> but where was its sweetness? I tasted gall.
> I am steeped in bitterness, as the seed
> of a bitter fruit in its juice.
> My heart smoulders.
> A fire without is plain to be seen
> but this fire flames within,
> it sears my breast.
> Desire burns the body—how can it be relieved?[29]

The other major form of selfless love is love in love in union, which is understood to be less intense—and thus less desirable, for intense passion is the ideal state. Here is an example of love in union between Radha and Krishna from the Bengali poet Jnana-dasa:

> Love, I take on splendor in your splendor
> grace and gentleness are mine because of your beauty.
> I remember,
> how I embraced your feet, holding them
> tight to my breast.
> Others have many loves, I have
> only you,
> dearer to me than life.
> You are the kohl on my eyes, the ornaments
> on my body
> you, dark moon.[30]

Another example of love in union comes from Vidyapati:

> O friend, there is no end to my joy!
> Madhava [Krishna] is home forever.
> The pain I suffered for the heartless moon
> Ended in bliss.
> My eyes live on his face.
> Lift up my dress, fill it with gold
> Yet never will I let him go again.
> He is my shelter in the rains,
> Ferry boat on the river.
> He is my warmth when the winter is hard,
> Cool breeze in the summer months,
> Nothing else I need.[31]

Bengali Vaishnavism also includes the complex of emotions known as *mahabhava*, in which the person experiences all possible emotions at once, especially the intensities of both union and separation. This poem by Govinda-dasa describes this state in Radha, a state that continually amazes Krishna:

> When they had made love
> she lay in his arms in the *kunja* grove.
> Suddenly she called his name
> and wept—as if she burned in the fire of
> separation.
> > The gold was in her *anchal* [the end of her sari]
> > but she looked afar for it!
> —Where has he gone? Where has my love gone?
> O why has he left me alone?
> And she writhed on the ground in despair
> only her pain kept her from fainting.
> Krishna was astonished
> and could not speak.[32]

For those devotees interested in the subtleties of *rasa*, there are poems that mix different emotions together. Sometimes Radha's love is mingled with fear, as Vidyapati states:

> O friend, friend, take me with you
> I am only a young girl
> No one can stop him
> So violent a lover is he.
> My heart shudders to go near him.
> How the black bee ravishes the lotus bud.
> He crushes my frail body
> Quivering like a drop of water
> On a lotus leaf.[33]

Sometimes love is combined with anger, as in this poem by the Tamil Vaishnava poetess Antal:

> If I see the lord of Govardhana
> that looting thief
> that plunderer,
> I shall pluck
> by their roots
> these useless breasts.
> I shall fling them
> at his chest,
> I shall cool
> the raging fire
> within me.[34]

Antal also writes from the perspective of the servant mood or *dasya bhava*:

> O Govinda, we have not come
> to ask for the ritual drum.
> We are your slaves,
> we serve only you.
> Forever and a day
> We shall be connected
> with you.
> Make all our desires
> flow to you alone.[35]

The god Shiva also has devotees who love him in various ways, though there is less language of union and separation. But we do have the poetry of these states: as the twelfth-century female poet Mahadeviyakka writes in loneliness:

> What do
> the barren know
> of birthpangs?
> Stepmothers
> what do they know
> of loving care?
> How can the unwounded
> know the pain
> of the wounded?
> O lord white as jasmine
> your love's blade stabbed
> and broken in my flesh,
> I writhe.
> O mothers
> how can you know me?[36]

In the state of longing, she also writes:

> Like a silkworm weaving
> her house with love
> from her marrow,
>   and dying
> in her body's threads
> winding tight, round
> and round,
>   I burn
> desiring what the heart desires.
> Cut through, O lord,
> my heart's greed
> and show me
> your way out,
> O lord white as jasmine.[37]

The Tamil poet Manikkavacakar describes love in mystical union:

> Could there ever be magic as wondrous as this?
> The lord let me serve his own loving servants,
> he released me from fear
> and took me for his own,
> he entered my being
> and so overwhelmed me with love
> my heart dissolved and flowed like nectar.
> Our father become man, woman
> and one without gender,
> sky, raging fire

> and the End of all things,
> Lord Siva
> with body red as a great *ceccai* blossom
> is king of the gods,
> our lord who stands on the other shore.[38]

The twelfth century poet Basvanna also writes of union:

> When
> like a hailstone crystal
> like a waxwork image
> the flesh melts in pleasure
> > how can I tell you?
> The waters of joy
> broke the banks
> and ran out of my eyes.
> I touched and joined
> my lord of the meeting rivers
> How can I talk to anyone
> of that?[39]

Many Shaiva writers also used the erotic *bhava* or mood for their poems, as does Manikavacakar here:

> I wear a cassia garland
> and cling to Siva's round shoulders,
> locked in his embrace, I swoon
> and then we quarrel like lovers.
> His red lips make me giddy with longing
> my heart melting, I search everywhere
> and fix my thoughts on his feet.
> I wither,
> then I blossom once more.
> Let's sing about the red feet of the lord
> who dances
> flame in hand.[40]

While both Vaishnava and Shaiva traditions of emotional *bhakti* emphasize passionate love, the goddess tradition of Shaktism emphasizes dependence on the mother, and the devotee is most often the child or servant of the mother. The erotic *bhava* is very rare in Shaktism (which may be surprising for those who equate Shaktism with tantra). Instead, we have such emotions as patriotism, parental love, and the desire for salvation. In this poem by Kazi Nazrul Islam (a poet who wrote both Muslim and Hindu religious poetry), we see the mother as patriotism and the force of revenge:

> How long will you be concealed
> Inside that clay image, O mother?
> Our paradise has been conquered
> By a tyrant, an evil monster.
> The divine children are being whipped
> Our young heroes are hanged daily
> All India has become a slaughter-house
> O goddess of catastrophe, why do you delay?...
> Who else but you can come to the battleground
> Holding your sword of lightning?...
> Save me, mother, save me.
> Only you should be at the front, with your sword in your hand.[41]

We also see the goddess as the daughter, and the devotee as her mother, in the *agamani* and *vijaya* songs traditionally sung during the Durga Puja holiday in West Bengal. In this poem by Jayanarayana Bandyopadhyaya, the goddess Shakti has been born on earth as the child Kalika, daughter of Menaka. Kalika has been married in an arranged marriage to the god Shiva Shankara, and Menaka is unhappy at the loss of her daughter, who is off living with her husband. She mourns in sad parental love:

> You have gone to the home of Shankara, on Kailash
> And you seem to have forgotten us.
> You do not miss me, your mother,
> To whom can I speak of this?
> I have spent my days crying
> For my child Kalika is far away from me.
> Look at me, I am weak, and unable to move,
> I am without Shakti, O wife of Shiva.[42]

Desire for salvation runs through the poetry of one of the most famous of the Shakta poets, Ramprasad Sen. He emphasizes the role of the goddess in saving the devotee from death, and bringing him or her to her paradise, or to a good rebirth. Kali is traditionally worshiped at the burning ground, amid the cremated bodies, to show her conquest of life and death:

> Because you love the burning ground
> I have made a burning ground of my heart
> So that you, dark goddess, can dance there forever.
> I have no other desire left, O Mother
> A funeral pyre is blazing in my heart.
> Ashes from corpses are all around me, my Mother
> In case you decide to come.
> Prasad prays, O Mother, at the hour of death
> Keep your devotee at your feet.
> Please come dancing with rhythmic steps
> Let me see you when my eyes are closed.[43]

These are some examples of emotion as shown in religious poetry. Emotion may also be seen in Bharat Natyam, or Indian dance, in which it is stylized in movement and facial expression, as well as in drama, where plays are structured so that specific moods are expressed in the performances.

NOTES

1. See *Yoga-Sutra* 1.2, in *The Yoga-Sutras of Patanjali, with the Exposition of Vyasa*, translated with commentary by Pandit Usharbudh Arya (Honesdale, Pa.: Himalayan International Institute of Yoga Science and Philosophy of the USA, 1986). All references to this work hereafter are to this edition.

2. Such waves are described in many Bengali biographies of *siddhas* or saints. For example, the Vaishnavite saint Vijayakrsna Gosvamin and his devotees were described as dancing in waves of *bhava*, which became a "sky-high typhoon." See his biography in June McDaniel, *The Madness of the Saints: Ecstatic Religion in Bengal* (Chicago: University of Chicago Press, 1989).

3. The following terms and definitions come from the *Samsad Bengali-English Dictionary*, ed. Sri Birendramohan Dasgupta (Calcutta: Sahitya Samsad, 1983).

4. In India, the dead are not buried but rather are burned at the *smasana* or burning ground. To compare the heart to a burning ground means that all earthly concerns have been left behind, as the corpse is left behind by the spirit, and a total devotion to the goddess has taken their place.

5. In the meditation system of *kundalini* yoga, the person is understood to have a body composed of energy (*shakti*), which exists invisibly within the physical body. This body is composed of seven centers (*chakras*) which are located along the spine and are foci of meditation. These centers are interpreted in different ways by different practitioners, but the heart center is usually associated with emotion, compassion and respiration.

6. We see a similar range of meanings to the term *raga* in the Japanese term *iro* (Chinese *se*). *Iro* means color and sensual pleasure, among other meanings, and includes such derivatives as *irogonomi* (sensuality, lust); *iroke* (coloring, shade, passion, romance); *irozome* (dyeing, dyed); and *irokoi* (love, sentiment). See the term *iro* in Andrew N. Nelson, *The Modern Reader's Japanese-English Character Dictionary* (Rutland, Vt.: Tuttle, 1974).

7. There is a special kind of madness in Bengal, colloquially known as "study-*pagal*," or study-insanity. Informants told me that too much thinking was dangerous, that it upset the balance of the mind, and could result in grave mental and physical illness. I was told quite firmly that I needed more emotion and less thought in order to be healthy. This is the "folk" view, which separates thought and emotion, and finds emotion to be especially important in women.

8. Visvanatha Kaviraja, *Sahityadarpana*, as cited by Jadunath Sinha. It may be noted that Visvanatha felt that philosophers were incapable of aesthetic enjoyment, as they are devoid of innate emotional dispositions. Dharmadatta echoes this opinion: persons devoid of emotional dispositions cannot appreciate art: they are "as good as a piece of wood, a wall, and a stone in the theatre hall." See Jadunath Sinha, *Indian Psychology*, vol. 2, *Emotion and Will* (Calcutta: J. Sinha Foundation, 1961), 166.

9. According to Dhananjaya's *Kavyasahityamimamsa*, erotic and comic emotions cause the blooming (*vikasa*) of consciousness; emotions of courage and wonder bring about the expansion (*vistara*) of consciousness; horror and fear cause the agitation

(*ksobha*) of consciousness, while fury and pathos produce the obstruction (*viksepa*) of consciousness. Ibid., 169.

10. The *Natyashastra* is usually dated not later than the sixth century C.E., but may have elements as old as the second century B.C.E. See Edwin Gerow, *Indian Poetics* (Wiesbaden: Otto Harassowitz, 1977), 245. Such divisions of basic emotions are also seen in Western thought, for example in Silvano Arieti's concepts of first-order emotions (protoemotions) and second- and third-order emotions. See his "Cognition and Feeling," in Arnold (1970). He includes tension, fear, appetite, satisfaction, and rage as first-order emotions.

11. Cited in Sinha, *Indian Psychology*, 2:175.

12. Ibid., 207.

13. *Rasa* theory also describes the causes and effects of emotion in great detail. Briefly, the dramatic emotions contain several aspects. The *vibhava* is the stimulus or cause of emotion (such as persons and events presented); the *anubhava* is the involuntary reaction or physical effect of emotion; and the *vyabhicharibhava* is the associated, temporary feeling or transitory state that may accompany the permanent emotion (*sthayibhava*).

14. According to Bharata, the moment of gustatory *rasa* occurs when the eater rests after the meal with a smile of satisfaction, appreciating the individual tastes merging into a general mood of happiness. This is similar to the aesthete appreciating the different aspects of a drama, which merge together.

15. See S. K. De, *Sanskrit Poetics as a Study of Aesthetics*, with notes by Edwin Gerow (Berkeley: University of California Press, 1963), 21.

16. This practice involves imitation of the *anubhavas*, or classical expressions of emotion, to generate passionate feelings within the practitioner, based on the emotions of the original Krishna devotees of Vrindavana. The goal of the practice is the generation of a new identity, that of a handmaiden of Krishna's consort Radha, composed of emotion (selfless love or *prema*). For a detailed analysis of this practice, see David L. Haberman, *Acting as a Way of Salvation: A Study of Raganuga Bhakti Sadhana* (Oxford: Oxford University Press, 1988)

17. O. B. L. Kapoor, *The Philosophy and Religion of Sri Caitanya* (Delhi: Munshiram Manoharlal, 1977), 210.

18. According to the *Govinda-lilamrta* of Krsnadas Kaviraj, the companions (*sakhis*) of Radha are "like flowers and buds of the vine of love which is Radha," and when Radha experiences the joy of Krishna's love, her companions' experience of that joy is one hundred times greater than her own. See Krsnadas Kaviraj (463 Gaurabda), *Govinda-lilamrta* (Navadvipa: Haribol Kutir, n.d.). Because they are detached from ego and desire, they are more open to deeper forms of love, and can experience these intensely. Thus, detachment (from ego and desire) paradoxically leads to intensity.

19. There are special meditations that lead to experience of these intense emotional states. In the *manjari sadhana*, the devotee identifies himself with one of Radha's handmaidens, while in the *gaur lila sadhana*, he identifies himself with the servants of Caitanya Mahaprabhu, a fifteenth-century Bengali saint believed by devotees to be a joint incarnation of Krishna and Radha. See McDaniel, *The Madness of the Saints*.

20. They differ in that the *sattvika bhavas* are composed only of *sattva guna*, and as such are purely spiritual emotions. There may be one or two at a time, or more than five may manifest themselves at once (in this case, the *sattvika bhavas* are said to be blazing or *uddipta*). While some of these may be caused by other events (such as sweating caused by heat or fear), the more of these bodily changes appear, the greater is the likelihood that the person is experiencing intense emotion.

21. In multiple personality disorder, the selves are highly segregated dissociative states, developed during childhood as a response to severe trauma, usually repeated abuse. Research indicates that for these personalities to develop, the trauma must occur relatively early, and that emotion and memory retrieval are bound to these dissociative states (thus protecting the child from a flood of painful memory and emotion). The most frequent "alter" personalities are frightened children, though the most common chief complaint is depression. See Frank Putnam, "The Switch Process in Multiple Personality Disorder and Other State-Change Disorders," *Dissociation* 1, 1 (March 1988), and B. G. Braun and R. G. Sachs, "The Development of Multiple Personality Disorder: Predisposing, Precipitating and Perpetuating Factors," in *Childhood Antecedents of Multiple Personality Disorder*, edited by R. P. Kluft (Washington D. C.: American Psychiatric Press, 1988).

22. See American Psychiatric Association *Diagnostic and Statistical Manual of Mental Disorders*, 3rd ed. (Washington D.C.: American Psychiatric Association, 1980).

23. *Yogasutra* 2.3. It is debated among scholars whether the sense of individuality is more a problem of ignorance (as personality and individuality are not ultimate truth) or of pride (too much focus on the illusion of individuality).

24. Mircea Eliade, *Yoga: Immortality and Freedom* (Princeton, N.J.: Princeton University Press, 1973), 42.

25. *Yogasutra* 1.2.

26. *Yogasutra* 1.12, Vyasa's commentary.

27. See my *Offering Flowers, Feeding Skulls: Popular Goddess Worship in West Bengal* (New York: Oxford University Press, 2004), for a discussion of the various forms of emotional worship of the goddess.

28. Deben Bhattacharya, trans., *Love Songs of Vidyapati* (New York: Grove Press, 1969), 72.

29. Edward C. Dimock, Jr., and Denise Levertov, trans., *In Praise of Krishna: Songs from the Bengali* (Garden City, N.Y.: Anchor Books, 1967), 31.

30. Ibid., 16. Krishna is called "dark moon" because of his dark skin.

31. Bhattacharya, *Love Songs of Vidyapat*, 52.

32. Dimock and Levertov, *In Praise of Krishna*, 23.

33. Bhattacharya, *Love Songs of Vidyapat*, 45.

34. Vidya Dehejia, *Antal and Her Path of Love: Poems of a Woman Saint from South India* (Delhi: Sri Satguru, 1990), 30.

35. Ibid., 60.

36. A. K. Ramanujan, trans., *Speaking of Siva* (Harmondsworth, England: Penguin Books, 1985), 138.

37. Ibid., 116.

38. Norman Cutler, *Songs of Experience: The Poetics of Tamil Devotion* (Bloomington: Indiana University Press, 1987), 163.

39. Ramanujan, *Speaking of Siva*, 89.

40. Cutler, *Songs of Experience*, 168–69.

41. Razaul Karim Talukdar, *Nazrul—The Gift of the Century* (Dhaka: Manam, 1994), 46–47. Rephrased.

42. Dasgupta, Sasibhusan. Bharater sakti-sadhana o sakta sahitya. Calcutta: Sahitya Samsad, 1393 BS (local dating, equivalent to our 1985),, 88, from the Bengali. We should note that there is a pun here—the word *shakti* means girl or woman, but also power. To be without *shakti* is to be without power or ability to act.

43. Ramprasad Sen, *Ramprasadi sangit* (Calcutta: Rajendra Library, n.d.), 46, from the Bengali.

BIBLIOGRAPHY

American Psychiatric Association. *Diagnostic and Statistical Manual of Mental Disorders.* 3rd ed. Washington, D.C.: American Psychiatric Association, 1980.

Arnold, Magda B., ed. *Feelings and Emotions: The Loyola Symposium.* New York: Academic Press, 1970.

Arya, Pandit Usharbudh, trans. *The Yoga-Sutras of Patanjali, with the Exposition of Vyasa.* Honesdale, Pa.: Himalayan International Institute of Yoga Science and Philosophy of the USA, 1986.

Braun, B. G., and R. G. Sachs. "The Development of Multiple Personality Disorder: Predisposing, Precipitating and Perpetuating Factors." In *Childhood Antecedents of Multiple Personality Disorder,* edited by R. P. Kluft. Washington D. C.: American Psychiatric Press. 1988, 37-64.

Dasgupta, Sri Birendramohan. *Samsad Bengali-English Dictionary.* Calcutta: Sahitya Samsad, 1983.

De, S. K. *Sanskrit Poetics as a Study of Aesthetics.* With notes by Edwin Gerow. Berkeley: University of California Press, 1963.

Eliade, Mircea. *Yoga: Immortality and Freedom* Princeton, N.J.: Princeton University Press, 1974.

Gerow, Edwin. *Indian Poetics.* Wiesbaden: Otto Harassowitz, 1977.

Haberman, David L. *Acting as a Way of Salvation: A Study of Raganuga Bhakti Sadhana.* Oxford: Oxford University Press, 1988.

Kapoor, O. B. L. *The Philosophy and Religion of Sri Caitanya.* Delhi: Munshiram Manoharlal, 1977.

Kaviraj, Krsnadas (463 Gaurabda). *Govinda-lilamrta.* Navadvipa: Haribol Kutir.

Lynch, Owen, ed. *Divine Passions: The Social Construction of Emotion in India.* Berkeley: University of California Press, 1990.

Marriott, McKim. "Constructing an Indian Ethnosociology." In *India through Hindu Categories,* edited by McKim Marriott. London: Sage, 1990.

McDaniel, June. *The Madness of the Saints*: Ecstatic Religion in Bengal. Chicago: University of Chicago Press, 1989.

Nelson, Andrew N. *The Modern Reader's Japanese-English Character Dictionary.* Rutland, Vt.: Tuttle, 1974.

Putnam, Frank. "The Switch Process in Multiple Personality Disorder and Other State-Change Disorders." In *Dissociation* 1 (March 1988): 24–32.

Siegel, Lee. *Fires of Love, Waters of Peace: Passion and Renunciation in Indian Culture.* Honolulu: University of Hawai'i Press, 1983.

Sinha, Jadunath. *Indian Psychology.* Vol. 2. *Emotion and Will.* Calcutta: J. Sinha Foundation, 1961.

Solomon, Robert. *The Passions.* Garden City, N.Y.: Doubleday, 1976.

CHAPTER 4

JAPANESE RELIGIONS

GARY L. EBERSOLE

THE topic of emotions in Japanese religions is a complicated one. Multiple religious traditions, each with its own privileged set of emotions or spiritual states, have taken root in the Japanese archipelago. These traditions include Shinto, Buddhism, Taoism, Confucianism, Christianity, and numerous so-called new religions from the nineteenth and twentieth centuries. In addition, the historical record in Japan covers over thirteen hundred years, during which tremendous changes in these religions occurred, not least in terms of the emotional states that were considered to be desirable and auspicious or undesirable and inauspicious.

Having said this, in some respects it would be misleading to treat the topic of emotion and religion in Japan serially, religion by religion. To do so would run the risk of suggesting that a given religion, such as Buddhism, was of a piece over time. Moreover, it would largely ignore the fact that over the centuries most Japanese have not identified with (or "belonged to") any single religion. Rather, aspects of multiple traditions were incorporated into their religious lives and value systems. This situation has led many scholars to speak of "Japanese religion" in the singular.[1] This term, though, suggests a certain homogeneity, which distracts due attention from significant differences among people, even as it ignores the anachronism in labeling religious phenomena "Japanese" before a national entity as such existed. To be sure, some Japanese have identified exclusively with one religion or sect (e.g., Nichiren Buddhism), as did some priests or nuns, especially in terms of ordination practices. However, most persons participated in diverse ritual practices and incorporated values identified primarily with more than one religious tradition. Rather than search for unique and essential emotions in discreet religions, such as Shinto, Buddhism, or Confucianism, I will focus attention on the shifting relative importance of selected emotional expressions or states for individuals enmeshed in specific social fields at specific moments in time.

Access to information concerning emotions in centuries past is largely through textual sources, although some pictorial and sculptural evidence is also available. The historian of religions who seeks to recover religious emotions from the past faces the inevitable problems that come with textual studies, along with some additional ones. These problems include the uneven number of written sources that are available for different periods of time and for individuals from different social levels, the uneven quality and reliability of specific documents, and questions as to how representative specific documents are of a religious group. In a recent study, *Bereavement and Consolation: Testimonies from Tokugawa Japan*, the historian Harold Bolitho had to grapple with these problems as he sought to understand how Japanese in the early modern period dealt emotionally with the deaths of persons close to them. As he notes for the Tokugawa period (1600–1864):

> in the written record bereavement and consolation necessarily remain elusive, their traces fugitive, and evidence of them oblique, amorphous, fragmentary, ambiguous—and sometimes mendacious. Brought under the historian's microscope, such materials can all too easily turn to dust.[2]

Even the three first-person accounts Bolitho has uncovered must be used with care, not least because they are so exceptional for the time period in speaking explicitly about the grief of the authors. Bolitho's position on the historical value of these documents is ambivalent and, perhaps, ultimately untenable. On the one hand, he suggests that the unusual nature of these documents means that they "cannot carry much weight." On the other hand, he suggests that "in the absence of anything else, these rare glimpses into the world of private sorrow are at least suggestive, on both an academic and visceral level."[3]

Bolitho's assumption that there is in fact such a thing as a "world of private sorrow" is problematic for several reasons. First, like too many scholars, he begins to go down a slippery slope by privileging individual and private emotions as real and authentic, whereas public and collective displays of emotion are suspect because they can be "faked" or performed for public consumption. This is then coupled with his unexamined assumption that grief is a universal emotional response to death, yielding the erroneous belief that his visceral response to the account of the death of a loved one must be the same as that of others. As a result of this circuitous reasoning, Bolitho can claim that the three admittedly exceptional accounts he has translated actually provide precious insight into the real emotional lives of the Japanese in the Tokugawa period—which, *voilà*, are found to be similar, if not identical, to our own!

The problems with a position such as this should be obvious. It ignores the extensive work on *habitus* by Pierre Bourdieu and others, which has demonstrated how social and cultural values are literally incorporated by individuals. However, societies do not replicate themselves perfectly; they are not static. In the realm of emotional displays and affect, too, changes happen or are effected by conscious activities. For instance, it is well known that some moral emotions, such as shame and embarrassment, are learned. Mothers and fathers around the world morally instruct their children by molding their emotions through admonitions such as "You should be embarrassed" or "You should be ashamed of yourself." It is my contention that, rather than attempting to recover private interior emotions, historians should focus their attention on the changing emotional display rules of different groups within a society, taking into full consideration issues of gender, class, age, and occupation. We should investigate how and why changes in emotional expression take place, as well as who is involved in the discourse on emotions at any given time and who the target audience for this discourse is.

The search for pure unadulterated emotions in the past is a vexed exercise doomed to failure. Rather than pursue such a task, in this essay I will focus on selected textual representations of emotions in religious texts from different historical periods in Japan. This will enable us to discern something about what emotions and emotional displays were valued either positively or negatively by a religious community at a given time and why. To adopt and adapt Clifford Geertz's terms, religious discourse on emotions often seeks to provide models for emulation, even as some texts mirror the social reality of the time by providing models of both appropriate and inappropriate emotional displays. The search for an essential religious feeling à la Rudolph Otto is also futile, since religious emotions are almost always blended with other social sentiments. For instance, the religious ritual aspects of expressions of grief, love, and longing for a deceased emperor or empress, understood to be a *kami* (deity) in human form, cannot be separated from the important sociopolitical roles such emotional displays played within the milieu of the court.[4] With these caveats, let me now turn to a few selected examples of the textual representation of emotions and emotional displays in Japan over the centuries.

ANCIENT JAPAN (EIGHTH CENTURY C.E.)

The primary texts for any study of religious emotions in ancient Japan are the *Kojiki* (712), the *Nihon shoki* (720), and the *Man'yōshū* (ca. 780)—all texts coming out of the imperial court, although some oral traditions are also preserved therein. In the oldest of these texts, the *Kojiki*, very few emotions are spoken of explicitly. In the myths, however, deities (*kami*) are sometimes depicted as becoming enraged, which leads them to pronounce curses, issue divine commands, or bring pestilence and suffering to the land. However, it is the affective response of humans to this sort of overwhelming power that bears our attention here. The terms used to describe the feeling of individuals confronted by such powerful deities center on the verb *kashikoeru* (*osoreru* in modern Japanese)—to be filled with awe, dread, or fear. Donald Philippi translates these emotion terms as "fearful reverence." Not surprisingly, in the human realm the same or similar terms are used to describe the proper attitude of subjects before the person of the emperor. In several cases, this feeling response leads individuals to build a shrine and to initiate ritual offerings and prayers in order to pacify the deity; in other cases, a daughter or daughters are presented to the deity or the emperor.

In general, though, in the *Kojiki* emotions are usually not explicitly pointed to as the causal source of action. Two emotions, however, are explicitly presented as motivating actors–shame and jealousy. Here I will limit my focus to shame. In the *Kojiki*, characters are motivated to act in dramatic ways in response to the shame felt when they are observed in a polluted state or otherwise find their public personas sullied. For instance, when the spouse of the *kami* Izanami breaks a taboo and views her in the land of the dead, Izanami is overcome with shame. This quickly turns into anger and provokes a curse, which brings mortality into the human world.[5] In other tales, when a woman is rejected by a man because of her looks, she also is shamed, sometimes into committing suicide. Similarly, women whose husbands take up with other females are both shamed and jealous[6] It is worth noting that both shame and jealousy are social emotions that are provoked when one's public image is compromised in some way. That is, they both are a response to a perceived broach of proper social relations in some way.

The poetic anthology the *Man'yōshū* (hereafter MYS) is filled with religious and other emotional expressions. In no case, though, should we fall into the trap of assuming that the poems re-present spontaneous expressions of emotions, even though traditional Japanese aesthetics has argued this to be the case. In a famous passage in the preface to the *Kokinshū,* the first imperial anthology of Japanese *waka* (thirty-one-syllable poems), Ki no Tsurayuki (884–946) wrote:

> The poetry of Japan has its roots in the human heart and flourishes in the countless leaves of words. Because human beings possess interests of so many kinds, it is in poetry that they give expression to the meditations of their hearts in terms of the sights appearing before their eyes and the sounds coming to their ears. Hearing the warbler sing among the blossoms and the frog in his fresh waters—is there any living being not given to song? It is poetry which, without exertion, moves heaven and earth, stirs the feelings of gods and spirits invisible to the eye, softens the relations between men and women, calms the hearts of fierce warriors.[7]

The conceit here that song or poetry is a spontaneous affective response to things and happenings in the world is based on earlier Chinese aesthetic theories. In fact, crafting a poem, be it orally or in written form, is precisely that—a craft, which is learned and honed through practice. Having said this, poems such as the following (MYS 1:32–33) are nevertheless useful documents for historians of religions and emotionology, for they present evidence of what was considered to be the appropriate affective (and verbal) display of a sensitive and cultivated person on viewing ruins of a bygone era—in this case, the poet Takechi Furuhito, sorrowing on the ruined walls of the capital at Ōmi (Sasanami is an older poetical referent for it):

inishie no hito ni	Am I one of the ancients?
ware are ya	Gazing on the ancient
Sasanami no	capital at Sasanami
furuki miyako o	by the rippling waves,
mireba kanashiki	I am filled with sorrow.
Sasanami no	The hearts of the gods
kunitsu mikami no	of the land of Sasanami
ura sabite	have withered with grief;
aretaru miyako	gazing on the ruined capital
mireba kanashimo	I am filled with sorrow.[8]

The religio-aesthetic sentiment glossed here as "filled with sorrow" is *kanashiki/kanashimo*. This emotional response to the sight of the ruined capital is repeatedly upheld as the appropriate response to the ravages of time and the ephemeral nature of human creations. This privileged affective response is modeled on Chinese precedents. It is impossible from this temporal distance to know whether this poet actually felt this emotion or not. What is clear is that in ancient Japan there was a certain cultural capital to be gained by expressing this form of sadness before ruins. That is, this form of sadness was not a private emotion but a public one, which linked one with the gods and with the poets and philosophers of old. As a physical remainder/reminder of the past, ruins function as *a katami*, a physical object marking both absence and presence. Whereas a rude peasant farmer might see the rubble of ruins only as an impediment to his work in the field, the person of sensibility finds his heart-mind (*kokoro*) moved by the ruins in a way that plumbs their deep significance. *Kanashimo*, then, has social, religious, and moral connotations akin to those of *mono no aware* in the Heian period (794–1185), as we will see later.

Ancient Japanese poets did not always have to name an emotion in order to convey it to readers or auditors, though. Students of religion have long noted that even common ritual acts (e.g., assuming the posture of prayer) can evoke a requisite emotion or an emotionally poised state in the actor. Yet we have paid less attention to the stylized ways people engage with specific items of material culture and emotionally charged places. In the following verse (MYS 2:216), for instance, the poet conjures up a powerful emotional scene by simply sketching his visual encounter with a household object that had belonged to his recently deceased wife:

ie ni kite	Coming home,
waga ya o mireba	when I looked in the house,
tamadoko no	on the haunted floor,
hoka ni mukikeri	facing me—
tsuma ga komakura	my wife's wooden pillow.[9]

In ancient and medieval Japan, ordinary objects, places, or even a child connected to a deceased individual could serve to ritually recall a dead person. Known as *katami* (literally "to see the form [of the deceased]"), when encountered, such memory-laden things or sites had the power to startle the living by making the absent other feel present. Here the poet is caught up short, as it were, by the shock of recognition of absence and presence when his eyes fall on his wife's night pillow. Like the ruins in the poem quoted earlier, this object collapses the distance between past and present through the immediacy of the poet's affective response.

Our own distance from this cultural world may be measured by the typical response today to a widow who continues to speak to her deceased husband. We are embarrassed by the behavior and write it off as a symptom of incipient Alzheimer's disease. In ancient and medieval Japan, though, such encounters with the spirit of a deceased loved one were common and were accepted as real visions. The dead were truly conjured up. Anthropologists and historians of religions, though, have recognized that embedding in objects and places associated with the deceased, emotional responses to death, which are then used to conjure up an affectively charged vision-memory of the deceased, is a fairly widespread phenomenon in the religions of the world.[10]

The ritual funeral laments (*banka*) of the *Man'yōshū* are filled with the verbal expressions of numerous emotions—regret, guilt, love and longing, loneliness, and grief to name but a few. The fact that some poems are almost identical suggests that these were stylized expressions of emotion, not spontaneous outpourings. Oral performative laments circulated among the people and were then adapted to specific circumstances. Ritual laments present socially expected emotions. Thus, *banka* enable us to glimpse the efforts of members of the court to deal with death socially—not only in individual emotional terms. Their affective responses to death were shaped and styled by the rituals and protocols of the court society.[11]

The *Man'yōshū* contains clear evidence of the increasing role Buddhism came to play in shaping the responses to death. For instance, the following remarkable long prose and poetic piece (MYS 5:793–99) traces the arc of the emotional experiences of the poet from the time he first learned of his wife's death to some time later. I will cite this passage in full before offering a brief analysis of it.

> *Poem by Lord Ōtomo Tabito, Commander of the Dazaifu, in Response to the Dreadful News*
>
> My brush is unable to express all I wish to say—the grief of ancient and modern alike.
>
> | yo no naka wa | When I realize |
> | munashiki mono to | that the world |
> | shiru tokishi | is an empty thing, |
> | iyoyo masu masu | more and more, evermore, |
> | kanashi karikeri | I am filled with sadness.[12] |

The sixth month, twenty-third day, of the fifth year of Jinki [728].

[794] Thus have I heard: that the birth and death of the four modes of life are comparable to the emptiness of all dreams, that the course of life through the three realms is like the endless spin of a cycle. Thus even the Elder Vimalakirti suffered the afflictions of pestilence in his priestly chamber, and even the great Sakyamuni could not stay the agonies of extinction as he sat in the sal forest. Who in the three thousand worlds has ever been able to escape from the intent clutch of darkness?

Day and night scramble away like a pair of racing rats. Life is the zip of a bird across the eyes—it can fly away in a single morning. The elements devour each other like four wrestling snakes. Man's existence is no more than the flash of a white steed across the evening as glimpsed through a crevice in a wall. Oh how painful it is! The maiden's crimson face is gone forever with the woman's three duties to obey, and young white flesh is destroyed forever with the wife's four virtues. Who ever expects the vows of husband and wife, that they shall be together until old age, to be betrayed, that one of them should be robbed of his mate halfway down the road of life, like a bird in solitary flight? To no purpose were screens set up around the Orchid Chamber, our nuptial suite—the gut-wrenching sorrow grows ever more painful. In vain was the bright mirror hung above her pillow—tears gather in a falling stream, enough to dye bamboo. Once the gate to the Underworld is shut, there is no way for us to meet again. Oh how sad it is!

> Waves on the river of love already collapsed,
> and agony never to thicken again over the sea of pain;
> I have always despised this tainted earth,
> my constant wish to entrust my life to the Pure Land beyond.

A Japanese Lament [Banka]

ōkimi no	She came yearning after me,
tō no mikado to	like a child in tears,
shiranui	to the land of Tsukushi—
Tsukushi no kuni ni	Tsukushi of the white weaving—
naku ko nasu	to our Lord's distant Kyushu Court.
shitai komashite	But before she could even
iki dani mo	catch her breath,
imada yasumezu	though months and years

toshi tsuki mo	have yet to pass—
imada aranuba	so suddenly it shocks
kokoro yumo	my very heart—
omowanu aida ni	she has collapsed,
uchinabiki	swaying, on her death bed.
koyashi nure	I do not know what to say,
iwamu sube	what to do.
semu sube shira ni	I do not know how to ask
iwaki o mo	the rocks and trees!
toi sake shirazu	If she had been at home,
ie naraba	at least I would have
katachi wa aramu o	her mortal form.
urameshiki	How cruel that my revered wife—
imo no mikoto no	what could she
are o ba mo	intend of me?—
ikani seyo yo ka	should betray the emotions
niotori no	we felt
futari narabinu	when we spoke to each other,
katarai shi	standing side by side
kokoro somukite	like a pair of grebes,
ie zakari imasu	and desert our home!
hanka	Envoys
[795] ie ni yukite	What would it avail me
ikani ka agasemu	to return home?
makura zuku	The marriage room
tsumaya zabushiku	where our pillows lie together
omoho yubeshi mo	will surely bring me desolation.
[796] hashikiyoshi	Helplessness of the heart:
kaku nomi kara ni	how my woman—
shitai koshi	oh my beloved!—
imo ga kokoro no	came yearning after me,
sube mo subenasa	and only for this!
[797] kuyashi kamo	How I regret it!
kaku shiramaseba	If only I had known
ao ni yoshi	it would come to this,

kunuchi kotogoto	I would have shown her every corner
misemashi mono o	of this beautiful land.
[798] imo ga mishi	The sandalwood blossoms
afuchi no hana wa	my wife once gazed upon
chiri nubeshi	seem to fall and scatter,
waga naku namida	while the tears I weep
imada inaku ni	have yet to dry.
[799] Ōno-yama	Mists rise and spread
kiri tachiwataru	over Ōno Mountain;
waga naku	mists rise and spread
okiso no kaze ni	on the wind
kiri tachiwataru	of my cries and sighs.

The seventh month, twenty-first day, of the fifth year of Jingi. Presented by Yamanoue Okura, the Governor of Chikuzen.[13]

It is impossible to deal here with all of the technical issues in this remarkable document; nor will we be able to address the various issues of dispute among scholars. For immediate purposes, it is enough to note several things. First, there is the composite nature of this document, which is multi-"authored." Second, it comes out of a period of secondary orality (i.e., a time when oral performative forms still survived alongside literacy). The beginning section includes poems and prose passages composed by Ōtomo Tabito on the death of his wife. The verses that follow make up a Japanese oral funeral lament (*banka*), apparently offered by a surrogate on behalf of the widower, Tabito.[14] *Banka* were ritual laments orally performed at the burial site or other locations associated with the deceased. *Banka* are often in the long verse form (*chōka*), as here, together with "envoys" or shorter verses that encapsulate the emotions already expressed. Third, although we do not know how these separate pieces were brought together, there is an integrity to the whole, which traces the arc of the poet's shifting emotions in the wake of his wife's death.

Although we do not have direct access to the poet's inner feelings, as historians we need not lament this fact. Rather, we should take this composite document for what it is—an important record of how emotions were publicly expressed in stylized form after the death of a loved one in the elite sector of Japanese society in the early eighth century. Oral poems, prose writings such as these, and *banka* committed to writing were all intended for public consumption. That does not mean that the emotions expressed therein are inauthentic or "false." Rather, in this prose and poetry sequence, we can glimpse something of the ways religious teachings, public rituals, and poetic exchanges all were used in an effort to shape and reshape emotions. Documents such as this provide valuable information about how the ancient Japanese sought to deal with a traumatic event. Corresponding with friends was one way of coping; another was expressing oneself though poetry. In stylized poetic expressions, a poet could even express his or her anger at the deceased ("How cruel that my revered wife...should betray the emotions we felt...and desert our home"), before dissolving his grief into nature. We should take care not generalize from the emotional expressions here to claim that all ancient Japanese responded to death in this manner. The elite provenance of the documents will not bear such a claim. Nor should we try to fit the affective responses depicted here into the modern psychological construction of a universal "grieving process."

Medieval Japan (Ninth to Sixteenth Centuries)

Our sources for the study of emotion in Japanese religions increase greatly in number and kind in the medieval period. In addition to *waka* poetry, we have diaries, travel journals, poetry and prose notebooks, epics, war tales, folk tales and folk songs, religious didactic works, plays, and works of narrative fiction, to name but a few. Here we will have to be very selective, limiting ourselves to only a few examples, although an effort will be made to pay attention to issues of class, gender, and occupational differences.

In the religio-aesthetic realm of the elite, there are a large number of emotion terms that would bear attention, but here we will confine ourselves to *mono no aware* and *sabi*. Both terms refer to an emotion evoked by a keen awareness and religio-aesthetic appreciation of the essential nature of the phenomenal world (*yo no naka*). The heavy influence of Mahayana Buddhist thought is evident here. The doctrine of nondualism was pushed to its logical extreme in Japan through the claims that *samsara* (this world of delusion) is nirvana and that buddhahood was to be realized in this very body (*sokushin jōbutsu*). As a result, many Japanese Buddhists came to see the natural world as a soteriological locus.[15] However, whereas Theravada Buddhism (or, at least, a popular image of it) stresses the goal of achieving a state of emotional equanimity or dispassion, epitomized by the figure of Gautama seated in meditation under the bodhi tree, medieval Japanese Buddhist poets sought to cultivate specific emotional states deigned to be proper and spiritually efficacious emotional responses to the things of the world. One of the best known statements on *mono no aware*—the power of the phenomenal world to move us emotionally by revealing the emptiness at its core—is found in the musings of a poet-priest, Kenkō (ca. 1283–1350), in *Tsurezuregusa* (Essays in Idleness). Kenkō suggests that human mortality is a blessing, rather than something to be lamented, precisely because it is the source of our religio-aesthetic sensibilities:

"If man were never to fade away like the dews of Adashino, never to vanish like the smoke over Toribeyama, but lingered on forever in the world, how things would lose their power to move us [*mono no aware mo nakaran*]! The most precious thing in life is its uncertainty."[16]

The religio-aesthetic sensibility of the cultural elite of medieval Japan was an achieved state, not a "natural" one. One had to work hard to achieve specific carefully controlled and modulated affective responses to things, events, the seasonal cycle, and so on. Often this involved realizing an at-oneness of one's emotional/spiritual state with the essence (*hon'i*) of a place and time. Let us take the feeling of loneliness as an example. In and of itself, loneliness (*sabishisa*) is not a religio-aesthetic emotion, yet as the following verses illustrate, it becomes such when an individual's emotion is identified with—and, thus, dissolved into—the essence of the phenomenal world. The first verse (*Goshūishū* 4:333) is by the priest Ryōzan (fl. 1040–1070):

sabishisa ni	When, in loneliness,
yado o tachiidete	I step outside my hut
nagamureba	and gaze around,
izuku mo onaji	it's the same everywhere...
aki no yūgure	autumn dusk.

A modern reader might be inclined to read this verse as an expression of deepening loneliness and despair,[17] but to do so would be to carry a modern sensibility into the medieval Japanese Buddhist world of meaning and religio-aesthetic practice. Identifying one's own emotional state with the essential nature of the world is not a negative act but a liberating one. The following *waka* from the *Sankashū* (Anthology of Mountain Poems) by the well-known poet-priest Saigyō (1118–1190) strikes a similar note, but more explicitly:

tou hito mo	Without the loneliness
omoitaetaru	of my mountain village,
yamazato no	where even passers by
sabishisa nakuba	are no longer expected,
sumiukaramashi[18]	life would be hard.

Ego-centered loneliness is, thus, transformed by these Buddhist poet-priests into a religiously efficacious state through its identification with, or dissolution into, the affective essence of the poetic *topoi* "autumn dusk" and "isolated mountain village."

Another often-cited poem (*Shinkokinwakashū* 4:361) by the poet-priest Jakuren (d. 1202) further locates *sabishisa* as the essence of autumn dusk in the deep mountains:

sabishisa wa	Loneliness
sono iro to shi mo	becomes the essential color
nakarikeri	of an inexplicable beauty...
maki tatsu yama no	autumn dusk falling
aki no yūgure[19]	on hemlock-covered mountains.

The emotion of loneliness (*sabishisha*) is aurally related to the verb *sabitaru*—to rust, decay, weather, or age. In medieval Japan, *sabi* became an important aesthetic term that pointed to the essential beauty of weathered objects, barren trees, and other things that showed the effects of time and age. Closely identified with Fujiwara no Shunzei and others, who cultivated a sense of quiet desolation in meditative practice, *sabi* also resonated with certain forms of Chinese verse and with the Taoist ideal of the hermit hidden in the deep mountains.

In the late seventeenth century, Matsuo Bashō, a master of *haikai* linked verse, revived widespread interest in *sabi*. One of his best known verses epitomizing *sabi* incorporates a popular subject in Chinese charcoal ink painting—crows perching on leafless trees in autumn. The verse thus invokes visual and aural elements. It reads:

kareeda ni	On barren branches
karasu no tomarikeri	crows settle down—
aki no kure	autumn dusk.

In this verse, Bashō participated in the ongoing process of distilling the religio-aesthetic emotional essence (*hon'i*) of the poetic *topos* "dusk in autumn." Originality as such was less a value in this tradition than was recreating a deeper sense of the religio-aesthetic essence of a place (*utamakura*). The true measure of one's emotional response, then, was its communion with that of other feeling men and women in previous times. Without this sort of association with earlier examples of valorized emotional expressions, individual feelings were suspect. Buddhist epistemology had long sought to undermine the faith of human beings in ordinary sensory perceptions, which could trap one in the world of illusion. In Japan, though, while individual affect was potentially idiosyncratic, certain emotional responses to the phenomenal world, such as *mono no aware*, came to be held to have salvific significance.

The sympathetic identification with the feelings of others was broadly valorized in the medieval period. Indeed, in an important but little recognized sense, this is an essential part of the definition of a *bodhisattva*, a *compassionate* being who has attained enlightenment but deigns to remain in the phenomenal world to assist all sentient beings to attain the same goal. The following description of an itinerant priest of the Lotus Sect, posthumously recognized to have been a *bodhisattva* in human form, is a typical instance of how compassion was viewed. It is from a tale in the twelfth-century collection *Konjaku monogatari-shū*:

At a time now past, there was a sutra chanter named Shunchū. He chanted the Lotus Sutra day and night. He had no fixed home but drifted from place to place, doing nothing but read[ing] aloud the sutra. His heart was full of compassion; when he witnessed another's suffering, he felt it as his suffering, and when he witnessed another's joy, he felt it as his own happiness.[20]

Innumerable tales from medieval Japan deal with a priest or some other person visiting a site associated with some notable person from the past. There the traveler recalls the verses and tale associated with the site, which usually moves him to compose a new poem. In many cases, the spirit of the deceased person is conjured up and a conversation between the visitor and the specter takes place. This scenario is found in numerous literary genres, but it became especially popular on the nō stage. A typical example is the play *Eguchi* by the famous playwright/actor Zeami (1363–1443).[21] The play builds on a venerable type of Buddhist tale in which a prostitute (later revealed to have been a *bodhisattva* in human form) lectures or otherwise enlightens an itinerant priest. In this case, Zeami built his play around numerous accounts of a famous encounter and a poetic exchange between the poet-priest Saigyō and an *asobi*. Originally, asobi were gypsy-like female dancers and singers associated with prostitution; by the medieval period, many of these outcaste women had taken on the role of lay nuns. They traveled on rivers and highways, performing popular songs (*imayō*), many of which conveyed Buddhist teachings.

In the nō play, a Buddhist monk visits the site of Saigyō's encounter with the *asobi*.[22] When he recites Saigyō's verse offered to the woman, a female figure suddenly appears and engages the monk in conversation. Together they recite the following poetic exchange:

Saigyō:

yo no naka o	It's hard to despise
itou made koso	the whole world
katakarame	as a borrowed lodging,
kari no yadori o	but that you should begrudge me
oshimu kimi kana	even one night's lodging!

asobi:

ie o izuru	Because I heard you were someone
hito to shi kikeba	who had left the household life,
kari no yado	my only thought was to warn you:
kokoro tonu na to	don't let your mind dwell
omou bakari zo	on this borrowed lodging![23]

The interest inherent is this exchange pivots on the double entendre of *kari no yado*. Literally, this means "a borrowed" or "temporary lodging," but the phrase was also widely used metaphorically in Buddhist discourse to refer to the human body. In the play, the *asobi*'s ghost claims to be "ashamed" when she recalls Saigyō's sexually suggestive language. Let us recall that this is the same emotion Izanami felt when her spouse, Izanagi, viewed her rotting body in the land of the dead. In both cases, the emotion of shame is produced in a character when someone views her in a way that does not match her own sense of identity or her public self-presentation. Note, though, that in the *Kojiki* and *Nihonshoki* myth, Izanami is ashamed when her true form is seen; in *Eguchi*, the reverse is the case. Initially Saigyō sees only the woman's temporary bodily form (*kari no yado*) as an *asobi*, rather than her real form as the *bodhisattva* Fugen. We may assume that actual *asobi* regularly faced the same problem: often people recognized *asobis'* sexual role but not their religious one.

Eguchi ends with the *asobi*'s true identity revealed. As Fugen flies westward into the clouds on a white elephant, the chorus reports her "leaving behind ... gratitude and joy" in all who had witnessed this revelatory moment. Medieval Japanese Buddhist tales frequently suggested that one's emotions were the result of one's perspective or, to put this another way, one's insight or lack thereof. Earlier I suggested that numerous ritual practices (e.g., *shikan* meditation, the composition/recitation of poetry, and the performance of *imayō*) were designed to help one to see through the superficial or phenomenal level of things to the essential and true nature of the world. When this insight was achieved, it produced the emotional sense of *aware*. Thus, *mono no aware* is the inherent and potential evocative power inherent in all things in the phenomenal world. The emotional response *aware! aware!* marks one's realization and an emotional at-oneness with the world (the *dharmakaya*) and all others who have previously had the same emotional response.

In more popular narratives and on the nō and kabuki stage, this change in one's emotional state/state of consciousness is embodied, as in *Eguchi*, in characters who exchange bodies at will, or, as in many Western sentimental novels, a character's true identity is finally revealed. For instance, in *zangemono*, a Buddhist genre Margaret Childs has called "revelatory tales," characters (male and female) often recount how they came to take the tonsure and "plant the seed of enlightenment."[24] A recurring theme in *Shichinin no bikuni* (Seven Itinerant Lay Nuns) is: "From times long past until today, sorrow has been a source of religious inspiration and a seed that will blossom in future lifetimes."[25] The natural state of women, it is noted, is to live lives filled with pain and suffering, yet these can be the source of ultimate salvation. The tragic deaths of a husband and only child, for instance, are declared to have been all for the best, since it led the then-grieving woman to take the tonsure. Indeed, we are told that both the husband and child had actually been temporary forms taken on by a compassionate *bodhisattva* in order to assist the woman in her own path to salvation. Thus, the emotions experienced by the wife/mother within the family were caused by mis-recognition, much like a person who feels fear when mistaking a rope on the ground for a snake. In *zangemono*, people do not think or reason their way to religious insight; rather, they *feel* their way through. In an almost alchemical process, base emotions are transmuted into soteriologically valuable ones. And not only are the ordinary emotional responses to the vicissitudes of life of the main character transmuted into gratitude and joy but also those listening to or reading the tale are portrayed as being so moved.[26]

Even these few examples of the representation of emotions in medieval texts suggest that historians of religions have paid insufficient attention to the ways religious communities seek to reform emotional responses to the world and the vicissitudes of life. A religious orientation to the world involves the achievement and maintenance of a certain affective disposition. To mention just one example, not unlike the lay Buddhist nun above, evangelical Christians work together to accept the death of a loved one by holding that God must have had a reason for taking this person, who is now in a better place. Consolation, like forgiveness, is not an intellectual achievement but an emotional one. Moreover, in both cases, the sense of the involvement of a greater power, a figure who has one's long-term interests in mind, is crucial. As we shall see below, the need to transform one's emotional response to life's difficulties is a common refrain in the so-called new religions (*shinshūkyō*) in modern Japan.

Not all emotions were valorized as spiritually efficacious in medieval Japan, of course. Many emotions were explicitly pointed to as detrimental to one's progress on the Buddhist path, including jealousy, avarice, and lust, to name a few. A tale in *Konjaku monogatari-shū* (20:35), for instance, describes an incident in the sometimes vicious politics of prestige within Buddhist ecclesiastical circles. A monk, motivated to outrageous behavior out of jealousy of another priest, is karmicly punished in this lifetime by a fall from grace and power and by contacting leprosy.[27] Numerous tales about Ōno no Komachi, the famous *Man'yōshū* female poet and lover, circulated in the medieval period, all describing how lust and other strong emotions led to her spirit being trapped in this world. The nō play *Sotoba no Komachi* famously deals with the negative karmic consequences of passionate emotion.

Having said this, it is important to repeat that not all emotions were negatively judged, nor was the practice of poetry widely condemned. Indeed, in the medieval period, the practice of poetry (*kadō* or *uta no michi*), along with many other arts, came to be considered a religious discipline (*michi* or *dō*). The religio-aesthetic practice of poetry could aid in the practitioners' search for enlightenment and salvation. In some cases, poetic composition and/or recitation was incorporated into Buddhist meditative practices; in other cases, for example, *renga* (linked verse), the composition of poetry as a social or collective ritual itself was considered to be religiously efficacious.

Two examples must suffice to suggest something of the practice of diverse arts as ritually and spiritually efficacious. Fujiwara no Shunzei (1114–1204) combined *waka* composition with a form of Tendai Buddhist meditation called *shikan*. For his part, the retired emperor Go-Shirakawa (1127–1192) scandalized some members of the court when he apprenticed himself to an *asobi*, an elderly female performer of popular Buddhist songs (*imayō*) and member of a marginalized social group. Go-Shirakawa performed *imayō* as part of his religious visionary practice, sometimes holding all-night vigils. He also believed that *imayō* performance was a means to attaining one's wishes and power.[28] A key aspect of the ritual practices of both of these men involved the recitation or singing of verses, the meditational concentration of mind, and reducing other sensory stimuli in order to evoke a powerful emotional state and tears. In broad terms, this is not unlike the ritual production of tears of compunction or contrition among the Christian Desert Fathers and in some forms of medieval meditative practice.

Emotion in the New Religions

In this last section, I will confine myself to a general overview of the newly founded religious groups in the nineteenth and twentieth centuries in Japan. Due to space limitations, I will further limit my characterization by relying on a single aspect of the work of one scholar, Helen Hardacre. Needless to say, a more detailed and careful analysis of each individual religion would yield a more complex and nuanced picture. According to Hardacre, Japanese new religions "display an orientation [to the world] that shapes and channels the experience and behavior of a large portion of the Japanese people. That orientation or world view in turn occupies a distinctive position in the history of Japanese religions."[29]

Hardacre defines "worldview" as "a characteristic conceptualization of the relation of the self to external levels of existence and stereotyped patterns of thought, action, *and emotion* based on that conceptualization."[30] One must applaud Hardacre's attention to stylized emotions, but question her assumption that such emotions are necessarily based on a prior conceptualization. Human beings are born into social systems that structure interpersonal relations *and* the emotional expressions of people enmeshed within a web of interpersonal relations. The first-born son (*chōnan*) in a Japanese family, for instance, feels himself to be such long before he conceptualizes the Japanese family structure and his position within it.

Be that as it may, Hardacre does an excellent job in showing how the leaders of new religions help adult members to deal with everyday problems. They "supply the links between [a problem's] constituent elements and events, attach labels to incoherent emotions, and specify the correct as opposed to the presently disordered relation among the actors." This redefinition of a situation (and the relative positions of the actors involved) ideally leads to, among other things, reformed "stereotyped emotions" that are valued by the religious community.[31]

Hardacre claims that the new religions of Japan share a common worldview or orientation to the world, even as they differ in terms of doctrine and beliefs. Specifically, she identifies four patterns of action and affect: "(1) the idea that 'other people are mirrors.' (2) the exchange of gratitude and repayment of favor, (3) the quest for sincerity [*makoto*],[32] and (4) the adherence to paths of self-cultivation."[33] In many important ways, neo-Confucian values inform this worldview and its patterns of action and affect. It assumes a hierarchical and patriarchal social structure within which the individual is subsumed into larger collectives (nuclear family, extended family, nation, cosmos). Since the social order and the order of the cosmos are assumed to be the natural order and thus set, when problems arise, it is incumbent on the individual to change his or her disposition rather than society. For instance, if a couple is having marital difficulties, the wife may be told that the husband's troubling behavior is in response to something she has done. The wife is instructed to search her own *kokoro* (heart-mind) for the cause and thus to accept part of the blame for the discord, as well as to realize that she has the power to solve the problem.

Hardacre points to gratitude (*kansha*) as a crucial emotion to be cultivated and circulated within the religious community. This is the same emotion we find in the conclusion of the tales in the late medieval Buddhist *Zangemono* (The Seven Itinerant Lay Nuns). According to Hardacre:

> religious leaders and especially founders are cast in the role of superiors, and the organization as a whole becomes the object of gratitude. ... Opportunities for the experience and expression of gratitude are plentifully provided and surrounded with strong emotion. ... The 'blessings' (*kudoku*), 'compassion' (*jihi*) of the founder, presented in [the] highly charged, emotional language of a mother's suffering for her children, stimulates the believer to experience gratitude. By sustained socialization of this kind, presented in sermons, testimony, dramatic presentations, movies and video tapes, and extended to lesser leaders and the organization as a whole, gratitude and the repayment of favor become a series of ongoing exchanges.[34]

Once again we see that a religiously valorized emotion—in this case "gratitude"—is an achieved affective state, not a "natural" or automatic response to stimuli. For members of the new religions, continuous cultivation of one's *kokoro* is required of each person. Hardacre cites a Japanese proverb as encapsulating the world view of the new religions: "To experience suffering and happiness both depend upon how one bears one's *kokoro*" (*kurushimu mo tanoshimu mo kokoro no mochiyō*).[35] In my terms, it depends on one's emotional and moral disposition. This leads me to my final point—the most highly valorized emotions for religious communities tend to be moral emotions. These are precisely those social emotions that are *learned* and, then, *internalized*. It is because of this that something "feels right" or "feels wrong" to an individual.

Conclusion

This all-too-brief overview of selected emotions in Japanese religious history may nevertheless be sufficient for me to make a significant point about how historians work. Historians have delineated historical ages by a number of different criteria. In the case of Japan, the prehistorical Yayoi period takes its name from a pottery pattern, the *kōfun* period from the keyhole-shaped artificial burial mounds of the elite, and other periods (the Nara, Heian, Kamakura, Edo) from their capital cities. For his part, William LaFleur has suggested that the medieval period may be defined by its Buddhist intellectual episteme:

> It was a period during which there was a general consensus concerning what kinds of problems needed discussion, what kinds of texts and traditional practices constituted authority worthy of citation and appeal, and what kinds of things constituted the symbols central to the culture and to the transmission of information within it. This means that we are able to come to an approximate definition of medieval Japan *in intellectual terms*.[36]

Another way of distinguishing ages in the history of religions, though, might be to critically analyze the shifts in the specific emotions that were held up by dominant religious communities. That is, rather than define "medieval Japan" in intellectual terms, as LaFleur does, one might define it as the period during which the sights, sounds, and events of the world evoked specific Buddhist-defined emotions in most persons in society, for example, the famous opening lines of the thirteenth-century *Heike monogatari*:

> The sound of the bells of Gion Shōja echoes the impermanence (*mujō*) of all things; the color of *śōla* flowers reveals the truth that the prosperous must decline. The high and proud do not endure, but are like a dream on a spring night. The mighty fall in the end and are scattered like dust before the wind.[37]

To say this is to suggest that a religious world of meaning is at base emotional as much as, if not more than, it is intellectual. In this manner of periodization, the end of the medieval period of Japan would be determined by the point in time when the sound of the bells of the Gion temple-shrine complex in Kyoto no longer evoked the sense of *mujō*. This would be to shift the focus of our attention from *mujō* thought primarily to *mujō* as a core broadly shared affective response to human existence in the world. I await with great anticipation a history of religions of this sort. The turn to the study of the body, gender, and emotion in many different disciplines in the past few decades, as well as the growing number of works on *habitus*, all bode well for future work in the history of religions on lived religion. Much work remains to be done, but it is clear that the critical historical study of emotion and religion will be of central importance to this enterprise.

NOTES

1. A typical and influential example is the textbook by H. Byron Earhart, *Japanese Religion: Unity and Diversity*, 4th ed. (Belmont, Calif.: Wadsworth, 2004).

2. New Haven, Conn.: Yale University Press, 2004, x. For a discussion some of the methodological issues involved in the study of emotions in the past, see my review of Bolitho's work, *Journal of Japanese Studies* 31, 1 (2005): 206–9.

3. Bolitho, *Bereavement and Consolation*, xii and xiii.

4. For analyses of copious examples of such verses, see my *Ritual Poetry and the Politics of Death in Early Japan*. Princeton, N.J.: Princeton University Press, 1989).

5. For an English translation of this mythic episode, see Donald L. Philippi, trans., *Kojiki* (Tokyo: University of Tokyo Press, 1968), 55–67. Several versions are also recounted in the *Nihon shoki*.

6. See Philippi, *Kojiki*, 224–25; for jealous wives of deities and humans, see 108–12 and 305–14.

7. Robert Brower and Earl Miner, *Japanese Court Poetry* (Stanford, Calif.: Stanford University Press, 1961), 3. For the original, see *Nihon koten bungaku taikei* (hereafter NKBT) 8, in *Kokinwakashū* (Tokyo: Iwanami Shoten, 1959), 93.

8. Translation adapted from Ian Hideo Levy, trans., *The Ten Thousand Leaves*. Princeton, N.J.: Princeton University Press, 1981), 55. For the original, see NKBT 4, 28–29.

9. NKBT 4, 88–89.

10. For a few examples, see Fred R. Myers, *Pintupi Country, Pintupi Self: Sentiment, Place, and Politics among Western Desert Aborigines* (Berkeley: University of California Press, 1991); Thomas Maschio, *To Remember the Faces of the Dead: The Plenitude of Memory in Southwestern New Britain* (Madison: University of Wisconsin Press, 1994); Steven Feld, *Sound and Sentiment: Birds, Weeping, Poetics, and Song in Kaluli Expression* (Philadelphia: University of Pennsylvania Press, 1982); and Alan Rumsey and James F. Weiner, eds., *Emplaced Myth: Space, Narrative, and Knowledge in Aboriginal Australia and Papua New Guinea* (Honolulu: University of Hawai'i Press, 2001.

11. See my *Ritual Poetry and the Politics of Death* for an extensive analysis of ritual funeral laments.

12. NKBT 5, 54–55.

13. NKBT 5, 54–59; translation from Levy, *The Ten Thousand Leaves*, 344, slightly adapted.

14. Here I follow the interpretation of Nakanishi Susumu, a leading *Man'yōshū* scholar.

15. For an early essay in English on these subjects, see William R. LaFleur, "Saigyō and the Buddhist Value of Nature," *History of Religions* 13, 2 (1973): 93–128, and 13, 3 (1974): 227–48.

16. Donald Keene, trans., *Essays in Idleness: The Tsurezuregusa of Kenkō* (New York: Columbia University Press, 1967), 7. The original may be found in NKBT 30, *Hōjūki, Tsurezuregusa*.

17. Indeed, Brower and Miner do precisely this in their famous early study *Japanese Court Poetry*. They suggest that here "loneliness is treated as a pathetic condition"; 260–61. This misses the specific medieval Buddhist understanding of the meaning and role of the human heart-mind in discerning the nonduality of the phenomenal world and the emptiness at its heart.

18. NKBT 29, *Sankashū*, no. 937, p. 167.

19. NKBT 28, *Shinkokinwakashū*, p. 100.

20. Marian Ury, trans., *Tales of Times Now Past: Sixty-Two Stories from a Medieval Japanese Collection* (Berkeley: University of California Press, 1979), 90. The original may be found in NKBT 24, *Konjaku monogatri-shū, san*, p. 222.

21. For an English translation and brief commentary, see Royall Tyler, trans., *Japanese Nō Dramas* (Harmondsworth, England: Penguin Books, 1992), 68–81.

22. This tale has been treated in English by, among others, William R. LaFleur. See *The Karma of Words: Buddhism and the Literary Arts in Medieval Japan* (Berkeley:

University of California Press, 1983), 70–74. LaFleur accepts Kan'ami as the play's author, while Royall Tyler favors his son, Zeami.

23. These poems are found in the *Sankashū* (7:752–53) and the *Shinkokinwakashū* (10:978–79). The translation here is slightly adapted from Burton Watson, trans., *Saigyō: Poems of a Mountain Home* (New York: Columbia University Press, 1991), 126–27.

24. See Margaret Helen Childs, *Rethinking Sorrow: Revelatory Tales of Late Medieval Japan* (Ann Arbor: Center for Japanese Studies, University of Michigan, 1991).

25. Childs, *Rethinking Sorrow*, 99.

26. If I am correct here, then Childs's title, *Rethinking Sorrow*, is misleading, insofar as it stresses cognition rather than emotion as the key.

27. See Ury, *Tales of Times Now Past*, 127–31; NKBT 25, pp. 199–202.

28. See my "The Poetics and Politics of Ritualized Weeping in Early and Medieval Japan," in *Holy Tears: Weeping in the Religious Imagination*, edited by John Hawley and Kimberley Patton (Princeton, N.J.: Princeton University Press, 2004).

29. *Kurozumikyō and the New Religions of Japan* (Princeton, N.J.: Princeton University Press, 1986), 4.

30. *Kurozumikyō*, 7, emphasis added.

31. *Kurozumikyō*, 11.

32. Although *makoto* is often translated as "sincerity," as Hardacre does here, I prefer "moral rectitude" or "propriety." In current English usage, "sincerity" tends to imply being true to oneself in word and deed. *Makoto*, though, means having one's *kokoro* (heart-mind) in line with what is right and proper.

33. *Kurozumikyō*, 21.

34. *Kurozumikyō*, 24–25.

35. *Kurozumikyō*, 19.

36. LaFleur, *The Karma of Words*, 9, italics added.

37. NKBT 32, *Heike monogatari, jō*, p. 83.

BIBLIOGRAPHY

Unfortunately, relatively little has been written on emotions in Japanese religions. This is true for scholarship in both Western languages and Japanese. Japanese scholarship on emotion tends to be from a psychological perspective. The work of Shinobu Kitayama, who has published extensively in English, is representative of the interesting work being done in psychology, although it sheds no light on cultural or historical issues.

The study of emotions in Japan began with stereotypes being legitimated by works such as Ruth Benedict's book *The Chrysanthemum and the Sword*, which purported to shed light on the Japanese character and motivation. Some recent work has attempted to debunk these racial and ethnic stereotypes. David R. Matsumoto, *Unmasking Japan: Myths and Realities about the Emotions of the Japanese* (Stanford, Calif.: Stanford University Press, 1996), is the best of this ilk, although it has little to say about religion. Matsumoto, *The New Japan: Debunking Seven Cultural Myths* (Yarmouth, Me.: Intercultural Press, 2002) continues this line of attack. Students might also consult Futoshi Kyobayashi, Diane L. Schallert, and Holly A. Ogren, "Japanese and American Folk Vocabularies for Emotions," *Journal of Social Psychology* 8, 1 (2003): 451–79, for a preliminary comparative study of emotion talk. Aviad E. Raz, *Emotions at Work: Normative Control, Organizations, and*

Culture in Japan and America (Cambridge, Mass.: Harvard University Press, 2002), compares differences in the expressions of emotion in American and Japanese work places.

Scholars of comparative philosophy have taken the lead in the study of emotions in Japan, although their work will not always satisfy historians or scholars of religion. Joel Marks and Roger T. Ames, eds., *Emotions in Asian Thought: A Dialogue in Comparative Philosophy* (Albany: State University of New York Press, 1994), contains two chapters on Japanese subjects, as well as some early discussion of important methodological issues. Thomas Kasulis, *Intimacy or Integrity: Philosophy and Cultural Difference* (Honolulu: University of Hawai'i Press, 2002), includes some discussion of relevance, although religious emotions are not a real focus. Works such as Alasdair Macintyre, "Individual and Social Morality in Japan and the United States: Rival Conceptions of the Self," *Philosophy East and West* 4 (1990), 489–97, may be of some interest, but this essay lacks a sophisticated grasp of Japanese religion and history.

No work in the history of religions focuses extensively on emotions in Japan. Gary L. Ebersole, *Ritual Poetry and the Politics of Death in Early Japan* (Princeton, N.J.: Princeton University Press, 1989), includes extensive information on the politics of public expressions of emotion and affect in the seventh- and eighth-century court. One might expect that a work such as Irit Averbuch, *The Gods Come Dancing: A Study of the Japanese Ritual Dance of Yamabushi Kagura* (Ithaca, N.Y.: East Asia Program, Cornell University, 1995), would deal with emotion, but such is not the case. Although Averbuch argues that ritual dance conveys and evokes emotions in the performers and audience, she does not critically study or analyze religious emotions per se. Similarly, in spite of the suggestive title, Scott Schnell, *The Rousing Drum: Ritual Practice in a Japanese Community* (Honolulu: University of Hawai'i Press, 1999), contains little to nothing on religious emotions in the festival studied here. One work by the anthropologist Emiko Ohnuki-Tierney, *Kamikaze, Cherry Blossoms, and Nationalisms: The Militarization of Aesthetics in Japanese History* (Chicago: University of Chicago Press, 2002), involves issues of religion, ideology, and emotion, although the focus is limited to an investigation of why young university students went to certain death as *kamikaze* pilots in the waning days of the Pacific War.

Because of the paucity of secondary studies, students interested in the study of emotions in Japanese religions would be well advised to turn to primary sources for literary representations of emotion. Works such as the *Nihonsoki (Nihongi)* and the *Man'yōshū* from the eighth century, for instance, are chock-full of depictions of emotional expressions. So, too, are many myths, folktales, *monogatari* (prose narratives), plays, travel diaries, poetic travel journals, and so forth. Students should also look at the writings of religious and philosophical intellectuals throughout Japanese history, from Kūkai, the founder of the esoteric Shingon sect of Buddhism, to twentieth-century figures, such as the Buddhist philosopher Nishida Kitarō. Similarly, the study of the works of nativist (*kokugaku*) scholars, such as Motoori Norinaga, and neo-Confucian scholars (e.g., Kamo no Mabushi) will shed light on the valuation of specific emotions in specific circles. H. D. Harootunian, *Things Seen and Unseen: Discourse and Ideology in Tokugawa Nativism.* Chicago: University of Chicago Press, 1988), contains scattered, but important, insights into issues related to emotion and nativist discourse.

Averbuch, Irit. *The Gods Come Dancing: A Study of the Japanese Ritual Dance of Yamabushi Kagura.* Ithaca, N.Y.: East Asia Program, Cornell University, 1995.
Benedict, Ruth. *The Chrysanthemum and the Sword: Patterns of Japanese Culture.* Rutland, Vt.: Tuttle, 1954.

Brower, Robert, and Earl Miner. *Japanese Court Poetry*. Stanford, Calif.: Stanford University Press, 1961.
Childs, Margaret Helen. *Rethinking Sorrow: Revelatory Tales of Late Medieval Japan*. Ann Arbor: Center for Japanese Studies, University of Michigan, 1991.
Earhart, H. Byron. *Japanese Religion: Unity and Diversity*. 4th ed. Belmont, Calif.: Wadsworth, 2004.
Ebersole, Gary L. "The Poetics and Politics of Ritualized Weeping in Early and Medieval Japan." In *Holy Tears: Weeping in the Religious Imagination*, edited by John Hawley and Kimberley Patton. Princeton, N.J.: Princeton University Press, 2004, 25–51.
———. *Ritual Poetry and the Politics of Death in Early Japan*. Princeton, N.J.: Princeton University Press, 1989.
Feld, Steven. *Sound and Sentiment: Birds, Weeping, Poetics, and Song in Kaluli Expression*. Philadelphia: University of Pennsylvania Press, 1982.
Harootunian, H. D. *Things Seen and Unseen: Discourse and Ideology in Tokugawa Nativism*. Chicago: University of Chicago Press, 1988.
Kasulis, Thomas. *Intimacy or Integrity: Philosophy and Cultural Difference*. Honolulu: University of Hawai'i Press, 2002.
Kyobayashi, Futoshi, Diane L. Schallert, and Holly A. Ogren. "Japanese and American Folk Vocabularies for Emotions." *Journal of Social Psychology* 8, 1 (2003): 451–79.
LaFleur, William R. *The Karma of Words: Buddhism and the Literary Arts in Medieval Japan*. Berkeley: University of California Press, 1983.
Levy, Ian Hideo. *The Ten Thousand Leaves*. Princeton, N.J.: Princeton University Press, 1981.
Macintyre, Alasdair. "Individual and Social Morality in Japan and the United States: Rival Conceptions of the Self." *Philosophy East and West* 4 (1990): 489–97.
Marks, Joel, and Roger T. Ames, eds. *Emotions in Asian Thought: A Dialogue in Comparative Philosophy*. Albany: State University of New York Press, 1994.
Maschio, Thomas. *To Remember the Faces of the Dead: The Plenitude of Memory in Southwestern New Britain*. Madison: University of Wisconsin Press, 1994.
Matsumoto, David R. *The New Japan: Debunking Seven Cultural Myths*. Yarmouth, Me.: Intercultural Press, 2002.
———. *Unmasking Japan: Myths and Realities about the Emotions of the Japanese*. Stanford, Calif.: Stanford University Press, 1996.
Myers, Fred R. *Pintupi Country, Pintupi Self: Sentiment, Place, and Politics among Western Desert Aborigines*. Berkeley: University of California Press, 1991.
Ohnuki-Tierney, Emiko. *Kamikaze, Cherry Blossoms, and Nationalisms: The Militarization of Aesthetics in Japanese History*. Chicago: University of Chicago Press, 2002.
Philipppi, Donald L., trans. *Kojiki*. Tokyo: University of Tokyo Press, 1968.
Raz, Aviad E. *Emotions at Work: Normative Control, Organizations, and Culture in Japan and America*. Cambridge, Mass.: Harvard University Press, 2002.
Rumsey, Alan, and James F. Weiner, eds. *Emplaced Myth: Space, Narrative, and Knowledge in Aboriginal Australia and Papua New Guinea*. Honolulu: University of Hawai'i Press, 2001.
Schnell, Scott. *The Rousing Drum: Ritual Practice in a Japanese Community*. Honolulu: University of Hawai'i Press, 1999.
Ury, Marian, trans. *Tales of Times Now Past: Sixty-Two Stories from a Medieval Japanese Collection*. Berkeley: University of California Press, 1979.
Watson, Burton, trans. *Saigyō: Poems of a Mountain Home*. New York: Columbia University Press, 1991.

CHAPTER 5

JUDAISM

JOEL GEREBOFF

THE emotions are an important feature of Jewish life and thought throughout the ages. From biblical descriptions of a God of pathos to early rabbinic and medieval works detailing the virtues (*midot*), to mystical tracts focused on the inner life, and occasionally portraying emotion filled religious experiences of the adept, to contemporary Jewish educational materials delineating techniques to foster the emotional intelligence of children, there have always been Jewish representations of the affective dimensions of life. In addition, the many ways Jews have actually participated in prayer and in the celebration of holidays, and in the construction of material objects and spaces in which such activities took place, also give evidence of emotional texture of the lives of Jews. Yet academic scholarship on Judaism and the emotions has been quite limited until the last several years. This recent turn to explicit examination of the emotions on the part of scholars (and of Jewish leaders) of Judaism is quite typical of the growing interest, charted by John Corrigan (in *Religion and Emotion: Approaches and Interpretations*), by academics in a number of disciplines in the emotions in general, and in the relation between religion and the emotions in particular.

The large bibliography on religion and the emotions compiled by Corrigan, Eric Crump, and John Kloos (*Emotion and Religion: A Critical Assessment and Annotated Bibliography*) contains barely twenty references to Judaism, the vast majority of these dealing with biblical sources. Although the bibliography in this chapter lists a number of items omitted from that book, it also makes clear that it is only in the last decade that scholars of Judaism have begun to discuss such topics as Jewish prescriptions for character formation, a topic that includes references to emotions. The reasons for the earlier lack of attention to emotions and for the recent rediscovery of them as an area of inquiry include both some factors internal to classical Jewish sources and modern Jewish self-representation and self-understanding and some typical of non-Jewish academic and social trends.

The character of Jewish texts composed before the Middle Ages is a key factor contributing to the limited amount of critical work on the range of Jewish thinking on the emotions. The Hebrew Bible and classical rabbinic sources consist of many genres of writing, redacted by anonymous editors into numerous documents, none of which is organized as a treatise on such topics as the good life and the place of the emotions in it. Such documentary features require a critical historical and literary approach that takes note of formal features of the texts and the contexts of their composition, as well as their subsequent transmission and reception, in order for one to distinguish developments in Jewish thinking on any given topic. In the case of early rabbinic sources, such modes of inquiry have become dominant in only the last thirty years. A second factor limiting the analysis of the relation between Judaism and the emotions is that until the Middle Ages, Judaic thinking did not develop a systematic psychology, nor did it thematize the emotions per se as a subject for analysis. Thomas Dixon's critique (*From Passions to Emotions: The Creation of a Secular Psychological Category*) of much of contemporary thinking on emotions is relevant here. Dixon asserts that until two centuries ago, "the emotions" did not exist. During the nineteenth century, the emotions came into being as a distinct psychological category, replacing existing psychologically related terms, such as *appetites, passions, sentiments,* and *affections*. In his view, this domination by one single descriptive category is not healthy, as it hampered attempts to argue with any subtlety about the enormous range of mental states and stances of which humans are capable. Most recent work also has failed to appreciate the religious underpinnings of much medieval thought on these matters. In a related way, then, in the study of emotions in Judaism, the lack of a comparably rich earlier discussion of mental states makes it difficult and in a way anachronistic to examine "Judaism and the emotions." A third factor contributing to prior omission of the study of emotions and Judaism is the intellectual biases and social and political concerns of Jewish scholars of the *Wissenschaft des Judenthums* (Scientific Study of Judaism) in the nineteenth century, and of other Jewish leaders throughout the twentieth century. One of the best bits of evidence of this oversight and omission is that nearly all books meant to introduce Judaism to Jews, to converts to Judaism, or even to students in introductory university classes focus on the ideas (beliefs), rituals, social institutions, and history of Jews but contain little in the way of Judaic reflections on the inner life, including the emotions. The characterization of Judaism as "ethical-monotheism," under the influence of Kantian and neo-Kantian views of ethics, highlighted the ways Jewish practices advanced a sense of the morally right rather than how Judaic views fostered the virtues and the emotions. Similarly, ritual life was described and analyzed to demonstrate how it conveyed great ideas, not how it stirred the heart. The mystical dimensions of Judaism, with their rich veins of emotive experience, also were not a serious subject of investigation until Gershom Scholem took up this matter. And even after Martin Buber presented collections of Hasidic tales to a more general audience, many modern Jews continued to be embarrassed by the highly emotive piety of the actual Hasidim of their day.

The recent interest in analyzing the place of the emotions in Judaism has grown out of the liberation of Judaic scholarship from an apologetic mission to represent Jews in terms that match the dominant cultural and aesthetic values of broader society. Moreover, refined methodological approaches to classical and medieval texts now recognize the importance of not overgeneralizing from a given source, of attempting to date strata and to identify different viewpoints within these sources, and of treating these documents as expressions of often competing elites within earlier Jewish societies who gave voice to their gender, intellectual, and social biases, for example. Recently revived interest in virtue ethics in general in academic circles has also had a major impact on the study of Jewish ethics and in its wake has led to some discussion of the connections between emotions and the moral life. These factors, coupled with the explosion of studies of emotions in numerous disciplines, now carried out often in interdisciplinary forums, have now begun to translate into a growing body of work on Judaism and the emotions. The following discussion surveys some of these trends, identifies important scholarly contributions, and notes suggestions for future research.

In examining this literature it is helpful to keep in mind several different foci for Jewish thought and practices related to emotions. As already noted, one expression of Jewish thinking about the emotions appears in numerous accounts of the deity as a god of pathos. Prescriptions for the way to interact with other human beings, including stories about ideal figures, are a second set of sources for examining Jewish thinking on the emotions. Prescriptions for how to act in relation to the divine in ritual conduct and, in addition, how to experience the divine are a third set of sources. Finally, ethnographic and biographical accounts of the lived Jewish life, including ways of engagement with material artifacts and with music and dance, yield significant data on the place of emotions in Jewish practice and experience.

Michael Fishbane, Daniel Boyarin, and Hava Tirosh-Samuelson have produced methodologically astute scholarship adding significantly to the understanding of aspects of Jewish thought on the emotions. Analyzing with intricate literary and nuanced substantive sensitivity numerous textual sources from biblical until modern times, each has made evident the diversity of Jewish thought on the emotions, though only Fishbane has made this topic a central focus on his studies. His essay "Joy and Jewish Spirituality" is the richest study of the changing understandings of this emotion. It serves as a model for scholarship on emotions and Judaism, at least in terms of how to analyze discrete sources and which questions to ask. Fishbane charts how new intellectual trends, for example, mysticism, philosophy, and changing social circumstances contributed to the reshaping of the notion and significance of joy. Thus for example, whereas in biblical times joy was an expression of the full willingness of the participant in the performance of commandments, in kabbalistic sources, the joy of the adept becomes part of the circulatory process activating particular cosmic-sephirotic elements within the godhead. This essay, however, is only suggestive of the rich potential such analyses have, for it examines only one or two sources from merely one thinker for each type of Jewish writing. Fishbane's new book-length study (*Biblical Myth and Rabbinic Mythmaking*) demonstrates the centrality of myth in biblical, rabbinic, and kabbalistic sources, highlighting their sense of a highly emotional (pathos-filled) deity who is moved by humans who are emotionally sensitive to this divine inner life. Fishbane also reveals how the elaboration of such notions results from changing life experiences of Jews mediated through their intricate exegetical endeavors.

Daniel Boyarin, in a large number of essays and books, through pointed readings, often against the grain, of talmudic and modern Jewish writings, has charted "cultural formations" that express a model for the Jewish male that is at odds with eventually dominant Christian and modern secular views. Informed by feminist and gay and lesbian scholarship, though not by works specifically on the emotions, Boyarin distinguishes among competing understandings of desire (*yeser*) and comments on how *edalkayt*, a gentle, timid, and studious but embodied and sexualized male "has something compelling to offer us in our current moment of search for a feminist reconstruction of male subjectivity."[1] In this account, emotions such as courage, timidity, and fear take on particular valuations and are joined with "desire" in rabbinic narratives about cultural heroes. Dixon's already noted observations on difficulties in the use of contemporary scholarly (and popular) terminology for the study of indigenous representations of the inner life are most relevant to the discussion of *yeser*. This term covers a range of inner states, including attitudes, desires, and emotions. Rabbinic sources explore, for example, how desire can be cultivated and channeled such that negative inclination and concomitant emotions can be directed to positive results.

Current scholarship on emotions, especially work on Aristotle's view, significantly informs Hava Tirosh-Samuelson's detailed and broad-ranging study *Happiness in Premodern Judaism*. Her book demonstrates, through careful readings of a selection of biblical, early rabbinic, medieval philosophical and kabbalistic sources, that "Judaism regarded itself primarily as a prescription for the attainment of happiness, and that the dynamic of the discourse on happiness captures the evolution of Jewish intellectual history from antiquity to the seventeenth century." According to Tirosh-Samuelson, these claims make sense

> if one understands happiness as human flourishing on the basis of Aristotle's analysis of happiness. Linking virtue, happiness and well-being, Aristotle's analysis of happiness can be traced in Jewish understanding of human flourishing as early as the Greco-Roman world, but the fusion of the Greek and Judaic perspectives on happiness reached its zenith in the Middle Ages in the thought of Moses Maimonides and his followers.... Properly understood... happiness is not a subjective feeling manifested in a given moment or for a short period of time. Instead, it means flourishing, thriving and experiencing well-being appropriate to a human being. It is an objective state of affairs that pertains to human nature and to the quality of human life as a whole from the perspective of its entire duration. Moreover, the intrinsically good life is inseparable from a set of religious beliefs,

the most important of which is that God, the creator of the world, has a special relationship with the People of Israel, to whom God revealed his Wisdom and Will in the form of law: the Torah.[2]

Tirosh-Samuelson often notes how and which emotions should or should not play a role in the life of the virtuous person in the course of her discussion, though the emotions are not the focus of her analysis. Like Fishbane, she correctly observes that biblical and early rabbinic sources contain a range of positions, but she makes a strong case that from Greco-Roman times forward, Jewish writers such as Philo and the editors of rabbinic documents like Abot de Rabbi Natan gave more systematic expression to the idea that cultivating certain emotions, especially humility, is necessary for the attainment of happiness. In terms of medieval developments, she makes the important contrastive observation that

> In contrast to the rationalist philosophers, for whom learning was a cerebral and ponderous intellectual activity, predicated on self-control and the extirpation of emotions, the crying and other expressions of extreme joy (for example hugging) make the Zohar a highly emotional text that portrays Torah study as an activity that involves enthusiasm, passion, emotion, sound, bodily movements, and physical contact, all of which culminate in a spiritual release when the secrets are revealed and received.[3]

Tirosh-Samuelson provides richly analyzed examples of many of these trends, but as she herself observes, much remains to be done in the study of other thinkers from these times. Her work, and that of Boyarin and Fishbane, has made evident the important contribution that the study of the emotions can make to the broader understanding of Judaism. We turn now to offer brief observations on other scholarship on different periods of Judaism.

A number of scholars have studied the terms for certain "emotions" in distinct types of biblical texts. By situating the usage of the terms for such emotions in select genres of biblical sources and by comparing them with earlier ancient Near Eastern and later rabbinic sources, the research of Yochanan Muffs and Gary A. Anderson has revealed the error of many other studies that were built solely around semantic analyses of individual terms and often with theologically grounded Western assumptions about the centrality of inner feelings in certain biblical understandings of the proper relationship with God. Muffs demonstrates that the terms for "love" and "joy" in some biblical (and rabbinic) legal texts focus on the will, not on an interior feeling. These sources indicate that covenantal obligations demand of the Israelites that they reciprocate God's grace without volitional reservation; that is, that one serve God with "love and joy." Anderson's analyses of a group of biblical and rabbinic texts complements Muffs's findings by criticizing previous studies of "joy" and "grief" in these works for their failure to discern that these notions require behavioral performances. "One does grief," "one does joy," and such actions in turn indicate one's status in the community. Though in certain instances these activities may engender feelings within the performer, they are primarily symbolic of one's status and one's relationships with other people and with God. In reaching these conclusions, Anderson draws on cross-cultural investigations of mourning practices, chiefly those of Peter Metcalf and Richard Huntington.

Kruger's several articles similarly engage current research on emotions and isolate cognitive elements in some biblical portrayals of anger, fear and shame. Meyer Gruber, like Muffs and Anderson, uses ancient Near Eastern materials to identify biblical views on anxiety and reverence. Milgrom's richly textured analyses of biblical cultic requirements, especially those of the Priestly source, show that an interior sense of "guilt" is a necessary feature for certain offerings to be efficacious.

The description of the pathos of the biblical God has its clearest discussion in Abraham Joshua Heschel's classic study of the literary prophets of the Hebrew Bible. For Heschel, this feature stands at the center of the biblical "prophetic" experience. Though Heschel's study has been criticized for importing his own theology, which is informed by Hasidic and Western romantic views of the nature of religious experience, his study does unapologetically foreground the mythic dimensions of the biblical deity, and it challenges earlier accounts that accentuated the *moral* import of the prophetic corpus. Fishbane's previously noted studies more carefully investigate this aspect of the emotions in biblical sources.

The foregoing overview of the study of emotions in the Hebrew Bible indicates the rich potential of properly framed analyses of biblical sources. Investigations of other "emotions" in various strata of the biblical text remain to be done. In addition, the introduction of the variable of "gender" would contribute to more nuanced understanding of the emotions and their correlation with the construction of gender, space, and time. The larger project of utilizing biblical and archaeological data to present reconstructions of the "emotional" dimensions of the actual lives of ancient Israelites remains to be undertaken. Finally, biblical texts as such, for example Lamentations, express and surely seek to engender certain emotional experiences, and such matters could also be the subject of future studies.

These comments on Muffs and Anderson, combined with my earlier observations on Fishbane, Boyarin, and Tirosh-Samuelson, demonstrate the growing attention by scholars to the meaning, significance, and historical background also of rabbinic discussions on emotions. Analyzing rabbinic sources with due concern for distinguishing among varying rabbinic documents by date and provenance, and taking into account differences between different genres of rabbinic writings, these studies, as well as those of Jonathan Schofer, Jacob Neusner, Jeffrey Rubenstein, and Eliezer Diamond, have charted dimensions of some emotions in early rabbinic documents. In addition, these scholars have, to varying degrees, engaged contemporary philosophical and historical studies of the emotions in other cultures. Citing the work of Robert Solomon and James Averill, Neusner lays out an account of the development of the "doctrine of emotions" in rabbinic sources spanning from Mishnah to the Palestinian and Babylonian Talmuds. In the only recent book-length study of the "virtues of the heart" and of the emotions in early rabbinic sources, Neusner correctly notes that these texts proscribe certain virtues, especially subservience, patience, generosity, endurance, and hope, as well as their correlative emotions, humility, love, and forbearance. He correctly and forcefully asserts on the basis of a documentary analysis of rabbinic sources that they view the emotions as articulating judgments, they present rules for the control and cultivation of emotions that should shape one's character and behavior, and they see the relationship between the people of Israel and God as inclusive of proper virtues and emotions. Finally, Neusner situates these views within their historical context, arguing that they were socially, politically, and psychologically meaningful to Jews so long as they found themselves a weak and subordinated people. Neusner overstates his case, in that he analyzes only a small portion of texts, ignores other important emotions (for example, shame, fear of God), and at times does not consistently distinguish between the virtues and their emotional components.

Jonathan Schofer's two recently published articles, which grew out of his dissertation and form part of his 2005 book, offer sharply focused literary and conceptual analyses of the views of a limited number of rabbinic documents on character formation.[4] Situating *Abot de Rabbi Natan,* in the context of Hellenistic efforts at forming character—studied previously by scholars such as Pierre Hadot—and locating it more generally in relation to Foucault's charting of cultural practices directed to the formation of the self, Schofer presents a carefully detailed, and not overstated, account demonstrating that "there were rabbis who reflected in subtle ways about the shaping of desire and emotion."[5] His discussion of *Abot de Rabbi Natan* builds on recent literary studies of rabbinic sources that treat larger literary units as compositions resulting from editorial work of selection, revision, and arranging, and he convincingly argues that sections of this document offer a large sequence, a treatise, on character formation. According to Schofer, for the arrangers of this unit,

> study is both an intellectual activity and a way of life that distinguishes the participant from the broader society. The disciple circle sets the context for the cultivation of virtue, particularly forms of self-restraint. Sages praise humility, patience and the control of speech, and they condemn in strong terms those who are arrogant or who engage in gossip and slander.[6]

Schofer's discussion of *yeser* distinguishes with care among virtue, impulse, and emotion, and as a result he makes a most valuable contribution to "strengthening our scholarly vocabulary for the study of rabbinic character formation" and "stimulating discussion about ethical themes in rabbinic sources, especially but not only the topics of human emotions, desires and ways to transform them."[7] One may build on such work, as well as that of Boyarin, by analyzing what were rabbinic depictions of "others,"—other male Jews, female Jews, and non-Jews–and how such notions gave voice to rabbinic self understanding.

Jeffrey Rubenstein's writings on rabbinic narratives also demonstrate the value of the focused analyses of distinct genres of rabbinic literatures for what they can contribute to knowledge about rabbinic notions of the emotions. Taking into account distinctions between Palestinian and Babylonian contexts and the respective Talmuds composed in each locale, and treating rabbinic sources as literary creations that give voice especially to the concerns of the redactors of those documents,

Rubenstein highlights that a good number of the longest stories contained in the Babli explore the tension between the commitment to the "warlike" atmosphere of the rabbinic academy and the concern for shame and honor. The redactors of the Babylonian Talmud, who in recent scholarship are dated to the saboraic period of the sixth and seventh centuries, reworked earlier stories to highlight that the greatest potential negative outcome of discussions and arguments between sages on matters of law and ethics was causing shame to a fellow rabbi. How to maintain deference to authority and commitment to correctly framed, passionate reasoning while at the same time not humiliating a fellow discussant stands out as a key concern of later rabbis. Though Rubenstein does not situate his studies within current scholarship on rabbinic ethics and the emotions, his findings indicate that these matters are important concerns for the redactors of important rabbinic documents and thus form part of their cultural formation.

The foregoing discussion demonstrates that a dominant message of early rabbinic sources is that all emotions are not to be eliminated but that certain ones are to be cultivated and enacted. Diamond's book-length study of early rabbinic views on asceticism provides data complementary to this conclusion. Focusing on fasting but including other types of restrained activity, Diamond identifies larger values informing rabbinic thinking on these matters. Like other scholars, Diamond distinguishes between different rabbinic documents and compares rabbinic views with culturally and contemporaneous notions, especially those of early Christian sources. He challenges earlier apologetic Jewish scholarship that celebrated the comparative merits of Judaism in relation to Christianity by depicting Christianity as entirely ascetic in its focus on the spiritual and its rejection of the sinful bodily existence, while portraying Jewish views as lacking any ascetic elements.

All of the aforementioned work has demonstrated rabbinic concerns for the emotions and for character formation, and has set the basis for studies of other emotions not yet investigated with the methodological and broader academic interests used therein. These recent works also furnish a fine foundation for tracing later developments of Judaic thinking about the emotions found in the diverse strands of medieval Jewish writings, including the philosophical, mystical, and pietistic.

In addition to the already noted studies by Tirosh-Samuelson and Fishbane, which do draw on portions of contemporary research on the emotions in biblical and rabbinic sources, other recent and some older scholarship have, in varying ways, addressed medieval Jewish thought on the emotions. The revival of interest in virtue ethics in the last several decades in academic and popular circles has had an influence on Jewish scholarship, and this work augments longstanding investigations into the *midot* (the moral virtues). The scholarly studies of Raymond L. Weiss, Raphael Jospe, Norbert Samuelson, Daniel Frank, Lenn Goodman, Warren Zev Harvey, and Lawrence Kaplan, many of which discuss with care aspects of Maimonides' ethical thought in the context of broader medieval Jewish moral thinking, especially in its "appropriation" of Aristotle, are now joined by more popular discussions of such writings. The academic investigations do not single out the emotions per se but make comments on them as relevant to the analysis of the position of these medieval philosophical writings on *midot* and character development as part of the moral/intellectual life. Tirosh-Samuelson's book pulls together much of this work and lays out competing Jewish views, for example, on the connections between moral character and the pursuit of intellectual-philosophical attainment. A number of writers have sought to make available these documents, and some of the insights of current scholarship on them, to a more general readership, Jewish and non-Jewish. Leonard S. Kravitz and Kerry M. Olitzky provide a commentary and study material on Maimonides' *Shemonah Peraqim*, and Niles Goldstein and Steven S. Mason do the same for the thirteenth-century text *Sefer Ma'alot HaMidot*, long popular within Jewish circles. Byron Sherwin, and more so Solomon Schimmel, present selections from biblical, early rabbinic, and later Jewish thinking on a number of virtues and vices. While neither writer systematically investigates the full range of comments on a particular emotion in any one writer or document, for example, the type of pointed work done by Schofer, nor does either discuss the thinking of such writers on all of the virtues, Schimmel's writings do indicate the importance of the emotions within such works. Schimmel brings to his discussions his training and practice as a psychologist, and in books directed to the general public, he brings some Jewish views into dialogue with selected Christian, philosophical, and psychological positions. He shows, for example, that the trend in much Jewish writing was to cultivate certain emotions while controlling others. In his recent book on forgiveness, he indicates that according to Jewish views, forgiveness requires the overcoming of the emotions of resentment and anger, but the wrongdoer must first seek out the aggrieved party.

Schimmel and Sherwin also make use of several key medieval Jewish mystical-ethical works, especially the encyclopedic volume *Reshit Chochmah* of Elijah Moses de Vidas. This work, written under the influence of the kabbalistic thinking of sixteenth-century Safed, has received some scholarly attention, but little has been done in the way of focused discussion of its full range of its views on the virtues, and especially on the emotions. Furthermore, of the existing scholarship only a small amount is in English. Joseph Dan provides a fine introduction to the genre of medieval ethical writing, arguing that its distinctive component is its spiritual-mystical underpinnings and goals. Pachter's Hebrew University dissertation on Safed moral writings has reached English readers only in a brief article ("Kabbalistic Ethical Literature in Sixteenth-Century Safed"). But neither author engages broader contemporary discussions on the emotions. Tirosh-Samuelson's analysis of the place of emotions within the Zohar, and within several later Jewish mystical works, indicates the centrality of the inner life in this strand of Jewish thought. She demonstrates how proper attention to the emotions and virtues was essential in interpersonal behavior and more so in practices, including mystical forms of study, directed at the attainment of mystical experiences. Such attention also served to activate the Sefirot, for they are in part divine cosmic passionate forces. Elliot Wolfson and Moshe Idel as well chart how the Jewish mystics' envisioning of the godhead as a pulsating, emotional being, who interconnects in a circulatory flow with the mystical adept, transformed Jewish devotional and moral behavior. Wolfson and Idel, like Tirosh-Samuelson, through careful study of certain passages, set within their broader context, demonstrate, for example, that weeping and joy are necessary for mystical ascent by the adept and for the activation of the flow of divine energy from above. These studies move beyond the earlier work of Scholem and of Isaiah Tishby by seeking to understand the experiential dimensions of kabbalistic works, no longer treating them primarily as intellectual accounts separated from lived experience.

Scholarship on Hasidism, a mystical form of Judaism, has offered rich insights regarding how different Hasidic works attend to the inner life as a central focus of Jewish thought and practice. Dan, Arthur Green, Idel, Rivka Schatz-Uffenheimer, and Norman Lamm have authored very detailed studies of such topics, though in nearly all cases comments on the emotions are noted in the course of larger discussions. More limited studies are those of Alan Brill, Niles Goldstein, and Don Seeman. Green's study of R. Nahman of Bratzlav serves as a model for bringing together psychobiography with analysis of complex ideas that are expressed, in this case, often very enigmatically. Sadness and depression are central features of Nahman's psychological makeup, and in turn, his views on the importance of joy in Jewish life take these into account. As Green and Fishbane make clear, the ideas of Nahman and other Hasidic leaders addressed the existential situation of Jews by identifying ways in which typical Jews in daily life could through proper inwardness and concomitant behavior find spiritual meaning and cosmic import in the commonplace. Recent scholarship on Hasidism has also distinguished among different genres of Hasidic writings, for example, guidebooks for behavior (*hanhaggot*), sermons delivered by *zaddikim* (Hasidic masters) on Shabbat and recorded only later, tales and more sophisticated treatises such as the *Tanya*, and different trends within Hasidic views. Those interested in Judaic views on the emotions can glean from these existing studies much about a segment of Hasidic thinking on the emotions. Lamm's collection of a broad range of primary texts, provided with fine introductions, can serve as a place to start.

Hasidic writings, discussed in these works, mostly date from the mid–eighteenth through the late nineteenth centuries and come from eastern Europe. The emergence of Hasidism lead to various reactions among eastern European Jews, one of which, the Musar movement, highlighted the inner life of Jews. Inaugurated by R. Israel Salanter, and in part an effort to fortify Jewish lay life in eastern Europe in its response to Hasidism, the growing forces of modernity and the Jewish Enlightenment, this movement resulted in what can be seen as a new Jewish psychology. Immanuel Etkes's book on Salanter identifies the development of Salanter's thinking, compares it with that of his immediate predecessors and contemporaries, and traces the translation of this thinking into institutional formations and personal practices. Although Etkes does not locate his historical study in conversation with recent work on the emotions, he does compare Salanter's views with emerging psychological views of his era and argues that Salanter's work, for the most part, does not grow out of them.

Salanter's response to emerging Jewish intellectual and social currents can be seen as an example of a much larger effort by Jewish thinkers and Jews in general to remake themselves in light of the opportunities and challenges of modernity. In the case of German Jews, for example, the articulation of *Bildung*, of a proper Jewish character, in many ways exhibiting the features of a cultured German, drove much of their efforts. American Jews also redefined Judaism in ways that, in their view, both preserved the "essence" of Judaism while also allowing for the participation and contribution of Jews to modern life. Numerous analyses of such developments are covered in many book- and article-length studies of Jews in the modern world. Such accounts analyze diverse types of evidence, including Jewish elitist and popular writings, educational materials, rules for synagogue membership and deportment, advertising directed at Jews, and newspaper and visual records of the behaviors of Jews. These data and studies are rich resources for exploring modern Jewish efforts in character formation, and in particular, for discerning the ways modern Jews thought about and lived out their emotions. Boyarin's *Unheroic Conduct* (1997) is in part an example of this type of research. But no specific secondary studies, as of now, analyze these modern data with attention to their position on the emotions.

Several recent constructive Jewish efforts, however, give primary attention to the emotions. Heschel's theological (and even historical) writings accentuate the importance of religious experience inclusive of such distinct religious emotions as awe, wonder, and amazement. Joseph Dov Soloveitchik, the doyen of modern Orthodoxy in America, in many of his works, including his thinking on Jewish law, notes how the observance of certain halakhot requires attention to the emotions. The influence of his views is evident in the writings of many of his disciples, including David Hartman, David Shatz, and Walter Wurzburger. Wurzburger, for example, argues that proper halakhic observance can take place only if a Jew has a well-formed character (*Ethics of Responsibility*). Virtues and emotions are thus integral to Jewish living. Reform Jewish thinking from nearly the same period, and led especially by the work of Eugene Borowitz, also has given renewed attention to Jewish virtue ethics. Borowitz's seminar in the 1990s at Hebrew Union College, in which this strand of Jewish literature was examined, has contributed to popular books by himself, Susan Freeman, Scott Mandel, and Olitzky and Rachel T. Sabath on *midot*, Jewish virtues, with some comments offered episodically on correlative emotions. Finally, Jewish educators at the Conservative-sponsored Jewish Theological Seminary, including Jonathan Cohen, Jeffrey S. Kress, and Carol Ingall, have discussed the importance of role modeling in Jewish education and the need for Jewish schools to address the "emotional" intelligence of students. These writers, however, have not yet made evident which emotions should be cultivated and which ones controlled.

Judaic thinking and practice has always taken into account in some way the inner life of the Jew. This discussion has made clear many of the different views on such matters and has noted the growing scholarly attention to this topic. This review also has suggested the rich potential contribution that systematic, carefully controlled, and properly contextualized studies of Judaic thought on the inner life, and on the emotions in particular, can make to the broader understanding of Judaism. Such scholarship, when informed by work on other religious traditions and, more generally, by the burgeoning research in numerous academic fields on the emotions, has much to add to these investigations. John Corrigan's concluding observations in his introduction to *Religion and Emotion*, in which he sets forth a model for future scholarship in this field, provides a standard against which to assess present investigations into Judaism and the emotions. He writes:

> The study of religion and emotion is in an early stage, well-begun, but still finding its feet.... It must avoid doctrinaire taxonomies. It must look beyond disciplinary boundaries in theory and method. It must remain sensitive to the differences and similarities between culturally constructed standards for emotion and actual emotional experiences of people. As investigation of religion and emotion from all of these perspectives progresses, it is likely to challenge current paradigms for the study of religion, and it may lead to the reconsideration of the study of religion as a whole.[8]

Much remains to be done in the study of Judaic materials. But recent scholarship now provides a basis on which to build, leading to the composition of both general introductions and more detailed accounts of Judaic thinking, and Jewish life that make evident that properly understanding these matters requires integrating analyses of emotions.

NOTES

1. Daniel Boyarin, *Unheroic Conduct: The Rise of Heterosexuality and the Invention of the Jewish Man* (Berkeley: University of California Press, 1997), 2.
2. Hava Tirosh-Samuelson, *Happiness in Premodern Judaism: Virtue, Knowledge and Well-Being* (Cincinnati: Hebrew Union College Press, 2003), 2–3.
3. Ibid., 307.
4. "The Redaction of Desire: Structure and Editing of Rabbinic Teachings Concerning Yeser ('Inclination')," *Journal of Jewish Thought and Philosophy* 12, 1 (2003): 19–53, and "Spiritual Exercises in Rabbinic Culture," *AJS Review* 27, 2 (2003): 203–25; book: *The Making of a Sage: A Study in Rabbinic Ethics* (Madison: University of Wisconsin Press, 2005).
5. Schofer, "The Redaction of Desire," 19.
6. Ibid., 25.
7. Ibid., 52.
8. John Corrigan, *Religion and Emotion: Approaches and Interpretations* (Oxford: Oxford University Press, 2004), 25–26.

BIBLIOGRAPHY

Alexander, Elizabeth Shanks. "Art, Argument, and Ambiguity in the Talmud: Conflicting Conceptions of the Evil Impulse in b. Sukkah 51b–52a." *Hebrew Union College Annual* 73 (2002): 97–132.

Anderson, Gary A. *A Time to Mourn, a Time to Dance: The Expression of Grief and Joy in Israelite Religion*. University Park: Pennsylvania State University Press, 1991.

Blau, Yitzchaq. "The Implications of a Jewish Virtue Ethics." *Torah u-Madda Journal* 9 (2000): 19–41.

Borowitz, Eugene B., and Frances Weimman Schwartz. *Jewish Moral Virtues*. Philadelphia: Jewish Publication Society, 1999.

Boyarin, Daniel. *Carnal Israel: Reading Sex in Talmudic Culture*. Berkeley: University of California Press, 1993.

———. *Unheroic Conduct: The Rise of Heterosexuality and the Invention of the Jewish Man*. Berkeley: University of California Press, 1997.

Brill, Alan. "Grandeur and Humility in the Writings of R. Simchah Bunim of Przysucha." In *Hazon Nahum: Studies in Jewish Law, Thought and History Presented to Dr. Norman Lamm*, edited by Yaakov Elman and Jeffrey Gurock. New York: Yeshiva University Press, 1997, 419–48.

Cohen, Ian J. "Classroom Climate in an Orthodox Day School: The Contribution of Emotional Intelligence, Demographics and Classroom Context." *Journal of Jewish Education* 68, 1 (2002): 21–33.

Cohen, Jonathan. "Focus on Social-Emotional and Jewish Education: Core Concepts and Effective Practice." *Jewish Educational Leadership* 1, 2 (2004): 27–30.

Corrigan, John. *Religion and Emotion: Approaches and Interpretations*. Oxford: Oxford University Press, 2004.

Corrigan, John, Eric Crump, and John Kloos. *Emotion and Religion: A Critical Assessment and Annotated Bibliography*. Westport, Conn.: Greenwood Press, 2000.

Dan, Joseph. *The Heart and the Fountain: An Anthology of Jewish Mystical Experience*. New York: Oxford University Press, 2002.

———. *Jewish Mysticism and Jewish Ethics*. Northvale, N.J.: Jason Aronson, 1996.

Diamond, Eliezer. *Holy Men and Hunger Artists: Fasting and Asceticism in Rabbinic Culture*. New York: Oxford University Press, 2004.

Dixon, Thomas. *From Passions to Emotions: The Creation of a Secular Psychological Category*. Cambridge: Cambridge University Press, 2003.

Etkes, Immanuel. "Humility." In *Midot u-Regashot*, edited by Asa Kasher and Aharon Namdar. Ramat Gan, Israel: Amutat Yehoraz, 1994, 13–31.

———. *Rabbi Israel Salanter and the Mussar Movement: Seeking the Torah of Truth*. Philadelphia: Jewish Publication Society, 1993.

Fishbane, Eitan. "Tears of Disclosure: The Role of Weeping in Zoharic Narrative." *Journal of Jewish Thought and Philosophy* 11, 1 (2002): 25–47.

Fishbane, Michael. *Biblical Myth and Rabbinic Mythmaking*. New York: Oxford University Press, 2004.

———. "Joy and Jewish Spirituality." In *The Exegetical Imagination: On Jewish Thought and Theology*. Cambridge, Mass.: Harvard University Press, 1998, 151–72.

———. *Kiss of God: Spiritual and Mystical Death in Judaism*. Seattle: University of Washington Press, 1994.

Frank, Daniel. "Humility as a Virtue: A Maimonidean Critique of Aristotle's *Ethics*." In *Moses Maimonides and his Times*, edited by Eric L. Ormsby. Washington, D.C.: Catholic University Press, 1989, 89–99.

Freeman, Susan. *Teaching Jewish Virtues: Sacred Sources and Arts Activities*. Denver: Alternatives in Religious Education, 1999.

Goldstein, Niles. *Forests of the Night: Fear of God in Early Hasidic Thought*. Northvale, N.J.: Jason Aronson, 1996.

Goldstein, Niles, and Steven S. Mason. *Judaism and Spiritual Ethics.* New York: UAHC Press, 1996.
Goodman, Lenn. "Determinism and Freedom in Spinoza, Maimonides and Aristotle: A Retrospective Study." In *Responsibility, Character and the Emotions: New Essays in Moral Psychology,* edited by Ferdinand Schoeman. Cambridge: Cambridge University Press, 1987, 107–64.
Green, Arthur. *Tormented Master: A Life of R. Nahman of Bratzlav.* Tuscaloosa: University of Alabama Press, 1979.
Green, Ronald. "Jewish Ethics and the Virtue of Humility." *Journal of Religious Ethics* 1, 1 (1973): 53–63.
Gruber, Meyer. "Fear Anxiety and Reverence in Akkadian, Biblical Hebrew and Other Northwest Semitic Languages." *Vetus Testamentum* 40, 4 (1990): 411–22.
Hartman, David. *Love and Terror in the God Encounter: The Theological Legacy of Rabbi Joseph B. Soloveitchik.* Vol. 1. Woodstock, Vt.: Jewish Lights Press, 2001.
Harvey, Warren Zev. "Maimonides on Human Perfection." In *The Thought of Moses Maimonides: Philosophical and Legal Studies,* edited by Ira Robinson. Lewiston, N.Y.: Edwin Mellen Press, 1996, 1–15.
Hauptman, Judith. "Death and Mourning: A Time for Weeping, a Time for Healing." In *Celebration and Renewal: Rites of Passage in Judaism,* edited by Rela M. Geffen. Philadelphia: Jewish Publication Society, 1993, 226–51.
Heschel, Abraham Joshua. *God in Search of Man: A Philosophy of Judaism.* New York: Farrar, Straus and Cudahy, 1955.
———. *Man Is Not Alone: A Philosophy of Religion.* New York: Farrar, Straus and Cudahy, 1951.
———. *A Passion for Truth.* New York: Farrar, Straus and Giroux, 1973.
———. *The Prophets.* New York: Harper and Row, 1962.
Idel, Moshe. *Hasidism: Between Ecstasy and Magic.* Albany: State University of New York Press, 1995.
———. "Hitbodedut as Concentration in Ecstatic Kabbalah." In Idel, *Studies in Ecstatic Kabbalah.* Albany: State University of New York Press, 103–69.
———. *Kabbalah: New Perspectives.* New Haven, Conn.: Yale University Press, 1988.
Ingall, Carol. *Transmission and Transformation: A Jewish Perspective on Moral Education.* New York: Melton Research Center, 1999.
Jospe, Raphael. "Rejecting Moral Virtue as the Ultimate Human End." In *Studies in Islamic and Judaic Traditions,* edited by William M. Brinner and Stephen D. Ricks. Atlanta: Scholars Press, 1986, 1:185–204.
Kaplan, Lawrence. "The Love of God in Maimoides and Rav Kook." *Judaism* 43, 3 (1994): 227–39.
Kravitz, Leonard S., and Kerry M. Olitzky, trans. *Shemonah Perakim: A Treatise on the Soul.* New York: UAHC Press, 1999.
Kress, Jeffrey S., and Maurice J. Elias. "Social and Emotional Learning in the Jewish Classroom: Tools for a Strong Jewish Identity." *Journal of Jewish Communal Service* 77, 1 (2001): 182–90.
Kruger, Paul A. "A Cognitive Interpretation of the Emotion of Anger in the Hebrew Bible." *Journal of Northwest Semitic Languages* 26, 1 (2000): 181–93.
———. "A Cognitive Interpretation of the Emotion of Fear in the Hebrew Bible." *Journal of Northwest Semitic Languages* 27, 2 (2001): 77–89.
———. "The Psychology of Shame and Jeremiah 2:36–37." *Journal of Northwest Semitic Languages* 22, 2 (1996): 79–88.

Lamm, Norman. *The Religious Thought of Hasidism: Text and Commentary.* New York: Yeshiva University Press, 1999.

Lauritzen, Paul. *Religious Belief and Emotional Transformation: A Light in the Heart.* Lewisburg, Pa.: Bucknell University Press, 1992.

Leighton, Stephen, ed. *Philosophy and the Emotions: A Reader.* Peterborough, Ontario: Broadview Press, 2003.

Mandel, Scott. *Wired into Teaching Jewish Virtues: An Internet Companion.* Denver: Alternatives in Religious Education, 2002.

Metcalf, Peter, and Richard Huntington. *Celebrations of Death: The Anthropology of Mortuary Ritual.* Cambridge: Cambridge University Press, 1991.

Milgrom, Jacob. *Cult and Conscience: The Asham and the Priestly Doctrine of Repentance.* Leiden: Brill, 1976.

Muffs, Yochanan. *Love and Joy: Law, Language and Religion in Ancient Israel.* New York: Jewish Theological Seminary of America, 1992.

Neusner, Jacob. *Vanquished Nation, Broken Spirit: The Virtues of the Heart in Formative Judaism.* Cambridge: Cambridge University Press, 1987.

Newman, Louis E. "Ethics as Law, Law as Religion: Reflections on the Problem of Law and Ethics in Judaism." *Contemporary Jewish Ethics and Morality: A Reader,* edited by Elliot N. Dorff and Louis E. Newman. New York: Oxford University Press, 1995, 79–93.

Nussbaum, Martha C. *Upheavals of Thought: The Intelligence of Emotions.* Cambridge: Cambridge University Press, 2001.

Olitzky, Kerry M., and Rachel T. Sabath. *Striving toward Virtue: A Contemporary Guide for Jewish Ethical Behavior.* Hoboken, N.J.: Ktav, 1996.

Pachter, Mordechai. "Kabbalistic Ethical Literature in Sixteenth Century Safed." *Binah* 3 (1994): 159–78.

Pliskin, Zelig. *Anger: The Inner Teacher.* Brooklyn: Mesorah, 1992.

Rubenstein, Jeffrey. *Talmudic Stories: Narrative Art, Composition and Culture.* Baltimore: Johns Hopkins University Press, 1999.

Samuelson, Norbert. "Revenge and Forgiveness in Jewish Virtue Ethics." In *Lesarten des judisch-shristlichen Dialoges,* edited by Silvia Kappeli. Bern: Peter Lang, 2002, 229–44.

Schatz-Uffenheimer, Rivka. *Hasidism as Mysticism: Quietistic Elements in Eighteenth Century Hasidic Thought.* Princeton, N.J.: Princeton University Press, 1993.

Schiendlin, Laurence. "Emotional Perception and Spiritual Development." In *International Journal of Children's Spirituality* 8, 2 (2003): 79–93.

Schimmel, Solomon. "Education of the Emotions in Jewish Devotional Literature: Anger and Its Control." *Journal of Religious Ethics* 8 (1980): 259–76.

———. "Gratitude in Judaism." In *The Psychology of Gratitude,* edited by Robert A. Emmons and Michael E. McCullough. New York: Oxford University Press, 2004, 37–57.

———. *The Seven Deadly Sins: Jewish, Christian and Classical Reflections on Human Nature.* New York: Free Press, 1992.

———. "Some Educational Uses of Classical Jewish Texts in Exploring Emotions, Conflict and Character." *Religious Education* 92, 1 (1997): 24–37.

———. *Wounds Not Healed by Time: The Power of Repentance and Forgiveness.* New York: Oxford University Press, 2002.

Schofer, Jonathan. *The Making of a Sage: A Study in Rabbinic Ethics* (Madison: University of Wisconsin Press, 2005).

———. "The Redaction of Desire: Structure and Editing of Rabbinic Teachings Concerning *Yeser* ('Inclination')." *Journal of Jewish Thought and Philosophy* 12, 1 (2003): 19–53.

———. "Spiritual Exercises in Rabbinic Culture." *AJS Review* 27, 2 (2003): 203–25.

Seeman, Don. "Martyrdom, Emotion and the Word of Ritual in Rabbi Mordecai Joseph Leiner's *Mei HaShiloah*." *AJS Review* 27, 2 (2003): 253–79.

Shatz, David, "Beyond Obedience: Walter Wurzburger's *Ethics of Responsibility*." *Tradition* 30, 2 (1996): 74–95.

Shatz, David, Joel B. Wolowelsky, and Reuven Ziegler. Introduction to *Out of the Whirlwind: Essays on Mourning, Suffering and the Human Condition*. Hoboken, N.J.: Ktav, 2003, ix–li.

Sherwin, Byron. "Fear and Awe of God." In Byron Sherwin, *Toward a Jewish Theology: Methods, Problems and Possibilities*. Lewiston, N.Y.: Edwin Mellen Press, 1991, 51–62.

———. "Fear of God." In *Contemporary Jewish Religious Thought*, edited by Arthur A. Cohen and Paul Mendes-Flohr. New York: Free Press, 1987, 245–54.

Sherwin, Nancy. *Making a Necessity of Virtue: Aristotle and Kant on Virtue*. Cambridge: Cambridge University Press, 1997.

Solomon, Robert C. *Not Passion's Slave: Emotions and Choice*. New York: Oxford University Press, 2003.

———, ed. *Thinking about Feeling: Contemporary Philosophers on Emotions*. New York: Oxford University Press, 2004.

Soloveitchik, Joseph B. "A Theory of Emotions." In *Out of the Whirlwind: Essays on Mourning, Suffering and the Human Condition*, edited by David Shatz, Joel B. Wolowelsky, and Reuven Ziegler. Hoboken, N.J.: Ktav, 2003, 179–214.

Stern, Josef. "Maimonides' Conception of Freedom and the Sense of Shame." In *Freedom and Moral Responsibility: General and Jewish Perspectives*, edited by Charles H. Manekin. Bethesda, Md.: University Press of Maryland, 1997, 217–66.

Stiebert, Johanna. *The Construction of Shame in the Hebrew Bible: The Prophetic Contribution*. London: Sheffield Academic Press, 2002.

Stiegman, Emero. "Rabbinic Anthropology." In *Aufstieg und Niedergang der Romischen Welt 19:2*, edited by Wolfgang Haas. Berlin: de Gruyter, 1979, 487–579.

Tirosh-Samuelson, Hava. *Happiness in Premodern Judaism: Virtue, Knowledge and Well-Being*. Cincinnati: Hebrew Union College Press, 2003.

Tishby, Isaiah. "The Doctrine of Man." In *The Wisdom of the Zohar: An Anthology of Texts*, edited by Isaiah Tishby. London: Littman Library, 1989, 2:677–776.

———. "Fear of God, Love of God and Communion." In *The Wisdom of the Zohar: An Anthology of Texts*, edited by Isaiah Tishby. London: Littman Library, 1989, 3:974–1016.

Weiss, Raymond L. *Maimonides' Ethics: The Encounter of Philosophic and Religious Morality*. Chicago: University of Chicago Press, 1991.

Wettstein, Howard. "Awe and the Religious Life." *Judaism* 46, 4 (1997): 387–407.

Wieselberg, Yael. "Awe, Love and Attachment: Religious Development and the Maharal of Prague." In *Wisdom from My Teachers: Challenges and Initiatives in Contemporary Torah Education*, edited by Jeffrey Saks and Susan Handelman. Jerusalem: ATID, 2003, 93–111.

Wolff, Hans Walter. *Anthropology of the Old Testament*. Philadelphia: Fortress Press, 1973.

Wolfson, Elliot. "Weeping, Death and Spiritual Ascent in Sixteenth Century Jewish Mysticism." In *Death, Ecstasy and Other Worldly Journeys*, edited by John J. Collins and Michael A. Fishbane. Albany: State University of New York Press, 1995, 209–47.

Wurzburger, Walter. *Ethics of Responsibility: Pluralistic Approaches to Covenantal Ethics*. Philadelphia: Jewish Publication Society, 1994.

CHAPTER 6

CHRISTIANITY

ANDREW TALLON

THIS essay focuses largely on philosophical and theological frameworks for the development in Christianity of notions of "head" religion and "heart" religion. Such notions are the product of a complex and sustained historical interplay of ideas about the soul, body, matter, spirit, thinking, acting, and feeling. While not exclusively the province of Christianity, ideologies of head and heart in religion nevertheless have developed distinctive forms within the Christian cultures of the West, changing over time and leading, at the beginning of the twenty-first century, to an engagement with scientific theories of emotion.[1] That engagement has been substantially shaped by rich traditions of Christian religious practice that have valued the cultivation and expression of emotion, even in contexts where official frameworks of theological ideas have offered little in the way of integrating such practice with official understanding of the nature of soul and body.

OVERVIEW

The history of emotion and Christianity may be approached as a record of how disagreements, some of which became heresies, even schisms, have influenced doctrine and practice. One such debate has focused on the nature of Christ: if for Christians God is pure spirit, for example, and pure spirit means being endowed with only the faculties of intellect and will, but without a physical body and associated feelings, then Christ as divine cannot suffer, and the incarnation, redemption, and salvation become problems since they involve bodily suffering and death (at least in one theory of why Christ died). Another example is Gnosticism, teaching salvation by *knowledge*, whereby those initiated into its secrets gain heaven—a heresy against the Christian teaching of salvation by *love*: Christians are saved by God's love, and commanded to love God and neighbor. Furthermore, if love comes from the "heart," as much of Christian history has it, then love cannot be exclusively an act of will, for how can love be commanded, since a person cannot command emotion? If love includes more than volition, namely, heart-felt emotion as well, then how much of love *is* emotion, and how much is will? Such disputes about mental states like love and the soul's relation to the body were once settled by conciliar decree but are more likely decided today by science. We will review some historical precedents for explaining the differing roles of emotion in Christianity as preparation for analyzing our present experience and anticipating what the near future may hold.

The current state of empirical knowledge about the role of emotion offers grounds for testing the philosophical and theological traditions dominant in Christianity. For nearly two millennia, neither philosophy nor theology was inclined or encouraged to listen or adapt to empirical investigation, which was thought to be so irrelevant that what we could call armchair philosophy could run unchecked. Nevertheless, the same basic perennial questions still dominate present life, even though the answers have evolved dramatically in recent years. The most important themes, both in their own right and because of their theological effects, are: (1) the effects of reducing emotion to cognition, volition, or embodiment; (2) experiencing faith as constituted partly by emotion; and (3) love as the core Christian virtue, not to be considered as solely a willed act but as including emotion. We could characterize the present, therefore, as the continuing contest between head and heart, reason and emotion, in Christian life.

A view of the place of emotion in Christianity in the wake of current scientific study, a possible future for Christianity, is glimpsed in strong present trends, especially in reference to recent science involving evolution, and understandings of both ethics and religion as emergent properties of the emotional and social brain.

Emotion and Christian History

There is both a *pre*history of emotion in human evolution and a *history* that includes biblical and secular pre-Christian sources. Emotion's story is older than the bible, of course, dating back before Abraham (ca. 1800 B.C.) and King David (ca. 1000 B.C.). According to recent evidence from anthropology and paleontology, *homo sapiens* goes back at least three million years, and our mammalian forebears, from whom evolved our emotional responses, date back much farther. Furthermore, the history of emotion within Christianity is part of the history of emotion's role in religion in general, as found in the Bible and in classical Greece and Rome before Christ. In the Greek classics, for example, we already find a religion of the "head" (Apollonian) and another of the "heart" (Dionysian), an apparently permanent distinction, still alive, for example, in von Hügel's "two religions,"[2] suggesting a contrast between the hierarchical, ecclesiastical, and institutional religion of the "head" and the mystical, personal, often more private religion of the "heart." There seem always to have been "heart religions,"[3] today perhaps more likely associated with distinctive worship services and forms of prayer, both personal and communal.[4] What some call "high church," with formal, rubric-controlled liturgies, uniform-like vestments, stylized ritual, classical-sounding music and chant, and a mostly passive, spectator congregation contrasts with lively meetings (revival style) sparked by hand-clapping, foot-stomping, dancing in the aisles, rousing gospel singing, and spontaneous exclamations from the active, participating congregation. This description hardly defines the "two religions" but serves merely to point out some more striking differences between cool and rational rather than warm and emotional kinds of services as lived in practice. Sometimes such rough-and-ready images do as well as real definitions to identify the broad outlines of the roles of emotion in religion, at least in presenting a case for the head-heart distinction. We need only search our own reactions, rational and emotional, to these descriptions of the "two religions" to assess our immediate appreciations of the difference between them.[5]

The evolution of human cognition has a more recent prehistory than that of emotion, probably because survival depended more on fear of predators and mating drives than on "higher" mental faculties like reason and intellect.[6] Compared with the evolution of emotion, Christianity's story is much shorter, being solely a human experience, with evolutionary roots in a religious sentiment going back at least to primitive burial rites (humans did not always bury their dead) and progressing to the ancient narratives, the cosmogonies, the myths of gods and demons, the sagas of birth and death, time and eternity, good and evil, light and darkness, love and hate. Evidence of religious practice more recent than what paleontology offers can be found in traces in ancient texts and practices documented in the immediate sources of the Christian religions: the Bible, older philosophical and mythological works of the Far East—China and India—and especially of the Near East and of ancient Greece and Rome, whose pantheons and Olympian myths pervasively influenced and radically formed Western civilization.[7] These forces bear witness to the depth and breadth of humanity's apparently natural openness and attraction to and irresistible fascination with the supernatural: to be human apparently is to experience a need to pursue the superhuman ceaselessly; questions about meaning and quests for the transcendent good, the sacred and holy, stir the emotions and lead persons on journeys they never expect to end.

Let us review a few key names and ideas that persist into the present, as follows.

Head and Heart, Apollo and Dionysius

In classical Greek represented by Euripides (*The Bacchae*, 404 B.C.) we find Apollo, god of reason, at one pole, and the heart religion of Dionysus, at the other. Dionysus is the divine son of Zeus and Bacchus. Some twenty-five centuries later, showing remarkable hardiness, "Apollonian" and "Dionysian" became Nietzsche's terms in *The Birth of Tragedy* for these two central principles in Western culture. Form, structure, rational thought are Apollonian. The Dionysian emerges in enthusiasm and ecstasy, where one trades, lends, or even loses individuality and submerges oneself in a greater whole: music is called the most Dionysian of the arts, since it appeals directly to instinctive chaotic emotions and not to the formally reasoning mind. Sculpture is called the most Apollonian of the arts, since it is so wedded to form.[8]

Nietzsche found both forces present in European culture in constant tension, appearing in drama, especially in the great tragedies. Apollo, the sun god, represents light, clarity, and form, whereas Dionysus, the wine-god, represents drunkenness and ecstasy. There are inevitable ambiguities: one person might seek self-expression in a religion that allows showing more emotion and shun services deemed too "cold" or passive because so very formal, conducted strictly "by the book"—for example, the *Roman Ritual*, the Catholic liturgical manual that prescribes every move made by clergy and faithful during the Mass; others might want to lose themselves in the same rigid ritual that deemphasizes the individual. Whatever the descriptions and definitions, what persists is an ambiguous polarity of "two religions."

Neither Objective nor Subjective but Interactive

Another approach to emotion's role is the common distinction between objective and subjective, usually misunderstood and falsely applied. In an era that favors scientific methods—characterized by leaning toward objectivity—art, ethics, and religion are often relegated to the subjective. The next "logical" step is then to dismiss them (as subjective) from serious consideration, from "reality" (always "objective"). So common a distinction must therefore be recognized before one can present emotion for serious discussion. One can, of course, romantically glory in the subjective and say that objectivists are benighted rationalists who miss the depth of feeling that, for romantics, is the most important part of reality. A better solution is to recognize that the mutual rejections of subjective and objective perspectives are both biased, and to propose a standpoint that includes and reconciles them. An *interactive* standpoint has solid basis in social neuroscience and goes a long way toward this goal. Essentially, this means accepting that human agents interact with one another and their world, and so their theories are always works-in-progress, permanently under revision.[9]

Representative Key Historical Figures and Their Theories

Historically, for the West the most important pre-Christian philosophers are Plato (427–347 B.C.) and Aristotle (384–322 B.C.) from classical Greece; next, leaping first about six hundred years into the centuries we broadly call medieval Latin, come

Augustine (354–430 C.E.), and, about eight hundred years later, Thomas Aquinas (1225–1274); then we arrive, in about three hundred years, in an accelerating explosion of knowledge out of the Renaissance, to the beginning of modernity, to Descartes (1596–1650), Hume (1711–1776), Kant (1724–1804), and Husserl (1859–1938). These figures are pivotal because of their influence on the dualism that still dominates so much prescientific thinking. Let us note the broad lines of the ideological standpoints inherited from these thinkers.

Plato and Augustine

Platonic dualism is of two beings with separate and independent existence. It is called substance dualism because soul and body are considered two separately existing entities temporarily conjoined in earthly life. This dualism represents the unexamined position of many whose folk psychology flows over into everyday ethics and religion. "The soul is in the body like a pilot in a ship" is a common way to imagine the body-soul relation; depending on the culture, an immortal spiritual soul is said to preexist in heaven with God, is infused at the moment of conception, or later, into the developing fetus, or at the time of birth, or even later, even some weeks, months, or longer after birth. Emotions were associated with the body, with consequent status.

Most important for Christianity, Plato's works were available during the first centuries of the Christian era and influenced the mentality of the New Testament writers, including Paul, whose writings are dualist. The Greek fathers of the church read and wrote in Greek, as did the New Testament writers, and drew inspiration from Plato's "spiritual" teaching. Whatever was associated with soul and spirit was better than whatever was associated with body and matter. Plato's idea-ism became Christian idealism.

The best known heresy expressing this dualism was Manichaeism, according to which soul and spirit were good, while body and the physical were evil. Augustine was an early Christian adherent. For Augustine and the Latin fathers of the church, Plato continued to be the favorite secular source of ideas considered friendly to Christian doctrines like immortality, heaven and hell, reward and punishment in a life after death for the immortal soul. Resurrection was easier to explain in Platonic terms, as were certain ways God could act directly on the soul, for example, by giving grace (usually with little or no detectable effect on the body), as infusing the gifts of the Holy Spirit (especially the virtues of faith, hope, and charity), and by speaking directly to the minds of prophets and evangelists. Again, the soul as a separate entity was the subject of the divine action (God is spirit and acts on spirit), sometimes by sacramental means, such as using water for baptism and oil for confirmation and the last rites; but even when physical healing occurred, the aegis of the miracle was repentance and conversion rather than something for the body itself for its own sake.

Disparagement of the physical body went hand in hand with its earthly (and earthy), temporal, spatial, material status, as compared with the spiritual soul, considered naturally immortal and created to spend eternity with God. The status of Jesus as God-man was much debated, and a succession of heresies, ecumenical councils, and creeds dealt with the incompatibilities between the role that essential embodiment played in Christ's salvific passion, death, resurrection, and ascension, and its second-class status in the philosophy and theology of Platonic and selected biblical sources. The councils "solved" the *problems* chiefly by declaring them to be *mysteries*, beyond mortal capacity to understand, and by stating in formally metaphysical language what Christians had to believe on faith; a defined creed became a litmus test of orthodoxy and church membership, with failure to profess it punished by excommunication.[10]

Aristotle and Aquinas

A major revolution occurred in the thirteenth century, however, when the recently discovered works of Aristotle, lost for centuries, began to be translated into Arabic and Latin. Thomas Aquinas had the audacity (which earned him condemnation by his bishop in Paris) to take the materialist ideas of the relatively (compared with Plato) unspiritual Aristotle and use them to address disputed questions previously settled mostly by quoting Plato, Augustine, sacred scripture, and assorted minor authors. The most significant difference was between the Platonic dualism of two separate *substances* or beings and the Aristotelian dualism, adopted by Aquinas, of two *principles* coconstituting *one substance* or being. This was a major epistemological move *away* from a kind of visual bias that took as model for the real what could be *sensed* (especially seen) *toward* a model of the real as what could be *understood*, as what was *intelligible* rather than only *perceptible*. The revolutionary nature of this shift from real as *sensible* to real as *intelligible* is still not recognized and accepted in some circles even today, since it is mistakenly confused with idealism. It is decidedly not a mere shift from one thing as *seen* to another thing as *seen*, from physical *objects* as seen to spiritual forms or *ideas* as seen, for that would still privilege intuition or seeing over understanding. It would remain a failed method based on a model of knowing as "taking a look" and just shift the looker from the senses as seeing or intuiting to a looker as the spiritual mind seeing or intuiting, that is, to the "vision of the soul." Historians of philosophy have noted that the hylomorphic synthesis achieved by Aquinas on the basis of Aristotle was largely ignored by those philosophers and theologians who leapt over the "Dark Ages" of medieval thought and began their philosophical reading with Descartes. Recent studies of language, especially on the dependence of thought on imagination (represented, e.g., by the virtually universal use of metaphor)[11] as well as recent scientific evidence have tended to favor a form of (emergent) *property dualism*. Hylomorphism can be taken as a historical precedent for property dualism, insofar as the body–soul relation is not something we imagine or picture as a literal description but is a metaphor used in aid of understanding. As soon as we fall back to taking images literally, we cease to operate at the level of understanding. Emotion's equal role in art, ethics, and religion is a casualty of substance dualism.

Descartes, Hume, Kant, and Husserl

The synthesis forged by Aquinas of Plato and Aristotle did not hold, and Descartes, rather than stand on the shoulders of giants, began all over again, falling back equivalently to where Plato had ended, about two thousand years earlier, and taking up substance dualism again. For Descartes, only the soul was the real person; the body was a machine, with the lower value and status, at best, of an animal temporarily dignified by being the soul's earthly vehicle.

Hume (1711–1776), with Locke (1632–1704) and Berkeley (1685–1753), represents the early modern empiricism that has become (to oversimplify) science today, thanks to gradual improvements in method. It is important to note that this empiricist approach consistently resulted in Hume's recognizing the central role of emotion in ethics. Despite their significant contributions in other domains, for what concerns emotion and Christianity, Kantian (1724–1804) and Husserlian (1859–1938) dualism made little advance over Cartesian, and this group represents the problem rather than the solution. For substance dualists, emotion was disparaged as merely bodily, and since only the soul was defined as rational and free (the essence of human nature), emotion was forcefully excluded from "serious" ethics and religion, from the inner sanctum of the human essence as discussed by academics and professionals, no matter how emotion figured in their lived aesthetic, ethical, and religious worlds. There were exceptions, but their influence has not been enough to dethrone the rationalist forces; among twentieth-century philosophers who included a role for emotion are Max Scheler (1874–1928), Dietrich von Hildebrand (1889–1977), and Emmanuel Levinas (1906–1995).

Dyadic or Triadic Soul?

To conclude this historical sketch, note that Plato's tradition, however, was more complex than the Aristotelian-Thomist tradition in one very important way: Plato's triadic concept of the soul was paradoxically more faithful to experience than the dyadic soul of Aristotle and Aquinas, despite the Platonic soul's separation from the body and the Aristotelian hylomorphic soul's essential oneness with embodiment. Plato's theory lost out because it was not adopted in the influential seminary theology, whereas Aquinas's works were canonical. In brief, for Aristotle, continued in Aquinas, the soul was two-part, comprising only the spiritual faculties of intellect and will (in Aquinas's terms), while for Plato the soul was tripartite, comprising in addition the thymus (*thumos*), variously rendered as anger or passion, or, in general, the affective, emotional part of the soul.[12] What Aristotle and Aquinas did was to relegate the emotions to the "lower," sensible, animal soul, having to do with the body, while reserving to the "higher" soul the "spiritual" faculties of reason and will.[13] The effect of this doctrine of the dyadic spiritual soul entered Catholic and Protestant theology through the influence of Aquinas and was woven into the fabric of Christianity's relation to embodiment and emotion from then on. This is the historical origin of theory and practice today. It is still dominant in Christian teaching, although signs of its demise are emerging as neuroscience enters mainstream education; despite the advances in science, however, the proverbial man on the street continues to live by a deeply rooted folk psychology.

Let us pause here to note the living effects then and today of these ideas that continue to play out "on the ground," for in the present we still feel the effects of the "age of faith," those centuries marked by the dominance of the church over social and political life, the rise of the religious orders, especially the monastic and cloistered communities, remembered for their Gregorian chant, the daily hours of the Holy Office (chiefly the Psalms) sung in choir. After the monks came the mendicant friars (e.g., the Franciscans), the orders of itinerant preachers freed from monasteries to travel (e.g., the Dominicans), and the missionary orders (e.g., the Jesuits), who not only did not live in monasteries but did not even sing or recite the hours of the Holy Office in common but did so in private, where, especially in the case of the Jesuits, feeling played a crucial role in religious meditation. The explorers of the New World were accompanied by missionaries who brought the fervor of their faith with them, and who enacted emotional dramas in their quest to evangelize indigenous peoples. This was the time of building the great cathedrals adorned with the stories of the Bible told in magnificent stained glass windows—"read" by the illiterate in images that illuminated the "heart"—and with decorated altars, façades, statues, and paintings (Fra Angelico, Michelangelo, Raphael, Leonardo). The Middle Ages brought the beginning of the universities, chiefly religiously inspired and staffed by clerics, and the later emergence of protestant Christianity as Catholicism was challenged by the Renaissance, by the Reformation, and by freethinking individualism and the beginnings of science. This was the era of the *Devotio Moderna*, of Thomas à Kempis (*The Imitation of Christ*), and of the contemplatives and mystics of France (including the Quietists), Flanders, the German-speaking countries, Spain (especially Teresa of Avila and John of the Cross), and England, who cultivated feeling in their religious practice. Many church feasts and holy days became civic holidays of society, more in Christian Europe than in the New World, for example, Christmas, Easter, All Saints (and Halloween), Corpus Christi, Mardi Gras, Lent. Practices such as the stations of the Cross, Holy Week services, the rosary, devotions to Mary and to the saints with novenas, parish missions, processions, Benediction, incense, and Nine First Fridays sprang more from an affective piety than strict theology. Devotions such as those centered around the Sacred Heart of Jesus and around the Virgin Mary (Immaculate Heart of Mary) clearly have emotional associations, and the theme of the heart has figured prominently in theology and spirituality. An entire world of popular piety that was saturated in emotion saw its birth during these centuries; so did the practice of indulgences and the reactions its abuse evoked.

We readily associate the great organs built for the cathedrals that flourished then, and much great music, with devotional feeling. Here is religious passion in the symphonic and requiem masses and oratorios of Bach, Handel, Mozart, Beethoven, Brahms, Berlioz, Verdi, Fauré, and others, as well as smaller works—such as Fauré's Requiem—that are products mostly of Christian and especially Protestant composers, representing an emphasis on the choir as a "big thing" eclipsing the sacramental liturgy. Protestant emphasis on the Word (the Bible as sacred text) and the sermon as a "big thing" arose as well, and took shape in connection with a distinctly Protestant "heart religion" that coalesced in Lutheran groups, in Presbyterian piety, and across a wide spectrum of separatist groups ranging from Moravians to Amish.

Emotional religion sometimes featured a focus on the body, which even in the case of bodily exertions provided occasions to link the body with feeling rather than to separate the body from it. One observes in Christian history the era of such pious practices as self-inflicted scourges and flagellations by penitents, privately and publicly, the wearing of the catena (chain) around the thigh as penance, not to mention the fasting, vigils, and perpetual adoration before the Blessed Sacrament practiced in chapels of some contemplative cloistered nuns. In the New World, Shakers and Quakers mixed attenuation of some emotional expression with heightened attention to others, and various forms of Protestant revivalism pioneered new expressions of religious feeling. It is possible to interpret the pervasiveness of religion in everyday life and the very scale of the cathedrals and less imposing churches as source and result of the high emotion of the religion of the people, for most of whom the daily acts of religion were inseparable from what we today call secular life, so intimately were they integrated. It would not be an exaggeration to say that the very "natural" way the medievals experienced their world was through the supernatural prism of Christianity, and it would risk even less exaggeration to emphasize that this experience was for most not a matter of reason, cognition, or intellectual work, even among the famous Scholastic theologians like Albert the Great, Bonaventure, and Thomas Aquinas, but essentially an affective and emotional one: indeed we can presume that the very mood of the times was one set by the blend of emotion with Christianity. The *faith* of the age of faith, therefore, shows how integral emotion is to faith (and to hope and love).

This is brought home forcefully by the controversies that arose among Protestant reformers who in some cases tried to distance themselves from the "mother church" represented by Roman Catholicism; they either combated the emotional element or, in other cases, resorted to more emphasis on the affections where they saw decline. The ambiguities evident in Luther himself, and then in Calvin and Wesley, show how crucial it became for the reformers to come to terms with an increasing intellectualism in the study of the faith in scripture and the reactions against it. Some gloried in theology (faith seeking understanding) while a fundamentalism resisted it as the work of the devil (the "whore reason"). We find these tensions still with us today, as well as the legacy of more recent attempts—such as those of the American colonial Congregationalist minister Jonathan Edwards and the early nineteenth-century Protestant writer Friedrich Schleiermacher—to approach religious experience as some blend of thinking, feeling, and doing. In the last two centuries, especially, Christian thought has been characterized by several different emphases in religion, that is, on whether Christianity is lived more by head, by heart, or by balancing both.

Science, Emotion, and Christianity

The human sciences have only for about the last quarter century become significant resources for understanding how emotion relates to human nature and life in the three value domains of art, ethics, and religion. Before relatively recent times, what passed for knowledge was anecdote and armchair philosophizing; when speculative and metaphysical philosophy became *natural* philosophy, it was because its method changed.[14] Science after the empirical revolution was set irreversibly in motion by Newton, Galileo, Copernicus, Kepler, and others who began to transform methodology toward what we call science today, marked by method based on testable theories, on hypotheses considered merely provisional until proved by experimentation that verified claims empirically. Since most (some estimates run higher than 95 percent) of what the brain does is beneath consciousness, only the very recent imaging instruments have begun to unlock the neural secrets of "the engine of reason."[15] Much of what once passed for knowing how to deal with emotion stems from a dualism that contemporary brain research refutes, so that for Christians whose thinking is affected by scientific advance (absorbed from culture or encountered directly), the meaning of human nature increasingly can depend on facing the question of whether one is primarily defined by a spiritual soul, independent of the body, or defined in a way other than by substance dualism.

In order to appreciate something of what recent brain science looks like, and to estimate its potential influence on traditionally Christian notions of head and heart, we might consider some interesting developments in understanding emotions and moods. Some researchers have focused on the frailty of received theories of emotion itself. For Leslie Brothers, there is insufficient evidence to establish emotions as distinct from other neural functions, despite folk psychology. Her theory does not deny emotions but affirms that the common-sense theory is more a result of acquired linguistic habit, custom, and usage than hypothesis confirmed by experiment. In other words, what is reduced is not emotion itself but a *theory* about emotion, about what emotions are and how they operate.[16]

Other research has offered alternative ways of viewing the relation of emotion and cognition. An image suggested by Silvan Tomkins's theory of affect as amplifier offers some perspective on how such research places emotion in relation to cognition and volition.[17] Think of a sound amplifier based on vacuum tubes. Simply described, a diode has two elements, a cathode (with heater) that emits electrons across a vacuum toward an anode (plate) that receives them. A triode adds a third element, between the cathode and anode, called a control grid, which adds a small voltage with the effect of increasing the current flow of electrons to the anode, resulting in amplification. If cognition resembles the cathode and volition the anode, we have a rough analogy whereby perceptions, ideas, and reasonings result in different choices, decisions, and actions when amplified by the grid of affections, emotions, and moods.[18]

Other approaches to investigating emotion draw on physiological data. Antonio Damasio, for example, has documented clinically that frontal lobe damage affecting the emotional centers of the brain interferes so much with good decisions that the patient's life practically falls apart.[19] Donald Norman and Susan Greenfield, imagining the created physiology of robots, state that to make good decisions, robots will need emotions.[20] Taken together, these various strands of research suggest that paradox might define the near future in the story of emotion: whereas on the one hand science questions the neural basis of folk psychology's distinctions among cognition, affection, and volition, on the other hand artificial intelligence and research in affective computing, neural nets, and cognitive and affective science are saying that we have to invest our robots (Kurzweil's "spiritual machines") with emotions so they can make good decisions. We have come full circle: we can hardly deny emotion a primary role in a *human* life enriched by art, ethics, and religion while affirming its necessity for *robots*. Observing the history of Christian practice, with its impressive emotional component, we might conclude that the categories by which Christians often have organized experience might be more fluid and their boundaries porous than we have supposed, at least enough to support some negotiation with the recent science. We might also conclude that scientific advance constitutes a direct challenge to formal Christian notions of experience divided into two parts, the head and the heart.

But isn't religion, one might object (like art and ethics), different from science, using different methods? And isn't emotion precisely where the major difference lies? The subhuman worlds of machines and robots have no emotions. Isn't emotion what makes us human, what defines art, ethics, religion—the humanities that science cannot explain? If cognition is to *truth* what emotion is to *worth*, then human access to the important, to values, to the good, is through what touches and moves us, what we feel deeply about, not just through what we know. Indeed, here enters the major role for emotion, for the affective dimension, for the "heart" in Christianity. Christian faith historically has been experienced as cognition *plus emotion*, as the addition of heart to head, emotion providing what knowledge alone cannot supply, making possible precisely those decisions and actions involving values, worths, good and evil, right and wrong, thus the realms of esthetics, ethics, and religion.[21]

Emotion and religion are both human properties that have emerged in our long evolution, and a method that attends to the underlying neurology of both emerged forms of consciousness informs us today and changes our perspective on emotion and religion, making both intelligible in a way not possible by a more timid historical recital of names and ideas. An evolutionary standpoint sets limits to speculation by bringing us back to the practical, for example, when we recognize that life aims at *action*, first to survive, and then, survival secure, to flourish. Cognition and affection both aim at volition, at action; both are means, not ends in themselves. Scientific investigation, and especially neuroscience, suggest that emotion is absolutely necessary for successful practical and ethical decisions, refuting the idea that an emotionless robot would be a perfect saint, devoid of unruly passions and lustful desires.

A perfect saint, in terms of Christian history, would model love. Love is a feeling, and through that feeling Christians have understood themselves to stand in some relation to God. But as the master emotion of Christianity, it also challenges an orthodoxy based, for example, on professing a creed (saying "Lord, Lord," but without action) and complements it with an orthopraxis (performing works of mercy such as visiting the sick, caring for widows and orphans, feeding the hungry). Love as shown in deeds is more than a pure act of will, as St. Paul suggests when saying that handing over one's body to the torturers without love avails nothing: for a Christian, if one's heart is not in it, despite a very strong will, something essential is nevertheless missing.

NOTES

1. Divisions loosely follow John Corrigan et al., *Emotion and Religion* (Westport, Conn.: Greenwood Press, 2000). I do not cover figures and themes covered *ex professo* elsewhere herein, with the exception of love, the master emotion of Christian life.

2. F. von Hügel, *The Mystical Element of Religion* (London: Dent, 1961).

3. See R. Steele, ed., *"Heart Religion" in the Methodist Tradition and Related Movements* (Lanham, Md.: Scarecrow Press, 2001). W. Wainwright, *Reason and the Heart* (Ithaca, N.Y.: Cornell University Press, 1995).

4. See the chapters on ritual and ecstasy herein for more on the subject.

5. While we continue to distinguish cognition and emotion in everyday speech and in "folk psychology," science tells us today that we need to recognize their common origin in the social brain; for clarity I use their usual names.

6. Cognitive science can mean, in a narrow usage, the science of human *knowledge*, or, in a wider usage, the science of human *behavior*, i.e., human *actions* as based on *both cognition and emotion*. Neuroscience sometimes specifies *affective* neuroscience (see J. Panksepp, *Affective Neuroscience* [New York: Oxford University Press, 1998], and P. Ekman and R. Davidson, eds., *The Nature of Emotion* [New York: Oxford University Press, 1994]) and sometimes *social* neuroscience, when clarifying that it is faulty methodology to study *individual* brains (rather than social interactions) as though we could learn everything about humanity from isolated brains alone (L. Brothers, *Friday's Footprint* [New York: Oxford University Press, 1997]).

7. See Joseph Campbell, *The Power of Myth* (New York: Doubleday, 1988).

8. Contrast this characterization of classical form with contemporary architecture's challenges to formal elegance (e.g., Gothic cathedrals) in designs by Santiago Calatrava and Frank Gehry.

9. See George Lakoff and Mark Johnson, *Philosophy in the Flesh* (New York: Basic Books, 1999).

10. Karl Rahner was famous for saying at the time of Vatican Council II that whereas conciliar definitions formerly were meant to *end* debate, what they actually did was *begin* it for theologians today.

11. See Lakoff and Johnson, *Philosophy in the Flesh*.

12. On the heart, see R. Wood's excellent introduction to his translation of S. Strasser, *Das Gemüt, Phenomenology of Feeling* (Pittsburgh: Duquesne University Press, 1977), 3–36.

13. An outdated debate for two reasons. First, faculty psychology was superseded by Husserl's phenomenological method of analyzing consciousness in terms of intentionality instead of in terms of faculties. Second, pattern recognition operating by neural nets' massively parallel distributed processing (PDP) has emerged as a more plausible explanation of the origin of universals than intentionality as an irreducible spiritual act of the soul.

14. Recall Newton's *Philosophiae Naturalis Principia Mathematica* ("mathematical principles of *natural* philosophy"), where natural meant empirical, not armchair.

15. Paul Churchland, *The Engine of Reason, the Seat of the Soul* (Cambridge, Mass.: MIT Press, 1995).

16. Leslie Brothers, *Friday's Footprint: How Society Shapes the Human Mind* (Oxford: Oxford University Press, 1997).

17. See Roslind Picard, *Affective Computing* (Cambridge, Mass.: MIT Press, 1997).

18. A more faithful model would include chemistry (neurotransmitters in synapses), but the basic triode illustrates that the three elements resemble the consciousness triad, even though its folk psychology terms (*cognition, emotion, volition*) reduce in the brain to action potentials across dendrites and axons in many different kinds of neurons; the image also omits the neural nets themselves and their massively PDP.

19. Antonio Damasio, *Descartes' Error* (New York: Grosset, 1994).

20. Donald Norman, *Emotional Design* (New York: Basic Books, 2004), 166; see chap. 6, "Emotional Machines." Susan Greenfield, *Tomorrow's People* (London: Penguin Books, 2003), 48–53.

21. Of course, the heart enters also into business, science, and technology, insofar as esthetic and ethical decisions and actions enter those realms, so this analysis is not exclusive but inclusive of those realms. The difference, as we know at least from Thomas Kuhn's *Structure of Scientific Revolutions* and the critiques it provoked, is not of kind but degree: it is not that "hard" mathematical science uses cognition alone whereas "human" science use cognition plus affection, but that both are done by humans with difference percentages of both cognition and emotion.

BIBLIOGRAPHY

Anderson, Peter Bøgh, et al., eds. *Downward Causation: Minds, Bodies, and Matter*. Aarhus, Denmark: Aarhus University Press, 2000.

Bracken, Joseph. *The One in the Many: A Contemporary Reconstruction of the God-World Relationship*. Grand Rapids, Mich.: Eerdmans, 2001.

Brothers, Leslie. *Friday's Footprint: How Society Shapes the Human Mind*. Oxford: Oxford University Press, 1997.

Chenu, M.-D. "Les catégories affectives dans la langue de l'école." In *Le Coeur*. Bruges, Belgium: Desclée de Brouwer, 1950, 123–28.

Churchland, Patricia. *Brain-Wise*. Cambridge, Mass.: MIT Press, 2002.
———. *Neurophilosophy*. Cambridge, Mass.: MIT Press, 1986.
Churchland, Patricia, and T. J. Sejnowski. *The Computational Brain*. Cambridge, Mass.: MIT Press, 1992.
Churchland, Paul. *The Engine of Reason, the Seat of the Soul*. Cambridge, Mass.: MIT Press, 1995.
Corrigan, John, Eric Crump, and John Kloos. *Emotion and Religion*. Westport, Conn.: Greenwood Press, 2000.
Damasio, Antonio. *Descartes' Error*. New York: Grosset. 1994.
———. *The Feeling of What Happens*. New York: Harcourt Brace, 1999.
———. *Looking for Spinoza*. New York: Harcourt, 2003.
Franks, David, and Thomas S. Smith, eds. *Mind, Brain, and Society*. Stanford, Conn.: LAI Press, 1999.
Greenfield, Susan. *Tomorrow's People*. London: Allen Lane, 2003.
Gregersen, Niels, ed. *From Complexity to Life*. Oxford: Oxford University Press, 2003.
Johnson, Mark. *The Body in the Mind*. Chicago: University of Chicago Press, 1987.
———. *Moral Imagination*. Chicago: University of Chicago Press, 1993.
Johnson, Steven. *Emergence*. New York: Scribner's, 2001.
Lakoff, George, and Mark Johnson. *Philosophy in the Flesh*. New York: Basic Books, 1999.
LeDoux, Joseph. *The Emotional Brain*. New York: Touchstone, 1998.
———. *Synaptic Self*. New York: Viking, 2002.
Lonergan, Bernard. *A Second Collection*. Toronto: University of Toronto Press, 1974.
Macmurray, John. *Reason and Emotion*. Atlantic Highlands, N.J.: Humanities Press, 1992.
McFadden, Johnjoe. *Quantum Evolution*. New York: Norton, 2000.
Norman, Donald. *Emotional Design*. New York: Basic Books, 2004.
O'Murchu, Diarmuid. *Quantum Theology*. New York: Crossroad, 1997.
Panksepp, Jaak. *Affective Neuroscience*. Oxford: Oxford University Press, 1998.
Picard, Roslind. *Affective Computing*. Cambridge, Mass.: MIT Press, 1997.
Rolls, Edmund. *The Brain and Emotions*. Oxford: Oxford University Press, 1999.
Tallon, Andrew. *Head and Heart*. New York: Fordham University Press, 1997.
Varela, Francisco, et al. *The Embodied Mind*. Cambridge, Mass.: MIT Press, 1991.
Vetlesen, Arne. *Perception, Empathy, and Judgment*. University Park: Pennsylvania State University Press, 1994.
Wallenstein, Gene. *Mind, Stress, and Emotions*. Boston: Commonwealth Press, 2003.
Young, J. Z. *Philosophy and the Brain*. Oxford: Oxford University Press, 1987.

CHAPTER 7

NEW RELIGIOUS MOVEMENTS

DOUGLAS E. COWAN

Emotion and the Study of New Religious Movements

The academic study of new religious movements (NRMs), which are often popularly and pejoratively labeled "cults," has been underway for several decades now. Despite the claims of some groups to be "the fastest growing religious movement on earth,"[1] their numbers remain statistically low, their membership marked by high rates of experimentation, temporary affiliation, and eventual disaffiliation. As Dawson argues, however, these groups continue to exercise a fascination for both the public and the academy that is distinctly out of proportion to their size and social influence.[2] For the public, NRMs usually come into view only when there is a significant problem, when there is sufficient conflict to warrant their media presentation as "news."[3] More often than not, this presentation reinforces the very concept of the NRM as a cultural metonym for "bad religion," little more than varied sanctuaries for the devious, the dangerous, and the dishonest. Most NRM scholars, on the other hand, have resisted this vastly oversimplified representation and sought to understand groups both on their own terms and as examples of the resilience of religious belief in the face of cultural (and academic) claims of the triumph of secularization. Rather than ask what is wrong with NRMs, scholars have tried to assess what they mean in society.

As a research problem, new religious movements are marked by a number of interrelated issues that have generated a large and growing academic literature: definition (what is a "new religious movement"?);[4] evolution (what factors affect the emergence and decline of NRMs?); recruitment (how and why do participants affiliate and disaffiliate with NRMs?); endurance (if it survives beyond its first generation, when does an NRM cease to be "new" in any reasonable sense of the term?); social relationships (what is the character of a particular group's relationship to the society in which it exists, especially the family and friends of members?); and, not infrequently, opposition (how has countermovement resistance to NRMs been organized and manifested?). In broad strokes, each of these larger issues has been conceptualized in both positive and negative terms. While defining groups as "new religious movements" is one way many scholars have sought to neutralize cultural antipathy, the groups we are concerned with in this chapter are still much more popularly known as "cults," with all the negative baggage the term carries. Positively, the growth of NRMs is seen as a response to the wider social and cultural availability of religious choice; negatively, it is regarded as the all but inevitable result of unscrupulous practices such as "brainwashing," "thought control," and emotional manipulation. While the long-term success of NRMs has been theorized as a confluence of factors, including the generational legitimation of leadership, the successful encoding and transmission of religious teachings, and the establishment of strong subcultural identity in the context of a religiously plural environment,[5] counter-movements (whether secular or religious)[6] often interpret NRM success as evidence of the failure of more traditional religions to meet the needs of adherents, lack of legal protection for potential recruits, and general social decline.

Emotion is undoubtedly a factor in the life cycle of every new religious movement, if only because the human beings involved have and experience emotions. This seems axiomatic. Contrary to counter-movement claims, however, there is no universal pattern of emotional experience, response, or performance in NRMs. Rather, within each group a different "emotionology" emerges, a different affective logic according to which NRM members both express their feelings and understand the feelings they express or, in some cases, seek to suppress.[7] Further, since participation in NRMs is a process that moves from initial contact through affiliation, involvement, and disaffiliation (to use David G. Bromley's model),[8] interpreting emotion in an NRM context requires sensitivity to a number of important factors. What is the dominant emotionology of the NRM? Different NRMs have widely differing understandings of the nature and function of emotional response. At what stage along the affiliation–disaffiliation continuum is the subject? Feelings of guilt or relief during the affiliation stage, for example, should not necessarily be interpreted in the same way as similar feelings that arise during disaffiliation or postaffiliation periods. Further to this, what is the relative emotional agency of the subject? That is, is she interpreting her feelings for herself, or is someone interpreting them for her as part of an externally imposed affiliation or disaffiliation strategy?

Because they so often result in a break with established social networks and patterns of behavior, NRMs frequently become the sites for a multitude of conflicting emotions; they are cultural lightning rods as much for anger, shame, and guilt as for joy, excitement, and a sense of release and relief. Throughout NRM narratives, however, whether primary sources or secondary, whether affirmative accounts of one's affiliation and conversion or postaffiliation critiques of the group in question, two principal affective aspects emerge: emotional fulfillment and emotional abuse. As a heuristic framework to consider these more specific aspects of emotion in NRMs, I will use the trajectory of participation suggested by Bromley's affiliation–disaffiliation model. That is, what roles do emotion and affect play in the *recruitment* processes of different groups? How do emotion and affect function during an affiliate's active *involvement* with the group? And what part do they play (or are they construed to play) during and after *exit* from the group by affiliates who either become dissatisfied or are forcibly removed? All of these, it should be noted, are elements of the emotional life of NRMs that are worthy of more intentional research.

Affect and Entrance: Emotion and Recruitment to New Religious Movements

One of the basic social dynamics that mark NRMs is the process of recruitment and affiliation, whether this means temporary experimentation with alternative religious beliefs and practices or the intentional and permanent exchange of one set of beliefs and practices for another.[9] Even the generational advance of such well-known nineteenth-century NRMs as the Church of Jesus Christ of Latter-day Saints (LDS; the Mormon church) and Jehovah's Witnesses has not diminished the evangelistic fervor of either group. Mormon missionaries and Witness Pioneers still diligently spread their respective teachings in the search for new members. And why individuals affiliate—as well as why so very many disaffiliate—has been at the heart of social scientific research into new religious movements for nearly four decades.[10]

As Max Weber noted, however, "all knowledge of cultural reality is always knowledge from *particular points of view.*"[11] Indeed, interpreting the nature and function of affect during the recruiting and affiliation process illustrates this thesis clearly. Particular emotional behaviors and performances are understood very differently by members of the NRMs themselves (including potential affiliates), by those who regard NRMs as dangerous and deceptive (whether family and friends or institutionalized countermovement groups), and by social scientists who are simply trying to understand the complex processes of affiliation and conversion that are at work. With this in mind, three conceptualizations of emotion and recruitment emerge.

Affective Enticement

This form of persuasion simply makes an appeal to the emotions of a potential affiliate, as opposed to presenting rational or propositional arguments for the plausibility of one religious worldview over another. It can be as simple as exaggerated personal interest in a potential member or as complex as an intentional, programmatic appeal to the affective component of personality. Members of the Unification Church, for example, were encouraged to "love bomb" potential new members, lavishing affection and attention on them during the recruiting process.[12] In the early years of the Children of God, now called The Family International, emotional (and often sexual) enticement was practiced through "flirty fishing."[13] The free vegetarian feasts offered weekly by smiling and gracious members of the International Society for Krishna Consciousness (ISKCON) and featuring consecrated food called *prasadam* appeal to what Paul M. Toomey calls "food as metaphor and metonym for emotion."[14] "The feast should be transcendentally sumptuous," writes Danavir dasa Vanacari in his recruitment training manual, *Fortunate Souls*. "With such a festive, pleasing atmosphere, guests will be attracted to become devotees."[15]

The Church of Scientology, on the other hand, one of the most controversial NRMs of the late modern period, has a very programmatic, rationalist approach to affective enticement. For decades now, from its storefront centers (called "orgs") to the click-and-answer ease of the internet, Scientology has used its "Free Personality Test" (called the "Oxford Capacity Analysis Test") as a primary recruiting tool. A two-hundred-item questionnaire that the church claims "would normally cost you $500.00 and up," the test contains nearly forty questions that relate directly to emotion and affect: "Do you find it easy to express your emotions?" "Have you any particular hate or fear?" and "Does emotional music have quite an effect on you?"[16] Inquirers fill out the test and either submit it online or mail it to a local org for evaluation. Test analysis inevitably suggests that the person will benefit from Scientological counseling, known as "auditing," and includes contact information for a local org.

In terms of affective enticement, two things are notable in this example. First, the test itself is offered "free of charge as a public service."[17] Simply put, people feel good when they believe that they are receiving something of value without cost. Though the courses and counseling that Scientology offers can run into the hundreds of thousands of dollars, the initial contact mechanism appeals to the emotional satisfaction of finding a bargain. Second, not unlike newspaper horoscopes, aspects of the test itself appeal to generalized emotional states that everyone is likely to experience at one time or another. Since each person taking the test will score something on affective questions such as these, every person can be evaluated as a potential beneficiary of Scientological counseling.

Affective Coercion

Seen through the interpretative lens of the brainwashing hypothesis, for members of the secular anticult movement, each of these examples is clear evidence of affective coercion, as opposed to enticement. That is, "love bombing," "flirty fishing," the sheer joy expressed by Hare Krishna devotees, and the concern for the emotional well-being of Scientology's auditing clients are regarded as a façade, a religious fraud perpetrated on an unsuspecting public. Each functions as part of an overall "thought control" strategy, and the loving attention showered on potential members is little more than a deceptive appeal to emotion designed explicitly to facilitate successful affiliation and bring the new adherent under the total control of the NRM.[18] Indeed, at the heart of the anticult position lies the belief that "people join cults, not because they make a rational, informed choice. They join because they are duped."[19] Once a successful affiliation has been effected, however, the anticult movement contends, the affection ceases, and the emotionally abusive aspect of involvement and control takes over. In this sense, the difference is between covert abuse that takes place during the recruitment and affiliation process and overt abuse that occurs once affiliation has taken place. As I will discuss later, this is not to say that emotional abuse does not occur in NRM contexts, simply that for the secular anticult movement, such covert and overt abuse is one of the defining characteristics of "cults."

Affective Bonding

Much of the social scientific literature of the past three decades has questioned the empirical validity of the brainwashing hypothesis,[20] and theorized considerably more complex and less prejudicial processes of recruitment and affiliation. In terms of emotional response, numerous scholars have pointed to the importance of affective bonding, the experience in which a new adherent's in-group ties gradually supersede and/or replace his out-group affiliations. Observing the early recruiting attempts of the Unification Church, for example, John Lofland and Rodney Stark noted that where interpersonal, affective bonds either did not exist or did not emerge in the affiliation process, affiliation was less successful. Those who joined the Unification Church did so because the bonds they formed within the group became stronger than with those outside the group or with individuals who opposed their affiliation.[21] Revisiting the problem some years later, Stark and William Sims Bainbridge contend that "interpersonal bonds are the fundamental support for recruitment."[22] While affective bonding is not the only effective component in an affiliation process, nor is such a bonding process limited to NRMs, as noted below, numerous studies have tested and confirmed its importance in recruiting new members, something that is validated regularly by affiliate testimony.

In 1990, the Fifth Ward of the Church of Jesus Christ of Latter-day Saints in Calgary, Alberta, collected over fifty conversion narratives from members of the church.[23] Some contributors had grown up either around Latter-day Saints (LDS) or as part of inactive LDS families; others did not encounter the faith until much later in life. Although these accounts are formulaic, in the sense that they are intended to present a rather uniform testimony to the truth of the LDS church, they do represent a rich tapestry of experiences, participants, and contributions. In terms of emotion and conversion to a new religious faith, two aspects stand out: (1) the affective response of those surveyed to the church members they met during the process of affiliation and conversion, and (2) the affective confirmation of the LDS home teachings that validated their conversion (this will be considered in the next section).

The following two examples are representative of the collection. When Olive Lindfield met her brother's new wife for the first time, she writes that she was "impressed" by a "glow" that seemed to surround her. Indeed, she continues, her "brother proceeded to immerse me in [LDS] church activities where the glow extended to everyone. I noticed that most people seemed very happy and radiated this happiness to everyone."[24] Soon afterward, she converted to the LDS church, and she remains a faithful member. In 1942, Gladys Matson and her young family moved to Calgary and began to build a new home. "Soon after we started construction," she writes, "the Kellough family started to build next door to the east of us. The Kelloughs were Mormons and what followed quite naturally was our children played together and went to school together. Our daughter Clare and Kathy Kellough also went to Primary together. This was my introduction to the Church of Jesus Christ of Latter-day Saints."[25] In both cases, nearly fifty years after the fact, both women recall the affective bonding they experienced as central to their eventual conversion.

Affect and Engagement: Emotion and Participation in New Religious Movements

Contrary to the reductionist claims of secular and religious counter-movement groups, the vast range of beliefs, practices, rituals, and group processes that cluster under the rubric "new religious movement" prevent any useful generalizing about the place of emotion in these groups. The full range of emotion—both positive and negative—is present, arguably in any group and at any point in its history. Rather, following the understanding that particular emotional logics are, to a large degree, culturally constructed and specific to time, place, and participant, I will present examples of the affective component of NRM participation in terms of two broad categories: affect and religious practice, and affect and the confirmation of religious belief. Since affect and abuse in the new religious context is so often claimed as the impetus for disaffiliation, I will consider it in the final section. Once again, these examples indicate where much more intentional research is needed.

Affect and Religious Practice

Emotion and affect have long been recognized as integral parts of religious experience and practice. Tears stream down the cheeks of Christian charismatics, and seemingly uncontrollable mirth accompanies the so-called laughing revival among

Pentecostals. The tenderness with which Roman Catholics in Mexico care for the graves of family members on the Day of the Dead speaks volumes about the emotional investment participants have in this simple ritual. In many religious traditions, prayer is as much an emotional category as a devotional or practical one. Part of the daily practice for devotees in Bhagwan Shree Rajneesh's ashrams involved ecstatic dancing and chanting that often left participants weeping and laughing. In the UFO-oriented Raëlian movement, one of the central religious practices is "sensual meditation," in which all things pleasurable are regarded as essential components of the experience. In other movements, however, the goal is the suppression or transcendence of affect. Sitting *zazen*, practitioners of Soto Zen seek release from all emotional attachment, while followers of the Rinzai school work to disconnect the rational mind through their often emotional wrestling with the numerous *koans* for which that meditative path is known. That emotion is present in NRMs, then, is not the issue; how particular traditions understand and manifest their individual "emotionology" is. In terms of particular logics of emotion, consider the following two examples, one the *performance of affect* as religious practice, the other its *analysis* as an integral part of religious counseling.

Though less obvious now than they were in the 1970s, Hare Krishna devotees (*bhaktas*) still gather regularly for *harinama-sankirtana*, the public chanting of the Hare Krishna mantra, which is accompanied by music, dancing, and literature distribution—all in the service of spreading Krishna-consciousness. According to one of the leading teachers in the ISKCON movement, this devotional *performance of affect* serves a number of functions. It creates a subcultural bonding, especially among new *bhaktas*. They share the joyful experience of chanting with other devotees and increasingly come to feel part of the group. Moreover, a joyous *sankirtana* attracts potential new affiliates, who see the joy with which the devotees chant and want to experience that joy for themselves.[26] Finally, it creates "favorable public relations for our movement."[27] Rather than be persuaded by countermovement portrayal of the ISKCON as emotionally abusive and spiritually fraudulent, the public is encouraged to interact with devotees during *harinama-sankirtana* and learn for themselves the positive aspects of chanting the divine names. "To summarize," writes Danavir dasa Vanacari, "the *harinama* party is an ecstatic adventure in presenting Krsna consciousness. . . . By glorifying the Lord in this way, we can experience love for Godhead."[28]

On the other hand, rather than a positive vehicle for the ecstatic performance of religious devotion, the Church of Scientology regards emotions—specifically negative emotions—as part of the human predicament, and contends that "until [Scientology founder L. Ron] Hubbard's examination of this matter, emotions were something we all suffered or enjoyed, but never fully understood."[29] The religious and therapeutic philosophy of Scientology is rooted in Hubbard's concept of the "engram," a stored mental image "which is a recording of an experience containing pain, unconsciousness, and a real or fancied threat to survival."[30] Negative emotion is regarded by Scientologists as a principal component of engram content. Scientological counseling—called "auditing"—is designed to clear these engrams of their negative "charge" and free the individual from their recurring influence. Pursuing this intentional *analysis of affect* even further, Hubbard devised what he called the emotional "Tone Scale," which, beginning with "Body Death" and rising to the "Serenity of Beingness," claims to plot "emotions in an exact ascending or descending sequence."[31] Scientologists not only use the Tone Scale to counsel practitioners but also maintain that "by knowing where a person falls on the scale, one can precisely predict his actions," and that "it is a true technology of helping others to better their conditions."[32]

AFFECT AND THE CONFIRMATION OF RELIGIOUS BELIEF

In addition to their place in religious practice, in some new religious movements emotion and affect also serve as powerful mechanisms of religious authorization and legitimation.

To return to the example of the Latter-day Saints, though we do not see so much an affective authorization (in the sense of legitimation), there is a clearly established process for affective confirmation of the truth of LDS teachings. That is, potential converts to the LDS church are not asked to make their decisions on the basis of a cognitive assent to LDS doctrine but on an emotional response to what they regard as the truth of church teachings. Many testimonies relate how converts "felt" that the teachings they received from missionaries were true, and on that basis made their decisions to be baptized. Others report feelings of guilt when, even during their preaffiliation phase, they began to contravene the tenets of the LDS "Word of Wisdom"—church sanctions against tea, coffee, alcohol, and tobacco. One convert reported an emotional response to encountering the LDS temple in Cardston, Alberta. "As I walked around this wonderful building, and imagined what sacred things must be going on inside, I felt an overwhelming sense of peace, reverence, and affirmation."[33] In most cases, missionaries urge potential converts to pray for this kind of affective confirmation—often referred to as a "burning in the bosom"—and many of these conversion narratives mention a sensation of peace and warmth when doing so. Perhaps the most eloquent statement of affect in the Calgary collection of conversion narratives, however, is from Andres Sanchez, an immigrant from Mexico. Watching a broadcast of the 1977 LDS General Conference, Sanchez writes: "President Kimball is talking on the television. His impressive voice immediately penetrates into the deepest of my heart, I feel a rain of tears inside my chest, even when my eyes are dry."[34]

Like the "burning in the bosom" experience by which many of the conversions to the LDS Church are marked, affect plays a key role in the emergence of modern Paganism. Unlike the LDS experience, however, in which participants experience an emotional confirmation of the texts, beliefs, and practices particular to the LDS church, modern Pagans often affectively authorize a set of beliefs and practices that are particular to them as individuals. "If someone wants to blend pantheons," writes one modern Pagan contributor to an online discussion forum, "if that's what feels right to them, then so be it." Indeed, this concept that "if it feels right, it must be right" epitomizes the understanding among modern Pagans that personal gnosis and the intuitive, intentional construction of one's own religious beliefs are the benchmarks by which an authentic modern Paganism is measured. As a non-rational imprimatur of religious experience, many modern Pagans have raised the affective authorization of belief and practice to the level of a statement of faith. In what I have called elsewhere the "open source" character of modern Paganism,[35] adherents are appropriating, manipulating, and reinventing religious resources from around the world and through time, and there are few if any of these resources that at least some do not see as potential candidates for both pantheon and practice. "I've been a witch since I was about 13," writes one young woman in her introduction to another online discussion group. "I practice a bit of everything I suppose though my main beliefs are in Vodou. However, I'm not yet initiated in it." Another contributor wrote that she discovered the goddess Tara at a meditation group and "now she is my goddess for my wiccan practise [sic]." This importation of a Buddhist deity into the spiritual understanding of a practicing Wiccan is only possible in a religious culture that values (indeed celebrates) this kind of affective authorization of belief and practice.

Affect and Exit: Emotion, Abuse, and Departure from New Religious Movements

In this final section, three important caveats must be kept in mind. First, although emotional abuse can occur at any stage in the affiliation-disaffiliation process, it is not the case, as secular and religious counter-movements contend, that it inevitably occurs at all stages. There is also no empirical evidence to suggest that it takes place in all NRMs. Nor is it limited to the new religious context; enough evidence certainly exists to declare that no religious tradition is free from the problem. Put simply, emotional abuse should not be used as a defining characteristic of NRMs (even when labeled "cults") while it is dismissed as an aberration in the life of more culturally dominant traditions. And when it does occur, it should be considered in its full social and historical context. This is not intended to minimize the trauma of emotional abuse when it happens, merely to suggest that accurate interpretation requires careful contextualization.

Second, whether they are found to be substantiated or not, given that charges of emotional abuse carry significant cultural resonance, they must be open to investigation and interpretation, rather than simple acceptance. Let me illustrate this by way of a personal example. When I was in graduate school, I was approached by a Protestant chaplain on campus and asked to provide information about a particular religious group in the area. Two students had complained to the chaplain that it was an emotionally abusive "cult," and he was seeking further clarification. A high-commitment, charismatic Christian sect, the group had attracted some negative attention from both the evangelical counter-cult movement and the secular mass media. As it turned out, though, there was no evidence of wrongdoing beyond the fears of the two students, who were not involved in the group themselves but were concerned for a mutual friend. The precipitating event was a Bible study during which the friend had been asked if she was sexually active. The two friends concluded this was emotionally abusive and went to the chaplain. My point is this: whether the affiliate felt "abused" by the question or not, or whether the friends later interpreted the experience that way or not, the question itself is not a priori abusive. It is quite easy to imagine that for any number of other participants, the same question would hardly show up on their affective radar. What feels abusive to one person registers with another not at all.

Third, all that said, emotional abuse in new religious movements does occur. There is ample legal, scholarly, and anecdotal evidence of that. Kate Strelley, for example, writes of her years as a follower of Bhagwan Shree Rajneesh, and the emotional abuse she witnessed at a number of levels in his organization.[36] While Miriam Williams tells of her years spent "flirty fishing" as a member of the Children of God,[37] Nori Muster chronicles the often emotionally turbulent and abusive history of the ISKCON following the death of its guru, A. C. Bhaktivedanta Prabhupada.[38] And Margery Wakefield, a former Scientologist who self-published her account of life in the Church, concludes her story: "It is not possible for me to see displays of Hubbard's books in the bookstores, especially the Dianetics book ... without feeling a sense of revulsion. I have the same reaction to the Scientology ads on television."[39] Bearing in mind the caveats already noted, similar stories could be multiplied across the annals of the secular anticult and evangelical counter-cult movements.

Affect and Disaffiliation

Broadly speaking, disaffiliation from new religious movements occurs in two ways: voluntary and involuntary.[40] In situations of voluntary disaffiliation, members choose to leave or to reduce their involvement in the group as a result of dissatisfaction that is either internally generated (arising within the group context and perceived by the adherent) or externally introduced (pointed out to the adherent by actors external to the group). Following Bromley's affiliation–disaffiliation model, internally generated tensions include "disruption of internal solidarity, destabilization of leadership and authority, and problems in organizational development."[41]

Externally introduced tensions range from questions posed to adherents by concerned family and friends to programmatic "exit counseling" conducted by putative therapists, to coercive, often violent deprogramming. In each case, it is not difficult to see how fear, anger, and guilt become common affective responses to the process of disaffiliation. Depending on the amount of time and energy an adherent has committed to a particular group, she may be leaving behind the only significant social support structure she has known for many years. Feelings of betrayal by leaders and coreligionists lead to anger and resentment. Self-reflexive anger can manifest in feelings of guilt—either at the thought of disaffiliation or an emerging awareness of the problematic situation in which the adherent has been living.

Involuntary exit is most clearly seen in situations of coercive deprogramming, when adherents are forcibly removed from the group, confined against their will, and subjected to long periods of emotional, psychological, spiritual, and often physical abuse in an effort to compel disaffiliation.[42] Though this has been quite rightly recognized as criminal conduct in North America and elsewhere, some countries, notably Japan, are slow to prosecute the kidnapping and coercive deprogramming of members of particular NRMs.[43]

Affect and Postaffiliation

Though the disaffiliation process itself is likely to be traumatic—"former members routinely experience continuing ambivalence about their exit decision and sometimes a sense of personal failure and loss of community"[44]—most former NRM members return, postaffiliation, to normal lives, emotionally and otherwise. Anger subsides, guilt fades, and the fear that often accompanies moving into a new social situation gives way to trust and acceptance. Indeed, one observer suggests that even when claims of extraordinary trauma as a result of one's involvement with an NRM are proposed (as in litigation brought by disaffiliates allegedly suffering from posttraumatic stress disorder), most of these claims should be reevaluated as evidence of factitious disorder, a situation in which "physical or psychological symptoms are intentionally produced or feigned."[45] To this we could easily add "emotional symptoms." In terms of voluntary and involuntary disaffiliation, however, there remain conflicting interpretations of the "success" of deprogramming and exit counseling in terms of emotion and affect. While the secular anticult movement obviously regards exit counseling (whether coercive or voluntary) as an important stage in the disaffiliation process,[46] social scientific research indicates that structured disaffiliation interventions actually prolong the emotional and psychological difficulties former members experience both during and after the disaffiliation process.[47]

Issues for Further Research

There is obviously an abundance of research questions implied in this very brief survey, and in closing I shall draw attention to three: (1) differences in emotionology across NRM generations; (2) comparative emotionologies when the new religious movement is a dominant tradition elsewhere; and (3) the dynamics of affective reinterpretation over the course of the affiliation–disaffiliation process.

First, many NRMs are advancing generationally and are struggling with a host of issues related to the rearing and enculturation of second-generation members.[48] How has the presence of children in particular NRM contexts affected the relative emotionologies of these groups? A number of groups, for example, from the Branch Davidians to the Hare Krishnas, have had to deal with allegations of child abuse. How has this impacted the emotional life of participants of all generations? On the other hand, with children in their midst, many modern Pagans have decided to amend the manner in which some religious practices are conducted, particularly with respect to ritual nudity. Has there been a similar shift in emotionology? Finally, some NRMs are struggling to retain the second (or third) generation of members. How does the emotionology differ when disaffiliation occurs for members raised in the group?

Second, what are the differences in emotionology when a religious group shifts from a position of social and cultural dominance to one in which it is a marginal faith? For example, is there a different logic of emotion for, say, evangelical Protestantism in India than in North America or western Europe? What would a historical study of emotion in missiology reveal, both in terms of the expectations of missionaries before they went to the field, and their experiences of religious dominance and marginalization once they arrived?

Finally, how do participants in new religious movements reinterpret their own emotional experiences and logics over the course of the affiliation–disaffiliation process? That is, since few people would submit voluntarily to emotional abuse and manipulation if they knew it was happening to them, how do former members reframe the affective character of their entrance and engagement processes, especially in light of the manner in which disaffiliation took place?

Notes

1. Church of Scientology International, *Scientology Effective Solutions: Providing the Tools for Successful Living* (Brussels: Church of Scientology International, 2004). Other new religious groups make the same claim. On the basis of certain statistical data, many modern Pagans claim that their religion is the fastest growing in both the United States and Australia (see Douglas E. Cowan, *Cyberhenge: Modern Pagans on the Internet* [London: Routledge, 2005]), and Carolyn Wah writes that "the Jehovah's Witnesses are one of the

world's fastest growing religious groups" ("An Introduction to Research and Analysis of Jehovah's Witnesses: A View from the Watchtower," *Review of Religious Research* 43, 2 [2001]: 161). Even the tiny United Nuwaubian Nation of Moors, which is clearly not a contender, maintains that it is "one of the fastest growing organizations on the planet" (www.geocities.com/Area51/Corridor/4978/unnm.html).

2. See Lorne L. Dawson, "The Sociocultural Significance of Modern New Religious Movements," in *The Oxford Handbook of New Religious Movements*, edited by James R. Lewis (Oxford: Oxford University Press, 2004), and "Teaching about the Meaning and Significance of NRMs," in *Teaching New Religious Movements*, edited by David G. Bromley (Oxford: Oxford University Press, 2007).

3. See Douglas E. Cowan and Jeffrey K. Hadden, "God, Guns, and Grist for the Media's Mill: Constructing the Narratives of New Religious Movements and Violence," *Nova Religio* 8, 2 (2004): 64–82; Stuart A. Wright, "Media Coverage of Unconventional Religion: Any 'Good News' for Minority Faith?" *Review of Religious Research* 39, 2 (1997): 101–15.

4. An often bewildering array of groups fall under the broader category "new religious movements." Reliable scholarly compendia of these include: J. Gordon Melton, *Encyclopedic Handbook of Cults in America*, rev. ed. (New York: Garland, 1992), and Timothy Miller, ed., *America's Alternative Religions* (Albany: State University of New York Press, 1995).

5. On this, see William Sims Bainbridge and Rodney Stark, "Cult Formation: Three Compatible Models," *Sociological Analysis* 40 (1979): 283–95; Lorne L. Dawson, "Antimodernism, Modernism, and Postmodernism: Struggling with the Cultural Significance of New Religious Movements," *Sociology of Religion* 59 (1998): 131–56; Rodney Stark, "Why Religious Movements Succeed or Fail: A Revised General Model," *Journal of Contemporary Religion* 11 (1996): 133–46.

6. By "counter-movement," I mean both the secular anticult movement, whose antipathy toward NRMs is based on allegations of thought control and emotional manipulation, and the evangelical Christian counter-cult movement, which regards NRMs as dangerous spiritual impostors. On the secular anticult movement, see Anson D. Shupe, Jr., and David G. Bromley, *The New Vigilantes: Deprogrammers, Anti-cultists, and the New Religions* (London: Sage, 1980); on the evangelical Christian counter-cult movement, see Douglas E. Cowan, *Bearing False Witness? An Introduction to the Christian Countercult* (Westport, Conn.: Praeger, 2003).

7. Peter Stearns and Carol Stearns, "Emotionology: Clarifying the History of Emotions and Emotional Standards," *American Historical Review* 90 (1985): 813–36.

8. See David G. Bromley, "Leaving the Fold: Disaffiliating from New Religious Movements," in *The Oxford Handbook of New Religious Movements*, edited by James R. Lewis (Oxford: Oxford University Press, 2004); James T. Richardson, *Conversion Careers* (Beverly Hills: Sage, 1978).

9. This situation comes closer to what Bromley understands as "conversion," "a designation that legitimates the affiliate-movement relationship. By designating themselves as converts, affiliates are indicating public acceptance of movement ideology and organization in orienting their behavior" (Bromley, "Leaving the Fold," 307). Those who convert to and are baptized in the Latter-day Saint church, for example, are converts, whereas the vast majority of those who call themselves Scientologists likely remain affiliates.

10. On affiliation and conversion, see, for example, Lorne L. Dawson, "Who Joins New Religious Movements and Why: Twenty Years of Research and What Have We Learned?" *Studies in Religion/Sciences Religieuses* 25 (1996): 141–61; John Lofland, "Becoming

a World-Saver Revisited," *American Behavioral Scientist* 20 (1977): 805–18; John Lofland and Norman Skonovd, "Conversion Motifs," *Journal for the Scientific Study of Religion* 20 (1981): 373–85, and "Patterns of Conversion," in *Of Gods and Men: New Religious Movements in the West*, edited by Eileen Barker (Macon, Ga.: Mercer University Press, 1983), 1–24; John Lofland and Rodney Stark, "Becoming a World-Saver: A Theory of Conversion to a Deviant Perspective," *American Sociological Review* 30 (1965): 862–74; E. Burke Rochford, Jr., *Hare Krishna in America* (New Brunswick, N.J.: Rutgers University Press, 1985); David A. Snow and Cynthia Phillips, "The Lofland-Stark Conversion Model: A Critical Reassessment," *Social Problems* 27 (1980): 430–47; Richardson, *Conversion Careers*; Rodney Stark and William Sims Bainbridge, "Networks of Faith: Interpersonal Bonds and Recruitment to Cults and Sects," *American Journal of Sociology* 85 (1980): 1376–95.

11. Max Weber, *The Methodology of the Social Sciences*, translated and edited by Edward A. Shils and Henry A. Finch (New York: Free Press, 1949), 81, emphasis in the original.

12. See Eileen Barker, *The Making of a Moonie: Choice or Brainwashing?* (London: Blackwell, 1984), esp. 172–88.

13. See William Sims Bainbridge, *The Endtime Family: Children of God* (Albany: State University of New York Press, 2002); James D. Chancellor, *Life in the Family: An Oral History of the Children of God* (Syracuse, N.Y.: Syracuse University Press, 2000).

14. Paul M. Toomey, "Krishna's Consuming Passions: Food as Metaphor and Metonym for Emotion at Mount Govardhan," in *Divine Passions: The Social Construction of Emotion in India*, edited by Owen M. Lynch (Berkeley: University of California Press, 1990).

15. Danavir dasa Vanacari, *Fortunate Souls, The Bhakta Program Manual: A Comprehensive Guide to Recruiting and Training New Devotees in Krishna Consciousness* (Moundsville, W.V.: Bhakta Program Institute, 1996), 348.

16. All questions from Church of Scientology International, "Oxford Capacity Analysis Test," www.scientology.org/oca.htm.

17. Ibid.

18. See Steven M. Hassan, *Combatting Cult Mind Control* (Rochester, Vt.: Park Street Press, 1990); Michael D. Langone, introduction to *Recovery from Cults: Help for Victims of Psychological and Spiritual Abuse*, edited by Michael D. Langone (New York: Norton, 1993), 1–21; Margaret Thaler Singer, with Janja Lalich, *Cults in Our Midst* (San Francisco: Jossey-Bass, 1995); Madeleine Landau Tobias and Janja Lalich, *Captive Hearts, Captive Minds: Freedom and Recovery from Cults and Abusive Relationships* (Alameda, Calif.: Hunter House, 1994).

19. Langone, introduction to *Recovery from Cults*, 6.

20. See, for example, the essays collected in David G. Bromley and James T. Richardson, eds., *The Brainwashing/Deprogramming Controversy: Sociological, Psychological, Legal, and Historical Perspectives* (New York: Edwin Mellen Press, 1983), and Benjamin Zablocki and Thomas Robbins, eds., *Misunderstanding Cults: Searching for Objectivity in a Controversial Field* (Toronto: University of Toronto Press, 2001). On the ongoing debate, see David G. Bromley, "Listing (in Black and White) Some Observations on (Sociological) Thought Reform," *Nova Religio* 1 (1998): 250–66; Benjamin Zablocki, "The Blacklisting of a Concept: The Strange History of the Brainwashing Conjecture in the Sociology of Religion," *Nova Religio* 1 (1997): 96–121; "Reply to Bromley," *Nova Religio* 1 (1998): 267–71.

21. Lofland and Stark, "Becoming a World-Saver."

22. Stark and Bainbridge, "Networks of Faith," 1389.

23. Carl H. Swendsen and Clark T. Leavitt, comps., *Wise Men Still Seek Him: Personal Accounts of the Conversion of Some Members of the Calgary Fifth Ward* (Calgary, Alberta: privately printed, 1990).

24. Olive Lindfield, "Testimony," in Swendson and Leavitt, *Wise Men Still Seek Him*, 18.

25. Gladys Matson, "My Conversion Story," in Swendson and Leavitt, *Wise Men Still Seek Him*, 22.

26. For an early explanation of this in the ISKCON movement, see International Society for Krishna Consciousness, *Chant and Be Happy... The Story of the Hare Krishna Mantra* (Los Angeles: Bhaktivedanta Book Trust, 1982).

27. Vanacari, *Fortunate Souls*, 213.

28. Ibid., 219. On changes in the practice of *harinama-sankirtana*, see Rochford, *Hare Krishna in America*, 171–89.

29. Church of Scientology International, *What Is Scientology?* (Los Angeles: Bridge, 1998), 74.

30. L. Ron Hubbard, *Dianetics: The Modern Science of Mental Health* (Los Angeles: Bridge, 1990).

31. Church of Scientology International, *What Is Scientology?* 74.

32. Ibid., 76.

33. James Kroeker, "Testimony of James Kroeker," in Swendsen and Leavitt, *Wise Men Still Seek Him*, 14.

34. Andres Sanchez, "Conversion of Andres Avelino Sanchez," in Swendsen and Leavitt, *Wise Men Still Seek Him*, 37.

35. Cowan, *Cyberhenge*, 27–50.

36. Kate Strelley, with Robert D. San Souci, *The Ultimate Game: The Rise and Fall of Bhagwan Shree Rajneesh* (San Francisco: Harper and Row, 1987).

37. Miriam Williams, *Heaven's Harlots: My Fifteen Years in a Sex Cult* (New York: Eagle Books, 1998).

38. Nori J. Muster, *Betrayal of the Spirit: My Life behind the Headlines of the Hare Krishna Movement* (Urbana: University of Illinois Press, 1997).

39. Margery Wakefield, *The Road to Xenu: A Narrative Account of Life in Scientology* (1996), available at www.cs.cmu.edu/~dst/Library/. This Web page—The Secret Library of Scientology—was created by Dean Benjamin.

40. On disaffiliation, see, for example, David G. Bromley, ed., *Falling from the Faith: Causes and Consequences of Religious Apostasy* (Newbury Park, Calif.: Sage, 1988), and *The Politics of Religious Apostasy: The Role of Apostates in the Transformation of Religious Movements* (Westport, Conn.: Praeger, 1998); Janet Liebman Jacobs, *Divine Disenchantment: Deconverting for New Religions* (Bloomington: Indiana University Press, 1989); Stuart A. Wright, *Leaving Cults: The Dynamics of Defection* (Washington, D.C.: Society for the Scientific Study of Religion, 1987).

41. Bromley, "Leaving the Fold," 300.

42. See Anson D. Shupe and Susan E. Darnell, "CAN, We Hardly Knew Ye: Sex, Drugs, Deprogrammers' Kickbacks, and Corporate Crime in the (Old) Cult Awareness Network," paper presented at the annual meeting of the Society for the Scientific Study of Religion, Houston, Texas, October 2000.

43. See, for example, the documents compiled in Lee Boothby, *White Paper Report and Call to Action to Uphold the Right of Thought and Conscience by Ending Forcible Deprogramming* (Falls Church, Va.: International Coalition for Religious Freedom, 2004); and Anson D. Shupe and Susan E. Darnell, "Agents of Discord: The North American-European ACM Connection," paper presented at the International Conference of CESNUR/INFORM (Center for Study on New Religions/Information Network Focus on Religious Movements), London, April 2001.

44. Bromley, "Leaving the Fold," 305.

45. H. Newton Malony, "Expert Testimony on Residual Effects of Participating in New Religious Movements," in, *Coercive Persuasion, Undue Influence, Mind Control: A Psychologist's Point of View* (Pasadena, Calif.: Integration Press, 1988), 71.

46. See Hassan, *Combatting Cult Mind Control*; Langone, *Recovery from Cults*; Singer, *Cults in Our Midst*; and Tobias and Lalich, *Captive Hearts, Captive Minds*.

47. Bromley, "Leaving the Fold," 310; see also James R. Lewis and David G. Bromley, "The Cult Withdrawal Syndrome: A Case of Misattribution of Cause?" *Journal for the Scientific Study of Religion* 26 (1987): 508–22, and Wright, *Leaving Cults*.

48. See Susan J. Palmer and Charlotte E. Hardman, eds., *Children in New Religions* (New Brunswick, N.J.: Rutgers University Press, 1999).

BIBLIOGRAPHY

Barker, Eileen. *The Making of a Moonie: Choice or Brainwashing?* London: Blackwell, 1984.

Bromley, David G., ed. *Falling from the Faith: Causes and Consequences of Religious Apostasy*. Newbury Park, Calif.: Sage, 1988.

Chancellor, James D. *Life in the Family: An Oral History of the Children of God*. Syracuse, N.Y.: Syracuse University Press, 2000.

Jacobs, Janet Liebman. *Divine Disenchantment: Deconverting for New Religions*. Bloomington: Indiana University Press, 1989.

Langone, Michael D., ed. *Recovery from Cults: Help for Victims of Psychological and Spiritual Abuse*. New York: Norton, 1993.

Muster, Nori J. *Betrayal of the Spirit: My Life behind the Headlines of the Hare Krishna Movement*. Urbana: University of Illinois Press, 1997.

Palmer, Susan J., and Charlotte E. Hardman, eds. *Children in New Religions*. New Brunswick, N.J.: Rutgers University Press, 1999.

Richardson, James T., ed. *Conversion Careers*. Beverly Hills, Calif.: Sage, 1978.

Rochford, E. Burke, Jr. *Hare Krishna in America*. New Brunswick, N.J.: Rutgers University Press, 1985.

Strelley, Kate, with Robert D. San Souci. *The Ultimate Game: The Rise and Fall of Bhagwan Shree Rajneesh*. San Francisco: Harper and Row, 1987.

Tobias, Madeleine Landau, and Janja Lalich. *Captive Hearts, Captive Minds: Freedom and Recovery from Cults and Abusive Relationships*. Alameda, Calif.: Hunter House, 1994.

Williams, Miriam. *Heaven's Harlots: My Fifteen Years in a Sex Cult*. New York: Eagle Books, 1998.

Wright, Stuart A. *Leaving Cults: The Dynamics of Defection*. Washington, D.C.: Society for the Scientific Study of Religion, 1987.

PART II
RELIGIOUS LIFE

CHAPTER 8

RITUAL

PAMELA E. KLASSEN

When I was twenty-two, newly graduated with a BA in political theory and religious studies, I set off on an extended trip through Australia and Southeast Asia. One of my goals for the journey was to undertake a twenty-six-day retreat at a Theravada Buddhist monastery in Chiang Mai, Thailand, which had been highly recommended to me by one of my uncles, a mystical type who had himself already visited the monastery. Arriving in Chiang Mai with only the name of the temple and no address (in an era before the internet), it took a while before my inadequate Thai pronunciation landed me at the proper place. Once there, however, it was clear from the handful of other backpackers, clothed all in white, that I had found the right place.

The retreat consisted of a progressively more intense schedule of daily sitting and walking meditation, which took place in a small room I was given as sleeping quarters in the nuns' section of the leafy compound. What began as six hours of alternating, short periods of sitting and walking—while paying attention to breathing in and out from the belly and mindfully acknowledging and letting go of passing thoughts and feelings—eventually culminated in "determination," a final three days and nights of continuous meditation in the form of one hour of sitting meditation and one hour of walking meditation, for seventy-two hours straight. An important part of the practice that worked up to determination was the daily "report" to the abbot of the monastery. After lining up with the other novices, all of whom had also taken on the eight Buddhist precepts upon entering the monastery, I waited for my turn to tell the abbot of my progress (or lack thereof). Once I had kneeled and prostrated before the abbot, I would describe my previous day's experience, and receive his counsel—whether it be the hoped-for advice of increasing the number of meditation hours, suggestions regarding technique, or reassurances that boredom and frustration were normal consequences of the practice.

During one of these visits, a little more than halfway through the retreat, I told the abbot about particularly vivid and terrifying dreams I had experienced the night before, and about how these images continued to hound me in my meditation practice. Worried that my nightmares and my inability to clear these images in my waking hours would mean that the abbot would dole out the most dreaded of rumored counsels—namely, the requirement to repeat a day of practice—I was relieved to find that my recounting of the grisly contents of my dream met with a smile. In the ancient and finely calibrated rhythms of this Vipassana ritual, I learned, my feelings of terror and my dramatic nightmares were right on schedule—my psychophysical reactions meant that I was progressing well on the way to the days and nights of determination. As unschooled as I was in Buddhist practice, my body and psyche, once living under the eight precepts and engaged in the regularity of Vipassana, seemed to know what to do.

The confidence of the monks and lay teachers that their teaching and my practice would result in a meditation experience that followed a universal physiological, emotional, and spiritual path raises one of the most controversial and longstanding questions for students of ritual and emotion: what is the relationship between physiology and culture in the practice of religious ritual? Does physically choreographed ritual engender universal emotional responses? What is the role of culture in the evocation as well as the expression of ritually produced emotion? And in the midst of the cross-cultural, interreligious eclecticism of the twenty-first century, in which outsiders seek to engage religious traditions while equipped with more or less intimate knowledge of those traditions, how do we determine the relationships among ritual, emotion, and the ambivalent notion of authenticity?

To answer these questions, one must first acknowledge that any discussion of the deeply personal and profoundly cultural phenomena of ritualized emotion is enmeshed in discourses that are themselves highly emotionally charged. "Sensitive" discussions of emotion and ritual take place within and between religious communities, as well as within and between academic communities—that is, both religious practitioners and scholars get worked up about what counts as authentic ritual emotion and about the significance of such emotions. For this essay, I will limit myself to considering two such realms of discourse: (1) politically motivated contests over the authenticity of ritualized emotion, such as weeping or visionary bliss, which can be contests internal to a community or between different communities, as in the context of charges of appropriation across traditions, and (2) scholarly debates over cognition and culture, or the relative importance of neurophysiological versus social and cultural influences on the origin, function, and meaning of ritual. Throughout, I will argue that the study of ritual and emotion needs to attend to embodiment and physicality, as well as to the social, historical, and cultural networks within which ritualized emotions "make sense."

Important to my argument is the underlying claim that discussions of both ritual authenticity and the relations of cognition and culture are situated within the larger contentious terrain of the relative status of emotion with regard to reason in Western scholarship and culture. Especially in the context of religion, charges of emotionalism have been used against a variety of groups construed as less evolved or more deprived, whether women undergoing possession, indigenous and colonized peoples involved in sacrifice, or the religiously devout in the West experiencing glossolalia or transubstantiation. Keeping these uses of emotion in mind, it is no surprise that discourses of ritual authenticity and of cognition and culture each have their own (often hidden) histories of emotional sedimentations. As such, they are helpful frames in which to question not only the relationship between emotion and ritual but also the ways we—whether as scholars and practitioners—think and feel about such relations.

Definitions of Ritual

Before venturing into these emotional discourses, I first attend to the necessary, albeit necessarily inconclusive, task of defining the term *ritual*. Perhaps because of its brevity, one of the most helpful characterizations of ritual is that of Jonathan Z. Smith, who suggested that ritual, occurring within a particular space, acts as a focusing lens, a call to pay attention to a particular person, deity, relationship, or transition.[1] Smith drew from the pioneering work of Arnold van Gennep, who coined the phrase "pivoting of the sacred" to describe how rites of passage (e.g., baptisms, initiations, weddings) mark off particular people for focused attention as they shift from one social category to another. For example, a bride is the focus of extraordinary family and community attention as she shifts from an unmarried woman to a wife.[2] While a seemingly obvious point, the acknowledgment of how rituals bestow social significance stresses the importance of the (often fleeting) power and status that come with ritual performances, in a way that definitions emphasizing the repetitiveness or the form of rituals do not.

Smith goes on to spell out the notion of ritual space as a focusing lens by describing ritual as a "controlled environment" in which the powerful uncontrollability of everyday life is acknowledged by the attempt to control it via performed actions—in one potential example, my neophyte meditation practice sought to overcome the everyday reality of distracting emotions and thoughts by acknowledging and letting go of them in a precisely choreographed ritual. This control, Smith argues, is not an attempt at sympathetic magic or the "translation of emotions" but is instead a display of and deliberation over the incongruency of ritual order and everyday disorder. In his words: "Ritual is a means of performing the way things ought to be in conscious tension to the way things are in such a way that this ritualized perfection is recollected in the ordinary, uncontrolled, course of things."[3] Central to Smith's definition, then, is the contention that ritual is about thinking, or about thoughtful consideration; it is about acknowledging and remembering the messiness and dangers of life through performing their opposite.

How does this definition, so focused on thinking, and seemingly less concerned with emotion, contribute to the task of understanding emotion and ritual? In some ways, one could argue that Smith's definition gives too much primacy to thinking as the route to displaying and performing ritual control over the uncontrollable everyday (and too much orderliness to ritual). After all, emotional engagement is almost always part of ritual behavior, whether in the outwardly dispassionate rhythms of Buddhist meditation or Anglican chants or in the dramatically visceral shivers of Pentecostals slain in the spirit or Vodou manbos possessed by Ogun. This, however, would position thinking and emotion in a false dichotomy, ignoring that emotions are themselves cognitive as well as embodied, in the vein of anthropologist Michelle Rosaldo's phrase "embodied thoughts."[4] Smith may have argued against understanding ritual as the translation of emotions; however, his notion of ritual as the thinking-through of incongruity does not necessarily leave us with a dichotomy that excludes emotion as part of the process of thinking ritual; in Smith's usage, thinking is more akin to pondering than reasoning.

Smith's and van Gennep's characterizations of ritual fluidity—in terms of their acknowledgment of the importance of social relations for the pivoting of the sacred—are helpfully paired with the anthropologist Victor Turner's discussion of ritual symbols. Turner's theory of ritual is highly focused on symbols as artifacts and natural elements that evoke emotional responses, personal memories, and social connections. Viewing symbols as the "basic unit of ritual," Turner argued that what he called "dominant symbols" have three formative properties: (1) they *condense* "many things and actions" into one representation; (2) they *unify* "disparate significata" along lines of association that are either factual or perceived; and (3) they have two *poles of meaning,* which they mediate: the *ideological pole* of moral and social orders, and the *sensory pole* of natural and bodily elements.[5] Turner's primary example of a dominant symbol was the milk tree of the Ndembu in Zambia, which, when the focus of girls' coming-of-age rituals, condensed, unified, and polarized elements such as breast milk, fertility, childhood, motherhood, and a mother's letting go of her child. A similar example would be iconic images of the Virgin Mary nursing the baby Jesus, in which fertility and virginity are both united and polarized.

According to Turner, it is at the sensory pole where emotions enter in with their fullest force, brought on by "those significata that may be expected to arouse desires and feelings."[6] Drawing from Durkheim's conception of symbols as "collective representations," Turner's placement of emotions firmly within the sensory pole of meaning may seem to be a predictable relegation of emotions to the irrational and eruptive body. His later comment, however, complicates such a picture. The polarization of meaning effected in dominant symbols, he argues, ends up bringing together the force of emotion with the compulsion of social norms:

> In the action situation of ritual, with its social excitement and directly physiological stimuli, such as music, singing, dancing, alcohol, incense, and bizarre modes of dress, the ritual symbol, we may perhaps say, effects an interchange of qualities between its poles of meaning. Norms and values, on the one hand,

become saturated with emotion, while the gross and basic emotions become ennobled through contact with social values. The irksomeness of moral constraint is transformed into the "love of virtue."[7]

For Turner, the interpenetration of emotion and norms within ritual is rarely a conscious or articulated process. Instead, ritual symbols are "suppressed from speech" as they do the complex work of bringing together norms, emotions, and signifiers for a socially diverse group. In Turner's view, ritual brings about a conjunction of incongruities similar to that described by Smith, but Turner, unlike Smith, does not focus on the thinking individuals who mull over such conjunctions. Instead, he seemingly grants agency to ritual itself; working with both body and society, "ritual adapts and periodically readapts the biopsychical individual to the basic conditions and axiomatic values of human social life."[8]

Along with his theories of liminality and communitas, in which ritual allows the inversion, mocking, and eventually reassertion of social hierarchies or relationships, Turner's understanding of ritual symbols has deeply influenced scholarship in religion. For example, Harvey Whitehouse, though he critically revises Turner's theory of communitas, has adopted the biopsychical aspect of Turner's definition, putting forward a cognitive theory of ritual and religion that is partly rooted in neurobiological understandings of emotion. Critiquing theories of ritual that ignore the conscious experience of its participants—a criticism that could be made of Turner's theory—Whitehouse argues for a theory that is deeply concerned with the emotional and cognitive processes of ritual participants.[9] To that end, he categorizes two kinds of modes of religiosity that are also modes of ritual: doctrinal and imagistic. Doctrinal ritual (such as liturgy) works largely with regular, repetitive performances that are usually tied to textually or orally recounted traditions of legitimation, and is less characterized by sharp memories of any singular event.[10] An example would be the ritual of the Eucharist or Communion within Christianity. Imagistic ritual, by contrast, is intermittent, more obviously emotionally arousing, and more memorable as a specific occasion peopled by particular actors. Whitehouse uses the example of the terror induced in male initiation rites in Papua New Guinea to clarify this ritual mode.[11]

The connection of ritual and emotion is central to Whitehouse's distinction, especially in terms of his view of the significance of memory for ritual processes. Doctrinal ritual, he argues, depends on a memory drawn from learning the texts and traditions of a religion, while imagistic ritual imposes memory on its participants by arousing intense emotions in a "flashbulb" moment, whether emotions of terror or (in the words of French theorists and not Whitehouse) *jouissance*. In a somewhat predictable turn, Whitehouse's categories end up with a religious typology in which doctrinal ritual is most commonly associated with "world and regional" religions, while imagistic ritual is tied to "small-scale religions and cults."[12]

Despite this provisional association of doctrinal ritual with world religions and imagistic ritual with small-scale "cults" (and the implicit association of small-scale religions with vivid emotionality, for good or ill), Whitehouse insists that doctrinal and imagistic rituals can coexist within a particular tradition. Although he argues that weddings are not among what he calls the "revelatory rituals" that are characteristic of the imagistic mode—that is, rituals that disclose cosmological knowledge and "trigger enduring religious revelations in the minds of novices"—his discussion of weddings is revealing of some of the limitations of his perspective. Speaking of weddings in the specific context of Papua New Guinea as well as more broadly, Whitehouse argues that weddings are not revelatory, in that they do not give the main participants "a new awareness of the structure of the cosmos and their place within it."[13] However, this seems to be an empirically uninformed view of the social relations involved in weddings in a variety of religious traditions—a view that is overly shaped by attention to the doctrinal, "official" part of the ritual. One could imagine a case in which a wedding ritual included the process of a woman moving from her family home to that of her husband, implying a strikingly memorable transformation of social relations, as well as the potentially strikingly memorable occasion of her first experience of sexual intercourse. Seen as an aspect of a larger ritual process, a wedding ceremony could easily become revelatory, bringing about a woman's new awareness of her place in the family, and even the cosmos. Whitehouse's reluctance to consider how gender might differentially affect the "comprehension" of "newlyweds" keeps him from considering the limits of his categorization.

Thinking even more specifically, a Christian wedding, though deeply doctrinal in many respects, could also be considered an imagistic ritual. Though the stress, and perhaps terror, of the couple on their wedding day may not always instill a "flashbulb memory" of enough depth to keep them adhering to their vows, the wedding ritual does show much of the singularity and memorability that Whitehouse ascribes to imagistic rituals. In fact, one could even argue that in contemporary North American wedding cultures (and their exported versions in Asia and elsewhere), the fetishization of singularity, emotional intensity, and creating "memories" within the wedding "script" makes weddings a consummate blend of imagistic and doctrinal rituals.[14]

The distinction between dogmatic and imagistic modes of religiosity also pays little attention to the importance of regular, annual, doctrinally inflected seasonal rituals, such as Christmas or Passover, and their ability to be memorable and filled with emotional resonance. For example, Joel Robbins writes of a community of Christians in Papua New Guinea, for whom one Christmas became a *hevi Krismas*— one burdened with sadness and strife—due to community rancor and disagreement propelled in part by the interventions of a multinational mining company. In response to the anger and distrust that had built up among the two sides of the community, one community member came up with an adaptation of an indigenous ritual, and in the days after Christmas the community engaged in a ritual exchange of goods and emotion, in which one party could "buy" the shame and anger of the other. The pain of the abnormally *hevi Krismas* was transformed by a ritual innovation developed in response to Christian and indigenous traditions, as well as to the interventions of capitalism and globalization, which memorably reoriented the participants both cosmologically and in their communities.[15]

Writing earlier than Whitehouse, and without his duality of imagistic and doctrinal, Talal Asad generated a theory of ritual with a focus on the power relations—both within cultures and within academia—that have shaped the concept of ritual as symbolic representations that can be read as texts. Asad contends that, particularly within anthropological conceptions of ritual as symbolic action, a distinction has been drawn "between 'feelings' as private and ineffable and 'ritual' as public and legible."[16] Though he recognizes that this distinction has been increasingly challenged by scholars' growing awareness of the ways language constructs emotion, Asad goes on to point out the ways anthropologists have considered emotion as a source of chaos that can be threatening or destructive to the representational structure of ritual—that unleashed emotion can overwhelm a ritual's carefully constructed symbols.

Asad questions the notion of ritual as symbolic representation by contrasting this notion with a model of ritual as the cultivation of the self within a particular community. Drawing from Marcel Mauss's 1936 essay "Techniques of the Body," Asad proposes that ritual, which he subdivides into discourse and gesture, could be "viewed as part of the social process of learning to develop aptitudes, not as orderly symbols that stand in an objective world in contrast to contingent feelings and experiences that inhabit a separate subjective one."[17] Situating his distinction between ritual as aptitude achieved through practice and ritual as symbols conveyed through representation, Asad continues:

> Clearly there is a fundamental disparity between a "ritual" that organizes practices aimed at the full development of the monastic self and a "ritual" that offers a reading of a social institution. We may speculate on the ways in which the increasing marginality of religious discipline in industrial capitalist society may have reinforced the latter concept.[18]

Asad's notion of ritual as the development of aptitude through practice (in addition to monasticism, he offers the example of the way a pianist learns to play music through practice that teaches both the hands and the memory) is not necessarily at odds with Whitehouse's categorization of doctrinal and imagistic modes of religiosity. Asad's sensitivity to the ways our categories of ritual, religion, and emotion are shaped by history and politics, however, does distinguish his work from Whitehouse's quest to think about ritual via a comprehensive dualism that is less interested in questions of context.

Though I cannot do full justice to any of these theories of ritual in the space of this chapter, I can point out that all these theorists set themselves the task of explaining why people enact rituals, what they hope to transmit through ritual and to whom, and what they do not recognize (or what, in the words of Catherine Bell, they misrecognize) in the process.[19] These theorists also hope to answer a larger question of how rituals work and, for some, how emotion contributes to efficacious ritual. The most ambitious of theorists (including Asad and Whitehouse) also call scholars to think about the politics behind our categorizations of ritual and emotion—to venture into thinking reflexively about what sorts of emotions and commitments we ourselves might imbue within our own analyses.[20]

Discourses of Emotion

In a recent survey of studies of emotion and religion, John Corrigan drew a distinction between universalistic and relativistic approaches to emotion. Arguing for the benefits of a middle ground between the two, Corrigan called for analyses of religion and emotion that can take in the insights of neurobiological thinkers such as Whitehouse, as well as those of culturally focused theorists such as Turner and Smith.[21] Such mediating attempts have increased in the last few years, as the work of Ann Taves, Peter Deeley, and even Whitehouse himself would suggest.[22] With several examples of this mediating work at hand, I now turn to my earlier claim that analyses of ritual and emotion are themselves implicated in complex, historically specific, emotion-laden discourses.

Studies of ritual have long considered emotion an element of inquiry, if not always explicitly. Durkheim's notion of "effervescence" in collective gatherings posited that group rituals could encourage sensations of community cohesion, in which the individual passions could be translated into dearly held concepts supporting social solidarity.[23] As we have already seen, emotion plays a central role in Victor Turner's analysis of the normative and sensory poles of ritual symbols. Similarly, Clifford Geertz's classic (though contested) definition of religion holds that "moods and motivations" are an important aspect of how ritual contributes to religion's persuasive force in a culture.[24]

In many ways, ritual has served as all things to all people in terms of the range of its emotional functions. In some analyses, ritual allows for the expressing of potentially disruptive emotions, such as grief or fear; in other cases, it makes room for conventionally harmonious emotions, such as love, filiality, or piety. For some scholars, the benefits of studying emotion within ritual lies in its qualities as a symbolic, pragmatic, "real" action in the world that can act as a filter, crystallization, or provocation of inner states that are notoriously difficult to pin down. Ritual provides an approach to the emotion and religion nexus that need not be limited to psychobiological or psychoanalytic approaches.[25] Considered both the instigator of social critique as well as the reproducer and creator of social hierarchies, ritual is itself the focus of shifting interpretations, just as it is the channel for pivoting notions of the sacred.

Several ritual theorists have made compelling cases for the situatedness of ritual studies and ritual critiques, drawing attention to the ways the study of ritual, similarly to historically and politically implicated constructions of the category of religion, also takes place within certain scholarly habits of mind.[26] As Catherine Bell contends, scholarly and popular interest in "ritual" in Europe and North America has made ritual into an important vehicle for experience and comprehension. The work of scholars to sift a variety of practices into the concept of ritual, she argues,

> suggests a certain drive toward transcending the particularities of place, time, and culture by means of the "higher learning" embodied in scientific, artistic, historical, and hermeneutical forms of analysis. This interest in transcending the particular suggests a fundamental drive toward world transformation and self-determination. It suggests an eagerness to find or forge spiritual-cultural commonalities among the heterogeneity of beliefs and styles in the world, but primarily in terms that extend our historical experiences as nearly universal.[27]

Considering this metacritique of ritual in the context of emotion (itself a historically and politically constructed category, whose construction I haven't room to consider here) calls for reflection not only on the ways ritual practices and emotion intersect but also on the ways ritual theories and emotion conjoin.

Crocodile Tears and the Authenticity of Ritual Emotion

To approach these two levels of reflection, I first turn to a discussion of authenticity in ritualized emotion. On the first level—the ways ritual practice and emotion intersect—studies of ritual authenticity have yielded fascinating insights. One of the most helpful cases for thinking about how people adjudicate the authenticity of ritually provoked or nurtured emotions is that of ritual weeping, particularly since it is an expression of emotion that has clear physiological effects. Returning to the risky terrain of autobiographical reminiscence, the first time I witnessed something I considered ritualized weeping was at the Hindu wedding of a friend. After the long Hindu wedding ritual, and before the North American–style reception, my friend took me aside to warn me that "the time for crying" was about to start. Accordingly, many of her female relatives gathered around her in the hotel lobby to weep publicly as a display of their grief over the loss of their sister/daughter/niece. To my unaccustomed (though tipped-off) eyes, the scene appeared to be entirely ritually provoked—that is, the women were crying because the schedule of the ritual called them to do so as they said a ritualized farewell to their beloved kinswoman whom they would see again at the reception in an hour. Perhaps due to its diasporic setting within a downtown Toronto hotel lobby and its timing in the middle of the wedding celebrations, and because I was warned of it by the bride, the weeping at first appeared to me as entirely contrived—as inauthentic tears that, though they might represent authentic feelings, were called on by ritual and not by the natural course of emotions.

Reflecting on this, of course, it is easy to see how my limited perspective of what counted as "natural" in the course of a ritual shaped my estimation of the authenticity of weeping. The "time for crying" provided a container to let out the grief of separation that comes with the maturing of a child in a way that the Christian weddings I was accustomed to did not. Though Christian weddings may not provide a "designated" time for the crying to begin, there are many such weddings where weeping—for a variety of complicated reasons—is copious. That the Hindu celebration actually made ritually prescribed space for these conflicting emotions is perhaps less a sign of the inauthenticity of the weeping than of the reluctance in many Christian (or Christian-influenced) weddings to recognize painful emotions on what—in some versions—is supposed to be the "happiest" day of (at least) a woman's life.

My skeptical and unaccustomed eyes aside, ritualized public weeping is a widespread practice, occurring during Catholic days of penance in early modern Spain and, in the late twentieth century, in evangelical Christian women's prayer meetings in the United States and Muslim women's mosque prayers in Egypt.[28] Gary Ebersole, in a discussion of ritualized weeping that warns against an overly scripted understanding of it, writes of the transgressive and productive role of "performative tears" shed in ritual contexts (and of socially expected tears going *unshed* in ritual contexts). Arguing, akin to Asad, that "moral human nature is not given but enacted," Ebersole insists that performative tears do "cultural work" that cultivates as well as constitutes a moral discourse.[29]

That said, ritual weepers must often contend with detractors, especially in contexts where competing notions of the relationship of ritual and emotion are at play. What one person considers crocodile tears, or the disingenuous disjuncture between inner emotions and outer display, another considers the cultivation of a pious self through ritualized practice. This conflict over the authenticity of emotion and its bodily display in ritual is compellingly depicted by Saba Mahmood in her study of the mosque movement among Egyptian Muslim women. Mahmood found that while most mosque participants valued the cultivation of weeping during prayer as a sign that one was achieving the proper level of devotion to Allah, their critics were suspicious of such weeping as mere self-interested performance. As one young woman charged: "I know from talking to many of these people that when they cry in prayer they do not really feel it from within; they do it because they think they will gain merits with God."[30] Partly offended by what they seemed to consider the scriptedness of the weeping, these critics held to a model of religious emotion that understood true emotion to well up unbidden and unpredictably "from within." In contrast to this model of interiority, Mahmood drew from Asad to argue that the weeping mosque participants considered that "outward behavioral forms were not only expressions of their interiorized religiosity but also a necessary means of acquiring it."[31]

Returning to Jonathan Smith's definition of ritual, we remember that ritual can act as a controlled environment, at least temporarily harnessing the unpredictability of everyday life. Though the devout Muslim woman who weeps at prayer may find her weeping provoked not only because of her devotion to Allah but also because of the trials of her own life—weeping, after all, has the voracious ability to call on and conflate multiple sources of distress to further itself—her weeping is not necessarily rendered less authentic to her simply because she has tried to cultivate it within ritualized conditions.

Mahmood's example demonstrates that critiques of the authenticity of emotion and ritual can emerge within traditions and communities. Critiques of authenticity, however, also foster emotionally wrenching debates across traditions and communities. One of the most prominent of such examples is found in Euro-American appropriations and adaptations (or fabrications) of First Nations rituals, whether the sweat lodge or the vision quest. These kinds of cross-cultural intersections, profoundly shaped by historical and political relations of oppression, can provoke potently emotional responses on both sides, in which debates over the authenticity of the ritual overshadow debates over the authenticity of the emotions. Bron Taylor shows this in his discussion of alliances and conflicts between Euro-American environmentalists and First Nation activists during gathering circles at a mountain considered sacred to the First Nations people. While some of the environmentalists thought that drinking and carousing were appropriate behaviors at the campfire the night before the morning circles, some First Nations activists were deeply offended by the use of alcohol at what they thought should be a composed, preparatory ritual, reverential of the mountain and in keeping with the seriousness of their task of protecting it as a sacred site.[32]

The debate around the limits and possibilities of sharing First Nations rituals and ritual spaces demonstrates most acutely the ways that ritualized emotions—of the Sun Dance or the sweat lodge, for example—are themselves encircled by highly emotional and historically grounded convictions about the morality of sharing a ritual tradition with members of a hegemonic, even when sympathetic, culture. That conflicts over emotional authenticity in ritual can be provoked both within religious communities and between historically opposed groups demonstrates the necessity to situate any analysis of emotions at multiple levels of analysis, from the individual to the historically embedded culture.

Cognition and Culture in the Analysis of Ritual and Emotion

Cognitive analyses of ritual espouse a very different approach to the study of ritual and emotion that is ultimately less concerned with differences and change over time and more interested in universals. With analyses focused on the role of the brain and its physiological effects, cognitively oriented scholars, such as Pascal Boyer, often contend that the real explanations for ritual can only be discerned "with the help of psychological experiments, anthropological comparisons, and evolutionary considerations."[33] Boyer goes on to argue that rituals are compulsive behaviors that are "*snares for thought* that produce highly salient effects by activating special systems in the mental basement."[34] Like Boyer, many scholars engaging in cognitive studies of ritual (and religion more generally) are doing so in the hope of establishing a scientific approach to their topic that will establish universally valid theories for the existence and function of ritual, and that will help answer questions such as "why ritual is a such a *general* human activity."[35]

In academia more widely, discussions of the relative weight of cognition and culture—or neurologically "hardwired" effects compared to outside influences—are notoriously contentious and even emotionally charged. Scholars specifically addressing the nexus of ritual and emotion are profoundly shaped by these emotionally freighted scholarly investments in explanatory frameworks that grant different levels of importance to biologically driven and culturally driven influences.[36] Motivated in part by the historical weight of racism and sexism that has burdened Western scholars' biological explanations of human behavior—including religiously oriented behavior—many anthropologists and religion scholars have been particularly wary of and opposed to biologically determined explanations.[37] Choosing instead to focus on the ways emotion is itself shaped by the language a certain culture offers to express emotions, or the social organization and cues that encourage or discourage emotional expression, culturally focused scholars set their task to be the analysis of emotion as an embodied response to culture that is shaped by complex historical factors such as the advent of colonialism, economic change, and changes in gendered expectations and roles.[38]

Another reason for these scholars' cautious approaches to cognitive theories of ritual is rooted in their concern that dichotomized views that offer two dominant explanatory modes (e.g., cognition and culture, or doctrinal and imagistic) effect a closure of explanatory possibilities. If the brain, and the way that it processes and remembers emotion, is thought to be at the center of ritual analysis, is culture then secondary? What about other explanatory (and socially constituting) categories such as gender, race, class, and religion? The brain, despite its seeming incontrovertibility as a physical fact and its continued dissection at the hands of scientists, is perhaps just as much of an unknown (or known) as culture, especially in terms of the ways it is shaped by and shapes emotion.[39] This is where humanists and scientists may demonstrate very different preferences: is the answer to a question determined by finding its prime cause—its independent variable—or is it discovered by finding multiple, intersecting causes? As we will see, part of the answer to this question lies in the scope of one's scholarly terrain.

A predominantly culturally focused analysis is that of Peter Burke, who, with his notion of "occasionalism," calls for an accounting of why people comport themselves differently in different occasions. Borrowing from Bourdieu, Burke argues for a more improvisational perspective on ritual that acknowledges that the "script" of a ritual is never the same as its enactment. Paying attention to the "gap between the script and the practice" of a ritual is a good methodological strategy that of course depends on having access to a script. Although Burke does not draw from the work of Whitehouse, it initially appears that his notion of occasionalism would fit more readily into a doctrinal mode of religiosity, which implies a certain scriptedness—more and less literally—to religious behavior. However, even under what Whitehouse considers to be imagistic modes of religiosity, there are those with the power to determine the process, timing, and placement of a ritual, suggesting that occasionalism—or the sense of knowing that one must act in a particular way in a particular time and place—would also be a helpful lens on imagistic rites, such as rites of initiation.[40] Mostly focusing on the exigencies of performance in the conditions of what Zygmunt Bauman has called "liquid modernity," Burke argues for an attention to ritual and emotion that understands conflict and multiplicity, and not cultural fixity, to be key elements of contemporary ritual performance.

A very different approach to the nexus of ritual and emotion has developed in recent years, in which some scholars have advocated a renewed approach to neurological explanations for religious activity, especially as research into the brain has offered more specific understandings of the relationship between emotion and cognition. An awareness of the emotional tenor of their work is heard in Robert N. McCauley and E. Thomas Lawson's preface to their 2002 work *Bringing Ritual to Mind: Psychological Foundations of Cultural Forms*:

> If our work seems tilted too far toward the scientific, it is only because we aim to redress an imbalance—an imbalance in strategy and approach that favors the particular over the general, the idiosyncratic over the systematic, and the interpretive over the explanatory (as if we could make sense of either item in each pair in isolation from the other). What we are out to do is to help bring an end to the defensive pronouncements of humanists and, especially, of scholars of religion concerning what the sciences can never address productively.... Instead of disdainful proclamations discouraging such initiatives, scholars of religion should welcome analyses that aim to increase simultaneously theoretical precision and empirical responsibility.[41]

McCauley and Lawson draw heavily from the work of Whitehouse, though they are careful to distinguish themselves from him. Characterizing Whitehouse's argument as a "ritual frequency hypothesis" that considers frequency the key variable determining the effects of ritual, they contend that "ritual form" is the most important determinant for understanding the importance of emotional arousal in religious ritual. By this they mean that the level of emotion a ritual evokes is determined by what form it takes in their categorization of "principles of superhuman agency and superhuman immediacy."[42] For example, a religious ritual—which for McCauley and Lawson (problematically) includes only a ritual in which an agent does something to someone else—has its most important and effective form when the agent is a "culturally postulated superhuman agent" (e.g., a god) or is very directly related to a superhuman agent, as in the case of a priest in the Roman Catholic Church.[43] This ritual form also arouses the greatest level of emotional response and ritual memory, both of which are central to the development and the cultural transmission of religious convictions, according to McCauley and Lawson: "Ultimately, only the gods can bring about such effects; thus, in these rituals the gods either act directly or certify the action indirectly."[44]

McCauley and Lawson repeatedly make the claim—often with recourse to competitive metaphors of hunting or gaming—that their theory outperforms that of Whitehouse. Their intent is to develop a theory of ritual that applies regardless of what religion they are considering and that can be tested in the ethnographic field.[45] Despite their confidence in the robustness of their theory, they do include one important caveat: "The ritual form hypothesis only addresses the comparative differences between the levels of sensory pageantry and emotional excitement that religious rituals possess within a specific religious community."[46] Qualifying the predictive ability of their hypothesis by stating that it "does not predict differences between different religious systems or even between different religious communities within the same religious system" effectively means that their hypothesis cannot account for the vast majority of contemporary (or even ancient) religious and ritual activity.[47] My Thai meditation experience (which I still consider a ritual, despite the fact that no "culturally postulated superhuman agent" was at work on me) was a crucible of different religious systems interacting: a Buddhist ritual in Thailand undertaken by a Canadian raised as a Christian. So, too, is the main ethnographic example McCauley and Lawson use to develop and prove their hypothesis, namely, a syncretic revival movement in Melanesia (as described in Whitehouse's ethnography).[48] Especially in a postcolonial, "globalizing" world, religious systems are intricately, sometimes subtly, intertwined with each other in relationships of hegemony, mutuality, and resistance. A theory of religious ritual that cannot attend to these historical and cultural conditions is seriously weakened as a result.

An approach of merging cognition and culture that does not set a universal theory as its goal will probably be more successful in accounting for the historical and cultural messiness of religious interaction while also trying to understand the role of neurology in religious and emotional experience. Whitehouse, in offering his theory of doctrinal and imagistic modes of religiosity, seems less invested in providing an ironclad answer to the origin or nature of all religious behavior than concerned to develop a theory that explains broad "tendencies" in different kinds of religious organizations. While also attending to political and historical contexts, he seeks to focus these tendencies at the individual, psychological level.[49] Similarly, recent articles by Margot Lyon, an anthropologist, and Peter Q. Deeley, a psychiatric researcher, argue for more common ground between culturally focused and cognitively focused studies of religion.[50] As Deeley contends, his approach is a

> social neuro-cognitive extension of the sociology of knowledge, in which the existence of all beliefs is taken as equally problematic (in the sense of equally requiring explanation). The focus of the inquiry is the Kantian question of "what cognitive capacities are presupposed by, and necessary for, the existence of beliefs?" This question can be asked of any beliefs, including those of scientists.[51]

Deeley's insistence that cognitively oriented scholars must engage "social anthropology, religious studies, and other humanities" when researching religion is refreshing; the first question such an engagement might provoke could be "Why must religion be reduced to a question of belief?"[52] Many considerations of ritual and emotion could quickly bring forth examples of participants with very complex, if not contradictory, emotional responses to religious ritual, and whose ritual participation does not imply a conviction—religious or otherwise—regarding the believability of a particular ritual's theological grounding or the legitimacy of its ritual practitioner. The conflicted emotions and ambivalent participation in the Catholic mass of many Roman Catholic women supportive of women's ordination, whether sisters or laywomen, is a prime example of the potential gap between ritual and belief. For these kinds of reasons, any theory of religious ritual and emotion that does not take into account gender, race, class, and other socially formative categories—categories with profound effects both at cultural and individual levels—will only answer very limited questions, for a very limited audience.

Scholars of emotion and ritual who seek to bring together cognition and culture would do well to remember that people and cultures are changeable—and that our scholarly attempts to categorize and analyze them are always efforts to provide maps, but not true descriptions of the territory.[53] They would also be well advised to remember, as Deeley suggests in his nod to the sociology of knowledge, that scholarly commitments to particular explanatory approaches are themselves shaped by emotional convictions—whether the passionate search for the all-explaining independent variable or the ardent commitment to consider the multiplicity of social categories that constitute historical and culturally laden traditions and individuals.

Conclusion

More than eighty years ago, Marcel Mauss called for a comparative study of ritual rooted in the body:

> I believe precisely that at the bottom of all our mystical states there are body techniques which we have not studied, but which were studied fully in China and India, even in very remote periods. This socio-psycho-biological study should be made. I think that there are necessarily biological means of entering into "communion with God."[54]

While my own experience of Buddhist meditation in a Thai temple could be viewed as proof of the validity and universality of the Asian study of "body techniques" that lead to a "mystical state" regardless of the cultural background of the practitioner, it could also be viewed as an exercise in appropriation. My retreat was feasible because of the historical, political, and economic conditions that made it possible for a young, unmarried, financially autonomous North American woman to travel to Thailand in search of a religious experience. Though my hosts at the temple openly and actively welcomed foreigners to their practice (and still do), the donations that they receive and the teachings that they convey are both relevant to their attitude of welcome.

To ignore these historical conditions in trying to make sense of the effects of ritual on the body or the emotions is, in effect, to limit our questions and sphere of analysis to a clinical gaze shorn of any awareness of the ambivalent emotional and moral discourses in which ritual is situated and which it participates in constructing. Our task as scholars, in my own admittedly emotional and reasoned view, is to self-reflexively search for generalities that can open up conversations and allow us to see commonalities and differences, while also attending to the particularities that shape not only the lives and emotions of those we study but our own lives and emotions as well.

NOTES

1. Jonathan Z. Smith, *Imagining Religion: From Babylon to Jonestown* (Chicago: University of Chicago Press, 1982), 54.
2. Arnold van Gennep, *The Rites of Passage*, translated by Monika B. Vizedom and Gabriel L. Caffee (Chicago: University of Chicago Press, 1960).
3. Smith, *Imagining Religion*, 63.
4. Michelle Rosaldo,"Toward an Anthropology of Self and Feeling." In *Culture Theory: Essays on Mind, Self, and Emotion*, edited by R. Schweder and R. LeVine (Cambridge: Cambridge University Press), 137–57.
5. Victor Turner, *The Forest of Symbols: Aspects of Ndembu Ritual* (Ithaca, N.Y.: Cornell University Press, 1967), 28–29.
6. Ibid., 28.
7. Ibid., 30.
8. Ibid., 43.
9. Harvey Whitehouse, "Rites of Terror: Emotion, Metaphor, and Memory in Melanesian Initiation Cults," in *Religion and Emotion: Approaches and Interpretations*, edited by John Corrigan (Oxford: Oxford University Press, 2004).
10. Ibid., 144.
11. See Harvey Whitehouse, *Arguments and Icons: Divergent Modes of Religiosity* (Oxford: Oxford University Press, 2000).
12. Ibid., 1.
13. Ibid., 20.
14. See Laurel Kendall, *Getting Married in Korea: Of Gender, Morality, and Modernity* (Berkeley: University of California Press, 1996).
15. Joel Robbins, *Becoming Sinners: Christianity and Moral Torment in a Papua New Guinea Society* (Berkeley: University of California Press, 2004).
16. Talal Asad, *Genealogies of Religion* (Baltimore: Johns Hopkins University Press, 1993), 72.
17. Ibid., 77.
18. Ibid., 78.

19. Catherine Bell, *Ritual Theory, Ritual Practice* (New York: Oxford University Press, 1992), 82.

20. For example, see Whitehouse, *Arguments and Icons*, 186.

21. John Corrigan, ed., *Religion and Emotion: Approaches and Interpretations* (Oxford: Oxford University Press, 2004).

22. Ann Taves, *Fits, Trances, and Visions: Experiencing Religion and Explaining Experience from Wesley to James* (Princeton, N.J.: Princeton University Press, 1999); Peter Q. Deeley, "The Religious Brain: Turning Ideas into Convictions," *Anthropology and Medicine* 11, 3 (December 2004): 264.

23. See Pickering, chapter 24 here, and Asad, *Genealogies of Religion*, 74.

24. Clifford Geertz, *The Interpretation of Cultures* (New York: Basic Books, 1973), 90.

25. See Margot Lyon, "Missing Emotion: The Limitations of Cultural Constructionism in the Study of Emotion," *Cultural Anthropology* 10, 2 (1995): 247; and Catherine Bell, *Ritual: Perspectives and Dimensions* (New York: Oxford University Press, 1997), 80.

26. Ronald Grimes, *Ritual Criticism* (Columbia: University of South Carolina Press, 1990); Asad, *Genealogies of Religion*; Bell, *Ritual Theory, Ritual Practice*.

27. Bell, *Ritual: Perspectives and Dimensions*, 267.

28. William Christian, "Provoked Religious Weeping in Early Modern Spain," in Corrigan, *Religion and Emotion*, 33–50; R. Marie Griffith, *God's Daughters: Evangelical Women and the Power of Submission* (Berkeley: University of California Press, 1997), 122–23. Also see Talal Asad, *Genealogies of Religion*, 64.

29. Gary L. Ebersole, "The Function of Ritual Weeping Revisited: Affective Expression and Moral Discourse," in Corrigan, *Religion and Emotion*. See also Kimberly Patton and John Stratton Hawley, *Holy Tears: Weeping in the Religious Imagination* (Princeton, N.J.: Princeton University Press, 2004).

30. Saba Mahmood, *Politics of Piety: The Islamic Revival and the Feminist Subject* (Princeton, N.J.: Princeton University Press, 2005), 146.

31. Ibid., 147.

32. Bron Taylor, "Earthen Spirituality or Cultural Genocide?: Radical Environmentalism's Appropriation of Native American Spirituality," *Religion* 27, 2 (1997): 183–215.

33. Pascal Boyer, *Religion Explained: The Evolutionary Origins of Religious Thought* (New York: Basic Books, 2001), 263.

34. Ibid.

35. Ibid., 231.

36. On emotional investment in scholarly analysis of religion more generally, see Daniel Gold, *Aesthetics and Analysis in Writing on Religion: Modern Fascinations* (Berkeley: University of California Press, 2003).

37. See, for example, Sander Gilman, *Difference and Pathology: Stereotypes of Sexuality, Race, and Madness* (Ithaca, N.Y.: Cornell University Press, 1985).

38. See Catherine A. Lutz and Lila Abu Lughod, *Language and the Politics of Emotion* (Cambridge: Cambridge University Press, 1990).

39. For example, see "Study Charts Origins of Fear" from the University of Toronto, available at www.news.utoronto.ca/bin6/050915-1631.asp.

40. On power and social position in the creation of ritualized emotion, see Randall Collins, "Rituals of Solidarity and Security in the Wake of Terrorist Attack," *Sociological Theory* 22, 1 (2004): 53–87.

41. McCauley and Lawson, *Bringing Ritual to Mind* (Cambridge: Cambridge University Press, 2002), ix.

42. Ibid., 7.
43. Ibid., 29, 33.
44. Ibid., 123.
45. Ibid., 37
46. Ibid., 119.
47. Ibid.
48. Harvey Whitehouse, *Inside the Cult: Religious Innovation and Transmission in Papua New Guinea* (Oxford: Oxford University Press, 1995).
49. Whitehouse, *Arguments and Icons*, 1.
50. Lyon, "Missing Emotion."
51. Peter Q. Deeley, "The Religious Brain: Turning Ideas into Convictions," *Anthropology and Medicine* 11, 3 (December), 2004: 264.
52. See also Amy Hollywood, "Practice, Belief, and Feminist Philosophy of Religion," in *Thinking through Rituals*, edited by Kevin Schilbrack (London: Routledge, 2004), 52–70.
53. Jonathan Z. Smith, *Map Is Not Territory: Studies in the History of Religions* (Chicago: University of Chicago Press, 1993).
54. Marcel Mauss, "Techniques of the Body," *Economy and Society* 2, 1 (1973): 70–88.

BIBLIOGRAPHY

Asad, Talal. *Genealogies of Religion*. Baltimore: Johns Hopkins Press, 1993.
Bell, Catherine. *Ritual: Perspectives and Dimensions*. New York: Oxford University Press, 1997.
———. *Ritual Theory, Ritual Practice*. New York: Oxford University Press, 1992.
Boyer, Pascal. *Religion Explained: The Evolutionary Origins of Religious Thought*. New York: Basic Books, 2001.
Christian, William. "Provoked Religious Weeping in Early Modern Spain." In *Religion and Emotion: Approaches and Interpretations*, edited by John Corrigan. Oxford: Oxford University Press, 2004, 33–50.
Collins, Randall. "Rituals of Solidarity and Security in the Wake of Terrorist Attack." *Sociological Theory* 22, 1 (2004): 53–87.
Corrigan, John, ed. *Religion and Emotion: Approaches and Interpretations*. Oxford: Oxford University Press, 2004.
Deeley, Peter Q. "The Religious Brain: Turning Ideas into Convictions." *Anthropology and Medicine* 113 (December 2004): 245–67.
Ebersole, Gary L. "The Function of Ritual Weeping Revisited: Affective Expression and Moral Discourse." In *Religion and Emotion: Approaches and Interpretations*, edited by John Corrigan. Oxford: Oxford University Press, 2004.
Geertz, Clifford. *The Interpretation of Cultures*. New York: Basic Books, 1973.
Gilman, Sander. *Difference and Pathology: Stereotypes of Sexuality, Race, and Madness*. Ithaca, N.Y.: Cornell University Press, 1985.
Gold, Daniel. *Aesthetics and Analysis in Writing on Religion: Modern Fascinations*. Berkeley: University of California Press, 2003.
Griffith, R. Marie. *God's Daughters: Evangelical Women and the Power of Submission*. Berkeley: University of California Press, 1997.
Grimes, Ronald. *Ritual Criticism*. Columbia: University of South Carolina Press, 1990.

Hollywood, Amy. "Practice, Belief, and Feminist Philosophy of Religion." In *Thinking Through Rituals*, edited by Kevin Schilbrack. London: Routledge, 2004, 52–70.

Kendall, Laurel. *Getting Married in Korea: Of Gender, Morality, and Modernity*. Berkeley: University of California Press, 1996.

Lutz, Catherine A., and Lila Abu Lughod. *Language and the Politics of Emotion*. Cambridge: Cambridge University Press, 1990.

Lyon, Margot. "Missing Emotion: The Limitations of Cultural Constructionism in the Study of Emotion." *Cultural Anthropology* 10, 2 (1995): 244–63.

Mahmood, Saba. *Politics of Piety: The Islamic Revival and the Feminist Subject*. Princeton, N.J.: Princeton University Press, 2005.

Mauss, Marcel. "Techniques of the Body." *Economy and Society* 2, 1 (1973): 70–88.

McCauley, Robert, and Thomas Lawson. *Bringing Ritual to Mind*. Cambridge: Cambridge University Press, 2002.

Patton, Kimberly, and John Stratton Hawley. *Holy Tears: Weeping in the Religious Imagination*. Princeton, N.J.: Princeton University Press, 2004.

Robbins, Joel. Becoming Sinners: Christianity and Moral Torment in a Papua New Guinea Society. Berkeley: University of California Press, 2004.

Rosaldo, Michelle. "Toward an Anthropology of Self and Feeling." In *Culture Theory: Essays on Mind, Self, and Emotion*, edited by R. Schweder and R. LeVine. Cambridge: Cambridge University Press, 137–57.

Smith, Jonathan Z. *Imagining Religion: From Babylon to Jonestown*. Chicago: University of Chicago Press, 1982.

———. Map Is Not Territory: Studies in the History of Religions. Chicago: University of Chicago Press, 1993.

Taves, Ann. Fits, Trances, and Visions: Experiencing Religion and Explaining Experience from Wesley to James. Princeton, N.J.: Princeton University Press, 1999.

Taylor, Bron. "Earthen Spirituality or Cultural Genocide?: Radical Environmentalism's Appropriation of Native American Spirituality" *Religion* 27, 2 (1997): 183–215.

Turner, Victor. *The Forest of Symbols: Aspects of Ndembu Ritual*. Ithaca, N.Y.: Cornell University Press, 1967.

van Gennep, Arnold. *The Rites of Passage*. Translated by Monika B. Vizedom and Gabriel L. Caffee. Chicago: University of Chicago Press, 1960.

Whitehouse, Harvey. *Arguments and Icons: Divergent Modes of Religiosity*. Oxford: Oxford University Press, 2000.

———. Inside the Cult: Religious Innovation and Transmission in Papua New Guinea. Oxford: Oxford University Press, 1995.

———. "Rites of Terror: Emotion, Metaphor, and Memory in Melanesian Initiation Cults." In *Religion and Emotion: Approaches and Interpretations*, edited by John Corrigan. Oxford: Oxford University Press, 2004.

CHAPTER 9

SEXUALITY AND THE EROTIC

JEFFREY J. KRIPAL

> If the mind remains in woman-and-gold, nothing will happen. Sex with a woman—what pleasure is there in that! When the vision of the Lord happens, the bliss is millions of times greater than sexual pleasure. Gauri used to say that when the great ecstasy occurs all the holes of the body—even down to the hair pores—become great vaginas. In each and every one of these holes one experiences the pleasure of sexual intercourse with the Self.
>
> —Sri Ramakrishna in *Kathamrita* 4.36

THE biological, psychological, cultural, and ethical complexities of what we today call sexuality, gender, sexual orientation, and sexual trauma have been the focus of intense research for well over a century now. It would be difficult to overestimate the importance of this corporate knowledge for how we have come to see "religion," and it is worth noting that both the modern categories of *religion* and *sexuality* as signs marking fields of rational discourse and critical study were born more or less together within the same time period (the nineteenth and twentieth centuries) and within the same cultural institution (the Western university). That is to say, our collective awakening to both sexuality and religion as fundamentally related semiotic fields amenable to rational analysis and hermeneutical insight is part of the same broad enlightenment that sets Western critical understandings of religion and sexuality apart from (and often in serious and irresolvable conflict with) all previous Western and virtually all historical and contemporary non-Western understandings of the same.

Very much related to the same modernist sense of the unprecedented is the intensely ethical tone and far-reaching social implications of much of the discussion and the degree to which analyses of sexuality and religion tend to question or transgress an otherwise assumed intellectual ideal of cultural relativism. It is, for example, exceedingly difficult to read very far into feminist studies of the world's religious traditions without getting a saddened, if not actually enraged, sense that modern forms of consciousness defined by the most basic moral standards of gender equity are incompatible with the past structures, doctrines and rituals of every major religious tradition on the planet.[1] And this leaves the sensitive reader in a profoundly uncomfortable, if also potentially creative, existential position.

Such a modernist moral sense, however, needs to be balanced by what Richard Shweder has poetically framed as a kind of ontological astonishment born from the postmodern realization that there are in actual anthropological fact multiple reality posits available to the human psyche, and that different cultural systems will elicit radically different experiences of reality from human beings who intentionally engage them (either as indigenous cultural actors or as cross-cultural hermeneuts— the anthropologist or historian of religions is also a potential mystic in this model). The goal here is "to recognize the other as a specialist or expert on some aspect of human experience, whose reflective consciousness and system of representations and discourse can be used to reveal hidden dimensions of our selves."[2] Shweder dubs this quest for the suppressed potentials of the human psyche via serial expeditions through different life-worlds a "cultural psychology," simply defined as "the study of the ways subject and object, self and other, psyche and culture, persona and context, figure and ground, practitioner and practice, live together, require each other, and dynamically, dialectically, and jointly make each other up."[3]

Such a cultural psychology seems particularly useful for the cross-cultural interpretation of erotic forms of religious emotion. Sexuality and its emotional fields, after all, are essentially dialectical, liminal, even nondual systems where psyche and culture, biology and society, spirit and body meet, meld, and merge and, in the process, provide both numinous power and gendered form to the symbolic worlds that make up the history of religions. "Emotion," here at least, encodes especially intense forms of experience that encompass both "consciousness" and "energy," both soul and sex, within a whole spectrum of possibilities, ranging from the radical dissociation of spirit and body in the ascetic transcendence of Jainism to the cosmic integration of the world-as-orgasm in some forms of Vajrayana Buddhism or Shakta Hinduism. The religions, moreover, may express any number of understandings of "the body," but it is usually the genitals (their strange morphing shapes, their specific acts, their anatomical contiguity to the "impurity" of menstrual blood, feces, and urine, their connection to fertility and procreation, and their astonishing powers to alter consciousness) that come to focus, order, and torment the same understandings.

And little of this can be adequately understood as "simply sexual." How could it, when each culture attributes different and multiple symbolic and ontological meanings to what we today call "sexuality"? Rather, the hermeneutical challenge consists in trying to understand other "astonishing" ontological conceptions of human sexuality, which are in turn embedded in elaborate webs of cultural practices and emotional fields, and allowing these to define and guide, at least initially, one's own interpretations. Something like erotic forms of mysticism, in other words, cannot be discussed comparatively, as if they were all minor variations on the exact same thing. Behind such a discourse lies the unspoken assumption that every time and culture has more or less agreed on the ontological natures of spiritual *and* sexual experience *and* on the manner in which they do or do not intersect. Such a discourse also ignores the very real possibility that different cultural systems set their actors up for radically different subjective and emotional experiences of the body and its energies, in effect creating different life-worlds with different social practices and symbolic systems.

This tension between the modernist and ethical sense that our critical theories are in many ways unprecedented and the postmodern celebration of polytheistic difference across all cultures and times that refuses to privilege modern rationality can be lessened somewhat, if hardly resolved, by the awareness that we can find meaningful resonances with our modern methodologies in many of the world's premodern mythological and mystical traditions. And why not? For all our perfectly legitimate concerns about difference and the social construction of emotion, do not all human beings share the same anatomical body, the same hormonal keyboard, the same swirling DNA pool? Even Shweder's cultural psychology, with its conviction that the reality posits of other cultures can awaken submerged or potential dimensions of our own modern selves, implies, indeed *requires*, a certain degree of psychic unity. Does this not at least suggest what Norman Brown argued, in a more poetic language, namely, that we all inhabit "one sea of energy or instinct; embracing all mankind, without distinction of race, language, or culture; and embracing all the generations of Adam, past, present, and future, in one phylogenetic heritage; in one mystical or symbolical body"?[4] Many might want to answer the latter American countercultural hymn to "love's body" in the negative, or at least qualify it heavily, but it is a question that our own sexual bodies, so astonishingly similar across cultures and often *literally* uniting with one another across these same alleged cultural boundaries, will continue to raise for us. Our bodies at least know that cultural boundaries are fictions, and that physical communion is quite possible between and beyond them.

This essay, anyway, proceeds through, and only through, this question, this tension between these two general patterns of sexual sameness and difference, themselves dialectically related within a larger whole, the whole or unity of the human species. Within this tensive field, we will look briefly at a few central emotional themes: the direction of sexual desire or love, the sexual dynamics of ascetic behavior and institution, the repression, expression, and sublimation of emotion in erotic ritual, and, finally, the fear, shame, and ecstasy of religiously expressed trauma.

From Mythos to Logos

Western religious reflection on sexuality and religion begins not with an encyclopedia entry or a scholarly monograph but with a myth about a transgressive desire for mature moral knowledge and a subsequent sexual emotion, namely, Adam and Eve's shameful sense of being naked after accepting the serpent's gift of the knowledge of good and evil. Modern readers, socialized by two millennia of orthodox theological readings, normally miss the rather clear sexual complexities of the story, but the ancient and medieval authors were generally not so naïve. Certainly sexual readings of the story were common in the rabbinic, gnostic, patristic, and medieval kabbalistic authors.[5] Here at least the fruit of the tree of knowledge of good and evil that God forbade the first couple to eat involved what we today call "sex"—"the forbidden fruit."

I begin with this early Hebrew myth, not to dwell on a single mythology or to pursue a particular sexual exegesis of it (I have committed those sins elsewhere[6]), but as a rhetorical device that can focus our discussion. Such a myth, after all, forces us to take seriously the highly conflicted emotional field in which this discussion seems always to take place, namely, that defined by the human desire to know (hence the serpent and the couple) and to *not* know (hence the prohibition and punishment) the truth about sexuality and religion. Precisely because the dialectical spirit-body realm of sexuality structures so much of religious institution, practice, and experience, any extended attempt to study the sexual dimensions of religion will likely reveal (and so implicitly deconstruct) some of the deepest psychological, biological, and social roots of piety, sanctity, and religion itself. Put mythically again, we should not expect the Gods of the religions to be terribly happy about this sort of inquiry. Quite the contrary: we should expect to be exiled.

The Body Social: Sexuality and Gender

The category of *sexuality* is usually understood to refer to a biologically driven instinct that, although genetically determined to varying degrees, is nevertheless open to the profound cultural conditioning and influences of the social environment in which it develops. Whereas the biological and cognitive sciences have generally focused on the "biologically driven instinct" (or alternately, on "the hardwiring of the brain"), the humanities and social sciences have turned to that "nevertheless open to...." The latter discourse, developed most fully in the last forty years from a variety of earlier and contemporary systems of thought, particularly psychoanalysis, feminism, and French philosophy, has been dominated by the category of *gender*, generally defined as a culturally variable model of masculinity or femininity, that is, the meanings, values, and practices normally associated with being a man or a woman in a particular social system.

More recent work has also begun to look at the heuristic category of the third gender, an umbrella term for all those alternative sexualities, bisexualities, or transsexualities that do not follow the traditional binary logic of male/female but break out into other "queer" modes of sexual being and religious experience.[7] Very significantly, in many cultures it is the latter category of the third gender or the queer figure that best captures the sexuality and charisma of the shaman, mystic, or saint who can most effectively mediate between the sacred and profane worlds. Indeed, sexual liminality that breaks the binarisms of a society's gender structure and the irruption of the numinous into human society are often more or less interchangeable moments.

It would be a serious mistake, however, to imagine that sexuality and gender are easily separable things that can somehow be abstracted from human experience and reduced to either the vocabularies of the natural sciences (sexuality) or to those of the social sciences and the humanities (gender), and the field of emotion is certainly a powerful example of just this impossibility. And indeed, this simple division between a biologically defined sexuality and a socially constructed gender has been problematized by historians, scientists, and philosophers alike. Some historians, for example, have begun to worry that the constructionist Foucauldian commitments to "discourse" and cultural relativism have actually resulted in the banishment of the flesh-and-blood body from historical understanding and so prevented us from deep encounters with other eras and their own forms of embodied consciousness.[8]

Evolutionary psychologists and sociobiologists have been particularly vocal in their rejection of absolute constructionist models of sexuality and gender that they believe are flatly contradicted by the biological evidence.[9] For these thinkers, both the actual content of religious teachings on sexuality (what sorts of sexual acts are encouraged and prohibited, who can have sex with whom, etc.) and the positive or negative emotional charges that surround these same codes cannot be properly understood as either finally textual or as historically relative. These features have rather been selected out through millions of years of evolutionary processes, and what survives—from the oft-noted pattern of male sexual promiscuousness, that is, the desire to impregnate as many women as possible with little emotional involvement and even less biological commitment (a few minutes and a teaspoon of sperm, as Steven Pinker humorously puts it) to the classic and curvaceous hourglass model of female attractiveness (a modal waist-to-hip ration of .67:.80) that we find so consistently from modern America's *Playboy* to ancient Indian iconography as a physiological sign of fertility and genetic quality—are *precisely* those sexual characteristics that best ensure the survival of the species (interestingly, this evolutionary model effectively reverses most traditional androcentric religious symbolisms, in which the woman is understood to be sexually voracious and the man stands in for stable spirit).

And indeed, to a very large degree, religious purity codes about proper sexual behavior can be explained by one simple biological fact: until very recently, a man could never really be certain of a child's paternity. But to ensure a smooth flow of inheritance and so guarantee the patriarchal order of society, he had to be more or less certain, and, moreover, he had to produce a son, hence the elaborate religious systems insisting on female (but not generally male) virginity, strongly preferring sons over daughters, and condemning any kind of sexual behavior that either cannot produce a proper son or confuses the proper lines of inheritance (adultery, incest, homosexuality, etc.). Hence also the elaborate emotional fields of shame, dirtiness, and guilt that the same purity codes produce. The body returns again for these sociobiological thinkers, then, this time on the micro level of the genes, and it is this invisible or subtle body that ultimately creates and sustains society, religion, and emotion, not the other way around.

In a very different spirit, humanists and philosophers have noted that sexuality and gender are implicated in an astonishing range of contemporary moral debates and global crises.[10] From the debates surrounding abortion and reproductive rights, homosexuality, gay marriage, clerical sexual scandal, and the ordination of women in the American Christian churches, to religious resistances to the education of women and birth control around the globe, from religious and cultural beliefs that encourage the spread of sexually transmitted diseases (including and especially AIDS) and exacerbate population problems to the twentieth-century "disappearance" (or cultural killing) of one hundred million women around the world that is attributable more to cultural practices and beliefs than economic realities,[11] the moral implications for such humanists are daunting. Such crises are also fundamentally unanswerable for these thinkers within any philosophical framework that balkanizes the species into separate solipsistic cultures, each with its own impenetrable and infallible moral, religious, and sexual norms. Foucauldian postmodern constructionism or cultural relativism are not just bad history or bad biology here; they are also bad political philosophy and bad ethics.

On the Different Directions of Desire

If the categories of sexuality and gender (and the related categories of race and class) taught us to adopt a wide range of perspectives on religious phenomena that had been otherwise erased or hidden from view by the standard male gaze and its tendency not to question (or even see) the patriarchal structures of tradition, that of *sexual orientation* honed this sense even further by warning us away from what look now like extremely naïve heterosexual assumptions about the religious texts and practices. What was always there, "right before our eyes," as it were, we did not see.

And then we saw. Consider, for example, all those ascetic practices, from Buddhist, Jain, and Christian monasticism to Hindu renunciation and Catholic clerical celibacy. Many have assumed that such practices are ascetic in both principle and psychology and require the effective suppression of sexual desire and affection. It is far more complicated than this. It all depends on how we imagine the man or woman doing the "renouncing." For a heterosexual male, traditional celibacy most certainly would be an ascetic move, as such a man likely truly desires a wife and generally feels at home in the heterosexual structures of society and its central institution, the heterosexual patriarchal family. But how does the abandonment of "this world" appear when we imagine it enacted by a homoerotically inclined man or almost any type of woman within a traditional society? It appears as *freedom*, as an abandonment of heterosexual structures that never fit the homosexual inclinations and desires of the male in the first place (or violated the individual wishes and safety of the woman) for a life of love and companionship in a close-knit, usually same-sex community. What appears, then, to be an ascetic denial of basic sensual and emotional needs turns out on closer inspection—that is, with the category of sexual orientation—to be an erotically motivated affirmation of the same within a society that allowed no other sexually meaningful outlets.

Although such hermeneutical "clicks" of the lens have found their greatest sophistication and effect in Biblical Studies,[12] similar re-focusing can be found in every major field of study, from ancient Greece, Judaism, early and medieval Christianity, and Islam to Indian, Tibetan, Chinese and Japanese Buddhism, Native American traditions, Jainism, Hinduism,[13] and modern Catholicism.[14]

Toward the Erotic

A biologically determined sexuality, a socially constructed gender, and a historically nuanced sexual-spiritual orientation: these three broad discursive domains have dominated much of the critical theory up to this point. What has been left out? Put simply: the specifically religious potentialities of human sexuality. It is a mistake, I believe, to imagine that what the mystical texts are reporting is identical or reducible to the modal sexual experience in any culture. As my opening Shakta Tantric epigram makes crystal clear, the mystico-erotic event is certainly an expression of human sexuality, but one now empowered by something quite out of the ordinary.

It is this astonishing amplification, occult empowerment, or hyperdimensionality of the sexual that the scholarship has yet to take seriously, that is, as an empirical phenomenological fact of religious texts across the comparative board. The philosophical work of Bataille and Foucault on the pleasures of prohibition and transgression and, in a very different mode, the Lacanian category of *jouissance* as developed by French feminism are happy exceptions here,[15] but they remain only beginnings, not yet fully developed theories that can take seriously the manner in which the mythologies and mystical traditions consistently connect sexuality to the terrifying and fantastically pleasurable experiences of divinization, visionary flight, magnetic, mesmeric, or electrical charge, literary and scriptural inspiration,[16] witchcraft,[17] magical influence,[18] occult encounter and sexual assault,[19] and, perhaps most commonly, immortality (a recurrent theme, from Adam and Eve to Chinese Taoist sexual yoga). However we want to judge the imaginary, imaginal, or realist status of these reality posits, one thing is certain: such emotionally complex events are an intimate part of the human record, and so no adequate history of sexuality and religion can afford to ignore them.

There are serious ontological questions here that call for another sexual category more open to some of the more fantastic and imaginative potentials of human sexuality, what I have called *the erotic*.[20] The erotic so defined is not simply "sexuality" (a very modern word with entirely secular and nonamplified connotations). From Plato's philosophical reflections in the *Symposium* on *eros* as a contemplative-ecstatic technique through India's philosophy of Being as *ananda*, or "ontological bliss,"[21] and the *ch'i* of Chinese Taoist sexual yoga to Bataille's *erotisme* and the Lacanian and feminist *jouissance*, what I am calling the erotic is rather an explicitly dialectical category that embraces all those advances made through the analytical categories of sexuality and gender but also reaches out to the phenomenological facts of intense mystical rapture, religious revelation, charismatic energy, and literary and philosophical creativity. It is a category, very much like that of emotion, that unites again what the religions have so often separated—the body and the soul, consciousness and energy.

Serpent Power: Drive Models and the History of Religions

What we need, then, is a comparative erotics that can integrate the scientific and ethical insights of sexuality, gender, and sexual orientation with the aesthetics and altered states of specifically religious forms of the erotic into a single rich spectrum of human experience. Psychoanalytic hermeneutics, now corrected and nuanced by feminist philosophy and sufficiently freed from its original scientific commitments, is a beginning foundation for this enterprise. Freud and his followers have seen further than most that originally sexual energies are routinely displaced or transformed (pick your loaded metaphor) into other forms of emotional, cultural, artistic, and religious experience. This central notion of sublimation or "making sublime" is a fundamental insight that can throw considerable light on any number of religious phenomena, from the common linkage of sexual continence and the intensely charged experience of piety to the oft-noted developmental pattern that conversion experiences often appear simultaneously with the onset of puberty. Indeed, one of the earliest findings of the American psychology of religion was that a psychological connection seems to exist between the biological awakening of sexuality at puberty and the intense emotional turmoil of the conversion experience.

The same model helps us understand the complex relationship between eroticism and asceticism in the history of religions that we examined earlier with relation to the category of sexual orientation. Religionists, committed to spirit-body dualisms and so anxiously concerned to protect transcendent truth claims (and their usually misogynist social implications) from the otherwise obvious influences of the gendered body, sometimes assert that the common religious requirement of celibacy establishes that there is no connection between the sexual and the sacred. But a more nuanced analysis can often show that asceticism is in fact a kind of intensified, sublimated, or transfigured eroticism. "The saint," Georges Bataille once wrote, "turns from the voluptuary in alarm; she does not know that his unacknowledgeable passions and her own are really one."[22]

Freud's psychoanalytic drive model is often criticized for its pseudophysical understanding of libido as a kind of material or quasi-material energy and for its mechanistic hydraulics metaphors, as if Freud's thought can be reduced to the crude mechanical metaphors of late nineteenth-century Europe. Certainly, there is much to question and correct in the Freudian corpus, but this particular reduction of theory to historical context is convincing only within a nearly total ignorance of the history of religions, where, it turns out, we can find a plethora of similar drive models that work through strikingly analogous hydraulic metaphors.

To take what are perhaps the most obvious cases, it has long been obvious to the remarkable Tantric subcultures of South Asia, the Himalayas, and China that one of the quickest ways to alter consciousness or produce religious emotion is to manipulate the body sexually. Sexual arousal and orgasm generate forms of consciousness and piety that, potentially at least, are more subtle and "higher," more sublime, than our normal banal fare. The medieval Kaula *siddha* traditions, for example, developed an elaborate hydraulics of the subtle body that worked through a series of breathing and visualization exercises, seminal retention and ejaculation, and muscular "locks" (anal and urethral contraction, for example) in order to raise the seminal fluids (really energies) from the genital region back up into the cranial vault, where they were believed to originate and where they could effect an alchemical transformation into the immortal nectar (*amrita*) that was the alchemist's goal and bliss (*ananda*).[23]

Similarly, the Bengali Vaishnava Sahajiyas explored a sophisticated theology of emotion through which they could transmute the powers of *kama*, or sexual desire, into the ecstasy of *prema*, or transcendent love, the latter archetypally expressed in Krishna's love-play with Radha and ritually reenacted in human sexual union.[24] So too, the various Hindu, Buddhist, and Taoist subtle body systems seem to be imaginal products of centuries of meditation and reflection on the human body-mind as an elaborate energy system through which different sensory, cognitive, emotional, and motor energies are sublimated into higher and higher forms or, in two popular symbolisms, as one immense thousand-petaled lotus growing directly out of the secret regions of the anus and genitals, or as a sleeping female serpent coiled around a secret *lingam* embedded in the base of the body awaiting activation so that she can travel up through the energy centers and unite with the male principle in the uppermost center above the head. Whatever the specific symbolism, however, the message is provocatively clear, namely, that the sexual and the mystical exist along a *single* organic developmental spectrum, and that the blooms of religious experience are rooted in the fundamentally esoteric, if also rather muddy, regions of the anus and the genitals. The lotus blooms only in low places, never on the mountains, as one Buddhist proverb has it.

Vajrayana Buddhism developed this same general mystico-erotic model of sublimation into a stunning array of philosophical, iconographic, ritual, and meditative traditions, some of which state quite clearly that the highest state of religious accomplishment, the union of emptiness and compassion, can be fully realized only through the act of sexual intercourse with a "seal," or female consort. Hence we arrive at the continuum of mind, emotion, and mystical experience in Tantric psychology and the consequent compatability of orgasm and reason:

> Both cognitive states and emotional states have the same basic nature, clear light, and thus are not separated off from each other in separate universes; both have luminosity as their core and exist within a continuum.... From this perspective, orgasmic pleasure is a type of mind, and the state of orgasm is even utilized to gain realization of the clear light nature of basic mind which is often compared to the sky.[25]

This same "mind of clear light" can be revealed erotically, since, phenomenologically speaking, "orgasm involves the ceasing of the grosser levels of consciousness and manifestation of the more subtle levels,"[26] and because "the consciousness that manifests in profound orgasm is deeper than reason, and is its basis."[27]

We find a very similar set of doctrines and practices yet again in the sexual yogas of Chinese Taoism, from which some historians suggest the Indian alchemical and Tantric traditions may have been partly derived. After quoting the *Wonderous Discourse* on how "the sexual union of man and woman is the *tao* of *yin* and *yang*," for example, Douglas Wile can observe that "sex is *yin* and *yang* in action; *yin* and *yang* are sex writ large" and, indeed, "one senses that much of Chinese metaphysics itself was actually inspired by the mundane physics of sex."[28] Hence the elaborate subtle body maps and mechanical techniques of simultaneous arousal and conservation that constitute Taoist sexual yoga, all of which appear to be designed to capitalize on the potentials of sexual and vital energy (as *ching* or *ch'i*, respectively) and their alchemical sublimation into pure spirit. Here, too, we find imaginal energy centers called "elixir fields" (the *tan-t'ien*) located along the spine or backbone, the hydraulic language of "gates" and "locks" to be manipulated through breathing techniques, various anal and genital contractions, and visualization instructions for precoital preparation and postcoital absorption.

None of this is meant to suggest that any such Asian sexology constituted some kind of sexual Shangri-La (as Jeffrey Hopkins warns us with respect to the Tibetan materials). The gender analyses that have been performed on these systems are particularly rich, and they have arrived at conclusions that are strikingly consistent in their insistence that such sexologies are androcentric models that grant little agency to the women who appear in their texts and rituals, and in the end the goal is the accumulation of energy for spiritual flight, not the (modern) ethical goods of gender equity, interpersonal reflexivity, and romantic love. The scholarship is thus now mature enough to warn us sternly away from any naïve or wishful notion that the Tantric traditions of Asia and modern Western notions of gender equity, reciprocity, and agency can somehow be easily reconciled. They cannot. Still, the point remains: it is both historically impossible and intellectually irresponsible to dismiss psychoanalytic hydraulic metaphors and drive models as somehow restricted to nineteenth-century European scientism. If the comparative witness of the world's religious cultures means anything, it is that what we find in Freud's psychoanalysis is a modern analogue to what we find in the historical mystical traditions, that is, a theorization of the relationship between the "dirty" depths of the human body and the highest flights of culture and contemplation.

Sacred Trauma

Very much related to this transformation of the sexual into the erotic within the history of religions is the topic of sexual trauma. Arguably, this is both the "cutting edge" and the most controversial aspect of the field.[29] This particular inquiry involves that broad range of ecstatic experiences, trance, possession states, and dissociative forms of consciousness that often display two seemingly contradictory features: they are often described as profoundly meaningful events, and they can be read as traumatically catalyzed (my terms are carefully chosen, as I think it must remain an open question whether the trauma "produces" these states or somehow breaks down the normal workings of the mind to "let in" other normally suppressed states of consciousness).[30] We are confronted here, in other words, with the dilemma of religious experiences that are psychosexually connected to violent, amoral, or even immoral events, a modern expression perhaps of what earlier writers such as Rudolf Otto taught us long ago, namely, that the phenomenological structure of human religious experience can seldom, if ever, be reduced to moral categories, and that human beings have long experienced the sacred as a *mysterium tremendum et fascinans*, that is, as numinous presence that displays both terrifying and astonishing features.[31]

Put differently, the emotions of fear, horror, and anxiety are as much a part of the historical record as those of love and security; indeed, probably more so. A car accident or operating table, for example, are probably far more likely to produce a dramatic religious event than a secure home or happy family life. Intense human suffering and profound religious experience are not only compatible, then; they often require one another. Hence, eerily, Otto's *mysterium tremendum et fascinans* as pointedly describes the psychology of sexual trauma as it is captured in the annals of mystical literature as accurately as it expresses the general phenomenology of the sacred in the history of religions.

The Two Ann(e)s

As a way of illustrating and summing up all of these rather abstract categories of sexuality, gender, sexual orientation, the erotic, and sexual trauma, let us end with two individual fields of sexual-religious emotion and, in this case, two historical female bodies, one (apparently) heterosexual, the other homosexual or bisexual: Mother Ann Lee (1736–1784), the charismatic founder of the American Shaker community, and the contemporary Hollywood actress, Anne Heche.

Mother Ann Lee quite literally identified the sin of Adam and Eve with sexual intercourse on the basis of an "open vision" she had around 1770 of the original couple engaging in the shameful sexual act: in other words, the Fall was not simply about sex; it *was* sex.[32] Lee herself took this traditional sexualization of sin to an unusually dramatic conclusion, insisting on complete celibacy for her community in order to restore the original bliss of Eden. The logic was simple: if sin was sex, then salvation was no-sex.

Practically speaking, this meant strict gender segregation in the Shaker communities, the breaking up of nuclear family attachments (children were raised communally), an obsessive concern with the control of sexuality and its many symbolic manifestations, and the famous marathon "shaking" and dancing sessions that were used to express devotion, cement community, and, by the self-descriptions of some of the Shakers themselves, spiritualize sexual desire. Lee also worked with a bisexual theology based on Genesis 1:26 ("Let us make man in our image"). Accordingly, God was believed to be both male and female (hence the "our"). If God were both male and female, moreover, it stood to reason that Christians could now expect a female incarnation of God. Accordingly, just as Jesus had been the male manifestation of God in the First Coming, Mother Ann was believed to be the female manifestation of God in the Second Coming (it is unclear whether Lee herself claimed this, but her followers certainly did).

Such an unorthodox theology had profound effects on the life of the community, where segregated men and women performed traditionally gendered work roles but also enacted a leadership and authority system that was dramatically egalitarian by the standards of the time. As in early Christianity, celibacy, and particularly female celibacy, had radical social and countercultural consequences, almost all of which worked to the advantage of the women, who were now free to pursue many cultural and religious ends that were both unthinkable and practically impossible within the hierarchical subordination and procreative burdens of the traditional patriarchal American family.

By all accounts, Mother Ann was absolutely terrified of sexual intercourse. And well she should have been. After all, according to the hagiographic accounts, she had lost all four of her babies in or shortly after birth and had almost died herself in the last and final of her birth-horror experiences. Little wonder, then, that she so feared intercourse, that she advanced a bald theological identification of sin and sex and a consequent insistence on total sexual continence, and that, finally, she resolutely refused to continue conjugal relations with her husband.

What role, if any, we might well ask, did her traumatic experiences of sexuality and birth play into her ascetic theology and her subsequent deification as the Second Coming or Daughter of God? And can we locate the source of the trauma even earlier, in her childhood and relationship to her own father perhaps? "It is remarkable that, in early youth, she had a great abhorrence of the fleshly cohabitation of the sexes," a very early biography tells us. "And so great was her sense of its impurity, that she often admonished her mother against it; which coming to her father's ears, he threatened and actually attempted to whip her; upon which she threw herself in to her mother's arms and clung round her to escape his strokes."[33] The historian attuned to psychosexual matters is allowed to be suspicious, particularly when we read that even later in life, "sometimes, for whole nights together, her cries screeches and groans were such as to fill every soul around her with fear and trembling," and that "by such deep mortification and sufferings her flesh wasted away till she became like a mere skeleton."[34]

Such questions are complicated further when we place them, in strong comparison, alongside another, more modern Ann(e). In her autobiography *Call Me Crazy*, Anne Heche chronicles a childhood of repeated sexual abuse at the hands of her father, whose sexual activities outside the home resulted in him contracting AIDS and dying in the early 1980s, when Heche was only thirteen. A family culture of total denial, an evangelical Christian piety in the home that wanted to translate everything into obfuscating patriarchal terms that both vaguely legitimated and successfully camouflaged her father's abusive activities,[35] and the lack of cultural and psychological resources to give Heche's experience an adequate voice outside the religious register led eventually to an almost complete breakdown of her mental functioning and a subsequent religious-psychotic experience in which God spoke to her audibly in order to inform her, rather matter-of-factly in front of Ray's Manhattan pizza parlor, that she was the daughter of God, just as Jesus had been the son of God.[36]

The traumatic catalysts and doctrinal content of the visions of these two Ann(e)s are eerily similar: both experienced serious and repeated trauma, and both came to see themselves as the Second Coming of Christ (again, historians debate whether this was Lee's self-understanding or that of her community). The differences seem to lie well outside the religious experiences themselves, that is, in the social contexts and final acts of their specific interpretations. Whereas Mother Ann may or may not have realized the connection between her early sexual life and her later religious experiences and found adequate meaning living entirely within a newly minted religious language, Heche, through years of therapy, learned to translate the religious phenomena into psychological categories and so moved beyond them in an act of healing and a defiant act of public speaking and self-affirmation. In the former case, the traumatized is literally divinized and healed within an otherwise partially liberatory religious worldview; in the latter, the traumatized speaks out against the silence and her own religious culture through an ethically imbued psychosexual code.

We might well imagine that it was often a wonderful experience to know Mother Ann as the Mother-God and to ritually enact in dance and song the androgynous nature of God as Mother-Father. The historical records are clear that a kind of "sensible" power emanated from the charismatic woman and could be transmitted into her disciples, who would subsequently experience a "new creation" through visions, revelations, and other altered states (the erotic appears). But the "shaking" sublimation of such amplified energies came with a very heavy price, namely, the bald and simplistic identification of human sexuality (and, by implication, children) with original sin. So, too, with Heche. Within the context of her conversation with God, she had known at last the presence of a loving father-substitute. Indeed, the vision clearly tried to suggest that her real father was God himself, and that she was a female Jesus or woman-man—in effect, she had been divinized, and in an implicitly queer form that nicely replicated her own psychosexual patterns. Things could not get much better than that. But again, as she herself so bravely came to realize, at what price? Mother Ann accepted the exchange. Heche finally refused it.

Concluding Thoughts

And what should we choose? Put differently, what is it that we now know after one hundred years of discourse on "sexuality" and "religion"? We know, in the words of Elliot Wolfson, that "matters pertaining to the spiritual have repeatedly been depicted in erotic images," and that the "consciousness of eros" is also the "eros of consciousness."[37] We know, moreover, that this consistent comparative pattern is almost certainly not a matter of simple "metaphors" or "symbols," that such erotic-noetic images have real physiological, emotional, genital, and ontological bases. We also know that these types of religious expressions are always informed by elaborate gender and sexual orientation dynamics, and that any reading that fails to take the directions of desire or the gendering of the religious expression into account will miss much. Finally, we know that some of the most idealized and most historically successful religious experiences were most likely catalyzed either through traumatic dissociative processes or within radically hierarchical and asymmetrical gender systems that many of us would now consider to be ethically problematic, if not actually oppressive.

It is exceedingly doubtful, though, that we have learned everything, that we will not again be surprised and astonished. The history of religions, after all, strongly suggests other truths, other possibilities, other reality posits that we, with all our contextualist, constructivist, political, and historical sophistication, have generally not seen, not accepted, not known. We still have much to learn. Our eyes, for example, have yet to open wide to what is perhaps the deepest and most important lesson of this history, namely, that human sexuality holds a secret, that sex is never just sex, that the sexual—empowered in the altered states of religious ecstasy, contemplative insight, and traumatic dissociation—merges imperceptibly but really into the erotic.

NOTES

1. Interestingly, this is decidedly less so with many of the minor, heterodox, or "heretical" religions, which often break from their orthodox source traditions on partly sexual or gendered grounds—there appears, in other words, to be some structural relationship between religious heterodoxy and gender experimentation.

2. Richard Shweder, *Thinking Through Cultures: Expeditions in Cultural Psychology* (Cambridge, Mass.: Harvard University Press, 1991), 108.

3. Ibid., 73.

4. Norman Brown, *Love's Body* (Berkeley: University of California Press, 1966), 89.

5. See Kristen E. Kvam, Linda S. Schearing and Valerie H. Ziegler, *Eve and Adam: Jewish, Christian, and Muslim Readings on Genesis and Gender* (Bloomington: Indiana University Press, 1999); and David Biale, *Eros and the Jews: From Biblical Israel to Contemporary America* (Berkeley: University of California Press, 1997), 109.

6. Jeffrey J. Kripal, *The Serpent's Gift: Gnostic Reflections on the Study of Religion* (Chicago: University of Chicago Press, 2006).

7. Gilbert Herdt, *Third Sex, Third Gender: Beyond Sexual Dimorphism in Culture and History* (New York: Zone Books, 1993).

8. See Lyndal Roper, *Oedipus and the Devil: Witchcraft, Sexuality, and Religion in Early Modern Europe* (London: Routledge, 1994).

9. See Steven Pinker, *How the Mind Works* (New York: Norton, 1997), 460–93.

10. See especially Martha C. Nussbaum, *Sex and Social Justice* (New York: Oxford University Press, 1999).

11. Amartya Sen advanced this famous thesis in a series of writings in the late 1980s. For a history, critical discussion, and update of the statistics, see Stephan Klasen and Claudia Wink, "'Missing Women': Revisiting the Debate," *Feminist Economics* 9, 2–3 (2003): 263–99.

12. The literature is immense here. For a realization of its potential, see especially the two-volume masterwork of Theodore W. Jennings, Jr., *The Man Jesus Loved: Homoerotic Narratives from the New Testament* (New York: Continuum, 2003); and *Jacob's Wound:*

Homoerotic Narrative in the Literature of Ancient Israel (New York: Continuum, 2005). With respect to the Hebrew literature, see also Steven Greenberg, *Wrestling with God and Men: Homosexuality in the Jewish Tradition* (Madison: University of Wisconsin Press, 2004).

13. For an impressive collection of same-sex readings across Indian literature (which is by no means restricted to the modern category of Hinduism), see Ruth Vanita and Saleem Kidwai, eds., *Same-Sex Love in India: Readings from Literature and History* (New York: Palgrave, 2000).

14. A single bibliography on Christianity alone (by far the most studied tradition) would run into hundreds of citations. For a relatively up-to-date sampling across the traditions, see Gary David Comstock and Susan E. Henking, eds., *Que(e)rying Religion: A Critical Anthology* (New York: Continuum, 1999).

15. See especially Catherine Clément, *Syncope: The Philosophy of Rapture*, translated by Sally O'Driscoll and Deirdre M. Mahoney (Minneapolis: University of Minnesota Press, 1994).

16. In the Tibetan traditions, a *terma*, or "mind treasure," is a hidden scriptural text that is "discovered" at an auspicious time by a trained yogi or *terton*. "Generally, before receiving their main revelations, *tertons* practice sexual yoga with a consort as a means of accelerating and enhancing their visionary powers" (Serinity Young, *Courtesans and Tantric Consorts: Sexualities in Buddhist Narrative, Iconography, and Ritual* [New York: Routledge, 2004], 155). Sexual experience and scriptural inspiration, in other words, are implicitly connected here.

17. Walter Stephens, *Demon Lovers: Witchcraft, Sex, and the Crisis of Belief* (Chicago: University of Chicago Press, 2002); Roper, *Oedipus and the Devil*.

18. Ioan P. Couliano, *Eros and Magic in the Renaissance* (Chicago: University of Chicago Press, 1987).

19. David J. Hufford, *The Terror That Comes in the Night: An Experience-Centered Study of Supernatural Assault Traditions* (Philadelphia: University of Pennsylvania Press, 1982). See also Paul Deane, *Sex and the Paranormal: Human Sexual Encounters with the Supernatural* (London: Vega, 2003).

20. I have developed this hermeneutical category in three separate books: *Kali's Child: The Mystical and the Erotic in the Life and Teachings of Ramakrishna* (Chicago: University of Chicago Press, 1998,); *Roads of Excess, Palaces of Wisdom: Eroticism and Reflexivity in the Study of Mysticism* (Chicago: University of Chicago Press, 2001); and *The Serpent's Gift*.

21. Patrick Olivelle has convincingly argued that the Vedic origins of *ananda* lie in the ecstatic experience of orgasm and phallic pleasure, in "Orgasmic Rapture and Divine Ecstasy: The Semantic History of Ananda," *Journal of Indian Philosophy* 25 (1997): 153–80.

22. Georges Bataille, *Erotism: Death and Sensuality* (San Francisco: City Lights, 1986), 7.

23. David Gordon White, *The Alchemical Body: Siddha Traditions in Medieval India* (Chicago: University of Chicago Press, 1996); and *Kiss of the Yogini: "Tantric Sex" in Its South Asian Contexts* (Chicago: University of Chicago Press, 2003).

24. Edward C. Dimock, Jr., *The Place of the Hidden Moon: Erotic Mysticism in the Vaisnava Sahajiyas of Bengal* (Chicago: University of Chicago Press, 1966).

25. Jeffrey Hopkins, *Sex, Orgasm, and the Mind of Clear Light: The Sixty-four Arts of Gay Male Love* (Berkeley: North Atlantic Books, 1998), 72.

26. Ibid.

27. Ibid., 91.

28. Douglas Wile, *Art of the Bedchamber: The Chinese Sexual Yoga Classics Including Women's Solo Meditation Texts* (Albany: State University of New York Press, 1992), 11.

29. Bessel A. van der Kolk, Alexander C. McFarlane, and Lars Weisaeith, eds., *Traumatic Stress: The Effects of Overwhelming Experience on Mind, Body, and Society* (New York: Guilford Press, 1996). For applications of the theory in religious studies, see, for example, Stevan L. Davies in New Testament studies (*Possession, Trance, and the Origins of Christianity* [New York: Continuum, 1995]), June Campbell in Buddhology (*Traveller in Space: In Search of Female Identity in Tibetan Buddhism* [New York: Braziller, 1996]), and Amy Hollywood in the history of Christianity (*Sensible Ecstasy: Mysticism, Sexual Difference, and the Demands of History* [Chicago: University of Chicago Press, 2001]). My own slandered work in Indology (*Kali's Child*) should also be located here.

30. This same question defined much of the early debate around the religious meaning of psychedelic states. Were these substances producing these experiences as pure illusions? Or were they somehow shutting down the brain's normal sensory filter to allow input in that is always "there" but normally excluded by the practical filters of the human brain? As with psychedelic states, so, too with mystico-erotic and traumatic ones, I think we would do well to leave the question generously open and not reduce these experiences to their psychosexual contexts-as-catalysts.

31. Rudolf Otto, *The Idea of the Holy* (Oxford: Oxford University Press, 1958).

32. Lawrence Foster, *Sex and Religion: The Shakers, Oneida Community, and Mormons* (Bloomington: Indiana University Press, 1981), 46.

33. *Testimonies of the Life, Character, Revelations and Doctrines of Our Ever Blessed Mother Ann Lee, and the Elders with Her; Through Whom the World of Eternal Life Was Opened in This Day of Christ's Second Appearing* (Hancock, Mass.: J. Tallcott & J. Deming, Junrs, 1816), 3. My sincere thanks to Lawrence Foster for sharing this historical document with me.

34. Ibid., 5.

35. This masking of sexual abuse in the language of piety is a common theme in the literature. See especially Donald Capps, *The Child's Song: The Religious Abuse of Children* (Louisville, Ky.: Westminster John Knox Press, 1995).

36. Anne Heche, *Call Me Crazy* (New York: Scribner's, 2001), 188-89.

37. Elliot Wolfson, *Language, Eros, Being: Kabbalistic Hermeneutics and Poetic Imagination* (New York: Fordham University Press, 2005), 261. Few, if any, scholars have done more than Elliot Wolfson to reveal the patterns I have summarized in the present essay.

BIBLIOGRAPHY

Bataille, Georges. *Erotism: Death and Sensuality*. San Francisco: City Lights, 1986.

Biale, David. *Eros and the Jews: From Biblical Israel to Contemporary America*. Berkeley: University of California Press, 1997.

Brown, Norman. *Love's Body*. Berkeley: University of California Press, 1966.

Campbell, June. *Traveller in Space: In Search of Female Identity in Tibetan Buddhism*. New York: Braziller, 1996.

Capps, Donald. *The Child's Song: The Religious Abuse of Children*. Louisville, Ky.: Westminster John Knox Press, 1995.

Clément, Catherine. *Syncope: The Philosophy of Rapture*. Translated by Sally O'Driscoll and Deirdre M. Mahoney. Minneapolis: University of Minnesota Press, 1994.

Comstock, Gary David, and Susan E. Henking, eds. *Que(e)rying Religion: A Critical Anthology*. New York: Continuum, 1999.
Couliano, Ioan P. *Eros and Magic in the Renaissance*. Chicago: University of Chicago Press, 1987.
Davies, Stevan L. *Possession, Trance, and the Origins of Christianity*. New York: Continuum, 1995.
Deane, Paul. *Sex and the Paranormal: Human Sexual Encounters with the Supernatural*. London: Vega, 2003.
Dimock, Edward C., Jr. *The Place of the Hidden Moon: Erotic Mysticism in the Vaisnava Sahajiyas of Bengal*. Chicago: University of Chicago Press, 1966.
Foster, Lawrence. *Sex and Religion: The Shakers, Oneida Community, and Mormons*. Bloomington: Indiana University Press, 1981.
Greenberg, Steven. *Wrestling with God and Men: Homosexuality in the Jewish Tradition*. Madison: University of Wisconsin Press, 2004.
Heche, Anne. *Call Me Crazy*. New York: Scribner's, 2001.
Hollywood, Amy. *Sensible Ecstasy: Mysticism, Sexual Difference, and the Demands of History*. Chicago: University of Chicago Press, 2001.
Hopkins, Jeffrey. *Sex, Orgasm, and the Mind of Clear Light: The Sixty-Four Arts of Gay Male Love*. Berkeley: North Atlantic Books, 1998.
Hufford, David J. *The Terror That Comes in the Night: An Experience-Centered Study of Supernatural Assault Traditions*. Philadelphia: University of Pennsylvania Press, 1982.
Klasen, Stephan, and Claudia Wink. "'Missing Women': Revisiting the Debate." *Feminist Economics* 9, 2–3 (2003): 263–99.
Kripal, Jeffrey J. *Kali's Child: The Mystical and the Erotic in the Life and Teachings of Ramakrishna*. Chicago: University of Chicago Press, 1998.
———. *Roads of Excess, Palaces of Wisdom: Eroticism and Reflexivity in the Study of Mysticism*. Chicago: University of Chicago Press, 2001.
———. *The Serpent's Gift: Gnostic Reflections on the Study of Religion*. Chicago: University of Chicago Press, 2006.
Kvam, Kristen E., Linda S. Schearing, and Valerie H. Ziegler, eds. *Eve and Adam: Jewish, Christian, and Muslim Readings on Genesis and Gender*. Indianapolis: Indiana University Press, 1999.
Nussbaum, Martha C. *Sex and Social Justice*. New York: University of Oxford Press, 1999.
Olivelle, Patrick. "Orgasmic Rapture and Divine Ecstasy: The Semantic History of Ananda." *Journal of Indian Philosophy* 25 (1997): 153–80.
Otto, Rudolf. *The Idea of the Holy*. Oxford: Oxford University Press, 1958.
Pinker, Steven. *How the Mind Works*. New York: Norton, 1997.
Robinson, James M., gen. ed. *The Coptic Gnostic Library: A Complete Edition of the Nag Hammadi Codices*. Leiden: Brill, 1995.
Roper, Lyndal. *Oedipus and the Devil: Witchcraft, Sexuality, and Religion in Early Modern Europe*. London: Routledge, 1994.
Shweder, Richard. *Thinking through Cultures: Expeditions in Cultural Psychology*. Cambridge, Mass.: Harvard University Press, 1991.
Stephens, Walter. *Demon Lovers: Witchcraft, Sex, and the Crisis of Belief*. Chicago: University of Chicago Press, 2002.
Testimonies of the Life, Character, Revelations, and Doctrines of Our Ever Blessed Mother Ann Lee, and the Elders with Her; Through Whom the World of Eternal Life Was Opened in

This Day of Christ's Second Appearing. Hancock, Mass.: J. Tallcott and J. Deming, Junrs, 1816.

van der Kolk, Bessel A., Alexander C. McFarlane, and Lars Weisaeith, eds. *Traumatic Stress: The Effects of Overwhelming Experience on Mind, Body, and Society.* New York: Guilford Press, 1996.

Vanita, Ruth, and Saleem Kidwai, eds. *Same-Sex Love in India: Readings from Literature and History.* New York: Palgrave, 2000.

White, David Gordon. *The Alchemical Body: Siddha Traditions in Medieval India.* Chicago: University of Chicago Press, 1996.

———. *Kiss of the Yogini: "Tantric Sex" in Its South Asian Contexts.* Chicago: University of Chicago Press, 2003.

Wile, Douglas. *Art of the Bedchamber: The Chinese Sexual Yoga Classics Including Women's Solo Meditation Texts.* Albany: State University of New York Press, 1992.

Wolfson, Elliot. *Language, Eros, Being: Kabbalistic Hermeneutics and Poetic Imagination* (New York: Fordham University Press, 2005).

Young, Serinity. *Courtesans and Tantric Consorts: Sexualities in Buddhist Narrative, Iconography, and Ritual.* New York: Routledge, 2004.

CHAPTER 10

GENDER

MELISSA RAPHAEL

If there has been very little study of religious emotion, there has been still less study of the role of gender in the occasion, quality, and expression of religious emotion. This is hardly to be wondered at. Not until the emergence of religious feminism in the late 1970s, the ordination of Jewish and Protestant women in increasing numbers, and the formulation of new rituals designed by and for women have women been speaking subjects in the major world religions. As women have been discoursed and legislated on but are not yet in many quarters themselves the subjects of religious discourse or the agents of religious legislation, the different scope and temper of women's religious emotion has still to become fully apparent.

Even so, the study of religion has produced, if indirectly, at least enough knowledge about masculine religious emotion and masculine views of female emotion for this essay to demonstrate that religious emotion is very fluidly gendered. The gendered rhetoric and expression of religious emotion is inherently prone to destabilization for two main reasons. First, religion's ordering of the world is at once rational and nonrational. Emotion is a necessary element of any theistic religion, in particular, insofar as love of and faith in a personal God are affective states whose meaning is elucidated by the transcendental operation of the reason.[1] Men are not necessarily emotionally detached from the object of their religious devotion, any more than they are from the human objects of their love. When subordinated to an ordered, disciplined masculine dispensation, religious emotion can be constitutive and expressive of mainstream theology and faith. Most traditions of Abrahamic theology are personalistic and therefore also predicate a range of emotions including not only wrath but also a (nonordinary) love and compassion even to an essentially and normatively masculine model of God.

Second, the gendering of religious emotion is unstable because religion often opposes the customary ordering of the world by its own prophetic social transgressions. Even where religious emotion is ascribed to one sex or another, it may still be subject to appropriation, inversion, and subversion on the part of both men and women, as well as to historical and cultural shifts in religious taste and sensibility. This means that religious emotion does not, in fact, always conform to the symmetrical dualistic pattern of masculine detachment and feminine affectivity that our cultural stereotypes would lead us to expect. Certain religious roles, narratives, situations, or styles will permit and elicit from men a variety of emotional responses.

In short, discussion of the gendering of religious emotion should be wary of transhistorical and cross-cultural generalizations. Not only is the postmodern academy properly cautious of comprehensive theories, but a relatively brief essay, referring to several different religions and on a topic as diffuse this one, will be necessarily eclectic and cannot note the myriad exceptions to very broad rule of the generalizations.[2] There is no single, normative historical or theological scheme by which to determine and theorize the gendering of religious emotion. Like emotion itself, the topic is unruly: it will conform to no one set of phenomenological rules. *Contra* Rudolf Otto's influential account of the sense of the holy or numinous, which he considered a *sui generis* religious emotion,[3] it may be that there is no essentially religious emotion but different emotions expressed in different religious contexts. It can be the factor of social class or ethnicity in a given religion, as much as gender, which inhibits or permits the release of religious emotion. Accordingly, whether or not women and men's emotional expression is either esteemed or denigrated by their religious communities is multiply determined.

Having noted, then, that the ascription of gender to religious emotion is not always culturally predictable and that male-dominated religions are hardly devoid of masculine emotional self-expression, this essay will argue that male-dominated religions tend to regulate, transcend, and thereby "masculinize" emotion by its accommodation in the sublime: in the narrative, ritual, dogmatic, and ethical scheme articulated by, and primarily for, men. Where emotion cannot be thus accommodated, male religious discourse often reduces "natural," "private" emotion to a function of sexual desire. After examining the male regulation of this "natural" emotion and the ways and contexts in which religious emotion is performed by men, I will close with a brief account of the religious feminist reclamation of the spiritually and politically transformative power of religious emotion.

FEMINIST CRITICISM AND THE GENDERING OF RELIGIOUS EMOTION

Although the romanticism of the late eighteenth and early nineteenth centuries found rationalism to be a taming and a sterilization of experience, it did not question the opposition between reason and emotion but thereby underscored it.[4] Even historians of religion of the romanticist tradition like Rudolf Otto regarded reason as the completion of religion and ranked religions that developed the rational faculties above those that did not. It is, for Otto, reason that distinguishes the human from the animal and faith from mere numinous apprehension and the (female) sphere of the flesh.[5]

As might be expected, feminist philosophers have criticized the gendered bifurcation and opposition of reason and emotion that has permeated Western philosophy from its ancient Greek origins and that has been both a cause and a result of the subordination of women to men in religion and culture.[6] Feminist theorists have qualified or dismissed the patriarchal philosophical assumption that women are more inclined to an embodied agitation or perturbation of feeling than they are to the reasoned response of the mind. They have rejected as partial and culturally conditioned the Cartesian model, where the defining characteristic of the normative (male) subject is the capacity for cerebration.[7] In her classic study *The Man of Reason: "Male" and "Female" in Western Philosophy*,[8] Genevieve Lloyd became one of the first feminist philosophers to criticize the casting of femaleness as the turbulent, mysterious power of nature that masculine reason must both exclude from its project and harness to the rational ends of religious and technological progress. More recently, Martha Nussbaum has argued that emotion plays a central role in the formation of identity and knowledge. We come to know who we are by being moved by the objects of our emotion, about which we have already made judgments of belief and value. Knowledge is produced in the processes of risky, vulnerable, embodied affective encounters, not by detached cognition alone.[9]

Feminist philosophical criticism of the derogation of female emotion informs and is informed by Western religious feminism's claim that the gendering of religious emotion is subsequent to the secondary status of women in religions. The patriarchal decertification of women's religious emotion is, above all, grounded in its androcentric or male-centered account of the nature of God and of persons. Both Christian and Jewish feminist theology has insisted that in religions of the textual word such as Judaism and Islam, where revelation is mediated through texts written by men for a primarily male readership, to be a prophetic allocutor of God or a priestly or scholarly interlocutor with men is the prerogative of men alone. Women are neither the allocutors of God nor the interlocutors of the divine-human conversation; therefore, their experience is not ordered or intellectualized by authoritative discourse. Women's religious emotion, being unarticulated, therefore falls outside, or to the side of, the logocentric ordering of the world that, in the classical philosophy of Western theism, is governed by an immutable, apathetic (nonsuffering), omnipotent God the freedom of whose attributes allows him to transcend the crude anthropomorphisms of reactive emotion.

Where women are regarded as incomplete or deficient persons (as in Judaism, where the legal category of full personhood is male), their affectivity may be construed as a symptom of their moral and rational deficiency, one that leaves them susceptible to temptation and transgression. The biblical Eve is, of course, the paradigmatic case of such. Eve's failings have been powerfully reinforced by Christian doctrine and Catholic theology's rehearsal of Aristotelian views of the female as a more or less aborted male. In all but the most radical sects of the Church, Eve's moral susceptibility has come to symbolize and justify women's subordination to men and their disqualification from religious and political leadership.

Since the early 1990s, religious feminist scholarship has offered a more nuanced criticism of religion than was previously the case: religion is acknowledged to be both oppressive and liberative, as countermanding its own injustices and as leaving women sufficient room to develop their own spirituality in spite of the sexual-political constraints placed on them.[10] It is clear that not all religions decertify domestic space and the mundane experiences associated with it: Judaism, for example, sacralizes the domestic sphere as well as the synagogue. Not only is the weekly peace of the Sabbath experienced at home but also the pivotal redemptive moment of the Exodus is celebrated at Pesach by a sacred meal (the Seder) prepared and eaten in the female space of the home.

Even so, Jewish women's religious devotion, because of being traditionally centered in the domestic sphere, has had little or no opportunity to engage in the study of religious law that is considered the Jew's highest act of service to God. Christian configurations of sacred space and the duties attending its sanctification are not the same as in Judaism. Yet again, without the opportunity to order emotion into authoritative forms of public expression, lay Catholic women's religious emotion has most often been directed toward a relatively unregulated private devotion to the saints and the Virgin Mary. And before the ordination of women in twentieth-century Protestant denominations, private prayers, devotional diaries, and occasionally preaching (sometimes dismissed as "ranting") were all instances of a generally unlettered "warm" religious self-expression commonly assigned to women's "little" or folk tradition in contrast to the "colder," "great" tradition of men's elite religious institutions.

Even where women's private devotion has effectively adapted public religious confession to the private, domestic, and familial situation, women's gender-specific grief and joy has rarely been engaged (or even addressed) in the traditional ritual provision. Male-dominated traditions—especially cultic or priestly ones—have been unwilling to sacralize the intimate life events that traditionally elicit women's most powerful emotions: romantic love, pregnancy, childbirth, and child-death.[11] In these traditions, the emotions attending these body-centered events have to be controlled and educated by the masculine tradition, especially by its rites of passage. In the Christian tradition, these rites of passage have been marriage, "churching" after childbirth (now widely fallen into disuse), and baptism. It is only since the end of the twentieth century that new religious rituals designed by religious feminists to meet women's gender-specific emotional needs have been developed. Rituals that both console and transcendentalize the trauma of, say, miscarriage, abortion, mastectomy, and divorce are now widespread on the liberal Left of the religious traditions and in alternative religious circles.[12]

The Sexualization of Female Religious Emotion

Across most of the world's religious cultures, women, like the emotion they hypostasize, represent chaos. In particular, the polluting menstrual cycle is held to generate periodic "natural" emotions whose flux corresponds with the natural cycles of the moon and tides, both of which signal the reversive pull of primal chaos. While excessive religious emotion in *male* saints and mystics may be regarded as the demonstration of supererogatory devotion or holiness, women's religious emotion may be pathologized as hysteria, echoing the early modern doctors who explained women's malaises as a detachment of the womb, whose wandering around the body causes unpredictable behavior. Women's emotional state, like their cultic impurity, is held to be beyond the control of either women or men's moral and spiritual will. As Majella Franzmann notes of Islam, loss of control of the body in menstruation and childbirth is considered among Muslims to indicate a general lack of emotional control. Women are open to irrationality and thus are unreliable spiritually. The general view among Muslims that women are too emotional and are controlled by passion rather than rationality adds to the reasons for their exclusion from any religious roles other than those available in their local indigenous, pre-Islamic practices.[13]

As in other religious cultures, a Muslim woman's sexual desire must be kept under control lest it bring dishonor to her family. Yet there is little Islamic discourse upon male sexual self-control despite expedient practices such as *mot'a*—temporary marriage—which is permitted to Shi'ite men whose visit to a prostitute or rape of women in war is an act of sexual and emotional incontinence that can be legitimated.[14] By contrast, silence and immobility are popular criteria for a desirable Muslim wife. For a wife to be *shaddaka*—talkative—is a serious flaw; it is a sign of her being emotionally expressive. Like other systems of religious law, Islamic law regulates pleasure and in doing so stigmatizes women as sources and seekers of pleasure. Correlating legal and erotic Islamic discourses, Fatna Sabbah argues that the representation of women in erotic Islamic literature as sites of unbridled desire makes female sexuality incompatible with the social roles of mother and wife. Female desire necessitates the veiling and seclusion of women so as to separate them from the male population.[15]

To exercise control over the chaos of emotion is at the same time to control the chaotic effects of female sexuality. As Jeffrey Hopkins points out, to hide or punish the body of the base other—whether female or, by extension, homosexual male—is to signify the control of the higher self over the base desires of the lower self.[16] In the most extreme cases of religious misogyny and homophobia, the object of desire is also the object of hatred and abuse, since she or he is the occasion of religious degeneration and loss of control. Conversely, when women (though not homosexuals) are idealized and elevated in religious systems, this can signify the triumph of sexual self-control, and therefore reason, over passion.[17]

A central element of any feminist critique of the gendering of religious emotion would therefore be criticism of the sexualization of female religious emotion. In misogynistic religious discourse, women's religious emotion is sexualized, that is, rendered a "natural" symptom of their embodiment that clouds their reason and provokes uncontrolled emotion (desire) in men. Male constructed and dominated religious systems fear the social and spiritual chaos—or at best, distraction—that results when men succumb to the passions aroused by the female body. Emotion comes to signify an actual or symbolic surrender of masculine autonomy to the temptation or heteronomy of female flesh. When men become susceptible to women, they, too, are "feminized," since they, too, become subject to, not masters of, desire. Women must therefore be controlled by the *ratio* of religious law and ethics if both a primal and historical reversion to moral chaos is to be avoided. It becomes necessary for male emotion to be theologized and redirected toward a proper divine object and for access to women's bodies to be legislated in such a way that they only elicit emotion in the (male) persons who control or are otherwise in authority over them: their fathers and, more especially, their husbands. Just as the physiological and instinctual heat of emotion must be sublimated and disciplined as spirituality, women, as the embodiments of "natural" or biological emotion, must be disciplined by the male spirit and polity. That is, as mere agitation, emotion is immanent and must, in men, be transcended by either autonomous or theonomous reason, virtue, and moral choice. When emotion is reduced to the distraction of sexual desire, there develops an antithesis between reason and sexual pleasure as well as between reason and emotion.

Of course the tropes—and sometimes practices—of desire as a state of spiritual captivity do not invariably conform to this pattern whereby a man must achieve sexual/emotional domination over himself as subject as well as over his feminine object. Although Buddhism, for example, generally enjoins nonattachment, in Indo-Tibetan Buddhist systems, intense (male) orgasm is held to produce the purest, deepest, and most blissful level of consciousness of reality—"the mind of clear light"—which dissolves the bifurcation between reason and experiential, bodily states and makes them continuous with one another.[18] Sexual bliss and the prolongation of pleasure with a woman therefore becomes a matter of technique, for "the aim of sexual yoga is . . . not mere repetition of an attractive state but revelation of the basic reality underlying appearances."[19]

Yet taking the example of Judaism, we can see that Hopkins's example is an exception to a very widespread rule. By custom, if not by law, the audibility of Jewish women's voices and their physical presence in a male space is held to sexually distract men from worship, and men's emotional response to women is controlled and socialized by laws pertaining to *tzniut* (modesty) and by marriage.[20] Since women arouse ungovernable (sexual) emotions in men, it is better, so the talmudic dictum goes, to walk behind a lion than a woman.

It quickly becomes apparent that the sexualization of a wide range of human emotions is not only a sociopolitical problem but a theological one. Men's resistance to their own affectivity can inhibit spiritual responsiveness to the divine object of love, as well as to women. As Charlotte Elisheva Fonrobert has noted, the rhetoric of passion structures the relation of God and Israel but also sets up a tension between men's love of God and love of their wives and families. Furthermore, how, asks Fonrobert, should Jewish men construe their passionate longing for God if emotion is female? If women are the objects of love and desire, and Torah is also the object of love and desire, then that not only feminizes Torah but also sexualizes it. This places women in a sexually asymmetrical relation to Torah and poses the question of how Judaism can ever construe women's desire for God and Torah if women's desire is always to be a function of their sexuality.[21]

SUBVERSION, POWER, AND FEMALE RELIGIOUS EMOTION

Women's heightened emotional sensibility has traditionally been attributed to their definitively feminine passivity and receptivity. And it is broadly true that male or female manifestations of "feminine" sensibility in public can be something of an embarrassment to religious elites and those of a more reserved religious disposition. If public religious authority has been the prerogative of elite men, then it would appear that women who strive for religious authority would have to renounce their embodied female emotion and desire. This was true of most of the women saints of the early and medieval Church, whose spirituality was markedly ascetic.[22]

However, not all Christian women saints have denied their bodily desires for children and for the love of men. In fact, female religio-emotional sensibility, heightened to the point of numinous ecstasy, could earn Christian women the esteem of their community. The life of the fifteenth-century British mystic Margery Kempe, described in the autobiography she dictated between 1432 and 1436, confirms the traditional association of female sexuality and affectivity, but it was one that conferred on her a considerable degree of popular authority—both then and now among contemporary Christian feminists. Although her emotional expressiveness did not always win approval (her loud weeping during church services was unpopular) Margery Kempe was the mother of four children whose affective piety allowed her to enjoy an erotic relationship with both God and Jesus.[23] Margery's was not a spiritual vision of the transcendental, metasexual union of the soul with the divine but a quasi-physical relation through which she cultivated a subversive Trinitarian theology of desire. Despite accusations of heresy from the Christian elite, Margery claimed to be adored by God. God, she believed, had promised obedience to her; his son Jesus was styled both as her son and husband.

Contemporary Christian feminists' celebration of Margery Kempe's affective piety also suggests that whether women's supposed greater excitability renders them the religious inferiors of men is a matter of perspective and priority. From an androcentric perspective, the apparently rational and ethical nature of masculine piety would rank it above women's more instinctual response to the divine.[24] Women's supposedly receptive affectivity appears to fit them for sacral roles such as lamentation or spirit manifestation: the untutored expression of emotion so often situated on the social and religious margins. Yet from a gynocentric perspective, that marginality may pertain only in relation to the male tradition, not to the more immediate female one, where such roles may be not marginal but central to women's lives. Where death from conflict or disease is common and funerary rituals are central to the culture of a community, women's lamentation for the dead is not peripheral to the practice of a religion, even if it is not always officially sanctioned. Lamentation allows women an unscripted but audible, visible, and relatively autonomous role in a public religious event. The uncontrolled expression of grief is not only cathartic for women but vicariously so for men, who may not be permitted the expression of grief in public.

The roles of public lamentation and spirit manifestation are worth attending to in a little more detail, not least because they further exemplify the patriarchal reduction of women's religious emotion to a function of their sexuality—or, more accurately in this instance, their biology. Women are associated with the expression of ritualized grief throughout the world's religions. The Hebrew Bible refers to professional or "skilled" women who composed and chanted lamentations (Jer. 9.16), and women also led public displays of grief in the rabbinic period. In other religions, the power generated by the sheer volume and volubility of grief can allow women to mediate between the worlds: the noise made by Korean women shamans, for example, permits them to make contact with the dead.[25]

Anthropologists of religion have variously explained women's association with public grieving for the dead. It is to be supposed that as a mother, a bereaved woman is more susceptible to grief than a bereaved man, since she brings life and therefore death into the world and, almost universally, has duties of bodily care to the living and the dead. Not only is a woman's relationship to a dead body more intimate than that of a man, she may, as a menstruant who can lose potential life each month, have affinities of pollution and impurity with a corpse that men do not. In short, women's marginal social status, their biological proximity to the beginning of life, and their cultural proximity to the end of life, as well as the relational intimacies afforded by a woman's socioreligious obligations to others, have together made lamentation a distinctively (but not exclusively) female religious role.

However, the religious establishment often frowns on an excessive display of female grief. The talmudic tract *Mo'ed Katan* is a warning to Jewish women of the risks of uncontrolled emotion: it records the death of a woman who lost all seven of her sons because she wept too copiously for each of them. In other cultures, too, women's emotional display is regarded with suspicion, since it can occasion a temporary suspension of social mores. That is, laments can present "subtheological" complaints from the social margins; they may lend women a political voice. I. M. Lewis, for example, describes how, in the male-dominated *zar* communities in

Somalia, ecstatic religion redresses the sexual-political balance for women and gives them opportunities to express transgressive views and make specific emotional and economic demands of their husbands.[26] Or again, in British spiritualism between the 1860s and 1890s, working- and middle-class Victorian women mediums subverted the ideal of feminine passivity and gained financial independence, status, and popular authority through the assumption of different (sometimes male) personae that addressed the grieving public in a sharply critical voice. Their speaking through the dead gave a supernatural voice to the period's campaign for women's rights.[27]

Susan Starr Sered has noted the prevalence of female spirit manifestation and its centrality in women's spirituality throughout the world's religions, and she attributes this to the relational, maternal posture: the symbolism and actuality of female embodiment that allows the biological presence of other persons inside a woman's pregnant body.[28] But there are other ways women's religious emotion can yield an ambivalent power within male-dominated religions. An important instance is when men in male-dominated religions claim that women's affectivity signals their "natural" disposition to religion. In ultra-Orthodox Jewish apologetics, it is women's refined sensibility and the immediacy of their response that makes them better qualified for an immediate, private relation with God.[29] Indeed, conservative religionists may consider men to be women's religious inferiors because they lack the heightened spiritual sensibilities that they suppose grant women a more immediate relation to the divine. Conservative religious rhetoric further insists that virtuous female emotion qualifies women for their traditional task, namely the tender care of children, other women, the sick, and the elderly. This domestication of female religious emotion has not been entirely disempowering for women. Women's emotion, sublimated as quasi-maternal compassion, is a quality that their religion may quite genuinely esteem: a dutiful, self-denying care for the vulnerable is a vocation that can offer women a place within the sphere of religio-ethical agency and ministry that may be public and is more often occupied by men.

Demonstrating the paradoxical interdependence of the radical and the conservative elements within a religion, romantic feminism from the nineteenth through to the late twentieth century has itself reinforced the sentimental association of women and religious emotion by its ascription of religious sensitivity and relational care to women. Religious feminism itself has also, thereby, judged men to be the spiritual and devotional inferiors of women. However, for feminists of a reformist inclination, this reversal merely regulates and domesticates disruptive female emotion by reallocating to women the nonintellectual, affective tasks of care traditionally ascribed to them by the traditional gendered economies of religious labor. The rhetoric of feminine affectivity may not serve women well. While, for example, female compassion appears to make even the most observant Jewish men women's religious "inferiors," men can, at the same time, exploit the practical services of women's compassion and exclude them from the privileges of normative religious practice enjoyed by men: the "rational," "objective" detachment of scholarship and public, time-bound prayer.

Rejecting this kind of religio-biological essentialism, liberal or reformist feminists would want to argue that, whatever its biological basis, emotion is gendered in the process of its socialization. A large, if controversial, body of research attests to how parents and others respond to girls more warmly than boys. Girls are taught more about feelings, are more exposed to the language of emotion, are more articulate in expressing emotion, and, being more empathetic and better able to "read" the emotional states of others, are also more adept at intimacy and the formation of interdependent relations.[30] For such reasons, few contemporary feminist scholars would venture to claim that women are innately prone to heightened religious emotion. Rather, the socialization of men and women permits each a different emotional repertoire and locale.

Permitted Masculine Religious Emotion

It should have become evident by now that despite the sexualization of female religious emotion and the eroticization of men's emotional response to women in most religious traditions, the gendering of religious emotion is far more complex than a sexually dichotomous theoretical framework would allow.

It is undoubtedly true that elite forms of hierarchical male-dominated religion temper emotion through reason, aesthetics, and ritual expression. With important exceptions—such as the relatively nonhierarchical charismatic churches, forms of sectarian religion such as the early Hasidic movement within Judaism, and native traditions dependent on spirit possession—it is usually the case that the higher the sacral status of the male individual, the less religious emotion is displayed. And since (elite) men occupy the upper end of almost all religious hierarchies, religious confession becomes more authoritative and more definitively masculine as it becomes less emotionally immediate, more removed from domestic space, and more intellectualized by dogma. Grief, longing, and joy are transcendentalized by Christianity through their accommodation in cosmic narratives of suffering and vindication—that of the cross and resurrection—whose eschatological ultimacy can trivialize the emotions experienced in the predominantly female domestic times and spaces that cannot compete with the sublime, as it is publicly witnessed and commemorated as a sign of God's redemptive self-revelation in history. While juridical religions such as Judaism or Islam temper divine and human justice with love and mercy, religious law is, by its nature, a personally disinterested system that is apprehensive of the tug and sway of emotion.

Even so, men do not always characterize their own religions as rational projects. Although Western philosophers of religion have been concerned to demonstrate that religious belief is not irrational and is at least reasonable, post-

Enlightenment Western religion has also been suspicious of rationalism as the cause of heresy, secularization, and the criticism of religion. Early Hasidic worship explicitly sacralized ecstatic over formal worship, and insisted that a life governed by Jewish law be undertaken with a joyous heart. And while the neo-Kantian Jewish philosopher Hermann Cohen celebrated Judaism as preeminently a religion of reason, other (male) Jewish philosophers have contested Jewish rationalism, regarding a predominantly ethical Judaism as (to use Michael Wyschogrod's term) merely "housebroken." So, too, Jewish thinkers have long and widely distrusted Maimonides' Aristotelian account of Judaism on that very count. In the twentieth century, Martin Buber, Abraham J. Heschel, and Emmanuel Levinas promulgated, instead, a profoundly relational Jewish philosophy and one that was the product of a male, not a feminist, religious tradition.

Daniel Boyarin's study of Jewish masculinity also warns us not to be too hasty in making gender-stereotypical assumptions about religious emotion. Rebutting a Western construction of gender that can be traced from Roman culture to Freud, Boyarin finds that in both ancient and modern religious texts the talmudic exemplar of the ideal male Jew is not aggressive and domineering but a gentle, receptive, and family-oriented figure who is, on that account, profoundly attractive to Jewish women.[31] The gendered bifurcation of religious emotion in Judaism is further confused by Howard Eilberg-Schwartz's observation that the male Jewish God—especially the anthropomorphic God of ancient Israel—invites men, not women, into a loving, monogamous, and surely quasi-homoerotic, quasi-marital relationship with him. If, in contemporary Judaism, the fatherhood of God is to be taken seriously, Eilberg-Schwartz urges that it should be conceived as that of a tender, embracing father whose love for his children affirms rather than derogates female love and as one that permits intimacy and tenderness in men.[32]

Just as grief might be orchestrated and aestheticized in a requiem mass, so, too, language, spectacle, and permitted intoxicants induce shifts in both men and women's emotional receptivity to the divine. Religious experience amounts, after all, to an altered emotional state whose very affectivity opens one to the sense of divine presence. As suggested earlier, theistic devotion may be said to be inherently feminine, insofar as it is an emotional attachment to an object of worship or transcendental love, demonstratively expressed in ritual and prayer. *Bhakti* Hinduism regards passionately loving devotion to one's chosen god as a means of liberation from the cycle of birth and death. Socially and sexually egalitarian in temper and practice, its poetic approach has been especially accessible to women who find role models in its women leaders and saints. Best known of these was the sixteenth-century Mirabai of Rajasthan, who was a devotee of Krishna and to whom are attributed fourteen hundred love songs addressed to the divine object of her passion. Nonetheless, *bhakti* is not a spirituality for women alone. It also attracts men and permits them the expression of powerful religious emotion.

In other traditions, too, emotion can be attributed to men's religious agency, especially if it is heroic. While Buddhism, like other traditions discussed in this essay, ascribes uncontrolled emotion to women, it may caricature Buddhism to claim that it seeks a state of pure wantlessness. More accurately, Buddhism seeks to control and craft emotion into tranquil, "skillful" emotion, to the end of experiencing joy without pain and without the sense of self that drives individualistic desire.[33] Just as Buddha's greatness lies in his infinite compassion, so, too, the paradigm of self-sacrificial love for Christians is the incarnate Christ, the man Jesus who wept at the news of his friend Lazarus's death. Indeed, the expression of male religious emotion is far from foreign to the Christian tradition: annually relived, the narrative pathos and drama of Christ's passion move all Christians, not just women, through a comprehensive range of profound emotions. Men perform religious emotion in the public realm of congregational prayer, preaching, and the rituals over which they officiate. Men as well as women express religious emotion when their role or relational situation permits it. In that care and compassion are required of those charged with responsibility for the spiritual and physical well-being of their flock, Christian priests and pastors share a common emotional orientation with mothers.

Male religious emotion can also be fashionable. Blurring the customary distinction between the church's "feminine" ethic of forgiveness and self-sacrificial love and its hierarchical masculine leadership, the so-called muscular Christianity of the nineteenth century permitted British men certain forms of public emotional display—as do contemporary evangelical Christian revival movements. Fashions, of course, can change, and by 1820, male evangelical weeping in public (considered vulgar by upper-class Christians in more established churches) was no longer acceptable, even in evangelical circles.[34] Nonetheless, in revivalist (just as in mystical) forms of religion, when male emotion is regulated and finds its proper nonnatural object in the divine other rather than in the body of the desired human other, it is not transgressive but virtuous. Nineteenth-century male evangelical preaching continued to endorse male sensitivity to women, and revivalists—as today—stirred ecstatic emotion among men as well as women by means of fervent singing and prayer. For this reason, in the nineteenth-century, working-class men, in particular, often dismissed Christian piety as "women's business," especially when many of the denominations' congregants were women.

However, the problem of male religious emotion in cultures that perceive emotion to be a sign of weakness or confusion continues to be negotiated. The contemporary men's spirituality movement, influenced by Jungian psychology, addresses the current postindustrial, postcolonial, and postfeminist "men's crisis," in which some men claim to find themselves unable to express intrinsically masculine emotion and bond with other men. This largely antifeminist movement reclaims "manly" emotion as a psychotherapeutic means for men to exercise their masculinity and to resist the "softening" effects of feminine religious emotion. One of the earliest and best known proponents of men's spirituality has been Robert Bly, who seeks to reconnect with the elementally masculine instincts of the pagan "wild-man-within" by means of men-only initiation rites that induct men into earthly and transcendent fatherhood and are intended to heal men's alienation from their selves and hence from nature and from a "neutered" God.[35]

The power of male religious emotion has also been reclaimed in some contemporary Christian circles. The Christian "Wild Man" of the biblical scholar Patrick Arnold repudiates the emasculating effects of the Christian spiritual and ethical valorization of feminine virtues. Arnold argues that feminized religion is disconnected from the eschatological ultimacies of judgment and the "harsh world [men] experience every day." He attacks the feminine "gushing," "fluttering," gentle, passive Christianity that "ignores the voracious appetite of men for the Great, the Wholly Other, and the Eternal" and the "tough, firm, and aggressive" love felt by men for Christ and for God.[36]

Rather differently, there are those in the men's movement who consider themselves to have been emotionally educated by the women's spirituality movement's criticism of the masculinist religious posture. The Christian ethicist and theologian James Nelson, for example, regrets the masculinist religious symbolic of the erect phallus and seeks to recover that of the soft penis, whose flaccidity could signify men's becoming more emotionally receptive to those around them.[37]

THE FEMINIST RECLAMATION OF RELIGIOUS EMOTION

Since the 1990s, neuroscientists, cognitive psychologists, educationalists, anthropologists, and ethicists have, like feminist theorists, revalorized the affective dimension as a significant contributor to decision-making, intelligence, and constructive behavior. "Emotional intelligence," once seen as a contradiction in terms, has come to denote not only the control of impulsion but also an aptitude or practical wisdom that enables people to relate empathetically and considerately to others (and thereby, in the business world, to become better managers).[38] As emotional skills and knowledge are cultivated in both feminist and nonfeminist philosophy and psychology, it is likely that—in educated Western circles at least—the derogatory association of emotion with femininity will be weakened.

Religious feminism has made a significant contribution to the current revalorization of emotion. It has done so through its refusal to conquer the passions, regarding the latter project as the legacy of a destructive gynophobic ascetic dualism. Feminist scholars of religion have argued that sacral role models for women such as the Virgin Mary have repressed women's negative emotions, such as rage, and overemphasized positive feminine emotions, such as self-sacrificial love and compassion. Consequently, both Christian and post-Christian religious feminists have reclaimed the transformative power of female emotion.[39] Since the late twentieth century, feminism's celebration of female difference and female knowing have led to the construction of relational, embodied spiritual paradigms that are considered more conducive to human flourishing than modernity's alienated rationalism, whose failings were amply evidenced in the twentieth century's capacity for military and ecological destruction.

Religious emotion has come to inform not only feminist spiritual politics but also, foundationally, feminist theology. The lesbian Christian feminist Carter Heyward is one through whom Christian feminism has come to creatively reaffirm the transformative power of religious emotion. She affirms that sexual pleasure can be an experience of the holy and, more than that, erotic desire is itself the creative love of God. In *Touching Our Strength: The Erotic as Power and the Love of God*[40]—a book that has widely influenced Christian feminist ethics and theology—Heyward draws on the Afro-Caribbean lesbian feminist Audre Lorde's account of the erotic as a dynamic female life force to argue that desire expresses women's power in and through embodied relation. While patriarchal religions have devised ethical codes that subdue or domesticate emotion, desire is not a private emotion but belongs to the public account we make of ourselves as individuals and as a society. When desire is distorted into sexual violence, it becomes a function of the alienated patriarchal power that maintains social hierarchy by sexual subordination and aggression. Yet when desire is a function of love, it becomes the generative ground of justice; the redemptive energy of social transformation, authority, and commitment. Desire, for Heyward, as for other feminist sexual theologians, is therefore not confined to the privacy of intimate relationships. Desire is the transformative power of justice and therefore of human becoming.[41]

It is significant, though, that only in the post-Christian tradition have women been able to reclaim and redirect the untamed reaches of female religious emotion long regarded by patriarchal religionists as a threat to the social order.[42] The radical post-Christian philosopher Mary Daly has insisted that patriarchal religion demands women's self-sacrifice and resignation in return for a salvation whose "pseudopassion" paralyzes and smothers spiritual and bodily desire, or "Female Fire." Female affectivity is, for Daly, a sacral power of "Pyrogenetic" or "Elemental" passion that can propel women into the "otherworld" of postpatriarchal freedom of consciousness where women learn, as it were, to fly. Daly urges that female emotion needs to become what she calls "E-motion": the driving force of their delirious departure (delirium being, literally, going off the track, from the Latin *de*, off, and *lira*, track). Female emotion will precisely "emote" or move women away (from the Latin *emovere*) from the "State of Stagnation" and allow them to enter into a separate, uncontained, "Other" space in which to experience their female authenticity.[43] Daly exhorts women to hypostasize their own emotion as "Volcanic Furies" whose wild and archaic venting of rage, despair, and joy will erupt through the "bore-ocratic" patriarchal taboos that have subdued not only women but the earth.[44]

After Daly, female prophetic rage has become a post-Christian feminist praxis in itself. Rage introduces female chaos as the prophetic subversion of the patriarchal religious order. Goddess feminism has done most to reinstate sacral female wrath, especially as hypostasized in the Crone Goddess and other revived images of dangerous or death-dealing female divine power such as Lilith, the Harpies, and the Furies.[45] Where feminists propose a somewhat better tempered deity, one who is neither the Crone-Goddess nor the patriarchal warrior-Lord, their emotional repertoire also accommodates the empathetic love of a co-suffering God/dess.[46]

NOTES

1. See further William Wainwright's proposal that trained passion and desire form our beliefs as much as does reason: *Reason and the Heart: A Prolegomenon to a Critique of Passional Reason* (Ithaca, N.Y.: Cornell University Press, 1995).

2. The primary focus of this essay will be on Judaism and Christianity, as it is within these two traditions that a feminist critique has been most comprehensively articulated and the religious meanings of emotion are more or less comparable.

3. *The Idea of the Holy: An Inquiry into the Non-rational Factor in the Idea of the Divine and Its Relation to the Rational*, translated by John W. Harvey (Oxford: Oxford University Press, 1958).

4. It is arguable that modern Western commentators interpret the gendered bifurcation of reason and emotion through the modern confrontation of rationalism and romanticism, where each are perceived to be in fundamental opposition to the other. But this is not entirely true of the relation of reason and emotion, even in the modern period. Hume, one of the most prominent philosophers of the Enlightenment, thought that (implicitly, male) emotion had a role to play in reason, and by the end of the eighteenth century it was not reason but sensibility that defined and divinized "man's" genius.

5. See Melissa Raphael, "Feminism, Constructivism, and Numinous Experience," *Religious Studies* 30 (1994): 511–26; Otto, *The Idea of the Holy*.

6. See Beverley Clack, ed., *Misogyny in the Western Philosophical Tradition: A Reader* (Basingstoke, England: Macmillan, 1999).

7. As Rosemary Radford Ruether puts it: "Feminism is a critical stance that challenges the patriarchal gender paradigm that associates males with human characteristics defined as superior and dominant (rationality, power) and females with those defined as inferior and auxiliary (intuition, passivity)." "The Emergence of Christian Feminist Theology," in *The Cambridge Companion to Feminist Theology*, edited by Susan Frank Parsons (Cambridge: Cambridge University Press, 2002), 3.

8. London: Methuen, 1984.

9. *Upheavals of Thought: The Intelligence of Emotions* (Cambridge: Cambridge University Press, 2001).

10. See Chava Weissler, *Voices of the Matriarchs: Listening to the Prayers of Early Modern Jewish Women* (Boston: Beacon Press, 1998), 89–171.

11. See, e.g., Susan Starr Sered, "Mother Love, Child Death, and Religious Innovation: A Feminist Perspective," *Journal of Feminist Studies in Religion* 12 (1996): 5–23.

12. For Jewish feminist-influenced rituals, see, e.g., Sylvia Rothschild and Sybil Sheridan, eds., *Taking Up the Timbrel: The Challenge of Creating Ritual for Jewish Women Today* (London, SCM Press, 2000). Serenity Young, *Anthology of Sacred Texts* (London: Pandora, 1993), offers a comparative selection of rituals and laments written by women for their own use. See, e.g., the feminist neo-Pagan ritual for healing the trauma of divorce and separation, 430–32.

13. See Majella Franzmann, *Women and Religion* (New York: Oxford University Press, 2000), 92.

14. Ibid., 90.

15. *Women in the Muslim Unconsciousness* (Oxford: Pergamon Press, 1984), 3, 4, 18.

16. It is notable that early second wave feminist theoreticians regarded sexual violence as the pivotal issue of sexual inequality.

17. "Reason and Orgasm in Tibetan Buddhism," in Joseph Runzo and Nancy M. Martin, eds., *Love, Sex, and Gender in the World Religions* (Oxford: Oneworld, 2000), 282–83.

18. Ibid., 271.

19. Ibid., 277.

20. Strictly speaking, women are not barred from reading the Torah or from reciting the blessings accompanying the chanting of a portion of the Torah lest their audibility and visibility prove to be a sexual distraction to the men of the congregation. Rather, it is the exhibition of female erudition that is problematic: it might shame the men of the community by suggesting that they are less educated than a woman.

21. "Taming the Powers of Desire: Love and Sex in Jewish Culture," in Runzo and Martin, *Love, Sex, and Gender in the World Religions*, 124.

22. The Church has, of course, demanded ascetic self-discipline of its male religious virtuosi. However, men have not been required to redeem the sin of Eve, which was long regarded as an ontological function of having been born a woman. It was women, not men, who sought to erase the sin of Eve through fasting and other practices that would diminish their female sexual characteristics, especially menstruality.

23. See *The Book of Margery Kempe*, translated by B. A. Windeatt (Harmondsworth, England: Penguin, 1985).

24. See M. H. Kleiman, "Masculine Sacrality," in *The Encyclopedia of Religion*, edited by Mircea Eliade (New York: Macmillan, 1987), 9:352–58; Melissa Raphael, *Thealogy and Embodiment: The Postpatriarchal Reconstruction of Female Sacrality* (Sheffield, England: Sheffield Academic Press, 1996). If this typology holds, then the symbolics of religious emotional performance correlates to the gendering of sacrality.

25. See further Gail Holst-Warhaft, "Mourning and Death Rites," in *The Encyclopedia of Women and World Religion*, edited by Serinity Young (New York: Macmillan, 1999), 2:682–85.

26. See Ivan Myrddin Lewis, *Ecstatic Religion: A Study of Shamanism and Spirit Possession* (London: Routledge, 1989), 66–71. See also Karen McCarthy Brown, *Mama Lola: A Voudou Priestess in Brooklyn* (Berkeley: University of California Press, 2001).

27. Alex Owen, *The Darkened Room: Women, Power, and Spiritualism in Late Victorian England* (London: Virago, 1989); see also Anne Braude, *Radical Spirits: Spiritualism and Women's Rights in Nineteenth-Century America* (Boston: Beacon Press, 1989).

28. Susan Starr Sered, *Priestess, Mother, Sacred Sister: Religions Dominated by Women* (New York: Oxford University Press, 1994).

29. See, e.g., Rav Aharon Soloveitchik, "The Attitude of Judaism towards the Woman," cited in A. Weiss, *Women at Prayer: A Halakhic Analysis of Women's Prayer Groups* (Hoboken, N.J.: Ktav, 1990), 3. In nineteenth- and twentieth-century Christian culture, this idealization of the feminine has sometimes resulted in the so-called feminization of religion, with piety being considered rather less than manly.

30. See Leslie R. Brody and Judith A. Hall, "Gender and Emotion," in *Handbook of Emotions*, edited by Michael Lewis and Jeanette Haviland (New York: Guilford Press, 1993), 338–49.

31. *Unheroic Conduct: The Rise of Heterosexuality and the Invention of the Jewish Man* (Berkeley: University of California Press, 1997).

32. *God's Phallus and Other Problems for Men and Monotheism* (Boston: Beacon Press, 1994), 5–6, 239–40.

33. David Webster, *Desire, Buddhism, and Philosophy: An Examination of Desire in the Buddhist Pali Canon and Beyond* (London: RoutledgeCurzon, 2005).

34. Leonore Davidoff and Carol Hall, *Family Fortunes: Men and Women of the English Middle Class, 1780–1850* (London: Hutchinson, 1987), 111.

35. *Iron John: A Book about Men* (Rockport, Mass.: Element, 1990).

36. *Wildmen, Warriors, and Kings: Masculine Spirituality and the Bible*. New York: Crossroad, 1992), 76–78.

37. "Embracing Masculinity," in *Sexuality and the Sacred: Sources for Theological Reflection*, edited by James B. Nelson and Sandra Longfellow (London: Mowbrays, 1994), 199–201.

38. See the foundational work of the Yale psychologists Peter Salovey and Robert J. Sternberg, *Beyond I.Q.* (New York: Cambridge University Press, 1985). One of the first proposals for "emotional intelligence" was Peter Salovey and John D. Mayer, "Emotional Intelligence," *Imagination, Cognition, and Personality* 9 (1990): 185–211. See also J. P. Forgas, ed., *Feeling and Thinking: The Role of the Affect in Social Cognition* (Cambridge: Cambridge University Press, 2000).

39. See, e.g., Kathleen Fischer, *Transforming Fire: Women Using Anger Creatively* (New York: Paulist Press, 2000).

40. San Francisco: Harper, 1989.

41. This insight also informed Lisa Isherwood's edited collection of essays *The Good News of the Body: Feminist Explorations in the Religious Construction of Female Sexuality* (Sheffield, England: Sheffield Academic Press, 2001).

42. See further Melissa Raphael, "Thealogy, Redemption, and the Call of the Wild," *Feminist Theology* 15 (1997): 55–72.

43. *Pure Lust: Elemental Feminist Philosophy* (London: Women's Press, 1984), 116.

44. Ibid., 225–26. The theme of female "elemental" emotion is developed throughout her subsequent work.

45. See further, e.g., Jane Caputi, *Gossips, Gorgon, and Crones: The Fates of the Earth* (Santa Fe, N.M.: Bear, 1993); Barabara B. Koltuv, *The Book of Lilith* (York Beach, Me.: Nicolas Hays, 1986).

46. Carol Christ's thealogy exemplifies this attempt to bridge the unhelpful gap between sanitized patriarchal representations of female divinity and subethical post-Christian representations of the Goddess. See, in particular, her most recent work, *She Who Changes: Re-imagining the Divine in the World* (New York: Palgrave Macmillan, 2003), esp. 86–91.

BIBLIOGRAPHY

Arnold, Patrick. *Wildmen, Warriors, and Kings: Masculine Spirituality and the Bible*. New York: Crossroad, 1992.

Bly, Robert. *Iron John: A Book about Men*. Rockport, Mass.: Element, 1990.

Boyarin, Daniel. *Unheroic Conduct: The Rise of Heterosexuality and the Invention of the Jewish Man*. Berkeley: University of California Press, 1997.

Braude, Anne. *Radical Spirits: Spiritualism and Women's Rights in Nineteenth-Century America*. Boston: Beacon Press, 1992.
Brody, Leslie R., and Judith A. Hall. "Gender and Emotion." In *Handbook of Emotions*, edited by Michael Lewis and Jeanette Haviland. New York: Guilford Press, 1993, 338–49.
Brown, Karen McCarthy. *Mama Lola: A Voudou Priestess in Brooklyn*. Berkeley: University of California Press, 2001.
Caputi, Jane. *Gossips, Gorgon, and Crones: The Fates of the Earth*. Santa Fe, N.M.: Bear, 1993.
Clack, Beverley, ed. *Misogyny in the Western Philosophical Tradition: A Reader*. Basingstoke, England: Macmillan, 1999.
Christ, Carol. *She Who Changes: Re-imagining the Divine in the World*. New York: Palgrave Macmillan, 2003.
Daly, Mary. *Pure Lust: Elemental Feminist Philosophy*. London: Women's Press, 1984.
Davidoff, Leonore, and Carol Hall. *Family Fortunes: Men and Women of the English Middle Class, 1780–1850*. London: Hutchinson, 1987.
Eilberg-Schwartz, Howard. *God's Phallus and Other Problems for Men and Monotheism*. Boston: Beacon Press, 1994.
Fischer, Kathleen. *Transforming Fire: Women Using Anger Creatively*. New York: Paulist Press, 2000.
Fonrobert, Charlotte Elisheva. "Taming the Powers of Desire: Love and Sex in Jewish Culture." In *Love, Sex, and Gender in the World Religions*, edited by Joseph Runzo and Nancy M. Martin. Oxford: Oneworld, 2000, 113–27.
Forgas, Joseph P., ed. *Feeling and Thinking: The Role of the Affect in Social Cognition*. Cambridge: Cambridge University Press, 2000.
Franzmann, Majella. *Women and Religion*. New York: Oxford University Press, 2000.
Heyward, Carter. *Touching Our Strength: The Erotic as Power and the Love of God*. San Francisco: HarperSanFrancisco, 1989.
Holst-Warhaft, Gail. "Mourning and Death Rites." In *The Encyclopedia of Women and World Religion*, edited by Serinity Young. New York: Macmillan, 1999, 2: 682–85.
Hopkins, Geoffrey. "Reason and Orgasm in Tibetan Buddhism." In *Love, Sex, and Gender in the World Religions*, edited by Joseph Runzo and Nancy M. Martin. Oxford: Oneworld, 2000, 271–85.
Isherwood, Lisa, ed. *The Good News of the Body: Feminist Explorations in the Religious Construction of Female Sexuality*. Sheffield, England: Sheffield Academic Press, 2001.
Kempe, Margery. *The Book of Margery Kempe*, translated by B. A. Windeatt. Harmondsworth, England: Penguin Books, 1985.
Kleiman, M. H. "Masculine Sacrality." In *The Encyclopedia of Religion*, edited by Mircea Eliade. New York: Macmillan, 1987, 9: 352–58.
Koltuv, Barabara B. *The Book of Lilith*. York Beach, Me.: Nicolas Hays, 1986.
Lewis, Ivan Myrddin. *Ecstatic Religion: A Study of Shamanism and Spirit Possession*. London: Routledge, 1989, 66–71.
Lloyd, Genevieve. *The Man of Reason: "Male" and "Female" in Western Philosophy*. London: Methuen, 1984.
Nelson, James. "Embracing Masculinity." In *Sexuality and the Sacred: Sources for Theological Reflection*, edited by James B. Nelson and Sandra Longfellow. London: Mowbrays, 1994, 195–215.
Nussbaum, Martha. *Upheavals of Thought: The Intelligence of Emotions*. Cambridge: Cambridge University Press, 2001.

Otto, Rudolf. *The Idea of the Holy: An Inquiry into the Non-rational Factor in the Idea of the Divine and Its Relation to the Rational.* Translated by John W. Harvey. Oxford: Oxford University Press, 1958.

Owen, Alex. *The Darkened Room: Women, Power, and Spiritualism in Late Victorian England.* London: Virago, 1989.

Raphael, Melissa. "Feminism, Constructivism, and Numinous Experience." *Religious Studies* 30 (1994): 511–26.

———. *Thealogy and Embodiment: The Postpatriarchal Reconstruction of Female Sacrality.* Sheffield, England: Sheffield Academic Press, 1996.

———. "Thealogy, Redemption, and the Call of the Wild." *Feminist Theology* 15 (1997): 55–72.

Rothschild, Sylvia, and Sybil Sheridan, eds. *Taking Up the Timbrel: The Challenge of Creating Ritual for Jewish Women Today.* London: SCM Press, 2000.

Ruether, Rosemary Radford. "The Emergence of Christian Feminist Theology." In *The Cambridge Companion to Feminist Theology*, edited by Susan Frank Parsons. Cambridge: Cambridge University Press, 2002, 3–22.

Runzo, Joseph, and Nancy M. Martin, eds. *Love, Sex, and Gender in the World Religions.* Oxford: Oneworld, 2000.

Sabbah, Fatna A. *Women in the Muslim Unconsciousness.* New York: Pergamon Press, 1984.

Salovey, Peter, and John D. Mayer. "Emotional Intelligence." *Imagination, Cognition, and Personality* 9 (1990): 185–211.

Salovey, Peter, and Robert J. Sternberg. *Beyond I.Q.* New York: Cambridge University Press, 1985.

Sered, Susan Starr. "Mother Love, Child Death and Religious Innovation: A Feminist Perspective." *Journal of Feminist Studies in Religion* 12 (1996): 5–23.

———. *Priestess, Mother, Sacred Sister: Religions Dominated by Women.* New York: Oxford University Press, 1994.

Wainwright, William. *Reason and the Heart: A Prolegomenon to a Critique of Passional Reason.* Ithaca, N.Y.: Cornell University Press, 1995.

Webster, David. *Desire, Buddhism, and Philosophy: An Examination of Desire in the Buddhist Pali Canon and Beyond.* London: RoutledgeCurzon, 2005.

Weiss, Avraham. *Women at Prayer: A Halakhic Analysis of Women's Prayer Groups.* Hoboken, N.J.: Ktav, 1990.

Weissler, Chava. *Voices of the Matriarchs: Listening to the Prayers of Early Modern Jewish Women.* Boston: Beacon Press, 1998.

Young, Serinity, ed. *An Anthology of Sacred Texts by and about Women.* London: Pandora, 1993.

CHAPTER 11

MUSIC

FRANK BURCH BROWN

Music has often been regarded as the most directly emotional of the arts and the art most intimately involved with religious and spiritual life. While frequently wedded to texts, music nevertheless seems to explore or express levels of awareness and kinds of feeling that elude words themselves. For that reason, and despite having important features that are susceptible to mathematical and rational analysis, music remains mysterious in many ways. Even the wisest thinkers have had difficulty finding words to explain how music works, emotionally—how it can move to tears or give unspeakable joy. It is not surprising that a modern French philosopher would give his most important publication on music the title *Music and the Ineffable*.[1]

In the endeavor to understand music's relation to emotion and religion, a variety of approaches and disciplines are relevant. There is, in the first place, the body of evidence provided by the history of music itself. In the second place, there are accounts of music provided by religious sources: myths, scriptures, worshipers, and religious thinkers of various traditions. Third, there are philosophical theories of music that, while not religious in character, pursue crucial questions. Finally, there are scientific and psychological studies that can yield insight into the character of musical and emotional response, and of music's access to the affective life. Multiple disciplines are pertinent, therefore—from musicology (including ethnomusicology) and history to philosophy, psychology, and various branches of religious studies, particularly theology and comparative religions.

This study is intended to map historical perspectives, major theories, and current issues regarding music, emotion, and religion. This interdisciplinary undertaking is necessarily exploratory as well as documentary. It begins by considering classic and exceptionally enduring images and ideas of music.

ORPHEUS: A CASE STUDY

Many of the perennial claims and questions about music, East and West, are captured by the ancient Greek myth of Orpheus, which is worth considering in some detail before exploring more formal theories of music and musical traditions themselves. While the story was transmitted in fragments, and by different sources, a composite version can be particularly suggestive.

As depicted in a wide array of stories from the sixth century B.C.E. onward, the legendary hero Orpheus was a singer, poet, religious teacher, and prophet who came from Thrace. A son of the god Apollo by the muse Calliope (according to most sources), Orpheus accompanied himself on a lyre and, in doing so, moved and enchanted all within the reach of his music. Even wild animals listened transfixed, or else moved in rhythmic response. Rivers changed course or stopped flowing at the sound; trees and rocks were charmed as well. Tragically, shortly after Orpheus married, his bride, Eurydice, was fatally poisoned by a serpent's bite. Grief-stricken, Orpheus descended to the underworld and with his lyre managed to move to tears even Pluto, the god of the realm of the dead; whereupon Plato agreed to allow Orpheus to lead Eurydice back to the land of the living, with the one condition that he not look back at her along the way. Eurydice almost regained her former life (or actually succeeded in doing so, in some versions). But as they were about to emerge from the underworld, Orpheus looked back to make sure she was following, and thereby lost his wife to death a second time, and forever. Disconsolate, he abandoned the company of women thereafter. Eventually, a band of Maenads—female followers of Dionysus who were frenzied and drunk with wine—came upon him, slew him, tore his body apart, and flung his severed head into a river, where even then it continued to sing.

For the Roman poet Virgil (70–19 B.C.E.) and many others in antiquity, Orpheus became the epitome of the singer-poet. Christians of the patristic and medieval eras adopted him as a symbol or "type" of Christ, the New Orpheus.[2] And when opera was revived in Italy in the late sixteenth and early seventeenth centuries, the first major musical creation in that genre was, appropriately, *L'Orfeo* (1607), by Claudio Monteverdi, which employed an alternative happy ending to the Eurydice episode, which was favored by Christians.

A number of significant themes about music's emotional powers emerge from the composite myth of Orpheus. The music of Orpheus, and implicitly the best music everywhere, is a great and miraculous gift of the gods and muses. Its qualities are identified with Orpheus's father and patron, Apollo, and are thus associated with the life-giving sun and with rational order and harmony. But implicitly the music of Orpheus also encounters, and in some traditions becomes allied with, the powers of Dionysus, the intoxicated and wild god linked both with procreativity and with the dark underworld.[3] The music that Orpheus sings and plays can be powerfully emotional and enlivening, but it can also be quieting. His music is able to change or stop the flow of rivers, hence the flow of ordinary time. In the underworld, it causes Sisyphus to rest on the stone he is otherwise destined to roll throughout the ages; it even stops the revolving wheel to which Ixion is bound forever. On the ship *Argo*, Orpheus's music invigorates weary sailors, yet it also soothes them when anger and quarreling threaten to get the best of them. In some instances, the music of Orpheus charms not by the expression of any emotion in particular but by certain appealing qualities inherent within the music itself, as when Orpheus saves the Argonauts from the lure of the Sirens' singing by playing his lyre in a fashion that compels the sailors' rapt attention and frees them to continue on their journey aboard the *Argo*. For this enchanting power of music the stories offer no explanation except the touch of divinity. But they suggest lines for further inquiry, extending from the ancient world to the present.

Among the questions about music that the Orpheus legend either raises or foreshadows, some of the more enduring are these: to what extent is the emotional impact of music due to the words? Orpheus, after all, is a poet *par excellence*; and ancient music was mostly vocal, even when accompanied by instruments. Some of the stories of Orpheus indicate that the music of his lyre has powers apart from any sung lyrics. But how can music alone express particular emotions? Isn't music by itself simply music *about* itself, lacking any definite point of reference? And if music, whether by itself or with words, somehow arouses emotions, need they be the emotions of either the maker or the performer? Might not music be beautiful and expressive without having to express personal feelings? In any case, to what extent are the emotions that music expresses like the emotions of real life? After all, who would ever want to feel the full weight of actual grief when listening, as is common, to mournful music? Does music not somehow transform what it expresses? Moreover, if music can sometimes comfort or heal, can it not also agitate and harm? Which of music's affective powers is more valuable, ritually—the power to stir up or the power to calm down? And what of the seeming paradox that, although music can be heard only in time and must sometime end, it can appear to make time stand still, or to flow differently, restoring what would otherwise die away? Finally, what is one to make of the effect of Orpheus's music on nature? Does it not suggest, at least symbolically, that music can affect or reflect the harmonies and creative principles at work in the larger cosmos? If so, can music, although apparently autonomous, relate our inner emotional life to the invisible (and perhaps inaudible) rhythms and creative forces beyond ourselves—to mysterious realities that are, at root, metaphysical and spiritual?

Such matters were pondered in various ways in antiquity itself, and in ways that were to exert a long-lasting influence. To these Western historical ideas, and their Asian counterparts, we now turn.

Ancient Perspectives: Background

It is impossible to know for sure how music actually sounded in ancient Greece, Rome, Israel, China, or India. Music notation in the ancient world, which was rare and relatively imprecise at best, has survived in very fragmentary form. Furthermore, few musical instruments from those times remain in existence. In large part, the major musical legacy of the ancient world consists in various traditions of thought concerning the nature and power of music and its influences on the soul and society, for good or ill.

In China, Confucius (sixth century B.C.E.) advocated the use of music in education, where it was to exemplify and instill moderation of the sort typified by his teachings overall. The Five Classics of the Confucian tradition speak of music as the harmony of heaven and earth. They acknowledge the importance of ritual music but tend to disapprove of the music of shamans and magicians. They also caution about the evil effects and bewitching powers of musical songs and dances, especially when carried to excess.

South Asian ideas of music and sound, from the ancient Vedas onward, likewise have both cosmological and spiritual overtones, reflecting a sense of the sacredness of sound (Nada-Brahman) as manifesting ultimate reality. While medieval Indian treatises recognize the pleasing qualities of music—music typically being combined with ritual, dance, and drama—they relate aesthetic perceptions to particular emotions and spiritual states. Abhinavagupta's eleventh-century commentary on the *Natyashastra*—which deals extensively with drama—stresses the importance of *rasas* (primary aesthetic effects, essential expressive qualities), which are also indirectly conducive to liberation. In such treatises, specific melodies or *jatis* (and, in later centuries, melodic types called *ragas*) are associated with emotions such as fear, pity, courage, and erotic desire.

In the West, the most important of the formative ideas about music and its religious and emotional powers go back to ancient Greece. To be sure, for Christians and Jews the primary norms and sanctions for the practice of music in worship are biblical. But the Bible includes relatively little speculation as to the nature and purpose of music. And the patterns of ancient biblical worship and music were radically disrupted with the fall of the second temple in 70 C.E. In relation to music, what Jews and Christians carried forward from biblical times was most of all a songbook—the Psalms—and an accompanying concept of the religious content and purpose of sung prayer.

When Islam established itself in the seventh century C.E., it made use of musical-sounding modes of reciting scripture (the Qur'an), just as Jews and Christians had continued to do. But, apart from the mystical Sufi traditions, Muslims, apparently following the example of the Prophet Mohammed, have typically regarded music per se as something inherently too secular in its moods and associations for use in worship.

During late antiquity, Jews and Christians alike had ample contact with pagan philosophical ideas of music, as did Muslims several centuries later. Although they rejected pagan music itself as immoral and idolatrous, they often found the more philosophical concepts of music to be congenial. Most of those ideas were Greek in origin—with Romans acting as relatively passive transmitters. It should be observed, in this connection, that the Greeks, like many other ancient peoples, did not think of music (*mousike*) as simply the art of working with sound. Rather, it was taken to be a mixed art combining dance, poetry, and tones (song and its accompaniment, or occasional instrumental performance). Music in this form was closely associated with drama. In its complex unity, music was meant to arouse and order feelings through words, gestures, movements, melodies, and rhythms. Greek thinkers also understood music as a science closely allied with mathematics, astronomy, and cosmology. Over a period of time, these philosophers and their successors came to believe that a kind of music was inherent in the creation and makeup of the cosmos itself, and is still produced constantly by the orbiting spheres. All of this, which pertains to the macrocosmos and its mathematically harmonious ordering, they understood as connected on a microcosmic level with the ordering of the soul and its emotions.

Musical Ethics and Metaphysics in the West: From Antiquity through the Renaissance

The orderly, calming, and Apollonian side of music was what the philosophical Pythagoreans found compelling. Led by Pythagoras (sixth century B.C.E.), who was evidently aware of the early Orphic traditions, those who followed this path were dedicated to Apollo and were exceptionally intellectual, as seen in their religious investigation of nature and mathematics. Pythagorean music theory centered on the discovery that the pleasing tones and harmonic intervals of the musical scale can be expressed, and perhaps explained, in terms of numbers and ratios. The observation that pleasing music can be analyzed in ways that are mathematically true and beautiful—a matter far too complex for brief exposition—was regarded with a kind of reverent wonder that continues to be expressed sometimes today.[4] In any case, the affinity between music and number was interpreted, early on, as a key to the divinely created harmony of the cosmos itself. The Pythagoreans taught, moreover, that music is unique among the arts in its capacity to shape the human soul, either by improving and healing or, on the contrary, by depraving and sickening. Music's rhythms, they said, are signs or expressions of character.[5]

Plato and Aristotle picked up this theme and explored more fully the ethical and soul-shaping implications of music within the context of ideals for a good society. In Plato's philosophical dialogue *The Republic*, which was written about 380 B.C.E., he has Socrates advocate an education that involves gymnastics for bodily discipline, and music for mental and moral development. At the same time, with respect to the training of those who are to govern, Plato's Socrates wants to exclude every musical mode except the Dorian and the Phrygian, which supposedly foster moderation and courage. Eliminating dirges and lamentations, he rejects kinds of music associated with drunkenness, softness, and idleness. Socrates warns that if a man allows sweet, plaintive, and melancholy tunes to pour endlessly into his soul through the funnel of his ears, such a person may in time become incapacitated as a warrior or ruler. It is important to be careful about music and poetry, he says, because "rhythm and harmony permeate the inner part of the soul more than anything else, affecting it most strongly and bringing it grace" (*Republic* 401e).[6] Books 2, 3, and 7 of Plato's *Laws* extend the same lines of thought, with Socrates in book 3 lodging a special complaint against those who ignorantly affirm that pleasure is the only standard of judgment in music.

Aristotle allows more latitude than his former teacher. In the *Politics*, from around 330 B.C.E., Aristotle envisions a place for music that is good for amusement and intellectual enjoyment as well as for education. He sees the sheerly pleasurable aspect of music as secondary, however, to moral and spiritual formation, to the right motivation of the will, and to a kind of musical therapy intended to bring about emotional balance and relief. Aristotle acknowledges that people are affected differently by the various musical modes and traditions. Nevertheless, he says, some modes of music tend to enfeeble the mind and soul, others to make listeners sad, and still others to inspire enthusiasm.[7]

What the ancient Greeks proposed is clearly an ethical view of music, both in the broad sense of being concerned to relate music to goals that are good for life as a whole and in the narrow sense of being concerned about music's impact on the conditions of the soul, and thus on moral or immoral habits. The metaphysical and mystical sides of music are downplayed in both Plato and Aristotle, in contrast to the Pythagoreans and their Orphic counterparts. Yet Plato in the *Timaeus* indirectly allows for the metaphysical aspects of music as well. There, without explicitly mentioning music, he describes the creation of the world in terms of the mathematical ratios of Pythagorean tuning—such as the perfect octave, fifth, and fourth—and suggests that the world and the human soul are both ordered according to a similar harmonic principle.

By the fifth century, with works such as Macrobius's *Commentary on the Dream of Scipio* (ca. 400 C.E.), the cosmological and metaphysical line of musical theory had given rise to a full-blown notion of the harmony of the heavenly spheres. Because that higher or deeper harmony was deemed to be inaudible to human ears, it was linked to the idea that the most elevated or profound levels of music, spiritually speaking, cannot in fact be heard physically but must be apprehended intellectually. The inaudibility of the supreme music had already been assigned great importance by Plotinus (ca. 205–270 C.E.) and other Neoplatonic philosophers. More explicitly than Plato himself, the Neoplatonists related the harmonious qualities of music to beauty itself, and considered audible music to be a kind of moving image or sensible shadow of truly divine beauty, the beauty of the One that is eternal and unchanging. Insofar as music of a more spiritual sort can produce emotions, those were understood to be refined in nature, reflecting the attunement of the soul through harmonies apprehended by the rational mind.

The great Christian theologian Augustine (354–430) reinterpreted in a Christian vein this sense of music and its effects. He did so theoretically (and mainly in terms of metrical theory), in book 6 of *De Musica*, and with more practical awareness in the *Confessions*. Thus, in book 10 of his *Confessions*, Augustine reports how in his first years as a committed Christian he was moved to tears by the singing of psalms in church. But he worries that sometimes he may be moved more by the music itself than by the truth of the words being chanted. He acknowledges that when the words of a psalm are chanted well, piety is kindled with warmer devotion than when the words are merely spoken. But physical delight, he adds, must be checked from enervating the mind. Consequently, Augustine concludes that he can welcome singing in church only when it is restrained and moderate—conceding, though, that music of some sort may be needed so that "weaker minds" may be stimulated to devotion through the "delights of the ear."[8]

Augustine in this passage provides a classic expression of the ambivalence that church fathers, like the pagan philosophers, typically felt about the emotional powers of music. Respecting music as God-given and good, Christian leaders of the patristic era were generally very guarded about music's effects on the emotions. They worried, as Christian theologians continued over the centuries to worry, about the bodily and erotic basis of certain emotions to which music and dance might appeal; and in general they advocated restraint rather than musical ecstasy or enthusiasm. Moreover, many a church father declared that what should give pleasure in sung prayer is not so much the singing itself as the words.

Because musical instruments were widely associated with frenzied or ecstatic pagan rituals, lewd dancing, and bawdy drama, early church leaders restricted church music to unaccompanied chanting—shortly ruling out even the voices of women. Judging from repeated warnings about the use of instruments and dance in church, it appears that music as practiced by Christians in late antiquity must have transgressed such norms with some frequency.[9] Even so, the use of instruments in church was mostly forbidden for the next thousand years or more; and in Eastern Catholic churches, Orthodox Jewish synagogues, and Islamic mosques, instruments (and often women's voices) continue to be proscribed to this day.

Over the following centuries, religious leaders also continued to be suspicious of the sensuous and emotional appeal of music even when vocal. It is true that, in the sixteenth century, Protestant reformers sought out overtly attractive and memorable melodies for congregational use. Luther is reported to have said that he did not want the devil to have all the good tunes. But that did not mean borrowing uncritically from bar and brothel. Nor did it imply that good music should necessarily be expressive of the full range of particular and powerful emotions.[10] The Swiss Protestant reformer John Calvin, who spoke of music as the greatest gift God has given human beings for rejoicing and pleasure, was more fearful than Luther of its abuse, explicitly recalling the admonitions of Plato and Augustine. Calvin thus endorsed a spirit of musical purity and restraint, which in worship meant restricting music almost entirely to the disciplined and unaccompanied unison singing of psalms. That pattern, too, had a lasting influence across denominational lines. In the twentieth century, the Lutheran pastor and theologian Dietrich Bonhoeffer judged that simple unison congregational singing has a purity and frugality that is more humane and less distracting than the more complex modes of worship music.[11]

Still another aspect of Augustine's musical restraint became a prominent feature of Christian attitudes toward music—namely, the priority he gave to words and their intelligibility. It is true that Augustine himself seemed to approve of occasionally singing to God in free jubilation, without always being able to understand or express in words what is sung in the heart—establishing a warrant for the long melismatic passages later given over to the "Alleluia" in the liturgy. Augustine claimed that because God is ineffable, it is sometimes fitting for the heart to rejoice wordlessly in singing God's praise.[12] Yet, as choral singing in Roman Catholicism frequently included polyphony from the High Middle Ages on, church leaders complained that the simultaneous sounding of multiple melodic lines of music inevitably tended to obscure the texts being sung. Thus the Council of Trent (1545–1563) placed more stress on the need for the words of a sung mass to be set in an intelligible way than on emotional fervor. Indeed, the documents of Trent caution against music that "delights the ears more than the mind" and excites the faithful to "lascivious rather than to religious thoughts." Instead, they say, the mass should be sung clearly, and in such a way that it "may reach tranquilly into the ears and hearts of those who hear" it, not giving "empty pleasure" but drawing listeners to desire heavenly harmonies and to contemplate the joys of the blessed.[13]

The complaint about the verbal havoc wrought by polyphony reappeared in the eighteenth century. John Wesley, for example, objected to Handel's way of setting texts in the polyphonic choruses of oratorios such as *Messiah*. But, significantly, Wesley did not worry that the emotion expressed in Handel's religious music might be too fervent; instead he argued that such polyphony is too artificial to engage the emotions fully.[14] Such a desire for musical expression to be more emotional rather than less was hardly something new under the sun; it was part of what originally gave rise to the opera at the end of the sixteenth century. But it did mark a change in emphasis that became characteristic of more modern approaches to music, including religious music.

Expression and Form: Toward Modernity, and Beyond

During the medieval period, and long after, thinkers inspired by Augustine, Boethius (ca. 480–ca. 524), and ancient philosophy had drawn extensively on the Platonic (mostly Neoplatonic) and Pythagorean traditions to maintain music's dual connection with ethics on the one hand and with metaphysics, mathematics, and cosmology on the other. That connection was presumed in university education by the inclusion of music in the medieval Quadrivium, or course of study, along with arithmetic, geometry, and astronomy. Both the ethical and the cosmological dimensions of music were likewise taken up in Islamic Neoplatonic theories of music. In the West such ideas persisted, to one degree or another, into the Renaissance and the early baroque period. They can be found in Shakespeare (1564–1616) and in Sir Thomas Browne (1605–1682), as well as in the influential writings on music theory and practice of Jean-Philippe Rameau (1683–1764). Related ideas of music, which had long flourished in China and in India, continued to exert an influence in Asia, even while evolving.

Because such thinking recognizes music's capacity to affect emotions, it is easy to forget that in the practice of Western religious music prior to the late Renaissance and early baroque, there was no consistent effort on the part of composers to bring out the affective qualities pertinent to specific texts in the liturgy. The main emphasis (with various important exceptions) was on supporting prayer and thoughtful contemplation through the chant or, in later times, on honoring God through the beauty and splendor of sometimes elaborate polyphony, which by its very radiance and sweetness (*suavitas*) provided a fitting setting for sacred texts, and a reflection of the higher harmony that ultimately derives from God. Inasmuch as emotion was involved, it typically consisted more in the delight taken in the sound, shape, and design of the music offered in service to God than in the listener's being moved to experience feelings specific to various texts and their musical settings.[15]

From the late Renaissance onward, the emphasis shifted dramatically, as musicians exploited the emotional and expressive resources of music to the fullest. With the ascent of Renaissance humanism, there was a revival of interest in classical rhetorical arts, and with that a growing desire for a closer relation between music and words. Accordingly, church leaders now expressed the wish that, when a mass is sung, the music not only match the particular meaning of the words but also truly move the affections to piety.

During the baroque era (ca. 1600–1750), musicians went on to maximize the expressive and rhetorical capacities of music, by paying special attention to the voice and the text and by employing instruments more fully and dramatically. When writing church music or sacred oratorios, composers from Claudio Monteverdi (1567–1643) and Carlo Gesualdo (1560–1613) to Georg Friedrich Handel (1685–1759) and Johann Sebastian Bach (1685–1750) drew freely from the emotive techniques of secular madrigals and opera itself (conceived of as a revival of Greek tragedy). Theorists, especially in Germany, joined with composers in developing the idea that every musical composition is to express or arouse a particular "affection" such as rage or wonder or mystical devotion.

But while baroque religious music was theatrical and expressive, and was sometimes criticized for sounding too worldly, it was rarely offered or received as a medium of intensely personal self-expression or subjective piety. Even cantata settings of pietistic texts were not meant primarily as a disclosure or exploration of the composer's own individual experience or inner emotional state. In that respect, it might be argued, baroque music paralleled contemporary musical developments in Mughal India, where the expressive potential of each kind of *raga* was being maximized, less as a form of self-expression than as a mode of making audible the aesthetic essence of this or that mood or emotion.

In the West, the next step, taken boldly during the era of Romanticism, was to make self-expression central to music. Beethoven, for example, anticipated that very move when he wrote on the first page of the score of his *Missa Solemnis* in D Major, "From the heart—may it go again to the heart." Such a move marked a wide-reaching (if sometimes subtle) shift in sensibility. Under the influence of Romanticism, music became, in large part, a window on the soul and a medium by which the heart of the musician and that of the listener could somehow commune. Music also became a means of discovering nuances and depths of subjective feeling for which words allegedly could not begin to be adequate. Hence the well-known assertion of the composer Felix Mendelssohn in a letter of 1842 that music expresses thoughts that, far from being vague, are too precise for words.[16] For philosophers such as Hegel (1770–1831) and Schopenhauer (1788–1860), the specific feelings music might appear to arouse were less important, however, than the musical expression of the inner emotional core, the experience of the soul.

Of course, intense religious feeling had been common to all sorts of mystical musical practices—Jewish kabbalistic and Hasidic traditions, Islamic Sufism, and Hindu *bhakti* movements, for instance. But whereas personal ecstasy and a feeling of transport were familiar to those on the path toward the goal of intense communion or union with God, that final goal was, and is, often envisioned in mystical traditions (particularly Asian) as so ineffable and mind-altering as finally to transcend emotions and thoughts altogether. Moreover, in both East and West, the outward musical expression of emotions was often seen as suitable only to the lower rungs of the ladder of spiritual ascent. It would be most unusual, for instance, for Buddhists involved in chanting sutras to expect the music itself to convey disciples to the highest states of right concentration and nondualistic consciousness, or enlightenment.

Any such reservations about music, or other signs of spiritual asceticism, were left far behind in the main streams of Romanticism, and not only in its more popular forms. Thus, in the realm of art music, the final paean to love as the eternal feminine in Mahler's Eighth Symphony (1906) completely fuses erotic and spiritual bliss in a concluding chorus—with words from part 2 of Goethe's *Faust*—which is ecstatic, emotionally climactic, and in no way self-effacing, let alone chaste and modest. Again, although Wagner's opera *Tristan und Isolde* (1859) finally lays the tumult of love's yearning to rest, and surrenders such striving in ways reminiscent of certain principles found in both Schopenhauer and Buddhism, there is no music that is more dependent on the ebb and flow of emotional tensions and resolutions.

In the realm of more popular religious culture, the desire to savor the expression of personal feeling made itself manifest, poetically, in the eighteenth century in the hymns of Charles Wesley. Personal emotion became still more central, however, to later evangelical hymns, spirituals, and gospel songs—evident not only in the words but in the music as well. In the Victorian era, the preferred mood of middle- and upper-class church music was a mild kind of reverence, gently touched by sentiment and sweetness, or uplifted in self-surrender and noble aspiration. By contrast, revival hymns were more casual, down-to-earth, and lively in style, using dotted rhythms and catchy melodies. The spirituals of African Americans gave voice to both lamentation and jubilation. And the successive styles of gospel music that came afterward grew increasingly demonstrative, making extensive use of percussion and, eventually, electronic instruments. In the twentieth century, a quality of raw emotion could be heard outside the church in the blues, which were personally and spiritually expressive even when religiously suspect.[17] Modern folk music as adapted for congregational song had an appeal that was nothing if not warmly social and personally bonding. More recently, contemporary rap has provided mostly youthful performers and listeners with a far more aggressive and confrontational style, often expressing protest and resistance,[18] increasingly in the context of religious gatherings. So-called contemporary Christian music has usually taken a sweeter tone, though branching out from soft rock and pop to include heavy metal.

Within the realm of modern art music, by contrast, the period after World War I saw a widespread rejection of overt emotionalism, especially on the part of formalists and neoclassicists. When modern "classical" composers became more emotional, their forbiddingly anguished avant-garde styles, even in religious music, primarily appealed to musical elites—the mystical dissonances of Olivier Messiaen, the jazz-influenced idioms of Leonard Bernstein, and the sometimes haunting lyricism or theatrical flourishes of Dmitri Shostakovitch being exceptions.

A later generation of composers such as Arvo Pärt, Giya Kancheli, Philip Glass, and John Adams has produced minimalist experimental works that tend to function like musical mantras or exercises in spiritual contemplation. Other spiritually inclined composers in the West, such as John Tavener, have turned to the ancient and mystical resources of Eastern Orthodoxy and religions of South and East Asia. This has been answered by Asian composers such as Toru Takemitsu and Tan Dun, who have looked West when producing spiritually evocative works.

Meanwhile, in the latter decades of the twentieth century and in the early twenty-first, spiritual seekers have also turned to various kinds of "world music" and "New Age" sound tapestries for solace, hope, and renewal. At the same time, churches and other religious groups have become increasingly identified with, and combative over, the styles of worship music, many of which have been borrowed from popular entertainment and commercial idioms.[19]

In view of such complex and conflicting developments, many religious leaders and scholars of religion and culture have found it ever more important, although also more challenging, to discern what music of different kinds has to offer, emotionally and spiritually. That requires, however, a keener understanding of the whole connection between music and emotion.

Remaining Issues and Unresolved Tensions

It has become increasingly clear that, in Western culture, theories of music since the Renaissance have left much unfinished business with respect to interpreting the value and function of music. Perhaps the most problematical yet important unresolved issues have to do with what exactly the role of emotion in music might be, and what relation musical expression can have to anything other than itself, including religion.

Because purely instrumental music was seldom prominent, let alone dominant, until the eighteenth century, it was not until then that the question of the powers of music alone emerged with full force. But once musical art had shown its potential for independence—which occurred about the time that the whole idea of the fine arts and aesthetic judgment caught hold in Europe—music was almost certain to become a prime candidate for "most autonomous art." For it was then recognized that no other art could be enjoyed so readily as a form without any identifiable subject matter. Because pure or abstract music seemed, nonetheless, to be tied to emotions, one way to describe music's simultaneous emotive power and aesthetic autonomy was to claim that music is a unique medium or language of emotions alone. And since most musicians and theorists from the Romantic era on have felt that the emotions expressed by music can never be expressed fully in words or rational concepts, music came to occupy a unique place among the arts.[20]

But if, as some have thought, genuine emotions are inevitably "intentional" and thus must be about something, it could be argued that music by itself does not, and cannot, represent anything about which to feel proper emotion. Eduard Hanslick (1825–1904) made such an argument in 1854, claiming that, although music may prompt us to use emotive terms when describing its features, in a figurative sense, it does not represent actual emotions, which must therefore be aesthetically irrelevant to the aims and values intrinsic to music.[21] Arthur Schopenhauer (1788–1860) took a different and more metaphysical tack, arguing that music represents nothing specific, emotionally, but presents us with the dynamics of the core emotions, those that are fundamental to the human experience of reality as Will.[22] A century later, in a related move, Susanne Langer theorized that music presents the listener not with the actual and particular feelings of life but with a "presentational" or nondiscursive symbol of the forms of feeling.[23]

Shortly thereafter, Deryck Cooke made a valiant effort to retrieve a union between music and real-life emotion when he published a detailed analysis of Western art music, treated as a language of specific emotions that employs a vocabulary of harmonic intervals, progressions, rhythms, and melodic gestures.[24] Many thinkers, however, have since questioned the extent to which music should be considered a language at all, even a language of feeling. At the very least, they have argued, the sheer variability in perceptions of the expressive qualities conveyed even by such common musical features as minor keys and their alleged sadness suggests that stylistic and cultural context, along with personal temperament and social construction, play a significant role in musical expression.[25]

Some influential theorists have argued that, while there may be some respects in which music is like a language (at least to the extent of having something like a syntax), it is not chiefly a language of or about emotions. Thus Peter Kivy argues that music itself is only secondarily emotional, being primarily a matter of artfully wrought sonic form and intrinsically rewarding structure. In fact, Kivy agrees with Hanslick that music in itself is not "about" emotions at all. Kivy goes on to argue that some music is intrinsically expressive in its features and gestures, just as a wrinkled and wizened face can be expressive without expressing what the person is really feeling, or expressing some very specific emotion.[26] But Kivy insists that even music that makes use of inherently expressive audible gestures typically employs them, finally, for its own ends. On those occasions when music does arouse emotions, those emotions are not to be thought of as exactly the same as the ones that the music is heard to express in itself. One can readily hear morbid despair in the last movement of Tchaikovsky's Sixth Symphony, for instance, without necessarily feeling the least bit suicidal. Kivy admits that if music alone is not about anything external to music, it is puzzling why certain works of pure music are perceived as profound and others less so. But, in Kivy's view, about the most one can say with respect to impressions of musical profundity is that some composers in their work exhibit not only consummate craft (which in itself can seem profound), but also discover through their compositions previously unimagined possibilities within the self-contained musical universe. Kivy does not think, however, that the musical universe of a "profound" work has anything to do with feelings about the world beyond the work, let alone with ultimate reality, in the way the ancients and many of their successors thought.[27] Orpheus charms with the lyre, one might say, but has no powers over anything beyond music itself.

What none of this answers satisfactorily is the question of what music alone could ever contribute to religious and spiritual life, if indeed we are to believe that music is finally an autonomous art—an art that, even when it moves the listener, does not move real life "affections" for any reasons other than its own, let alone connect any emotions with religious beliefs or with actual devotion. Such a theory of musical autonomy seems powerless to address adequately the widely shared conviction that some music is profoundly moving precisely *because* it conveys a deeper or fuller sense of human and spiritual realities, thereby revealing itself—as even the avowedly formalist Igor Stravinsky said—as a form of communion with other human beings, "and with the Supreme Being."[28]

Problems remain even with the more moderate purism represented by thinkers such as Susanne Langer. For if Langer and others are right that the forms of feeling entailed in music are strictly virtual, not actual, then it is hard to see that the emotions expressed "virtually" in music could ever be experienced as lively and fulfilling, which Langer herself seems to think they are. And if the expressive aspect of music supposedly exists in a domain of feeling that is completely removed from ideas and commitments, how can one explain why Bach's Cantata no. 140, *Sleepers,*

Wake, or Benjamin Britten's *War Requiem*, appears, to many listeners, to interpret religious or moral insights and convictions, and in a profoundly musical way that is not ascribable to the words alone?

The problem may be, in part, that most theorists have worked with a relatively one-dimensional notion of the nature of emotion, and an insufficiently flexible concept of the range of possibilities and aims within music itself. Too few who connect music with language have taken care, for example, to explore the metaphoric dimensions of musical imagination—emotive and cognitive at once—though some attempts have been made.[29] Even postmodern theorists, who have repeatedly opened music up to cultural and ideological critique, have been restricted in the factors they seem willing to consider in the analysis of musical meaning—primarily politics, gender, race, and class.[30]

One begins to see why one contemporary philosopher concludes his book on music and the emotions by writing: "A new theory of music is needed; and if this theory is to be revealing it will, I believe, have to be less monolithic than the theories I have rejected."[31] This same philosopher, who declines to proffer such a theory himself, insists nonetheless that any relatively adequate theory of music and emotions must honor the (relative) autonomy and integrity of music. Many other theorists would agree, at least to the extent of claiming that there should be no denying that what music provides emotionally cannot be provided any other way, or abstracted or translated without remainder into some other medium. To see where this line of thought might lead, it is necessary to fill in some of the details and to point to new trends and resources.

Reconsiderations: Restoring the Powers of Orpheus

Although much has been written about music and emotion, relatively little of this thought has been devoted to the nature of emotions themselves, in relation to music. Back in the nineteenth century, a number of poets, musicians, and philosophers reacted against the rationalistic and pragmatic deprecation of emotion by arguing (in an extension of Pascal) that the heart has reasons, too. This was partly to say that what one most deeply intuits and enjoys may elude clear concepts and rational propositions. The Romantic position hearkened back in various ways to ancient ideas of the capacity of music to provide a moving image of a higher, eternal reality and to touch the depths of the soul. But the Romantics' way of supporting this kind of claim (which had fallen on hard times during the Enlightenment) had difficulties of its own. Indeed, the difficulty with Romantic theories of musical expression was twofold. First, they fashioned too tight a link between the emotional impulse of the artist or composer, the expression embodied in the work, and the experience of the listener, as though there would always be a strict correspondence between all three. Second, they worked with too vague a notion of aesthetic emotions and their relation to ideas and extramusical values, which made it hard to account for how such emotions could be so penetrating when expressed musically.

When modern theorists of art and music tried to clarify how music and other art is emotionally expressive, they typically offered finely honed analyses of musical structure and style but rarely differentiated much between the various kinds of emotions themselves, or sorted out the different ways emotions interact with volitions and thoughts—not only in music but in the rest of life. Psychology was not as helpful in this regard as one might suppose, not least because psychotherapy was, after all, a "talking cure" (Freud and Jung had little to say about music), and experimental psychology was still too crude a tool.[32] Yet even a philosopher such as John Dewey (1859–1952), who wrote little about music but emphasized connections between art and life, was inclined to treat the emotional experience art affords as essentially one kind of process: the creation, intensification, and then resolution of tensions, yielding a sense of emotional equilibrium and satisfaction.[33] Leonard Meyer took a similarly uniform approach to emotion in music when he employed the tools of information theory to support his analysis of the emotionally rewarding anticipations and deferred resolutions of musical experience.[34]

In various ways, scholarship since the latter part of the twentieth century has made it possible to move beyond such limitations and toward a more integralist aesthetic of music and emotion, and of religion as well—one that nevertheless preserves important distinctions and declines to privilege absolutely any one particular form of music, emotion, or religion. Here it must suffice to point to a few works and theories that appear most promising.

First, in the broadly Anglo-American tradition of analytical philosophy, there has been renewed philosophical interest in the emotions and their artistic expression. Much of this thinking, sometimes with a hidden affinity with phenomenological and existentialist thought, has developed a sophisticated, if not entirely satisfactory, theory of emotions. This is a cognitive theory according to which emotions are fundamentally "intentional"—that is, judgments about, and evaluative reactions to, something or someone: some object of consciousness. On this view, one's idea or evaluation of a person, object, or event defines—or at least decisively colors—one's very emotion (such as shame or embarrassment), which in terms of sheer physiological response may be relatively indistinguishable and unspecific.[35] A related theory, claiming precedent in Aristotle, downplays the element of judgment per se by describing emotion as basically "thought experienced with pain or pleasure."[36] As we have seen in the work of Peter Kivy, such philosophies of emotion, in either form, challenge the standard emotivist understanding of music, which equates the emotions intrinsic to musical expression with those of everyday experience, supposedly transferred directly into a musical medium by the composer or performer and aroused directly in the audience. Since music in its purer forms presents consciousness with no primary object of attention but music itself, the emotivist theory seems unlikely to be true as stated. What does seem likely, and not just to cognitive theorists, is that music itself is, at the very least, the focal reason for whatever emotions or expressive traits are identified with the work or its performance. Geoffrey Madell, in a recent study, challenges the cognitive view of music and emotion, accusing it of falsifying or denying the immediately emotional response one actually feels in relation even to purely instrumental music. But he, too, concludes that "musical events" are what musical expression and emotion is all about.[37] But this brings us back to the question of whether music directs us only to itself. If we are moved by music, need our emotions be only about the music? If that were true, it would be extremely difficult to explain the potentially intimate connection between music and such things as texts, values, and rituals.

Philosophers such as Aaron Ridley, therefore, have begun to challenge in fresh ways such a purely self-referential view of music.[38] But among those who claim no special expertise as music theorists, Martha Nussbaum is perhaps the most notable. She claims that music experienced fully and attentively invites the "implied listener" to respond emotionally in ways embedded in the music itself. Unlike Kivy, she affirms that some music, at least, is intimately linked with our deepest strivings and most powerful emotions. But she agrees with the cognitive theorists that judgment, or something like that, is necessary for emotion, and she therefore finds it "tempting" to think that music can indeed contain, and cause, beliefs by being "about" something other than itself. She then suggests that one can see how this might indeed be true, but only if one gives up on the idea that music is a language per se, and if one can see how music nevertheless has a way of becoming "emotional material" that is distinctively musical and therefore in a sense indispensable. Nussbaum suggests that, among other things, what musical works are somehow able to embody is the idea of our "urgent need for and attachment to things outside ourselves that we do not control," and thus the hope for transcending the pettiness of daily life. Then she goes further by equating what she has just said with Mahler's reference, in a letter, to the musical possibility of being "raised on angels' wings to the highest heights."[39] This is all very tentative, however, and cries out for fuller development and further modification.

It is worth observing, in this regard, that the major cognitive theory of emotions that Antonio Damasio has recently advanced from the standpoint of neurobiology has quite a different emphasis from the philosophical theories just described. This difference becomes evident when Damasio states, "the essence of sadness or happiness is the combined perception of certain body states with whatever thoughts they are juxtaposed to, complemented by a modification in ... the thought process."[40] This emphasis on the bodily basis of primary emotions and of subsequent conscious feelings and reflective judgments is almost the reverse of Malcolm Budd's idea of emotion as essentially "thought experienced with pain or pleasure," where it is the thought and not any bodily response that is featured as determinative. Damasio's work in neurobiology and brain research appears to demonstrate that emotional responses to images and situations need not, in many instances, pass through a reflective or conscious process first before being registered in the body. He shows, or tries to show, that the body and the multipart prereflective brain, with their complex array of neurological and chemical responses, strongly affect how an emotion (which in his account is initially unconscious) is eventually registered by the mind as a preconscious feeling and then, potentially, made the subject of reflective awareness.[41] He says little about the possibility that an evaluative judgment or complex idea might itself shape emotions to begin with, or later result in more reflective emotions, feelings, or emotion-laden thoughts. But Damasio argues that unconscious emotions, which in stages emerge as conscious feelings, do interpret the world and guide our behavior and values in crucial and often reliable ways. His theory of emotions, then, like that of our recent philosophers, is cognitive. Both camps agree that emotions and thoughts or judgments are intimately connected, and that emotions therefore relate us to the world as judged and understood. But the philosophical and neurobiological theories describe the driving and determinative forces behind the specific character of emotions and feelings quite differently.

Perhaps each approach is true in important respects, but in need of qualification. Perhaps it is the case that some of the feelings expressed in music, and some of the emotions aroused by music, are taken in by the brain and body in such a way that they first register on us without any questions being asked, so to speak, and thus at an inarticulate but formative level. Exactly how that happens, and what makes those feelings distinctively musical while also genuinely related to life, remains something of a mystery, though Damasio provides suggestive scientific data. Part of an answer supplementary to his may be that such "primal" responses are constantly colored and modified by more reflective perceptions and feelings related to conscious observations and ideas, including fictive imaginations and metaphors. There may be a feedback loop between perception, body, brain, and reflective mind that is more extensive and sensitive than could previously be imagined.

In any case, one might make more of the idea that awareness itself does not operate on only one level; even in aesthetic response there is foreground awareness and background awareness; there is focal awareness and peripheral awareness.[42] Thus, even when one is attending to specific features of a musical work and responding to it in the manner invited, one brings to the experience all sorts of ideas that have an emotional component literally embodied within oneself. And when one responds at a "gut level" to musical rhythms and purely instrumental sounds, one is still a being whose whole embodied mind is the main organ of musical perception. And that mind brings thoughts and words as part of the peripheral or background awareness, even when focusing on the experience of music without words or entertaining imaginative possibilities through the elaboration of "purely" musical worlds. This helps explain why it has always seemed so natural in virtually all cultures to bring words and music together, or music and religious ritual. The emotions and expressions of music have their home in the experience of the self as a whole, in relation to society and the world. And since religion can be described as concerned, at root, with vital and harmonious relations between the self, others, world, and God/the Whole, one can see why religion has a vested interest in music. Acknowledgments of this sort of integral approach to music, religion, and emotion have recently come from scholars in both world religions and ethnomusicology, as well as in music therapy.[43] Such works increasingly recognize the rich internal heterogeneity of music and the complex cultural factors shaping the experience of the emotions that music can express and arouse not only personally but also socially. One can see a related development in theologies of music as well. Thus Albert Blackwell, in his book *The Sacred in Music*, reintroduces Pythagorean and cosmological thought while revisiting the possibility that, at least for those listeners of a certain religious inclination, there is a deeply felt and audible ontological depth to musical harmony.[44] Blackwell goes on to explore the sacramental potential within music, and the particular relations of music to Christian doctrines of creation, fall, salvation, and ultimate beatitude or bliss. Gone, however, is the inclination to claim that all listeners and makers of music will experience music in the same way. Finally, Jeremy Begbie, in his book *Theology, Music, and Time*,[45] may have less to say about emotions as such, but he gives close attention to the rhythmic and temporal structures of music and how they can convey various theologically resonant senses of temporality: of time's possibilities, liabilities, and rewards in relation to "God's good time." Begbie thus expounds on music's potential gift of liberation, healing, and wholeness. Such approaches as these suggest that Orpheus can be welcomed back not merely as musician but also, in that very role, as prophet and as celebrant of the most vulnerable and vital feelings, of death and life.

NOTES

With thanks to Joyce Krauser, Bharat Gupt, and Sunthar Visuvalingam for timely assistance.

1. Vladimir Jankélévitch, *Music and the Ineffable* (1961), translated by Carolyn Abbate (Princeton, N.J.: Princeton University Press, 2003).
2. John Block Friedman, *Orpheus in the Middle Ages* (Cambridge, Mass.: Harvard University Press, 1970).
3. See E. R. Dodds, *The Greeks and the Irrational* (Berkeley: University of California Press, 1951), 171; and W. K. C. Guthrie, *Orpheus and Greek Religion*, reprint, with a foreword by Larry J. Alderink (Princeton, N.J.: Princeton University Press, 1993), 41.
4. See Edward Rothstein, *Emblems of Mind: The Inner Life of Music and Mathematics* (New York: Random House, 1995).
5. See Wladyslaw Tatarkiewicz, *History of Aesthetics*, edited by J. Harrell, 3 vols. (The Hague: Mouton, 1970), vol. 1; and Edward Lippman, *A History of Western Musical Aesthetics* (Lincoln: University of Nebraska Press, 1992), 3–18.
6. Plato, *Republic*, translated by G. M. A. Grube (1974); revised by C. D. C. Reeve (Indianapolis: Hackett, 1992), 78.
7. Aristotle, *Politics* 8.1339a–1340a.
8. Augustine, *Confessions* 10.33.49–50, translated by Henry Chadwick (Oxford: Oxford University Press, 1991), 207–8.
9. See James McKinnon, *Music in Early Christian Literature* (Cambridge: Cambridge University Press, 1987); and Johannes Quasten, *Music and Worship in Pagan and Christian*

Antiquity, translated by Boniface Ramsey (Washington, D.C.: National Association of Pastoral Musicians, 1983).

10. See Friedrich Blume et al., *Protestant Church Music* (London: Gollancz, 1975), 3–123.

11. See Frank Burch Brown, *Good Taste, Bad Taste, and Christian Taste: Aesthetics in Religious Life* (New York: Oxford University Press, 2000), 40.

12. McKinnon, *Music in Early Christian Literature*, 156, 158–59.

13. Robert F. Hayburn, *Papal Legislation on Sacred Music 95 A.D. to 1977 A.D.* (Collegeville, Minn.: Liturgical Press, 1979), 27.

14. John Wesley, app. 1, in *Works*, vol. 7, *A Collection of Hymns for the Use of the People Called Methodists* (Nashville: Abingdon, 1983), 766–69.

15. See Quentin Faulkner, *Wiser Than Despair: The Evolution of Ideas in the Relationship of Music and the Christian Church* (Westport, Conn.: Greenwood Press, 1996), 93–105.

16. Leo Treitler, ed., *Strunk's Source Readings in Music History*, rev. ed. (New York: Norton, 1998), 1201.

17. See Jon Michael Spencer, *Sacred Music of Black Religion* (Minneapolis: Augsburg Fortress, 1990).

18. See Tricia Rose, *Black Noise: Rap Music and Black Culture in Contemporary America* (Hanover, N.H.: Wesleyan University Press, 1994).

19. See Brown, *Good Taste, Bad Taste, and Christian Taste*, 230–51.

20. Enrico Fubini, *The History of Music Aesthetics*, translated by Michael Hatwell (Basingstoke, England: Macmillan, 1990), 261–308.

21. Eduard Hanslick, *The Beautiful in Music* (1854), translated by Gustav Cohen and edited by Morris Weitz (New York: Liberal Arts, 1957).

22. Arthur Schopenhauer, *The World as Will and Representation* (1819), translated by E. F. J. Payne, 2 vols. (New York: Dover, 1966).

23. Susanne K. Langer, *Philosophy in a New Key* (Cambridge, Mass.: Harvard University Press, 1951), and *Feeling and Form* (New York: Scribner's, 1953).

24. Deryck Cooke, *The Language of Music* (London: Oxford University Press, 1959).

25. See Stephen Davies, *Musical Meaning and Expression* (Ithaca, N.Y.: Cornell University Press, 1994); Roger Scruton, *The Aesthetics of Music* (Oxford: Oxford University Press, 1997); and Joseph P. Swain, *Musical Languages* (New York: Norton, 1997).

26. Peter Kivy, *Sound Sentiment: An Essay on the Musical Emotions, Including the Complete Text of "The Corded Shell"* (Philadelphia: Temple University Press, 1989).

27. Peter Kivy, *Music Alone: Philosophical Reflections on the Purely Musical Experience* (Ithaca, N.Y.: Cornell University Press, 1990), 202–18.

28. Igor Stravinsky, *Poetics of Music* (Cambridge, Mass.: Harvard University Press, 1947), 146.

29. See, for example, Donald Ferguson, *Music as Metaphor: The Elements of Expression* (Minneapolis: University of Minnesota Press, 1960); and Michael Spitzer, *Metaphor and Musical Thought* (Chicago: University of Chicago Press, 2004).

30. See Richard Leppert and Susan McClary, *Music and Society: The Politics of Composition, Performance, and Reception* (Cambridge: Cambridge University Press, 1987); and Peter J. Martin, *Sounds and Society: Themes in the Sociology of Music* (Manchester, England: Manchester University Press, 1995).

31. Malcolm Budd, *Music and the Emotions: The Philosophical Theories* (London: Routledge, 1985), 176.

32. See Patrik N. Juslin and John A. Sloboda, *Music and Emotion: Theory and Research* (Oxford: Oxford University Press, 2001).

33. John Dewey, *Art as Experience* (1934; reprint, New York: Putnam, 1958).

34. Leonard B. Meyer, *Emotion and Meaning in Music* (Chicago: University of Chicago Press, 1956).

35. For an existentialist and phenomenological anticipation of such claims, see Robert C. Solomon, *The Passions: The Myth and Nature of Human Emotion* (Garden City, N.Y.: Doubleday, 1976); analytical philosophical theories, proper, appear in Solomon, ed., *What Is an Emotion? Classic and Contemporary Readings* (New York: Oxford University Press, 1993).

36. Malcolm Budd, *Music and the Emotions: The Philosophical Theories* (London: Routledge, 1985), 4–5.

37. Geoffrey Madell, *Philosophy, Music, and Emotion* (Edinburgh: Edinburgh University Press, 2002), 149; compare similar claims in Derek Matravers, *Art and Emotion* (Oxford: Clarendon, 1998).

38. Aaron Ridley, *Music, Value, and the Passions* (Ithaca, N.Y.: Cornell University Press, 1995).

39. Martha C. Nussbaum, *Upheavals of Thought: The Intelligence of Emotions* (Cambridge: Cambridge University Press, 2001), 249–94.

40. Antonio Damasio, *Descartes' Error: Emotion, Reason, and the Human Brain* (1994; reprint, New York: HarperCollins, 2000), 146–47.

41. Antonio Damasio, *The Feeling of What Happens: Body and Emotion in the Making of Consciousness* (New York: Harcourt, 1999), 283–84.

42. See Michael Polanyi, *The Tacit Dimension*, (1966; reprint, Garden City, N.Y.: Doubleday, 1967); and Frank Burch Brown, *Religious Aesthetics: A Theological Study of Making and Meaning* (Princeton, N.J.: Princeton University Press, 1989), 50–76.

43. See, for example, Lawrence E. Sullivan, ed., *Enchanting Powers: Music in the World's Religions* (Cambridge, Mass.: Harvard University Press, 1997); and Judith Becker, *Deep Listeners: Music, Emotion, and Trancing* (Bloomington: Indiana University Press, 2004).

44. Albert L. Blackwell, *The Sacred in Music* (Louisville, Ky.: Westminster John Knox, 1999).

45. Jeremy S. Begbie, *Theology, Music, and Time* (Cambridge: Cambridge University Press, 2000).

BIBLIOGRAPHY

Augustine. *Confessions*. Translated by Henry Chadwick. Oxford: Oxford University Press, 1991.

———. *De Musica*. http://www.chmtl.indiana.edu/tml/3rd-5th/3RD-5TH_INDEX.html.

Beck, Guy L. *Sonic Theology: Hinduism and Sacred Sound*. Columbia: University of South Carolina Press, 1993.

Becker, Judith. *Deep Listeners: Music, Emotion, and Trancing*. Bloomington: Indiana University Press, 2004.

Begbie, Jeremy S. *Theology, Music, and Time*. Cambridge: Cambridge University Press, 2000.

Blackwell, Albert L. *The Sacred in Music*. Louisville, Ky.: Westminster John Knox, 1999.

Blume, Friedrich, et al. *Protestant Church Music*. London: Gollancz, 1975.

Brown, Frank Burch. *Good Taste, Bad Taste, and Christian Taste: Aesthetics in Religious Life*. New York: Oxford University Press, 2000.

———. *Religious Aesthetics: A Theological Study of Making and Meaning*. Princeton, N.J.: Princeton University Press, 1989.

Browne, Sir Thomas. *Religio Medici: In the Prose of Sir Thomas Browne*. Edited and with an introduction by Norman J. Endicott. Garden City, N.Y.: Doubleday, 1967.

Budd, Malcolm. *Music and the Emotions: The Philosophical Theories*. London: Routledge, 1985.

Cooke, Deryck. *The Language of Music*. London: Oxford University Press, 1959.

Damasio, Antonio. *Descartes' Error: Emotion, Reason, and the Human Brain*. 1994. Reprint, New York: HarperCollins, 2000.

———. *The Feeling of What Happens: Body and Emotion in the Making of Consciousness*. New York: Harcourt, 1999.

———. *Looking for Spinoza: Joy, Sorrow, and the Feeling Brain*. New York: Harcourt, 2003.

Davies, Stephen. *Musical Meaning and Expression*. Ithaca, N.Y.: Cornell University Press, 1994.

Dewey, John. *Art as Experience*. 1934. Reprint, New York: Putnam, 1958.

Dodds, E. R. *The Greeks and the Irrational*. Berkeley: University of California Press, 1951.

Faulkner, Quentin. *Wiser Than Despair: The Evolution of Ideas in the Relationship of Music and the Christian Church*. Westport, Conn.: Greenwood Press, 1996.

Ferguson, Donald N. *Music as Metaphor: The Elements of Expression*. Minneapolis: University of Minnesota Press, 1960.

Friedman, John Block. *Orpheus in the Middle Ages*. Cambridge, Mass.: Harvard University Press, 1970.

Fubini, Enrico. *The History of Music Aesthetics*. Translated by Michael Hatwell. Basingstoke, England: Macmillan, 1990.

Gnoli, Raniero. *The Aesthetic Experience According to Abhinavagupta*, including portions of Abhinavagupta's commentary on the *Natyashastra* of Bharata, in Sanskrit and English. Serie Orientale Roma 11. Rome: Istituto Italiano per il Medio ed Estremo Oriente, 1956.

Guthrie, W. K. C. *Orpheus and Greek Religion* (1933). Reprint, with a foreword by Larry J. Alderink, Princeton, N.J.: Princeton University Press, 1993.

Hanslick, Eduard. *The Beautiful in Music* (1854). Translated by Gustav Cohen and edited by Morris Weitz. New York: Liberal Arts, 1957.

Hayburn, Robert F. *Papal Legislation on Sacred Music 95 A.D. to 1977 A.D.* Collegeville, Minn.: Liturgical Press, 1979.

Hjort, Mette, and Sue Laver. *Emotion and the Arts*. New York: Oxford University Press, 1997.

Hoffman, Lawrence A., and Janet R. Walton, eds. *Sacred Sound and Social Change: Liturgical Music in Jewish and Christian Experience*. Notre Dame, Ind.: University of Notre Dame Press, 1992.

Idelsohn, Abraham Z. *Jewish Music: Its Historical Development*. 1929. Reprint, New York: Dover, 1992.

Irwin, Joyce, ed. *Sacred Sound: Music in Religious Thought and Practice*. Chico, Calif.: Scholars Press, 1983.

Jankélévitch, Vladimir. *Music and the Ineffable* (1961). Translated by Carolyn Abbate. Princeton, N.J.: Princeton University Press, 2003.

Jourdain, Robert. *Music, the Brain, and Ecstasy: How Music Captures Our Imagination*. New York: Morrow, 1997.

Juslin, Patrik N., and John A. Sloboda. *Music and Emotion: Theory and Research*. Oxford: Oxford University Press, 2001.
Kivy, Peter. *Music Alone: Philosophical Reflections on the Purely Musical Experience*. Ithaca, N.Y.: Cornell University Press, 1990.
———. *Sound Sentiment: An Essay on the Musical Emotions, Including the Complete Text of "The Corded Shell."* Philadelphia: Temple University Press, 1989.
Lang, Paul Henry. *Music in Western Civilization*. New York: Norton, 1941.
Langer, Susanne K. *Feeling and Form*. New York: Scribner's, 1953.
———. *Philosophy in a New Key*. Cambridge, Mass.: Harvard University Press, 1951.
LeDoux, Joseph. *The Emotional Brain: The Mysterious Underpinnings of Emotional Life*. New York: Simon and Schuster, 1996.
Leppert, Richard, and Susan McClary. *Music and Society: The Politics of Composition, Performance, and Reception*. Cambridge: Cambridge University Press, 1987.
Lippman, Edward. *A History of Western Musical Aesthetics*. Lincoln: University of Nebraska Press, 1992.
Madell, Geoffrey. *Philosophy, Music, and Emotion*. Edinburgh: Edinburgh University Press, 2002.
Martin, Peter J. *Sounds and Society: Themes in the Sociology of Music*. Manchester, England: Manchester University Press, 1995.
Matravers, Derek. *Art and Emotion*. Oxford: Oxford University Press, 1998.
McClellan, Randall. *The Healing Forces of Music*. San Jose, Calif.: toEcel, 1991.
McKinnon, James. *Music in Early Christian Literature*. Cambridge: Cambridge University Press, 1987.
Meyer, Leonard B. *Emotion and Meaning in Music*. Chicago: University of Chicago Press, 1956.
Nussbaum, Martha C. *Upheavals of Thought: The Intelligence of Emotions*. Cambridge: Cambridge University Press, 2001.
Plato. *Republic*. Translated by G. M. A. Grube (1974). Revised by C. D. C. Reeve. Indianapolis: Hackett, 1992.
Polanyi, Michael. *The Tacit Dimension*. 1966. Reprint, Garden City, N.Y.: Doubleday, 1967.
Quasten, Johannes. *Music and Worship in Pagan and Christian Antiquity*. Translated by Boniface Ramsey. Washington, D.C.: National Association of Pastoral Musicians, 1983.
Ridley, Aaron. *Music, Value, and the Passions*. Ithaca, N.Y.: Cornell University Press, 1995.
Rose, Tricia. *Black Noise: Rap Music and Black Culture in Contemporary America*. Hanover, N.H.: Wesleyan University Press, 1994.
Rothstein, Edward. *Emblems of Mind: The Inner Life of Music and Mathematics*. New York: Random House, 1995.
Rouget, Gilbert. *Music and Trance: A Theory of the Relations between Music and Possession*. Translated and revised by Brunhilde Biebuyck. Chicago: University of Chicago Press, 1985.
Rowell, Lewis. *Music and Musical Thought in Early India*. Chicago: University of Chicago Press, 1992.
Rust, E. Gardner. *The Music and Dance of the World's Religions: A Comprehensive, Annotated Bibliography of Materials in the English Language*. Westport, Conn.: Greenwood Press, 1996.
Sadie, Stanley, and John Tyrell, eds. *New Grove Dictionary of Music and Musicians*. 2nd ed. 29 vols. New York: Oxford University Press, 2003.
Schopenhauer, Arthur. *The World as Will and Representation* (1819). Translated by E. F. J. Payne. 2 vols. New York: Dover, 1966.

Scruton, Roger. *The Aesthetics of Music.* Oxford: Oxford University Press, 1997.
Shiloah, Amnon. *Music in the World of Islam: A Socio-cultural Study.* Detroit: Wayne State University Press, 1995.
Solomon, Robert C., ed. *What Is an Emotion? Classic and Contemporary Readings.* New York: Oxford University Press, 1993.
———. *The Passions: The Myth and Nature of Human Emotion.* Garden City, N.Y.: Doubleday, 1976.
Spencer, Jon Michael. *Sacred Music of Black Religion.* Minneapolis: Augsburg Fortress, 1990.
Spitzer, Michael. *Metaphor and Musical Thought.* Chicago: University of Chicago Press, 2004.
Stravinsky, Igor. *Poetics of Music.* Cambridge, Mass.: Harvard University Press, 1947.
Sullivan, Lawrence E. *Enchanting Powers: Music in the World's Religions.* Cambridge, Mass.: Harvard University Center for the Study of World Religions, 1997.
Swain, Joseph P. *Musical Languages.* New York: Norton, 1997.
Tatarkiewicz, Wladyslaw. *History of Aesthetics.* Edited by J. Harrell. 3 vols. The Hague: Mouton, 1970.
———. *A History of Six Ideas: An Essay in Aesthetics.* The Hague: Nijhoff, 1980.
Treitler, Leo, ed. *Strunk's Source Readings in Music History.* Rev. ed. New York: Norton, 1998.
Weiss, Piero, and Richard Taruskin. *Music in the Western World: A History in Documents.* New York: Schirmer, 1984.
Wesley, John. *A Collection of Hymns for the Use of the People Called Methodists.* In *Works,* vol. 7. Nashville: Abingdon, 1983.

CHAPTER 12

MATERIAL CULTURE

JOHN KIESCHNICK

DESPITE the burgeoning of material culture studies in recent decades and the enormous amount of data available regarding religious objects from all time periods and all parts of the world, the role objects play in evoking and shaping emotion in religious contexts remains largely unexplored. Most religious activity involves objects of some sort, whether they be the elaborate gowns and imposing cathedral of a medieval Christian priest or the inexpensive wooden prayer beads of a shopkeeper in modern Bangkok; few experience religion alone and empty-handed in the desert. There is much to be gained by resisting the temptation to dismiss objects such as gowns and prayer beads as peripheral to authentic, elevated religious experience and hence insignificant. For many, particular types of clothing, food, or devotional objects are essential for establishing a religious identity or cultivating religious sentiments. A Korean Buddhist monk, for instance, is instantly recognizable by his robes and shoes, the objects he carries about with him, and the food on his table. Those familiar with other religions can similarly assess the region of origin, status, and even degree of piety of a given figure all on the basis of mute objects. More than an almost unconscious assertion of identity, objects are used in religion to instruct, to persuade, and even more fundamentally to transform the emotional state of religious adherents, whether it be to calm an angry man with an image of a serene saint or conversely to provoke to anger with the destruction of a sacred thing held dear. And while some scholars and theologians may disparage recourse to external things for achieving religious ends, the prevalence of objects in religion suggests that the antimaterialist stance is a radical, minority interpretation of how religion *should* be perceived rather than an honest description of how most practice it.

A focus on how objects affect emotions sheds light on culturally specific aspects of religion. A German Lutheran faced with a Tibetan painting of a fierce protector deity or a Tibetan monk faced with a Lutheran sculpture of a suffering Christ on the cross are more likely to be baffled than moved, reflecting the importance of knowledge of iconography and artistic tradition before such works can have their intended emotional effects. Even within a given culture, though the object may remain the same, reactions to it may change significantly over time; in Chinese Buddhism, scriptures written in blood once evoked a sense of awe and wonder and were put on display in monasteries, whereas modern Buddhists are more likely to feel uneasiness and even disgust when confronted with the same scripture in the same setting. The same holds true for gruesome images of Christian saints. And similar examples readily come to mind for other religious traditions, underlining the importance of historical as well as cultural context for shaping emotions.

At the same time, attention to material culture reveals generally shared responses across cultures to size, light, and representations of the human form, outgrowths perhaps of spontaneous physiological responses. Even without specific cultural knowledge, monumental sculpture tends to provoke a sense of awe and small dark spaces a sense of foreboding and mystery. For this reason, whether for small-scale studies of individual practices or events or for comparative religion on a grander scale, attention to material culture has great explanatory potential—potential we can only hope will be exploited in the coming years as specialists in religion overcome a longstanding prejudice against material culture and embrace the growing interest in artifacts so evident in other disciplines in recent decades.

Before returning to the value of an appreciation of objects for understanding emotion and religion, I begin with a brief introduction to the term "material culture" and problems specific to the study of the material culture of religion.

Material Culture and the Study of Religion

Unlike discussion of the terms "religion" and "ritual," years of debate over the definition of material culture seem to have produced consensus. "Material culture" is now generally defined as artifacts, as well as ideas about and conduct related to artifacts, with "artifacts" limited to material objects made or altered by human beings. According to this definition, attitudes toward, say, bagpipes—their price, their prestige value in comparison with other instruments, the manner in which they are played, their regional and ethnic associations, and even jokes about them—are all as much a part of their place in material culture as their manufacture and appearance. By the same definition, "material culture" would not include a natural forest or a river, though it could include a garden or a manmade canal.[1]

While art historians, archaeologists, historians of technology, and, to a certain extent, anthropologists founded their disciplines on the study of artifacts and hence can be said to have been studying material culture all along, "material culture studies" as a self-conscious discipline with its own journals and conferences has only taken shape in recent decades. Social historians have been slow to incorporate the research of art historians and archaeologists into their own work, but there are exceptions, that is, historians who have made ample use of artifacts in their research; and even those who haven't have at least acknowledged the importance of objects in history. Specialists in the history of religion, however, have made a conscious effort to place objects outside of their field of study, generally considering the study of artifacts to be peripheral to more central concerns of theology, ritual, mysticism, and ideology, all of which seem at first to consist primarily of ideas and behaviors rather than objects. Outside of painting, sculpture, and architecture, which are given special aesthetic value, most religious objects have received surprisingly little scholarly attention, considering their prevalence and the importance religious practitioners accord them. The study of the history and symbolism of religious clothing, ritual implements, food consumed in religious settings, and popular religious art is, with rare exceptions, weak and sketchy. There is, for example, no solid accessible scholarship for first-time visitors to Lhasa or Jerusalem looking for reliable information on the history and significance of the dizzying array of unfamiliar clothing, food, art, and devotional objects that surround them. In short, despite the substantial body of research now available for the study of material culture, the study of material culture *in religion* has barely begun.[2]

Part of the reason for this disinterest in the material aspects of religion may stem from Protestant critiques of material mediation in the relationship between the individual and the divine. That is, although the suspicion of material things in religion is not limited to Protestantism, some have laid blame for the tendency of modern scholarship to ignore the material culture of religion on Protestant theology, with its emphasis on faith and doctrine as opposed to crass devotional objects and other such "external things."[3] It has even been suggested that in the study of ancient Indian Buddhism, the overreliance on textual doctrines, even when they contradict archaeological evidence, is rooted in Protestant assumptions.[4] Hence it is not surprising that the pioneers in the study of religion and emotion, emerging as they did from a Protestant tradition, took scant notice of the role of objects in provoking or shaping emotions. None of the leading scholars who are discussed in the subsequent chapters of this book addressed the question of the place of objects in religion directly. At the opening of the nineteenth century, Friedrich Schleiermacher, for instance, though emphasizing the importance of feeling in religion, expressed less enthusiasm for the way devotional objects or religious symbols might elicit religious feelings, stating that "everything that is religion spurns and easily dispenses with every external aid."[5] This same tendency to dismiss material aids to emotion as, at best, uninteresting appears in the works of more modern scholars of emotion and religion as well. Objects figure in only a handful of the accounts of intense encounters William James describes in *The Varieties of Religious Experience*. Indeed, many of the figures he discusses would have considered religious encounters mediated by objects adulterated and hence less authentic. James's enthusiasts tend to experience their most emotional moments while walking in nature or while alone in empty rooms.

Similarly, while Rudolf Otto in *The Idea of the Holy* makes repeated reference to the ability of music and poetry to evoke religious sentiments, he only mentions objects in passing in a few pages on refined, elite religious art, curiously citing as an example the simplicity and "emptiness" of Chinese landscape painting, as if he were drawn to this type of art precisely because of its airy, less material, qualities.[6]

The rejection of material things is itself a part of material culture, and it is worth exploring the implications of valuing only emotions elicited by the most ethereal abstractions. More important, once we leave the genre of fervent, introspective Protestant reflections on religious experience and look more generally at how religion and emotion interact in the everyday lives of people in a wide variety of contexts and time periods, we find objects everywhere. Pilgrimage and public ritual are almost always closely linked to a set of carefully considered objects, and even the most private devotional practices often involve things. Close examination reveals that even those who espouse the rhetoric of the rejection of "external things" at the same time place great importance on material culture in the day-to-day practice of their religion. It is revealing, for instance, to examine the history of the Bible as object among Protestants who were otherwise suspicious of ritual and devotional paraphernalia.[7] Nor should it surprise us that objects play a role in the emotional life of even the most ardent Puritans or determined ascetics; for objects are a part of the basic vocabulary of human communication. When a Puritan rejects a Catholic rosary, or a Jain refuses to wear clothing, material culture forms the syntax of their arguments.

Objects as Triggers for Emotion

Now that the term "material culture" has gained currency, it is a simple matter to return to classics in the study of emotion and religion and point out their failure to consider the role of objects. And few would object to the general observation that material culture plays an important role in the history of religion. What is needed now is, on a general level, analysis of attitudes toward the material world in various cultures and religions; and, on a more specific level, descriptions of which objects tend to evoke emotional responses in a given culture, which emotions are evoked, and what factors are responsible for shaping emotional responses. The study of material culture is perhaps most fruitful when, in addition to attention to the historical development of mentalities associated with particular things, it takes into consideration the nature of particular categories of objects and the emotions they evoke, that is, how certain physical properties tend to affect us emotionally. Below I look at four types of sacred things that trigger emotions: icons, relics, architecture, and clothing, beginning with icons.

Puzzled by those Christians who hold images in disdain, Teresa of Avila once commented on the importance of religious images for stimulating and cultivating her own religious sensibilities:

> I had so little ability to represent things in my mind, except for what I could see. I could profit nothing from my imagination, [unlike] other persons who can see things in their minds wherever they pray... for this reason I was such a friend of images. Unhappy those who by their fault lose this good! It surely seems that they do not love the Lord, for if they loved him, they would delight in seeing his portrait, just as here one is still happy to see someone one loves dearly.[8]

Unlike modern Protestant and even Catholic thinkers uncomfortable with emotions evoked by material things, Teresa was attracted to images precisely because of their materiality, so useful for stimulating the senses and cultivating feelings. In Teresa's case, images caused delight, but Juan de Avila, also writing in sixteenth-century Spain, speaks of images provoking the opposite reaction: "When they want to take out an image, to make people weep, they dress it in mourning and arrange it so it provokes sadness."[9] In Chinese hagiography, the most common response to images is neither sorrow nor joy but wonder. Devotees are forever marveling at images attributed with miraculous powers and "sighing in wonder" at images that perspire or weep or speak to them in dreams. In these cases, the responses to icons, though ranging from sorrow to joy, reverence to fear, are nonetheless all positive. But negative reactions to icons are at least as visceral. Nineteenth-century Christian missionaries railing in the streets against the evils of idolatry in China, twenty-first-century Taliban purists dynamiting ancient Buddhist statues in Afghanistan, and even the more detached distaste for depictions of the religious figures in refined Islamic and Jewish theological discourse, though rooted in carefully reasoned doctrine, betray at the same time a more immediate, emotional reaction to icons, suggesting something fundamentally disturbing in the creation of artificial human forms. While some preliminary work has been done on the place of icons in various religions and cultures, the emotions they provoke, and how such experiences relate to attitudes toward these same emotions in other contexts have received little attention.[10]

In addition to documenting the links between icons and emotions in cultural context—why, for instance, in the presence of icons devotees of a certain time and place weep or smile, while others tremble with fear—it is useful to consider the nature of the icon, a human shape that appears real yet at the same time we know has been manufactured. Daniel Freedberg has noted perceptively that in most cases when the mentally unbalanced have attacked images in modern museums, they have targeted first the eyes, for these are the part of the icon that seem to give it life. Religious artisans in Asia have given equal importance to the eyes of their icons, only completing them in a special ceremony, at which point the lifeless piece of clay or wood is transformed into the abode of a god. In the same way, icons usually face directly outward, forcing the devotee to engage the gaze of the image as a living thing. Thorough study of icons should take into account not only the ritual and theological context of images in a given culture but also more generally how images were viewed outside of these contexts. In principle, the "decay of the aura" of art in modern times with the explosion of mechanical reproductions of human forms should have had a profound effect on the power of religious images as well, but whether it has or not can only be determined by careful historical study that has not yet been done.[11]

Another material locus of emotion, again prominent in Christianity and Buddhism, is relics or, more precisely, the body parts of holy figures. Scholars have long recognized the importance of relics in the history of Christianity, and scholars of Buddhism have followed suit in recent decades with studies of relic worship throughout Buddhist history. As in the case of icons, much of the research has focused on documenting the importance of relic worship, its geographic spread, and its historical development and prevalence in religious writing, with less attention to the forms of response to relics by individuals and why relics should evoke an emotional response. Again, we can easily find cases of Christians weeping before the relics of saints and of Chinese expressing wonder or, in one famous incident in the ninth century, burning and mutilating themselves in a state of ecstasy before a relic of the Buddha. To a certain extent, responses to bodily relics mirror those to "contact relics" such as pieces of the cross on which Christ died, or the bowl used by the Buddha. But scholars have suggested that the response to bodily relics stems in part from the nature of the objects themselves, and that the fascination with parts of the bodies of holy figures emerges from uncertainty about the boundaries between life and death and the destination after death of the powers attributed to sacred beings.[12] Again, then, some of the most exciting research on the place of relics in material culture involves questioning what it is about the shape and substance of relics that triggers emotional responses in devotees.

There is little point in attempting to assign the effect of certain objects to physiological elements or, conversely, to social construction; it is more rewarding to consider both in the stew of ingredients that make up an emotional event—an approach now commonplace in material culture studies. Religious architecture is in this respect particularly interesting both for its ability to evoke emotions and for the variety of possible responses to the same structure, depending on the expectations the visitor brings to the site. While I may feel the same sensation walking into a Romanesque chapel in the hills of Catalonia as I do entering a Buddhist temple in the mountains of Tibet, whether or not this is in part a physiological response to the height of the ceilings and manipulation of light is extremely difficult to demonstrate, though neurological research may shed light on at least part of what makes sacred architecture work. It is much easier, and at least as interesting, to show how a similar building may be experienced in radically different ways, depending on belief and other cultural preconceptions.[13] Buildings provide a useful measure of the range of religious emotions and how they relate to social background and divergent expectations. Elites, peasants, natives, foreigners, lay people and religious professionals, construction workers and tourists may all have different emotional responses to the same space or be attracted to particular aspects of a religious structure. Just as important are distinctions between group and individual, festival and everyday, all of which play key roles in shaping emotional experience. The strong sense of community imbued by religious architecture, in addition to providing a locus for solace and pride, has a dark side in the acerbic and often violent contests between rival groups for sacred land and the buildings it contains. Distinctions between festive and ordinary time are equally important for the study of the role of sacred architecture in stirring feelings. Architecture can, then, present the scholar with a neat composite of the emotional expectations of a religious community, providing as it does a relatively open invitation for interpretation when compared to, say, doctrine or ritual, which tend to be more tightly controlled by elite interpretation.

If one of the distinguishing characteristics of architecture is its immobility—the fact that it establishes a stable sacred space to be shared or contested by those who occupy it—religious clothing is appealing in part because of its mobility, its ability to communicate religious sentiments and identity silently wherever one goes. A Muslim woman in Toronto, an orthodox Jew in Jerusalem, a Buddhist nun in Taipei may be instantly recognized by their clothing, symbols that in turn evoke varied responses from those they encounter, ranging from respect and admiration to ridicule and scorn. Conversely, the undergarment worn by many Mormons may be completely invisible to outsiders; indeed, some Mormons go out of their way to cover it, while at the same time finding a sense of security and spirituality in the knowledge that they constantly wear a religious garment beneath their secular clothing.[14]

One specialist in material culture has pointed out that while it is commonplace to use linguistic metaphors when speaking about the capacity of clothing to "communicate," even at its most sophisticated, clothing is a weak and crude medium of communication when compared to spoken language.[15] While a Muslim woman who chooses to wear a headscarf may do so out of a general sense of modesty or longing for tradition, her act may be misconstrued as a sign of radical, even violent fundamentalism.[16] Similarly, few outside of the Mormon community and a handful of specialists understand the significance of Mormon undergarments. In other words, without ample explanation, clothing seldom communicates with any degree of precision. Perhaps it is out of the same sense of uncertainty about the intentions of those who wear particular clothes that the robes of Buddhist monks and Catholic priests have for centuries been the subject of intense debate and heated criticisms.[17] At the same time, the tenacity of tradition in the history of clothing suggests that it has a special role to play as a medium of communication, despite its inherent limitations. But beyond the histories and significance of particular types of clothing in particular religious traditions, precisely what it is about religious clothing that makes it a magnet for emotions is an open question.

The Manipulation of Emotions through Material Culture

To this point I may have given the impression that emotions arise spontaneously when sparked by the presence of mute, neutral objects—a purely natural process, whether the result of physiological responses or of slowly developing, barely perceived social norms; one wanders into a temple and is suddenly taken unawares by a flood of religious feelings. Normally, however, emotional responses are *planned* in a process in which all are complicit, from artisans and religious leaders to the devotees themselves. The devotee feels a sense of reverence in a temple or of sorrow when contemplating a painting because that is what he or she is supposed to feel. In Europe, medieval monks and nuns went to great lengths to cultivate emotional states—be they sorrow or joy—before images of Christ or of saints, or before symbolic objects like the cross. Those who manufactured devotional images and those who wrote about them contributed to the effect, ensuring that the devotee would achieve the state he or she pursued. For this reason, unraveling the dynamics involved requires the combined talents of art historians, theologians, and social historians.[18]

Buddhist monks similarly have laid down detailed instructions for how to achieve blissful visions from guided contemplation of icons or mandalas.[19] And like prayer in a Christian context, meditative states in Buddhism (which we normally think of as being entirely internal) are often achieved with the help of particular settings, such as the meditation hall or cell; or devices, such as the meditation chair or pillow, or the stick carried by the master of the meditation hall, an ever-present warning against falling asleep.

Shamans, too, frequently employ ritual objects—costumes, drums, bells, swords, mirrors—in order to enter into trance.[20] The symbolism and function of these objects vary. They may serve a direct, physiological purpose. Taiwanese mediums, for instance, use a sword to lacerate their backs, inflicting physical pain that is endured only because of the trance into which they have entered, at once demonstrating the validity of their state while perhaps at the same time contributing to it. The physiological effect of drugs used to elicit particular states is of course even more apparent. Less direct, though no less vital, are articles of clothing, such as the cap worn by shamans among the Nenets of Siberia. When, in a secular context, Nenet shamans performed ceremonies for interested outsiders, they did so without the caps, signaling a very different approach to the ritual, accompanied no doubt by a different emotional state.[21]

In addition to such voluntary processes in which specific emotions are carefully cultivated by the individual, material culture provides a useful entry point as well for understanding the more sinister manipulation of emotion on a larger scale for political, ideological, and even military ends. Assemblies are enthused and troops mobilized with physical and mental images of banners, temples, crosses, and photographs, stirred by the public destruction of the most sacred objects of their enemies, or enraged by the decimation of their own sacred things. Objects are as much a part of the vocabulary in public religious settings as words are.

On a more subtle level, rulers of varying degrees of sincerity employ religious objects to assert their legitimacy and authority. Two examples from China illustrate the twin poles of pious commitment and disinterested manipulation. The greatest public project to reverence Buddhist relics in Chinese history was carried out in the sixth century by Emperor Wen of the Sui, who distributed relics thought to be of the Buddha to various far-flung parts of the empire in an elaborate, carefully orchestrated campaign that at once demonstrated his position as highest caretaker of the religion and his authority over a vast geographic empire that he had only recently unified. While the political motivations for carrying out the campaign are manifest—local and central officials from throughout the empire were required to participate in the ceremonies—we have no reason to doubt the emotional responses of local devotees who witnessed the installation of the relics, or the personal sincerity of the emperor, who openly professed his devotion to Buddhism. Similar examples of religious leaders from various times and places who encouraged pilgrimage to sacred sites out of a blend of pious and practical motivations readily come to mind. At the other motivational extreme, in the 1950s Chairman Mao and Zhou Enlai also encouraged a tour of a Chinese Buddhist relic to Burma and Ceylon. Again, the emotional response of Buddhists in those countries was no doubt genuine, but the motivations of Mao and Zhou (who hoped to solidify international relations) were completely devoid of any religious sentiments; indeed, both had on repeated occasions expressed their contempt for Buddhism and all religion.[22] This second case illustrates how the distance objects supply at times makes them more appealing than language. One can hardly imagine Mao delivering a Buddhist sermon to the people of Burma, while it was a simple matter for him to allow the transport of a Buddhist relic there. Objects, that is, are less contaminating and, in a sense, more readily disposed of than language or ritual behavior.

Less obviously, imposing religious architecture, monumental sculpture, and the elaborate garments or precious ritual objects of a religious elite convey a sense of authority and may in turn provoke a sense of cowed submission among ordinary devotees. The dynamics in this relationship between authority, religious objects, and emotion is subtle, and the hardened cynic can miss as much as the wide-eyed naïf when assessing the motivations of those in authority who employ objects with religious associations to elicit emotional responses from their followers; while the pope may derive much of his authority from the material culture that surrounds him, he ultimately has little choice in the matter, since the vestments and ritual paraphernalia are as much a part of the post as the doctrinal training and ritual procedures that secured it for him. Regardless of motivation, objects often provide a crucial link between emotions and ideology, religion and politics; they supply the lubricant that makes this complex and ever-changing mechanism run smoothly.

Emotions Attributed to Objects

On occasion, instead of eliciting emotions in people, objects are said to themselves embody sentiments. More than literary device, the attribution of feelings to objects assumes the miraculous presence of divinity in what are normally inanimate things. This is particularly common in the case of images that are frequently described, in various religious traditions, as rising to anger, grief, joy, and other emotions. Images weep, sweat, shout, and bleed. This is readily understandable: since images are made to look like people and are often thought to be in some sense alive, it is natural that they should express human emotions; this is particularly the case for religious images, since they represent people extraordinary in life and powerful still after death. Here, though, while there may be some correspondence between the emotions exhibited by the icon and the figure it represents, the correspondence is, curiously, often a loose one. While images of the Virgin have, from medieval times to the present, been seen to weep, no biblical passage refers to Mary weeping. And while the biblical Mary certainly had cause to weep, the prevalence of this particular characteristic is more closely related to her postmortem legacy, and more specifically to the biography of her icon, than it is to the character of Mary as presented in the Gospels. It is precisely this disjunction between the literary-historical figure and his or her icon that makes the history of the icon useful for the study of the history of emotions; for the weeping icon responds to the emotional needs of its contemporaries rather than to the demands of artistic or theological accuracy. At the same time, the meaning of the icon's tears is subject to interpretation, as it can be read as a sign of joy, sorrow, pity, or even anger.

We encounter a more striking example of the incongruence between an icon and the historical figure on which it is based in the case of the Buddha. Accounts of images of the Buddha in China describe how an image perspired nervously when bandits approached the monastery in which it was housed, or how an image of the Buddha appeared in a dream to angrily rebuke a disciple who had not kept him in good repair. Such stories are surprising since in accounts of the Buddha himself, the Buddha is in complete control of his emotions, never becoming angry and certainly never sweating from fear of a physical threat.[23] Both cases illustrate the subtle interplay between literary tradition, objects, history and the emotional needs of devotees that constitute the material culture of literate religious traditions. That is, just as material culture allows for distance in the manipulation of emotions by religious and secular authorities, so, too, does it allow room for maneuvering between canonical doctrine and everyday belief—the subject of the following section.

Everyday Objects, Ordinary Feelings

My focus thus far has been on intense emotions in extraordinary contexts: the ecstasy of a shaman in trance, the anger of a crowd driven to violence, the weeping of saints, and the wonder of devotees in the presence of the miraculous. Objects tend to play a role in all of these emotional experiences. But objects play a role in more pedestrian, though not necessarily less important, feelings as well. In his studies on household goods, Mihalyi Csikszentmihalyi explores the psychological dangers of a world without objects. The natural state of the mind, he argues, is "psychic entropy," disconnected ruminations leading to anxiety and emotional instability. In the struggle to avoid this state, objects help to give a sense of direction and stability, providing continuity of time (in, for instance, photographs and mementos) and help as well to consolidate the fragmentary self by providing markers of identity.[24] What is important in such objects is not their aesthetic or economic value, or even their value as status markers, but their ability to evoke emotional connections to one's past and to others. The same holds true for ordinary religious objects. That is, if the objects discussed above represent in large measure the quest for excitement in religion, another set of more prosaic things are necessary to satisfy the need for stability and routine.[25]

Colleen McDannel begins her book *Material Christianity* with a picture of a poor, rural American family in a humble government-built home. The room pictured contains what are clearly religious paintings—an image of Jesus (*Ecce Homo*), and the *Infant Samuel*—but hung next to an obviously secular image of a child playing with a dog on a calendar. McDannel points out that there is no separate, sacred space in the house. The same holds true for other images of the interiors of houses in her book. Such images are not normally thought to contain sacred power and are often not the objects of worship or prayer, at least not when hung on the wall in the home, over a sofa or next to a piano. That is, while in other contexts a painting of a suffering Jesus may be the focus of prayer, contemplation, empathy, and intense emotion, in the household it often provides a much more subdued, consistent emotional experience.

The same holds true, for instance, for the Buddhist prayer beads hanging from the mirror of a taxi in Taipei. Buddhist prayer beads have a history of close to two thousand years. The standard modern Buddhist rosary conforms to prescriptions given in ancient Buddhist scriptures that stipulate that the string of prayer beads is to have 108 beads. Each of the beads signifies one of the "108 afflictions." Buddhist scriptures describe how devotees are to use the rosary to count various sorts of recitations, most commonly the name of the buddha Amitabha, to accumulate religious merit and to calm the mind.[26] But the busy taxi driver, swerving to miss the bus crowding his lane, does not employ the rosary hanging from his rear-view mirror for recitations, to contemplate the 108 afflictions, accumulate merit, or even cultivate his mind. For some, such rosaries serve an apotropaic function, to protect car and driver from accident, as well as an aesthetic function, but, more important, they serve a less explicit, poorly defined emotional function, providing a vague sense of spiritual comfort. A wide range of religious articles fall into this category of objects, as prevalent as it is nebulous, that has thus far largely eluded the attention of scholars of religious studies.

Conclusion

Ideally, an essay in a handbook such as this should summarize the relevant research and highlight recent scholarly trends. In the case of religion, emotion, and material culture, however, the best I can do is to point to the general trend toward the study of material culture in religion in general. The subdiscipline of the role of the material culture of religion in emotional experience does not yet exist. I hope that the preceding has shown that this lack of scholarly literature is not because of the inherent insignificance of the topic but stems instead from the tendency to see religion in general, and emotions in particular, as essentially internal phenomena, whether they be the cerebral reflections of the theologian or the emotional states of an illiterate devotee. And while my emphasis here has been on what specialists in the study of emotions can learn from attention to objects, art historians and archaeologists have at least as much to gain by exploring the role of emotions in the objects of their research as well.

Notes

1. For a brief survey of definitions of "material culture" see Thomas J. Schlereth, ed., *Material Culture Studies in America* (Nashville: American Association for State and Local History, 1982), 1–75; for a more sustained discussion of the term, see Michael Brian Schiffer, *The Material Life of Human Beings: Artifacts, Behavior, and Communication* (London: Routledge, 1999).

2. For examples of works that *have* addressed the role of material culture in religion, see Colleen McDannell, *Material Christianity: Religion and Popular Culture in America* (New Haven, Conn.: Yale University Press, 1995); David Morgan, *Visual Piety: A History and Theory of Popular Religious Images* (Berkeley: University of California Press, 1998); John Kieschnick, *The Impact of Buddhism on Chinese Material Culture* (Princeton, N.J.: Princeton University Press, 2003).

3. McDannell, *Material Christianity*, 4–8.

4. Gregory Schopen, "Archaeology and Protestant Presuppositions in the Study of Indian Buddhism," chap. 1 in *Bones, Stones, and Buddhist Monks: Collected Papers on the Archaeology, Epigraphy, and Texts of Monastic Buddhism in India* (Honolulu: University of Hawai'i Press, 1997).

5. Friedrich Schleiermacher, *On Religion: Speeches to Its Cultured Despisers* (Cambridge: Cambridge University Press, 1988), 119.

6. Chinese landscape painting was primarily the provenance of literati who tended to look askance at temple murals and religious statuary, both of which, in contrast to the more restrained, minimalist landscapes, are filled with color and detail.

7. For discussion of the Bible as object, see "The Bible in the Victorian Home," in McDannell, *Material Christianity*, 67–102. More generally, on the way even those who profess a distaste for material things of necessity employ them, see Birgit Meyer, "Christian Mind and Worldly Matters: Religion and Materiality in the Nineteenth-Century Gold

Coast," *Journal of Material Culture* 2, 3 (1997): 311–37; and Allan I. Ludwig, *Graven Images: New England Stonecarving and Its Symbols, 1650–1815* (Middletown, Conn.: Wesleyan University Press, 2000); I have made a similar argument for Buddhist suspicion of the material world in *The Impact of Buddhism*.

8. Quoted in William A. Christian, Jr., "Provoked Religious Weeping in Early Modern Spain," in *Religious Organization and Religious Experience*, edited by J. Davis (London: Academic Press, 1982), 110.

9. Christian, "Provoked Religious Weeping in Early Modern Spain," 100.

10. One notable exception being Christian, "Provoked Religious Weeping." For a general study of icons in the West, see Hans Belting, *Likeness and Presence: A History of the Image before the Era of Art*, translated from the German by Edmund Jephcott (Chicago: University of Chicago Press, 1994).

11. For the classic presentation of the "decay of aura" of artwork in modern times, see Walter Benjamin, "The Work of Art in the Age of Mechanical Reproduction," in *Illuminations: Essays and Reflections* (New York: Harcourt Brace Jovanovich, 1968). For discussion of the problem in a Buddhist context, see Bernard Faure, "The Buddhist Icon and the Modern Gaze," *Critical Inquiry* 24 (1988): 768–813.

12. Robert H. Sharf, "On the Allure of Buddhist Relics," *Representations* 66 (1999): 75–99.

13. This is one of the major themes of Lindsay Jones, *The Hermeneutics of Sacred Architecture: Experience, Interpretation, Comparison* (Cambridge, Mass.: Harvard University Press, 2000).

14. "Mormon Garments: Sacred Clothing and the Body," in McDannell, *Material Christianity*, 198–221.

15. Grant McCracken, "Clothing as Language: An Object Lesson in the Study of the Expressive Properties of Material Culture," in *Material Anthropology: Contemporary Approaches to Material Culture*, edited by Barrie Reynolds and Margaret A. Stott (New York: University Press of America, 1987), 103–28.

16. For a useful collection of essays on the Muslim veil, see Sajida Sultana Alvi et al., eds., *The Muslim Veil in North America: Issues and Debates* (Toronto: Women's Press, 2003).

17. I have discussed the history of monastic clothing in Chinese Buddhism in *The Impact of Buddhism*, 86–115. For priests' robes in Christianity, see Louis Trichet, *Le costume du clergé: Ses origines et son évolution en France d'après les réglements de l'Eglise* (Paris: Cerf, 1986).

18. See Eugène Honée, "Image and Imagination in the Medieval Culture of Prayer," in *The Art of Devotion in the Late Middle Ages in Europe*, edited by Henk van Os (Princeton, N.J.: Princeton University Press, 1994), 157–72.

19. Peter Harvey, *An Introduction to Buddhism: Teachings, History, and Practices* (Cambridge: Cambridge University Press, 1990), 264–65; Stanley K. Abe, "Art and Practice in a Fifth-Century Chinese Buddhist Cave Temple," *Ars Orientalis* 20 (1990): 1–31.

20. For some examples, see "Symbolism of the Shaman's Costume and Drum" in Mircea Eliade, *Shamanism: Archaic Techniques of Ecstasy* (1951), translated by Willard R. Trask (Princeton, N.J.: Princeton University Press, 1972), 145–80.

21. Ibid., 154.

22. I discuss these two cases in more detail in *The Impact of Buddhism*, 36–44.

23. Ibid., 63–69.

24. Mihalyi Csikszentmihalyi, "Why We Need Things," in *History from Things: Essays on Material Culture*, edited by Stephen Lubar and W. David Kingery (Washington, D.C.:

Smithsonian Institution Press, 1993), 20–29. This essay draws on Csikszentmihalyi's longer work (together with Eugene Rochberg-Halton) *The Meaning of Things: Domestic Symbols and the Self* (New York: Cambridge University Press, 1981).

25. On the two poles of routine and excitement, see Norbert Elias and Eric Dunning, *Quest for Excitement: Sport and Leisure in the Civilizing Process* (Oxford: Blackwell, 1993). On "prosaic objects" in religion, see Morgan, *Visual Piety*.

26. Kieschnick, *The Impact of Buddhism*, 116–137.

BIBLIOGRAPHY

Abe, Stanley K. "Art and Practice in a Fifth-Century Chinese Buddhist Cave Temple." *Ars Orientalis* 20 (1990): 1–31.

Belting, Hans. *Likeness and Presence: A History of the Image before the Era of Art*. Translated by Edmund Jephcott. Chicago: University of Chicago Press, 1994.

Benjamin, Walter. "The Work of Art in the Age of Mechanical Reproduction." In *Illuminations: Essays and Reflections*, translated by Harry Zohn. New York: Harcourt Brace Jovanovich, 1968, 211–44.

Christian, William A., Jr. "Provoked Religious Weeping in Early Modern Spain." In *Religious Organization and Religious Experience*, edited by J. Davis. London: Academic Press, 1982, 97–114.

Csikszentmihalyi, Mihalyi. "Why We Need Things." In *History from Things: Essays on Material Culture*, edited by Stephen Lubar and W. David Kingery. Washington, D.C.: Smithsonian Institution Press, 1993, 20–29.

Csikszentmihalyi, Mihalyi, and Eugene Rochberg-Halton. *The Meaning of Things: Domestic Symbols and the Self*. New York: Cambridge University Press, 1981.

Eliade, Mircea. *Shamanism: Archaic Techniques of Ecstasy* (1951), translated by Willard R. Trask. Princeton, N.J.: Princeton University Press, 1972.

Elias, Norbert, and Eric Dunning. *Quest for Excitement: Sport and Leisure in the Civilizing Process*. Oxford: Blackwell, 1993.

Faure, Bernard. "The Buddhist Icon and the Modern Gaze." *Critical Inquiry* 24 (1988): 768–813.

Harvey, Peter. *An Introduction to Buddhism: Teachings, History, and Practices*. Cambridge: Cambridge University Press, 1990.

Honée, Eugène. "Image and Imagination in the Medieval Culture of Prayer." In *TheArt of Devotion in the Late Middle Ages in Europe*, edited by Henk van Os. Princeton, N.J.: Princeton University Press, 1994, 157–72.

Jones, Lindsay. *The Hermeneutics of Sacred Architecture: Experience, Interpretation, Comparison*. Cambridge, Mass.: Harvard University Press, 2000.

Kieschnick, John. *The Impact of Buddhism on Chinese Material Culture*. Princeton, N.J.: Princeton University Press, 2003.

Ludwig, Allan I. *Graven Images: New England Stonecarving and Its Symbols, 1650–1815*. Middletown, Conn.: Wesleyan University Press, 2000.

McCracken, Grant. "Clothing as Language: An Object Lesson in the Study of the Expressive Properties of Material Culture." In *Material Anthropology: Contemporary Approaches to Material Culture*, edited by Barrie Reynolds and Margaret A. Stott. New York: University Press of America, 1987, 103–28.

McDannell, Colleen. *Material Christianity: Religion and Popular Culture in America*. New Haven, Conn.: Yale University Press, 1995.

Meyer, Birgit. "Christian Mind and Worldly Matters: Religion and Materiality in the Nineteenth-Century Gold Coast." *Journal of Material Culture* 2, 3 (1997): 311–37.

Morgan, David. *Visual Piety: A History and Theory of Popular Religious Images*. Berkeley: University of California Press, 1998.

Schiffer, Michael Brian. *The Material Life of Human Beings: Artifacts, Behavior, and Communication*. London: Routledge, 1999.

Schleiermacher, Friedrich. *On Religion: Speeches to Its Cultured Despisers*. Cambridge: Cambridge University Press, 1988.

Schlereth, Thomas J., ed. *Material Culture Studies in America*. Nashville: American Association for State and Local History, 1982.

Schopen, Gregory. "Archaeology and Protestant Presuppositions in the Study of Indian Buddhism." Chap. 1 of Schopen, *Bones, Stones, and Buddhist Monks: Collected Papers on the Archaeology, Epigraphy, and Texts of Monastic Buddhism in India*. Honolulu: University of Hawai'i Press, 1997, 1–22.

Sharf, Robert H. "On the Allure of Buddhist Relics." *Representations* 66 (1999): 75–99.

Trichet, Louis. *Le costume du clergé: Ses origines et son évolution en France d'après les réglements de l'Eglise*. Paris: Cerf, 1986.

PART III
EMOTIONAL STATES

CHAPTER 13

ECSTASY

ANGELIKA MALINAR AND HELENE BASU

Among the many emotions that may be evoked and sought after in religious practice, ecstasy is an emotional state reserved by definition for extraordinary occasions and fields of performance and discourse. In this case, the demarcation line between daily life and the unusual is clearly drawn and serves as a precondition for ecstasy's manifestation. However, it often shares the space that many cultural contexts concede for extraordinary experiences with adjacent emotional states like aesthetic rapture or sexual ecstasy. This explains the fluidity of religious ecstasy, which time and again is not only expressed in poetic language using erotic metaphors or at least metaphors of desire but also evoked in the context of textual recitations and musical performances.[1] This inclusion of erotic and aesthetic aspects can be regarded as enhancing the potential attraction of this emotion for those who practice a religion. On the other hand, this is also one reason why the guardians of religious doctrines and ethics have tended to regard ecstatic practices with skepticism. This is especially true of religions that base the success of religious life on the control of the emotions and the study of scripture. Often this is combined with creating a congregational hierarchy of representatives who pass judgments on individual or collective behavior as more or less conforming to what is regarded as the true teaching. Therefore, ecstatic practices are frequently deemed heretic or subaltern, especially when practiced in groups that include individuals from the margins of religious orthodoxy on a more egalitarian basis that is temporarily oblivious to social or gender distinctions.[2] This does not preclude the possibility that ecstatic practices may be at the center of a religious community and in certain local contexts followed by many believers of religions that otherwise reject ecstasy.[3] Compared to other religious paths, some ecstatic practices allow for an intensification of certain emotions that may overwhelm groups as well as individuals and result in behavior that is otherwise regarded as transgressing the rules of decency, thus evoking emotions of shame and embarrassment. However, to be capable of this emotional intensity was often regarded as a sign of religious achievement and even as a proof of the reality of the absolute or the divine. Certain similarities between the expression of ecstasy and the symptoms of what was often interpreted as mental or emotional disturbance or as signs of disobedience and nonconformity have made these practices a contested topic in both religious and scholarly discourses. At stake in many of these arguments have been questions that touch on the very relationship between religion and emotion. Should emotions be activated, or should they be suppressed or sublimated in order to reach the final goal? Can the transcendent entity be experienced while remaining in the body, and can intensive emotionality be accepted as proof of it? Or do we just meet people indulging in self-induced enthusiasm over their own feelings?[4]

Academic Approaches

In a great deal of academic research, ecstasy has been if not equated with then often juxtaposed to (spirit-) possession or seizure on the one hand and "shamanistic journeys" outside the body on the other. Perhaps the original meaning of the Greek word, namely, "placed outside or beside" or "being dislocated" has influenced this association, as both possession and ecstasy are phenomenologically related. To the outside observer, the person may display symptoms of a loss of self-control, of not being oneself or of being "beside" oneself, that resemble each other, such as glossolalia, uncoordinated gestures, the uncontrolled or unmotivated expression of other emotions like laughter, tears, and so on. This convergence is one of the reasons that ecstasy has now become an "umbrella" term that seems to cover too many phenomena to allow a definition. Moreover, the word "ecstasy" is quite often used without any explanation or just serves as a catchword in the title of a publication though it is not prominent in the running text.[5]

Early research stressed the connection between possession and ecstasy from a psychiatric point of view, classifying it together with other forms of "hysteria," "trance," or "altered states of consciousness" and distinguishing it according to what incites its manifestation (prayers, dancing, drugs etc.). While some scholars have defined its convergence with trance as "suggestive absorption," others have interpreted it as a state of consciousness characterized by "overalertness."[6] Some researchers have also pointed to certain similarities between ecstasy and trance as sharing qualities of the so-called flow experience, that is, a pleasant, self-forgetful merging of activity and mental concentration without losing self-control.[7] This line of research, stressing the similarity of ecstatic practices on the basis of general human psychology, has now become fused with studies of the medical and biophysiological aspects of emotions. Thus, for instance, possession has been traced back to nutritional deficiency.[8]

By the 1950s, ecstasy had also become a well-established topic in anthropological, sociological, and religious studies. Ecstatic practices were not only ethnographically documented but also analytically embedded within their respective cultural and historical contexts. The sociocultural factors that make ecstasy a multiform phenomenon embedded in divergent practices and both scholarly and popular discourses were explored. Seminal for many studies is Ioan M. Lewis's examination of how possession cults converge and relate to the power structures within a society. Ecstasy (equated by Lewis with possession) is seen as a way of expressing and dealing with the concerns of those groups that find themselves at the lower end or on the margins of the social hierarchy.[9] It is argued that ecstasy is the preferred religious practice of women and of the afflicted and is used as a means to achieve goals normally denied them. In this connection, the therapeutic dimensions of ecstasy and possession are stressed, in that they help an individual to overcome a crisis and to continue with his or her life. Recent studies, conversely, rejecting the hypothesis of marginality, focus on ecstatic possession as a means of negotiating social roles, questions of gender and cultural constructions of the "self" and the "other." According to V. Crapanzano, possession can be regarded as a "cultural idiom" that allows specific forms of experience to be communicated.[10] Following this perspective, possession and ecstasy can be viewed as an event in which cultural texts are produced.[11] As a form of communication, possession was also studied as a mimetic reproduction or enacting of individual and collective histories.[12]

While psychological explanations tend to focus on the similarity of ecstasy and stress that it is a capacity rooted in the human organism, anthropological studies explore the diversity of the phenomenon that emerges from the situated nature of emotions, their experience and expression in specific social and cultural contexts. Oscillating between the two approaches are studies of literary documents of ecstasy.[13] In many traditions, oral and written texts are not only important media that are used to evoke ecstatic states but also modes of expression and interpretation. There are also studies of mystical language, or rather the language of mystics, that emphasize that it not only aims to express ecstatic experience mimetically but also often explores the limitations of language itself. Thereby language is turned into a medium of the desired mystic union with the transcendent entity. Research on "ecstatic literature" provides an insight not only into how ecstasy was interpreted but also into how it was modeled and transmitted as a desirable mode of experience.[14] Hagiographies and autobiographies of ecstatics have proved crucial in shaping and advertising ecstasy as traditions of emotionality. In the following discussion, the different approaches as well as levels of studying ecstasy will be referred to, although another perspective will be offered that treats the place of ecstasy in relation to the larger framework in which religions interpret and deal with the emotions. This implies a focus on concepts of the body, cognition, and experience that are developed in diverse religious traditions. As we have pointed out, the convergence of ecstasy, shamanism and possession has created analytical and definitional difficulties that lead us to plead for maintaining terminological distinctions.[15] Thus, all three shall be regarded as related but distinct phenomena, the aim being to qualify the usual equation between possession and ecstasy that is characteristic of many studies, especially anthropological ones. Having drawn these distinctions, we will reserve the word "ecstasy" for the experience of an emotional state that is self-referential: ecstasy is experienced as such. Ecstasy as an emotional experience thus is based on awareness, not on amnesia, although its intensity may result in a loss of consciousness and is thereby brought to its end. In this regard, ecstasy as an emotion differs from possession, hypnosis, or trance, of which the person often has no memory. However, we will show that there are no insurmountable boundaries between the different forms and practices but that they can be experienced alternately by the same groups or individual; this will be analyzed by studying texts as well as living traditions of performance. Their classification is based on differences in the physical reactions, the degree of awareness, and self-control. In this way, the term "ecstasy" is retained as a common denominator for an emotional state that is characterized by intensity and awareness and is embedded in a complex and heterogeneous field of practices and experiences that unfolds in many cultural contexts and is probably based on a psychophysical capacity that all human beings share but do not all necessarily activate.

Ecstasy, Possession, and Shamanism

It is not only for analytical purposes that it seems useful to maintain a terminological distinction between ecstasy and possession but also because, in most religious traditions, these two modes of experience are regarded as different on the terminological, doctrinal, and ritual levels. However, especially in ritual contexts, blending and oscillation allow participants to have different experiences. Many religious traditions explain these distinctions by referring to the objective and subjective sides of ecstasy. Thus one finds on the one hand comments on specific forms of emotional self-perception, consciousness, and bodily expression of the subject and on the other classifications of emotional states according to the object of the ecstatic experience for example, (a) god, spirit, ancestor, demon, angel, saint, the self, or the void. Accordingly, one can distinguish these states according to (1) the degree of consciousness and self-perception that go along with either ecstasy or possession, and (2) the intensity of bodily reactions, which, in religious discourse, are often related to notions of the absence or presence of self-control and power.

Thus, what has variously been termed seizure, possession or, more neutrally, embodiment is frequently seen as a temporary relinquishing of one's body to another who can be a deity, an (ancestor-) spirit or a demon. Characteristic of this state is the fact that the "host" has no memory of what happened during the embodiment but can only describe the moments of arrival and departure and the consequences of the contact. In some contexts the host-body acts as a medium addressed for divination or consultation by the members of the ritual group that is participating in the occasion.[16] In many cultural contexts, the spirit is encountered during a therapeutic session in which the ritual specialist controls and channels the contact with embodied spirits. These sessions are focused on the individual who is undergoing treatment, which may be directed toward either reestablishing good relationships with the spirit or its exorcism. Both contexts indicate a purposeful exploitation of the capacity and desire of gods, spirits, or demons to reside temporarily in a human body. In yet other ritual contexts, the group invites spirits to a celebration that serves the purpose of social bonding by sharing its pleasure. This "positive" form of possession has also been called "ceremonial" or "ritual" possession,[17] which is often related to ancestor spirits. Practices related to these spirits are often connected with notions of the memory and history of the performing group,[18] and may therefore also include the spirits of outsiders—for example, foreigners, colonizers, or oppressors—and may reflect the advent of new techniques in a familiar cultural setting (for example, railways, planes, etc. in the *zar* cult of Northern Sudan). Possession is frequently either a dialogical process between the client and the ritual specialist or an intragroup interaction in which those who are not in direct contact with a spirit see the embodiment and take care of it, while those who in the course of the ritual surrender their body to possession go through it rather unconsciously and feel the consequences, like well-being or empowerment, only afterward. This is very different from ecstasy, an emotional, cognitive, and physical experience that is perceived while and as it happens.

However, "possession" also differs from another form of contact with non-human beings, which, since Eliade's seminal study, has been called shamanistic ecstasy.[19] In this case, the individual shaman is said to leave his or her visible body in order to travel to some otherwise hidden region "out there" and to meet spirits, ancestors, or gods to obtain knowledge or other forms of power. The shaman usually remembers these journeys or reports the contact in "sacred signs," which may be poems, songs, paintings, and so on. These journeys are often associated with dreaming, which is often regarded as a state in which the body opens itself up to contact with the outer world and its inhabitants. This ecstatic state is often induced by using certain instruments like ritual coats, musical instruments, or drugs (e.g., Siberian mushrooms, Vedic *soma*, Mexican peyote). Interest in the latter, in particular, has led to research on the chemical effects of hallucinogens that cause this altered state of consciousness. The use of "Ecstasy," the "designer drug" of the late twentieth century, recalls this dimension (for a second time, following the mid-twentieth-century discovery of LSD and revival of esoteric subcultures), while at the same time narrowing contemporary popular perceptions of ecstatic experience to club-nights, love-parades, and their aftermaths in the form of addiction or mental disturbance. In contrast to so-called possession, the attraction of these states consists in the experience of an expanded consciousness and alertness, often accompanied by a surge of physical empowerment and sensual intensity that, for instance, give one the feeling that one can fly or perceive otherwise invisible phenomena. The ecstatic quality of this experience consists in the overflowing of those emotions that are valued as pleasant and positive—feelings of bliss, love, desire, and lightness. These signs of what psychological research has called "over-alertness" connect the shamanistic mode of ecstasy with ecstasy as an emotional state that mediates and at the same time consists in a direct encounter with the very goal that is central to any religious tradition. This can be regarded as a temporary realization of the soteriological teachings of the religious tradition the adept is following. Often, this implies a direct use and even training of the desired emotional capacities of the adept. Rather than embodying "another" being, one is called on to embody one's own emotions, and this experience is thus regarded as a way one not only meets the object of its quest but undertakes a highly pleasant journey into oneself that in most cases leaves one asking for more. This form of ecstasy results in bodily and emotional transformations and provokes scholarly theological interpretations that allow religious ecstasy to be studied as an emotional state of its own. Therefore, it has often been connected to mysticism as a special branch of religious activity and emotionality. This has often been related in its turn to concepts of power and empowerment, inspiration, and the production of charisma (like the Hindu *shakti*, the Sufi *barakat*, or the Christian *charismata*).

Ecstasy as an Emotional State

As an emotional state, ecstasy is characterized by a double-sidedness, since it comprises surrendering to both object- and subject-experiences. Thus, ecstasy can be regarded not only as a specific reaction to an experience of the religious object but also as an intense mode of self-perception and awareness by the ecstatic subject. In contrast to other emotions that may be regarded as obstacles to the realization of religious aspirations, the ecstatic intensification of certain emotions is, in certain contexts, welcomed as a bridge that connects the adept to that very absolute, divine, and transcendent entity, realm, or state taught in the religious doctrine. The ecstatic experience results in temporal contact with that realm in terms of direct experience (as in Hindu *darshana*, Sufi *hal* or *wajd*, or Catholic *visio beatificatia*), immersion (as in Vedantic *brahman* or Christian *unio mystica*), release of the "self" from the body (as in some yogic practices), or the vanishing of notions of "self" to open up the space of a blissful emptiness (as in some Buddhist meditation practices). All these practices arise from the quest for an immediate and sensual experience of the absolute, of "tasting" or "touching" a salvation that is usually considered to be dependent on leaving the body and the world for good. This synaesthetic character of ecstasy has often been stressed, as ecstatics not only hear God's voice, for example, but also taste it, they feel colors, and so on. In order to account for this extraordinary sensuality, the Catholic tradition, for instance, teaches specific "spiritual sensations." This quest for an experiential knowledge of God (what Thomas Aquinas called *cognitio dei experimentalis*) results in ecstasy as a temporal accomplishment of eternity and divinity that may only emphasize the transience and boundaries of worldly existence. Paradoxically, the experience of union may also imply the realization of an unbridgeable distance and result in a more or less permanent state of unfulfilled desire and longing that may take different forms, ranging from depression or love-sickness to an intense longing for death.

Ecstatic experiences create an emotional reality that may change an individual's mode of being by turning him or her into an ascetic, hermit, monk, nun, or stranger in this world. The last term would most precisely recall the Greek and then Latin notions of ecstasy as dislocation and even alienation, of living in the world while possessing contact with the otherworldly that works like a fissure. This is also one of the reasons why ecstatics or mystics not only are delving into happiness and bliss but also are often seen as suffering from depression and alienation, from feeling displaced in this world yet not being a fully-fledged resident of the other world. Often they are confused with other alienated "strangers" like madmen, fools, or lunatics.[20] More often than not, the symptoms of ecstasy, madness, and possession are hard to distinguish while they are being manifested. The ecstatic, however, is able time and again to function in the world and take on the role of a specialist—as a religious leader, prophet, teacher, healer, or singer. Many religious traditions acknowledge the paradoxical nature of ecstasy and highlight the particular blend of physical, emotional, cognitive, and performative dimensions that ecstasy calls for. This can be put in more concrete terms with the help of certain aspects of yogic traditions that can be regarded as mapping recurrent themes and methods of mystic ecstasy and empowerment, which are not only applied in the Buddhist and Jain traditions but also come to the fore in many Hindu and Sufi ecstatic practices in India.

The Silent Ecstasy of Meditation

In many religions, contemplation and meditation are taught as means to achieve the intense sensual and cognitive awareness that is devoid of ego-centered reflections and interest and allows for the immediate presence of the object of meditation. These objects may vary according to the spiritual stage of the adept, but in each case their appearance is regarded as an intense experience that may not only provoke pleasant emotions but also involve an encounter with pain, terror, and anxiety. Although ecstatic practices aim at contact with an entity or realm that is regarded as providing ultimate and indescribable happiness and bliss, so that the emotions chosen for intensification are among the happier ones, other emotions must be dealt with along the way. As a spiritual path, the quest for contact with the divine or with one's essential self in an earthly body implies an encounter with its limitations. Thus, in contrast to temporary experiences of ecstasy at festivals or in ritual or therapeutic contexts, ecstasy as a religious path is based on enduring individual practice. The practice is often modeled on cultural traditions related to exceptional individuals who represent the technique and its success for later followers. Although these practices allow for comparison, they and the traditions related to them differ widely, again showing that the ways emotions are defined, selected, and dealt with in ecstatic practices are dependent on the cultural context and language of their articulation.

Yoga is one of those religious traditions that epitomize certain aspects of ecstasy and can even be regarded as a mapping of its preconditions. Yogic traditions encompass a wide range of techniques that bear different fruits, which have been variously interpreted.[21] As a repertoire of useful methods of sensual and mental control, yoga has been used not only in many Hindu traditions but also in Buddhism and Jainism. The oldest extant codification of yoga techniques, the *Yogasutra* of Patanjali, can be dated back to the fourth to fifth centuries C.E. This treatise incorporates different traditions of yoga that are not all based on meditation but also allow the use of external means, such as the consumption of certain herbs. The primary aim of yogic practice is to expel the grip of the ego-related emotions and conceptions that bind the immortal soul (*atman*) to the body. This is achieved by introducing a tight regime of practices to govern the autonomous and thus normally uncontrolled activity of the physical organism, the senses, and the cognitive organs. This results in gaining power over the bodily self, in turning it into "crystal," as the *Yogasutra* puts it, which indicates both invulnerability and transparency (for the subtle light of the immortal self). Correspondingly, a major and enduring task of the practice consists in fighting those emotions that are regarded as obstacles to the perception of the essential self and to the enjoyment of its limitlessness and freedom. The *Yogasutra* mentions three emotions, called "afflictions" (*klesha*) that constantly need counteracting: passion (*raga*), hatred (*dvesha*), and attachment to one's life (*abhinivesha*). Since these emotions are, apart from ignorance (*avidya*), regarded as the most powerful chains between the soul and its body, they pervade and determine the individual's mode of being (*svabhava*) at all levels. Until a yogin has achieved ultimate release, he is threatened by the ever-present temptation to surrender again to one of these emotions and thus lose all his "ascetic capital" and fall back to some lower level of practice (*yogabhrasta*, as he is called in the Bhagavadgita). Indian literature abounds in stories of fallen yogins who have been defeated by intense and powerful outbursts of fury or sexual desire and thus lost the power they had accumulated during their "conquest" (*jaya*) of their physical, sensual, and cognitive nature. A successful yogin experiences ecstasy in quietly enjoying the "ultimate bliss" (*ananda*) in the vision of either his essential self or, in so-called theistic yoga, the god or goddess he believes in. In Buddhism, this happiness consists in discovering the limitlessness and emptiness of one's consciousness, which is normally hidden by the confinements produced by the cardinal emotions and false ideas of the world. The experience of the vastness of time and space, which occurs in the final stages of yogic meditation (*jhana*), indicates the nearness of *nirvana*, of final release, and is praised as a culminating experience that can only be surpassed by *nirvana* itself. In contrast to the performative and highly expressive character of other forms of ecstasy, during this experience the yogi remains "unmoved like a flame in the absence of wind," as one favorite metaphor puts it, and he cannot be disturbed by the outer world—as is illustrated, for instance, by stories about birds nesting on a yogin's head. In all these practices, ecstasy stands at the end of a long path, although it may have been tasted or touched on time and again on the journey.

Counteracting undesirable emotions and attempting to stop the ever-lasting movement of consciousness are characteristic of this practice. In theistic contexts, it is recommended to use textual formulas (*mantras*) or songs of praise (*stotra*) that serve to evoke the deity whose powerful presence one desires. Often, *mantras* and *stotras* are practiced in the context of the so-called *bhakti* traditions, in which the mutual love and affection (*bhakti*) between the god or goddess and the devotee is the basis of the contact and the desire to be in each other's presence. "Vision" (*darshana*) is therefore the declared aim of religious practice, which is focused on the cultivation and expansion of love as a religious emotion. However, the yogic dimension of this emotionality is indicated by the necessity of power and self-control that allows both the overflow of emotion and the overwhelming sensual quality of the appearance of the divine (often described as fiery or dazzling) to be physically endured. Ecstatic vision is thus not only a "state" but also a capacity, and it shows the power and empowerment of anyone who goes through it; sometimes this is regarded as a sign of God's grace. Therefore, the mastery of the physical self results in yoga, as in other traditions, in the acquisition of special powers that indicate that the adept has surmounted his physical limitations. In yoga these are called *siddhis* and are regarded as an inevitable consequence of successful practice. They enable a yogi to fly and to change his size or vulnerability to injuries. However, in the end the yogin must leave these behind if he wants to find the ultimate happiness of release. Ascetic yogic techniques result in an experience of the extra-ordinary happiness of being close to ultimate liberation, which is based in the conquest of certain emotions and results in an overflow of just one feeling: the intensity and joy of insight and vision. More often than not, it has no expression, since it is the intense awareness of absolute consciousness that pervades the individual completely. This self-contained and yet encompassing awareness is not embedded in performative contexts[22] and thus contrasts with the ecstatic performance, as will be shown in the following discussion of the Hindu and Sufi religious traditions.

Ecstasy as the Embodiment of Religious Emotions in Ritual Performances

The Hindu Caitanya Tradition

While some elements of yoga are also used in Hindu ecstatic traditions of *bhakti*, the emphasis is more often on the direct cultivation and intensification of certain emotions through already mentioned methods of *mantra* practice (*japa*), meditation (*dhyana*), and so on. Most important, however, is the expression of these emotions in singing, dancing, or theatrical and ritual performances. Here, the ability to display one's feelings is appreciated as an indicator of the degree to which internal emotions have progressed. In many Hindu traditions, these emotions are called *bhava*, a term that comes from the ancient Indian aesthetic tradition and includes emotions that are interpreted as both "positive" and "negative" (love, heroism, disgust, fear, etc.). By contrast, religious traditions are more selective in their choice of the emotions that should be intensified as much as possible. It is thus no coincidence that emotions are chosen that allow for an enduring presence (love, desire) and do not follow the curve of emotional peak experiences like fury or fear. In most cases, the emotion that is cultivated mirrors the nature of the desired object, in that it is regarded as providing bliss and happiness. Nevertheless, the decisive aspect seems to be that it must be an emotion that may determine one's whole life. What would otherwise be called, from a pathological point of view, an "obsession" is here taken as a sign of a complete emotional surrender to religion.[23] We will show how such a surrender is produced in the Caitanya tradition in Orissa.

This religious community (*sampradaya*) traces itself back to its charismatic founder, Caitanya Mahaprabhu of Navadvipa (1486–1533), who developed a practice of emotional intensification that is transmitted through an ideally uninterrupted succession of teachers. As in other parts of India, the community is institutionalized in monastic centers whose members follow the path as ascetics in most cases. They are organized in different spiritual lineages (*parivara*) that are supported by the lay community. The religious doctrine teaches its followers how to unfold the feeling of love (*srngara* or *prema*) toward Lord Krishna and his divine consort, the goddess Radha. Love as the principle emotion is, however, differentiated according to the actual emotional disposition of the adept. Thus, the devotee can chose between five different types of love relationships and the corresponding emotion. While some concentrate on the development of parental love, others prefer the affection that unfolds with same-sex friends and companions, and others strive to become ecstatic in fulfilling their duties as a servant of the beloved. The highest form, however, is seen in the development of a heterosexual erotic relationship. This points to the gendered character of these emotions, which in turn highlight the cultural notions that determine the perception and expression of feeling. The Caitanya tradition shares with its cultural context the interpretation of love as an emotion that reaches its highest form in women. Love is regarded as a prominent feature of *stribhava*, that is, of the way women exist. As a consequence, the ultimate goal of a male adept is to develop this female emotionality and ultimately to turn into a woman physically, too. Moreover, this practice of transgender emotionality is also necessitated by the prohibition of homosexual desire, which would arise if the male adept began to love his god erotically. Whatever style one adopts, the emotion should be intensified in such a way that one surrenders fully to it and relinquishes all ego-related emotions. Then the intensified emotion turns into *rasa*, its depersonalized relish, which culminates in a state called *unmada* (intoxication), which leads to tears, trembling, stammering, or fainting. Again, the power of the adept is tested and confirmed by the fact that he or she is capable of tolerating this surge of emotion. The occasions and symptoms of a successful intensification of the emotions are described and transmitted in the religious community by personal instruction from a teacher and through written and oral texts. These states are mostly expressed during festivals or song-and-dance performances in which participants may experience and embody ecstasy as an overflow of their cherished emotion which means to encounter the beloved god and experience his grace.

In Orissa, major occasions for public ecstatic performances are the birthday of the founder Caitanya and the annual car-festival for the god Jagannatha and his two siblings in the sacred city of Puri. Since within the Caitanya tradition Jagannatha is regarded as being an incarnation of the god Krishna, and since Caitanya himself spent half of his life in Puri, participation in this all-Orissa festival is indispensable. Followers from all over in India visit Puri at this time and sing and dance all along the route taken by the deities in their huge cars from Jagannatha's temple-palace to his "summer-residence," where they stay for several weeks. *Nama-sankirtana*, the singing and the name and praising of Lord Krishna and his divine consort, Radha, are, apart from the repetitive recitation of *mantras* related to them, the most important practices for a member of the *sampradaya*. This is publicly displayed in a moving group performance that should take place as close to the cars as possible.[24] The heads and members of the monastic institutions, accompanied by male and female lay members, take their allotted place in the procession with groups belonging to other religious communities. Musicians play drums and cymbals, others sing, and yet others dance. The performance consists in evoking the "name" of God (Krishna) by chanting his *mantras* and singing poems that praise and remember the stories of God's presence on earth. Teachers become famous when they compose new poems under the influence of the surge of feeling caused by the presence of Jagannatha-Krishna. Here, ecstasy is connected with enabling poetic and musical creativity. Other members are famous for their dancing in which they try to enact the mythic "circle-dance" (*ras lila*) that, according to tradition, Lord Krishna performed with his female consorts (*gopi*). This dance is a celebration of that love that unfolds in an extramarital love relationship, which is taken as the epitome of love because it will never result in marriage and thus in the final union of lovers living happily ever after. Rather, the emotion of love is regarded as being continuously intensified because of the change between the momentary happiness of the union and the longer periods of suffering from separation. This is especially true for women, as they both risk and tolerate more than their ever-mobile lover; however, this is exactly why women are said to love more. The dancing reaches its peak when all lose themselves in the joy of its performance. People may laugh, smile, shed some tears, jump around clapping their hands, or display perfect female grace. With regard to participation in the car-festival, some hagiographical texts, also about teachers in recent times, report that they have embodied the emotion and the power of love and desire so intensely that the car of Jagannatha has stopped right in front of them, thus testifying to the fact that the love in this case is mutual. However, this has not happened in recent decades, which points not so much to a lack of important charismatic teachers as to certain skepticism regarding the possibility of reaching ecstasy in contemporary circumstances. This mirrors the widespread religious notion that one lives at present in the last "world age" (*kaliyuga*) that is characterized by signs of decay which makes it difficult to realize this goal. This shows that ecstatic practices are not just regarded by outsiders and skeptics, but also by followers of the tradition as a rare religious achievement.

The Sufi Rafa'i Brotherhood

Like many Hindu religious communities, Sufi orders or brotherhoods, in India as elsewhere in the Islamic world, distinguish themselves not only with reference to a specific founder of a spiritual lineage or "chain," but also through different ritual experiences that often involve ecstatic experiences called *hal*. In scholarly discourse, *hal* means a certain stage or phase in approaching God. Although the adept's efforts are regarded as a precondition, *hal* is finally brought about by God's grace and is seen as a sign of his approval. In more popular discourse, *hal* is an unexpected and unpredictable contact with God. It is often experienced by participants in a performance of Quawwali (Sufi devotional music) and is described as an intense joy that is evoked by feeling the nearness to God that is brought about by the songs, the music, and being together with other believers.

Hal may make listeners raise their arms and shake their bodies in self-abandonment, but it may also be experienced as an extreme form of bodily discipline, such as that practiced by members of the Rifa'i brotherhood in Gujarat, who ecstatically pierce their bodies with sharp instruments without inflicting wounds on themselves. The invulnerability of the Rifa'i body is held to be the manifestation of the spiritual power (*baraka* or *karamat*) of the founder saint, the twelfth-century Sufi saint Ahmed Rifa'i of Baghdad. Contemporary spiritual representatives of the Rifa'i brotherhood in Gujarat closely relate the spiritual power to overcome ordinary bodily constraints (such as bleeding when the skin is penetrated with a sharp object) with channeling or purifying the emotion of love or, more specifically, devotional love. In local hagiographic accounts, the manner in which Ahmed Rifa'i was born, leaving his mother's womb with folded hands covering his genitals, foreshadows his later acquisition of spiritual power (*baraka*). As a boy he was instructed in the Qur'an and developed a great interest in the teachings of Sufi masters. He became a disciple of Abdul Quadir Jilani. After becoming a Sufi master in his own right, Abdul Quadir Jilani sent one of his servants to Ahmed Rifa'i to pose the question: "What is love [*ishq*]?" Ahmed Rifa'i replied: "Love is a fire which consumes everything but Allah." While he was speaking these words, the tree under which Ahmed Rifa'i was sitting began to burn, and he was devoured by the flames. Then the fire turned into ice. The servant, distraught at observing what was happening, returned to his master and reported it. Abdul Quadir Jilani told the servant to burn amber and musk and thus to consecrate the place under the tree where Ahmed Rifa'i had been sitting. The servant did as he was told. As soon as the ice melted, Ahmed Rifai's body emerged unscathed. By overcoming the vulnerability of a perishable body, Ahmed Rifa'i had demonstrated that in order to experience pure love (*ishq*), physical passions must be burnt first.

The Rifa'i brotherhood is widely dispersed throughout the Indian Ocean world. In Gujarat (India), it is represented by several shrines (*dargah*) dedicated to the graves of spiritual successors (*pir*) of Ahmed Rifa'i. Annual shrine celebrations commemorating the death of the *pir* provide a ritual framework for a variety of performances of ecstatic love. The celebrations of the anniversaries of saints' deaths are called '*urs*, a term derived from the Arabic for "marriage" or "nuptials." Since the relationship between a *pir* and God is metaphorically expressed as that of a bride longing for her lover, '*urs* rituals celebrate the death of a saint as his mystical union with the divine, that is, as a spiritual marriage to God. In the case of the Rifa'i brotherhood, the "spiritual marriage" ('*urs*) is orchestrated by different kinds of performer, as follows.

The spiritual successor *pir* and *sajjada nishin* (spiritual head of Rifa'i): This person mediates the *baraka* of the founding saint Ahmed Rifa'i by applying his saliva to the bodies of performers of *zarab*. Representing the invulnerability of the Rifa'i body, the posture of the *sajjada nishin* is one of absolute stillness during the '*urs* celebrations.

An "intoxicated" member of the spiritual lineage: In every generation, one male member of the spiritual cum inherited saintly lineage of the Rifa'i dignitaries turns into a *mastan*, that is, is "intoxicated with love." This intoxication is paradoxically expressed by behavior that violates social norms and expectations. During '*urs*, a *mastan* embodies the ecstatic love of God. His unpredictable behavior (for example, sitting around in a stupor, or gesticulating wildly) does not conform to any ritual pattern, thus drawing attention to the spiritual power (*baraka*) that runs in the lineage and is transmitted as a capacity for emotional intoxication.

Musicians playing the *daf* (tambourine): They evoke the sound associated with the Rifa'i brotherhood that helps to bring about a state of *hal* in the performers.

Rifa'i fakirs and lay disciples performing *zarab*: In the contemporary practices of the Rifa'i brotherhood, the spiritual power of Ahmed Rifa'i is realized and his message is manifested in ecstatic performances of body piercing (*zarab*) displayed by both individual male disciples (*murid*) and professional fakirs. Rifaʻi fakirs remain unmarried, having dedicated their life to the devotion of Ahmad Rifaʻi. As a sign of their ritual status, they wear black cloths and live on alms (*bhik*). During the annual shrine celebrations (*ʻurs*), fakirs and lay disciples publicly perform *zarab* at Rifaʻi shrines (*dargah*). Fakirs as well as individual *murids* (followers) step into a circle formed by the musicians and display their skills at using swords, chains, and daggers on their bodies (*zarab*). Some use chains of nails, beating themselves for some minutes without chapping the skin; some pierce their arms and necks with long sharp needles without shedding a drop of blood; others may also lie on a mat strewn with sharp pieces of broken glass, apparently numb; yet another may balance a heavy iron rod on his forehead. Each performance is carried out in a state of *hal*, accompanied by the rhythm of the tambourine (*daf*). Thus, the message of the saint is embodied in emotional experiences of devotion and love in the state of *hal*. Disciples are therefore able to perform *zarab*, that is, violating the body without becoming injured. This is regarded as mirroring the physical invulnerability that demonstrates the spiritual power (*karamat*) of the Rifaʻi, which is based on the capacity to control one's physical nature. At the end, each performer kneels down before the *pir* and receives his blessing in the form of saliva put on his body.

Women from the Sidi community of Bava Gor:[25] While the performers mentioned so far are all male, the Rifaʻi *ʻurs* also provides space for female performers of ecstatic love. Women watch *zarab* performances from a balustrade behind a screen. Toward the end of the ritual sequence, female fakirs from the Sidi community enter the scene "behind the veil," performing for the women. The Sidi women begin to beat drums, shake rattles, and clap their hands, invoking their ancestor-saints who received a share of the Rifaʻi *baraka* through the master-disciple relationship (*pir-murid*). Alluding to the eroticism associated with a wedding, the devout mood gives way to increasing exuberance. The Sidi women sing songs performed at weddings that allude to erotic attractions and sexual acts. One of the Sidi women starts to dance by imitating male movements in the sexual act, while the spectators amuse themselves by cheering on the dancing woman with suggestive questions. The mood lifts, laughter rings out, and the rhythm becomes quicker and wilder until the mood suddenly changes, as most of the Sidi women present experience *hal*. In this case, *hal* is experienced as embodying a male or female ancestor-saint. According to the interpretive scheme of the Sidi, *hal* refers to the practice of embodying an ancestor-saint, that is, women (and men) become "possessed" by her or him. Those who are in *hal* dance wildly. Nobody follows formal rules as to how to dance. In this case, it is not the individual controlling the body in order to channel pure emotion but the reverse: a divine agent has taken possession of the body of a person as an expression of its love toward him or her. In contrast to the *zarab* performers, who never lose consciousness, a Sidi embodying an ancestor-saint has no memory of his or her actions afterward. Thus, in the final sequence of the Rifaʻi *ʻurs*, ecstatic performances dissolve the boundaries between subject and object, ecstatic emotion and possession that have so carefully been set up and maintained during preceding sequences of the ritual.

Final Remarks

Both these performative traditions show some striking similarities with regard to the development of love as a religious emotion that overflows in states called rapture or intoxication and effects comparable bodily reactions. However, their differences are no less remarkable, for example, in the strongly gendered interpretation of the love and relationship between the teacher and God that culminates in a marriage in the case of the Sufi Rifaʿi and in a striving for the persistent suspense of an extramarital love relationship that, within the Caitanya tradition, is notable for its ever-lasting intensity. Embodying ancestor spirits is a possibility in a certain stage in the Sufi ʿ*urs* ascribed to a special community of followers. This shows the fluidity of the emotional states that may find a place in one ritual event, while testifying to the distinctions that are socially, conceptually, and experientially drawn between them. As an individual path, meditative ecstasy of absolute consciousness, represented by the unmoved and indescribably happy yogin, is rarely expressed in spectacular performances. In the ʿ*urs,* this dimension is indicated by the *pir,* who is in control of his senses and his emotions. However, the ʿ*urs* also provides space for ecstatic group performances that show ecstasy as the capacity to intensify emotions of love, affection, and desire until their overflow results in complete surrender. This capacity is used, provoked, and channeled in specific religious traditions as a religious path in its own right. Although it never seems to be the path of the many, it was nevertheless not just a choice for groups and individuals at the margins. Rather it may be regarded as a practice of exceptional individuals or important minority groups that have managed to assert themselves as a religious option for those who are seeking direct experience of the entities and realms taught in religions and of the power of its intensity. The interpretation and performance of ecstasy is embedded in the different cultural contexts in which a religion develops. In this case, the fact that ecstasy appears in many forms does not so much hint at an underlying unity of emotion or experience as point to its refracted and occasional presence in the larger maps that mirror the dissemination of religions. More often than not, the majority of religious specialists and lay followers welcome the phenomenon as a distant relative who may arouse curiosity and admiration as well as irritation and a lack of understanding—an ambivalence that is made easier to tolerate by the fact that his or her home is somewhere else.

Notes

1. For the relationship between trance and music see Gilbert Rouget, *Music and Trance: A Theory of the Relations between Music and Possession* (Chicago: University of Chicago Press, 1985).

2. For example, the participation of women in Sufi rituals, Christian women ecstatics, and Hindu *bhakti* religions that abolish caste distinctions.

3. As is the case with Muslims participating in rituals celebrating the presence of sprits in East Africa.

4. This concern has been nicely put by William P. Alston: "One nagging worry is the possibility that the phenomenal content of the mystical perception wholly consists of affective qualities, of various ways the subject is feeling in reaction to what the subject takes to be the presence of god." *Perceiving God: The Epistemology of Religious Experience* (Ithaca, N.Y.: Cornell University Press, 1991), 49.

5. Rouget already complained about this state of the arts, *Music and Trance*, 5.

6. For an overview see Nils G. Holm, "Ecstasy Research in the Twentieth Century," in *Religious Ecstasy*, edited by Holm (Stockholm: Almquist and Wiksell, 1982), 1–26. See Rouget, *Music and Trance*, 4–25, on the use of trance and ecstasy in academic studies.

7. M. Huppertz, "Mystische Erfahrung und Trance," in *Profane Mystik? Andacht und Ekstase in Literatur und Philosophie des 20. Jahrhunderts*, edited by W. Amthor et al. (Berlin: Weidler, 2002), 23–50.

8. For example, D. Roybeck et al., "Women, Stress and Participation in Possession Cults: A Reexamnination of the Calcium Deficiency Hypothesis," *Medical Anthropological Quarterly* 3, 2 (1989): 139–61.

9. Ioan M. Lewis, *Ecstatic Religion: An Anthropological Study of Spirit Possession and Shamanism* (London: Routledge, 1989).

10. V. Crapanzano and V. Garrison, eds., *Case Studies in Spirit Possession* (New York: Wiley, 1977).

11. Janice Boddy, *Wombs and Alien Spirits: Women, Men, and the Zar Cult in Northern Sudan* (Madison: University of Wisconsin Press, 1989).

12. F. Kramer, *The Red Fez* (London: Verso, 1993). Helene Basu, "Theatre of Memory: Ritual Kinship Performances of the African Diaspora in Pakistan," in *Culture, Creation, and Procreation: Concepts of Kinship in South Asian Practice*, edited by M. Böck and A. Rao (New York: Berghahn, 2000), 243–70.

13. These studies are rarely included in research surveys, although textual traditions are important sources. Future research on ecstasy could profit from interdisciplinary research, for example, on the language of ecstasy.

14. Cf. Annemarie Schimmel, *Mystical Dimensions of Islam* (Chapel Hill: University of North Carolina Press, 1975).

15. We thus share Rouget's concern about terminological clarification, while we retain the term "ecstasy" also for performative contexts. Rouget, *Music and Trance*, 3–31.

16. For instance, *bhuta* cults in South India, *sheitani* sessions in East Africa, or spiritual media and trance sessions in modern Euro-American culture.

17. Cf. Sheila S. Walker, *Ceremonial Spirit Possession in Africa and Afro-America: Forms, Meanings, and Functional Significance for Individuals and Social Groups* (Leiden: Brill, 1972), 5.

18. Like the *goma* of Sidi in Gujarat, *n'goma* practices in East Africa, or *candomblé* in Brazil.

19. Mircea Eliade, *Shamanism: Archaic Techniques of Ecstasy* (New York: Pantheon Books, 1964). For modern movements see Robert J. Wallis, *Shamans, Neo-Shamans: Ecstasy, Alternative Archaeologies, and Contemporary Pagans* (London: Routledge, 2003).

20. Cf. June McDaniel, *The Madness of Saints: Ecstatic Religion in Bengal* (Chicago: University of Chicago Press, 1989).

21. See, for instance, Mircea Eliade, *Yoga: Immortality and Freedom* (Princeton: Princeton University Press, 1970); Ian Whicher, David Carpenter (eds.), *Yoga: The Indian Tradition* (London: Routledge, 2003).

22. In order to emphasize the introverted character of this awareness and to distinguish it from expressive "ecstasy," *samadhi*, the final stage of yogic practice, has been rendered by M. Eliade and others as "enstasy." However, this suggests that ecstasy be expressed through physical reactions which implies an unnecessary conceptual and phenomenological restriction.

23. How seriously pervasion by a certain emotion is taken as a criterion for devotion can be seen in what is called in the Hindu tradition *dvesha-bhakti*, that is, the love or affection for a god or a goddess that consists in hatred. In several myths it is narrated that the worst enemies of a god, who have no other thought than seeing the god's annihilation, in the end obtain direct salvation though the grace of the very god or goddess they had hated so much. This is because that hatred has consumed their lives in a way that is comparable to the experience of an ecstatic devotee who cannot but think and live in terms of his or her love. However, hatred is not an emotion that is selected for traveling along the religious path.

24. For other performances of *nama-sankirtana*, a special tent is erected that houses a temporary, free-standing shrine or *pitha* (lit. seat or throne) on which images of gods and important teachers are placed and worshiped before and after the performances. Usually, the *nama-sankirtana* group dances around this seat. See Angelika Malinar, "Mantra-Recitation as a Religious Institution: Sri Kalpataru Seva Asrama in Bhubaneswar" in *Text and Context in the History, Literature, and Religion of Orissa*, edited by A. Malinar et al. (Delhi: Manohar, 2004), 175–202.

25. The Sidis are a community of African origins who became followers of the Rifaʻi *pirs* as fakirs of their ancestral saint Bava Gor. See Helene Basu, "Hierarchy and Emotion: Love, Joy and Sorrow in a Cult of Black Saints in Gujarat, India," in *Embodying Charisma*, edited by Pnina Werbner and Helene Basu (London: Routledge and Kegan Paul 1998), 117–39.

BIBLIOGRAPHY

Alston, William P. *Perceiving God: The Epistemology of Religious Experience*. Ithaca, N.Y.: Cornell University Press, 1991.

Basu, Helene. "Hierarchy and Emotion: Love, Joy, and Sorrow in a Cult of Black Saints in Gujarat, India." In *Embodying Charisma*, edited by Pnina Werbner and Helene Basu. London: Routledge and Kegan Paul, 1998, 117–39.

———. "Theatre of Memory: Ritual Kinship Performances of the African Diaspora in Pakistan." In *Culture, Creation, and Procreation: Concepts of Kinship in South Asian Practice*, edited by M. Böck and A. Rao. New York: Berghahn, 2000, 243–70.

Boddy, Janice. *Wombs and Alien Spirits: Women, Men, and the Zar Cult in Northern Sudan*. Madison: University of Wisconsin Press, 1989.

Crapanzano, V., and V. Garrison, eds. *Case Studies in Spirit Possession*. New York: Wiley, 1977.

Eliade, Mircea. *Shamanism: Archaic Techniques of Ecstasy*. New York: Pantheon Books, 1964.

———. *Yoga: Immortality and Freedom*. Princeton: Princeton University Press, 1970.

Holm, Nils G. "Ecstasy Research in the Twentieth Century." In *Religious Ecstasy*. Stockholm: Almquist and Wiksell, 1982, 1–26.

Huppertz, M. "Mystische Erfahrung und Trance." In *Profane Mystik? Andacht und Ekstase in Literatur und Philosophie des 20. Jahrhunderts*, edited by W. Amthor et al. Berlin: Weidler, 2002, 23–50.

Kramer, F. *The Red Fez*. London: Verso, 1993.

Lewis, Ioan M. *Ecstatic Religion: An Anthropological Study of Spirit Possession and Shamanism*. London: Routledge, 1989.

Malinar, Angelika. "Mantra-Recitation as a Religious Institution: Sri Kalpataru Seva Asrama in Bhubaneswar." In *Text and Context in the History, Literature, and Religion of Orissa*, edited by A. Malinar et al. Delhi: Manohar, 2004, 175–202.

McDaniel, June. *The Madness of Saints: Ecstatic Religion in Bengal*. Chicago: University of Chicago Press, 1989.

Rouget, Gilbert. *Music and Trance: A Theory of the Relations between Music and Possession*. Chicago: University of Chicago Press, 1985.

Roybeck, D., et al. "Women, Stress and Participation in Possession Cults: A Reexamnination of the Calcium Deficiency Hypothesis." *Medical Anthropological Quarterly* 3, 2 (1989): 139–61.

Schimmel, Annemarie. *Mystical Dimensions of Islam*. Chapel Hill: University of North Carolina Press, 1975.

Walker, Sheila S. *Ceremonial Spirit Possession in Africa and Afro-America: Forms, Meanings, and Functional Significance for Individuals and Social Groups*. Leiden: Brill, 1972.

Wallis, Robert J. *Shamans, Neo-Shamans: Ecstasy, Alternative Archaeologies, and Contemporary Pagans*. London: Routledge, 2003.

Whicher, Ian, and David Carpenter, eds. *Yoga: The Indian Tradition*. London: Routledge, 2003.

CHAPTER 14

TERROR

HARVEY WHITEHOUSE

In a book about religion, what topics should a chapter on "terror" cover? Some readers might expect a discussion of religious "fanaticism" and its role in terrorist atrocities. Or perhaps such a chapter might focus on fears of damnation and other supernatural punishments. Or should it be an essay about religion as a response to (rather than a cause of) terror, building on the common notion that "there are no atheists in the trenches"? Such topics would no doubt be interesting to explore, but they concern, arguably, somewhat trivial or tangential connections between religion and emotion. If religious commitments inspire terrorism (and that would of course be a contentious claim),[1] then its targets are primarily located outside the religious coalition itself. If fear inspires sudden conversion, then all too often the circumstances of fear are said to originate in causes outside the belief system (e.g., "the trenches"). The notion of dogma as a cause of terror may seem to be more promising, insofar as it requires us to focus on the emotionality of religion itself. But this topic also belies some thorny problems. For in order to explain why supernatural sanctions inspire fear, we first have to explain why people believe in the efficacy of such sanctions. To live in dread of damnation, for instance, is to accept that it is possible to be damned; to fail to explain the belief is to fail to explain the emotion. Moreover, not all religions inspire terror by means of supernatural threats. If we allow ourselves to be distracted by that idea, we may lose sight of issues of general significance in the study of religion.

The principal focus of this chapter will be on ritual ordeals that inspire terror *regardless of the participants' preexisting beliefs*. Indeed, in such traditions, the relationship between belief and emotion is more or less the converse of that entailed by fears of supernatural punishment. It is not so much that one's beliefs inspire fear but that fear is a major part of the psychological processes that *give rise* to the gradual formation of mystical knowledge. Understanding the nature of such practices may, in a roundabout way, help us to answer the question of where religious beliefs come from, and why these sometimes (in turn) elicit anxieties. But focusing on terrifying rituals, at least as a starting point, also has the advantage of picking out a generalizable feature of religion—not a feature of all religions, to be sure, but a "mode of religiosity" that is probably as ancient as our species and is still found in every corner of the globe.[2] Given the shocking nature of the rituals in question, it is not unreasonable to refer to these practices as "rites of terror."[3]

Although archeological evidence on ancient ritual practices is more often suggestive than conclusive, it seems likely that many of our earliest fully modern human ancestors experimented with terrifying ritual ordeals. In the famous caves at Tuc D'Audoubert, France, there are signs of ritual activities dating back up to fifteen thousand years, in which cohorts of adolescents appear to have undergone traumatic rituals that made full use of the dangers of the subterranean environment and the special acoustic and visual effects that those surroundings afforded.[4] Steven Mithen has recently pointed to the widespread occurrence of similarly frightening and often very violent rituals during long periods of prehistory in western Asia.[5] From the time of the classical civilizations, we have increasingly detailed evidence for such practices.[6] But of course it is from the contemporary ethnographic record that our most detailed studies of such rituals derive.

Traumatic ritual ordeals feature in all the world religions, at least as locally or regionally distinctive traditions rather than universal features. Examples might include the rituals of the *penitentes* of New Mexico or their Filipino or Mexican counterparts; Sufi performances of mortification; Opus Dei flagellations; or Buddhist and especially Zen monastic initiations. A particularly rich source of illustrations comes from anthropological research on small-scale traditional societies and their local cult practices. Aborigine groups, for instance, are famous for their practice of circumcision and subincision, involving the ritualized mutilation of boys' penises. But Aboriginal initiations traditionally involved a much wider range of tortures. For instance, Strehlow has described how Aranda boys were obliged to suffer sadistic episodes of head-biting, evulsions of their fingernails, showering with red-hot coals, and other agonizing procedures from which they were not permitted to flinch or take flight, on pain of death.[7] The caves of Aranda totemic groups were permanently spotted with the blood of generations of novices who had endeavored to paint sacred pictures with their mutilated fingers. Similarly grisly practices have been widely reported in studies of cult rituals in Amazonia, Melanesia, Africa, and elsewhere.[8]

Rites of Terror: Some Established Approaches

Two strategies, broadly speaking, have been developed in an attempt to understand the nature and origins of rites of terror. The first strategy is sociological in orientation, focusing mainly on the social consequences of participation (such as social integration, political domination, distinctive patterns of group interaction, the reproduction of cosmological knowledge, and so on). A strength of this approach is that it places rites of terror in a broader context, which is obviously necessary in order to understand them on their own terms but may also deliver important clues as the causes behind their recurrence cross-culturally and their persistence historically. De-contextualized descriptions of rites of terror have a somewhat lurid character, encouraging us to make sense of what is going on with reference to cultural schemas remote from the practices at hand (an error roundly deplored by social and cultural anthropologists as ethnocentricism). Relativism has its limitations, however. Some of the psychological implications of these ritual ordeals can be tacitly inferred on the basis of universal cognitive capacities that are little colored by local cultural knowledge: for instance, the obvious but important fact that these practices are terrifying, dangerous, and painful and (perhaps more contentiously) that they activate moral anxieties (for even if they are construed as being desirable or necessary for initiates to endure, they involve forms of cruelty that exact a toll on perpetrators as well as "victims"). But there are also many features of local sociocultural environments that do have important implications for our understanding of what is going on in rites of terror. The crunch question is *what* features of the context should really be taken into account, and *why*. As noted, it is reasonable to hope that at least some potentially generalizable features of the sociocultural context will help to *explain* what is going on. But, again, this is something to be demonstrated rather than assumed. I shall presently consider how some sociological approaches to the problem have tackled these issues.

The second major strategy is a psychological one: asking, for instance, about the motivations, conscious or otherwise, that induce people to participate in such traumatic and costly types of religious activities. A strength of this approach is that it takes us to the heart of problems of explanation. Unlike sociological theories, which generally have more to say about consequences and rationalizations than about causes and motives, psychological theories focus unashamedly on the primary unit of interest—human subjects and the mechanisms driving their behavior. But many of the psychological approaches currently available also have their limitations. Following a brief consideration of some prominent analyses of rites of terror, both sociological and psychological, I will set out the key features of a new theory that seeks to combine the strengths of both approaches: one that drives us more deeply in the ethnographic contexts at the same time that it identifies generalizable cognitive causes.

To begin with the sociological approaches, these come in a dazzling array of varieties, but those with serious explanatory ambition (rather than primarily interpretive objectives) are broadly concerned with issues of political and cultural reproduction. Some of the most searching of these approaches may have become unfashionable, but that is no reason to overlook them (indeed, the problems they address have often been avoided rather than solved or, as is more commonly asserted, "transcended" by recent scholarship). A particularly promising theoretical tradition in anthropology, delivering significant insights into the ethnography of rites of terror, was instigated by Emile Durkheim and Arnold van Gennep, among others.[9] There were several distinct (though often closely interconnected) strands to this scholarship, of which two of the most influential may be described as "functionalist" and "symbolist." Although these perspectives were developed in a number of fruitful directions over the course of the twentieth century, some core features can be illustrated briefly by considering Edward Norbeck's work on ritual inversion in African religions and Maurice Bloch's theory of "rebounding violence," which is applicable to a wide range of rites.[10] Both approaches offer intriguing insights into the nature of violent ritual ordeals.

Norbeck observes that a great variety of traditional African rituals express themes of *conflict* between social groups and categories: between the sexes, between superiors and inferiors, between the relatives of bride and groom at weddings, between political coalitions, between people who hold grievances toward each other, and so on. In many cases, such rituals serve to exaggerate or caricature social tensions in ways that, although largely symbolic, are liable to spill over into actual violence. Conflict between the sexes might be expressed, for instance, in ritualized role reversal, whereby women would arm themselves with weapons, normally only handled by men, or use phallic objects to simulate male masturbation and sexual penetration. Such practices form part of a wider pattern of ritual transvestism in African religion. Conflict between people of different social rank might be expressed in ritual abuse of persons of high rank, for instance by means of symbolic regicide, commonly in traditional African states through the installation and symbolic (or actual) slaughter of a mock king.[11] It is also common in African societies for weddings to entail ritualized conflict between the relatives of the bride and groom, expressed in such practices as symbolic bride abduction, exchanging of insults among affines, and so on. Larger scale rituals, involving entire descent groups or other major coalitions, might involve mock battles and duels. And in many African societies it is common for outpourings of grievances to occur at sacrifices. In short, religious rituals are often occasions when social tensions are emphasized. Although some anthropologists, including Norbeck, have been tempted to interpret these practices as a form of emotional catharsis (a way of letting off steam and releasing pent-up frustration and aggression), a strong functionalist tradition in the study of such rituals has understood them to contribute to the stable reproduction of *society*, by publicly demonstrating enduring cohesion in the face of destabilizing conflicts. A classic example of this argument is to be found in Max Gluckman's interpretation of Swazi royal rituals in which he argued that structural tensions in the kingdom are symbolically expressed and then transcended through culminating ritual acts that emphasize the unity and loyalty of the king's subjects.[12]

Although not primarily focused on terror, as such, it is clear that functionalist theories of ritualized conflict seek to explain the violent character of many ritual traditions, of which "rites of terror" might be considered a subset. After all, like other rituals of conflict, the kinds of initiation rites noted in the previous section all involve expressions of intergenerational tensions, and many emphasize gender opposition (often in an explicitly violent fashion), intergroup warfare, and other kinds of confrontational themes. A drawback with all functionalist arguments, however, is that they do not specify the mechanisms that would lead to the emergence of rituals that reinforce the status quo, in this case by caricaturing and then symbolically overcoming the tensions that threaten to disrupt it.

Maurice Bloch's theory of ritualized violence takes up a rather different strand of the Durkheimian legacy, in a way that explicitly eschews its functionalist aspects.[13] Bloch's approach is premised on the symbolist notion that images of the "other world" are more or less coded expressions of the transcendent quality of society. This notion, that institutions can have a transcendent quality (a kind of sacredness), lay at the heart of Durkheim's conception of the "elementary forms" of religion, which pivoted on a distinction between the sacred and the profane. In many ways, the sacred/profane dichotomy in Durkheim's writings was just another expression of his more pervasive distinction between the social and biological aspects of people. This is easiest to understand in a concrete way by thinking about the biological life cycle. In terms of their bodies, human beings go through irreversible phases of life: after being born, they grow and eventually reproduce, deteriorate, and die. These processes are biologically fixed, and all human beings are aware of the fact that they can't somehow "stop the clock" or turn it back. These biological realities constitute the essence of that which is profane or "worldly." Durkheim saw objects of religious worship, by contrast, partly as ways of grappling with a sense that social institutions transcend these biological limitations: they outlive us; we are socialized into them rather than creating them ourselves; they regulate our behavior. Religious ideas dwell on the notion of a state of permanent order and of transcendental power—something more powerful than the individual, something that is creative and is fundamentally unchanging. This, for Durkheim, was the essence of sacredness. But what these religious images refer to (or symbolize) is the unchanging and transcendent order of society itself. Building on these insights, Bloch argues that many religious rituals enact a dramatic conquest of the transcendental realm (Durkheim's category of the "sacred") over this world (the "profane"). Using examples from a great range of traditional religions across several continents, Bloch makes a strong case for the view that the ritual process begins by constructing a dramatic bifurcation of worldly vitality (images of biological processes) and their typically violent annihilation by agents of the sacred realm (images of the spiritual or sacred realm symbolizing the abiding authority of society). Thus, the rites of initiation briefly described earlier (and thousands of others like them) generally begin with a violent assault on the bodies of novices, symbolizing the overwhelming power and transcendence of the social/sacred realm over earthly vitality.

Bloch's account of the ritual process, however, is rather more complex (and more interesting) than that. If the symbolic destruction of the flesh constitutes a victory of sacred over profane (and thus of social reproduction over the impermanence of biological process), then rituals that end at this point would abandon their patients to the realms of the sacred. This, of course, is the purpose of the funeral, and perhaps of some millenarian rituals, but most rituals go further: far from delivering us into the transcendental domain (the afterlife or some heaven on earth), they must bring us back into "this world" somehow invigorated by the powers we have absorbed. In most traditional religions around the world, ritualized "reentry" into this world is expressed as a violent conquest—an act of "rebounding violence," to use Bloch's apposite phrase. In the case of initiations, novices are symbolically brought back from the dead in the guise of heroic conquerors (warriors, hunters, and the like). Whereas the ritual process began with the destruction of their bodies, it ends with a reclaiming of those bodies, but in a way that emphasizes the enhanced spiritual/sacred power of their owners. We see similar symbolism in many royal rituals, ordinations, and other rites that are intended to imbue their patients with worldly authority. In Bloch's scheme, violence becomes an indispensable feature of the ritual process in general.

Unlike functionalist approaches to "rites of terror" Bloch's theory does not presuppose some mechanism of self-preservation at the level of society itself. The challenge is not to explain how the social order established rituals to maintain its stability but rather to explain how people come to imagine society as a transcendent force ("the gods" or "the ancestors") whose powers can be tapped in the reproduction of worldly authority. For the purposes of this discussion, the argument is interesting, in that it promises to explain the extremely violent character of many rituals but does not provide an entirely satisfactory explanation of the role of terror. Rituals could involve *symbolic* violence, thereby meeting the expectations of the "rebounding violence" theory, without requiring participants to endure *real* acts of violence. In most initiation rites, for instance, not only are novices obliged to endure genuine physical assault but also the agonies and horrors of their predicament are typically maximized and exacerbated.

Psychological approaches to the subject tackle the issue of terror more directly, by drawing analogies between ritual torture and overt acts of terrorism. In a classic study of extremely violent male initiations in New Guinea, Donald Tuzin identifies striking parallels between the initiator–novice relationship and way hostages in airplane hijackings and similar scenarios sometimes come to feel about their captors.[14] It has long been recognized by social psychologists that, following their release, hostages are liable to emphasize acts of compassion on the part of their captors and even to defend their actions in a systematic way (in extreme cases, converting to their cause).[15] Tuzin observes that the traumatic ordeals of initiation are punctuated by acts of kindness on the part of initiators, apparently inspiring feelings of "love," "gratitude," and "deep identification."[16] This process of identification with the oppressor may, Tuzin suggests, play a key role in the reproduction of the rituals. Novices may be "converted" to the cause of the ritual experts and motivated to assume the role of initiators themselves, when their time arrives.

The cognitive anthropologist Pascal Boyer more recently notes strong parallels between the ritual groupings formed through rites of terror and other kinds of coalitions.[17] He observes that the most violent rituals tend to be associated with groups that face exceptionally acute dangers (e.g., on the battlefield or hunting grounds) and where the temptation to abandon one's fellows is in consequence very considerable. In selecting members for coalitions of this sort, one intuitively seeks reassurance that recruits will prove trustworthy when the going gets tough. An obvious way to put prospective recruits to the test is to require them to make a massive sacrifice in advance and see if they will stand firm. According to Boyer, this is the main purpose of rites of terror: it is a way of testing the loyalty of members of endangered coalitions in circumstances where the costs of failure are not too damaging to the group.

An advantage of these sorts of psychological theories is that they seem to explain the emphasis on terror, rather than merely on violence per se, in certain rituals. As such, these approaches potentially complement (rather than contradict or replace) sociological ones. But they also have their limitations, perhaps the most serious of which stem from the fact that they are based on analogies with rather distant kinds of social situations. Initiation rites have some similarities with acts of terrorism in which hostages are taken, but there are also dangers in carrying the analogy too far. Terrorists do not take hostages with the aim of spiritually and physically transforming them or transmitting a set of secret mystical revelations. Likewise, the ritual groupings formed through initiations are not quite the same as other kinds of endangered coalitions where there is a need to put potential recruits to the test. Consider the situation confronted by a gang of youths or a crime ring that faces constant threat from its rivals, from the police, and perhaps from other locally powerful organizations. In such coalitions, potential recruits could be required to undergo "tests" of a kind that might well be reminiscent of initiation rituals. But there are also crucial differences: recruits would typically have the option to "keep their noses clean" rather than to get involved with gangs or the mob. There is, at least in principle, an assumption of voluntary involvement, and this is crucial to the intuitive effectiveness of any test new recruits may be required to pass. In the case of most initiation rites (indeed, all those mentioned earlier), there is no such voluntarism, even in principle. It is axiomatic that those undergoing initiation have no choice other than to comply and indeed would be killed if they attempted to resist or run away. The price of defection is invariably much higher than the price of compliance, and so such ordeals cannot be construed by any stretch of the imagination as genuine tests of loyalty.

Existing attempts to makes sense of rites of terror may well capture some salient elements of what is happening, in both sociological and psychological terms but also leave a lot to be explained. Sociological approaches have explored some general features of the symbolic character and institutional consequences of violent rituals, and a major point in their favor is that they encompass a wide range of ritual phenomena. Nevertheless, such approaches do not satisfactorily explain why symbolic violence so often turns into *actual* violence. Psychological approaches have begun to penetrate possible causes of the terrifying character of certain violent rituals. In doing so, however, they have tended to focus more heavily on initiations than on other kinds of religious phenomena and have done so in ways that underestimate some features that might make religious initiations different from other forms of corporate recruitment. In the next section, I consider a new approach that attempts to combine a number of cognitive and sociopolitical features of these rituals, while trying also to draw on some of the strengths of existing theories.

Rites of Terror: Ritual, Memory, and Motivation

To understand why a significant class of religious rituals elicits strong, negatively valenced emotion—typically "terror"—we first need to appreciate some basic features of ritual *in general*. What makes ritualized actions different from other kinds of behaviors is the fact that the choreography and speech is stipulated in advance, not by the performer him- or herself but by some other agent (often of unknown origin) for reasons that are not capable of being inferred intuitively. Rituals are actions for which almost any rationale could in principle be given (even if in practice the exegetical meanings are supplied by religious authorities). In nonritual actions, by contrast, we presume that the intentional system driving the performance is firmly located inside the actor: even if the actions are somewhat fixed by convention, rather than being the spontaneous creations of those carrying them out, we know that the actor is making each move according to means-end calculations. As soon as such calculations cease to be relevant—that is, as soon as we start to suspect that the action is selected purely for reasons of stipulation rather than because of the actor-driven goals and decisions—then the behavior appears progressively ritualized. Humphrey and Laidlaw, who pioneered this line of argument, describe ritual actions as lacking "intrinsic intentional meaning."[18] Thanks to recent breakthroughs in those fields of cognitive science that focus on the way humans try to "read" the intentions of those around them, we are now able to formulate increasingly precise psychological theories of (at least this aspect of) ritualized behavior.

Experimental psychologists have shown that cognitively normal adults possess a distinctive repertoire of highly sophisticated mechanisms for making sense of other people's behaviors. These mechanisms, collectively referred to as "theory of mind" (TOM),[19] develop during childhood according to a fixed series of stages, regardless of cultural differences. Infants and toddlers all around the world rapidly come to appreciate that animate beings are driven by invisible states (intentions) rather than having to be acted on by external forces (as would be the case with all inanimate objects, like natural kinds and artifacts). Only around age three or four, however, do children begin to realize that these intentions can be based on erroneous premises. Up to this point in development, children assume that whatever they know about the state of the world is also known to everyone else, even if many of the people around them couldn't possibly have seen or heard the same things that they have witnessed. But four-year-olds realize that other people are not quite so omniscient: they can be mistaken about things and, perhaps more important, they can be tricked or misled. Although this capacity, sometimes described as "first-order TOM," develops quite automatically in most young children, one of the defining features of autism is the failure of such mechanisms to become properly established (in people with this condition, all further development of TOM likewise seems to be arrested).[20] Around middle childhood, a major new development occurs: children now begin to realize that other people are constantly playing the mind-reading game and that their actions are therefore often selected with the aim of communicating and concealing information. This development, sometimes called "second-order TOM," marks the maturation of an extremely sophisticated intention-reading system (or set of systems) that continues to operate throughout adulthood. Every time adults observe other people doing something, they automatically (if largely unconsciously) interpret the intentional states of the actor, with greater or less degrees of accuracy. And this is also what makes ritualized behavior possible.

Ritual actions, like any other actions, trigger our TOM mechanisms. But then we immediately run into problems. The actions carried out in rituals are not driven by the actors' intentions in any normal way. When people put on special clothes (not any clothes, but something very deliberately stipulated) and start carrying out odd procedures (not any procedures, but specifically prescribed ones in a predetermined order) that have no obvious technical motivations, we find that our TOM capacities cannot deliver satisfactory explanations for what is happening. We might start to speculate that, even if the present actor is not the author of this peculiar behavior, there must be an intelligent agent at the root of it. Perhaps the previous generation, who taught us to behave in this way, or the generation before them? Such a search for meaning is a search for ritual exegesis, but its outcomes are uncertain and problematic. As Bloch has recently observed:

> Exegesis, that is the search for original intentionality, is in itself perfectly reasonable, and although frustrating, almost inevitable. After all, we are dealing with human minds, that is, with animals whose minds are characterized by an intentionality-seeking device that is normally exercised ceaselessly, one might almost say obsessively, sometimes consciously but often unconsciously, and that enables them to read the minds of others and thus coordinate their behavior with them. But in a ritual, these poor little animals, amongst them poor little anthropologists, appear to be faced with an impossible situation because the search for intentionality leads them ever further back, to ever more remote authorities, but without ever settling anywhere with any finality.[21]

There are two major ways this search for meaning unfolds.[22] One possibility is that the rituals become so habituated, through frequent repetition, that they no longer trigger TOM mechanisms to any significant extent. Performative competence becomes largely a matter of procedural fluency at an unconscious level, and once we find that we no longer need to reflect explicitly on the question of *how* to perform the rituals, there will be a corresponding reduction in our efforts to reflect on *why* we perform them. In the case of many such actions, such as the Roman Catholic practice of crossing oneself, exegetical concerns simply evaporate, and hardly anyone knows (or cares) any more what the actions mean. In other cases, religious authorities step in and tell us how to interpret the rituals. Since their pronouncements are not, by and large, challenged by competing interpretations (based on independent reflection), and to the extent that the authoritative exegesis is effectively policed and regulated (via the monitoring functions of ecclesiastic hierarchies and the use of routinized sermonizing), the official version of what the rituals mean is likely to stick. But we need not concern ourselves here with the details of such forms of religious transmission. Our present interest is in rites of terror. So what happens to our TOM mechanisms when ritual experiences are really shocking and upsetting?

The short answer to this question is that our TOM mechanisms go into overdrive. And to understand why, we also need to understand how our memory systems respond to traumatic situations. A very substantial body of psychological research, over an appreciable period of time, has revealed that elevated arousal, coupled with shocks to the cognitive system (triggered by events that do not conform to expectations), give rise to special kinds of long-lasting memories, commonly referred to as "episodic" memories.[23] What is special about this kind of remembering is that it enduringly encodes details of the unique event or episode, identifying it as a distinct experience in space and time, in contrast with the kinds of memories that pertain to bits and pieces of information we have picked up without ever being able to recall when or where we first learned them. Recollections that are particularly detailed and haunting are sometimes referred to as "flashbulb memories,"[24] because they seem to be etched in our minds with photograph-like vividness, encoding all kinds of details in our perceptual systems (visual, tactile, auditory, olfactory, and so on). One of the key features of flashbulb memory, and of episodic memory more generally, is that it is an explicit system, delivering outputs that are accessible to conscious inspection and report. This also means that the things we remember as distinctive episodes are liable to become a focus for conscious rumination, often over many years or even a lifetime. If we think of life-changing events in general, it is hardly surprising that they give rise to intermittent rumination, particularly in periods of stress. When we are very unhappy with our lives, for instance, we may be prone to "what if" kinds of thoughts, focused on junction points in our lives when we might have made different choices "if only..." or when things might have happened slightly differently. But all of this pales into insignificance when we consider the long-term effects of participation in life-changing *rituals*. Why? Because of all the *problems* ritualization presents to our TOM mechanisms.

Ritualization, uniquely among all other kinds of human behavior, both activates and frustrates our TOM mechanisms. In the case of rituals that are frequently repeated and elicit relatively low levels of arousal, the potential frustration is offset by habituation, which effectively suppresses the need for exegetical interpretation, as noted. But high-arousal rituals, rarely enacted, trigger lasting episodic recall (often exhibiting all the classic features of "flashbulb memory") that thrusts itself on our conscious awareness, particularly in religious traditions that contrive continually to remind us of the traumas we have had to endure. In initiation cults, for instance, reminders of the tortures and privations of novices are always amply present in the physical and social environment, and the agonies of flagellants, ascetics, and visionaries are perpetually triggered by religious discourse and iconography. The wounds, so to speak, are forever being "reopened" in consciousness, or in semiconscious modalities. Consequently, there is no rest for our TOM mechanisms, and we are condemned to an endless search for interpretative meaning. I have argued at length elsewhere that exegesis based on internal rumination of this kind results in highly motivating religious ideologies, typically idiosyncratic and hard to convey in words but nevertheless deeply implicated in the formation of attitudes and beliefs. One of the key psychological features of this sort of exegetical knowledge is analogical thinking, which uses both affect and semantic structure to generate connections between the possible intentional meanings of rituals and other domains of knowledge and understanding. In unraveling the processes involved, we have not only ethnographic evidence to draw on but also some experimental evidence.[25]

Note, however, that this enriches rather than displaces the arguments surveyed in the preceding section. For instance, it is certainly the case that many rituals express themes of conflict, and functionalist analyses of this phenomenon have raised some important issues. Gluckman and Norbeck, as noted, have observed that the expression of social tensions in a ritualized fashion provides a way of managing emotional (and perhaps also social structural) challenges, without having to deal with a backlash of recriminations from aggrieved parties. The explanation for this lies precisely in the cognitive properties outlined here: it is in the nature of rituals that the persons performing them are not (at least not wholly) the intentional agents behind it all. They are perceived to be acting in a way that absolves them of responsibility, since they are not really the authors of their actions. This line of argument also supports the central insights of the symbolist school. Authority is indeed reproduced and distributed through ritual action, but this is mainly because ritualization confounds our TOM mechanisms and so continually refers us back to prior intentionality, construed variously as "the ancestors," "tradition," or "the gods." Bloch describes this as the essence of deference: when people assert that a ritual must be performed in this or that particular way, even though it is hard to say why, "they are surely telling us that what they are doing, saying, singing, is above all *deferring*."[26] Yet these potentialities are part and parcel of all kinds of ritualized behavior and do not account specifically for rites of terror.

To understand why some rituals are terrifying, we need to appreciate their motivational consequences. Patterns of experimentation with ritualized behavior that drive us in the direction of high-arousal, low-frequency performances have major consequences for our motivational systems and ultimately, therefore, for the transmission of ritual traditions over time. The rich and revelatory exegesis that develops in the wake of ritual traumas has profound and enduring effects on our levels of religious commitment, especially when compared with the effects of exegetical transmission based on verbal testimony. At the core of this process is the activation of episodic memory, which ensures the persistence of problems of exegetical meaning in the consciousness of ritual participants. But episodic memory for rites of terror has other consequences, too. It ensures that participants will always recall who else was present during a given ritual ordeal, thereby establishing enduring and cohesive bonds between those who went through the experience together.[27] This, in turn, provides a powerful foundation for coalitional thinking, as noted by Boyer (see above). And this line of argument is also compliant with Tuzin's observation that violent and frightening initiations may encourage novices to identify with their ritual persecutors. The point would be *not* that these earlier theories are wrong but that they are not sufficient in themselves to uncover the dynamics that drive the transmission of rites of terror over time.

Conclusions

"Rites of terror" are an ancient and cross-culturally recurrent feature of religion primarily because they trigger powerful motivational states through the activation of episodic memory and "theory of mind" mechanisms. The significance of lasting episodic memories for ritualized ordeals is that they encourage people to dwell on the possible *meanings* of their experiences and so to construct elaborate cosmological knowledge based on processes of "spontaneous exegetical reflection." Such knowledge, resulting from internal processes of explicit rumination, hardens into elaborate (if largely esoteric and mystical) cosmology. Such knowledge forms the core of the belief systems of ritual experts and leads to the overriding conviction that others must acquire the knowledge in their turn, via the same costly processes of revelation. This conclusion would seem to be supported by the ethnographic record, and in particular by a number of recent attempts to evaluate the model presented here against a wide range of cases.[28] Assuming the approach continues to withstand empirical scrutiny and testing, where is this likely to leave us in relation to more established hypotheses, both sociological and psychological?

In some respects, Durkheim's original characterization of the "elementary forms" of religion still seems remarkably penetrating. Durkheim took seriously the role of emotional arousal in Aboriginal ritual, for instance, producing what he called "collective effervescence"—the affective intensity of group identity and cohesion. Moreover, he was among the first to appreciate the identity-conferring aspects of imagistic ritual, expressed most famously in his symbolist interpretation of Aboriginal totemism:

> The totem ... expresses and symbolizes two different sorts of things. In the first place, it is the outward and visible form of what we have called the totemic principle of god. But it is also the symbol of a determined society or clan ... so if it is at once the symbol of god and of the society, is that not because the god and the society are only one?[29]

Nevertheless, a limitation of Durkheim's argument, and with subsequent functionalist and symbolist interpretations more generally, was that the cognitive or conceptual dimensions of identity-conferring ritual cannot be reduced to simplistic forms of correspondence or isomorphy between religious classificatory schemes and the constitution of social organization or worldly authority. Such approaches bypass the most compelling aspects of the imagistic mode of religiosity, especially the traumatic and revelatory nature of ritual, and consequently fail to integrate these into a theory of group formation. The focal imagery of Aboriginal ritual is not a set of "emblems" or "flags" but a repertoire of loosely associated concrete metaphors, generated through long-term reflection on the meanings of emotionally haunting ritual experiences.

This is also what makes "rites of terror" different from the experience of being taken hostage by terrorists or being recruited by the mob. After hostages are released, or after people have been violently inducted into a criminal gang, they are certainly likely to remember their ordeals for a long time to come (in fact will probably take these memories to the grave). They may even reflect to some extent on what might have been, had not certain chance events occurred, or key decisions been taken, at various points leading up to the events in question. But when traumatic experiences are heavily ritualized, this kind of reflection becomes very much more complex and fertile. Ritual is, after all, a somewhat vexing phenomenon in that it refuses to yield simple and obvious meanings. The place of intentionality and technical motivation remains forever elusive—a problem that most of the time is easy enough to overlook. But when rituals are also deeply shocking, leaving scars in memory that can never completely heal, we are condemned not only to reflect on what happened but also to repeat it, for the benefit (or perhaps to the detriment) of succeeding generations.

NOTES

This article was written during a period of sabbatical leave funded by the British Academy in the form of a two-year research readership.

1. See Pascal Boyer, *Religion Explained: The Evolutionary Origins of Religious Thought* (New York: Basic Books, 2001).
2. See Harvey Whitehouse, *Inside the Cult: Religious Experience and Innovation in Papua New Guinea* (Oxford: Oxford University Press, 1995), *Arguments and Icons: Divergent Modes of Religiosity* (Oxford: Oxford University Press, 2000), and *Modes of Religiosity: A Cognitive Theory of Religious Transmission* (Walnut Creek, Calif.: AltaMira Press, 2004).
3. For a fuller justification of this term, see Harvey Whitehouse, "Rites of Terror: Emotion, Metaphor, and Memory in Melanesian Initiation Cults," *Journal of the Royal Anthropological Institute*, n.s., 4 (1996): 703–15.
4. See John E. Pfeiffer, *The Creative Explosion: An Inquiry into the Origins of Art and Religion* (New York: Harper and Row, 1982); Whitehouse, *Arguments and Icons*.
5. Steven Mithen, "From Ohalo to Çatalhöyük: The Development of Religiosity during the Early Prehistory of Western Asia, 20,000–7,000 B.C.E.," in *Theorizing Religions Past: Archaeology, History, and Cognition*, edited by Harvey Whitehouse and Luther H.

Martin (Walnut Creek, Calif.: AltaMira Press, 2004), 17–43; Karen Johnson, "Primary Emergence of the Doctrinal Mode of Religiosity in Prehistoric Southwestern Iran," in Whitehouse and Martin, *Theorizing Religions Past*, 45–66.

6. See for instance Luther H. Martin, "Performativity, Discourse and Cognition: 'Demytholo-gizing' the Roman Cult of Mithras," in *Persuasion and Performance: Rhetoric and Reality in Early Christian Discourses*, edited by Willi Braun (Waterloo, Canada: Wilfrid Laurier University Press, 2005), 187–217; Douglas Gragg, "Old and New in Roman Religion: A Cognitive Account," in Whitehouse and Martin, *Theorizing Religions Past*, 69–86; Roger Beck, "Four Men, Two Sticks, and a Whip: Image and Doctrine in a Mithraic Ritual," in Whitehouse and Martin, *Theorizing Religions Past*, 87–103; Anita Leopold, "Syncretism and the Interaction of Modes of Religiosity: A Formative Perspective in 'Gnostic Christian' Movements in Late Antiquity," in Whitehouse and Martin, *Theorizing Religions Past*,105–21.

7. T. G. H. Strehlow, "Culture, Social Structure, and Environment in Aboriginal Central Australia," in *Aboriginal in Australia: Essays in Honour of Emeritus Professor A. P. Elkin*, edited by Ronald M. and Catherine H. Berndt (Sydney: Angus and Robertson, 1965), 116–17.

8. Whitehouse, *Inside the Cult* and *Arguments and Icons*.

9. Emile Durkheim, *The Elementary Forms of the Religious Life* (1915) (London: Allen and Unwin, 1964). Arnold van Gennep, *The Rites of Passage* (1908) (London: Routledge and Kegan Paul, 1965).

10. Edward Norbeck, "African Rituals of Conflict," *American Anthropology* 65 (1963): 12254–79; Maurice Bloch, *Prey into Hunter: The Politics of Religious Experience* (Cambridge: Cambridge University Press, 1992).

11. For a classic discussion, see James Frazer, *The Golden Bough* (1922) (London: Macmillan, 1976).

12. Max Gluckman, "Rituals of Rebellion in South East Africa," in *Order and Rebellion in Tribal Africa* (London: Cohen and West, 1963), 110–36.

13. Bloch, *Prey into Hunter*.

14. Donald F. Tuzin, *The Voice of the Tambaran: Truth and Illusion in Ilahita Arapesh Religion* (Berkeley: University of California Press, 1980).

15. For a recent critical appraisal of work in this area, see Ian K. McKenzie, "The Stockholm Syndrome Revisited: Hostages, Relationships, Prediction, Control, and Psychological Science," *Journal of Police Crisis Negotiations* 4, 1 (2004): 5–21.

16. Tuzin, *The Voice of the Tambaran*, 77–79.

17. Pascal Boyer, "A Reductionistic Model of Distinct Modes of Religious Transmission," in *Mind and Religion: Psychological and Cognitive Foundations of Religiosity*, edited by Harvey Whitehouse and Robert N. McCauley (Walnut Creek, Calif.: AltaMira Press, 2005), 3–29.

18. Caroline Humphrey and James Laidlaw, *The Archetypal Actions of Ritual: A Theory of Ritual Illustrated by the Jain Rite of Worship* (Oxford: Oxford University Press, 1994).

19. See Susan A. Gelman, Gail M. Gottfried, and John Coley, "Essentialist Beliefs in Children: The Acquisition of Concepts and Theories," in *Mapping the Mind: Domain Specificity in Cognition and Culture*, edited by L. Hirschfeld and S. A. Gelman (Cambridge: Cambridge University Press, 1994), 341–66; Alan M. Leslie, "Pretending and Believing: Issues in the Theory of ToMM," *Cognition* 50 (1994): 211–38.

20. See Simon Baron-Cohen, *Mindblindness: An Essay on Autism and Theory of Mind* (Cambridge, Mass.: MIT Press, 1995).

21. Maurice Bloch, "Ritual and Deference," in *Ritual and Memory: Toward a Comparative Anthropology of Religion*, edited by Harvey Whitehouse and James Laidlaw (Walnut Creek, Calif.: AltaMira Press, 2004), 63–64.

22. My own views on this matter contrast somewhat with Bloch's. See Whitehouse and Laidlaw, *Ritual and Memory*.

23. For an authoritative overview, see Alan Baddeley, *Human Memory: Theory and Practice*, rev. ed. (Hove, England: Psychology Press, 1997).

24. See Martin Conway, *Flashbulb Memories* (Hillsdale, N.J.: Erlbaum, 1995).

25. See, for instance, Fredrik Barth's classic ethnographic research: *Ritual and Knowledge among the Baktaman of New Guinea* (New Haven, Conn.: Yale University Press, 1975), and *Cosmologies in the Making: A Generative Approach to Cultural Variation in Inner New Guinea* (Cambridge: Cambridge University Press, 1987). For some experimental evidence, see Rebekah Richert, Harvey Whitehouse, and Emma Stewart, "Memory and Analogical Thinking in High-Arousal Rituals," in Whitehouse and McCauley, *Mind and Religion*, 127–45.

26. Bloch, "Ritual and Deference," 65.

27. See Harvey Whitehouse, "Memorable Religions: Transmission, Codification, and Change in Divergent Melanesian Contexts," *Man*, n.s., 27 (1992): 777–97.

28. A particularly significant body of wider ethnographic, historiographical, and archaeological evidence is assembled in the following collections of essays: Whitehouse and Laidlaw, *Ritual and Memory*; Whitehouse and Martin, *Theorizing Religions Past*; Luther H. Martin and Harvey Whitehouse, *History, Memory, and Cognition*, special issue, *Historical Reflections/Réflexions Historiques*, 31 (2005): 195–200.

29. Durkheim, The Elementary Forms of the Religious Life, 206.

BIBLIOGRAPHY

Baddeley, Alan. *Human Memory: Theory and Practice*. Rev. ed. Hove, England: Psychology Press, 1997.

Baron-Cohen, Simon. *Mindblindness: An Essay on Autism and Theory of Mind*. Cambridge, Mass.: MIT Press, 1995.

Barth, Fredrik. *Cosmologies in the Making: A Generative Approach to Cultural Variation in Inner New Guinea*. Cambridge: Cambridge University Press, 1987.

———. *Ritual and Knowledge among the Baktaman of New Guinea*. New Haven, Conn.: Yale University Press, 1975.

Beck, Roger. "Four Men, Two Sticks, and a Whip: Image and Doctrine in a Mithraic Ritual." In *Theorizing Religions Past: Archaeology, History, and Cognition*, edited by Harvey Whitehouse and Luther H. Martin. Walnut Creek, Calif.: AltaMira Press, 2004, 87–103.

Bloch, Maurice. *Prey into Hunter: The Politics of Religious Experience*. Cambridge: Cambridge University Press, 1992.

———. "Ritual and Deference." In *Ritual and Memory: Toward a Comparative Anthropology of Religion*, edited by Harvey Whitehouse and James Laidlaw. Walnut Creek, Calif.: AltaMira Press, 2004, 65–78.

Boyer, Pascal. "A Reductionistic Model of Distinct Modes of Religious Transmission." In *Mind and Religion: Psychological and Cognitive Foundations of Religiosity*, edited by

Harvey Whitehouse and Robert N. McCauley. Walnut Creek, Calif.: AltaMira Press, 2005, 3–29.

———. *Religion Explained: The Evolutionary Origins of Religious Thought.* New York: Basic Books, 2001.

Conway, Martin. *Flashbulb Memories.* Hillsdale, N.J.: Erlbaum, 1995.

Durkheim, Emile. *The Elementary Forms of the Religious Life* (1915). London: Allen and Unwin, 1964.

Frazer, James. *The Golden Bough* (1922). London: Macmillan, 1976.

Gelman, Susan A., Gail M. Gottfried, and John Coley. "Essentialist Beliefs in Children: The Acquisition of Concepts and Theories." In *Mapping the Mind: Domain Specificity in Cognition and Culture,* edited by L. Hirschfeld and S. A. Gelman. Cambridge: Cambridge University Press, 1994, 341–66.

Gluckman, Max. "Rituals of Rebellion in South East Africa." In *Order and Rebellion in Tribal Africa.* London: Cohen and West, 1963, 110–36.

Gragg, Douglas. "Old and New in Roman Religion: A Cognitive Account." In *Theorizing Religions Past: Archaeology, History, and Cognition,* edited by Harvey Whitehouse and Luther H. Martin. Walnut Creek, Calif.: AltaMira Press, 2004, 69–86.

Humphrey, Caroline, and James Laidlaw. *The Archetypal Actions of Ritual: A Theory of Ritual Illustrated by the Jain Rite of Worship.* Oxford: Oxford University Press, 1994.

Johnson, Karen. "Primary Emergence of the Doctrinal Mode of Religiosity in Prehistoric Southwestern Iran." In *Theorizing Religions Past: Archaeology, History, and Cognition,* edited by Harvey Whitehouse and Luther H. Martin. Walnut Creek, Calif.: AltaMira Press, 2004, 45–66.

Leopold, Anita. "Syncretism and the Interaction of Modes of Religiosity: A Formative Perspective in 'Gnostic Christian' Movements in Late Antiquity." In *Theorizing Religions Past: Archaeology, History, and Cognition,* edited by Harvey Whitehouse and Luther H. Martin. Walnut Creek, Calif.: AltaMira Press, 2004, 105–21.

Leslie, Alan M. "Pretending and Believing: Issues in the Theory of ToMM." *Cognition* 50 (1994): 211–38.

McKenzie, Ian K. "The Stockholm Syndrome Revisited: Hostages, Relationships, Prediction, Control, and Psychological Science." *Journal of Police Crisis Negotiations* 4, 1 (2004): 5–21.

Martin, Luther H. "Performativity, Discourse and Cognition: 'Demythologizing' the Roman Cult of Mithras." In *Persuasion and Performance: Rhetoric and Reality in Early Christian Discourses,* edited by Willi Braun. Waterloo, Canada: Wilfrid Laurier University Press, 2005, 187–217.

Martin, Luther H., and Harvey Whitehouse. *History, Memory, and Cognition.* Special issue, *Historical Reflections/Réflexions Historiques* 31 (2005): 195–200.

Mithen, Steven. 2004 "From Ohalo to Çatalhöyük: The Development of Religiosity during the Early Prehistory of Western Asia, 20,000–7,000 B.C.E." In *Theorizing Religions Past: Archaeology, History, and Cognition,* edited by Harvey Whitehouse and Luther H. Martin. Walnut Creek, Calif.: AltaMira Press, 2004), 17–43.

Norbeck, Edward. "African Rituals of Conflict." *American Anthropology* 65 (1963): 12254–79.

Pfeiffer, John E. *The Creative Explosion: An Inquiry into the Origins of Art and Religion.* New York: Harper and Row, 1982.

Richert, Rebekah, Harvey Whitehouse, and Emma Stewart. "Memory and Analogical Thinking in High-Arousal Rituals." In *Mind and Religion: Psychological and Cognitive*

Foundations of Religiosity, edited by Harvey Whitehouse and Robert N. McCauley. Walnut Creek, Calif.: AltaMira Press, 2005, 127–45.

Strehlow, T. G. H. "Culture, Social Structure, and Environment in Aboriginal Central Australia." In *Aboriginal Man in Australia: Essays in Honour of Emeritus Professor A. P. Elkin*, edited by Ronald M. and Catherine H. Berndt. Sydney: Angus and Robertson, 1965, 116–17.

Tuzin, Donald F. *The Voice of the Tambaran: Truth and Illusion in Ilahita Arapesh Religion*. Berkeley: University of California Press, 1980.

van Gennep, Arnold. *The Rites of Passage* (1908). London: Routledge and Kegan Paul, 1965.

Whitehouse, H. *Arguments and Icons: Divergent Modes of Religiosity*. Oxford: Oxford University Press, 2000.

———. *Inside the Cult: Religious Experience and Innovation in Papua New Guinea*. Oxford: Oxford University Press, 1995.

———. "Memorable Religions: Transmission, Codification, and Change in Divergent Melanesian Contexts." *Man*, n.s., 27 (1992): 777–97.

———. *Modes of Religiosity: A Cognitive Theory of Religious Transmission*. Walnut Creek, Calif.: AltaMira Press, 2004.

———. "Rites of Terror: Emotion, Metaphor, and Memory in Melanesian Initiation Cults." *Journal of the Royal Anthropological Institute*, n.s., 4 (1996): 703–15.

Whitehouse, Harvey, and James Laidlaw, eds. *Ritual and Memory: Toward a Comparative Anthropology of Religion*. Walnut Creek, Calif.: AltaMira Press, 2004.

Whitehouse, Harvey, and Luther H. Martin, eds. *Theorizing Religions Past: Archaeology, History, and Cognition*. Walnut Creek, Calif.: AltaMira Press, 2004.

Whitehouse, Harvey, and Robert N. McCauley, eds. *Mind and Religion: Psychological and Cognitive Foundations of Religiosity*. Walnut Creek, Calif.: AltaMira Press, 2005.

CHAPTER 15

HOPE

W. WATTS MILLER

FORMS OF HOPE

Hope is obviously about an object of concern and something hoped—that a friend will get well, that winter will soon be over, that all is not lost. Yet hope is not just *hope-that*. To explore why, a place to start is with the work of the French Catholic philosopher Gabriel Marcel. Writing during the occupation of France in the 1940s, he sees the core authentic form of hope as "I hope in thee for us."[1] Writing in the uneasy years of the 1950s, he says, "Hope is perhaps nothing but an active struggle against despair."[2]

In effect, these are ways to stress hope as a *virtue*, anchored in *relation*. Hope, as a virtue, is an *active personal struggle* to hold on, against the going-to-pieces of despair. Hope, as a personal struggle to hold on, needs anchorage in relation, and *solidarity* and *communion*. It is a holding on through the solidarity of *hope-for*—where one's own hope is bound up with hope "for us," and the self escapes isolation in forming, through attachments with others, the "city" of the individual personality.[3] But the foundation of this "city" and of our interrelation with one another is the commonality and totality to do with the communion of *hope-in*—hope in a "thee" at once inside and beyond each individual, an inner immanent force and a transformative, transcendent power.

In wanting an account that is nonsectarian, Marcel draws a veil over the identity of this "thee." But it is clear enough that for him it entails a religious hope in the power that is "god." It cannot be the pure secularism of a Durkheimian hope in the power that is "society" or a Marxist hope in the "dynamics of history" or a general hope in "humanity." Yet it is not pure otherworldliness either. It involves hope in a "thee" that is an active presence in our lives, helping us to keep going in the here and now. And so it is a religious hope that is in a way "secular," but it is in the sense that it invokes an immanent "god" at work in this world, and not just limited, transcendentally, to another realm.

We can now come to a possible criticism of Marcel. A strength of his account is that it drives home the importance of *hope-in* and *hope-for*, against preoccupation with *hope-that*. The trouble is that he then marginalizes hope-that, in a worry over its vulnerability to defeat and in a quest for an absolute hope. But how can the hope of limited humans be unfaltering and absolute, even if it is hope in a "god" who is absolute? In any case, how can hope have much meaning, without anything hoped-that?

Structures and Dynamics of Hope

Marcel in fact emphasizes and interlinks two quite general hopes-that—rock-bottom hope that all is not lost, and transcendent hope of salvation. He also sees imprisonment—by illness, in a land under occupation, in an actual jail—as a paradigmatic case of hope's struggle against despair. And this involves not only general but particular hopes to do with emancipation—however much "prisoners of hope" still need the stronghold of a core source of hope.[4] Yet he remains worried over hope-that. Why? A basic reason, of course, is if it disconnects from hope-in and hope-for, through preoccupation just with objects of hope. At the same time it is because pinning everything on a particular object of hope is a recipe, if this fails, for despair. But it is also because of the "objectivity" telling us to calculate our chances of success as if detached spectators, and in a confusion of hope with expectation.

This ignores our role as agents, and how adopting "objectivity" is an active internal way of going to pieces in despair. Hope is an active internal empowerment precisely because it is *not* "objective realism" about our situation but a way to transform it and keep together the "city" of a basic personal integrity. So this is also *not* to see hope as instrumental psychological magic and a technique for success in any object if the individual sufficiently wills it. It is about a deep structure of hope, with "I hope in thee for us" at its core and as an anchorage of general and particular concerns that interact in a capacity to hold on but also to let go of some hopes and discover others. And in going beyond "objectivity," this approach is still about a difference between the realm of hope and the realm of the utopian dream. The object of a dream can be admitted as altogether "unrealistic," in its very creativity and power as an illuminating vision of things. The object of a hope is bound up with the possibility of its actualization, thanks to the transformative power of a fundamental source of hope.

In sum, Marcel does not give up on hope-that but instead worries over it in certain forms. And this links with his wider philosophy, but especially his distinction between the worlds of "being" and "having."[5] The hope he defends is embedded in a communitarian world of being and belonging. The hopes he criticizes concern an individualistic world of having and possessing. These are the hopes that are a fast track to despair—but not just due to fortune's ups and downs. These kinds of hope are associated with the vulnerability of isolated atomistic selves, and of individuals centering life around material things, calculating rational interest and gripped by the tyranny of desire.

Accordingly, there are important similarities with Durkheim's classic account of the two main modern routes to suicide.[6] One is the *egoism* of a cold intellectual atomistic world of the self, cut off from the warmth of social feelings. The other is the *anomie* of a raging bonfire of desires, impossible to dampen down and bring under conscious control. Thus, a good question is whether for Marcel and Durkheim the real modern killer is the Arctic of intellectual detachment, not the Sahara of unquenchable desire. But whatever the answer, it is necessary to recognize a systematic ambivalence in their view of emotion. Both of them dislike *desire*—in a modern hostility to it, carrying over from traditional condemnations of *lust*. Yet both of them, in worries about the ice-man of reason, rally around the feelings of *warmth, attachment, solidarity, communion,* and indeed *love* bound up in interrelation in a life in common.

There is a difference, however. Durkheim is almost carried away, in *The Elemental Forms*, by the force of collective effervescence—with its "total bodily and mental highs" of a "surexcitation de toute la vie physique et mentale."[7] Marcel does not share this enthusiasm.[8] In fact, he makes little or no reference to the explosive upsurges of hope in millenarian and messianic movements throughout the history of religion. These are central to the concern with the dynamics of hope in the work of both the neo-Durkheimian Henri Desroche[9] and the Marxist Ernst Bloch.[10] Marcel's account of structures of hope is also in a way concerned with dynamics—and how the struggle against despair depends on a patient, stubborn, obdurate hope. This might let in the emotional intensity of *longing* and *yearning*. But what he clearly distrusts is the emotional intensity plus impatient expectation of *desire*, and the dynamics of the sort of hope that climaxes in a "high" and then goes to pieces. Nor is he alone in this view.

The particular moment when a people set out to change a system of ideas is a time when they can well believe, in an outburst of enthusiasm and youthful confidence, that the task is easy. But it does not take them long to experience all the difficulties, and the illusions they might have had serve only to make their disenchantment more bitter.[11] What is important here is not just how Durkheim himself criticizes effervescence but his concern above all not just with individual but also with collective hope. So in developing an account of structures and dynamics of hope, a very basic Durkheimian point is to include "we hope."

True, a Marcellian "I hope" entails "I hope for us." And like Marcel, Durkheim also rethinks the individual personality, replacing the individual as atom with what could be called the "liberal-communitarian self." Yet even a liberal-communitarian "I hope" is not the same as a collective "we hope."

A way to see this takes us to 1893 and Durkheim's first major publication, *The Division of Labor*. A key problematic, stated at the outset, is how the individual can be both autonomous and solidary. And a key solution is the distinctively individual yet social personality of the liberal-communitarian self. But when we get to the end of the work, what we get to is a grand vision of collective hope. This includes how *individual autonomy is itself a collective ideal*, built into the modern world's structure and dynamic. But it is above all about a whole interlinking set of modern collective aspirations. These recall the motto of the French Revolution, "Liberté, Egalité, Fraternité"—readopted by the Third Republic in 1880, appearing everywhere in public buildings, and emblazoned above every school entrance as an inspiration to future citizens. And in fact Durkheim began work on his book at just around this symbolically optimistic time, completed the first full draft in 1886, and was still busy on it during celebrations of the centenary of the revolution in 1889, when he wrote an article about its "new audacious faith."[12] In his book, this audacious faith expands into the interlinked modern collective ideals of freedom, equality, justice, solidarity, human rights, and human fraternity—and how modern society must work to achieve all these together. So it is little wonder that in his grand concluding vision of things there will always be "a field wide open to our efforts."[13] Nor is it hard to understand why, in reviewing the new edition, a member of his group saw all this as so utopian that it stirred up pessimism.[14] And in his new preface itself, the bright hopes can come across as a whistling in the dark, thanks to his picture of the gulf separating the ideal from the actual existing society.[15]

The upshot, then, is another candidate for the hope that creates despair—a vast, sweeping idealism. Accordingly, it is also another case of the Marcellian problematic of a kind of hope against hope—"false" hope versus authentic hope. Yet how might we sort out what is authentic? The Marcellian strategy is to look for a core *form* of hope. But this is at the same time to base it in a core *job* of hope. When it is asked what this core job is, a Marcellian response centers around "my" hope to hold on against going to pieces as an individual, while a Durkheimian response centers around "our" hope to hold on against despair as a group or society. Perhaps, through the interpenetration of individual and society in the liberal-communitarian self, these are two sides of the same answer. And perhaps it is not the only answer. But it is enough to go forward with.

"Give Us This Day Our Daily Bread"

It is not altogether fair to sneer at the idealism of *The Division of Labor* and its nineteenth-century vision of progress. This is partly because Durkheim might be right, that ideals come interconnected in a living web of belief, which survives picking to pieces by mere theorists. But it is also because he himself repeatedly criticizes a vast, abstract idealism. Again and again, in a lifelong campaign for what he calls "intermediate groups," he insists on anchorage of grand horizons in definite milieux and a network of concrete meaningful relationships—which translates, in *The Elemental Forms*, into anchorage of religion's grand horizons in a network of particular rituals, symbols, myths, and beliefs. These help to make the ideal concrete, and a living hope.

In a way, this is encapsulated in the verse, in the Lord's Prayer, "Give us this day our daily bread." It is not just theology and a thin, abstract intellectualist discourse about a vast abstract idea of "god." It is religion, and embeds a sense of the transcendent in a web of ritual, story, and symbolism creating a living hope in "god"—a hope at work in ordinary as well as special times, and at once individual as well as collective, material as well as spiritual, particular as well as fundamental.

Thus a limitation of Marcel's attempt to lay bare the fundamental is how, even in its insights, it is a philosophy of hope. True, it is developed through examples from experience; yet these remain the thin descriptions of abstract discourse. And it is essential to involve the thick-textured descriptions of narrative. This can take us to "fiction"—including his own efforts, escaping philosophy, at drama.[16] Or it can take us to "real-life" stories—both iconic, such as the story of Anne Frank,[17] and little known, such as the story of Gerhard Durlacher.[18] For what is also important is how narrative, in all its modern diversity, circulates among an immense public as a modern sacred body of myth. Even if it is no longer collected together in a common sacred text such as the Bible, it does a similar job. It is not just that various basic themes run through modern stories to do with hope and despair. Beyond an individual author's construction of experiences, there is a collective construction of a "fictional" or "real-life" story's mythic significance. And beyond the different stories, there is narrative as a genre, mobilizing the power of thick-textured description to explore, through the particular, the fundamental. But also—in reading the Bible or a biography or a novel—narrative is itself a rite, concretely acting to create in life, as in its stories about life, a sense of the fundamental.

Emphasizing all this is the context for continuing, here, with abstract enquiry into hope, and its job as the integrity of keeping things together, holding on, not going to pieces. What is hope keeping together? A basic hope is keeping body and soul together. And a basic topic of myth is the facing of a choice between these. A classic way to go to pieces is the Faustian bargain of purchasing life through selling the soul. A classic hope is strength to surrender life and keep care of the soul. But twentieth-century stories of the death camps are about a terror that aims to deny even this choice and, in killing the physical individual, to smash the personality. In the mythic power of stories of endurance in the face of terror, it is sometimes forgotten how they also bear witness to those who were worn down, and crushed. An important step in destroying people is to take away their names and reduce them to numbers. Yet it is only part of an entire assault on identity. For identity is a key to integrity, and holding out against going to pieces. Identity, however, has two aspects. It involves deep-rooted feelings of attachment, defining the self through a group, an ethic, a religion. But it also involves a whole concrete symbolism, including all the emotive significance of a ("mere") name. And together these are a source of vulnerability, as well as strength. It is how—in an act of affirmation *or* a recipe for collapse—it is possible to pin everything on what has come to mean everything, as a make-or-break symbol of the soul. Yet it is also how it is possible to keep finding space in a network of symbols and a web of identity, to keep going with a succession of particular hopes, each serving a fundamental purpose for a time, and to realize that the world does not cease with one's own death and there is still hope "for us." It is the atomistic self that in the end is much more vulnerable. It is identity, with its resilience, that is the greater stronghold.

It is not a stronghold come what may, and twentieth-century stories make it hard to believe in Marcellian "absolute" hope. But they also make it hard to believe in Durkheimian Jerusalems. Indeed, faced with brave new worlds, a way to hold on is rock-bottom hope that all is not lost.

"There Is a Happy Land, Far, Far Away"

There are many arguments against unutopian hope. Every society comes with its own dream. There is little chance of any social reform without great social movements and an inspiring vision of things. There is no logic in sticking at a minimum without an ideal to define it, and no sense in fighting against the world without an aspiration to fight for. Indeed, it is absurd—a hope without reason of revolt without a cause.

Albert Camus is a good candidate as the champion of such hope, with his publication, in the 1940s and 1950s, of *The Plague, The Myth of Sisyphus,* and *The Rebel*.[19] Michel Foucault is a more recent contender, with a mass of similar criticism hurled at him—for example, as a theorist of "hopelessness," paralyzing action for reform.[20] Yet is this fair? Where Camus lashes out, in *The Rebel*, against grand ideological visions as a route to terror, Foucault systematically articulates a not-unjustified skepticism about institutions of power. In addition, as defenders remind us, his later work turns to ethics and the hope involved in "care of the self." But this might have little to do with a liberal-communitarian self's hope "for us," or Camus's declaration "I rebel, therefore we are."[21] Foucault's suspicion of institutions can come across as extending to every aspect of social life, including solidarity. It could even be that his "postmodern" philosophy recycles the modernism of the atomistic self. In any case, another way into these issues is through the work of the sociologist Michel Maffesoli and his bright, seemingly hope-filled announcement of a "veritable *re-enchantment of the world.*"[22] It is only seemingly hope-filled because he also sees a veritable power struggle nowadays—but between different kinds of power, which he calls *pouvoir* and *puissance*. In effect, this struggle is between the Foucaultian power/*pouvoir* of institutions and apparatuses and the Durkheimian power/*puissance* of solidarity and the sacred. And the upshot is that Maffesoli's initial rousing optimism ends in rock-bottom hope. On the one hand, the power of the sacred can never be completely crushed by the power of institutions. On the other, it can never completely conquer and transform their power. All it can do is rebel against it.

This way of thinking about hope picks up on a key feature of the "Australia" evoked in *The Elemental Forms*—a sacred land, far, far away, with nothing remotely resembling institutions such as the state. But it remains a rock-bottom hope. It does not resurrect nineteenth-century anarchist ideals of a modern world without machineries and apparatuses, just as it also ditches long-running modern hopes in the coming of a commonwealth. These were still powerful in the time of Camus. And when people sang battle hymns of a republic—*The Marseillaise* or *The Red Flag*, it does not much matter—it was still with some belief. Maffesoli represents a generation who have said goodbye to all that.

Perhaps this is only a phase, in the fortunes of an idealism that Durkheim, peering into the future in *The Division of Labor*, saw as built into modernity's dynamic. Or there is the view of his contemporary, the Catholic convert and quintessential rebel Charles Péguy. In an impassioned essay of 1910, Péguy observes, famously, "Everything begins in mystique and ends in politics"[23]—whether it is the mystique of a republic or of socialism or of Christianity that inevitably becomes a home to ways of the world and normal betrayal from within. For mystique is a sort of daily bread of politics, which it needs to live on, even as it eats away at it. The essay is in fact an affirmation of an ideal's power to survive, and how "mystique is not consumed by the politics born from it."[24] So this is not quite the same as other versions of rock-bottom hope. For Camus, "the bacillus of the plague never dies" but "can lie around for years and years."[25] For Péguy, the germ of mystique never dies but bides its time until the day comes "*when they will see what we are still capable of doing for the Republic.*"[26]

What is at stake, then, is not just a history of the ups and downs of modern idealism. Pèguy is concerned with how, even in the conflict between the world of politics and the realm of mystique, there is interdependence. This is especially evident in the case of the church—the secular institution of power and politics that exists only in claiming that it is *already* a sacred mystic church. It is *not* simply that the church might one day realize the ideal of a church, which, anyway, as a this-worldly institution, it never can. Indeed, Péguy's whole notion of mystique ties in with the religious problematic of immanence as opposed to transcendence. For mystique involves commitment to what is *already* a sacred republic, *not* simply a future republic that somehow escapes politics and actualizes an ideal. So it is again important to relate Péguy to Christianity, with its belief in a reign already here yet still to come. *Immanent*, rock-bottom hope that all is not lost in this world combines with *transcendent* hope of salvation and a coming of the kingdom in a total transformation of things.

This is how prayer for "our daily bread" combines with hymns about "a happy land, far, far away."[27] But it is also how the connection falls apart with secularism. In a first bright dawn, hope in the kingdom converts into hope in a republic, while

Christian mythic narrative converts into rational philosophical history. Then comes fragmentation. Forms of rock-bottom hope reemerge, but disjoined from whatever idealisms survive. For without the glue of the transcendent, is there any way to link them?

"Praise the Lord and Pass the Ammunition"

It was the American naval chaplain Howell Forgy who urged, at Pearl Harbor, "Praise the Lord and pass the ammunition."[28] And it is the American philosopher Richard Rorty who attacks faith in "god" but also an unfolding history to see hope as "a matter of weapons and luck."[29] However, this perspective fails to understand religious hope, its conversion into philosophical history, and the birth of modern secular "luck."

In its mainstream traditions, Christianity is not about a "god" ruling us with iron law and necessity. It is about a "god" gifting us with free will. Accordingly, it involves hope in ourselves, and—whether "passing the ammunition" or waiting to show "what we are still capable of doing for the Republic"—hope in our own determination as free moral agents. At the same time, it is hope in "god" as an inner presence in our lives, rather than just as an external power. And this one-and-manifold "god" is at the center of a set of interrelated problematics. There is the hope that is at once *both* hope in "thee" *and* hope in ourselves. There is the vast complex hope involving *both* a realm of justice, law, necessity, and an order of things *and* a realm of grace, love, spontaneity, and the free bonds of a gift-relationship. Not least, there is the anchorage of these hopes in a narrative that is in various ways *both* revealed and accessible to us *and* hidden, mysterious, unseen.

So a task is to explore how all this converts into secular philosophies, each picking out different elements. But a special puzzle is how religion generates notions of luck and the contingent—which secularists like Rorty habitually invoke, as if they were part of the furniture of the world. "Luck" has no place in religious cosmologies. Yet once we ask where the idea comes from, we see it must have some roots in religion. Indeed, the problem is that it might have so many: hidden narrative, the free spontaneity of grace, or even the determinism of a preordained destiny. Thus it may be a sign of its religious origins that "luck" is sometimes confused with "fate." In any case, it is not hard to see affinities. When there are no gods deciding for their own impenetrable reasons our *lot*, what is left is an arbitrary *lottery*. True, it comes with the rationalism of a theory of chance—but a rationalism that forbids questions such as *Why me?* and replaces mystical explanation of particular life-events with the black hole of "the contingent." In the same basic way, the "luck" idea might originate in ideas of grace, above mere law, or in hidden narrative, or in whatever else involves a power beyond limited human understanding. Dropping the enigma of "god" turns up the enigma of "luck," in an exchange of one mystery for another. And both are to do with an absurd hope. One is in a power that is not understandable yet makes total sense. The other is in a contingency that is understandable only in making no sense.

It is in its specific form of absurdity that "luck" runs into trouble as a source of hope. But it is also in ending up as a single source, as against all the diverse, even contradictory elements adhering together in religion. And it heads that way when, after deconstructions of "god," "man," "society," "grand narrative," "science," and so on, there is little left except the atomistic individual in a vast universe of the contingent. True, this sweeping intellectualism might not have much impact. There is still a need to recognize some sort of "luck" as a more or less well-entrenched notion in modern Western culture. But it is inadequate just to add it into the set of problematics already touched on, if this is just to add it into abstract discourse about them. It is again essential to recognize how—among the religious or the secular—hope is embedded in symbolism, narrative, drama, and, in fact, all kinds of art.[30]

The Aesthetics of Hope

Durkheim's *Elemental Forms* discusses something he calls the "mimetic rite." But we could see it as prayer. It is above all about ways to fix the mind on an object of concern, "to say the thing wished to happen, to call up and evoke it," and so it provides ways people focus on a hope, and "concentrate on it the force of their attention and will."[31] Prayer can come in various forms—requests to "god," hymns, mantras, the imitative actions of the "mimetic rite," and so on. Yet at bottom prayer is action that concentrates thought on key concerns. At the same time, it is action that not only expresses but creates hope. And it does this through the power of ritual and symbolism, but also art.

Durkheim looks for basic forms of ritual, each with their own basic job—while seeing an overall dynamic in which the same action can come to do different things, and the same thing is done by different actions. This is why it is difficult to identify prayer with only one way of hoping, yet also why particular ways of hoping draw power from an entire religious world of ritual, symbolism, and aesthetics. But it is why, too, a special importance attaches to sacred drama's enactment of sacred myth.

He calls this the "representative or commemorative rite." Yet it is not just a representation, and not just a commemoration. He stresses that it is a *dramatic representation*. And what it dramatizes is *mythology*—at once "an ethic and cosmology, as well as a history."[32] So myth is at once collective memory *and* collective hope—in how it creates solidarity between the generations through an ethic of a continuing moral community, through a worldview spanning all of time, and through a story linking past, present, and future times. Like prayer and other rites, the enactment of myth is thus a form of communion of people both with one another and with the vast moral-cosmic power that is "god." Yet sacred drama is still special. It is less about particular practical concerns, more a way to explore a whole human-divine relationship.

But it is also that *drama brings myth to life* and, in continuing new enactments, *helps to keep it alive*. A common intellectualist preoccupation is just with the structure and content of myth's stories—as though they are a mere "text." Yet even if myth has some such existence in the human mind, it is not how it grips the human imagination. It owes its power to the actual social-aesthetic forms creating and recreating it through the generations. These include the traditional skill of collective oral storytelling, while nowadays there is the impact of repro art—the art made possible by mass reproductive techniques, such as the novel, the film, the television soap. Yet Durkheim still seems right to emphasize live drama, with its fusion of the power of assembly, the power of symbolism, and the power of a whole combination of art forms—not just narrative, verse, song, music, dance, painting, or costume but also the creative collective interaction and electricity of an entire atmospherics.

And this sets the scene for radical views. His account of drama involves what we might call "practical aesthetics"—how art is social sacred symbolism. But he then highlights what we might call "pure aesthetics"—how art goes beyond symbolism, in sheer inventive energies of a *surplus* and enjoyment of "free creations of the mind."[33] There is always a mixture of these elements. Art, at its most playful, still secretes an underlying symbolism. Yet art, at its most somber, also generates pure aesthetic *surplus* and *jouissance*. Indeed, when he insists on art as a necessity, it is to insist on the necessity of *surplus* and on a transcendent *jouissance* inhering in life—which is why "there is a poetry inherent in all religion."[34]

All of this opens up the issue of an aesthetic of hope. Thus something is missing from various familiar lines on religion's hope in a transcendent realm—its dismissal as illusion, its defense with abstract theological argument, its rereading as social symbolism, and so on. These leave out the poetry in religion. And so it is all very well to look down on "There Is a Happy Land." It is not in the same league as the "high art" of Péguy's work *The Portal of the Mystery of Hope*,[35] or Messiaen's work *The Transfiguration of Our Lord Jesus Christ*.[36] Yet in all three there is the same fusion of the religiousness of hope in a transcendent realm with an aesthetic that, in giving this power, also creates—through the energy and *jouissance* of art itself—another reechoing realm of transcendence. All kinds of questions arise to do with secularism. But it is crucial to ask about works such as *The Plague*. For there is not so much a fusion as a contradiction of energies, in which a story of the bleakness of the world lifts up into something else through the creativity and *jouissance* of the novel's own aesthetics. And it must have something to do with this transcendence that Camus, in *The Myth of Sisyphus*, says he senses in the work of Kafka: an "immense cry of hope."[37] After all, their stories do not just describe "reality," as if we are left to manage through the same feelings of hope or despair as before. Hope can also exist through the transfigurative power of art—not least its transfiguration of the "real" world of power and institutions into a grim, laughable world of the Kafkaesque.

Let us finish, then, with a rough guide to the modern landscape of hope. Marcel and Péguy represent, in their very differences, continuation of a protean religious hope. But it is important how—even if Marcel's theatre does not compare with Péguy's verse—both of them embed this hope within art. For it is through art and a whole mythic web of problematics—not least immanence-transcendence—that religion creates a mystique that is able to bind together rock-bottom hope and a vision of a transcendent realm's total transformation of things. Even in interlinking art, symbolism, and the sacred, Durkheim could never recognize how secularism unravels this web and decouples rock-bottom and idealistic hope.

At one stage, in his work, effervescence's explosive hope is a route to despair. Later, in *The Elemental Forms*, it is the way to an idealism that overcomes present-day "mediocrity."[38] But the lesson of Péguy is that it is a route, if not to despair, certainly to a new "mediocrity." And no amount of secular ritual, mimicking religion, can keep politics out of this-worldly Jerusalems. Indeed, the basic trouble with Durkheim's changing searches for a new secular idealism is his continuing hope in a new "secular religion"—as if just the same as traditional religion, minus belief in the transcendent.

God become man is not man become god; given Durkheim's own stress on human finitude, and limits to what we can know, do, or will, such "secular religion" is at most a scene of the semisacred. This lets in a key continuity with religion, to do with feelings of communion as the feelings of solidarity central to "we hope" and "I hope for us." Yet there remain key discontinuities. After "god," there is "luck." And there is a gap, which "luck" cannot bridge, between the rock-bottom and the visionary. True, there are different forms of secular idealism. The most common, as well as most slippery, of all is the form that views the ideal as something not to actualize but only to aim at. There is still an unmistakable brightness of hope in a radical transformation of institutions, so that they might live up to mystique, instead of living off it. And such idealism still contrasts with the rock-bottom hope that manages to resist, hold on, and keep care of the soul, despite the "real" world of politics and everyday apparatuses of the Kafkaesque.

In a way, however, all hope is escape from "reality," and holding on through the power of imagination. Difference over belief in a transcendent realm is fundamental to modern varieties of hope. Yet these are also varieties of imagination, and of the realm of transcendence that is art. There is a "poetry" inherent in all vision, even the most secular, while it is "poetry" that, in the religiosity of Péguy as in the secularism of Camus, helps to save rock-bottom hope from mere despair. And it is the same with feelings of communion with "god" or of solidarity with one another. These are at the same time feelings of uplift, with roots in the transfigurative and aesthetic.

Perhaps religion was once everywhere. In any case, art is now everywhere. Some of it is avowedly religious, yet with a power that reaches far beyond the ranks of the faithful. Some of it is card-carrying secularism, yet just to place it on an index does not rise to the challenge. All or almost all of it is open to our own different imaginative responses, which are themselves part of the *jouissance* of the creative. Art, in this protean energy, is an elemental modern source of feelings of hope.

NOTES

1. Gabriel Marcel, *Homo Viator: Proléégomènes à une métaphysique de l'espérance* (Paris: Aubier, 1944), 81.
2. Gabriel Marcel, "Structure de l'espérance," in *Dieu vivant* (Paris: Seuil, 1951), 71. For an introduction to Marcel on hope, see Joan Nowotny, "Despair and the Object of Hope," in *The Sources of Hope*, edited by Ross Fitzgerald (Oxford: Pergamon Press, 1979). For a full-length study, see Simonne Plourde, *Gabriel Marcel: Philosophe et témoin de l'espérance* (Québec: Presses de l'Université de Québec, 1975).
3. Marcel, *Homo Viator*, 82.
4. See "Return to the stronghold, ye prisoners of hope," Zec 9:12.
5. See Plourde, *Gabriel Marcel*, chaps. 1 and 2.
6. Emile Durkheim, *Le suicide* (Paris: Alcan, 1897).
7. Emile Durkheim, *Les formes élémentaires de la vie religieuse* (Paris: Alcan, 1912), 310.
8. Cf. his remark, during the German occupation, "It is difficult to interpret as hope the idolatry shown by vast collectivities, bewitched by their leaders"; Marcel, *Homo Viator*, 75.
9. Henri Desroche, *The Sociology of Hope*, translated by Carol Martin-Sperry (London: Routledge and Kegan Paul, 1979).
10. Ernst Bloch, *The Principle of Hope*, 3 vols., translated by Neville Plaice, Stephen Plaice, and Paul Knight (Oxford: Blackwell, 1986).
11. Emile Durkheim, "Sur l'œuvre de Taine," in *Textes*, (Paris: Minuit, 1975), 1:174—article of 1897.
12. Emile Durkheim, "Les principes de 1789 et la sociologie," in *La science sociale et l'action* (Paris: Presses Universitaires de France, 1970), 224.
13. Emile Durkheim, *De la division du travail social*, 2nd ed. (Paris: Alcan, 1902), 336.
14. Célestin Bouglé, "Revue générale des théories récentes sur la division du travail," *Année sociologique* 6 (1903): 107.
15. Durkheim, *Division du travail*, ii–v.
16. See Joseph Chenu, *Le théâtre de Gabriel Marcel et sa signification métaphysique* (Paris: Aubier, 1948).
17. Anne Frank, *The Diary of Anne Frank: The Critical Edition*, translated by Arnold J. Pomerans and R. M. Mooyaart-Doubleday (London: Viking, 1989).
18. Gerhard Durlacher, *The Search: The Birkenau Boys*, translated by Susan Massotty (London: Serpent's Tail, 1998).
19. Albert Camus, *La peste*, in *Théâtre, récits, nouvelles* (Paris: Gallimard, 1962); *Le mythe de Sisyphe* and *L'homme révolté*, in *Essais* (Paris: Gallimard, 1965). For two recent studies, see Jeffrey Isaac, *Arendt, Camus and Modern Rebellion* (New Haven, Conn.: Yale University Press, 1992), and Tony Judt, *The Burden of Responsibility: Blum, Camus, Aron, and the French Twentieth Century* (Chicago: University of Chicago Press, 1998).

20. Richard Rorty, *Achieving Our Country* (Cambridge, Mass.: Harvard University Press, 1998), 37. For a relevant collection of essays *pro* and *contra* Foucault, see David Hoy, ed., *Foucault: A Critical Reader* (Oxford: Blackwell, 1986).

21. Camus, *L'homme révolté*, 432.

22. Michel Maffesoli, *Le temps des tribus* (Paris: La Table Ronde, 2000), 59.

23. Charles Péguy, *Notre jeunesse* (Paris: Gallimard, 1969), 31.

24. Ibid., 32. For studies, see Jean Bastaire, *Péguy l'insurgé* (Paris: Payot, 1975), and Géraldi Leroy, *Péguy entre l'ordre et la révolution* (Paris: Presses de la Fondation Nationale des Sciences Politiques, 1981).

25. Camus, *La peste*, 1472.

26. Péguy, *Notre jeunesse*, 254.

27. Andrew Young, "There Is a Happy Land," hymn 608 in *The English Hymnal* (London: Oxford University Press, 1906).

28. Reported in *New York Times*, November 1, 1942, and the title of a popular song composed later that year.

29. Richard Rorty, "Private Irony and Liberal Hope," in *Contingency, Irony, and Solidarity* (Cambridge: Cambridge University Press, 1989), 91.

30. The discussion that follows draws on and develops W. Watts Miller, "Total Aesthetics: Art and *The Elemental Forms*," *Durkheimian Studies*, n.s., 10 (2004): 88–118.

31. Durkheim, *Formes élémentaires*, 512.

32. Ibid., 536.

33. Ibid., 545.

34. Ibid., 546.

35. Charles Péguy, *Le porche du mystère de la deuxième vertu*, in *Œuvres poétiques complètes* (Paris: Gallimard, 1967).

36. Olivier Messiaen, *La transfiguration de Notre-Seigneur Jésus-Christ*, Orchestre Philharmonique et Chœur de Radio France dir. Myung-Whun Chung, Deutsche Grammophon, DGG4715692.

37. Camus, *Mythe de Sisyphe*, 208. See also the discussion of art in *L'homme révolté*, 657–80.

38. Durkheim, *Formes élémentaires*, 610.

BIBLIOGRAPHY

Bastaire, Jean. *Péguy l'insurgé*. Paris: Payot, 1975.

Bloch, Ernst. *The Principle of Hope*. Translated by Neville Plaice, Stephen Plaice, and Paul Knight. 3 vols. Oxford: Blackwell, 1986.

Bouglé, Célestin. "Revue générale des théories récentes sur la division du travail." *Année sociologique* 6 (1903): 73–122.

Camus, Albert. *L'homme révolté*. In *Essais*. Paris: Gallimard, 1965.

———. *Le mythe de Sisyphe*. In *Essais*. Paris: Gallimard, 1965.

———. *La peste*. In *Théâtre, récits, nouvelles*. Paris: Gallimard, 1962.

Chenu, Joseph. *Le théâtre de Gabriel Marcel et sa signification métaphysique*. Paris: Aubier, 1948.

Desroche, Henri. *De la division du travail social*. 2nd ed. Paris: Alcan, 1902.

———. *Les formes élémentaires de la vie religieuse*. Paris: Alcan, 1912.

———. "Les principes de 1789 et la sociologie." In *La science sociale et l'action*. Paris: Presses Universitaires de France, 1970, 215–25.

———. *The Sociology of Hope*. Translated by Carol Martin-Sperry. London: Routledge and Kegan Paul, 1979.

———. *Le suicide*. Paris: Alcan, 1897.

———. "Sur l'œuvre de Taine." In *Textes*. Paris: Minuit, 1975, 1:171–77.

Durlacher, Gerhard. *The Search: The Birkenau Boys*. Translated by Susan Massotty. London: Serpent's Tail, 1998.

The English Hymnal. London: Oxford University Press, 1906.

Frank, Anne. *The Diary of Anne Frank: The Critical Edition*. Translated by Arnold J. Pomerans and R. M. Mooyart-Doubleday. London: Viking, 1989.

Hoy, David, ed. *Foucault: A Critical Reader*. Oxford: Blackwell, 1986.

Isaac, Jeffrey. *Arendt, Camus, and Modern Rebellion*. New Haven, Conn.: Yale University Press, 1992.

Judt, Tony. *The Burden of Responsibility: Blum, Camus, Aron, and the French Twentieth Century*. Chicago: University of Chicago Press, 1998.

Leroy, Géraldi. *Péguy entre l'ordre et la révolution*. Paris: Presses de la Fondation Nationale des Sciences Politiques, 1981.

Maffesoli, Michel. *Le temps des tribus*. Paris: La Table Ronde, 2000.

Marcel, Gabriel. *Homo Viator: prolégomènes à une métaphysique de l'espérance*. Paris: Aubier, 1944.

———. "Structure de l'espérance." In *Dieu vivant*. Paris: Seuil, 1951, 71–80.

Messiaen, Olivier. *La transfiguration de Notre-Seigneur Jésus-Christ*. Myung-Whun Chung, with Orchestre Philharmonique et Chœur de Radio France. Deutsche Grammophon, DGG4715692.

Nowotny, Joan. "Despair and the Object of Hope." In *The Sources of Hope*, edited by Ross Fitzgerald. Oxford: Pergamon Press, 1979, 44–66.

Péguy, Charles. *Notre jeunesse*. Paris: Gallimard, 1969.

———. *Le porche du mystère de la deuxième vertu*. In *Œuvres poétiques complètes* Paris: Gallimard, 1967.

Plourde, Simonne. *Gabriel Marcel: Philosophe et témoin de l'espérance*. Québec: Presses de l'Université de Québec, 1975.

———. "Private Irony and Liberal Hope." In *Contingency, Irony, and Solidarity*. Cambridge: Cambridge University Press, 1989, 73–95.

Rorty, Richard. *Achieving Our Country*. Cambridge, Mass.: Harvard University Press, 1998.

Watts Miller, W. "Total Aesthetics: Art and *The Elemental Forms*." *Durkheimian Studies*, n.s., 10 (2004): 88–118.

CHAPTER 16

MELANCHOLY

JULIUS RUBIN

An examination of the relationship of religion and melancholy must begin with Clifford Geertz's oft-cited definition of religion, which provides an excellent point of departure. He writes in "Religion as a Cultural System" that a religion is

> (1) a system of symbols which acts to (2) establish powerful, pervasive, and long-lasting moods and motivations in men by (3) formulating conceptions of a general order of existence and (4) clothing these conceptions with such an aura of factuality that (5) the moods and motivations seem uniquely realistic.[1]

Theologies and sacred symbols constitute worldviews, cosmologies, and ontologies, compelling images of what is really real—the fundamental realities of human existence for various groups. Thus religion as a cultural system provides what Benjamin Nelson terms a dramatic design and a directive system, "complexes of instructions charging us to feel, think and perform in desired ways."[2] Geertz explains that sacred symbols induce, in varying times and places, a seemingly endless variety of emotional states, moods, and feelings ranging from exaltation to melancholy. The textures of religious experience and distinctive religious emotions like melancholy are constituted by concepts, beliefs, rituals.[3] This perspective on religion and emotion follows the *Annales* School of French Social History that explores the interconnection between *existence* (religion as worldview), *experience* (the social phenomenology of religious experience as mediated to believers by symbolic codes and ritual practice) and *expression* (the typical modalities of emotion prescribed by this directive system of meanings).[4]

Max Weber's concept of religious ethos proves important to the study of religion and emotion. He did not focus on the intellectual-theoretical dimensions of ethics, dogma, or systematic theology: "we are interested rather in something entirely different: the influence of those psychological sanctions which, originating in religious belief and the practice of religion, gave direction to practical conduct and held the individual to it."[5] Weber was interested in religious ideas that form the foundation for coherent worldviews and result in the rationalization of practical conduct. He introduces dogma only to demonstrate its contribution to practical rationalism and the formation of a life-order and corresponding type of personality. Through the concept of religious ethos, Weber developed a structural phenomenology of religious experience, emotion, personality, and life-order.[6] Believers who embrace a distinctive religious ethos will attempt to forge religiously grounded personalities, conduct their lives in conformity to religious dictates, pursue prescribed religious experiences, and struggle to attain emotional states (including melancholy) in pursuit of the promises of salvation.

In the spirit of Max Weber, we will investigate a variety of religious ethics and their affinity with melancholy. These ethics include inner-worldly asceticism (Protestant evangelical pietism), other-worldly asceticism (Christian monasticism), and inner-worldly mysticism (apophaticism and quietism among Christian mystics, in Hasidism, and in Sufism).

This is a daunting task, given the limitations of a chapter-length essay. We will proceed using Weber's concept of the ideal type, where each religious ethos is articulated with clarity and precision, in a logically consistent form that accentuates or exaggerates certain aspects of religious experience and expression. In this manner, ideal types create "logical utopias" that are not intended realistically to describe or to depict, photographically, the lived religion of peoples in concrete settings. Ideal types serve as helpful organizing concepts that we employ when examining actual case studies. Using this ideal type methodology as applied to types of asceticism and mysticism, we hope to realize John Corrigan's challenge to create "more precise characterizations of the emotional lives of religious individuals and groups within a historical setting rendered as a system of feeling rules."[7]

The concept of melancholy is a culturally and historically specific form of depressive disorder (dysphoria) that originates in Western medicine and thought. Melancholia as a clinical psychopathology was first identified by the Hippocratic writers in the fifth century B.C. as a disease of humoral imbalance, an excess of black bile—the melancholy humor produced by the spleen. Afflicted persons suffered a fear added to sadness, aversion to food, despondency, and sleeplessness. Galen, in the second century A.D., systematized humoral medicine, creating the clinical standard through which melancholia would be perceived for the next two thousand years. Melancholia represented a chronic, nonfebrile form of madness marked by fear, sadness, world-weariness, and suicidal inclinations.[8]

Jennifer Radden explains:

> For most of western European history, melancholy was a central cultural idea, focusing, explaining, and organizing the way people saw the world and one another and framing social, medical, and epistemological norms. Today, in contrast, it is an insignificant category, of little interest to medicine or psychology, and without explanatory or organizing vitality.[9]

We must avoid seeing despondent souls merely as patients suffering from a psychological disorder where the religious content of their suffering is considered epiphenomenal to an underlying organic pathophysiology. They would be viewed simply as depressed individuals, afflicted with a neurophysiological disease—as categorized in the *Diagnostic and Statistical Manual (DSMR-IV)* of the American Psychological Association—who express their symptoms using the idioms and vocabulary of religion.

Rather, we need to recover the meanings and experiences associated with melancholy states and religion in past times, before the advent of modern psychiatric nosology in the twentieth century. We need to examine literature, memoirs, poetry, spiritual diaries, theology, and writings about spiritual direction and the cure of souls.[10] Melancholy states must be understood in the context of Geertz's definition where religious systems of meaning instill powerful emotions and motivations in the hearts and minds of believers. Thus, melancholy as an emotion associated with religious states refers to an affect (fear, sadness, hopelessness), a distinctive stance toward life, a grieving over the loss of God's love, and an obsession and psychopathology associated with the spiritual itinerary of conversation and the path to salvation. By developing historical ideal types of the religious ethics of asceticism and mysticism and recovering how various religions have called on the faithful to seek paths to salvation that resulted in melancholy, we will develop the tools of analysis to examine case studies of religion and emotion without committing the errors of medical or social scientific reductionism.[11]

Religious Melancholy and Evangelical Pietism

Max Weber developed the historical ideal type of inner-worldly asceticism, the "Protestant Ethic," to refer to that ethos of life regulation whereby the isolated believer struggled to achieve an inner, psychological assurance of God's election and grace. Motivated by a wholly irrational concern for salvation, the believer worked ceaselessly, methodically, in a mundane calling to fulfill the God-willed demand that each person must serve as God's instrument and express brotherly love in service to the commonweal. Each individual was bound to consider himself or herself chosen and to combat all doubts, to create the inner, psychological conviction of election.[12] Work became the technical means of dispelling doubt, of actively constructing a life doing his will, increasing his glory, and seeking the highest good: *certitudo salutis*, the certainty of salvation.

According to Weber, following the Protestant Reformation, in the Occident, and particularly within Calvinist and Puritan sects, a new concept of religious personhood emerged. However, while Weber emphasized vocational asceticism as the center point of personality, it is also possible to reconstruct the ideal type of inner-worldly asceticism by devaluing vocational asceticism and accentuating dimensions of spirituality that Weber ignored. He might have examined "the Protestant ethic and the spirit of melancholy" as constituted by an inward spiritual pilgrimage in warfare against the self in search of the assurance of God's caress.[13] Here the self was organized around a central core of ultimate values, driven to achieve an inner consistency of motive and action. As an instrument of these transcendent purposes, embracing the concept of the ascetic warrior, the Christian soldier battled in *auto-machia*, or battle within, against the natural self and rejected the world in order to remake it according to God's will.

Early Puritan spiritual autobiographies such as Richard Baxter's *Reliquiae Baxterianae* and John Bunyan's allegorical tale *The Pilgrims's Progress* recorded the forging of lives in the crucible of incessant spiritual warfare against the self. George Goodman captures the motif of life as a pilgrimage of *auto-machia* in this poetic lament:

> I sing my SELF; my *civil-warss* within,
> The *Victories* I howeverly lose and win;
> The dayly *Duel*, the continuall strife,
> The *Warr* that ends not, till I end my life.
> And yet, not Mine, not onely Mine,
> But every-One's that under th'honnon'd Signn
> Of Christ his Standard, shal his Name enrole,
> With holy Vowes of Body and Soule.[14]

A life that is pursued as an inner pilgrimage and founded on warfare against the self necessarily encourages believers to turn anger and aggression inward through acts of repentance of sin and sorrowful grieving over their natural imperfections. In this manner, the Puritan theology of conversion, the practice of piety, and the ethos of inner-worldly asceticism structured experiences of melancholy. Believers viewed these emotional states as indispensable and authentic signs of the soul's progress from sin to election.

The other-worldly asceticism of medieval monasticism, in comparison, promoted a different religious complex of symptoms, sorrow-dejection-despair, known as the sin of *acedia*, or sloth in regard to spiritual duties. John Cassian first identified this despondency among the Desert Fathers in his work *The Conferences* (ca. 420), observing that "dejection and accidie generally arise without external provocation.... they often harass solitaries, and those who have settled themselves in the desert without any intercourse with other men."[15] Likening it to the noonday demon, Cassian observed a form of melancholy associated with solitary monastic discipline. Jackson relates that "the spiritual authors of the twelfth century and the Scholastics of the thirteenth century had tended to emphasize the state of mind of acedia (weariness, disgust, lack of fervor, sorrow), but, influenced by the increased activity of confessors and preachers, the common man's image of acedia came to center on spiritual idleness or neglect in the performance of spiritual duties."[16] The spiritual lassitude and deadness of acedia differed markedly from the holy desperation of the evangelical pietist experience of melancholy, where the penitent collapsed in self-abnegation and terror attendant to the conviction of desertion by God.

Martin Luther's Theology of the Cross and doctrine of *Anfechtung*, Jean Calvin's writings on solicitude, and other Reformation theologians introduced a type of religiosity that spread from the Reformation on the Continent into Puritan England, and found its most consistent expression in the nonconformist sectarians who settled in New England.[17] Known as evangelical pietism, this variant of Protestant belief emphasized: (1) experiential oneness with God; (2) the quest for spiritual perfection through the *ordo salutis* of conversion; (3) reliance on the objective authority of the biblical Word as interpreted by the prepared heart of the new man, himself transformed by the "ingrafting" of a dynamic, organic relationship between the believer and Christ; and (4) the opposition to and endeavor to transform, by evangelical means, the sinful nature of the unregenerate and the world.[18]

Evangelical pietism fused together disparate elements, including mysticism-illuminism, narcissism, inner-worldly asceticism, evangelical fervor to convert the masses and transform the world in God's image, and a particularism of grace founded on the doctrine of predestination. Wherever these five elements coalesced, one found the propensity for souls to suffer protracted melancholy.

The marrow of divinity for the Cambridge Calvinists in late Tudor England, for divines such as William Perkins (1158–1602), Richard Rogers (1550–1618), and Richard Greenham (1535–1594), centered on the question of the assurance of election (*certitudo salutis*). The methodical practice of piety included self-examination, repentance of sin, private prayer, and reading scripture and devotional works. This spiritual itinerary from sin to salvation (*ordo salutis*) provided devotional exercises where the faithful would experience an initial godly sorrow for sin that progressed in severity by means of the "inquisition of self-examination" into despair and the desired state of selfless ecstasy—holy desperation. Peter Iver Kaufman characterizes the assurance of election as a "pious dis-ease" that combined melancholy and vertigo as prefatory to the rapturous reception of grace that signaled the seal of election and salvation.[19] He explains: "The pietists wanted to structure character and desire and took a special interest in the therapeutic value of despair."[20]

This approach envisioned the soul caught in the dialectic between melancholy and hope. Each person needed to lose himself or herself in despair, and thus seek redemption and healing as a child of God. Kaufman presents John Donne's *Holy Sonnets* as an example of the soul's spiritual exercise of welcoming holy discontent, continual suffering, and vehement grief. Sonnet 3 begins:

> O might those sighes and tears return againe
> Into my breast and eyes, which I have spent,
> That I might in this holy discontent
> Mourne with some fruit, as I have mourn'd in vaine; . . .

> To (poore) me is allow'd
> No ease; for, long, yet vehement griefe hath beene
> Th' effect sand cause, the punishment and sinne.[21]

Timothie Bright (1550?–1615) in his *Treatise of Melancholie* identifies a type of melancholia consistent with the therapeutic despair and holy discontent of pietistic Puritans who suffered from a "salvation panic"—whose consciences oppressed them with an overwhelming sense of sin. Sufferers lived in fear of God's wrath and eternal damnation and were obsessed with their sinfulness.

Robert Burton published *The Anatomy of Melancholy* in 1621 and first identified the malady of "religious melancholy" as a distinct form of love-melancholy caused by a defect in man's relation to God. Through excesses and religious enthusiasm and through doctrinal error, Satan has polluted individuals' hearts with temptations and sinful obsessions and thus they remain alienated from God's love. Those afflicted with religious melancholy suffered the terrors of conscience, despair, and hopelessness. Only the infusion of faith—the assurance that God's love abides in the soul of the believer—could justify the sinner, and turn the depraved one toward God by renewing his or her mind, will, and heart.

Burton recounts the problems of devotional piety: weakness of faith, misunderstood scripture, the scrupulous conscience, excessive meditations, doubt and despair over one's status of election. His descriptions of the symptoms of "Despair, Fear, Sorrow, Suspicion, Anxiety, Horror of conscience, fearful dreams and visions," derived from the work of Felix Plater, reveals the seriousness of religious melancholy as a mental alienation that frequently resulted in suicide or madness. Plater explains:

> Never was any living creature in such torment before, in such a miserable estate, in such distress of mind, no hope, no faith, past cure, reprobate, continually tempted to make away [with] themselves.... that they are compelled against their will to harbour impious thoughts, to blaspheme against God, to the committing of many horrible deeds, to laying violent hands upon themselves, &c.[22]

Burton identified a new form of spiritual desolation among Puritans. He "invented a new name for pathological doubt about one's spiritual state, religious melancholy, and he charged that the Puritans were tearing and wounding people's consciences, so that they were almost mad with fear and sorrow."[23] Religious melancholy reportedly prevailed among Cambridge Puritans in the period from 1580 to 1600. Richard Napier, an Anglican minister and astrological physician who practiced in the English Midlands from 1597 to 1634, treated nearly three hundred religious melancholiacs, Puritans who suffered from what Napier regarded as "Puritanical consciences," "salvation panic," and obsessions with sinfulness.[24] The true incidence of religious melancholy is unknowable. However, by the late 1500s, Puritan practical divinity had incorporated suicidal crisis as an integral part of the morphology of conversion. Pastoral works defined suicidal despair as the work of Satan tempting the godly into doubt or blasphemy.

The Oxford Movement, begun by John and Charles Wesley in the 1730s and championed through the transatlantic revivalism of George Whitefield, added the important dimension of "heart work" to the religious ethos of evangelical pietism. Now itinerant evangelists and exhorters in the Great Awakening (1737–1740s) preached extemporaneous sermons designed to awaken the slumbering sinners assembled before them en masse, at open field revivals. The faithful whose hearts had grown cold expected to be awakened, and anticipated that the Holy Spirit would descend on their communities.[25]

Timothy D. Hall argues that Whitefield's revival campaigns "provided personal, representative contact with what was soon to become a vast 'imagined community' of saints that transcended geographical and denominational lines through a common experience of the New Birth."[26] This morphology of religious revival, written in narrative form and printed in newspapers and Thomas Prince's *The Christian History*, sustained the impression that each American locality was indeed participating in a transatlantic work of the Holy Spirit.[27] Correspondents from the field proclaimed the wondrous work of the Spirit, the sinners brought through the morphology of conversion and into the New Birth.[28]

Thomas Prince offers this account of Whitefield's labors in Boston in September 1740: "He distinctly applied his exhortations to the elderly people, to the middle aged, the young, the Indians and Negroes; and had a most winning way of addressing them."[29] Itinerants, imitators, and other "New Lights" emulated Whitefield; chief among them was Gilbert Tennent, whom Whitefield designated to prosecute the revival after Whitefield returned to England.

Tennent preached a farewell sermon in Boston on March 2, 1741, before sixty people, who included boys and girls, young men and women, Indians, African Americans, heads of families, aged persons, those in full communion, and the unchurched. Prince recorded this revival narrative of Tennent's masterful power in exciting the religious affections:

> Some under slight, others under strong convictions of their sins and sinfulness, guilt and condemnation, the wrath and cure of God upon them, their impotence and misery; some for a long time, even for several months under these convictions: some fearing lest the Holy Spirit should withdraw; others having quenched His operations, were in great distress lest he should leave them for ever.[30]

During March, Tennent arrived in Lyme, Connecticut, and fostered an awakening in the congregation of Reverend Jonathan Parsons. The revivalist opened the cold hearts of sinners to the terrors of the Lord, to a true and awful sense of the enormity of their sins, and the wrath of a "sin-hating God." Parsons marveled at the work of the Spirit and wrote: "I observed many of the assembly in tears, and heard many crying out in very great bitterness of soul.... Alas! I am undone! I'm undone! O my sins!"[31]

Jonathan Edwards, in his work *A Faithful Narrative*, relates the spiritual narratives of the Northampton revival in 1737, where the Holy Spirit awakened this community and brought showers of grace to sinners who found New Birth in the "white heat" of the revival. Edwards provides definitive clinical accounts of religious melancholy, which he viewed as the authentic work of the God in transforming the hearts of awakened men and women and transforming them into regenerate Christians.

The machinery of revival in the nineteenth century included Methodist camp meetings and Charles G. Finney's invention of protracted meetings; the "anxious bench," where awakened sinners might come forward to receive exhortation; and the calling out of the names of the unredeemed. Religious melancholy had become so prevalent among Methodists that Phoebe Palmer struggled to find a "shorter way," to assuage those who "feel that their *convictions* were not deep enough to warrant an approach to the throne of grace."[32] Palmer wrote *The Way to Holiness* in 1843 following years of domestic tragedy and spiritual struggle. Through mystic exercises in self-abnegation, she wrote, she attained a heart emptied of self and experienced an epiphany. In her earlier prophetic writing, the Altar Covenant (July 27, 1837), Palmer had said: "The Lord reigns unrivaled in my heart.... I *will* be holy *now*."[33] Ironically, Palmer's teachings of self-annihilation as the path to holiness, sanctification, and perfect love brought about yet another version of religious melancholy so prevalent among inner-worldly mystics, to which we now turn.

INNER-WORLDLY MYSTICISM AND THE DARK NIGHT OF THE SOUL

Max Weber's essay "Religious Rejections of the World and Their Directions" provides the following comparison of inner-worldly asceticism and mysticism, as abnegations of the world. He contrasts the active asceticism that is a God-willed action of the devout who are God's tools with the contemplative possession of the holy as found in mysticism. Mysticism intends a state of "possession," not action, and the individual is not a tool but a "vessel" of the divine. Action in the world must thus appear as endangering the absolutely irrational and other-worldly religious state. Active asceticism operates within the world; rationally active asceticism, in mastering the world, seeks to tame what is creatural and wicked work in a worldly "vocation" (inner-worldly asceticism).[34]

Wherever inner-worldly mysticism has articulated the path to salvation as the ecstatic union with God (*unio mystica*), the faithful, especially among Christian monastic orders, have embraced a life dedicated to methodical renunciations. These renunciations include what Weber termed the formation of a religious ethos that requires a withdrawal from the mundane world—from active participation in the domestic household and from economic, political, and aesthetic pursuits. The seekers were largely drawn from a "religious aristocracy" of monastics and religious virtuosi, not lay men and women or householders. Only a minority could seek contemplative flight from the world and find the path toward God by renouncing the false and inauthentic self of the "natural man." This self was stained by sin, pride, and concupiscence. Contemplative prayer, withdrawal into solitude, and ascetic mortification of the body aided the mystic in achieving the goal of self-annihilation. Quietism championed this principle of *annihilatio*, whereby the way to God necessitated complete self-abnegation. Only the person who had cleared this inner space and had achieved "divine nothingness" could become an empty vessel that would subsequently be filled by the godhead.[35]

Apophaticism, the Christian mystical tradition of darkness and negation, has informed the spiritual lives of countless men and women, including the Desert Fathers (John Cassian), Gregory of Nyssa, Pseudo-Dionysius, Meister Eckhart, St. John of the Cross, and the contemporary Trappist monk Thomas Merton.[36] St. John of the Cross (1542–1591), a Spanish monk who led a reform movement among mendicant Discalced (shoeless) Carmelites, best articulated the ideals of apophaticism. He developed a spiritual discipline of contemplation intended to open the soul to God, who would cleanse and purify the soul and eradicate sin. This "passive" purgation stripped the soul naked of all sensation, stifling mental activity and plunging the believer into a bitter and terrible dark night. The mystic viewed the melancholy dark night as an indispensable spiritual exercise that was essential to wean the soul from worldliness and sin and prepare the soul for the ultimate and complete assimilation to God.[37] This spiritual itinerary first involved the awakened soul, who was afflicted with spiritual dryness, filled with anxiety, and languishing in mental and emotion torpor. Bereft of God's love and unable to feel joy or hope, the soul succumbs to a protracted melancholy: "the dread that besets them that they have gone astray along this road, thinking that spiritual goodness has deserted them and that God has forsaken them."[38] As the melancholy of the Dark Night proceeded, it left the mind in darkness, the will stranded, and the memory voided. Drawing on the examples of the suffering and travail of Job and Noah and the castigations of the prophet Ezekiel, St. John argues that purgations and purifications produce self-annihilation and create the possibility for unity with God. He writes: "In order to purify and cleanse away the rust of the affections which remain in the center of the soul, it is necessary that she herself co-operate in this self-annihilation and disintegration.... Whence, in this furnace the soul is purified like as gold in the crucible."[39]

Teresa of Avila (1515–1582) allied with St. John in reforming the Discalced Carmelites. As a contemplative mystic and Doctor of the Church, she authored numerous works of spiritual direction regarding the pastoral care for melancholy nuns. Although she argues that Satan tempts the faithful to doubt and afflicts them with the sickness of melancholy, she offers another explanation of the propensity for inner-worldly mystics to suffer melancholy: the loss of God's favor. She writes in *The Interior Castle* (1577): "It then seems to the soul that it has never been mindful of God and never will be; and when it hears His Majesty spoken of, it seems to it as though it were hearing about a person far away."[40]

On the basis of the writings of Madame Guyon and St. John of the Cross, Evelyn Underhill formulated a spiritual itinerary of apophatic mysticism that she called the Mystic Way. This included (1) the awakening of the self, (2) the purification of the self, (3) the illumination of the self, (4) the dark night of the soul, and (5) the unitive life.[41] The religious virtuosi devoted to the Mystic Way methodically turned anger and aggression inward and relentlessly attacked the self. They wished to eradicate pride, ambition, and desire. In their quest for divine nothingness and humility, they embraced regimes of extreme mortification, privation, and melancholy. Catherine of Sienna (1347–1380) thus practiced "digging up the root of self-love with the knife of self-hatred."[42]

Mystical union (*unio mystica*) was a Roman Catholic theological concept originating in the Pauline and Johannine Gospels, where the believer's new life in Christ constituted a dynamic union.[43] The religious state and experience of mystical union, however, was central to the development of Jewish mysticism and Islamic Sufism. In these disparate milieux, distinctive religious ethics fostered spiritual itineraries (mystic paths) that structured unique experiences and expressions of melancholy.

While we cannot attempt an examination of Jewish mysticism from ancient Judaism through the emergence of postexilic rabbinic Judaism of the diaspora, we can identify the relationship of melancholy to mysticism with the formulation of kabbalism in Provence and northern Spain in the twelfth century and the rise of Hasidism as a popular religious movement among eastern European communities in the eighteenth century.

Moses Maimonides (1135–1204) systematized the tradition of rabbinic commentary on sacred texts and law (the oral Torah, Mishnah) by codifying Jewish law. In *The Guide of the Perplexed* he asserts the existence of a transcendental, incorporeal, remote, and inaccessible deity. How could believers know an unknowable God? How could the faithful overcome the abyss that separated them from God?[44] Rabbi Moshe de Leon, who authored the Zohar, and the many contributors to the Kabbala—a compendium of theosophy on the nature of God that included contemplative, devotional, and magical practices—attempted to resolve Maimonides' questions through the *via negativa*. All that could be stated about God was what he was not. The esoteric, secret tradition purportedly given to Moses at Mount Sinai was expressed in the Sefirot, the commentaries and contemplations of God as he is.[45] Kabbalists emphasized that daily prayer and practical piety, newly charged with spiritual efficacy, became the path to know God. Other mystics, following the writings of Abraham Abulafia (1240–1291), incorporated elements of Sufism (world-renunciation, indifference, solitude (*hitodedut*), repetition of God's name, and communion with God) to seek ecstatic, prophetic, and unitive experiences.[46]

Spiritual autobiographies of medieval Jewish mystics are rare; little is known about the interiority of the experience of their mystical path.[47] We can infer from this religious ethos that the structure of the *via negativa* and the fervency of mystical prayer and daily pietism fostered intense experiences of self-annihilation as prefatory to ecstatic union. In addition, following this transitory rapture, the mystic frequently succumbed to profound despondency associated with the return of a state of sinful alienation and separation from God.

Hasidism offers a more complete picture of the inward experiences and emotional economy of Jewish mysticism. Hasidism began as a popular religious movement in eastern Europe in the middle of the eighteenth century where the faithful devalued the traditional Jewish ethos of strict compliance with Talmudic law and ritualized obedience to God's mitzvoth (commandments). Instead, Hasidic mystics devoted their lives to the founding zaddiq (charismatic, righteous leader), Rabbi Ba'al Shem Tov (ca. 1700–1760), also known as the Besht (an acronym derived from the words forming his name). He introduced a doctrine of pan-sacramentalism inviting the worship of God whose "sparks of holiness" and immanence were found everywhere in the world.[48] The mystic sought self-annihilation (analogous to quietism) to achieve the desired devotional state of *devengut*, or "divine nothingness." "Self-abnegation is the precondition for ethical life in the presence of God."[49] The humble and modest seeker adopted a stance toward the world and conduct by adopting a *kavuanah*, or devotional intention, of ceaseless meditation on God. Whether through work, dancing, singing, sexuality, or communal activities, the Hasid was instructed to seek joy in a world filled with God's presence. No matter the activity, each believer "sanctified the profane," as the Ba'al Shem Tov stated: "In all your ways know him."[50]

The Hasidic mystic encountered the godhead through the experience of *hislahavus*, holy intoxication and ecstasy, which transcended all anxiety and worldly concerns. Feelings of despair over past sins and mistakes and sadness at the inability to attain perfection were prohibited as surrender to the "Evil Urge" that was characteristic of undue focus on self and not the obligation to serve God in all things.[51] Despite the importance of *Bitahon* (trust in God) and a disinterested stance toward the world, Hasidic mystics stumbled into melancholy in their quest to identify with the divine through acts of self-annihilation and in the dynamic tension of striving to find God in the sanctified profane. Elie Wiesel identifies the ubiquitous melancholy in the spiritual biographies of the founding generation of Hasidic masters and their successors, including the Besht, Rebbe Levi-Yithak, and Rebbe Elimeloch. It appears that these zaddiqs succumbed to melancholy during their old age when they became fearful of impending death, weary of the pastoral duties of guiding and consoling the faithful, and overwhelmed with angst at the deteriorating social and political status of Jewish communities. The Besht's grandson, Rebbe Baruck (d. 1811), agonized when the redemptive ascent and union with the Creator eluded him. He struggled with the possibility that "man and the Creator would remain strangers forever."[52] Yaakov Yitzhak Horowitz (1745–1814), known as the Holy Seer of Lublin, would lament to his disciples: "I stay with my sadness; mine is a black fire."[53] Hasidic communal prayer, dance, sacred music, and festivals such as Simhat Torah (the Jewish holiday that sponsors an annual birthday party given to celebrate the completion of the reading of the five books of Moses) obligated the faithful to rejoice. The Holy Seer of Lublin reportedly instructed the faithful: "Rejoice on this festival event, let yourself go, let your spirit soar.... And if your ecstasy is pure enough, contagious enough, it will last forever—I promise you that."[54] However, those seeking inner-worldly mystical union by following the path of descent into self-abnegation and seeking ascent toward God discovered that ecstasy was transitory. Not infrequently the pious lamented that God had removed his countenance, and the believer who would know God succumbed to black fire.

This proclivity for melancholy as a prefatory stage on the path to religious ecstasy is particularly prominent in the Habad movement, founded by Rabbi Shneur Zalman of Liadi (1745–1813) and systematized in his work of dialectical theosophy, the *Tanya*, published in 1796. The *Tanya* taught that each person needed to wage a ceaseless inner war between the animal soul and the divine soul. Each believer needed to embrace a state of brokenhearted melancholy, in the spirit of: "a broken and contrite heart, O God, Thou wilt not despise."[55] Communal worship fostered a state of self-annihilation, *bittul ha'yesh*, that "is likened to a ladder of spiritual ascent that begins with contemplation and rises to mystical ecstasy."[56] In this manner, melancholy continually punctuated the spiritual journey of Jewish mystics.

Sufism represents a hybrid form of Islamic popular religion that combined elements of asceticism and mysticism to foster an emotion-laden daily piety, inwardness, and spiritual journey that intensified and perfected the knowledge of God.[57] The first Sufi mystic-ascetic, Hasan al Basri (d. 801) lived during the era of the Prophet and suffered profound melancholy analogous to the despair of Martin Luther, who could not find forgiveness of sin. Hasan al Basri forged a penitential devotionalism that including wearing woolen garments (*soofs*) that became the distinctive garb of the faithful. In his *Prayers for Forgiveness*, with its seventy prayers, he instructing those overwhelmed by sinfulness to turn to Allah as a baby would seek the comfort of a loving mother.[58] He cited the authority of the Qur'an (39:53–54) as the basis for the spiritual direction of the sinful and melancholy soul. "O My servants—those who have committed excess against their own souls—never despair of the mercy of Allah! For, indeed, Allah forgives sins, one and all. Indeed, it is He who is the All-Forgiving, the Mercy-Giving. So turn in penitence to your Lord. And submit yourselves to Him."

Al Basri's disciples in Persia and Baghdad, most notably Abd al-Wahid, forged a distinctive Muslim religiosity of voluntary poverty, self-mortification, extreme fasting, contrition, and ceaseless mourning over the threat of divine retribution for even minor lapses in the observance of *sharia* (divine law). Known as the "weepers" (*bakkaun*), these "beggars of the spirit" appropriated the Christian concept of *gratia lacrimarum* of Coptic and Syrian monks and the woolen robe of Nestorian monasticism.[59] As Margaret Smith explains, during the formative centuries of Sufism, when Islamic civilization extended to Spain, North Africa, and the Middle East, Muslims found themselves "almost everywhere in a Christian environment, in close contact with Christian forms of worship and Christian culture."[60] Not surprisingly, Sufism was a syncretism of Neoplatonism, Christian asceticism and mysticism, elements from Hebrew scripture and the medieval Kabbala, and Gnosticism.

Early ascetical Sufism articulated a penitential stance of renunciation of self and world that structured a life devoted to what Ibrahm Ibn Adhan (d. 777) taught as the quietistic path to God through contrition and sadness.[61] The weepers understood that the "gift of tears" signified contrition. In this manner, a religiously grounded melancholy served as the foundation of charismatic piety.[62]

Fritz Meier's essay "A Book of Etiquette for Sufis" explains the religious significance of the distinctive patchwork frock of the Sufi virtuoso. "If one has overcome the concupiscent soul (*nafs*), killed it with the sword of the *vita purgativa*, and one now sits mourning the soul's demise, then one should wear black."[63] The faithful wore a "thousand-needle robe" which symbolized how the virtuosi had worn themselves down and wounded themselves through a thousand blows of spiritual combat, torturing themselves with "the needle of despair."[64]

The penitential act of purification of the soul (*tazkiyat al nafs*) was simultaneously an exercise in the cultivation of the soul—destroying the carnal self to become the mirror of God. Instructed to seek pain and self-torture for religious ends, the Sufi theologian Ibn al-ʿArabî (d. 1240) would write: "Whoever is more awake has greater pain, / Whoever is more aware has a paler face."[65]

Henry Corbin argues in *The Man of Light in Iranian Sufism*, examining the life and theology of Sufi masters like Alaoddawleh Semnani (d. 1336), that the "spiritual therapeutics" of self-annihilation (*fana*) plunged each seeker into the mystical station of the black light or luminous darkness. Without careful spiritual direction, the faithful easily lapsed into delirium and melancholy.[66] Thus the Sufi culture hero was "the man of light, held captive by the Darkness and struggling to free himself from the Darkness" so as to transform himself by the attainment of Perfect Nature in the knowledge of God.[67]

Ibn al-ʿArabî is another important Sufi thinker who codified the practical divinity of Wujud—the stations of the mystic path and the corresponding emotional states of abandoning the self in order to come to God. While only a minority might achieve perfection and traverse the seven levels of self-annihilation, the masses who embraced Sufism understood that "to be annihilated from the Unreal is to subsist through the Real."[68]

By the eleventh and twelfth centuries, Sufism had become a mature movement allied to the doctrinal orthodoxy of Sunni teachings, with communities spread throughout Islam, including India and Asia. Religious brotherhoods of mendicant monks pursued the path toward God, shifting the focus from penitence and fear of divine justice to the doctrine of ecstatic communion with God that was articulated through the language of erotic passion first introduced through the love mysticism of Rabi'a al-Adawiyya (d. 801) and Abu Yazid al-Bistami (d. 874). Jalal al-Din Rumi (d. 1273) systematized forms of poetry, singing, and ritual dance (*sama*) that produced entranced, intoxicated, ecstatic experiences of ascent and unity with God. This addition to Sufi mystical experience made world-renouncing piety the first stage to the spiritual attainment of total annihilation in God.[69]

Sufi mysticism is founded on the concept of *dhikr*, the ceaseless recollection and contemplation of God ("There is no god but God"). It is practiced through communal ritual devotions by prepared souls who have achieved "servanthood" through self-annihilation and surrender to God's will.[70] This doctrine derives from Qur'an 55:27: "All that dwells on the earth is annihilated, and there subsists only the face of your Lord, the possessor of majesty and generosity." The inward melancholy sobriety of the *dhikr*—the prescribed emotions of sadness and fear—alternate with the dervish dance (*samra*), which is marked by intoxication, weeping, shouting, rapture, and the selfless ecstasy of stupor.[71]

Incorporating elements of Christian mysticism, Sufism resembled the "purgative way" of apophaticism and the spiritual itinerary of repentance, abstinence, renunciation, poverty (awareness of human inadequacy), patience, trust in God, satisfaction.[72] The Wujud also incorporated the *via illuminativa* and *unio mystica* of Christian mysticism. The path began with Islam (the total surrender of the seeker to the will of God), followed by *iman* (the stations of self-annihilation, poverty, patience, and trust in God), and culminated in *ihsan* (serving God as if you see him).[73] The path of mystical ascent represented a prolonged spiritual warfare characterized by emotional states in dialectical tension that include fear/hope, separation/union, drunkenness/sobriety, contraction/expansion, and annihilation/subsistence.

Conclusion

This examination of religion and melancholy has provided a framework to understand how varieties of mysticism and asceticism have structured religious ethics where the path to God and salvation has an elective affinity to melancholy. The few examples provided are illustrative, not a comprehensive treatment of the subject. This essay has provided an ideal typical analysis of the relationship between a religious ethos and melancholy. This methodology is intended to assist us in future research in investigations of religion and melancholy that is focused on concrete instantiations of religious groups, situated in unique culture areas and in particular times and locales.

We close with the understanding that wherever believers have committed themselves to the heroic pilgrimage of forging a life consistent with the ultimate values of devotional piety, of pursuing the achievement of a religious grounded personality that demanded the rationalization and renunciation of the self and the body, and accepted as the seal of grace the inward assurance of God's love, melancholy has afflicted them. With life cast as a continual rejection of the "natural man," in pursuit of *unio mystica* or as an instrument of divine will, melancholy has been an important dimension of their lived religion and spiritual journeys.

NOTES

1. Clifford Geertz, "Religion as a Cultural System," in *The Interpretation of Cultures* (New York: Basic Books, 1973), 90.
2. Benjamin Nelson, *On the Roads to Modernity: Conscience, Science, and Civilizations* (Totowa, N.J.: Rowman and Littlefield, 1981), 23.
3. Wayne Proudfoot, *Religious Experience* (Berkeley: University of California Press, 1985), 77, 219.
4. Nelson, *On the Roads to Modernity*, 7. See Lucien Febvre, *A New Kind of History*, edited by Peter Burke and translated by K. Folca (New York: Harper and Row, 1973), 12–43.
5. Max Weber, *The Protestant Ethic and the Spirit of Capitalism*, translated by Talcott Parsons (New York: Scribner's, 1958), 97.
6. Wolfgang Schluchter, *Rationalism, Religion, and Domination: A Weberian Perspective* (Berkeley: University of California Press, 1989) 156–66.
7. John Corrigan, *Business of the Heart: Religion and Emotion in the Nineteenth Century* (Berkeley: University of California Press, 2002), 280.
8. Stanley W. Jackson, *Melancholia and Depression: From Hippocratic Times to Modern Times* (New Haven, Conn.: Yale University Press, 1986), 3, 383. See also John Owen King, *The Iron of Melancholy: Structures of Spiritual Conversion in America from Puritan Consciousness to Victorian Neurosis* (Middletown, Conn.: Wesleyan University Press, 1983).
9. Jennifer Radden, *The Nature of Melancholy: From Aristotle to Kristeva* (New York: Oxford University Press, 2000), vii.
10. John Corrigan, *Business of the Heart*, 280. See John T. McNeill, *A History of the Cure of Souls* (New York: Harper and Row, 1951); and William A. Clebsch and Charles R. Jaekle, *Pastoral Care in Historical Perspective: An Essay with Exhibits* (New York: Harper and Row, 1964).
11. For an example of this type of analysis applied to a case study see Julius H. Rubin, *The Other Side of Joy: Religious Melancholy among the Bruderhof* (New York: Oxford University Press, 2000). Donald Capps, *Men, Religion, and Melancholia: James, Otto, Jung, and Erickson* (New Haven, Conn.: Yale University Press, 1997), explores the loss and separation from the mother as a key developmental and intrapsychic explanation for the spiritual longings and melancholy of key religious writers who suffered from alienation from God's love.
12. For a more complete discussion of Weber and these questions, see Julius H. Rubin, *Religious Melancholy and Protestant Experience in America* (New York: Oxford University Press, 1994), 3–51. For a secondary analysis of Weber's sociology of religion, see Schluchter, *Rationalism, Religion, and Domination*. Benjamin Nelson, "Weber's Protestant Ethnic Thesis: Origins, Wanderings, and Foreseeable Futures," in *Beyond the Classics? Essays in the Scientific Sociology of Religion*, edited by Charles Y. Glock and Philip E. Hammond (New York: Harper and Row, 1973), 71. Harvey Goldman, *Max Weber and Thomas Mann: Calling and the Shaping of the Self* (Berkeley: University of California Press, 1988).
13. Charles Lloyd Cohen, *God's Caress: The Psychology of Religious Experience* (New York: Oxford University Press, 1986).
14. Owen C. Watkins, *The Puritan Experience: Studies in Spiritual Autobiography* (New York: Shocken Books, 1972), 13–14.
15. John Cassian, "The Dynamics of Sin," quoted in William A. Clebsch, *Pastoral Care in Historical Perspective* (New York: Harper and Row, 1964), 141–42.

16. Jackson, *Melancholia and Depression*, 71.

17. Won Young Ji, "Significance of Tentatio in Luther's Spirituality," *Concordia Journal* 15, 2 (1989): 181. Alister E. McGrath, *Luther's Theology of the Cross: Martin Luther's Theological Breakthrough* (London: Blackwell, 1985), 61.

18. Ernest F. Stoeffler, *The Rise of Evangelical Pietism* (Leiden: Brill, 1965), 15.

19. Peter Iver Kaufman, *Prayer, Despair, and Drama: Elizabethan Introspection* (Urbana: University of Illinois Press, 1996), 1, 6.

20. Ibid., 36.

21. John Donne, *Complete Poetry and Selected Prose*, edited by John Hayward (Bloomsbury: Nonesuch Press, 1929), 280.

22. Robert Burton, *The Anatomy of Melancholy*, edited by Floyd Dell and Paul Jordan-Smith (New York: Farrar and Rinehart, 1927), 948.

23. Michael MacDonald and Terrence Murphy, *Mystical Bedlam: Madness, Anxiety and Healing in Seventeenth-Century England* (Cambridge: Cambridge University Press, 1981), 64.

24. Ibid., 39.

25. Frank Lambert, *Inventing the "Great Awakening,"* (Princeton, N.J.: Princeton University Press, 1999), 21–53.

26. Timothy D. Hall, *Contested Boundaries: Itinerancy and the Shaping of the Colonial American Religious World* (Durham, N.C.: Duke University Press, 1994). 33.

27. Ibid., 17. Nathan Cole, "Spiritual Travels," in *Great Awakening: Documents on the Revival of Religion, 1740–1745*, edited by R. L. Bushman (New York: Atheneum, 1970) 183–84.

28. Michael J. Crawford, *Seasons of Grace: Colonial New England's Revival Tradition in Its British Context* (New York: Oxford University Press, 2001), 141. Crawford writes: "an international network for exchanging revival news sustained the impression that the Holy Spirit was unusually active among congregations throughout Protestantism."

29. Thomas Prince, *Account of the Revival of Religion in Boston in the Years 1740–1743* (Boston: Samuel T. Armstrong, 1823), 8.

30. Ibid., 18–19.

31. Joseph Tracey, *The Great Awakening: A History of the Revival of Religion in the Time of Edwards and Whitefield* (Boston: Tappan and Dennet, 1842), 137.

32. Phoebe Palmer, *Selected Writings*, edited by Thomas C. Oden (New York: Paulist Press, 1998), 167.

33. Ibid., 115, 118. See also Randy L. Maddox, "A Change of Affections: The Development, Dynamics, and Dethronement of John Wesley's Heart Religion," in*"Heart Religion" in the Methodist Tradition and Related Movements*, edited by Richard B. Steele (London: Scarecrow Press, 2001), 3–32.

34. Max Weber, "Religious Rejections of the World and Their Directions," in *From Max Weber: Essays in Sociology*, edited by Hans Gerth and C. Wright Mills (New York: Oxford University Press, 1946), 325.

35. Rivka Schatz Uffenheimer, *Hasidism as Mysticism*, translated by Jonathan Chipman (Princeton, N.J.: Princeton University Press, 1993), 67.

36. William H. Shannon, *Thomas Merton's Dark Path* (New York: Farrar, Straus, Giroux, 1981), 10.

37. St. John of the Cross, *The Dark Night of the Soul*, translated by Gabriela Cunninghame Graham (London: John M. Watkins, 1922), 71.

38. Ibid., 79.

39. Ibid., 139.

40. Jennifer Radden, *The Nature of Melancholy: From Aristotle to Kristeva* (New York: Oxford University Press, 2000), 113.

41. Evelyn Underhill, *Mysticism* (New York: Dutton, 1930), 463.

42. Ibid., 476.

43. Louis Dupré, "*Unio Mystica*: The State and the Experience," in *Mystical Union in Judaism, Christianity, and Islam*, edited by Moshe Idel and Bernard McGinn (New York: Continuum, 1996), 4–6.

44. David S. Ariel, *The Mystic Quest* (Northvale, N.J.: Jason Aronson, 1988), 51–59.

45. Joseph Dan, *The Heart and the Fountain: An Anthology of Jewish Mystical Experiences* (New York: Oxford University Press, 2002), 2–8. Dr. Rabbi Louis Jacobs, *The Via Negativa in Jewish and Christian Thought: The Zohar and The Cloud of Unknowing Compared* (Essex, England: Centre for the Study of Theology in the University of Essex, 1997), 20.

46. Moshe Idel, *Studies in Ecstatic Kabbalah* (Albany: State University of New York Press, 1988), 107–8.

47. Moshe Idel, preface to *Jewish Mystical Autobiographies: Book of Visions and Book of Secrets*, translated by Morris M. Faierstein (New York: Paulist Press, 1999), xi.

48. Uffenheimer, *Hasidism as Mysticism*, 17.

49. Ibid., 81.

50. Ibid., 57–58.

51. Ibid., 93–95.

52. Elie Wiesel, *Four Hasidic Masters and Their Struggle against Melancholy* (Notre Dame: University of Notre Dame Press, 1978), 53, 90.

53. Ibid., 89.

54. Ibid., 62.

55. Rabbi Zalman Schachter-Shalomi, *Wrapped in a Holy Flame* (San Francisco: Jossey-Bass, 2003), 174.

56. Rachel Elior, *The Paradoxical Ascent to God* (San Francisco: Jossey-Bass, 2003), 175.

57. William Chittick, "Between the Yes and the No: Ibn al-'Arabî on Wujud and the Innate Capacity," in *The Innate Capacity*, edited by Robert K. C. Forman (New York: Oxford University Press, 1988), 95.

58. Mircea Eliade, *A History of Religious Ideas*, translated by Alf Hitelbeitel and Diane Apostolos-Cappadona (Chicago: University of Chicago Press, 1988), 123. Hasan Basri, *Prayers for Forgiveness*, translated by Abdur-Rahman Ibn Yusuf (London: White Thread Press, 2004).

59. Alexander Knysh, *Islamic Mysticism: A Short History* (Leiden: Brill, 2000), 13–14.

60. Margaret Smith, *Studies in Early Mysticism of the Near and Middle East* (Oxford: Oneworld, 1995), 123.

61. Knysh, *Islamic Mysticism*, 19.

62. Smith, *Studies in Early Mysticism of the Near and Middle East*, 157.

63. Fritz Meier, "A Book of Etiquette for Sufis," in *Essays on Islamic Piety and Mysticism*, translated by John O'Kane (Leiden: Brill, 1999), 68.

64. Ibid., 71.

65. William C. Chittick, *Sufism: A Short Introduction* (Oxford: Oneworld, 2000), 69, 40.

66. Henry Corbin, *The Man of Light in Iranian Sufism* (London: Shambhala, 1978), 122–29.

67. Ibid., 14.

68. Chittick, "Between the Yes and the No," 108.

69. Knysh, *Islamic Mysticism*, 43–68, 71.
70. Chittick, *Sufism*, 4.
71. Fritz Meier, "The Dervish Dance," in O'Kane, *Essays on Islamic Piety and Mysticism*, 30–39.
72. H. A. R. Gibb, *Mohammedanism* (New York: Oxford University Press, 1962), 135–51.
73. Knysh, *Islamic Mysticism*, 301–3.

BIBLIOGRAPHY

Ariel, David S. *The Mystical Quest: An Introduction to Jewish Mysticism*. Northvale, N.J.: Jason Aronson, 1998.
Basri, Hasan. *Prayers for Forgiveness*. Translated by A.-R. I. Yusuf. London: White Thread Press, 2004.
Burton, Robert. *The Anatomy of Melancholy*. Edited by F. D. a. P. Jordan-Smith. New York: Farrar and Rinehart, 1927.
Capps, Donald. *Men, Religion, and Melancholia: James, Otto, Jung, and Erikson*. New Haven, Conn.: Yale University Press, 1997.
Chittick, William. "Between the Yes and the No: Ibn al-'Arabî on Wujud and the Innate Capacity." In *The Innate Capacity, Mysticism, Psychology, and Philosophy*, edited by R. K. C. Forman. New York: Oxford University Press, 1998, 95–110.
———. *Sufism: A Short Introduction*. Oxford: Oneworld. 2000.
Clebsch, William A., and Charles R. Jaekle. *Pastoral Care in Historical Perspective: An Essay with Exhibits*. New York: Harper and Row, 1964.
Cohen, Charles Lloyd. *God's Caress: The Psychology of Religious Experience*. New York: Oxford University Press, 1986.
Cole, Nathan. "The Spiritual Travels of Nathan Cole." In *The Great Awakening: Documents on the Revival of Religion, 1740–1745*, edited by R. L. Bushman. New York: Athenaeum, 1970, 67–71.
Corrigan, John. *Business of the Heart: Religion and Emotion in the Nineteenth Century*. Berkeley: University of California Press, 2002.
Crawford, Michael J. *Seasons of Grace: Colonial New England's Revival Tradition in Its British Context*. New York: Oxford University Press, 1991.
Dan, Joseph, ed. *The Heart and the Fountain: An Anthology of Jewish Mystical Experiences*. New York: Oxford University Press, 2002.
Donne, John. *Complete Poetry and Selected Prose*. Edited by J. Hayward. London: Nonesuch, 1929.
Dupré, Louis. 1996. "Unio Mystica: The State and the Experience." In *Mystical Union in Judaism, Christianity, and Islam*, edited by M. Idel and B. McGinn. New York: Continuum, 1996), 3–23.
Edwards, Jonathan. *A Faithful Narrative: A Narrative of the Late Work of God, at and near Northampton, in New-England*. Bristol, England: Felix Farley, 1744.
Eliade, Mircea. *A History of Religious Ideas: From Muhammad to the Age of Reforms*. Translated by A. H. a. D. Apostolos-Cappadona. Vol. 3. Chicago: University of Chicago Press, 1988.

Elior, Rachel. *The Paradoxical Ascent to God: The Kabalistic Theosophy of Habad Hasidism.* Albany: State University of New York Press, 1993.
Ellwood, Robert S. *Mysticism and Religion.* 2nd ed. Chappaqua, N.Y.: Seven Bridges Press, 1999.
Febvre, Lucien. *A New Kind of History.* Translated by K. Folca. Edited by P. Burke. New York: Harper and Row, 1973.
Geertz, Clifford. *The Interpretation of Cultures.* New York: Basic Books, 1973.
Gibb, H. A. R. *Mohammedanism.* 2nd ed. New York: Oxford University Press, 1962.
Goldman, Harvey. *Max Weber and Thomas Mann: Calling and the Shaping of the Self.* Berkeley: University of California Press, 1988.
Hall, Timothy D. *Contested Boundaries: Itinerancy and the Shaping of the Colonial American Religious World.* Durham, N.C.: Duke University Press, 1994.
Hoffman, Edward. *The Way of Splendor: Jewish Mysticism and Modern Psychology.* Northvale, N.J.: Jason Aronson, 1989.
Idel, Moshe. *Studies in Ecstatic Kabbalah.* Albany: State University of New York, 1988.
Idel, Moshe, and Bernard McGinn, eds. *Mystical Union in Judaism, Christianity, and Islam.* New York: Continuum, 1989.
Jackson, Stanley W. *Melancholia and Depression: From Hippocratic Times to Modern Times.* New Haven, Conn.: Yale University Press, 1986.
Jacobs, Rabbi Dr. Louis. *The Via Negativa in Jewish and Christian Thought: The Zohar and the Cloud of Unknowing Compared.* Vol. 14, *Essays in Theology and Society.* Essex, England: Centre for the Study of Theology in the University of Essex, 1997.
Jewish Mystical Autobiographies: Book of Visions and Book of Secrets. Translated by M. M. Faierstein. New York: Paulist Press, 1999.
Ji, Won Young. "Significance of *Tentatio* in Luther's Spirituality." *Concordia Journal* 15, 2 (1989): 181–89.
John of the Cross, St. *The Dark Night of the Soul.* Translated by G. C. Graham. London: John M. Watkins, 1922.
Kaufman, Peter Iver. *Prayer, Despair, and Drama: Elizabethan Introspection.* Urbana: University of Illinois Press, 1996.
King, John Owen. *The Iron of Melancholy: Structures of Spiritual Conversion in America from Puritan Conscience to Victorian Neurosis.* Middletown, Conn.: Wesleyan University Press, 1983.
Knysh, Alexander. *Islamic Mysticism: A Short History.* Leiden: Brill, 2000.
Lambert, Frank. *Inventing the "Great Awakening."* Princeton, N.J.: Princeton University Press, 1999.
MacDonald, Michael, and Terrence Murphy. *Mystical Bedlam: Madness, Anxiety, and Healing in Seventeenth Century England.* Cambridge: Cambridge University Press, 1990.
McGrath, Alister E. *Martin Luther's Theology of the Cross: Martin Luther's Theological Breakthrough.* London: Blackwell, 1985.
McNeill, John T. *A History of the Cure of Souls.* New York: Harper and Row, 1951.
Meier, Fritz. "The Dervish Dance." In *Essays on Islamic Piety and Mysticism*, edited by B. Radtke. Leiden: Brill, 1999, 23–48.
———. "A Book of Etiquette for Sufis." In *Essays on Islamic Piety and Mysticism*, edited by B. Radtke. Leiden: Brill, 1999, 49–92.
Nelson, Benjamin. *On the Roads to Modernity, Conscience, Science, and Civilizations.* Edited by T. E. Huff. Totowa, N.J.: Rowman and Littlefield, 1981.

———. "Weber's Protestant Ethic: Its Origins, Wanderings, and Foreseeable Futures." In *Beyond the Classics? Essays in the Scientific Study of Religion*, edited by C. Y. Glock and P. E. Hammond. New York: Harper and Row, 1973, 71–103.

Palmer, Phoebe. *Selected Writings*. Edited by T. C. Oden. New York: Paulist Press, 1998.

Prince, Thomas. *Account of the Revival of Religion in Boston in the Years 1740–1743*. Boston: Samuel T. Armstrong, 1823.

Proudfoot, Wayne. *Religious Experience*. Berkeley: University of California Press, 1985.

Radden, Jennifer, ed. *The Nature of Melancholy: From Aristotle to Kristeva*. New York: Oxford University Press, 2000.

Rubin, Julius H. *The Other Side of Joy: Religious Melancholy among the Bruderhof*. New York: Oxford University Press, 2000.

———. *Religious Melancholy and Protestant Experience in America*. New York: Oxford University Press, 1994.

Schachter-Shalomi, Rabbi Zalman. *Wrapped in a Holy Flame: Teachings and Tales of the Hasidic Masters*. San Francisco: Jossey-Bass, 2003.

Schluchter, Wofgang. *Rationalism, Religion, and Domination: A Weberian Perspective*. Berkeley: University of California Press, 1989.

Shannon, William H. *Thomas Merton's Dark Path: The Inner Experience of a Contemplative*. New York: Farrar Straus Giroux, 1981.

Smith, Margaret. *Studies in Early Mysticism in the Near and Middle East*. Oxford: Oneworld, 1995.

Steele, Richard B., ed. *"Heart Religion" in the Methodist Tradition and Related Movements*. London: Scarecrow Press, 2001.

Steinsaltz, Rabbi Adin. *Opening the Tanya: Discovering the Moral and Mystical Teachings of a Class Work of Kabbalah*. Translated by R. Y. Tauber. San Francisco: Jossey-Bass, 2003.

Stoeffler, Ernest F. *The Rise of Evangelical Pietism*. Leiden: Brill, 1985.

Tracy, Joseph. *The Great Awakening: A History of the Revival of Religion in the Time of Edwards and Whitefield*. Boston: Tappan and Dennet, 1842.

Uffenheimer, Rivka Schatz. *Hasidism as Mysticism: Quietistic Elements in Eighteenth-Century Hasidic Thought*. Translated by J. Chipman. Princeton, N.J.: Princeton University Press, 1993.

Underhill, Evelyn. *Mysticism: A Study in the Nature and Development of Man's Spiritual Consciousness*. New York: Dutton, 1930.

Watkins, Owen C. *The Puritan Experience: Studies in Spiritual Autobiography*. New York: Shocken Books, 1972.

Weber, Max. *The Protestant Ethic and the Spirit of Capitalism*. Translated by Talcott Parsons. New York: Scribner's, 1958.

———. "Religious Rejections of the World and Their Directions." In *From Max Weber: Essays in Sociology*, edited by H. Gerth and C. W. Mills. New York: Oxford University Press, 1946, 323–59.

Wiesel, Elie. *Four Hasidic Masters and Their Struggle against Melancholy*. Notre Dame, Ind.: University of Notre Dame Press, 1978.

CHAPTER 17

LOVE

NANCY M. MARTIN
AND JOSEPH RUNZO

RELIGIOUS iconography is replete with paradigmatic images of love: Krishna playing his flute to entice the love of devotees, the passion of Jesus dying on the cross out of love for humankind, and the benevolently extended hand of the *bodhisattva* of compassion, who is the male Avalokiteshvara in Indian tradition, becoming the female figures of Kuan-yin in China and Kannon in Japan. Love lies at the heart of the religious life, as a principle mode of relationship between the human and the transcendent, as a guiding motivation for the moral life, and, for many, as a defining attribute of the transcendent. The Latin root of "religion," the verb *religare*, means to re-bind or bind together, and for those who follow the "way of love" rather than the "way of the intellect," *bhakti* yoga rather than *jnana* yoga, that relational bond is love. For those following the "way of love," shared understandings of the way the world is (worldviews) and shared views of the way the world ought to be (normative moral principles) may form the cognitive structure of this bond, but it is love that secures, animates, and empowers this bond.

Love is arguably the most potent and, by that very fact, also the most dangerous of the human emotions. Love can overcome powerful negative emotions such as fear, anger, and hatred, and it can bring ecstatic fulfillment. Among all the emotions, love is the most transformative. Indeed, as Robert Nozick says, "in love's bond, we metamorphose."[1] Yet the transformative power of love can be highly disruptive, contravening the careful conceptual apparatus of religion, undermining institutional religious authority, and upsetting social expectations and hierarchies. And if the power of the emotion of love is not harnessed for self-transformation, then rather than enhancing the other-regarding perspective prescribed by religion, this emotion can increase attachment, partiality, and self-centeredness.

In theistic traditions such as Judaism, Christianity, Islam, Baha'i, *bhakti* Hinduism, and Sikhism, love is considered an essential defining attribute of God and a definitive mode—if not the single definitive mode—of relationship between humans and the divine. Moreover, in theistic traditions love is understood as flowing from the abundance of the divine to inform not only human-divine but also human-human relationships. In nontheistic traditions like Buddhism and Confucianism, close relatives of love have a similar role in human-human relationships. In Mahayana Buddhism, compassion complemented by wisdom forms the heart of the Buddhist path, and in Confucianism, love informs *jen*, or human-heartedness, which is a key attribute of the fully realized human being and inseparable from *li*, the ordering principle that structures all relationships and indeed all reality. Thus in these nontheistic traditions, love is an attribute of the transformed person who becomes congruent with the nonpersonal transcendent.

The Nature of Love and Emotion

In its broad usage, "love" encompasses the dependency of children on parents, the fierce protectiveness of parents for children, the intense passion of erotic love, and the deep affection of friends, and even extends to a universal benevolence toward all human beings, as well as the utter devotion of humans toward God. How these relationships are understood varies considerably across cultures, religions, and time, yet there are fundamental shared features. The *religious* emotion of love, while equally variant, shares important features with romantic love, as is evident in, for example, the eros dimension of the Islamic poetry of Jalal al-Din Rumi, the Christian poetry of St. John of the Cross, and the Hindu songs of Mirabai.

Robert Solomon offers an extensive analysis of romantic love in which he asserts that "Love is an emotion, nothing else."[2] Though many, both religious and nonreligious, might hold that love is not wholly reducible to an emotion, Solomon does offer an incisive analysis of emotion and of love insofar as it is an emotion. He rejects the view that emotions are primitive "intrusions in our otherwise orderly, rational lives," arguing instead that "love, like all emotions ... is a reaching *out*, the projection of a structure, a meaning, a way of personally relating to the world."[3] Indeed, according to Solomon,

> every emotion defines a world for itself.... The world defined by love—or what we shall call the *loveworld*—is a world woven around a single relationship, with all else pushed to the periphery. To understand love is to understand the specifics of this relationship and the world woven around it.[4]

Such an understanding corresponds to the view, taken by those who follow the "way of love" in religious traditions, that the intellect is not superior to the heart and that the loving relationship of greatest importance is between the individual and God.

Solomon explains the loveworld this way:

> What love is about—the poles of the loveworld and goal of its development—is the creation of self. But ... the self that is created through love is a *shared* self, a self that is conceived and developed together.... In love, what is so peculiar is that the self that is created in the development of the emotion is a shared self ... whereas in most emotions the self is set up in opposition to or in isolation from other people.[5]

Thus he concludes that a "component of the loveworld is oneself.... We are not in love *at*, but rather *with*, another person ... there is no emotion without self-involvement."[6] Both we ourselves and the world we inhabit are transformed in the experience of love.

As Robert Nozick points out:

> Intimate bonds change the contours and boundaries of the self, altering its typology.... Alterations in the individual self's boundaries and contours also are the goal of religious quest: expanding the self to include all of being (Indian Vedanta) [i.e., *advaita vedanta*], eliminating the self (Buddhism) [i.e., the empirical self], or merging with the divine. There are also modes of general love for all of humanity, often religiously enjoined ... that greatly alter the character and contours of the self, now no longer so appropriately referred to as "individual."[7]

A principle goal of religion is the transformation of self, whether the self is understood as soul, *atman*, or *anatman* and whether the underlying problem is understood as willful disobedience of God's will or ignorance of the self's true nature. Further, the human shared self that emerges through love can alternately be conceived of as (1) in love with God and thus loving that which God loves; (2) fully aware of being empty of independent existence and of being radically interdependent with other selves, a realization marked by compassion for all other beings, as in the case of Buddhism; or (3) fundamentally defined through relationships marked by human-heartedness or *jen*, as in Confucianism.

In view of this positive transformative power, why would the emotion of love be dangerous? The transformation of self brought about by and/or fully realized in love and compassion necessitates the radical passing away of former notions of the self for a relationally defined, interdependent and so vulnerable, self. Speaking about romantic love, Solomon suggests,

> it should be clear why the process of love tends to be so explosive, makes us feel so vulnerable, and fills us with such joy and terror. Romantic love ... involves nothing less than a change of self, and suddenly we find ourselves precariously dependent on one another, exhilarated by our discovery but inevitably terrified as well ... halfway between two identities.[8]

The change of self that occurs in romantic love is greatly amplified when that love is the love between the individual human and the transcendent. So it should be no surprise that we find Christian mystics, Muslim Sufis, and Hindu devotees speaking of this experience as an "affliction," or an all-consuming fire, or the crushing of the self in the crucible that is love, or annihilation. As the Sufi poet Rumi puts it, "the way of love is not a subtle argument. The door there is devastation."[9] Allah is reported in a well-known *hadith* as saying "I am with those whose hearts are broken for my sake,"[10] and Jesus says to those who would follow his call to love, "If anyone would come after me, let him deny himself and take up his cross and follow me" (Matthew 16:24).

This transformation of the self—awe-inspiring in its attraction and explosive in its results—is a testament to both love's power and its danger. In religious contexts, the desire for this transformation through love leads to an intentional cultivation of this emotion by means of ritual and other practices designed to elicit religious experiences and create moods and motivations that reinforce a particular "religious loveworld," as it were. Yet by the very institutionalization of such practices, religions seek to discipline and channel the explosiveness of love. A line is often drawn between human–human love, especially romantic love or eros, and a "purer" human-divine love, even as the language of human love is employed to speak metaphorically about the human-divine relation. Moreover, religions often seek to separate universal love and/or compassion, as an attitude expressing care for others, from the emotion of love. Yet a love that can be institutionally controlled and does not transform the self is not fully love and would not result in a fully realized loveworld. Indeed, apart from the institutional desire to control, theistic religions speak of love as an attribute of the transcendent that comes to humans as an unbidden gift. Thus, Sufis will say that when the guard intellect is asleep, love comes as a thief in the night and steals everything.[11] For as the Catholic theologian Bernard Lonergan says, one "falls in love with God."

Love as an Attribute of the Transcendent

The monotheisms of the West—Judaism, Christianity, and Islam—speak of love as an attribute of God. The love of human beings analogically mirrors divine love, though it also includes dimensions of need and duty, particularly in the context of familial relations. God does not need human reciprocity, so the love of God—or the Love which is God—is a grace, an overflowing abundance that is experienced by humans and is the source of the human capacity to love. Jewish daily prayers speak of God's deep love and "boundless tender compassion" for his people Israel, evidenced by his giving of the Torah and the mitzvot, or commandments, and the classic text of the Jewish mystical tradition of kabbalah, the Zohar, portrays "God's love as the operative principle governing the universe."[12] Islam lists ninety-nine names of God, and one of those names is al-Wadūd, "the Loving One," though it is Allah's compassion and mercy that are invoked at the beginning of every *surah* of the Qur'an.[13] Within the Christian tradition, the New Testament book of 1 John states that "God is love and he who abides in love abides in God and God in him."[14] God is likened to a father whose love is demonstrated in acts of loving kindness toward human beings who are God's children. As the story of the prodigal son makes clear, the father loves the profligate son without regard for whether he deserves that love and without an expectation of being loved in return.[15]

In Hinduism, the transcendent is Brahman, the one Reality behind all that is, whether conceived of ultimately as impersonal (*advaita vedanta*) or as personal (*bhakti*). In either case, this world, including the human, is a manifestation of Brahman. Brahman encompasses all things, including all emotions and their opposites, and is variously characterized in the Upanishads as no one thing or all things, as source and end of all things, as both immanent and transcendent, and as *sat-chit-ananda* (being, consciousness, and bliss). The Kena Upanishad further describes Brahman, the Supreme Spirit:

> He is seen in Nature in the wonder of the flash of lightening, He comes to the soul (*atman*) in the wonder of the flash of vision.
> His name is Tadvanam, which translated means "the End of love-longing." As Tadvanam he should have adoration. All beings will love such a lover of the Lord.[16]

This personalistic understanding of Brahman comes into much sharper focus in the Bhagavad Gita in the person of Krishna, and throughout the development of devotional Hinduism or *bhakti*, we find the One Reality continuously described as loving Lord. In contrast, in the nontheistic Asian traditions of Buddhism and Confucianism, the transcendent is nonpersonal and indeed in Buddhism is characterized as the fullness of emptiness rather than the fullness of being. In this context, love, or more accurately compassion, is an attribute of the enlightened or fully realized person who knows and aligns him or herself with the transcendent.

Love as the Response to the Transcendent

Love is a principle human response to the transcendent in theistic traditions, love both for God and for our fellow humans. In Judaism, our ability to love is a principal dimension of our being created in God's image, and we are first and foremost called to love God. The *shema*, the fundamental statement of faith in Judaism, begins "The Lord our God is one Lord, and you shall love the Lord your God with all your heart, and with all your soul, and with all your might."[17] This foundational love is marked by respectful awe coupled with fear before the majesty of God, and is demonstrated in action—upholding the laws of holiness and justice and studying the Torah, which allows one to come to know God ever more deeply.

Moses Maimonides (1135–1205) writes of the emotional depth and proper form of this love:

> And what is the proper love? It is that a person shall love the Lord with a very mighty and overflowing love so that his soul shall be attached to the love of God, constantly dwelling on it, as one who is lovesick and cannot take his mind away from his love for a particular woman, but dwells on it at all times, on lying down and on rising up, when eating and when drinking. Even more than this must be the love for God in the hearts of His lovers, dwelling on it constantly as we have been commanded (Deut. 6:5): "with all your heart and all your soul," and this was conveyed in a parable by King Solomon, when he said (Song of Songs 2:5), "I am lovesick." The entire *Song of Songs* is a parable dealing with this theme.[18]

Even though Maimonides follows the "way of the intellect," he sees that it is romantic love that most deeply captures the depth of human-divine love. The Song of Songs, with its celebration of the passionate love of a young man and young woman, came to be interpreted as a parable of the love of God for Israel and is read regularly in synagogues to commemorate God's act of love in the historical Passover.

Maimonides' suggestion that this text also portrays the individual's impassioned love for the divine is further developed in the kabbalistic and Hasidic mystical strands of Judaism. In the Mishnah, Rabbi Akiba refers to the Song of Songs as the "Holy of Holies" among the writings of the Torah, and kabbalistic interpretations find in it a description of the human–divine relationship—a relationship marked by mutual desire, intense attachment, and the pleasure of union,[19] with an exclusivity such that one relationship comes to dominate the lover's entire world, corresponding to Solomon's description of romantic love. The line between lover and beloved fades as the young lover in the Song of Songs asks her beloved to "bind me as a seal upon your heart, a sign upon your arm" and describes this love as "fierce as death, its jealousy bitter as the grave. Even its sparks are a raging fire, a devouring flame. Great seas cannot extinguish love, no river can sweep it away."[20]

The study of the Torah, for both the ordinary Jew and the practitioner of kabbalah, also occasions a free emotional expression of love directed at the text itself, which is likened to a beautiful woman. The Zohar speaks of this intimacy not only as an attitude of the student toward the text but as a way in which God, through feminine Wisdom (the Shekhinah), draws the student into love.[21] To her lovers, the Torah reveals the secrets of the universe and of God's true nature which is concealed from others. Knowledge and love merge for the (male) Torah student, who is alternately lover and child suckling at its mother's breast.[22] Yet in spite of the intense love enjoined for the Torah, care must be taken not to let the love of the Torah displace the love for God, who is its source.[23]

The later Hasidic tradition that came to flower in eighteenth- and nineteenth-century eastern Europe embraced the emotional experience of love in a wider way, even as it opened up the mystical path to the common person. The loveworld that emerges from this encounter is one in which human beings work with God to free the divine spark of love within each person. For Hasidism, according to Maurice Friedman,

> the world was created out of love and is to be brought to perfection through love. Love is central in God's relation to [humans] and is more important than the fear of God, justice or righteousness. The fear of God is only a door to the love of God—it is the awe which one has before a loving father. God is love and the capacity to love is man's innermost participation in God. This capacity is never lost but needs only to be purified to be raised to God himself. Thus love is not only a feeling; it is the godly in existence. Nor can one love God unless he loves his fellow man. For the same reason the love of God and the love of man is to be for its own sake and not for the sake of any reward.[24]

For Judaism the heart must be conditioned to love all people even as God does, including those who are wrongdoers. The sixteenth-century kabbalist Moses Cordovero writes that a person

> is to cultivate in his heart a love even for the wicked, saying: Would that these people become righteous, turning from their course in penitence, and then they would all become great and acceptable to God, as the faithful friend of the Jewish people.... And how he would get himself to love them if he learnt to focus his mind on their good points, overlooking their defects, concentrating not on the aberrations but on their good attributes.... In God's eye [someone I might look down on] is more important than I since he is troubled with privation and suffering by which a person is cleansed from sin. Why should I dislike one whom God loves?"[25]

Another sixteenth-century practitioner of kabbalah, Isaac ben Solomon Luria, addresses the nature of the love of neighbor that is to be cultivated before entering the synagogue—a love that takes another's troubles to heart in identification, and is accompanied by an understanding of one's self as part of a group so that if any suffer, then all suffer.[26] This is a love of neighbor that leads to a sense of communal and interpenetrating identity.

The experience of love of which Hasidism speaks also softens the boundary between the individual identity and God. That love has two distinct levels. The first is "love with delights," which is "a state of wondrous delight in God, with a great, a mighty joy, the joy of the soul to the very limits of its strength." The second level is marked by "the soul's yearning to cleave to God, to be included in the source of life."[27] For the soul, in the words of Shneur Zalman of Lyady,

> the nearness of God is her good, and she desires it; and it is painful for her to be separated from Him by a barrier formed by worldly involvements. This love is hidden in the heart of every Jew, even the wicked.

And for the devoted follower of Hasidism:

> As the mind contemplates God, according to his intellectual capacity and the state of his culture, how He is the life of all life, and the life of his own soul in particular,

he will naturally desire to cleave to Him and to be near Him, as the son always yearns to be near his father and as fire always tends to rise upward.[28]

The desire to cleave to God (*devekut*) carries with it a range of meanings, "from imitating divine behavior to total fusion with the divine."[29] The one who cleaves to God experiences a transformation like that of romantic love, moving into a shared self, open to and bound to God, while still retaining a distinct existence.

Turning to Christianity, the complex set of divine commandments in the Hebrew Bible are distilled into the foundational love commandments of the New Testament:

> You must love the Lord your God with all your heart, with all your soul, and with all your mind. This is the greatest and the first commandment. The second resembles it: You must love your neighbor as yourself.[30]

It is not enough merely to love those who love you (the person-person realm of ordinary emotional love); you are called to love even your enemies,[31] and your love must be manifested in helping those in need and acting for good rather than evil.[32] This "Christian" love was taken to be *agape* rather than *eros*. During the formative early period of Christianity, the term "eros" had negative connotations, given its use by the licentious Roman Dionysian cults and the salaciousness associated with the Greek god Eros. This undoubtedly influenced the choice to employ agape rather than eros in key New Testament scriptures, such as 1 Corinthians 13.[33] In contrast to eros, or passionate love, agape is defined as unconditional other-regarding love, given without expectation and universally and impartially applied to all. By the third century, Augustine advocates a Christian Platonic love, in which we love God because God loves us and we love both neighbor and enemy because they are in God, rather than for themselves. God's love, which does not partake of need or reciprocity, is *agapeistic*, and Augustine holds that human-human relations ideally should mirror God's love, agape, as closely as possible.

In the twentieth century, the Swedish Lutheran theologian Anders Nygren reemphasized this distinction in his influential work *Agape and Eros*, drawing a sharp dichotomy between eros and agape. According to Nygren, "*Eros* is an upward movement ... *agape* comes down."[34] Consequently, for Nygren, "there is thus no way for [human beings] to come to God, but only a way for God to come to [human beings]: the way of divine forgiveness, divine love. *Agape* is God's way to [human beings]."[35] Thus for Nygren, while eros arises out of need or desire, agape flows out of abundance as a grace, and while eros is conditional and can be earned or merited, agape is given unconditionally. Consequently, agape is a higher kind of love, since "*eros recognizes value* in its object—and loves it ... [while] *agape* loves—and *creates value* in its object."[36] But agape is also a higher kind of love, he thinks, because eros is self-love and agape excludes self-love.

Nygren's rejection of eros is based, as Julius Lipner has observed, on an assumption of "the inherent depravity of human nature," which not all Christians would share,[37] even though there is a discomfort in much Christian theology with both the emotional attachment and sexuality encompassed by eros. Further,

Nygren's rendering of agape as the polar opposite of eros leaves no room for the transformative potential of the emotion of love to create a new and shared self, which is expressed by many in the Christian tradition who write of their experience of God's love.

In contrast to Nygren, a modern Christian thinker who follows "the way of love" is C. S. Lewis, who writes:

> In one high bound [eros] has overleaped the massive wall of our selfhood; it has made appetite itself altruistic, tossed personal happiness aside as a triviality and planted the interest of another in the center of our being. Spontaneously and without effort we have fulfilled the law.... It is an image, a foretaste of what we must become to all if Love Himself rules in us without rival.[38]

In its truest sense, eros has this other-directed quality, rather than being purely self-interested, as Nygren supposes. Moreover, the love of God (of which Lewis claims human eros offers a foretaste) is not, it may be argued, the sort of disinterested love Nygren's characterization suggests but rather reflects, in part, the key elements of eros: reciprocity, vulnerability, surrender, integration, union, and equality of acceptance.[39] To incorporate these elements of eros into the Christian understanding of the nature of divine love and to avoid the limitations of past polarized definitions of agape and eros, it has been proposed that a new term be used, that of "seraphic love," with agape and eros in a dynamic tension as its two poles: "On the one side, the motive for *agape* is the passionate love of *eros*. And on the other side, true *eros* is not manipulative—for *agape* is the counter-balancing pole within seraphic love."[40]

Christian mystics across the centuries have written about their experiences of the love of God in terms that fit this notion of seraphic love, integrating eros with agape. In the monasteries of medieval Europe, the scripture most often recited and commented on was the Song of Songs, and it was understood to describe the intensely passionate love between the soul and God, much as Jewish mystics understood the text.[41] In his *Sermons on the Song of Songs*, the twelfth-century Cistercian abbot Bernard of Clairvaux affirms that "of all the motions, the senses, the affections of the soul, it is love alone in which the creature is able, even, if not on an equal basis, to repay the Creator for what it has received, to weigh back something from the same measure."[42] To initiate the cultivation of this love of God that will eventuate in so-called "spiritual marriage," sensual human love provides the powerful and proper starting place. For, as M. Corneille Halflants observes, Bernard of Clairvaux

> does not believe it possible to suppress with impunity the indestructible force of sense love.... What is to be done? Present to carnal love an object which is proportionate to it and more delightful than any sinful creature.... Here is the advantage of attaching one's sense love to the humanity of Christ. It directs the vital strength of such love toward a more attractive sensible object. This new sensible object is the dwelling place of the divinity, which will gradually reveal itself as it draws the soul into holiness.[43]

The love which thus grows between the soul and God is emotional, not merely intellectual, as the humanity of Christ opens up the way to love with the seeds of ordinary sensual love. Indeed, the soul which reaches the highest level becomes love, loving as it is loved, conforming its nature and its will to that of God in a spiritual marriage marked by mutuality.

The image of the bride soul and the divine bridegroom continues to imbue the language of later Christian mystics. St. John of the Cross in his *Spiritual Canticle* writes in the voice of the bride soul speaking of the divine Beloved:

> I gave myself to him indeed, reserving nothing; There I promised him to be his bride. My soul has employed itself And all my possessions in his service: Now I guard no flock nor have I now other office, For now my exercise is in loving alone.[44]

The soul "divine and deified" in the experience of loving union with God is completely dedicated to the divine beloved.

Yet that love at times bewilders and overwhelms the soul, overtaking it in an experience of piercing pain or burning conflagration. St. Teresa of Avila speaks of such love piercing her like

> an arrow... driven into the very depths of the entrails, and sometimes into the heart, so that the soul does not know either what is the matter with it or what it desires. It knows quite well that it desires God and that the arrow seems to have been dipped in some drug which leads it to hate itself for the love of this Lord so that it would gladly lose its life for Him.... It sees so clearly that this love has come to it through no act of its own, but that, from the exceeding great love which the Lord bears it, a spark seems suddenly to have fallen upon it and to have set it wholly on fire.[45]

For the soul in love with God, that love includes a willingness to give up all that it formerly held dear, even life itself, for the Beloved. It requires dying to the past, as the soul is engulfed in a purifying conflagration, emptied of egoistic self even as it is filled with the overwhelming abundance of divine love. Yet while this experience is emotionally intense, Teresa is careful to point out that the love about which she speaks is not an overflowing of superficial emotion expressed through exterior weeping. Instead it is a welling up of deep affection that has its source outside the individual even as it manifests interiorily, and she counsels that great discretion is needed in developing this religious emotion.

In medieval Europe, expressions of the religious emotion of love develop alongside the tradition of courtly love, which is an impassioned and "pure" love marked by longing and carefully separated from mundane and duty-bound conceptions of marriage.[46] Antedating St. Teresa of Avila, mystics from the twelfth through the fourteenth centuries speak of a pure and *agapeistic* eros and explore in great detail the nature of this intimate, emotional, and transformative experience of love, from the beguines Hadewijch of Antwerp and Mechthild of Magdeburg to Catherine of Siena and the English mystics Julian of Norwich and Richard Rolle. French beguine Marguerite Porete, writing of a culminating passing away of the self into the Beloved, addresses Love this way: "Ah, most sweet, pure, and divine Love, what a suave transformation it is to be transformed into what I love more than myself. And I am so transformed that I have lost my name in order to love, I who can love so little; it is into Love that I have been transformed; for I love nothing but Love."[47] The radical nature of this love renders the hierarchy of gender and religious authority irrelevant. Perceiving this as a grave danger, Christian authorities called many mystics to appear before the Inquisition, though great figures like Teresa of Avila would be recognized as saints in later centuries. Marguerite Porete did not fair as well, for she was burned at the stake for daring to speak of such love. Islamic Sufi mystics sometimes suffered a similar fate.

In Islam, the orthodox tradition speaks of the human-divine relation principally in terms of submission, yet Allah has placed signs revealing Allah's nature in the human heart, so that human love reveals the nature of God's love. In the Qur'an, Allah is shown to be responsive to human action, for "only he who surrenders to God with all his heart and does good, will find his reward with his Lord, and will have no fear or regret," and Allah admonishes the believer to "do good—for God loves those who do good"—and warns that "God does not love the unjust."[48] Yet to this one must add another well-loved *hadith* in which Allah says:

> My servant continues to come near to me by piety beyond what is required so that I love him.... And if my servant approaches a hand's breadth, I go toward him and arm's length; and if he approaches an arm's length, I go forward the space of outstretched arms; and if he comes toward me walking, I go toward him running. And if my servant should bring to me sins the size of the earth itself, my forgiveness will be more than equal to them."[49]

Indeed Allah is always, the Qur'an says, "closer than the jugular vein," dwelling in the heart and revealed to those who would do good and reach out toward Allah.[50] The Sufis especially pursue this closeness to God, and the emotion of love takes center stage as a radically transformative force, annihilating the self so that only an awareness of God remains.

Rabi'a Al-'Adawiyyah of Basra, the eighth-century woman mystic credited with bringing the emotion of love into the mystical practice of Islam, is famously said to have gone through the streets with a burning torch in one hand and a bucket of water in the other—to pour water on the fires of hell and to set fire to heaven, so that no one might mistakenly follow Islam out of fear of hell or desire for heaven but only because of the beauty of God, to which the human response must be absolute love, modeled by the love of Potiphar's wife Zulaikha for Joseph.[51] This love of God is experienced as affliction, suffering, and poverty. Indeed the Sufis speak of the martyrdom of love, referring not only to the complete annihilation of self but also to literal martyrdom at the hands of those who hear, in the mystic's description of his or her experience, *shirk*, or "the placing of another beside God," which is the only unforgivable sin. The tenth-century Sufi al-Hallaj was executed after he was heard publicly proclaiming in ecstasy, "I am the Absolute Truth." For in the experience of the extreme nearness of God and the annihilation of the egoistic self, only an awareness of God remains. Indeed, al-Hallaj claims: "I am He whom I love, and He whom I love is me."[52]

In this context, the meaning of the central tenet of Islam that God is one (*tauhîd*) and the creedal statement of the *shahadah* ("There is no God but God and Muhammad is his prophet") take on new meaning. Annemarie Schimmel describes this meaning in the Sufi conception of the mystical path this way:

> They spoke of the different stages on the mystical path, of intoxication and sobriety, of gnosis and love, of finding and being found in ecstasy; and the experience of the central concept of Islam, that of *tauhīd*, was hidden under verbal play. For *tauhīd* has both a declarative and a factitive meaning: it means in the first instance "to declare God as one," i.e., to profess that He is the sole Agent, Creator, Sustainer, and Judge who works without secondary causes, and that He is the sole and only goal of man's life.... But among the mystics the feeling soon grew stronger that man had "to render God One," i.e., to annihilate himself before the only real Being who alone has the right to say "I." Finally the formula of the creed "There is no deity save God" could be converted by radical mystics into the phrase *la maujūda illā Allāh*, "There is nothing existent save God."[53]

The Sufi path of love is that of the moth drawn to the flame: one must give up everything but God, even the self, until only an awareness of God remains. Indeed Ibn al-'Arabî writes: "When my Beloved appears, with what eye do I see Him? With His eye, not with mine, For none sees Him except Himself."[54] Thus the creature is not identical with God but is a reflection of God's attributes, yet "Lover, beloved and love—all the three are one. When union comes in, what has separation to do?"[55]

Beginning in the tenth century, the language of romantic love becomes a principle mode of speaking about this experience. Indeed Sufism comes to affirm the value of human love relationships as "the ladder leading to the love of the Merciful," so much so that "the soul needs the wings of human love to fly toward divine love."[56] It became more and more popular

> to see the Divine beauty reflected in or manifest in a human being, ideally in a boy of fourteen.... The veneration of young boys—branded by the orthodox as a kind of manicheism—developed into a highly refined spiritual art.... The sober Sufis were always aware of the danger of "looking at the unbearded." ... The lovers, however, maintained that such love was licit, provided that the chastity of the glance was preserved.[57]

Not surprisingly the Sufis endured accusations of homosexuality and licentiousness from their critics because of these ideas and practices, since their poetic expressions intentionally "oscillat[ed] between the two levels of experience," without placing an absolute distinction between the love of humans and of the divine.[58] For the most part, the orthodox had an uneasy truce with Sufi ideas and practice but recognized, as Schimmel says, "the danger of breaking out of the well-ordered world of the *nomos*, the Divinely inspired law, into the vast fields of *eros* in all its shades," and at times this disintegrated into violent suppression.[59]

The life of perhaps the most famous of the Sufi saints, the thirteenth-century Julaluddin Rumi, was marked by such loving relationships, which were for him ladders to divine love, making his life "a paradigm of the ideal mystical biography."[60]

Love stands at the center of Rumi's writing, and he draws on a wide range of images, portraying love as a fire that burns away all human faults, as the wind that fans the flames or as purifying water, as an ocean, a garden, a kingdom, and a cave for monks, as a trap or net with no way out, and as a man-eating monster slaughtering the lover for the feast of 'Id.[61] For Rumi, the love of human and divine is characterized as much by affliction as by ecstasy, as much by separation as by union. Thus, in the opening stanzas of Rumi's *Mathnawi*, we hear the voice of the reed, empty yet filled with the fire of love, consumed by longing, having been cut loose from its source in the reed bed, and playing a haunting melody.

In his own life, his initial encounter with his teacher, Shamsuddin (Shams), led him to forget all else as he experienced through him the love of God in the eighteen months they spent together. It appeared that Rumi's former self had passed away, much to the distress of his family and disciples, who eventually forced Shams to leave, but Rumi's poems are filled with his praise and love of Shams, and the identities of Rumi, Shams, the Prophet, and God merge in his verses.[62] He then developed a deep friendship with the goldsmith Salahuddin, marrying his son to Salahuddin's daughter, and his love stabilized during this period. After Salahuddin's death he became particularly close to his disciple Hasamuddin, in a "return to the created things," and composed his *Mathnawi* for his benefit.[63]

The Sufi master, the *shaikh* or *pir*, remains a key figure in Sufi practice, though the orthodox are still uneasy with the incorporation of the veneration of *pirs*, past and present, into Islam. In contrast to ordinary love,

> the love of the [disciple] for the sheikh, the divine love in Sufi belief, is de-caged from the temporality of space and time. It seeks the immortal and endures. Rather than isolate the self, it restores to the self its divine destiny. Rather than destroy, divine love dissolves the self into divinity. When it grows, it doesn't bear its opposite, but begets itself. The love for the sheikh is an endless longing that culminates with ever increasing intensity.[64]

To some extent, the *shaikh* fulfills the same role as the humanity of Christ in the writings of a Christian mystic like Bernard of Clairvaux, where love expands even as the individual soul contracts in a process that allows a radically transformed shared self to emerge.

In Hinduism, although the way of knowledge, *jnana* yoga, dominates in the literature of the Upanishads, the way of love, *bhakti* yoga, evolves as the dominant mode of Hindu religiosity, even more so than the more peripheral mystical traditions of Christianity and Islam. For the *bhakta* (devotee), love is the ideal human response to the transcendent, a transcendent perceived as loving Lord. That loving Lord comes to the human in multiple incarnational forms, for it is far easier for humans to love one whom they can see and in whose presence they can stand than to love the Unmanifest.

The Bhagavad Gita (composed ca. 200 B.C.E.) offers the first fully developed discussion of the merits of the way of love. This text explicitly advocates that loving devotion to God is equally valid, if not superior, to the way of knowledge as a path for moving beyond a false sense of the self to reach liberation. Arjuna's charioteer, Lord Krishna, tells him first to act without attachment to the fruits of his actions (*nishkama* karma), doing what is right, or dharmic, simply because it is right. This includes fulfilling his duties as a righteous ruler but also includes universal virtues such as "compassion for all creatures, patience, lack of envy... generosity and lack of greed," enumerated in Gautama's *Dharma Sutra*—qualities that are much like those of Christian love advocated in 1 Corinthians 13. Acting with detachment and not acting for self in fulfilling these dharmic responsibilities requires a difficult transformation of the self, which may be accomplished by following either the way of knowledge or the way of love. The former is especially hard, while selfless action is enabled by turning to God in devotion and love, offering up one's actions as a sacrifice. Indeed, Krishna tells Arjuna, "By devotion alone can I, as I really am, be known and seen and entered into" (Bhagavad Gita 11:54).[65] Yet though the Gita advocates the way of love, Krishna counsels detachment and equanimity rather than impassioned emotion. In later *bhakti* literature, however, the transformative power of the emotion of love in a reciprocal loving intimacy between human and divine comes to full bloom. In this context, human relations of love provide an emotional training ground and a language for human–divine love.

Beginning in South India in the sixth century C.E. and sweeping across the subcontinent over the next millennium, a series of religious movements arose that embraced the emotion of love as the very heart of the religious life. *Bhaktas* within these movements immerse themselves in the love of God, and their poet-saints speak of a human-divine romance marked by mutuality, ecstatic union, and devastating separation, a romance in which the divine longs for the human as much as the human for the divine. Representatively, the ninth-century Tamil poet-saint Nammalvar speaks in wonder of the mystery of loving a God who is at once all in all and the great god Vishnu who incarnates in the world in multiple forms and can be encountered in the temples that dot the landscape, yet who is also enshrined in the human heart. Drawing on the Tamil literary traditions of romantic love poetry, Nammalvar speaks of the soul as feminine, in love with and possessed by the Beloved, devouring and being devoured by love, overcome with longing so that even when she is with him, she suffers because she knows that in a split second he will quickly be gone again.[66]

In the tradition of *bhakti*, every type of human love becomes a model and provides a language for the love of God. The North Indian Vaishnava saint Surdas speaks in parental terms of loving the divine incarnate baby Krishna and of taking on the persona of his adoptive mother, Yashoda, while devotees of the Goddess speak in the voice of child to a divine and all powerful mother.[67] Entering into the dramatic world of Krishna's incarnation in particular allows the devotee to love him as friend, as servant, and, most intimately, as lover. In portraying the latter role, poet-saints can draw on the full range of emotions that accompany erotic love—the ecstatic joy of union, the piercing pain of longing, the excitement at the anticipated return of the lover, and jealousy, anger, regret, and sorrow. Here a distinction is made between *kama*, "the erotic love of marriage with its attendant responsibilities and obligations, social acceptance, and resulting procreation" and divine love, or *prema*, "the delight of hearts that meet freely, risking social sanction, with no end but love itself."[68] In the words of the twelfth-century Kannada devotee of Shiva Mahadeviyakka, the soul is a "woman of love for her Lord," and she cries out: "He bartered my heart, looted my flesh, claimed as tribute my pleasure, took over all of me."[69]

Yet love's union is always in dynamic tension with the inevitable separation that is essential for love to flourish, so the fifteenth-century North Indian Vaishnava saint Mirabai compares her Lord to a renouncer, and she cries out to him not to leave her. In order not to be plunged into separation again, Mirabai would have her Lord Krishna build a funeral pyre of fragrant sandalwood and aloe, lighting it with his own hand: "When I am burned away to cinders," she says, "rub this ash upon your limbs. Let flame be lost in flame."[70] Unlike the Abrahamic faiths, where the separateness of God and humans is the clear one of creator to creation, for Mirabai and in Hinduism generally the human is a manifestation of the divine and so is, in this sense, one with the divine. At the same time, the separateness of the One manifesting and the manifestation makes love possible. Hence, in a metaphysical as well as an emotional sense, human existence is fundamentally characterized for the *bhakta* by both union and separation, equal grounds of love.

Religious emotion is highly valued in the Hindu context, in part because emotion in general is valued: "India finds emotions, like food, necessary for a reasonable life, and like taste, cultivatable for the fullest understanding of life's meaning and purpose."[71] An elaborate theory of emotion has been developed in Indian culture within the context of the cultivation of aesthetic sensibilities, where the goal is an ever deepening capacity for a universal emotional experience. Laid out in Bharata's *Natyasastra*, the emotions are divided into eight major *bhavas*, of which love is one, with a wide range of attendant secondary emotions. These emotions are to be tasted, relished, refined in experience, and transformed into a universal experience (*rasa*) that touches on the divine bliss. Hindu *bhaktas* expand this aesthetic theory into a religious discipline designed to cultivate religious emotion, refined in Vaishnava traditions into the practice of *raganuga bhakti*, in which the devotee enters into the dramatic realm of Krishna's incarnation. "Through physical action and imaginative visualization, the devotee builds a soul, a spiritual body composed of love, which can experience emotion more intensely than can the ordinary personality."[72] For the *bhakta*, June McDaniel suggests,

> emotion is the path to God and is thus sacred. Rather than trying to eliminate emotion, the goal is to intensify emotion until it becomes powerful, overwhelming, the center of the devotee's being.... Human emotion is transformed into divine emotion; it is boiled, thickened, purified, and redirected.[73]

In this *bhakti* religious loveworld, there is no room for hierarchies of caste, gender, or religious authority. Women and those of low-caste birth can as easily enter this world as can men and those of high-caste birth, and the leaders of these *bhakti* movements include people from all these groups. For if love can bring the human and divine into a relationship of equality, then there is no room for human inequality. Though sometimes this equality has been relegated strictly to the religious realm, from its inception to the present, *bhakti* has offered a radical democratizing force within Hinduism. Attempts to instantiate this loveworld of equality in the social realm have at times evoked violent suppression, as in the case of the twelfth-century community of Kalyana in the Kannada-speaking region of South India.[74] The songs composed by the great devotees of the tradition, popularly acclaimed as saints, are the principle texts of the *bhakti* tradition, and many nameless devotees across the centuries have composed additional songs in their names and styles. These devotional songs are sung in communal gatherings with the explicit purpose of eliciting and deepening the love of God both in those who perform them and in those who hear them, offering a language for the expression and exploration of the Hindu loveworld. And these songs also continue to provide a language of resistance for those oppressed by the social system, as that love moves out into the realm of human–human relations.

In Buddhism, the enlightened mind, which fully realizes that reality is radically interdependent and that all things are entirely made of nonself elements—the Buddhist *anatman*, or "no-self"—experiences compassion for those who suffer under the delusion of self. Compassion, which is a quality of the Dharmakaya (reality as it is in itself) and of the enlightened mind, is coupled with three additional virtues—loving-kindness, magnanimous joy, and equanimity. Together they form a broad perspective of universal love.

This universal compassion and love stands in sharp contrast to the emotional attachments of family, and indeed the historical Buddha, Siddhartha Gautama, leaves his young wife Yashodhara and his son to pursue enlightenment. A body of literature did arise that was sympathetic to his wife's consequent feelings of both sorrow and anger, but the tradition ultimately affirms the Buddha's action, since the emotion of romantic love is wed to attachment and, as such, is an impediment to the pursuit of liberating wisdom unless it is transformed into a universal love.[75] The Dalai Lama affirms this teaching:

> Compassion should be cultivated toward all sentient beings. To identify a particular group of sentient beings as friends or relatives and maintain a special feeling of closeness toward them is actually attachment, not genuine compassion. And the result of obsessive attachment is suffering. Therefore we should cultivate a sense of equanimity toward others, free of feelings of partiality, attachment and hatred. The next step is to see all sentient beings as our relatives.[76]

Compassion grows in importance in Buddhism with the advent of Mahayana Buddhism, beginning half a millennium after the Buddha's death, and with the Mahayana emphasis on the *bodhisattva* rather than the enlightened monk or *arhat* as the ideal practitioner. The *bodhisattva* is one who vows to work for the liberation of all beings, not just for self- liberation, and addresses the suffering of fellow creatures, not with an objectifying attitude of pity but with an abiding empathy that perceives the pain of others as one's own. Compassion involves both an intentional cognitive orientation and a naturally arising sentiment—a habit of thought to be cultivated and a capacity to be deepened through action and the development of wisdom. For the Buddhist, the true enemy is the negative emotions like anger, hatred, and desire with their power to destroy.[77] Negative emotions arise suddenly, flaring out at whoever is near, and often dissipate quickly, but the positive emotions of compassion and love are abiding, and arise in concert with reason and a "purposive commitment to adopt a complex pattern of actions and attitudes" toward the one who is loved.[78] Buddhists recognize the power of the loving mind and seek to develop *bodhicitta*, translated as both "the mind of enlightenment" and "the mind of love."[79]

The ideal of the *bodhisattva* in Mahayana Buddhism emphasizes not only compassion but also that enlightenment can perhaps most effectively be pursued in the midst of the world rather than in monastic isolation and renunciation. With this affirmation of the world comes a positive valuation of emotion. The *Vimilakirti Nirdesha Sutra* affirms that even as lotuses do not grow in the dry ground but in the swamps and mudbanks, so the Buddha-qualities of compassion, generosity, and sensitivity grow in those living beings who are like swamps and mudbanks of passions.[80] The later strand of tantric Buddhism, often intermingled with Mahayana, goes even further, asserting that the purity and power that lie at the heart of the emotions are aspects of the enlightened mind. Thus entering into the depths of passion, particularly of erotic love, "provides the fuel and energy of meditation on emptiness," which can lead to a transformation of passion into enlightened bliss.[81] While recognizing the danger of impassioned emotional love, tantric practitioners seek its power, for "love, enjoyed by the ignorant, becomes bondage. That very same love tasted by one with understanding, brings liberation."[82]

Tantric practices designed to cultivate this enlightened bliss move practitioners into the full realization of a boundary-less shared self and a mutual enlightenment. For them, to deny desire and impassioned emotion is "to live a lie," leading away from realization rather than toward it. Because of the power of emotion, a teacher who can especially help one deal with any negative emotions that may arise in the process of meditation is essential for this tantric path, while a human partner with whom one shares love is arguably essential to reach the highest levels of transformation of the self that are required for full enlightenment.

Confucianism offers yet another alternative for self-transformation. On the Confucian view, self-transformation or, more accurately, the cultivation of the self is the fundamental task of human beings. The transcendent is Tien, or Heaven, an ordering power manifest in the world through the structuring principle of *li* and in the dynamic matter-energy continuum of *ch'i*. Human beings belong to this vast interrelated reality, and Confucianism asserts the unity of humanity and Tien. For humans to realize their full humanity, they must act in concert with "heaven, earth and the myriad things," acting according to *li* and with *jen* or human-heartedness. Like Buddhist compassion and wisdom, *li* and *jen* are inseparable.[83]

Jen or human-heartedness entails being able to put oneself in another's place so that the fully human person is "an indivisible continuum between 'self' and 'other,' between 'I' and 'we,' between 'subject' and 'object,' between 'now' and 'then' "[84]—a description that comes very close to the Buddhist notion of compassion. Confucius himself refers to "loving others" (*ai jen*) as integral to the process of becoming fully human, but this love is a graduated rather than universal love, beginning with family and moving out in successively wider circles to one's community, one's nation, and then to humanity more generally. For Confucius, filial love with its emphasis on reciprocal roles is the key to developing the capacity for wider love.[85] Universal love, as advocated by Confucius's contemporary Mo-Tzu, was untenable on Confucius's view because one can only achieve the desired "loveworld" in which love is relationally instantiated throughout society by means of immediate and specific love relationships supported by a deliberately structured, shared understanding of attendant reciprocal social responsibilities.

Ai jen is a taking-in of another "into one's sphere of concern, and in so doing mak[ing] him an integral aspect of one's own person [and w]here this taking in is reciprocated, *ai* is a bond that allows one's own person to be defined by reference to those he loves."[86] This Confucian conception of love contrasts with understandings of Christian agape because it originates from the human. Comparing agape and *jen*, David Hall and Roger Ames suggest that in Christianity, "persons are channels of *agape* and can only approximate it in their relationships to the extent that they are vehicles of God's love. *Jen*, by contrast, originates with personal judgment (*yi*) exercised in community."[87]

In addition to this cognitive dimension, *jen* has an affective dimension, a dimension that is often absent in Christian notions of agape, particularly in the wake of Nygren's analysis. William LaFleur reports, in his insightful study of the difference between American and Japanese attitudes toward cadaveric organ transplantation, that agape (the principle rationale for organ donation among American Christians), when viewed from the perspective of Japanese Confucian understandings of *jen* in familial relations, appears inhuman, unnatural, and even unethical *because* it can contravene emotional love.[88] The graduated love of Confucianism is marked by a strong emotional bond ideally modeled on the parent-child relation and consequently is closer to eros than to agape. Finally, Confucianism assumes that we come into the world unshaped, needing to be made into full human beings, and that the process of person-building includes the development of *jen*, such that the secular, including the secular emotion of love, becomes sacred and *jen* grows outward from familial love relationships expanding to a universally encompassing human-heartedness.

Love as Transformation of the Self

The importance of the religious emotion of love lies in its unfathomable power to transform the self. Religious practitioners may come to understand the need for transformation through the doctrinal teachings of their tradition, but transformation requires a change of heart, a new perception of being self-and-the-divine-Self or self-and-world, and a new way of being in the world, all gifts of love. In the Western traditions, Saint Bernard of Clairvaux employs a marvelous metaphor to illustrate this: "Man and God... are with strict truth called 'one spirit' if they adhere to one another with the *glue of love*... [and] this unity is effected... by concurrence of wills."[89] The parallel transformation in Buddhism entails developing *bodhicitta* or "cultivating the mind of love," where heart and mind are inseparable and are awakened through meditation to the realization (not simply the intellectual grasping) of the radical interdependence and impermanence of all things, resulting in compassion for all other beings. Similarly for the Hindu *bhakta*, religious practices are focused on deepening the capacity for love of the divine—with its seat in the *man*, or heart/mind—until the devotee becomes the embodiment of love, seeing the divine in all things and manifesting love toward all beings.

Emotion is an essential aspect of the transformative power of this experience, for radical transformation of the self requires an open vulnerability (as the notion of seraphic love emphasizes), a complete vulnerability that a mere act of willed love alone cannot provide. By its very nature, the unrestricted emotion of love breaks down the barriers of an isolated, individual self, enabling one to embrace a new shared self. This transformed self is not simply characterized by love and compassion; rather it extends its loveworld to the wider world while finding ultimate fulfillment in relationship to the transcendent, however that is conceived. Participation in this encompassing religious loveworld of relationships is the *telos* of the religious path, whether it be Jewish, Christian, Islamic, Hindu, Buddhist, or Confucian. The emotional dimensions of love, so often associated with self-centered eros, here take on the added other-regarding dimension of seraphic love, the heart of the religious path.

NOTES

1. Robert Nozick, *The Examined Life: Philosophical Meditations* (New York: Simon and Schuster 1989), 86.
2. Robert C. Solomon, *Love: Emotion, Myth, and Metaphor* (Garden City, N.Y.: Doubleday, 1981), 34.
3. Ibid., 35, 40.
4. Ibid., 126.
5. Ibid., 142, 143.
6. Ibid., 132.
7. Nozick, *The Examined Life*, 85–86.
8. Solomon, *Love*, 149.
9. Rumi, *The Essential Rumi*, translated by Coleman Barks (San Francisco: HarperCollins, 1995), 243.
10. Quoted in Annemarie Schimmel, *As through a Veil: Islamic Mystical Poetry* (New York: Columbia University Press, 1982), 123.
11. Ibid., 127.

12. Ben Zion Bokser, *The Jewish Mystical Tradition* (New York: Pilgrim Press, 1981), 117. The hidden godhead, the En-Sof or the Infinite, manifests in ten aspects, the Sefirot, and among them are Love (Hesed) and Compassion (Rahamim, sometimes also called Beauty or Tifereth) which mediates between God's love and God's power.

13. Sheikh Tosun Bayrak al-Jerahi al-Halveti, *The Most Beautiful Names* (Putney, Vt.: Threshold Books, 1985), 60–61.

14. 1 Jn 4:16b (RSV).

15. Lk 15:11–32.

16. Kena Upanishad, in *The Upanishads*, translated by Juan Mascaro (Harmondsworth, England: Penguin Books, 1965), 53–54.

17. Dt 6:4–5 (RSV).

18. Maimonides, *The Guide to the Perplexed*, in Bokser, *The Jewish Mystical Tradition*, 80–81.

19. Mishnah, tractate Yadayim 3:5, cited by Charlotte Elisheva Fonrobert, "Taming the Powers of Desire: Love and Sex in Jewish Culture," in *Love, Sex, and Gender in the World Religions*, edited by Joseph Runzo and Nancy M. Martin (Oxford: Oneworld, 2000), 120.

20. Song of Songs 8:6–7.

21. Moses de Leon, *Zohar*, in Bokser, *The Jewish Mystical Tradition*, 121.

22. Charlotte Elisheva Fonrobert, "To Increase Torah Is to Increase Life: Poetics of the Mind and Poetics of the Everyday in Jewish Culture," in *The Meaning of Life in the World Religions*, edited by Joseph Runzo and Nancy M. Martin (Oxford: Oneworld, 2000), 81.

23. Judah Loew of Prague (1512–1609), *Tiferot Yisrael*, introduction, in Bokser, *The Jewish Mystical Traditions*, 163.

24. Maurice Friedman, *Martin Buber: The Life of Dialogue*, 3rd rev. ed. (Chicago: University of Chicago Press, 1955), 22.

25. Moses Cordovero (1522–1570), *Tomer Devorah*, chap. 2, in Bokser, *The Jewish Mystical Tradition*, 133.

26. Isaac ben Solomon Luria (1534–1572), *Shulhan Arukh, Hillhot Bet Hakeneset*, in Bokser, *The Jewish Mystical Tradition*, 145.

27. Shneur Zalman of Lyady (1745–1813), in *Iggeret haKodesh* 18, in Bokser, *The Jewish Mystical Tradition*, translated by Bokser, 218.

28. Ibid.

29. Moshe Idel, "Universalization and Integration: Two Concepts of Mystical Union in Jewish Mysticism," in *Mystical Union in Judaism, Christianity, and Islam: An Ecumenical Dialogue*, edited by Moshe Idel and Bernard McGinn (New York: Continuum, 1996), 28. See also Moshe Idel, *Kabbalah: New Perspectives* (New Haven, Conn.: Yale University Press, 1988).

30. Mt 22:34–40 (RSV).

31. Mt 5:43–38; Lk 6:27.

32. E.g., 1 Jn 3:17–18.

33. Joseph Runzo, "Eros and Meaning in Life and Religion," in Runzo and Martin, *The Meaning of Life in the World Religions*, 194.

34. Anders Nygren, *Agape and Eros*, translated by Philip S. Watson (reprint: London, 1982), 210, quoted in Vincent Brümmer, *The Model of Love* (Cambridge: Cambridge University Press, 1993), 128.

35. Nygren, *Agape and Eros*, 80–81, quoted in Brümmer, *The Model of Love*, 128.

36. Nygren, *Agape and Eros*, 210, quoted in Brümmer, *The Model of Love*, 130.

37. Julius Lipner, "The God of Love and the Love of God in Christian and Hindu Traditions," in Runzo and Martin, *Love, Sex, and Gender in the World Religions*, 68.

38. C. S. Lewis, *The Four Loves* (New York: Harcourt, Brace and World, 1960), 158.

39. Runzo, "Eros and Meaning in Life and Religion," 194–95.

40. Ibid., 195.

41. Jean Leclercq, *The Love of Learning and the Desire for God: A Study of Monastic Culture* (New York: Fordham University Press, 1982), 84.

42. Sermon on the Song of Songs 83.2, quoted by Bernard McGinn, "The Human Person as Image of God: Western Christianity," in *Christian Spirituality: Origins to the Twelfth Century*, edited by Bernard McGinn, John Meyendorff, and Jean Leclercq (New York: Crossroad, 1988), 325.

43. M. Corneille Halflants, introduction to Bernard of Clairvaux, *On the Song of Songs 1*, translated by Kilian Walsh, Cistercian Fathers Series no. 4, Bernard of Clairvaux, vol. 2 (Kalamazoo, Mich.: Cistercian, 1977), xx.

44. St. John of the Cross, *Spiritual Canticle*, edited and translated by E. Allison Peers (New York: Image Books, 1962), stanzas 18b–19, 45.

45. St. Teresa of Avila, *The Autobiography of St. Teresa of Avila: The Life of Teresa of Jesus*, edited and translated by E. Allison Peers (Garden City, N.Y.: Image Books, 1960), 273.

46. Brümmer, *The Model of Love*, 83–106.

47. Marguerite Porete, quoted in Emilie Zum Brunn and Georgette Epiney-Burgard, *Woman Mystics in Medieval Europe* (New York: Paragon, 1989), 154.

48. Qur'an 2:112. Ahmed Ali, trans., *al-Qur'ān: A Contemporary Translation* (Princeton, N.J.: Princeton University Press, 1988).

49. John Renard, *Seven Doors to Islam: Spirituality and the Religious Life of Muslims* (Berkeley: University of California Press, 1996), 16–17.

50. Qur'an 50:16.

51. Schimmel, *My Soul Is a Woman: The Feminine in Islam*, translated by Susan H. Ray (New York: Continuum, 1997), 34–36, 60–68.

52. Schimmel, *As through a Veil*, 32.

53. Ibid., 21–22.

54. Ibid., 38.

55. Ibid., 70, as quoted in 'Iraqi, *Kulliyāt*, Lama'āt, no. 2.

56. Ibid., 68.

57. Ibid.

58. Ibid.

59. Ibid., 24.

60. Ibid., 94–95.

61. Ibid., 83–133.

62. Ibid.

63. Ibid., 94–95.

64. Bikram N. Nanda and Mohammad Talib, "Soul of the Soulless: An Analysis of the Pir-Murid Relationships in Sufi Discourse," in *Muslim Shrines of India*, edited by Christian W. Troll (Delhi: Oxford University Press, 1992), 129.

65. *The Bhagavad Gita: Krishna's Counsel in Time of War*, translated by Barbara Stoller Miller (New York: Bantam, 1986), 108.

66. A. K. Ramanujan, trans., *Hymns for the Drowning: Poems for Visnu by Nammalvar* (London: Penguin Books, 1992).

67. See Nancy M. Martin, "Love and Longing in Devotional Hinduism," in Runzo and Martin, *The Meaning of Life in the World Religions*, 201–19, and "Loving the Goddess in Hinduism," in Runzo and Martin, *Love, Sex, and Gender in the World Religions*, 89–111.

68. Nancy M. Martin, "Love and Longing in Devotional Hinduism," in Runzo and Martin, *The Meaning of Life in the World Religions*, 212.

69. A. K. Ramanujan, trans., *Speaking of Siva* (London: Penguin Books, 1973), 125.

70. Translated by Nancy M. Martin.

71. Owen Lynch, *Divine Passions: The Social Construction of Emotion in India* (Delhi: Oxford University Press, 1990), 23.

72. June McDaniel, "Emotion in Bengali Religious Thought," in *Religion and Emotion: Approaches and Interpretations*, edited by John Corrigan (New York: Oxford University Press, 2004), 259–60.

73. Ibid., 262.

74. Ramanujan, *Speaking of Siva*, 61–64.

75. For an example of literature exploring the Buddha's wife's feelings, see Donald K. Swearer, "Bimba [Yashodara]'s Lament," in *Buddhism in Practice*, edited by Donald S. Lopez, Jr. (Princeton, N.J.: Princeton University Press, 1995), 541–52. The transformation of romantic love into universal love is the subject of Thich Nhat Hanh, *Cultivating the Mind of Love* (Berkeley: Parallax Press, 1996), in which he recounts his early experience of falling in love with a nun.

76. His Holiness the Dalai Lama, *The Joy of Living and Dying in Peace* (Hammersmith, England: Thorsons, 1998), 14.

77. Ibid., 73–78; 108–9.

78. Brümmer, *The Model of Love*, 153.

79. See Hanh, *Cultivating the Mind of Love*.

80. Miranda Shaw, *Passionate Enlightenment: Women in Tantric Buddhism* (Princeton, N.J.: Princeton University Press, 1994), 24.

81. Ibid.

82. *Cittavisuddhiprakarana*, v. 42, quoted in ibid., 140.

83. For a detailed discussion of *ch'i* and *li*, see Mary Evelyn Tucker, "Confucian Cosmology and Ecological Ethics," in *Ethics in the World Religions*, edited by Joseph Runzo and Nancy M. Martin (Oxford: Oneworld, 2001).

84. David L. Hall and Roger T. Ames, *Thinking through Confucius* (Albany: State University of New York Press, 1987), 119.

85. Tucker, "Confucian Cosmology and Ecological Ethics," 334.

86. Hall and Ames, *Thinking through Confucius*, 121.

87. Ibid., 120.

88. LaFleur, "From *Agapé* to Organs: Religious Difference between Japan and America in Judging the Ethics of the Transplant" in Runzo and Martin, *Ethics in the World Religions*, 277.

89. Bernard of Clairvaux, *Sermons on the Canticles*, no. 71, quoted in Pike, *Mystic Union*, 36.

BIBLIOGRAPHY

Brümmer, Vincent. *The Model of Love*. Cambridge: Cambridge University Press, 1993.

Hall, David L., and Roger T. Ames. *Thinking through Confucius*. Albany: State University of New York Press, 1987.

Hanh, Thich Nhat. *Cultivating the Mind of Love*. Berkeley: Parallax Press, 1996.

John of the Cross. *Spiritual Canticle*. Edited and translated by E. Allison Peers. New York: Image Books, 1962.

Martin, Nancy M. "Love and Longing in Devotional Hinduism." In *The Meaning of Life in the World Religions*. Oxford: Oneworld, 2000.

Nozick, Robert. *"Love" in The Examined Life: Philosophical Meditations*. New York: Simon and Schuster, 1989.

Ramanujan, A. K., trans. *Hymns for the Drowning: Poems for Visnu by Nammalvar*. London: Penguin Books, 1992.

———, trans. *Speaking of Siva*. London: Penguin Books, 1973.

Rumi. *The Essential Rumi*. Translated by Coleman Barks. San Francisco: HarperCollins, 1995.

Runzo, Joseph. "Eros and Meaning in Life and Religion." In *The Meaning of Life in the World Religions*. Oxford: Oneworld, 2000.

Runzo, Joseph, and Nancy M. Martin, eds. *Love, Sex, and Gender in the World Religions*. Oxford: Oneworld, 2000.

Schimmel, Annemarie. *As through a Veil: Islamic Mystical Poetry*. New York: Columbia University Press, 1982.

Shaw, Miranda. *Passionate Enlightenment: Women in Tantric Buddhism*. Princeton, N.J.: Princeton University Press, 1994.

Solomon, Robert C. *Love: Emotion, Myth, and Metaphor*. Garden City, N.Y.: Doubleday, 1981.

Teresa of Avila, St. *The Autobiography of St. Teresa of Avila: The Life of Teresa of Jesus*. Edited and translated by E. Allison Peers. Garden City, N.Y.: Image Books, 1960.

CHAPTER 18

RELIGIOUS HATRED

JOHN CORRIGAN

Religious ideologies and institutions historically have served as backgrounds that condition the performance of hatred by individuals and groups. The record of religious hatred in the West is visible across the sweep of the history of civilizations, from the centuries in which Judaism took root in the eastern Mediterranean through medieval holy wars, and into the twenty-first century. Some religious hatred arises from intellectual cultures characterized by an absolutizing worldview, in which reality is parsed into clearly bounded categories of holy and unholy, good and evil, saved and damned. In some settings, religious hatred finds expression in the identification of a scapegoat, a group whose sacrifice is judged essential for the overcoming of troubles and for the restoration of order. Ignorance of the religious beliefs and practices of others likewise plays a role in religious hatred, sometimes in combination with tendencies to absolutize and to scapegoat. Worldviews that distinguish, in absolute terms, one group of persons from another historically run the risk of insulating themselves and therefore increasing the likelihood of their ignorance of the ideas and behaviors of others. Religion is a marker of group identity, and is frequently interwoven with other aspects of identity, including nationalistic, ethnic, and cultural elements. Religious hatred, accordingly, is sometimes mixed with hatred having to do with ethnicity or nationalistic fervor. Religious hatred is most easily observed in violence, and it is through violence that it is most effectively expressed. It takes shape particularly with regard to cycles of violence, in which groups trade hateful words and violent acts on a reciprocal and sometimes escalating basis. Religious hatred nevertheless is not a foregone consequence of cultural encounter, and can be addressed through education, broadening of contact, legal intervention, the promotion of competing religious emotions, and other means.

Religious hatred has appeared throughout history and in virtually every culture where encounter between different religious groups has taken place. The history of

Judaism is especially marked by outbursts of religious hatred against Jews, and Jewish response, ranging from the conflicts with hostile rulers that are related in Old Testament stories through the Middle Ages, when Pope Innocent III explained in a letter to Christian clerical authorities that "the Jews, by their own guilt, are consigned to perpetual servitude because they crucified the Lord.... As slaves rejected by God, in whose death they wickedly conspire, they shall by the effect of this very action, recognize themselves as the slaves of those whom Christ's death set free," and into the twentieth-century Holocaust. Judaism remains a lightning rod for religious hatred in many parts of the world, especially the eastern Mediterranean.[1]

In the history of religious hatred in the West, Judaism shares the center stage with Christianity and Islam, although an assortment of other religions, including ancient Roman religions and the religions of their various antagonists across the Danube, in England, and in North Africa, play important roles in that history as well. The persecution of Christians by the empire from the late first century to the early fourth century was at times carried out under the umbrella of Roman legal reasoning that identified Christian practice as sacrilegious, and in some cases painted Christians as immoral as well. But earlier, in the late Roman republic, religious crime was not a familiar category of law, and violence against Christians, as well as Jews, tended to be sporadic rather than systematic.[2] For the outspoken historian Edward Gibbon, religious intolerance and its fruit—the violent campaigns of religious hatred that Christian "fanatics" launched against Jews, Muslims (eventually), and Roman polytheists—arose as part of the theological and political coalescence of Christianity in the fourth century. According to Gibbon, "in almost every province of the Roman world, an army of fanatics, without authority, and without discipline, invaded the peaceful inhabitants; and the ruin of the fairest structures of antiquity still displays the ravages of those Barbarians, who alone had time and inclination to execute such laborious destruction."[3]

Subsequent medieval conflicts between the monotheistic religions took the form of holy wars undergirded by the rhetoric of religious hatred. Christian armies that assembled to battle Muslims in the Holy Land, imbued with a strong sense of "us versus them," made their way through the Rhineland, during the opening phase of the First Crusade, slaughtering entire populations of Jews. Arriving in Jerusalem, the Crusaders enacted a ritual of bloodletting, the reports of which were enhanced for European audiences, whose religious viewpoint welcomed descriptions of horses knee-deep in blood and Muslim and Jewish bodies stacked in cremation pyramids as high as houses. Muslims, for their part, managed their own performances of religious hatred in massacres of Christians in later campaigns led by the Egyptian sultans Baybars and Kalavun. In the wake of the Protestant Reformation, rival Christian factions expressed their hatred for one another in events such as the Bartholomew's Day Massacre, which destroyed virtually all of the Huguenot leadership during the Wars of Religion (1562–1598) and in the butchery of the Thirty Years' War (1618–1648), which reduced the population of Germany by one-third.

The manifestation of religious hatred in persecution and warfare is also apparent in cultural settings where monotheistic religions do not predominate. In some such contexts, hatred directed at religious groups has arisen from concern that a multiplicity of worldviews was dangerous to the survival of a national or imperial culture. Such was the case in China in 844–845, when Confucian Tang dynasty authorities undertook a campaign against Buddhism, during which forty-six hundred monasteries and as many as forty thousand Buddhist temples were destroyed.[4] According to Chinese chronicles, the citizens of the empire were to bring about "the extermination of evil," to "drive out those idlers and sluggards" and "demolish those red-painted useless buildings" in order to "help the government in its task to perfect the one and only system of (archaic Confucian) manners and customs."[5] Elsewhere in Asia, the persecution of Old Believers by the Orthodox Church in Russia in 1688–1694 led to the suicides of as many as twenty thousand followers of Avvakum, who imitated his execution by walking into fires.[6] In the twentieth century, the colonial and postcolonial religious history of the South Asian subcontinent has been marked by religious hatred between Hindus and Muslims. Colonialism itself has incited religious hatred in virtually every place it has a history, from Northern Ireland to the Americas, in Africa and the Pacific. The end of the age of colonial expansion, like the end of the Crusades, has brought little relief from outbursts of religious hatred. The late-twentieth-century war in Bosnia, which pitted Christians against Muslims, differed little from previous embodiments of religious hatred in its scale of atrocities.

Hatred is a powerful emotion, and the species of emotion with which we are concerned, religious hatred, has been said to be the most potent form of hatred, described by a nineteenth-century American magazine as "the fiercest passion that rages in the breast of man."[7] Religious hatred is not always easy to recognize apart from other kinds of hatred between groups, however. As Sudhir Kakar has written, the conflict between Hindus and Muslims in the territory that today is India and Pakistan often has been seen by historians as the consequence of competing economic interests or as the negotiation of political power. For the Hindu nationalist, however, the conflict "is squarely religious, indeed theological."[8]

We see this diversity of viewpoint about conflict between religious groups in other instances as well. The antagonism that characterized relations between Mormons and non-Mormons in nineteenth-century America reached its peaks in murders, massacres, "extermination" decrees, and pitched battles. It has not been hard to identify it as an episode of religious hatred. But, as Kenneth H. Winn has shown, it is possible to assign hatreds arising from religious difference a supporting role in the ongoing Mormon conflicts, while viewing the heart of the matter as a falling-out over "republican ideology," each side branding the other as antirepublican because of perceived failures to embrace a small constellation of political and social ideals having to do with virtue, character, power, self-reliance, and property ownership.[9] Thirteenth-century warfare between Roman Catholic authorities and the heretical Cathars of Beziers has given the history of religious hatred one of its most recognized (but unsubstantiated) linguistic markers: "Kill them all; God will sort them out." But the battles between the victorious papal forces and the subdued peoples of southern France also have been interpreted as the consequence of frictions over civil authority and economic issues, with religion as window dressing for those more urgent problems. The massacre of "ghost-dancing" Native Americans at Wounded Knee likewise has been seen alternately as a chapter in the history of religious hatred and as the predictable result of ethnic difference, language impasses, white people's desires for access to land, and other factors.

The overlapping of religious hatred with hatred grounded in other kinds of difference—ethnic, for example—does not mean that religious hatred is simply dissolved into a more generic, encompassing hatred, however. Acts of religious hatred are often still recognizable precisely as that. The Bosnian war in the 1990s was reported in the media virtually worldwide as a horror that emerged out of a fanatical campaign for "ethnic cleansing." References to "Muslim" in that reportage took it to be preeminently an ethnic category. Often lost in this characterization of the war was the profoundly religious character of the hatreds between Christian and Muslim rivals. Serbian Christians conceived the war as profoundly religious, and, as one scholar has observed, they "identified themselves and their cause through explicit religious symbols," including uniform insignia, hand gestures representing the Christian Trinity, religious song, kissing the ring of a priest before and after acts of persecution of Muslims, and "in the formal religious ceremonies that marked the purification of a town of its Muslim population." For Michael A. Sells, "the term 'ethnic' in the expression 'ethnic cleansing,' then, is a euphemism for 'religious.'"[10]

Debate about the role of religion in conflicts such as those in Bosnia turns up an assortment of issues having to do with structural features of religion. More precisely, it leads to further debate about whether there are certain elements inherent in religion that foster the growth of hatred, directly or indirectly. In some cases, statements of religious belief are clearly antagonistic to other religions and so have the potential to directly affect the emotional orientation of adherents toward those other religions. When the Southern Baptist leader Reverend Jerry Vines delivered a public address in 2002 in which he declared Mohammed to be a "demon-possessed pedophile," he was promoting an orientation of Christian hatefulness toward Muslims.[11] The long history of similar statements from outspoken religious leaders—including the tragic consequences of such statements—illustrates the potential of religious rhetoric for fostering religious hatred.

More problematic is the investigation of potential ways religions can encourage hatred in indirect fashion. Some scholars have argued that the way religion absolutizes reality sets the stage for the growth of religious hatred. Religions that organize the world into clearly defined territories of good and evil can lead to a religious conceptualization of "us" versus "them." The monotheistic traditions of Judaism, Christianity, and Islam emerged, in terms of their most distant origins, from ancient Zoroastrian dualism, from the radical religious division of the cosmos into good and evil, and opposed spirits at war with each other in an ongoing struggle. In as much as these three Abrahamic traditions incorporated such an absolutizing tendency, they conceptually separated believers from unbelievers, clearly demarcating the social world into two camps, the holy and unholy. One obvious corollary believers might draw from such a scheme was that contact with unbelievers amounted to contact with the impure. Viewing such contact as a threat, persons would create rationales and strategies for protecting themselves from the dangers it posed. Observing the history of religious hatred with respect to theological notions of purity, Barrington Moore has written that for the believer, "it is necessary to define the polluting enemy as nonhuman or inhuman, ... as a demonic threat to the existing social order," on the way to a "morally approved infliction of death with cruelty." In certain instances, the absolutistic mentality of fixed boundaries comes to include, as Mark Juergensmeyer has argued with regard to the roots of terrorism, the believers' perceptions that "their communities are already under attack—are being violated" and that violent responses to such perceived attacks are justified.[12] Short of violence, persons might attempt to convert others to their beliefs, but the starkly dualistic nature of some theological worldviews can incline away from rapprochement should evangelization fail. Such was the opinion of Jean Jacques Rousseau, who, observing religion in eighteenth-century France, declared: "It is impossible to live in peace with people whom one believes are damned. To love them would be to hate God who punished them. They must absolutely be either brought into the faith or tormented."[13]

Debate about whether monotheistic religions are inherently prone to religious hatred has raged for a long time, perhaps since the reign of the Roman ruler Julian.[14] What is clear is that religious hatred is not limited to monotheistic religions. Historically it can be found in polytheistic religions as well, and in religions sometimes thought to be oriented away from hatred. One need only consider the historical outbreaks of violence between sects of Tibetan Buddhists (in which the Dalai Lama has played a role) in order to appreciate the potential for religious hatred to appear in any context, even among groups that are generally thought of as essentially peaceful and tolerant.[15]

Religious identity can be rigidly constructed, or it can be fluid. In the case of the former, boundaries can be drawn so sharply between oneself and those who are not part of one's group that identity itself becomes an exercise in aggression toward others. In her scholarly exploration of "the violent legacy of monotheism," Regina Schwartz locates "the origins of violence in identity formation," arguing that "imagining identity as an act of distinguishing and separating from others, of boundary-making and line drawing, is the most frequent and fundamental act of violence we commit."[16] For Schwartz, the construction of identity as itself an act of violence, preceding violence actually enacted by one group against another, is modeled in biblical stories, so that for Jews, Christians, Muslims, and others who have inherited the categories of thought and the cultural mapping redolent in monotheism, religious identity is inherently hateful and violent.[17]

Groups for whom identity is a matter of highly articulated group boundaries must police those boundaries, turning back as threats any kinds of crossings of those boundaries that they imagine to be underway. Moreover, such groups typically oppose in active fashion persons or groups whom they imagine might have reason to attempt to cross the line, even in the absence of evidence that such a transgression is actually taking place. Religions (including religious scriptures), however, often encompass what appear to be a range of theological and cultural perspectives, so that support for contradictory ideological positions can emerge within the same religion, or be claimed as the expression of what is revealed in a holy book. Religiously grounded notions of group identity accordingly can develop in ways that to some degree offset the difficulties that arise when rigid boundaries and obsessive policing of those boundaries are the norm. In some cases, religious identities can be more fluid, and therefore less likely to end in hatred and violence. Such situations sometimes arise in connection with polytheistic religious practice, as opposed to monotheistic. But all religions, regardless of their theological details, to a certain extent run the risk of setting the stage for hatred as they shape identity.

To speak of identity, of boundaries and their maintenance, does not, however, directly provide insight into the problem of why people hate others in such a way as to determine that others must be tormented or killed. Discussion of identity offers a broad view of an intellectual and emotional landscape on which acts of religious hatred take place—and it is important to see that landscape—but it stops short of analysis of religious hatred at the level of the violent act. Understanding religious violence as specific acts of violence involves consideration of a multitude of factors, many of which are distinctly local. In order to make sense of religious hatred and violence between Mormons and non-Mormons in nineteenth-century Missouri and Illinois, for example, we must take a broad view of historical processes ranging from economy to demography, marriage customs, western migration, mass media, political aspiration, notions of authority, and popular intellectual culture, alongside the various religious elements: revelation, authority, forms of organization, the role of charisma, theodicy, sin, and so forth. Analysis of acts of violence requires a focus on motivation as it arises from such factors.

Bearing in mind the complexity of religious hatred as embedded locally, we nevertheless can view something of the linkage between religious hatred and violence in terms of the overview offered by René Girard, who has proposed that religious sacrifice is fundamental to the production of the "sacred." According to Girard, "violence and the sacred are inseparable."[18] But the violent nature of religious sacrifice—whether, in the past, that has meant the slaughter of lambs in the ancient Mediterranean or, at various times, human sacrifice[19]—is for the most part concealed by ritual, which shapes the consciousness of participants in such a way as to cause them to see religious violence not as vengeance but as a kind of purifying judicial episode, an event undertaken for the good of the community, to overcome social pollution by means of sacrifice. That sacrifice is the scapegoat, the person on whom the sins of the community are heaped, who is killed in order to restore to a community that has experienced social friction some measure of stability. The community views "this member as the single 'polluted' enemy who is contaminating the rest," religion providing the theological and ritual machinery that enables the community "to convince themselves that all their ills are the fault of a lone individual who can be easily disposed of."[20]

As Girard points out, however, religious scapegoating, though in its origins and through at least some of its history a process that identifies specific individuals as scapegoats, can develop into campaigns against entire populations, as in the case of lynchings, pogroms, and similar large-scale enterprises.[21] The dynamics of these larger movements illustrate two aspects of the linkage between religious hatred and violence. First, religion as a cult of sacrifice—all religion for Girard—historically has failed to preserve the fiction that the killing of a scapegoat is sacrifice rather than violence, that it is not vengeance but rather a substitution for violence of a larger and more blatant sort. By the same token, religion has failed to limit sacrificial violence to the case of the substitutionary individual. Religious cultures have in fact historically modeled violence as a means of addressing perceived pollution of the social world, and the ritual remedy for this, which calls forth a world of theological argument and social drama, has proven translatable to massive social encounter, under various secular ideological banners. Second, the application of a theology of human sacrifice to broad arenas of social encounter—where social pollution is identified as entire groups rather than as individuals—emerges in concert with the formation of group identity. That is, the kinds of social hostilities described by Schwartz as a product of the formation of rigid religious identities might here be seen in their connection to the violent drive for social purity that is the focus of Girard's analysis. The picture of religious hatred that such an intersection conjures is the religious movement aimed at "cleansing," a project taken up *both* as a performative means of asserting identity *and* as a means by which to destroy those who are viewed as pollution. In terms suggested by sociologist Mark Jurgensmeyer as part of his survey of the "logic of religious violence," religiously motivated terrorist acts "can be both *performance events*, in that they make a symbolic statement, and *performative acts*, insofar as they try to change things."[22]

In many cases, long-simmering social tensions between groups and unresolved claims for power eventually appear incapable of solution through negotiation, and differences that began as quarrels over geographical boundaries or political process are translated into religious engagements. For example, since the 1950s the Reverend Ian Paisley, founder of the Free Presbyterian Church of Ulster and his own political party, the Democratic Unionist Party, has explicitly joined politics to religion in Ireland, casting the political struggle there as a matter of resistance to "Rome rule," that is, the potential danger of Roman Catholic influence over government in Northern Ireland.[23] Similar cases are the disputes between Muslims and Hindus in India, and between groups that have a stake in the rule of Palestine, both ongoing conflicts that participants have constructed as religious out of what initially were experienced as largely social altercations. When disputes are cast as religious, the situation deteriorates. As Sudhir Kakar has noted, "the involvement of religious rather than social identities does not dampen but, on the contrary, increases the violence of the conflict" because it brings to the conflict "a greater emotional intensity and a deeper motivational thrust than language, region, or other markers of ethnic identity."[24]

The eruption of religious hatred into violence, a process in which the emotional tenor is extreme, often occurs under a conceptual umbrella that views differences between groups as a representation of battle between good and evil on a cosmic scale. In cases where a group has lost confidence in the possibility of political settlement, where there is a strong sense of corruption of processes by which groups might negotiate their differences, that group imagines resolution of its problems in the sacred realm. Everyday events acquire cosmic significance, and the struggle between a group and its opponents is recast as a battle between cosmic good and cosmic evil. This investing of social conflict with a religious quality of absoluteness and rigidity in turn hardens the identities of those involved on each side of the conflict. Subsequently, persons come to believe that their situation is unlikely to improve without the intervention of divine personages, and their expectation of such intervention takes shape as apocalyptic hope. The complexity of their hatred is apparent in their conflicted view of the future: they are deeply pessimistic about a just conclusion to social discord in terms of everyday life, but optimistic about the ultimate outcome of the conflict, in cosmic terms.

Hatred, when considered against a background of religious belief, appears complex in other ways. Hatred, first of all, is sometimes viewed in religion as a desirable emotion. Christian writers over the centuries have cited the New Testament declaration of Jesus that if "any one comes to me and does not hate his own father and mother and wife and children and brothers and sisters, yes, and even his own life, he cannot be my disciple."[25] For Jews, God himself hates liars, haughty eyes, and troublemakers, and "the wicked and those who love violence his soul hates."[26] Referring to those who are against God, the Psalmist says: "I hate them with perfect hatred; I count them my enemies."[27] In the Bhagavad Gita, Arjuna declares in exasperation: "Lo, I hate triumph and domination, wealth and ease" (Bhagavad Gita 1:91–92).[28] English Puritans cultivated "hatred of sin," and there is an abundance of instances illustrating the strength of such hatred in persons' lives, including parents killing children whom they believe to be possessed by evil or at risk of being influenced by it. Love of God, often linked with hatred of sin, is frequently involved in such incidences, as in the case of the Old Testament patriarch Abraham attempting to kill his son Isaac.

Love and hate are not present together only in religious contexts and not only as hatred of sin/love of God. Hate as an emotion, while not exactly the same in all instances, manifests in certain ways regardless of whether the context is religion, ethnicity, sexuality, gender, or other kinds of difference. Across that broad front of situations and environments, there is the likelihood, as Gordon W. Allport has written, that "love is a precondition of hate." As an emotion, hatred arises in settings where an "affiliative relationship" has been interrupted. That is, hate emerges when there is a disruption in the relationship with what one loves, and the agent responsible for that disruption becomes the object of hatred. In such circumstances, love does not "turn to" hate. One does not suddenly hate what one loved. Rather, the strong feelings of hatred grow out of the same rich soil that supported feelings of love.[29]

Religious hatred as the hatred of a group of persons is a different kind of feeling from anger, which is directed largely toward individuals. Anger passes, Aristotle observed, but hatred, imbedded in a web of cultural practices, often grows stronger, so that it "desires the extinction of the object of hate."[30] This quality of the emotion—religious hatred as the impetus for a campaign of extinction against its object—develops, as Sudhir Kakar has observed, alongside a strengthening of love for one's own group of like-minded religionists.[31] Such love is often expressed in connection with rhetoric about the importance of devotion to a certain god, or faithfulness to scripture, or holding fast to traditional forms of religious practice.

Religious hatred, like several other emotions, is best thought of as collective emotion. This is not to say that hatred felt by individuals toward other individuals is an entirely distinct species of emotion. There are profound connections between individual feeling and collective feeling. But it is appropriate to recognize that hatred, fear, terror, hope, or joy as experienced in collective settings is both similar to and different from the emotional experience of an individual in everyday life. Collective identity is shaped by emotion and serves as a standpoint for group emotional performance in the same way that more personal identities are constructed in emotion.[32] "Emotional climates" can be of various sorts—hopeful or fearful, joyful or hateful—and can change rapidly, over the course of a generation, depending on political, religious, economic, and educational factors.[33]

Religious hatred is most visible when it has reached the point at which it fuels cycles of violence. The hatred between Christians and Muslims that characterized the hostilities in Bosnia in the 1990s developed over centuries of conflict between those two groups. For Michael A. Sells, the cataclysm of violence in Bosnia was deeply rooted in ongoing religious hatred, and the severity of the conflict, and the scale of genocide in Bosnia, emerged out of a cycle of hatred. That cycle, brought to a fever pitch by years of antagonism and the construction of Christian mythologies about the region's past and its destiny, reached a point where violence seemed justified to the aggressor Serbian nationalists. The same kind of cycling of hatred and its violent consequences is clear in the difficult relations between Muslims and Hindus in India, and in the previously mentioned Irish troubles. The rhetoric of radical Muslim groups in the twenty-first century contributes to the escalation of hatred between Christians and Muslims, although in the West there have been successful attempts to identify such radicals as distinct from Islam as it is practiced in most places. Many Muslim leaders decry religious hatred and violence, but Islam, like Christianity, is characterized by diverse religious styles, and so presents a wide range of opinion about relations with Christians and Jews. Cycles of religious hatred are subject to the same kinds of factors that lead to relatively rapid change in emotional climates generally. But collective religious hatred differs from other emotions—for example, from a collective emotion, or emotional climate, of fear— in that it frequently demands the extinction of the object of hatred. It motivates to action in ways that other emotional climates do not.

Religious hatred incubated to violence through cycles of antagonisms is the same religious hatred that can be forgotten. The same Bible that models the construction of identity as a violent act offers a view of forgetting identity, of letting go of collective memory, and collective emotion. Regina Schwartz has argued that biblical paradigms of "violent" collective identities are complemented by biblical stories demonstrating that sometimes "forgetting offers more of an opportunity than a threat to the community."[34] Forgetting, historians and social scientists have pointed out, can be decidedly constructive. Jennifer Cole has described, for example, how the "art of memory" in Madagascar is practiced in such a way as to forget the ghosts of the nation's painful colonial past.[35] People think in partnership with others, utilizing means provided by culture for doing so.[36] People feel with others as well. Collective memory, which keeps alive ideas and feelings,[37] can become cultural forgetting, a process of losing certain memories—of feeling as well as of ideas, people, things, and so forth—when such a course is sensed as likely to bring about a desirable outcome.

Groups that have been engaged in religious conflict for generations cannot easily forget their feelings. It is hard to forget, just as it can be hard to remember. When the potential rewards are great enough, a group can forget how it has felt. When the consequences of remembering religious hatred are catastrophic, when they are so terrible as to make the retention of a cultural climate of hatred an impediment to the survival of a group, a people can forget their feelings. But one of the lessons of history is that the tipping point, at which hatred is conceived as counterproductive to the survival of that group, is set high. That is, groups will risk their own annihilation, and repeatedly so, before disinvesting in a destructive religious emotional culture. Particularly in cases where religion has supplied a transcendental ideal in the form of heaven or some other rewarding afterlife, hatred and violence that leads to the deaths of many persons can be considered necessary in implementing a long-term plan for victory over one's religious enemies. Suicidal acts of terrorism and mass military engagement alike, generated from religious visions of holy struggle and joyous afterlife, have been a fact of religious conflict throughout history. Religious hatred, of all the different kinds of hatred that are present in conflicts between groups, is the least likely to be forgotten because it is explicitly constructed on a platform of belief in the eternal, not the temporal, and the cosmic, not the worldly. In eternity, there is no past, nothing is forgotten.

Short of taking religion entirely out of politics—a scenario that is not likely, judging by what has happened in the past—there are few promising avenues toward defusing religious hatred. Education, always a potential solution, might be possible in some instances. Increased secure contact between groups that are opposed to each other, in particular, offers possibilities for educating groups about their similarities as well as differences. Legal interventions and the judicial use of force present themselves as options as well. The heart of the problem, however, is the religious hatred that motivates violence. Historically, it has been the case that cycles of religious hatred and violence have been limited or prevented in instances where the collective emotion of religious hatred has been kept in check by more powerful emotional climates, in which emotions and sentiments such as love and compassion hold sway, or where religiously inflected ideals of justice or fairness are preeminent. If it is hard for a group to forget religious hatred, it is also hard to forget more constructive spiritualized emotion that is similarly framed by ultimate concerns. Religious promotion of the latter, accordingly, could prove to be an option for overcoming religious hatred. For such an enterprise to succeed, however, it would have to be carried forward by religionists, not imposed by secular government. In the imagined world of cosmic dramas, it is the religious imagination that must take the lead.

NOTES

1. Innocent II, Letter to the Archbishops of Sens and Paris, July 15, 1205.
2. Simeon L. Guterman, *Religious Toleration and Persecution in Ancient Rome* (London: Aiglon Press, 1951), 41–47.
3. Edward Gibbon, *Decline and Fall of the Roman Empire*, chap. 27, pt. 2. See also Graham N. Stanton and Guy G. Stousma, eds., *Tolerance and Intolerance in Early Christianity and Judaism* (Cambridge: Cambridge University Press, 1998).
4. Barrington Moore, *Moral Purity and Persecution in History* (Princeton, N.J.: Princeton University Press, 2000), 115–28.
5. Quoted in J. J. M. De Groot, *Sectarianism and Religious Persecution in China* (Taipei: Literature House, 1963), 66–67.
6. Thomas Robbins, "Apocalypse, Persecution, and Self-Immolation: Mass Suicides among the Old Believers in Late-Seventeenth-Century Russia," in *Millennialism, Persecution, and Violence: Historical Cases*, edited by Catherine Wessinger (Syracuse, N.Y.: Syracuse University Press, 200), 205–6.
7. *North American Review* 66, 138 (January 1848), 215–16.
8. Sudhir Kakar, *The Colors of Violence: Cultural Identities, Religion, and Conflict* (Chicago: University of Chicago Press, 1996), 13.
9. Kenneth H. Winn, *Exiles in a Land of Liberty: Mormons in America 1830–1846* (Chapel Hill: University of North Carolina Press, 1989).
10. Michael A. Sells, *The Bridge Betrayed: Religion and Genocide in Bosnia* (Berkeley: University of California Press, 1998), 15.
11. Susan Sachs, "Baptist Pastor Attacks Islam, Inciting Cries of Intolerance," *New York Times*, June 15, 2002, A10.
12. Moore, *Moral Purity and Persecution in History*, 57; Mark Juergensmeyer, *Terror in the Mind of God: The Global Rise of Religious Violence*, 3rd ed. (Berkeley: University of California Press, 2003), 12.
13. Jean Jacques Rousseau, *On the Social Contract with Geneva Manuscript and Political Economy*, translated by Judith R. Masters and edited by Roger D. Masters (New York: St. Martin's Press, 1978), 131.
14. Guy S. Stousma, "Postscript: The Future of Intolerance," in Stanton and Stousma, *Tolerance and Intolerance*, 356.
15. On Tibetan Buddhists, see George Dreyfus, "The Shuk-den Affair: History and Nature of a Quarrel," *Journal of the International Association of Buddhist Studies* 21 (1998): 227–70.
16. Regina M. Schwartz, *The Curse of Cain: The Violent Legacy of Monotheism* (Chicago: University of Chicago Press, 1997), 5.
17. Ibid., 6, 8. Schwartz also notes that the Bible can be read in various ways, including as a criticism of identity grounded in violence. See her discussion, for example, on 103.

18. René Girard, *Violence and the Sacred*, translated by Patrick Gregory (Baltimore: Johns Hopkins University Press, 1979), 19. For Girard, religion at its best serves to deflect social violence through focus on ritual.

19. On the lynching of African Americans in the South as a religious ritual of human sacrifice see Donald G. Mathews, "The Southern Rite of Human Sacrifice," *Journal of Southern Religion* 3 (2000): http://jsr.as.wvu.edu/mathews.htm.

20. Girard, *Violence and the Sacred*, 79, 80.

21. Ibid., 80, 82.

22. Juergensmeyer, *Terror in the Mind of God*, 127.

23. See Steve Bruce, *God Save Ulster: The Religion and Politics of Paisleyism* (Oxford: Clarendon Press, 1986).

24. Kakar, *The Colors of Violence*, 192.

25. Lk 14:26.

26. Zec 8:17; Prv 6:16; Ps 11:5.

27. Ps 139:22.

28. In *The Harvard Classics*, vol. 45, pt. 4 of 51, edited by Charles W. Eliot and translated by Sir Edwin Arnold (New York: P. F. Collier and Son, 1909–1914).

29. Gordon W. Allport, *The Nature of Prejudice* (Garden City, N.Y.: Doubleday Anchor Books, 1958), 32.

30. Aristotle, *Rhetoric* 2.1382a.

31. Kakar, *The Colors of Violence*, 190–94.

32. J. H. de Rivera, "Conceptualizing and measuring Emotional Climate," proceedings of the 8th International Conference of the International Society for Research on Emotions, edited by N. H. Frijda (Storrs, Conn.: International Society for Research on Emotions, 1994), 161–170.

33. J. H. de Rivera, "Emotional Climate: Social Structure and Emotional Dynamics," in *International Review of Studies on Emotion*, edited by K. T. Strongman (New York: Wiley, 1992), 199; also see de Rivera, "Aggression, Violence, Evil, and Peace," in *Comprehensive Handbook of Psychology*, vol. 5, *Personality and Social*, edited by T. Millon and M. J. Lerner (New York: Wiley, 2005).

34. Schwartz, *The Curse of Cain*, 159.

35. Jennifer Cole, *Forget Colonialism: Sacrifice and the Art of Memory in Madagascar* (Berkeley: University of California Press, 2001).

36. Gavriel Salomon, *Distributed Cognitions* (Cambridge: Cambridge University Press, 1996).

37. On the role of emotion in the construction of memory, see Daniel Schachter, *Searching for Memory: The Brain, the Mind, and the Past* (New York: Basic Books, 1996); Robert Brown and James Kulik, "Flashbulb Memories," *Cognition* 5 (1977): 73–79; Ulric Neisser, ed., *Memory Observed: Remembering in Natural Contexts* (San Francisco: Freeman, 1982).

BIBLIOGRAPHY

Girard, René. *Violence and the Sacred*. Translated by Patrick Gregory. Baltimore: Johns Hopkins University Press, 1979.

Juergensmeyer, Mark. *Terror in the Mind of God: The Global Rise of Religious Violence*. 3rd ed. Berkeley: University of California Press, 2003.

Kakar, Sudhir. *The Colors of Violence: Cultural Identities, Religion, and Conflict*. Chicago: University of Chicago Press, 1996.

Moore, Barrington. *Moral Purity and Persecution in History*. Princeton, N.J.: Princeton University Press, 2000.

Schwartz, Regina M. *The Curse of Cain: The Violent Legacy of Monotheism*. Chicago: University of Chicago Press, 1997.

Sells, Michael A. *The Bridge Betrayed: Religion and Genocide in Bosnia*. Berkeley: University of California Press, 1998.

Stanton, Graham N., and Guy G. Stousma, eds. *Tolerance and Intolerance in Early Christianity and Judaism*. Cambridge: Cambridge University Press, 1998.

Winn, Kenneth H. *Exiles in a Land of Liberty: Mormons in America 1830–1846*. Chapel Hill: University of North Carolina Press, 1989.

PART IV

HISTORICAL AND THEORETICAL PERSPECTIVES

CHAPTER 19

AUGUSTINE

JAMES WETZEL

A man who casts his affections as his soul's feet and who envisions his life's journey as his heart's quest for repose is not likely to neglect the emotions in his philosophy. The dazzling display of emotional intelligence that gives the *Confessions*, Augustine's most famous work, its resonance for students of the inner life is evident, albeit in more muted hues, in nearly everything that he wrote: sermons, letters, scriptural commentaries, polemical and apologetic works, theological meditations. Augustine made it his practice to use his heart as an organ of illumination.

There is of course an important difference between speaking from the emotions and speaking about them. Theorists of the emotional life will find much that is of interest in Augustine, but it would be misleading to attribute the theorist's ambitions directly to Augustine himself. In one of his earliest works, the *Soliloquies*, he claims to want to know only two things: God and soul. The conjunction is important to him. There is no disclosure of soul that is not God's disclosure of soul. Whatever Augustine has to say about the emotions (a matter of soul) will have to be read, then, in the context of his theology. Apart from that context, his invocation and use of some classical theories of emotion—most if not all of which he would have taken from Cicero's attempt, late in his political career, to Latinize Greek philosophy—will seem disappointingly derivative. Set within its proper context, Augustine's insights into the emotions form part of his strikingly original attempt to confess to the ambivalence of his soul's love of God.

Take, for instance, Augustine's general characterization of emotion in book 14 of *City of God*. He opens that book with his influential distinction between two cities, one ruled by flesh (*secundum carnem*), the other by spirit (*secundum spiritum*). The first kind of rule is really an abdication of rule, a surrender to a chaos of mind and body that is sometimes driven, but not always, by bodily appetite. It is possible to be under the rule of the flesh and abstemious if carnal restraint is serving the vices of a malign intelligence. Because Augustine does not equate living by the flesh with sensual indulgence, he is quick to distance his sense of rule by the spirit from a Manichean hatred of sex and from even the milder contempt of the body that Platonists exhibit when they blame the body for subjecting the soul to emotional disturbances. "It is the quality of a person's will that matters to emotion," he writes. "If the will is perverse, then so are the person's emotions; if upright, then those emotions are not only innocent but praiseworthy as well. Will is in all emotions; emotions are indeed nothing other than expressions of will."[1]

If we want to know how something as seemingly involuntary as an emotion can express willfulness, Augustine will explain to us that emotions have two aspects to them. There is first the involuntary impression that something about to happen or happening is an object of aversion or attraction; then comes a judgment. We either agree or disagree with the value—good or bad—that has impressed us involuntarily. It is the mind and its judgment, not bodily reflex, that finally determines the quality of an emotion. On the face of it, Augustine is adopting a Stoic account of emotion, where there is a clean distinction between an impression (*phantasia*) of some good or evil and consent (*sunkatathesis*) to that impression. The original inspiration of this view is likely to have been Chrysippus, Zeno's successor among the early Stoics, but Augustine gets his Chrysippus by way of Cicero. Witness Cicero in book 4 of *Tusculan Disputations*, encapsulating the Stoics on emotions: "It seems to me that the whole argument about the mind's susceptibility to emotion comes down to this, that emotions are all in our power, all of them express judgment, all are voluntary."[2]

So far the Augustine I have described is blandly Stoic in his understanding of emotion. To leave the matter there, however, is to miss altogether the theological involvement of Augustine's notion of will. In some of his earliest writings, notably the first book of *On Free Choice* (*De libero arbitrio*), Augustine invokes an unanalyzed and relatively unencumbered kind of consent to account for human responsibility. The view of that particular book is that we are free, and most free, when consenting to wise desires; when we consent to foolish ones, full of false promise, we are less free, having wed ourselves to delusory happiness, but still accountable. Consent, whether to wisdom or foolishness, is our own. This early Augustine *is* blandly Stoic, at least when it comes to his ethics, but Augustine soon comes to outgrow his Stoicism.

Certainly by the time he ascends in middle-age to the episcopate of Hippo, he has ceased to presume on the innocence of consent. It becomes his habit to look intently at the motives behind consent, the sources of delight and aversion that land human beings in one of the two cities. Undoubtedly the turn in Augustine's thought has come with his set of responses to Simplician, an aged priest, soon to be Ambrose's successor in the See of Milan, and a man who, a decade back, had helped Augustine find the will to convert. Augustine is asked by his old friend to tackle some exegetical problems, the toughest coming from Paul and the ninth chapter of Romans: what is it about Jacob, and not Esau, that finds favor with God? Augustine ponders the mystery of election in his response, and he comes to the conclusion—a surprising one for him at the time—that election has to remain a mystery. There is no basis of merit that distinguishes a Jacob from an Esau, a saint from a lost soul. God elicits and elects the whole of the good will, leaving nothing of independent worth for a human being to contribute. Consent to a wise desire is not, then, what a human being adds to divine gift (Augustine's earlier view); it is part of what is given with grace. To suppose otherwise would be, by the reckoning of the new bishop, to leave the soul a veto of its election—a denial of God's capacity to delight.[3]

Despite the thorny problems of accountability that his revised view of consent left unresolved, particularly in regard to unelected souls, Augustine never reverts to a quasi-Stoic concept of consent. When he identifies emotions with expressions of will in *City of God*, a work that extends well into his episcopate, he is presupposing that redemptive consent, the kind that commends us to our better selves, is divinely mediated and no longer simply up to us. Consequently he will make the substitution of love for will in his definition of emotion, as if love and will were somehow the same thing: "And so a straightened will is love that is good, and a twisted one is bad love."[4] Good love, an expression of delight in the good, and good will, a resolve to work goodness, are naturally one only in God. For human beings, it takes a labor of love to bring together the two, whose usual separation feels like a split in will: wanting the good and not wanting it. The labor, thinks Augustine, is both God's and ours, but the initiative, he insists, is solely God's.

Again, no study of Augustine on the emotions can do him justice and not engage directly with his theological animus. His God is infinitely distant from his flesh-and-blood feel for his own humanity, and yet, at the same time, his God is his humanity. The mystery of the incarnation—of the intimacy between a divine and a human way of being—is tied in his mind to the mysterious perversity that both necessitates and denies him his confession: he loses himself in self-love, and, worse, he is blind to many of the forms his self-love can take (some look patently self-denying). If Augustine has to generate self-love on his own, it will be hard for him to envision external sources of delight and dismay—the lodestones of emotion—other than as threats to his personal integrity. Augustine evades this trap only because he encounters God as a mediating presence in his self-love.

In the relatively brief compass of this essay, I hope to open a window on Augustine's theology of the emotions. Basically this will be a two-part undertaking. In the first part I take a closer look at Stoicism in *City of God* and Augustine's eventual rejection of its theory and practice of emotion. Augustine's rejection of Stoicism is importantly symptomatic of a shift in his notion of will, from a facility for consent to a focus of internal conflict and incoherence. In the second part, I attend to the connection between sin and self-undoing by entering into Augustine's fascination with a first or original will to sin. My primary resources here are his psychological analysis in *City of God* of the Adam and Eve of Genesis and his parallel analysis of himself in *Confessions*, where he describes a fall of his own. I conclude my essay with a reflection that bridges its two parts.

A Stoic Stalking Horse

The eminent classicist Richard Sorabji delivered his 1997 Gifford Lectures on the theme of emotion in ancient philosophy. The book that came of his lectures is mostly devoted to the Stoics, whom Sorabji calls "the driving force of the whole ancient discussion," but the final part ventures into early Christian transformations of Stoicism, where Augustine plays the dominant role in the narrative. Sorabji presents us with an Augustine who thinks of what the Stoics called "first movements" or "pre-passions" as *emotional* responses, laden with implicit value judgments. This is a misreading of the Stoics, Sorabji argues, but one that will allow Augustine to construct a sinful experience of temptation out of what counts, for Stoics, as simple bodily agitation.[5]

Sorabji's provocative reading of Augustine focuses primarily on Augustine's use of anecdotal evidence in *City of God*, book 9, chapter 4, to discredit Stoicism. The anecdote comes from *Attic Nights*, the journal compiled by the second-century amateur philosopher Aulus Gellius during his visit to Athens. Gellius tells of being on board a storm-tossed ship in the company of a Stoic who turned pale, apparently with fright. When the storm passed, Gellius asked the Stoic to explain the meaning of his pallor, since actual fright would have been inconsistent with the equanimity of a true Stoic, able to discount adversity. In response, the Stoic fetched from his bags a compendium of Stoicism composed by the first-century Stoic luminary Epictetus. The relevant part covered how everyone, wise or foolish, experiences involuntary impressions (*phantasiae*) of what seems desirable or not. Only the fool, however, acquiesces to the impression; the wise person consents only to reason. The Stoic wanted Gellius to know that his pallor, fleeting and involuntary, gave no reliable indication of what he was really thinking or valuing at the time.

Augustine invokes the anecdote to decide a question about the emotions that had left the various schools of philosophy divided. Namely, does a wise person feel passion? Read "passion" in this context (Greek *pathê*, Latin *perturbatio*) to refer to feeling that tends to subvert a person's better judgment. Aristotelians and Platonists (Augustine lumps them together on this issue) concede that a wise person sometimes experiences passion but, being wise, never gives into it. The Stoics, by contrast, deny that the sage ever has passions. The crucial difference between the two sides is that the passion-touched sages of Aristotelian wisdom are willing to call "good" (*bonum*) goods that are beyond a person's ability to control fully, whereas the passionless sages of Stoic wisdom call the same goods "advantages" (*commoda*) and refuse to lament their loss. Take the case of our Stoic at sea. He does not have full control over either his physical well-being or his material possessions, both of which can be taken from him by storm. He presumably does have control over his own virtue (his courage, for instance), which he cannot lose except by consenting to its loss. All things being equal, our Stoic finds it preferable to have both his virtue and his health, but if he cannot have both, he continues to define his virtue as his *whole* happiness. His Aristotelian counterpart would define *most* of his happiness that way, but if he loses some vulnerable good, natural for a person to want (his health, for instance), he will feel the pinch. More relevant than the feel of the pinch, though, is that the pinch is powerless to induce our Aristotelian to compromise his virtue, the better part of his happiness.

Along with Cicero, who argues the point at length in *On Ends* (*De finibus*), Augustine takes the distinction between "goods" and "advantages" to be a distinction without a difference. Rather than rehearse Cicero's argument, Augustine is content to draw a simple moral from an anecdote: "Surely if the philosopher in the story were giving no weight to what he felt he was about to lose by shipwreck—his life and limb—he would not have so shuddered at the danger as to give witness to fear with pallor."[6] The pallor Augustine has in mind is not like a pang or an ache or the pastiness that comes of having the flu: it is pallor bound to fear, fear bound to an impression of impending harm. This impression, Augustine insists, discloses the philosopher's sense of value, albeit without his consent. Consent is not necessary because (if Augustine is right) a person's sense of value is not always, and perhaps not even usually, a deliberate judgment. It lodges in involuntary feelings. In subjecting one representative Stoic to such feelings, Augustine seeks to deny the philosophical schools their last best hope of finding happiness in personal integrity and perfectly controlled judgment. Even assuming—as Augustine would not—that virtue is the part of happiness that a person controls, the virtuous life is never all the life that a virtuous person values.

Sorabji's point against Augustine and on Stoicism's behalf is that Augustine begs the question against Stoicism when he builds fear into his description of the shipboard Stoic's involuntary state of mind. Pallor does not, in and of itself, indicate fear. Sorabji notes that Aulus Gellius is not so careful as to distinguish between two verbs—*pallescere* (to become pale) and *pavescere* (to begin to quiver)—in his paraphrase and gloss of Epictetus. Augustine has a vested interest in not making that distinction clear. When "becoming pale" is allowed to slip into the more emotionally invested notion of "quivering," the Stoic becomes subject to involuntary emotion. Sorabji reminds us that Augustine needs to do more than presuppose the emotive content of involuntary impressions. He needs to argue the point.

It is not clear to me, and perhaps it was not so clear to Augustine either, how an impression could be an object of assent or dissent without also having some propositional content (at least implicitly). I do not dissent from an itch, although I may choose not to scratch it; I can dissent from a fear. My fear tells me that some danger or unpleasantness is impending. If I discredit that perception, I go some way, if not all the way, toward dissolving the fear. If the Stoic sage really did not consider his physical safety a good, but only an optional advantage, would he have grown pale during the storm (assuming, of course, that he was not just seasick)? Sorabji's reminder is nevertheless perceptive. If Augustine is arguing against the possibility of Stoic *apatheia*[7]—freedom from passion—in book 9 of *City of God*, he is not going to convince many Stoics with his anecdotal argument. They can always conclude either that the situation has been misdescribed or that the Stoic, thus described, is not a very good Stoic. The argument of book 9, construed as a case against *apatheia*, is a poor one.

But what if Augustine hoped to discredit less the possibility of *apatheia* than its desirability? Chapter 4 of book 9 is still not that argument. Augustine's ambition there is to use the issue of the passions to house the various schools of philosophy under one roof. There they will all be heard to preach the gospel of virtue against the chaos of passion. They will all seek to reshape and refine a person's value commitments, to the point where he or she may hope for a reasonably consistent happiness, secure in its core values. Augustine's composite portrait of the genius of philosophy as it flourished in the polytheistic culture of Greece and Rome is designed to be attractive. Stoicism's loss of its claim to perfect *apatheia* is everyone's gain of a reasonable hope. It is still reasonable, as of chapter 4, book 9, for philosophers—Stoics included—to marshal their virtues to restrain and diminish their passions. The passions may never be eliminated entirely, but real progress is possible.

In book 9 of *City of God*, Augustine includes within his account of the origins of human sinfulness an attack on the ideal of *apatheia*. He aims his ire squarely at the desirability of a passionless life. Stoics continue for him to be the chief promoters of *apatheia*, being the self-described purists of reason, but we already know from book 9 that Augustine has denied them their purist credentials. So why then does he bother to critique a way of life that he believes no one lives in practice? A balloon, once deflated, is hardly worth bursting.

Stoicism in *City of God* plays the role of stalking horse for any philosophy that adopts an ethics of autonomy and so turns the pursuit of virtue into an essentially self-referential affair. It falls to the Stoics to display the deadly logic of this pursuit. Because Stoics refuse to call good what has yet to elicit their consent, they affect not to be affected by unacknowledged sources of value. Informed and voluntary consent to an impression of something desirable or repellent is taken by them to determine the entire range of their emotional possibilities. Although in theory, it is possible to consent to the goodness of a good that can be lost involuntarily, in practice the Stoics would restrict their consent to the one good that seems unassailable to them: the reasonableness of the world's order. The terrible irony of Stoic practice, as Augustine describes it in book 19, chapter 4, of *City of God*, is their sanctioning of a reasonable suicide—for the loss of goods whose goodness they would (in theory) disown.

The obvious alternative to Stoicism is for a person to acknowledge goods whose goodness exceeds or has nothing to do with an exercise of self-possession. Augustine's Platonists and Aristotelians do this explicitly; his Stoics repress the acknowledgment and are constantly compelled to disown their own involuntary impressions of value. Any acknowledgment of such goods, sometimes called "external goods" (*bona externa*), is bound to move a self out of self-containment. Cicero calls this movement a *perturbatio*; the word means passion or emotion and connotes a shake-up. Augustine uses the word in book 14 to enumerate the passions that *apatheia* is meant to eliminate. His presentation there of the four cardinal movements of soul, the *perturbationes*, parallels Cicero's in book 4 of *Tusculan Disputations*. In both accounts, the soul is moved in one of two basic ways: by attraction or by repulsion. When the soul anticipates what attracts it, it experiences desire; when its desire is satisfied, it feels joy. When the soul shrinks from what repels it, it feels fear; when its fear is realized, it knows grief. The four cardinal movements of soul are desire and joy, the two modes of attraction, and fear and grief, the corresponding modes of repulsion.

It may seem odd for a Stoic or anyone else to want to live a life free of desire and joy. Even fear has its uses, as a tonic for mental clarity and a call to avoid avoidable grief. If any of the cardinal passions is worth missing, it would be grief itself, the passion that weds the soul to loss. Cicero spends all of book 3 of *Tusculan Disputations* making the case that Stoic sages are strangers to grief. When in book 4 he takes up the question of the remaining passions, he imagines ideal Stoics not to be free of joy, desire, and fear, but to be free of the *disorder* of those affects. Grief is not redeemable, but apparently the three other *perturbationes* are. When a *perturbatio* no longer perturbs, the Stoics call it a *eupatheia*, a well-tempered passion. Cicero's Latin designation for the good kind of passion is *constantia*, a condition of constancy. The idea behind his choice of term is that a soul can be both constant and emotional if its emotions admit of measure: fear, when measured, becomes prudent caution, joy becomes just satisfaction, desire enlightened resolve. Augustine notes that when Cicero speaks of grief, he uses the word *aegritudo*, a term that can signal physical as well as emotional distress. Augustine prefers *tristitia*, in order to narrow distress to pain of soul. "Regarding grief" (*tristitia*), he writes, "the tough question is whether there is a good experience of it."[8]

His eventual answer to that tough question, based in part on scriptural evidence (Paul and Jesus both seem to have grieved for others), is that grief can be a good thing. He does not mean by this that grief is ideal. As he reads the story of the human start in Genesis, humanity's parents could have inaugurated a tradition of obedience to God and passed it on to their descendents, who would have led happy, immortal lives, untouched by loss. Instead Adam and Eve looked for a greater life in a break from God, and their willfulness injected loss into human happiness. It is now too late for those born to history to live beyond loss and, Augustine would add, too ungenerous for them to try. The three *constantiae*, when made to serve a private, impregnable integrity, define smallness of soul.

Augustine's rehabilitation of grief marks his profoundest break not only from the cognitive therapy of Stoicism but from all the various forms of philosophical self-help he associated with classical culture.[9] Even his beloved Platonists, who seemed to him to love the one God, desired too blithely the soul's separation from the body, as if this were a liberation of life and not the disintegration of personality that comes of sin and death.[10] They failed to comprehend, as would any school of philosophy untutored in scriptural wisdom, the first form of grief: the soul's lack of God.

My next section on Augustine explores the willful element of that lack and its effect on human affect.

Three Degrees of Disaffection

The story of the man, the woman, Yahweh, and the serpent, as recounted in Genesis (2:4b–3:24), was a source of constant meditation for Augustine. The story begins with Yahweh, a heavenly deity, fashioning a human being, Adam, out of the clay of the earth. Yahweh breathes life into Adam's clay and places him in a garden where two trees are singled out—one of knowledge, the other of life. In his first words to Adam, Yahweh tells his creature not to eat from knowledge, as even a taste would bind Adam's life to death. Adam's humanity is differentiated into male and female when Yahweh sends Adam into a deep sleep and sculpts a woman out of one of his ribs. A shrewd serpent soon appears on the scene and convinces the woman that eating from knowledge is life, not death, and that she will come to know as a god knows. She eats and then offers the fruit of her knowing to the man, who also eats. When Yahweh discovers that the man and woman have both tasted of knowledge, at the serpent's instigation, he curses the three of them and expels the human couple from the garden. The man and woman are not to have access to the tree of life. Yahweh consigns humanity's parents to labor in the soil of human origins, where they and their descendents will know life conjoined to death.

In *Genesis According to the Letter* (*De Genesi ad litteram*), his most extensive commentary on the creation narrative, Augustine insists that it was disobedience, not knowledge, that rendered mortal a potentially immortal human nature and caused other troubles: "The more I consider the matter, I can hardly express how strongly I agree with the view that food from the tree of knowing was not harmful to humans—for the one who had made all things very good would not have planted an evil in paradise—but disobeying the command not to eat was."[11] Augustine's decision to put the entire burden of mortality on an original, transhistorical act of human defiance was to have fateful consequences for his theology and the history of its reception, including the part that pertained to emotions.

In book 14 of *City of God*, right after his critique of *apatheia*, Augustine begins to speculate about the emotions of the first man and woman in the time prior to their disobedience. He believes that neither of the two would have been subject to emotional disturbances, the *perturbationes* that so concerned the Stoics: "Their love for God and for one another, as they lived in a true and trusting partnership, knew no disturbance, and this love brought them great satisfaction, since what they loved was never denied them. Their avoidance of sin was peaceful, and while it remained so, no evil of any kind broke in to cause them sadness."[12] If his speculation is to be credited, then Augustine is describing characters with no motive to break faith with their creator and risk losing their already complete and secure happiness.

He does pause, if only briefly, to consider an alternative possibility. Given his somewhat convoluted assumption that the original man and woman were not created immortal, but only provisionally not mortal (their ultimate status to be determined), Augustine wonders whether fear of death and desire for an immediate immortality may have been motives for the original disobedience. The motives he is considering would be reasonable motives were it reasonable for a human being not to believe Yahweh, who is for Augustine the one God. Augustine cannot bring himself to conceive of a situation in which this would be reasonable. Were he then to attribute desire and fear of the above sort to the newly created couple, he would be reading *perturbationes* into sinless human psyches. He adamantly refuses this option and insists instead on the perfect contentment of Eden's Adam and Eve.

As Augustine's analysis of original felicity progresses, his portrait of emotional life in Eden begins to resemble an exaggerated Stoicism. In the beginning Adam and Eve have all of their desires completely under rational control, their sexual desires included. In chapters 23 and 24 of book 14, Augustine ventures his audacious theory that Adam must have been able to command his erections with the facility that most men have now for raising or lowering a finger. He has less to say specifically about Eve on this topic, perhaps out of modesty, but clearly he believes that she too commands her arousal at will. The moral he wishes his readers to draw from his excursion into the sex lives of Adam and Eve is that conflict between will and desire entered human life only after sin.

Now that we have one side of Augustine's sketch of emotional life in Eden, it is time to consider the other: two reasonably contented people, with no emotional baggage to unload, are moved to disobey a divine command and invite death and chaos into their lives. Taking his cue from Paul in 1 Timothy 2:14 ("It was not Adam, but Eve, who was seduced"), Augustine reads different motives into their joint act. The woman, he says, was driven by sensuality. She saw a kind of carnal beauty in the fruit of knowing and wanted to add the fruit's life to her own; the serpent's lies encouraged her in her desire. The man acted out of pity and condescension. He knew that the serpent was lying (and so was not seduced), but he had no wish to be parted from his partner, whom he believed too weak to manage on her own. Consequently he favored his flesh-hewn bond to her over his spirit-infused bond to God. Augustine uses the difference in motive to suggest the alliance of a weakened will to unthinking appetite, but differences aside, he places pride (*superbia*) at the root of all sin and preeminently the first sin. The man and woman, he concludes, sinned because of pride.

It is not easy to grasp what Augustine means by pride. It is harder still to motivate the turn from reason to folly that he attributes to supposedly reasonable beings. Of the latter difficulty at least, Augustine was keenly aware. In several of the chapters of book 12 of *City of God*—6 through 8—he carefully develops the idea that the cause of an evil will, or a disposition to desire a lack of goodness, is always deficient (*deficiens*), never effective (*efficiens*). Although the specific case he has in mind is that of the fallen angels, who turned from God's light to pursue Satanic illusions of power, he intends his analysis of deficient motivation to apply equally well to the human case. The pride that deficiently caused Adam and Eve to sin may not tell us why they sinned, as it would were it a sufficient motive, but it does tell us what genuine good they obscured in their twisted attempt to acquire it. "Pride," observes Augustine, "is not a vice that belongs to the administering of power or to power itself, but to the soul's perverse love of its own power, in contempt of power that is higher and more just."[13] Deficient pride is not effective because, in distorting the good of power, it finally loses the good it seeks. The vices that are heir to pride—lust, greed, anger, vanity, to name a few—are bound to do likewise.

Augustine's best explication of deficient motivation takes the form of a gloss on a sin of his own, confessed in book 2 of his *Confessions*. In itself the sin seems remarkably unremarkable. Augustine is sixteen years old at the time and in Thagaste, his home town in his native North Africa. One particular evening, he and his gang, all adolescent males, conspire to steal pears from a nearby orchard. They carry off armfuls, food to be thrown to pigs. Although there is no reason to doubt the historicity of the episode Augustine describes, he clearly intends his theft and waste of pears to carry allegorical significance. The pears, as forbidden fruit, recall the fruit of first knowledge and humanity's original sin; as wasted food, thrown to pigs, they have their association with the prodigal son of Luke's Gospel (15:11–32). Anxious to live by his own devices, the younger of two sons in this parable leaves his father's house, squanders his resources, suffers impoverishment, and resolves to return home when he finds himself coveting the food of pigs. As Augustine looks back at his youthful transgression and its prodigal outcome, he tries to bring his original motive into focus and discovers, in ways scarcely imaginable to his adolescent self, a shifting affection.

More specifically he recollects three degrees of disaffection in his theft and waste of pears, each degree a rejection, in ascending order of ambition, of a value-sanctioning authority. Disaffection of the first degree is criminal in nature. "When the motive for a crime is being sought, the motive is not credible," Augustine writes, "unless it takes the form of an appetite for having or an aversion for losing some one or another of the goods we have been calling the lowest."[14] The goods he refers to as "lowest" (*infima*) include material wealth, social prestige and position, physical beauty and power, and pleasures of the flesh; in short, they are just those goods that Stoics think of as advantages but not goods in and of themselves. Seeking one's own advantage is not a crime, but doing so at the expense of the public good is. Augustine considers his petty theft a crime in the sense that any crime is a crime: it violates communal standards of value. He also remembers all too well what made his petty theft peculiar. Most thieves want what they steal. Augustine cared not a whit for the pears: "I threw away the ones I picked, with only the delightful taste of injustice to enjoy; if any one of those pears did make it into my mouth, it was my crime that was the flavoring."[15]

The love of crime for crime's sake puts a person at the extremity of a criminal disaffection. Even there, however, the disaffection is still serving an apparent good, in this case the good of being subject to no authority alien to one's own—a negatively defined autonomy. The hard part about getting one's autonomy that way is having to determine who or what is alien to oneself. Augustine recognizes that he never would have behaved so meanly that evening in Thagaste had he been alone and facing no prospect of feeling shame, but he also recognizes that he was in no position back then to consider his fellow instigators his soul's kin. They were just so many threats to his criminally defined autonomy. Tyrannize or be tyrannized: there is no other logic to a criminal disaffection.

From the perspective of his confession, Augustine sees this logic well enough, which is why he takes so little consolation from the pettiness of his theft. But he is also able to see past the logic, to the next degree of disaffection. The instability of criminal disaffection lies in its excessive dependence on competition for self-definition; it opposes the self that is one's own against all other selves, without ever defining an alternative principle of selfhood. Eventually the disposition must fold before this paradox: if I am to recognize some self as a self to be opposed, I must first know what self I am; but I cannot come to know what self I am except as a self to be opposed. The next degree of disaffection, emerging out of this paradox, belongs to the perverse or evil will. It is disaffection felt toward the authority of any self, whether corporate or individual. Augustine recalls that he was insufficiently motivated to steal the pears—meaning not that he refrained from stealing them (he did not refrain) but that his motives somehow failed to convey *him* in his act of theft. He had become to himself "a place of emptiness" (*regio egestatis*).

Being a deficient cause, the evil will has to present itself in the guise of what it is not. Mostly it looks like criminal disaffection. It looks that way to Augustine too, until he tries to confess to criminality. His motives for theft lose for him their expected, albeit criminal, intelligibility, and where he would expect to find a confident selfishness in himself, he discovers instead a strangely evacuated desire for selfhood. That place of emptiness, somewhere between a womb and an open grave, remains undetermined. He senses that he has insufficient motive to love himself—regardless of which self he takes himself to be, the one he was or the one he could be. His love's deficiency, when made into the object of his confession, puts him in mind of his third and final degree of disaffection, felt toward God.

As the self behind any pretended self, God is present in both criminal (selfish) and evil (self-undoing) disaffection as the unconfessed object of attraction. When it becomes apparent to Augustine that the first two degrees of disaffection are forms of the same disaffected love, he is able to begin his confession. What is it, he wonders, that his soul feels it lacks from God? He contemplates a variety of his human vices, all illustrative of the disparity between his pathetically independent efforts at happiness and God's perfect goodness. It is power, apparently, that his soul wants from God, specifically the power to live beyond loss: "Grief pines over the loss of goods that were desire's diversion. My soul does not want it so, but would have it be true, as it is for you, that nothing can be taken away."[16]

Augustine goes on to lament his soul's fornication, its stepping out on God to seek pleasure in a world of God's absence. In confessing to this degree of disaffection, he admits to the element of theft and distortion that is present in all breakaway human desire. The theft lies in affecting to take from God what only God can bestow: a fruitful way of desiring. The distortion shows up in what is actually taken: a love of nothing, sin. A soul that loves nothing is beyond loss, but also beyond love. Augustine's God has nothing to lose by loving, but also, and unlike the human case, nothing to gain. It is a sign of generosity that his God loves anyway. It is a sign of pride that his soul forgets this generosity and seeks to be secure in its own desires.

Pride in Augustine's analysis ultimately comes down to faulty self-regard and the desire not to be beholden to the love of others. The cause of this pride, being deficient, has to remain a mystery for him, but he is confident of the love that is pride's undoing. To love himself humanly and well, Augustine knows that he must learn to love more than himself—a lesson that is generosity's gift. There is grief in the lesson as well as delight. To will away the grief, as his Stoics try to do, is to learn the hard way that there are things in this mortal life worse than grief.

The Will's Apocalypse

Over the course of this essay, I have used Augustine's construct of Stoicism as a measure of his willingness to admit emotions, especially the unsettling ones, into the saintly life. When I speak of his "construct" of Stoicism, I do not mean to imply that his Stoicism has been solely his mind's invention and so carries no force against the schools of philosophy—Stoic and the rest—that he took to task. I happen to think that Augustine is an astute but not scholarly critic of the core ambitions of historical Stoicism. Be that as it may, the student of Augustine on the emotions still needs to see his Stoicism essentially for what it is: a temptation Augustine resists. He is especially tempted, as he looks to Genesis for some hint of a lost human integrity, to turn *apatheia*, a vice in desperate and corrupted times, into an original virtue: if only Adam had felt no grief at the prospect of losing Eve, the flesh of his flesh, he might have resisted his impression that something unique would be lost to him and stayed his course. What is remarkable, however, about Augustine's ultimate reading of Adam's motives is that it is *precisely* as a man of upright will, able not to sin, that the first man stumbles and wills deficiently to follow his heart.

Augustine is sometimes credited with having invented or significantly clarified the notion of will.[17] I am more inclined to think that he helpfully obscures a notion of will, the one that puts a person in a secure position to survey his or her desires and choose one to follow. Many a philosopher has pondered the means for determining the rightness of that choice. Augustine takes a step back and wonders about the security that he or anyone else has in choosing. Maybe *apatheia* would seem to be the ideal kind of internal security, were it possible to see outside of time and free of the claims of conflicting desires. But Augustine thinks that no one can. Our best Adam falls.

It is surely no coincidence that Augustine receives his "light of security" (*lux securitatis*) when he stumbles on these words of Paul's, while agonizing over the conversion he kept postponing: "Not in revelries and drunken bouts, nor in debauchery and shameless pursuits, nor in contention and rivalry, but put on the lord, Jesus

Christ, and make no provision for the flesh in its desires."[18] The citation is just as it appears in the *Confessions*; it is not Paul's complete thought, but an imperative, broken off in mid-sentence—a fitting metaphor for Augustine's sense of his own will. Paul's words suggest to Augustine a contrast of desires: there is what the flesh desires, and there is what the flesh desires when Christ is doing the desiring. To put on Christ is to will one kind of flesh rather than another, but what is the difference? One kind dies, the other dies and lives again—a difference between death and death conjoined to life.

Based on the evidence of the remaining books of the *Confessions*, it is doubtful whether Augustine thought his light of security gave him any special insight into the difference between abandoning his life to death and offering his life to others. His security seems to have come from his confidence that he would be taken into a greater wisdom by not presuming on his own. That included his wisdom about himself. Lack of presumption, at its best, is neither a willed humility nor an affected ignorance, but an openness to the good that is yet to be known. This is the openness that makes emotion genuinely a motion toward something. Augustine called that movement grace.

NOTES

My essay has benefited from the eyes of well-informed friends and colleagues. I thank especially Stanley Stowers, Jesse Couenhoven, Wayne Proudfoot, John Cavadini, and Coleman Brown.

1. *De Civitate Dei* 14.6. The translation, here and elsewhere, is my own. My sources for Augustine's Latin are indicated in the bibliography. I have also listed there some readily available translations.

2. *Tusculanae Disputationes* 4.65. I follow Margaret Graver in translating *perturbatio animi* as "emotion" rather than "disturbance of the mind" or "affective disorder." Although the term *perturbatio* can carry a negative connation, in this context it clearly does not: the proffered account of a *perturbatio* applies to desirable as well as undesirable movements of the mind. Later Latin authors, Augustine included, will tend to use *affectus* or *affectio* to designate "emotion" in the neutral sense, leaving *perturbatio* to its negative connotations. See *Cicero on the Emotions: Tusculan Disputations 3 and 4*, translated with commentary by Margaret Graver (Chicago: University of Chicago Press, 2002), 80.

3. For a moving description of Augustine's turn of mind and some further sense of its context, consult the chapter entitled "The Lost Future" in Peter Brown's now classic biography *Augustine of Hippo*, new ed. with epilogue (Berkeley: University of California Press, 2000). Martha Nussbaum develops an important qualification to Brown's interpretation in her *Upheavals of Thought: The Intelligence of Emotions* (Cambridge: Cambridge University Press, 2001), 535–43.

4. *De Civitate Dei* 14.7.

5. See pt. 4 of *Emotion and Peace of Mind: From Stoic Agitation to Christian Temptation* (Oxford: Oxford University Press, 2000), especially 375–84.

6. *De Civitate Dei* 9.4.

7. The Greek word *apatheia* is the root of the English word "apathy." I am nevertheless going to refrain from making the translation. Apathy connotes lethargy and inner deadness and is generally accounted a vice; *apatheia* does not carry any of this baggage.

8. *De Civitate Dei* 14.7.

9. Augustine's break from Stoicism on the issue of grief is well described in Marcia L. Colish, *The Stoic Tradition from Antiquity to the Early Middle Ages* (Leiden: Brill, 1985), 2:221–25. For the broader matter of Augustine's break with classicism, I recommend two works especially: Charles Norris Cochrane, *Christianity and Classical Culture: A Study of Thought and Action from Augustus to Augustine*, rev. ed. (New York: Oxford University Press, 1944), and more recently, Carol Harrison, *Augustine: Christian Truth and Fractured Humanity* (Oxford: Oxford University Press, 2000).

10. Augustine valued soul over body, but unlike other Christian Platonists, he put no value on the soul's separation from the body, or what Plato defined as death. For an illuminating discussion of Augustine's attitude toward death, see John Cavadini, "Ambrose and Augustine *De bono mortis*," in *The Limits of Ancient Christianity*, edited by William E. Klingshirn and Mark Vessey (Ann Arbor: University of Michigan Press, 1999), and "Ambrose to Augustine," pt. 3 of Peter Brown, *The Body and Society: Men, Women, and Sexual Renunciation in Early Christianity* (New York: Columbia University Press, 1988).

11. *De Genesi ad litteram* 8.6.12.

12. *De Civitate Dei* 4.10.

13. *De Civitate Dei* 12.8.

14. *Confessiones* 2.5.11.

15. *Confessiones* 2.6.12.

16. *Confessiones* 2.6.13.

17. Albrecht Dihle elaborates an argument for this in *The Theory of Will in Classical Antiquity* (Berkeley: University of California Press, 1982).

18. *Confessiones* 8.12.29; Rom 13:13–14.

BIBLIOGRAPHY

Augustine: Latin Sources

Confessions. Edited by James J. O'Donnell, with introduction and commentary. 3 vols. Oxford: Clarendon Press, 1992.

De Civitate Dei. Edited by Bernard Dombart and Alphonse Kalb. Corpus Christianorum Series Latina. Vols. 47 and 48. Brepols: Turnholt, 1955.

De Diversis Quaestionibus Ad Simplicianum. Edited by Almut Mutzenbecher. Corpus Christianorum Series Latina. Vol. 45. Brepols: Turnholt, 1970.

De Libero Arbitrio. Edited by Klaus-Detlef Daur. Corpus Christianorum Series Latina. Vol. 29. Brepols: Turnholt, 1970.

La Genèse au sens littéral. Edited by P. Agaësse and A. Solignac. Oeuvres de Saint Augustin. Vols. 48 and 49. Paris: Institute d'études augustiniennes, 2001.

Soliloquia. Edited by Wolfgang Hörmann. Corpus Scriptorum Ecclesiasticorum Latinorum. Vol. 89. Vienna: Hoelder-Pichler-Tempsky, 1986.

Augustine: Recommended Translations

The City of God against the Pagans. Translated by R. W. Dyson. Cambridge: Cambridge University Press, 1998.

Confessions. Translated by Henry Chadwick. Oxford: Oxford University Press, 1991.

The Literal Meaning of Genesis. Translated by John Hammond Taylor. 2 vols. New York: Newman Press, 1982.

On Free Choice of the Will. Translated by Thomas Williams. Indianapolis: Hackett, 1993.

Saint Augustine's Sin (bk. 2 of *Confessions*). Translated by Garry Wills. New York: Penguin Books, 2003.

Soliloquies: Augustine's Inner Dialogue. Translated by Kim Paffenroth. Hyde Park, N.Y.: New City Press, 2000.

To Simplician—On Various Questions. Bk. 1. Translated by John Burleigh. In *Augustine: Earlier Writings.* Philadelphia: The Westminster Press, 1953, 370–406.

References

Brown, Peter. *Augustine of Hippo: A Biography.* New ed., with an epilogue. Berkeley: University of California Press, 2000.

———. *The Body and Society: Men, Women, and Sexual Renunciation in Early Christianity.* New York: Columbia University Press, 1988.

Cavadini, John. "Ambrose and Augustine *De Bono Mortis*." In *The Limits of Ancient Christianity*, edited by William E. Klingshirn and Mark Vessey. Ann Arbor: University of Michigan Press, 1999, 232–49.

Cicero. *Cicero on the Emotions: Tusculan Disputations 3 and 4.* Translated with commentary by Margaret Graver. Chicago: University of Chicago Press, 2002.

———. *De Finibus Bonorum et Malorum.* Translated by H. Rackham. Cambridge, Mass.: Harvard University Press, 1983.

———. *Tusculan Disputations.* Translated by J. E. King. Cambridge, Mass.: Harvard University Press, 1960.

Cochrane, Charles Norris. *Christianity and Classical Culture: A Study of Thought and Action from Augustus to Augustine.* Rev. ed. New York: Oxford University Press, 1944.

Colish, Marcia L. *The Stoic Tradition from Antiquity to the Early Middle Ages.* 2 vols. Leiden: Brill, 1985.

Dihle, Albrecht. *The Theory of Will in Classical Antiquity.* Berkeley: University of California Press, 1982.

Harrison, Carol. *Augustine: Christian Truth and Fractured Humanity.* Oxford: Oxford University Press, 2000.

Nussbaum, Martha. *Upheavals of Thought: The Intelligence of Emotions.* Cambridge: Cambridge University Press, 2001.

Sorabji, Richard. *Emotion and Peace of Mind: From Stoic Agitation to Christian Temptation.* Oxford: Oxford University Press, 2000.

Further Reading

O'Daly, Gerard. *Augustine's Philosophy of Mind.* Berkeley: University of California Press, 1987.

Rist, John M. *Augustine: Ancient Thought Baptized.* Cambridge: Cambridge University Press, 1994.

Wetzel, James. *Augustine and the Limits of Virtue.* Cambridge: Cambridge University Press, 1992.

CHAPTER 20

MEDIEVAL MYSTICISM

NIKLAUS LARGIER

Is it possible to speak of "emotions" in Medieval Christian mysticism? Is not "emotion" a modern psychological concept that cannot but lead us to misunderstand the medieval ways of speaking about objective passions and affections of the soul (*passiones* or *affectus animae*), especially with regard to the experience of the divine?[1] In fact, many of the documents of medieval spirituality and of the texts that testify to mystical intimacy and ecstatic union between man and God thematize this relation exactly in terms not merely of affections (referring primarily to voluntary, possibly virtuous movements of the will) or of passions (referring to involuntary, overwhelming powers of the soul) but instead often in terms of subjective and deeply emotional experience (referring to specific, complex, and highly intense voluntary states of mind). How else could we understand the following text from the fifteenth-century *Book of Margery Kempe* than in terms of an essentially emotional piety that tries to narrate and depict the state of mind in which Margery experiences herself as deeply moved:

> You may boldly, when you are in bed, take me to you as your wedded husband, as your dear darling, and as your sweet son, for I want to be loved as a son should be loved by the mother, and I want you to love me, daughter, as a good wife ought to love her husband. Therefore, you can boldly take me in the arms of your soul and kiss my mouth, my head, and my feet as sweetly as you want. And as often as you think of me or would do any good deed to me, you shall have the same reward in heaven as if you did it to my own precious body which is in heaven.[2]

In this late medieval text, the figure of Christ speaks to the woman using a language that implies an emotional engagement between the soul and God. It is an engagement based on the woman's desire and on the mediation of this desire through the figure of Christ. However, the text at the same time makes use of several topical situations that help to understand the dynamics of the feeling of love in terms of a phenomenology of emotion, referring to multiple forms of love (husband, wife, daughter, mother, lover). As we know, the guiding rhetorical and psychological model for this enactment of desire—the role of Christ as the bridegroom, the church or the soul as the bride—is to be found in the Song of Songs and in a long tradition of interpretations of this biblical text, going back to Jewish readings of the Song of Songs. The Christian exegetical tradition starts in the third and fourth centuries with the church fathers Origen and Gregory of Nyssa, and it leads to innumerable examples of texts portraying the experience of God in a highly emotional way inspired by the Song of Songs. Before turning to this tradition, however, I would like to go back to the epistemological question of how we should understand the concept of "emotion" in the context of premodern texts. It is indeed not obvious that early Christian thinkers would turn to models of emotional expression in their attempts to understand and describe Christian beliefs and practices. Inheriting the Stoic precept that passions (*passiones, affectus*) should be controlled and repressed, early Christian thinkers had to deal with the idea that philosophical freedom and spiritual return to the divine origin could only be found in a state of *apatheia*. Not only was a moderation of the unruly nature of the passions (sorrow, fear, desire, joy) the goal of the Stoic philosophers but also a liberating suppression of the passions themselves.[3] Although some of the theologians followed this way of thinking about and dealing with the passions, it became increasingly clear that the Stoic ideal as such could not be adopted by Christians and that it had to be transformed into something quite different, with the help of the direction of the will and love.[4] Thus, addressing the question of how to interpret the Song of Songs (390–394 A.D.), Gregory of Nyssa writes:

> The most acute physical pleasure (I mean erotic pleasure) is used mysteriously in the exposition of these teachings. It teaches us the need for the soul to reach out to the divine nature's invisible beauty and to love it as much as the body is inclined to love what is akin and like itself. The soul must transform passion into passionlessness so that when every corporeal affectation has been quenched, our mind may seethe with passion for the spirit alone and be warmed by the fire which the Lord came to cast on earth [Luke 12:49]. (*In Canticum Canticorum* 27.5–15)[5]

Like Origen in his commentary on the Song of Songs (about 290 A.D.), in his teachings about mystical contemplation of this important text Gregory postulates that readers should be free of "earthly, irrational passions" and "passionate, fleshly thoughts."[6] This does not mean, however, that they were called on to turn toward a state of Stoic *apatheia* and an absolute negation of the passions. Instead, Gregory's position implies that the transformation of "passion into passionlessness" is not only an act of control but at the same time a "metamorphosis of passion."[7] The paradoxical figures of "passionless passion" and of "erotic *apatheia*" are thus not primarily part of a rhetoric of repression but of a spiritual transformation of the passions. This rhetoric of transformation stands at the beginning of a tradition of affective piety and mysticism. It is a tradition that articulates the challenge of the transformation in terms of a metamorphosis of the passions by means of a Christian rhetoric largely inspired by the Song of Songs. It is also a tradition that thematizes and problematizes the relation between "eros" and "agape," "love" and "charity,"[8] as well as between "intellect" and "love," leading from Gregory the Great's statement that identifies love and knowledge (*amor intellectus ipse*)[9] to a long tradition of medieval discussions concerning the significance of knowledge and love in the soul's search for God.[10]

The affective mysticism that follows from this early turn toward a metamorphosis of the passions includes both teachings about the evocation and transformation of affections and passions and a phenomenology of emotional states of mind. In particular the medieval commentaries written by Bernard of Clairvaux and William of Saint Thierry on the Song of Songs, but also mystical texts inspired by it, explore this realm of emotional states of mind, practicing a scriptural exegesis that is closely linked to emotional experience and that includes techniques of sensual and emotional stimulation. In other words, the metamorphosis of the passions implies not only a control of their disorderly nature and a positive concept of specific affections but also prepares the ground for ever new ways of exploring the possibilities for emotional arousal of the human soul. Nourished by the never-ending desire for God mentioned by Gregory of Nyssa, the engagement of medieval Christian mystics with the biblical texts has to be seen in the light of this transformation of the passions. Speaking of Moses and of the bride of the Song of Songs, Gregory of Nyssa points out: "they never cease to desire, but every enjoyment of God they turn into the kindling of a still more intense desire" (*In Canticum canticorum* 32.2–5).[11] Speaking of this "kindling of desire," he prepares a way for a culture of religious emotions that will deeply mark medieval contemplative practices.

The metamorphosis of the passions—taking shape, as Gregory of Nyssa pointed out, in an ever growing desire (*epektasis*)—is based on practices that include the reading of the scriptures and mystical contemplation, but also liturgy and prayer. These forms of engagement with the biblical text and the message of the gospel can not be fully understood if we consider them only in the context of memorial practices, that is, a pious remembering of the narrative content of the biblical message.[12] Rather, we have to look at them in terms of a spiritual reading that relies on mimetic practices and on "sacramental mimesis,"[13] that is, on a translation of the meaning of the texts into a fact of sensual and emotional experience.

Memory and Prayer

The practice of memory through reading, liturgy, and prayer that is at the center of the Christian life is for the most part also a practice of emotional stimulation. This becomes obvious when we look at the history of prayer.[14] It is also a key to understanding the affective nature of a large part of medieval Christian mysticism. Essentially, contemplation and mystical union have their place in the context of prayer that is inspired by the reading of the scriptures, that is, a practice that leads toward the desired moment of unity in love. As many textual examples show, prayer enacts a situation of dialogue, a space of interaction between the soul and God, evoking at the same time the possibilities for intellectual knowledge and emotional stimulation of the divine. The best examples for this form of prayer can be found in the *Confessions* of Saint Augustine, a text that inspired religious writers throughout the Middle Ages, providing a model for a dialogic engagement of the soul with itself and with the divine. The emotional experience of the divine has its place often within such a setting, where the biblical model from the Song of Songs converges with Augustine's philosophical and theological form of intellectual and emotional search for the self in the face of God and the scriptures. Acknowledging in many cases at the starting point that God is incomprehensible and that God's existence is beyond the reach of human rational understanding, the theories of prayer address a specific problem, namely, the inadequacy of the human mind in its finitude on one hand and its desire for communication with the divine on the other. Responding to this challenge, an important tradition of Christian spirituality relies on Augustine's rhetoric of dialogic structures wherein a self is portrayed as exploring its relation to the divine in a soliloquy or an inner dialogue. This tradition, often expressed in terms of a *confabulatio*, a "conversation" between the soul and God, represents a most interesting territory for research on the history of emotional experience, also because it builds on practices of staging and fashioning the self in specific ways. From Augustine through Bernard of Clairvaux, William of Saint Thierry, Mechthild of Magdeburg, Marguerite Porete, and up to the Spanish mystics of the "golden age" of Spanish mysticism, such dialogic structures have been explored in spiritual and poetic ways, emphasizing the importance of emotional experience and exploring its different shades.

As I have pointed out, in the texts we are dealing with, the setting for the encounter between the human and the divine is often a dialogic one. Largely inspired by the Song of Songs, this dramatic setup serves as a rhetorical device of amplification, stressing moments of desire and distance, familiarity and alienation, joy and melancholy, deprivation and fruition. Nearly all the authors mentioned earlier place their reflection on the inner senses within this pattern of a basic tension that is evoked by the text of the Song of Songs and that is reproduced in the rewriting of the Song of Songs in many shapes. The *St. Trudperter Hohelied* is one example of this rewriting; texts from Mechthild of Magdeburg's *Flowing Light of the Godhead* or Marguerite Porete's *Mirror of Simple Souls* could figure as other such examples. In each case, the sensory and emotional experiences of the divine we are told about unfold in a process of reading, or, more precisely, in the practice of the meditation of the text, in its contemplative reproduction, and finally in the rewriting of the text. Within and through these practices, sensory experiences of vision, taste, touch, hearing, and odor are evoked, and together with the arousal of the senses goes an arousal, a stimulation, of emotions.[15]

In order to illustrate this point, I turn to David of Augsburg, a late medieval Franciscan author whose texts exist both in Latin and in the vernacular. David can be seen as a writer who is at the source of a specific circle of spirituality and of the production of vernacular texts.[16] In his book *Septem gradus orationis* (in Middle High German, *Die sieben staffeln des gebets*) David of Augsburg writes:

> Because the *words* of truth are *spirit and truth*, the soul has to create and nourish a spiritual life while she is wandering in exile, until she will *see* the word of God, through which everything lives, *from face to face*. Therefore she has to chew and ruminate these sounding and corporeal words, so that the spirit extracts the sweetness that inhabits these words. Thus the spirit tries to suck his life with pain out of them. This is the way... the words of prayer, which appear dry and tasteless from the outside, unfold their taste in devotion. The work of prayer turns into delightful pleasure, so that we now "throw up" with delight from the overflowing fullness of our heart what we used to recite with pain and like a foreign thing.[17]

This description of prayer focuses from the beginning on the inner experience of taste. *Ruminare*, "to ruminate," is not only seen as a technique of repetition of the text and of memorization, but as a perception of the word that goes hand in hand with *pulsare*, that is, with a rhythmical movement of the body (quoting the "knocking at the door" from Matthew 7:7 and Luke 11:9). In this rhythmical movement, we experience the sensual and emotional sweetness of the word: "pulsando experiamur quam suavis" (through knocking we experience the sweetness). Let us examine this line in its context:

> Non enim curat Deus, cum nos orare iubet, ut cum verbis ei nostram petitionem aperiamus, quippe qui per se scit quid nobis necesse sit, *antequam petamus eum* (Matthew 6:8). Hoc magis intendit, ut ipsum orando *pulsemus* (Matthew 7:7; Luke 11:9), pulsando experiamur quam suavis et bonus... et inde eum amemus et amando [ei] inhaeremus, inhaerendo unus cum ipso spiritus efficiamur.

> When he tells us to pray, God does not mean that we should tell him with our words what we wish, since he anyway already knows what we need before we ask him for it. He rather means that we should *knock*. Through knocking we experience how sweet and good he is and thus we love him and join him in love and become one spirit with him.[18]

Not the praise of God—not the petitioning of God—are at the center of this understanding of prayer. What *pulsare*, the gesture of "knocking at the door," refers to is the practice of inserting the verses of the scriptures into meditation and prayer. It is through this that—alluding to Luke 11:9—human claims will be heard: "knock, and it shall be opened unto you." "Rumination" and "mastication" refer to this way that the hidden meanings of the biblical verses are made present and take shape as inner sensory and emotional experiences. This is the *excitatio*, which is based on the practice of the inner senses and leads to the emotional intensity of the experiences of both the desolate state of exile and the joy of fulfilled desire. The different shades of emotions are ultimately of secondary interest; the stimulation is indeed at the center, leading to this final moment of excitement. David of Augsburg quotes Hugh of Saint Victor at this point: "It is the power of love to make you into the thing you love, and through this society of love you will be transformed into an image of that with which you are joined in affection."[19]

Spiritual Sensation and Emotion

As we have seen in the passages quoted, the emotional engagement of the soul with God and Christ implies not only a transformation of the passions but in most cases sensual experience as well. It is important to keep in mind that considerations of the transformation of the passions were developed by Origen and by Gregory of Nyssa not in the context of theories about the human soul but in the context of questions addressing the hermeneutic engagement with the biblical text. Using the Greek term *aisthesis*, Origen indicates that he speaks about a faculty or an experience that transcends the rational and discursive operations of our intellect. In fact, Origen translates the biblical verse Proverbs 2:5 ("Then shalt thou understand the fear of the Lord, and find the knowledge of God") in such a way as to introduce the term *aisthesis* where other translations, for example the Septuagint and the Vulgate, use *gnosis* or *scientia* ("knowledge" or "understanding").[20] As Karl Rahner has shown, Origen's choice of word is to be seen in the light of his teaching about what he—referring to a number of scriptural passages—in several places in his works calls "senses of the soul," "divine senses," "senses of the inner man," "senses of the heart," or "spiritual senses." Thus Origen emphasizes that Christ and the Christian message is the object of each sense of the soul, such as light for the eyes, words for the ears, bread for the taste, tactile sensation for the touch (*Commentarium in Canticum Canticorum* 2.9, 12).[21] Although it is clear that in Origen the possession of the inner senses is seen as something belonging to the hierarchy of those who have reached higher stages in the contemplation of the divine, he does not define his teaching as strictly esoteric. Rather, he emphasizes that practice and exercise (*gymnasía*) are key elements leading to the constitution of this inner realm of experience. Where this happens is above all in prayer. Prayer is the place, as well, where the rational, discursive, and practical level of the life of the soul is left behind in favor of the contemplative aesthetic experience of the divine.

In many cases, starting with Gregory of Nyssa and essentially on the basis of a number of biblical verses, the emphasis of this contemplative prayer lies not on the inner vision—as one might expect from a modern perspective and from the Greek philosophical basis of a large part of Christian theology—but on inner taste and finally inner touch as well. Taste refers above all to the sweetness that is experienced in the perception of the divine. Honey is the expression used in many of these cases, quoting from the Bible and its uses of "milk and honey" with regard to the experience of paradise or eternal life, but reference is also made to bitterness and other terms, evoking the culinary realm and allowing for the exploration of a variety of experiences of taste.[22] Innumerable authors who use this terminology could be quoted here, especially those who comment on the Song of Songs, the text that is at the basis of most elaborations on the sensory and emotional experience of the divine. Among these, William of Saint Thierry plays an important role in the medieval tradition, and the *St. Trudperter Hohelied* (written in Middle High German) testifies to the importance of the theory of the inner senses.[23]

Often the approach these authors chose was not systematic. It does not take shape in the form of a clearly elaborated theory of the hierarchy of the senses, but rather in the form of comments on different approaches to the divine that have their reality in the perfume, the sound, the touch, or the taste that is perceived by the soul while praying, that is, in other and more concrete words, while it is "chewing" and "ruminating" the words. In most cases, biblical verses expressing such moments of taste figure prominently in these texts. Quite often, these verses are used as the stimuli, the rhetorical means that call forth specific sensations and emotions, producing states of mind that can be characterized as "mystical union" or "ecstatic rapture."

Major attempts to systematize this practice of prayer and contemplation can be found in Albert the Great and in Bonaventure. Albert relates sight, hearing, and odor to knowledge of truth, that is, to the more cognitive intellectual realm; he relates taste and touch to the experience of the good, that is, to the realm of love and will. Inspired by Dionysius the Pseudo-Areopagite, he emphasizes the passivity of this form of experience and the fact that the soul is "suffering" it and that the inner sensory phenomena are aspects of the reality of this suffering of the divine. Speaking of *tactus* and *sapor* with regard to the divine, he accentuates the "experiential," purely "receptive," and "passive" character of this kind of perception.[24]

It should be pointed out that the perception of the divine in terms of a highly emotional experience of taste and touch becomes most significant in Franciscan traditions, in David of Augsburg's *Septem gradus orationis*, in Bonaventure's *Itinerarium mentis ad Deum* and *Breviloquium*, but even more so in later medieval texts, for example, in Rudolf of Biberach's treatise *De septem itineribus aeternitatis*, a text that has been handed down under the name of Bonaventure. Other examples where the emotional, gustatory, and tactile experience is very important could be added, for example the works of Peter of Ailly and the *Imitatio Christi* by Thomas à Kempis. *Delectatio* (pleasure), and *suavitas* (sweetness) are the key words these authors use when discussing the ways by which human beings can reach the divine in an experiential way, referring to a sensation of taste and touch that evokes a state of high emotional arousal. Peter of Ailly speaks in this context of a way "to reach already in this life the pleasures of the eternal rewards in an experiential shape, and to taste their sweetness with delight."[25] Rudolf of Biberach uses the following words, largely inspired by treatments of the inner senses by Alcher of Clairvaux, Bernard of Clairvaux, Hugh of Saint Victor, and Bonaventure: "reaching the inner sense of taste, it opens it up toward the tasting of eternal sweetness."[26]

The eschatological structure of this concept is to be stressed, since it is in the inner experience that the senses are rehabilitated and dignified in a way unknown since the loss of paradise.[27] In the texts of the authors discussed here, such experiences are characterized as an anticipation of the eternal and a reconciliation with the ideal existence of human beings beyond the state of sin. It is also, however, more than that. In the Franciscan tradition, this rehabilitation of the senses and of experience leads to a new affirmative mode with regard to sense experience itself and to an aesthetic justification of the world as it is to be found in Franciscan poetry and science of the late Middle Ages.

Like other authors of the thirteenth century who refer to the theory of the five inner senses, for example Albert the Great, Bonaventure stresses that we should not consider these senses inner faculties but aspects of an inner dialogue. They are to be seen as acts that constitute and call forth their reality in the context of spiritual practices, that is, during prayer and contemplation. It could be said that they draw their reality from prayer and contemplation, more precisely, from the insertion of biblical verses into the daily practice of *confabulatio* with the divine. This is the place where the text of the Bible turns into experience and nothing else. This is the place where the sensory and arousing experiential quality of the repetition of the text transcends all intellectual attempts. With regard to this experience of the text, Bonaventure clearly privileges the inner experience of taste and—maybe at a first glance surprisingly, but certainly also under the influence of the image of the stigmatization of Saint Francis—of touch, connecting these two senses to the realm of the affective communication with God that is so important for Franciscan spirituality. Bonaventure explains that the ultimate goal of this perception is Christ, the *Verbum increatum, inspiratum, incarnatum,* the "uncreated, inspired, incarnated Word." The inner ear perceives the *Verbum increatum* in the form of Christ's voice and of most sublime harmonies; the inner eye perceives the light and beauty; the inner nose perceives the *Verbum inspiratum* in form of a sublime perfume; finally taste and touch perceive the sweetness and pleasantness of the *Verbum creatum*.[28] *Splendor, harmonia, fragrantia, dulcedo, suavitas* are words that express the moments of this inner aesthetic experience of the sublime divine, which includes the ascent of the soul and a growing emotional satisfaction. The *excessus extatici* are the peak of this experience of the divine. As Bonaventure points out, this is not what theology calls the *raptus*, but what he calls "in caligine sentire Deum in se" (to experience the presence of God in darkness within oneself). It is a moment of sensory and emotional immediacy and intensity entirely different from an intellectual vision (*tantum in affectu,* "in the affect"). This is the place where inner touch and excessive emotion (*amor extaticus,* ecstatic love) converge, love being actually one with touch.[29] It is also the place where the sensory experience of the world is theologically justified, insofar as it is nothing else than the experience of the divine. From the artifact of prayer we return to the experience of nature—an experience that now is also highly sensual and emotional.

Most treatments of the inner senses in the later Middle Ages follow this theory of Bonaventure. Some of them, however, include interesting accents. Thus, for example, Rudolf of Biberach creates an intimate link between the Eucharist and the theory of the inner senses,[30] reflecting the growing importance of the Eucharist for late medieval spiritual experience. Another example for the connection between the emotional life, sensation, and liturgy may be found in texts where medieval authors discuss the impact of church music and liturgic song on their souls.[31] Listening and singing, the experience of music, are portrayed as having a corporeal effect that produces sensations of an intense sensory and emotional character.

In this context, it must be recalled again that a theory of the "spiritual senses" has been elaborated by Origen and Gregory of Nyssa in their respective exegeses of the Song of Songs, with the intention to avoid a literal and sensual reading of this text in favor of a spiritual reading. However, this step toward a radical spiritualization of the textual meaning neither overlooks nor eliminates the deep sensuality and emotionality of this text. On the contrary, one might argue, Origen's and Gregory's interpretative efforts liberated the sensual from its primary and compulsive relation to objects of sensation and its submission to intellectual and rational evaluation. They did so through the construction of a "higher," "interior," "spiritual" level of sensation; a level of sensation that seems to be disconnected from everyday sensory experience, from its determination through the object as well as from its orientation toward the intellectual and discursive grasp and control. By emphasizing that the true realm of the sensory is "within" the soul, by stressing that it forms a realm of experience independent from the outer senses, they made it possible for sensation itself to be experienced as an excessive form of intensity free from the binding force of a determining object. With regard to God, all experience could be nothing else than excessive. Thus, Origen and Gregory prepared the way for a mainly experiential and heavily emotional form of spirituality during the Middle Ages, allowing ultimately for the intense depictions of the encounter between the soul and God that can be found in medieval mysticism from Bernard of Clairvaux and William of Saint Thierry to Ruusbroec, Julian of Norwich, and Margery Kempe.

Negative Theology and Affective Mysticism

We have seen that already in Gregory of Nyssa the metamorphosis of the passions is linked to negative theology. Insisting on the unknowable character of God, Gregory points out that it is in love where—through the metamorphosis of their passions and desires—men and women are able to compensate for this lack of intellectual understanding and approach "divine beauty." In his commentary on the Song of Songs, Thomas Gallus, abbot of the Victorine house at Vercelli in Piedmont beginning in 1226, draws his own conclusions from this fundamental theological observation and concludes that "affectivity tends to *exclude* rather than *subsume* human knowledge in the highest stages of the mystical itinerary."[32] Based on his knowledge of the twelfth-century mystical interpretations of the Song of Songs and on "the Dionysian commentary tradition begun by his Victorine predecessor, Hugh of Saint Victor, he combined Dionysian apophaticism with an affective reading of the Song of Songs to form a potent new mystical theory that had a major influence in the later Middle Ages."[33] In his reading, he understands the Song of Songs as the "practical part" of the mystical theology of Dionysius the Pseudo-Areopagite. As Bernard McGinn has pointed out, the influence of his "affective Dionysianism" extended not only to the Franciscans (Bonaventure, Rudolf of Biberach, and David of Augsburg) but also to the Carthusian Hugh of Balma, to Hendrik Herp, and to the author of *The Cloud of Unknowing*.[34]

Inheriting the emphasis on an "experiential" reading of the Song of Songs from Bernard of Clairvaux and William of Saint Thierry, Thomas Gallus not "only sees the Song as a key to unlock the central meaning of the Bible," but he also sees Dionysius as the key that "unlocks" the Song of Songs.[35] Since God is unknowable to the intellect, he can be only experienced in love, which is above intellect and mind. The apophatic rhetoric in Dionysius is thus reinterpreted in such a way as to emphasize the significance of negative theology as a form of acknowledging the finitude of human understanding. In the eyes of Thomas Gallus, the intellect had to be disqualified and cut off, before "the amorous *unitio deificans*" could happen that in turn would inform all the lower powers of the soul.[36] Providing the later Middle Ages with this theory of superintellectual love, Thomas Gallus also influences the creative rewriting of the Song of Songs I have already mentioned. The close dialogue he establishes between the Dionysian texts and the Song of Songs gives a new shape to the Cistercian tradition of interpretation, and it emphasizes the possibilities of a phenomenology of emotional life within the framework of the formation of the powers of the soul through the engagement with the text. Authors like Hadewijch of Antwerp, Mechthild of Magdeburg, or Marguerite Porete explore this framework in similar ways, using the bridal scenario of Song of Songs as a blueprint for their own texts, emphasizing the absoluteness of love, including dramatic enactments of the interplay between the powers of the soul and a phenomenology of their own emotional life, and making use of the affective language of courtly literature to reinforce the lively character of their emotional experience in their dealings with the unknowable God and the mediating images they use.

The Passion of Christ and the History of Emotions

An overview of the significance of emotions in medieval mysticism would not be complete without an account of two other paradigms of affective arousal, namely, the suffering of Christ and the sacrifice of martyrdom. A mysticism of the passion of Christ, and of martyrdom as an imitation of the passion of Christ, emerged already in the early times of the church (Acts 7:59–60; Lk 23:34–46). In many ways, monastic asceticism follows this pattern, emphasizing acts of self-mortification, of spiritual martyrdom, and of mystical death, often invoking—for example in the life of Saint Anthony—a psychomachy that includes the investment of the passions as well. The eleventh century sees a remarkable shift, however, that would have a major impact on the understanding of the imitation of the passion of Christ. Contemplative practices as well as visual and textual representations focus now more prominently on the suffering of Christ, emphasizing at the same time a type of devotion that is more emotional than before. After Jean of Fécamp and Anselm of Canterbury, Bernard of Clairvaux and William of Saint Thierry focus most on this "school of Christ" and on the teaching of Christ in his suffering.[37] For both of them, true love is taught by Christ in his suffering, and it is through the imitation of Christ's suffering that the human soul can be assimilated to true love. Elisabeth of Schönau, Beatrijs of Nazareth, Hadewijch of Antwerp, Mechthild of Magdeburg, Mechthild of Hackeborn, and Gertrude the Great follow this path, making the imitation of the suffering of Christ a centerpiece of their devotional practices and evoking time and again minute details of this suffering with the goal of producing sensations of emotional intimacy with Christ in their own lives. New motives appear in this history of dramatic enactment with Saint Francis and the Franciscan movement, especially with regard to the poverty and nakedness of Christ, the suffering of Mary, and finally the stigmatized body. To be crucified with Christ meant not only to contemplate the suffering body of the savior but at the same time to emulate it, to make it present through the imagination, to feel the suffering in terms of sensation and emotion, and to embody it psychologically and physically. Thus, the image of the suffering Christ became the image that shapes the desire for God, that is, the mediating form that allows for an emotionally rich enactment of the drama that links human being and God in the incarnation. During the later Middle Ages, this tradition tends to turn into a realistic and highly expressive form of spirituality. Angela of Foligno experiences in her visions the passion in a way that implies the investment of all the senses and of a deep emotional commitment, as do Henry Suso and his disciple Elisabeth Stagel, Christine and Marguerite Ebner, or Catherine of Siena. Often the practices of arousing the emotions include not only ascetic exercises—for example, self-flagellation[38]—but also the use of images and the enactment of plays.[39] In a less spectacular way, the *Vita Jesu Christi* of Ludolf of Saxony offers a version of the biblical narrative of the passion that inspires a contemplation with the "eyes of the heart,"[40] that is, an emotional form of private contemplation for a larger audience of pious Christians, and anticipating the techniques of sensual and emotional arousal explored by Ignatius of Loyola in his *Spiritual Exercises*.

NOTES

1. Cf. Thomas Dixon, *From Passions to Emotions: The Creation of a Secular Psychological Category* (Cambridge: Cambridge University Press, 2003). For questions of terminology and translation, see especially 39–48.

2. *The Book of Margery Kempe*, translated by Barry Windeatt (Harmondsworth: Penguin, 1985), 126–27.

3. Cf. Richard Sorabji, *Emotion and Peace of Mind: From Stoic Agitation to Christian Temptation* (Oxford: Oxford University Press, 2000).

4. For Augustine's criticism of Stoic thought compare Dixon, *From Passions to Emotions*, 40–41.

5. Gregory of Nyssa, *In Canticum Canticorum*, edited by Hermann Langerbeck, in *Gregorii Nysseni Opera*, vol. 6 (Leiden: Brill, 1960); translation from Gregory of Nyssa, *Commentary on the Song of Songs*, translated by Casimir McCambley (Brookline: Hellenic College Press, 1987), 49.

6. McCambley, *Commentary on the Song of Songs*, 43.

7. Bernard McGinn, "Topics of Desire," in *That Others May Know and Love: Essays in Honor of Zachary Hayes, OFM*, edited by Michael F. Cusato and F. Edward Coughlin (St. Bonaventure, N.Y.: Franciscan Institute, 1997), 144.

8. See Bernard McGinn, "God as Eros: Metaphysical Foundations of Christian Mysticism," in *New Perspectives on Historical Theology: Essays in Memory of John Meyendorff*, edited by Bradley Nassif (Grand Rapids, Mich.: Eerdmans, 1996), 189–209.

9. Gregory the Great, *XL Homiliarum in Evangelia libri duo*, in *Patrologia Latina*, edited by Jean-Paul Migne (Paris: Migne, 1849), 76: 1207A.

10. See Bernard McGinn, "Love, Knowledge, and Mystical Union," in *Mystical Union in Judaism, Christianity, and Islam: An Ecumenical Dialogue*, edited by Moshe Idel and Bernard McGinn (New York: Continuum 1996), 59–86, and McGinn, *The Presence of God*, vols. 1–3 (New York: Crossroads, 1992–98).

11. McCambley, *Commentary on the Song of Songs*, 51.

12. See Mary Carruthers, *The Craft of Thought: Meditation, Rhetoric, and the Making of Images, 400–1200* (New York: Cambridge University Press, 1998).

13. Catherine Brown Tkacz, "Singing Women's Words as Sacramental Mimesis," *Recherches de théologie ancienne et médiévale* 70 (2003): 275–328. Tkacz uses the term "sacramental mimesis" to "describe the liturgical imitation that was described and experienced by Christians as bringing them into likeness with Christ and the Saints, and examining such sacramental mimesis enlarges the modern understanding of the patristic, medieval and Byzantine Church" (275).

14. See Patrick Henriet, *La parole et la prière au Moyen Âge: Le Verbe efficace dans l'hagiographie monastique des onzième et douzième siècles* (Brussels: De Boeck and Larcier, 2000). Piroska Nagy, *Le don des larmes au Moyen Age: Un instrument spirituel en quête d'institution* (Paris: Albin Michel, 2000). McGinn, *The Presence of God*, 1: 277–81.

15. For an analysis of the act of reading and its relation to emotions in Richard of Saint Victor, Hugh of Saint Victor, and William of Saint Thierry, see: Ineke van 't Spijker, "De ordening van affecten: Kloosterleven in de twaalfde eeuw," in *Emoties in De Middeleeuwen*, edited by R. E. V. Stuip and C. Vellekoop (Hilversum: Verloren, 1998), 115–33.

16. Kurt Ruh, *Geschichte der abendländischen Mystik*, vol. 2, *Frauenmystik und Franziskanische Mystik der Frühzeit* (Munich: Beck, 1993), 524.

17. David of Augsburg, *Septem gradus orationis*, in Jacques Heerinckx, "Le 'Septem gradus orationis' de David d'Augsbourg," *Revue d'ascétique et de mystique* 14 (1933): 160. The passage ends with the quotations that follow in the text, evoking the praying of the psalm and Bernard of Clairvaux.

18. Ibid., 161. The Middle High German translation of the text (in *Die sieben Staffeln des Gebets in der deutschen Originalfassung*, edited by Kurt Ruh [Munich: Artemis, 1965]) replaces this reference to the specifically physical *pulsare* with the more general expression

mit gebette suochen (to seek in prayer), responding most likely to the habits of a non-monastic audience.

19. Hugh of Saint Victor, *Soliloquium de arrha animae*, in *Patrologia Latina*, edited by Jean-Paul Migne, vol. 176 (Paris: Migne, 1854), quoted in Heerinckx, "Le 'Septem gradus orationis' de David d'Augsbourg," 162.

20. See Karl Rahner, "Le début d'une doctrine des cinq sens spirituels chez Origène," *Revue d'ascétique et de mystique* 13 (1932): 116. The important translations are: Origen: *kai aísthäsin theían heuréseis*. Septuagint: *kai epígnosin theou heuréseis*; Vulgate: *et scientiam Dei invenies*.

21. *Commentaire sur le Cantique des cantiques*, vol. 1, edited by Luc Brésard, Henri Crouzel, and Marcel Borret (Paris: Cerf, 1991), 442.

22. Langerbeck, *In Canticum Canticorum* 14, 425–26.

23. See *Das St. Trudperter Hohelied: Eine Lehre der Liebenden Gotteserkenntnis*, edited by Friedrich Ohly (Frankfurt: Deutscher Klassiker Verlag, 1998), 922–23.

24. Albertus Magnus, *In quattuor libros Sententiarum* 3 d. 13 a. 4, edited by Stephanus Borgnet, in *Opera omnia* (Paris: Vivès, 1894), 28: 240. See *Super Dionysium De caelesti hierarchia* 15.5, edited by Stephanus Borgnet, in *Opera omnia* (Paris: Vivès, 1894), 14: 414.

25. Peter of Ailly, *Compendium contemplationis* 3.11, in *Opuscula spiritualia* (Douai, 1634), 134.

26. Rudolf of Biberach, *De septem itineribus aeternitatis* 6.5, edited by Margot Schmidt (Stuttgart: Frommann-Holzboog, 1985), 467.

27. In his long treatment of the inner senses, Rudolf makes the experiential (emotional and sensual) aspect very explicit; ibid., 464–72.

28. See Rahner, "La doctrine," 275–76. Rahner refers to the following texts of Bonaventure: *Collationes in Hexaemeron* 9.1–4; *Itinerarium mentis in deum* 4.3; *Breviloquium* 5.6.

29. See Rahner, "La doctrine," 280–90. He notes: "le toucher est l'acte de l'amour dans l'extase" ("Touch is the act of love in ecstasy," 290).

30. See Margot Schmidt, introduction to Rudolf von Biberach, *Die siben strassen zu got* (Stuttgart: Frommann-Holzboog, 1985), xxv.

31. See the reference to Saint Gertrude of Helfta in Tkacz, "Singing Women's Words," 277–78. Further references in Niklaus Largier, *Lob der Peitsche: Eine Kulturgeschichte der Erregung* (Munich: Beck, 2001), 29–33.

32. McGinn, "Topics of Desire," 85. See Jeanne Barbet, *Thomas Gallus: Commentaires du Cantique des Cantiques* (Paris: Vrin, 1967).

33. McGinn, "Topics of Desire," 82.

34. Ibid., 84.

35. Ibid., 87.

36. Ibid., 89.

37. Bernard of Clairvaux, *Sermones super Cantica Canticorum* 44.1, *Sermones super Cantica Canticorum*, edited by Jean Leclercq et al., in *Sancti Bernardi Opera*, vols. 1–2 (Rome: Editiones Cistercienses, 1957–58); *De diligendo Deo* 3.7 and 8, *De diligendo Deo*, edited by Jean Leclercq et al., in *Sancti Bernardi Opera*, vol. 3 (Rome: Editiones Cistercienses, 1963). William of Saint Thierry, *De contemplando Deo* 9–11, edited by Jacques Hourlier (Paris: Cerf, 1959).

38. See Niklaus Largier, *In Praise of the Whip: A Cultural History of Arousal*, translated by Graham Harman (Brooklyn, N.Y.: Zone, 2007).

39. See Jeffrey Hamburger, *Nuns as Artists: The Visual Culture of a Medieval Convent* (Berkeley: University of California Press, 1997), and *The Visual and the Visionary: Art and Female Spirituality in Late Medieval Germany* (New York: Zone Books, 1998). For an

analysis of the broader connection between religious plays and the stimulation of emotions in the later Middle Ages see Ingrid Kasten, "Ritual und Emotionalität: Zum Geistlichen Spiel des Mittelalters," in *Literarisches Leben: Festschrift Volker Mertens zum fünfundsechzigsten Geburtstag*, edited by Matthias Mayer and Hayo Schiewer (Tübingen: Niemeyer, 2002), 335–60.

40. See Fritz Oskar Schuppisser, "Schauen mit den Augen des Herzens: Zur Methodik der spätmittelalterlichen Passionsmeditation, besonders in der Devotio Moderna und bei den Augustinern," in *Die Passion Christi in Literatur und Kunst des Spätmittelalters*, edited by Walter Haug and Burghart Wachinger (Tübingen: Niemeyer, 1993), 169–210.

BIBLIOGRAPHY

Albertus Magnus. *In quattuor libros Sententiarum*. Edited by Stephanus Borgnet. In *Opera omnia*, vol. 28. Paris: Vivès, 1894.

———. *Super Dionysium De caelesti hierarchia*. Edited by Stephanus Borgnet. In *Opera omnia*, vol. 14. Paris: Vivès, 1894.

Barbet, Jeanne. *Thomas Gallus: Commentaires du Cantique des Cantiques*. Paris: Vrin, 1967.

Bernard of Clairvaux. *De diligendo Deo*. Edited by Jean Leclercq et al. In *Sancti Bernardi Opera*, vol. 3. Rome: Editiones Cistercienses, 1963.

———. *Sermones super Cantica Canticorum*. Edited by Jean Leclercq et al. In *Sancti Bernardi Opera*, vols. 1–2. Rome: Editiones Cistercienses, 1957–58.

Bonaventure. *Breviloquium*. Edited by Adolphe C. Peltier. In *Opera omnia*, vol. 7. Paris: Vivès, 1866.

———. *Collationes in Hexaemeron*. Edited by Wilhelm Nyssen. Darmstadt: Wissenschaftliche Buchgesellschaft, 1964.

———. *Itinerarium mentis in deum*. Edited by Adolphe C. Peltier. In *Opera omnia*, vol. 12. Paris: Vivès, 1868.

Carruthers, Mary. *The Craft of Thought: Meditation, Rhetoric, and the Making of Images, 400–1200*. New York: Cambridge University Press, 1998.

David of Augsburg. *Septem gradus orationis*. In Jacques Heerinckx, "Le 'Septem gradus orationis' de David d'Augsbourg." *Revue d'ascétique et de mystique* 14 (1933): 146–70.

———. *Die sieben Staffeln des Gebets in der deutschen Originalfassung*. Edited by Kurt Ruh. Munich: Artemis, 1965.

Dixon, Thomas. *From Passions to Emotions: The Creation of a Secular Psychological Category*. Cambridge: Cambridge University Press, 2003.

Gondreau, Paul. *The Passions of Christ's Soul in the Theology of St. Thomas Aquinas*. Munich: Aschendorff, 2002.

Gregory the Great. *XL Homiliarum in Evangelia libri duo*. In *Patrologia Latina*, edited by Jean-Paul Migne, vol. 76. Paris: Migne, 1849.

Gregory of Nyssa. *Commentary on the Song of Songs*. Translated by Casimir McCambley. Brookline, Mass.: Hellenic College Press, 1987.

———. *In Canticum Canticorum*. Edited by Hermann Langerbeck. *Gregorii Nysseni Opera*, vol. 6. Leiden: Brill, 1960.

Hamburger, Jeffrey. *Nuns as Artists: The Visual Culture of a Medieval Convent*. Berkeley: University of California Press, 1997.

———. *The Visual and the Visionary: Art and Female Spirituality in Late Medieval Germany*. New York: Zone Books, 1998.

Henriet, Patrick. *La parole et la prière au Moyen Âge: Le Verbe efficace dans l'hagiographie monastique des onzième et douzième siècles*. Brussels: De Boeck and Larcier, 2000.

Hollywood, Amy. *Sensible Ecstasies: Mysticism, Sexual Difference, and the Demands of History*. Chicago: University of Chicago Press, 2002.

Hugh of Saint Victor. *Soliloquium de arrha animae*. In *Patrologia Latina*, edited by Jean-Paul Migne, vol. 176. Paris: Migne, 1854.

Kasten, Ingrid. "Ritual und Emotionalität: Zum Geistlichen Spiel des Mittelalters." In *Literarisches Leben: Festschrift Volker Mertens zum fünfundsechzigsten Geburtstag*, edited by Matthias Mayer and Hayo Schiewer. Tübingen: Niemeyer, 2002, 335–60.

Kempe, Margery. *The Book of Margery Kempe*, translated by Barry Windeatt. Harmondsworth, England: Penguin, 1985.

Largier, Niklaus. "Inner Senses—Outer Senses: The Practice of Emotions in Medieval Mysticism." In *Codierung von Emotionen im Mittelalter/Emotions and Sensibilities in the Middle Ages*, edited by C. Stephen Jaeger and Ingrid Kasten. Berlin: de Gruyter, 2003, 3–15.

———. *In Praise of the Whip: A Cultural History of Arousal*. Translated by Graham Harman. Brooklyn, N.Y.: Zone, 2007.

McGinn, Bernard. "God as Eros: Metaphysical Foundations of Christian Mysticism." In *New Perspectives on Historical Theology. Essays in Memory of John Meyendorff*, edited by Bradley Nassif. Grand Rapids, Mich.: Eerdmans, 1996, 189–209.

———. "Love, Knowledge, and Mystical Union in the Western Christian Tradition." In *Mystical Union in Judaism, Christianity, and Islam: An Ecumenical Dialogue*, edited by Moshe Idel and Bernard McGinn. New York: Continuum 1996, 59–86.

———. *The Presence of God*. Vols. 1–3. New York: Crossroads, 1992–98.

———. "Topics of Desire: Mystical Interpretation of the *Song of Songs*." In *That Others May Know and Love: Essays in Honor of Zachary Hayes, OFM*, edited by Michael F. Cusato and F. Edward Coughlin. St. Bonaventure, N.Y.: Franciscan Institute, 1997, 133–58.

Mommaers, Paul. "Is Hadewijch Emotioneel?" In *Emoties in de Middeleeuwen*, edited by R. E. V. Stuip and C. Vellekoop. Hilversum: Verloren, 1998), 135–56.

Nagy, Piroska. *Le don des larmes au Moyen Age. Un instrument spirituel en quête d'institution*. Paris: Albin Michel, 2000.

Origen. *Commentaire sur le Cantique des cantiques*. Vol. 1. Edited by Luc Brésard, Henri Crouzel, and Marcel Borret. Paris: Cerf, 1991.

Peter of Ailly. *Opuscula spiritualia*. Douai, 1634.

Rahner, Karl. "La doctrine des 'sens spirituels' au Moyen-Age, en particulier chez Bonaventure." *Revue d'ascétique et de mystique* 14 (1933): 263–99.

———. "Le début d'une doctrine des cinq sens spirituels chez Origène. *Revue d'ascétique et de mystique* 13 (1932): 113–45.

Rudolf of Biberach. *De septem itineribus aeternitatis*. Nachdruck der Ausgabe von Peltier 1866 mit einer Einleitung in die lateinische Überlieferung und Corrigenda zum Text, edited by Margot Schmidt. Stuttgart: Frommann-Holzboog, 1985.

———. *Die siben strassen zu got*. Revidierte hochalemannische Übertragung nach der Handschrift Einsiedeln 278 mit hochdeutscher Übersetzung. Synoptische Ausgabe, edited by Margot Schmidt. Stuttgart: Frommann-Holzboog, 1985.

Rudy, Gordon. *Mystical Language of Sensation in the Middle Ages*. London: Routledge, 2002.

Ruh, Kurt. *Geschichte der abendländischen Mystik*. Vol. 2. *Frauenmystik und Franziskanische Mystik der Frühzeit*. Munich: Beck, 1993.

Schuppisser, Fritz Oskar. "Schauen mit den Augen des Herzens: Zur Methodik der spätmittelalterlichen Passionsmeditation, besonders in der Devotio Moderna und bei den Augustinern." In *Die Passion Christi in Literatur und Kunst des Spätmittelalters*, edited by Walter Haug and Burghart Wachinger. Tübingen: Niemeyer, 1993, 169–210.

Sorabji, Richard. *Emotion and Peace of Mind: From Stoic Agitation to Christian Temptation*. Oxford: Oxford University Press, 2000.

Spijker, Ineke van 't. "De ordening van affecten. Kloosterleven in de twaalfde eeuw." In *Emoties in De Middeleeuwen*, edited by R. E. V. Stuip and C. Vellekoop. Hilversum: Verloren, 1998, 115–33.

Tkacz, Catherine Brown. "Singing Women's Words as Sacramental Mimesis." *Recherches de théologie ancienne et médiévale* 70 (2003): 275–328.

Turner, Denys. *Eros and Allegory: Medieval Exegesis of the Song of Songs*. Kalamazoo, Mich.: Cistercian, 1995.

William of Saint Thierry. *De contemplando Deo*. Edited by Jacques Hourlier. Paris: Cerf, 1959.

———. *Das St. Trudperter Hohelied: Eine Lehre der Liebenden Gotteserkenntnis*. Edited by Friedrich Ohly, in collaboration with Nicola Kleine. Frankfurt: Deutscher Klassiker Verlag, 1998.

CHAPTER 21

KIERKEGAARD

DAVID KANGAS

THIS essay explores the intersection of religion and emotion in the thought of Søren Kierkegaard (1813–1855). Kierkegaard's thought has been enormously influential, having inspired twentieth-century existentialism (Heidegger, Sartre), neoorthodox theology (Barth, Bultmann), as well as various strands of postmodernism (Levinas, Derrida). Central to this inspiration, no doubt, is the extraordinary role the emotions—or, more generally, affectivity—play in Kierkegaard's analyses of human existence. Coming after German idealism and Romanticism, and giving extraordinary new life to the heritage of pietism, Kierkegaard finds in the affective life of human beings the key disclosures concerning our being-in-the-world. The emotions are philosophically central. Not only that, but Kierkegaardian "religion" takes shape in terms of certain affects and virtues that emerge in face of such existential disclosures.

A full account of Kierkegaard's thinking on religion and emotion, especially in relation to contemporary discussions, is not possible here.[1] However, it is possible to focus on certain key moments in his thought in order to illuminate at least the general horizon of a larger picture.

I shall begin by exploring how Kierkegaard frames the problem of emotion in terms of his understanding of selfhood. In particular, I look at the way Kierkegaard's phenomenology challenges an understanding that links emotions to judgments (whether cognitive or evaluative). The latter understanding, an inheritance of Aristotle, though reprised within Stoicism and neo-Stoicism, depends on a classical ontology that privileges determination, measure, presence, and intentionality. For the "classical" tradition, emotions offer thematic content about the world, guide moral reasoning and decision-making, predispose one toward certain virtues or vices, and can be altered by a resolution toward right thinking.

By contrast, Kierkegaard situates his analysis of emotion within an entirely different world: that of philosophical modernity—whose first decisive statement is to be found in the philosophy of Kant. Philosophical modernity signifies that self-consciousness cannot be analyzed through ontological categories derived from the world of things, that is, from what is simply given, present at hand. The analysis of self-consciousness must proceed through an immanent analysis of self-consciousness's own laws of reflection. However, as soon as self-consciousness can no longer discover a measure or norm for itself in what is given (worldly reality on hand), once it becomes a law unto itself, it opens itself to an experience of *indetermination*—Kierkegaard will say, an experience of "nothing"—that breaks the contours of the classical account of emotion.

Important for Kierkegaard are emotions, such as anxiety, boredom, and despair, that lack an "aboutness" or intentionality. To remain faithful to the phenomenology of such emotions is, for Kierkegaard, finally to contest the fundamental ontology of the classical world: namely, the one that links reality to *determination* (measure, form, limit, ideality). What cannot be captured within the categories that determine something in terms of its ideal "whatness," or essence—above all, the "singularity" of the person—emerges as central. One could say Kierkegaard's account of emotions, then, "deconstructs" classical ontology. That is the first point.

More constructively, though, Kierkegaard keys his understanding of "transparent" human existence—which is to say, existence not deceiving itself concerning its basic reality—off of the experience of indetermination. The transparent self is for Kierkegaard the religious self. Yet we should not too quickly assume we know what "the religious" means. The religious self is for Kierkegaard, as I shall show, the self that lets itself be guided by the "nothing that interlaces human existence" into a dis-illusioned understanding of the finitude of the self. The religious attitude is one that "makes use of," so to speak, the nothing disclosed in objectless emotions in order to disabuse the self of its illusions of infinitude. Put the other way, the religious attitude does not flee or suppress the disclosure offered in the experience of nonbeing. Nonbeing becomes a reliable teacher if a person is capable of letting go of what is for Kierkegaard, following a long tradition in Lutheran pietism and reaching back at least to Meister Eckhart, the most stubborn of self-deceptions: that the self possesses itself.

The latter, however, is an idea that is powerfully reinforced, even driven to its extreme expression, in the philosophies of German idealism (Kant, Fichte, early Schelling, and Hegel). Thus to make sense of Kierkegaard's thinking on emotion and its connection to religious consciousness, it will be necessary to consider, however briefly, the intellectual context of German idealism. To that I turn now.

Emotions in Kierkegaard

The Modern Subject: Kierkegaard's Self in Context

As is any theory of emotion, Kierkegaard's is deeply embedded within a metaphysical problematic: more exactly, within a conception of what the self is. It must first be said that, in the context of German idealism, the meaning of the self (or "subject") is not merely one problematic among others, but a radical and primary problematic. If I could summarize the movement of German idealism, what Richard Kroner has called the greatest period of intellectual accomplishment since the Greeks, within a single sentence, it would be this: it is the effort to justify the radical priority of *self-consciousness* to any *consciousness of* an object. In many ways, J. G. Fichte provides the clearest statement of the governing idea of idealism: "I can be conscious of any object only on condition that I am also conscious of myself, that is, of the conscious subject. This proposition is incontrovertible."[2] Consciousness depends on and presupposes self-consciousness. But self-consciousness, precisely as such, seems to offer radical possibilities for explanation: if consciousness is conditioned by self-consciousness, and if, on the basis of the immediate access one seems to have with one's own consciousness, one exhaustively could set forth the basic operations of the latter (presumably they are not infinite), then one could articulate a total "system" of self-consciousness. A "science" (*Wissenschaft*) of consciousness would be possible. The early Schelling and especially Hegel were the main inheritors of this quest.

Though few today hold out hope for such a science, one should avoid dismissing the attempt simply as an act of intellectual hubris. What Fichte is after is something very simple and very powerful: namely, to articulate the basis for a radical critique of "dogmatic" thinking, by which he means a thinking that attaches itself to a standpoint that is simply "given" and thus arbitrary. One has to show, thought Fichte, how meaning is *made* through the activity of self-consciousness and not merely *found*. One has to discover the *interests* that underlie knowledge—that alone is the critical task of the thinker.

Fichte was thus perhaps the first thinker in the West systematically to link meaning in a radical way to the *meaning-making* of self-consciousness. He thus opens the door simultaneously to Marx's critique of ideology and to twentieth-century existentialism's notion of radical choice. Perhaps more broadly, he articulates and tries philosophically to justify the modern sentiment that the subject has the capability to, and is in any case bound to, shape, determine, and even "create" itself. In his aptly named text *The Vocation of Man*, Fichte is utterly clear about the implications of his position:

> I am, therefore, to shape my own way of thinking for myself and, under that presupposition, will do so necessarily. I will then be absolutely independent... the

innermost spirit of my spirit is not an alien spirit but is simply produced by myself in the truest sense of the word. *I am thoroughly my own creation.*[3]

The culture of modernity is the culture of the self-defining, self-creating subject, that is, one who decides radically concerning the meaning of human being, its possibilities, limits, social and political organization, and so on. Subjectivity decides concerning itself in every way.

This excursus on idealist metaphysics, however brief and inadequate, has been necessary to provide the conceptual and historical context for Kierkegaard's discussion of the self and emotion.

The opening passages of *Sickness unto Death* provide a thumbnail sketch of Kierkegaard's psychology. As will be seen, he develops a conception of selfhood that is deeply related to those found within German idealism. What is more important, however, is to see how he contests and even deconstructs this framework even while he appropriates it. The language is technical and the issues are thorny, but it is absolutely necessary to wade into them in order to have a sense of what, for Kierkegaard, constitutes the *origin* of emotions.

I will quote the famously tricky but crucially important passage, make a few comments, and then situate and explicate it within the context of German idealism. Kierkegaard writes:

> A human being is spirit. But what is spirit? Spirit is the self. But what is the self? The self is a relation that relates itself to itself or is the relation's relating itself to itself in the relation; the self is not the relation but is the relations' relating itself to itself. A human being is a synthesis of the infinite and the finite, of the temporal and the eternal, of freedom and necessity, in short, a synthesis.[4]

This can be translated as follows: the self is first of all not some underlying "thing" that then is capable of relating to itself, to objects, to others, and so on. The self is first of all and originally a *relating* of itself to itself, a reflexive turning toward itself. The self is a verbal rather than a substantive. Relating to itself is what the self is, not what it does; or rather, it *is* what it *does*, and what it does is reflexively turn upon itself. In addition—and this is the first decisive complication—the self's reflexive turning toward itself accomplishes a "synthesis" of elements that cannot, in fact, be synthesized (finite and infinite, temporal and eternal, freedom and necessity). Without entering into all of the complications of this notion, which have to do with the relation of Kierkegaard's thought to Lutheran pietism and Christian Neoplatonism, we could say simply this: the self is essentially *ambiguous*. It can never simply identify itself with any definite object (anything finite) or lose itself in a sea of indeterminacy (the infinite). It can neither possess itself nor lose itself; it can never simply *be*, but must always forge its being by synthesizing opposing elements.

The self is thus essentially active, originally self-relating, but always also in question concerning itself. So far, this puts pressure on idealist notions, but does not go beyond the idealist conception of selfhood as self-creative. There is however one final qualification in Kierkegaard's conception of the self: "Such a relation that relates itself to itself, a self, must either have established itself or have been established by another."[5] This is the passage where Kierkegaard opens up something really new.

The core of the idealist notion of the self is that the self establishes or "posits" itself through its radical reflexivity. Its power to posit itself—which means not only to endow itself with predicates but also, more originally, to found itself in being— is crucial to upholding the metaphysics of an autonomous ego. More basic, more original, more founding than its relation to anything "other," the self relates reflexively to itself. Now, on the one hand, Kierkegaard does clearly appropriate this idea: the self only is in relating to itself, and by the latter Kierkegaard can only mean that the self must posit itself. There is an "I" only in *saying* "I." On the other hand, Kierkegaard raises the possibility that even the self-positing, autonomous subject might—without ceasing to be that—refer to some *further condition* for its act of self-positing. He raises the possibility that what idealism takes to be radically first, the movement of self-positing, might in fact be enabled by some "other." He questions, in other words, how original and autonomous the domain of self-consciousness really is. If self-consciousness itself is conditioned and enabled by an other, then its power to create itself will run into an essential limit.

What is important for our purposes here, however, is that Kierkegaard pursues this question, arguing for a position which finds self-consciousness enabled by an "other" it cannot control or integrate, by way of laying out a phenomenology of despair, that is, in his account of emotions. In *Sickness unto Death*, for example, he tries to show how despair, which for him is something like the panic that ensues from the sense of being unable to be rid of oneself, cannot be understood or explained except on condition that self-consciousness *both* posits itself radically *and* finds itself posited by an "other" it cannot assimilate. It is the suffocating experience that "a person cannot rid himself of the relation to himself any more than he can rid himself of his self, which, after all, is one and the same thing, since the self is the relation to oneself."[6] The emblem of despair is the terminally ill patient who cannot die, the person for whom life persists, beyond any meaning, almost in defiance of the person's will to persist. Despair is "death dying," the persistence of life beyond meaning. The autonomous subject, primordially active, cannot despair; nor could a subject without the radical power to posit itself. The despairing subject knows itself as cleft in two at a point it cannot master. It experiences the torment of being unable either *to be* or *not to be* itself.[7]

For Kierkegaard, then, that the self is "spirit" means that it stands face to face with the tragic double bind that the self can neither *be* nor *not be* anything determinate. The self hovers between being and nonbeing and has to "synthesize" them. Yet, owing to the specific philosophical heritage of the West, being (determination, form, limit, objectivity, etc.) has always received a definite priority. The self desires to be; the modern self desires to be through its own effort. Thus the impossibility to be, announced where the *indeterminate* steals into situations and projects, becomes in modernity the "object" of a particularly intimate horror. Hamlet, for Kierkegaard the paradigmatic figure of the tragic double bind, cannot even become nothing through suicide without considering the "rub" of an inexorable return to being.

In a moment I will consider other examples of emotion in Kierkegaard's works. What I wish especially to underscore at the moment is this: the emotions that interest Kierkegaard philosophically and religiously are those that disclose such a tragic double bind within the self—in particular, by bringing it to an affection of itself as originally enabled by a factor it can never possess, catch sight of, bring under its reflective control, and so on. This factor, referred to simply as what is "other" to self-positing consciousness, is for it an abyss of indetermination. To speak of it is to speak of "the nothing that interlaces all human existence." The *critical* emotions for Kierkegaard (i.e., the philosophically and religiously interesting ones), then, are those that disclose "the nothing." This, we shall see, implies a different understanding of the place of emotions within philosophy and religion than is often given in contemporary accounts.

To continue, then, I will consider some contemporary accounts of emotion, most of which reprise the classical ontology of Stoicism, and then show how Kierkegaard's thought differs.

Undoing (Neo-)Stoicism

According to a dominant strand of contemporary theory (e.g., Martha Nussbaum, Robert Solomon, Robert Roberts) emotions constitute a fundamental tie-in to reality. Proper listening to emotions puts one in sync (though not infallibly, for emotions can deceive and can be manipulated) with *what is*; emotions attune one to the key of the world. They are always "about" something; they have "intentionality." Thus, emotions have cognitive or precognitive value (similar to sense perceptions). They embed certain cognitive and evaluative *judgments* about the world. Judgments of whatever sort—cognitive, perceptive, emotive, transcendental—serve what may be called an "apophantic" function: that is, they determine something *as* something. Judgments are thus at bottom acts of intellection. And for precisely this reason, as Stoics and neo-Stoics have emphasized, if emotions are judgments, they can be altered depending on the direction of one's thinking.

The ethical task for the human being in this context is to achieve, through right thinking—which is to say, thinking anchored to the logos, or universal intelligibility, of the world—a well-ordered emotional life. Having appropriate emotions leads to appropriate estimation of the world and thus to appropriate virtues and actions.

One point should be underscored about the Stoic and neo-Stoic theory: it depends on an understanding of reality that privileges the Greek experience of logos. What is real of reality, as opposed merely to what appears, is what has definition, form, limit, determination—in general, the real is the intelligible. Emotions are so important for the Stoics because it is there where the basically Greek philosophical experience, that is, drawing the distinction between what merely *appears* and what *is*, plays itself out. Appropriate emotions, and the dispositions toward them (i.e., the "virtues"), must therefore always be intentional, value-appraising, goal-directed, and limit-setting. Excessive, objectless, a-teleological emotion would prima facie indicate either moral aberration, an epistemic glitch, or a failure of will.

The emotions that interest Kierkegaard philosophically, however, involve a relation to what *cannot be* determined as something and thus to what can only be named as "nothing." Because they are emotions concerning "nothing," they are perhaps more accurately called "moods."[8] Here, however, it is important to notice how moods are generally handled by "classical" accounts of emotion: owing to their objectlessness, which makes them indeterminate and limitless, they are more or less systematically downgraded to the status of the secondary.[9] Moods don't provide us with the propositional content, the evaluative appraisals, or the teleological thrust that emotions do. One can get bogged down in moods that seem to have no bottom. On Greek presuppositions, the bottomless (*apeiron*) *eo ipso* does not coincide with the real. Therefore emotions (taken in the Stoic way) are regarded as the primary, governing phenomena, the real clue to our being-in-the-world.

Although there are, as Robert Roberts argues,[10] "classical themes" in Kierkegaard, his "theory of emotions" embeds a metaphysical horizon that privileges the indeterminate over the determinate, possibility over actuality, hence nonbeing over being. This will be the decisive difference.

Emotions as Existential Disclosures

The emotions that grab Kierkegaard's philosophical and religious interest are those that don't seem capable of closure, the emotions in which a person finds himself or herself suspended between beginnings and endings (e.g., in grief, anxiety, despair). The feeling of not being *able* to come to closure, except through either bad faith or violence, constitutes for Kierkegaard a kind of primordial affectivity of one's own existential reality. Indeed, it would not be too much to say that Kierkegaard's "theory of the self" as a self-relating relation that is enabled by an other is simply an effort to thematize, in terms of the conditions of its possibility, such existential affectivity. What I wish to do now is consider certain specific emotions in Kierkegaard in order to show how he exploits their disclosive possibilities for an analysis of human existence. I will consider three: boredom, anxiety, and despair.

As a way into Kierkegaard's thinking on emotions, however, I would like first to consider a short story he wrote and included in his book *The Stages on Life's Way* entitled "A Possibility."[11] It is the story of a deranged bookkeeper who is obsessed over a youthful indiscretion—namely, visiting "one of those places where, strangely enough, one pays money for a woman's contemptibleness." Drunk at the time, he cannot recall exactly what he did. Yet after a serious illness there arises for him, in the midst of this uncertainty, a far more radical concern. Kierkegaard writes:

> He was restored to health, but when he rose from his bed cured he took along with him a *possibility*, and this possibility pursued him, and he pursued this possibility in his passionate investigation, and this possibility incubated in his

silence, and this possibility animated the features of his face in many ways when he saw a child—and this possibility was that another being owed its life to him.[12]

The possibility that he *may* have fathered a child, that he can *neither* confirm it *nor* disconfirm it, pursues him to the point of derangement. And why? Because it is an event, intimately connected to his self-understanding, that can neither be said to have happened nor not to have happened; it neither is nor is not. It is an event or rather quasi event, definitive for his sense of being-in-the-world, that he cannot catch up with. He finds himself thrust into a tragic double bind from which there is no exit. What makes his situation so "dialectical" (i.e., intractably ambiguous), we are told, is that "he could never know for sure whether [his anxiety] was a result of the illness, a feverish hallucination, or whether [his illness] had actually come to the aid of his memory with a recollection of an actuality."[13] Like a disappearance for which there are no clues, his self-understanding is dominated by a void. The void, nonbeing, *pursues him* in the form of an indeterminate and indeterminable possibility that he can neither take in hand nor let go.

What, we may wonder, does this have to do with a theory of emotions? In this story the concern, anxiety, and even obsession of the bookkeeper mediates to his self-consciousness the fundamentally indeterminate character of reality itself. Reality is for Kierkegaard not "rational," it is "absurd," *in the sense that* the point of coincidence between self-consciousness and the eventfulness of the world cannot be secured in and for self-consciousness—not, at least, where existential concerns are at issue. In the above case, the event that determines the fate of the bookkeeper cannot be recollected. To recollect something presupposes that it has been. But where a quasi event is at issue, where being can neither be affirmed nor denied, recollection cannot get started—or, what is the same, it can never finish.

The intentional acts of consciousness, directed toward the world—that is, in representing it, imagining it, knowing it, judging it, remembering it, valuing it, and so on—are, it was said, ways of *constituting* meaning. Such acts neither merely presuppose meaning in the world nor passively reflect it; rather, they *make* meaning in the world. Such, at least, is the conviction of the metaphysics of modernity. What Kierkegaard's little narrative presents, however, is a case where self-consciousness bumps up against its own limit. In the obsessive, interminable concern of the bookkeeper—perhaps like the infinite passivity of Bartleby—the difference between the real and the acts of self-consciousness that attend to the real "manifests" itself. A gap appears that cannot be closed in the form of a possibility that can neither be confirmed nor disconfirmed. The gap between self-consciousness and reality manifests itself *within* self-consciousness, however, precisely in its *affective* life.

This, then, is where emotions, or at least certain emotions, function decisively in Kierkegaard's thought: they put the self in touch with that *of reality* that resists the meaning-making function of self-consciousness (the indeterminable slipperiness of reality). The emotions that really interest Kierkegaard are those that grant reality, but not meaning—that is, those where the self is deprived of its power to act as a spontaneous (i.e., self-causing) origin of meaning. Where the self cannot exit itself via some worldly meaning or an attachment to some object, it finds its own uncanny reality disclosed to it. Emotions like boredom, anxiety, and despair are the disclosure of the self to itself.

One might say this is to make too much of Kierkegaard's bookkeeper (or Melville's scrivener, for that matter). Why should such an aberrant, plainly pathological figure do such "normative" work? Yet for Kierkegaard, not unlike Freud later, the aberrant is an irreducible part of the everyday. The everyday phenomena I will consider now point to a similar disclosure of the excess of reality over meaning that Kierkegaard places at the center of his account of emotions.

Boredom

In an essay entitled "The Rotation of Crops" in *Either/Or I* (1843), Kierkegaard's first literary production, he explicitly thematizes boredom as a crucial emotion for the understanding of the self in modernity.[14] "People with experience maintain that proceeding from a basic principle," he writes, "is supposed to be very reasonable; I yield to them and proceed from the basic principle that all people are boring. Or is there anyone who would be boring enough to contradict me in this regard?"[15] Boredom so shapes the cultural horizon of modernity that it constitutes something like an invulnerable first principle: one cannot speak against it without thereby witnessing to it and reaffirming it.[16] Who would be so boring as to offer three reasons why all people are not boring? Boredom, in short, can't be argued with. Reasons for not being bored simply become fuel for the boredom machine. To combat boredom, one has to "rotate the crops"—in other words, continually vary one's routine.

But what does boredom as an emotion show concerning a human being's being-in-the-world? How can one account for boredom as a phenomenon? What generally characterizes boredom is the inability to have one's attention engaged, an inability to derive meaning from one's projects. In boredom the world manifests itself as devoid of meaning. For Kierkegaard, however, this disclosure is highly significant: boredom must be seen, he thinks, as an affective state in which the void, that is, nonbeing, is disclosed. Kierkegaard writes: "Boredom rests upon the nothing that interlaces existence; its dizziness is infinite, like that which comes from looking down into a bottomless abyss [*Afgrund*]."[17] The nothing, the abyss, signifies what interrupts the engagement in the world according to projects. The bored subject is the subject who can no longer regard projects as fundamental, that is, who is unable any longer to relate to projects as a source of meaning. Projecting ends, or projecting oneself as an end, in a goal-directed movement of actualization—something that in modernity a "subject" does par excellence—is seen as a ludicrous response to the unending reality of time.

Thus in boredom the excess of time over meaning opens up and manifests itself. This involves the experience of discovering the way that self-consciousness *is not* the origin of meaning, does *not* reign sovereignly over its temporality, *cannot* enable itself. It is the experience of being *un-able* to flee oneself toward an object (an interest) and so of being "stuck" to oneself. In boredom, the self cannot not be. It is forced to relate to itself without the support of a "meaning," hence forced to deal with its own nonbeing. Boredom is a kind of death the subject nevertheless cannot die (hence the appropriateness of the expression "dying of boredom").

This account of boredom differs sharply from accounts in the contemporary theory of emotion. Actually, in the literature on emotion, especially that of neo-Stoicism, boredom is rarely analyzed. No doubt this is because it cannot so easily be taken into the judgment paradigm of emotion.

Robert Roberts, however, is one contemporary theorist who does discuss it. He interprets boredom in light of his own account of emotions as "concern based construals" as follows: "Let us say that the defining proposition for boredom is, *It is very important for me to be interested, absorbed, to have my attention engaged, but everything I currently behold, and everything I currently might do, is uninteresting; may I soon be free from this state of mind.*"[18] By allowing boredom to speak, as it were, he turns it into an interested, goal-directed subject. He interprets the disinterestedness of boredom, in other words, as only another modality of interest. This would say that consciousness stands always in relation to being, to what is, and is never a relation to what is not, the nothing. It is an account of boredom is entirely in keeping with a classical account of emotions as ways of construing or making judgments about reality.[1]

We cannot pause too long to criticize Roberts's account on Kierkegaardian grounds, except to say that Kierkegaard's bored aesthete may find it a touch boring.[20] The point to emphasize is that he treats boredom as an emotion in which nonbeing is disclosed. This is true also for *anxiety*.

Anxiety

As a second example, let us look briefly at Kierkegaard's influential discussion of anxiety in his book *The Concept of Anxiety*. Again, Kierkegaard's author (one "Vigilius Haufniensis") distinguishes anxiety from fear on the basis of the fact that it is an emotion that lacks an object (intentionality): "I must point out that [anxiety] is altogether different from fear and similar concepts that refer to something definite, whereas anxiety is freedom's actuality as the possibility of possibility."[21] Kierkegaard raises the question of anxiety in a dogmatic theological context in order to account for the irruption of "sin." Nevertheless, he resolutely sticks to anxiety as a "psychological" (we would say "phenomenological") problematic. At issue in his analysis is how to account for the transition from the nondifferentiated identity of subject and object in "immediacy" to self-consciousness aware of itself in its distinction from everything else. What allows self-consciousness reflexively to grasp and explicitly to posit itself as a (unique) self?

According to Kierkegaard, anxiety is an emotion that draws the self simultaneously out of itself and into itself, so to speak. Anxiety solicits (or rather seduces) the undifferentiated self into an explicit positing of itself. It is, and not only in the "first" instance, but throughout life, the engine of self-definition. As with boredom, Kierkegaard's analysis focuses squarely on the way anxiety manifests nonbeing in the form of indeterminate possibility. Anxiety is "freedom's disclosure to itself," the disclosure that "freedom is infinite and arises out of nothing."[22] The infinitude of freedom becomes manifest in the emotion of anxiety.

Yet what does it mean that freedom is "infinite"? It only means that freedom, the power of the self to posit and determine itself, to decide concerning the meaning of its being, is not intrinsically keyed into any determined order of things. Freedom, in short, has no intrinsic goal or telos. Yet this is not an antinomian motif. It signifies, rather, that freedom has to suffer the excess of its own possibility. Freedom is a burden to itself.

This notion of freedom is completely opposed to the classical ontology of freedom (found in Aristotle, Stoicism, Aquinas and neo-Stoicism) according to which freedom signifies acting in accordance with already given ends, that is, some "natural order" of things. The actuality of freedom, that is, of selfhood, is constituted not vis-à-vis some definite possibility (even vaguely conceived) but vis-à-vis "the possibility *of* possibility." In anxiety, according to Kierkegaard, the self affectively grasps and is grasped by its absolute difference from an "order of things." It finds itself exposed to a radical ambiguity, a double bind, in the face of which it is simultaneously drawn and repulsed. Kierkegaard describes this dynamic:

> How does spirit relate itself to itself and to its conditionality? It relates itself as anxiety. Do away with itself, the spirit cannot; lay hold of itself, it cannot, as long as it has itself outside of itself. Nor can [the human being] sink down into the vegetative, for he is qualified as spirit; flee away from anxiety, he cannot, for he loves it; really love it, he cannot, for he flees from it.[23]

With the relation to the nothing disclosed in anxiety—that is to say, in freedom's relation to itself as the possibility of possibility—the self becomes entangled in a "sympathetic antipathy" and an "antipathetic sympathy."[24] As an emotion, then, anxiety has the same structure as boredom: it is an affect that mediates that of reality that remains indeterminately suspended between being and nonbeing. Yet, even more than boredom, anxiety puts the screws on the self by forcing it to deal with an ambiguity that can neither be eliminated nor reduced.

For Kierkegaard, anxiety constitutes the milieu in which "sin" is enacted as a fundamental will toward controlling the abyss of indeterminate possibility. In the face of the latter, the self wills violently either to be or not to be; it refuses the position of being unable either to be or not to be. It refuses the tragic double bind. Religion, I will show now, is for Kierkegaard the *nonrefusal* of the tragic double bind. It lets itself be taught by it. Yet the problem of relating to the nothing is not for Kierkegaard a narrowly religious problem. Much of modern culture, he thinks, can be understood as the effort, more or less systematically, to ward off the torments of anxiety and boredom. Above all he finds this, almost a century before Heidegger's critique of "das Mann," in the tendencies toward homogenization, bureaucratization, mass entertainment, and in general in the powerful will toward *quantifying* all phenomena. Modern culture remains fixated on the domain of what is calculable. *Everything* must be made calculable and so made safe for self-consciousness and its projects. And yet to the extent that everything cannot be made calculable, modern self-consciousness will remain afflicted by boredom, anxiety, and despair. The deranged bookkeeper, very capable of balancing accounts, will perhaps still walk among us.

Religious Affection: Being Today

The task now is to consider how Kierkegaard's account of emotions plays out in his account of "the religious." In his *Concluding Unscientific Postscript*, Kierkegaard makes a distinction between "religion A," which signifies religion as a human phenomenon apart from any particular dogmatic context, and "religion B," which signifies Christian religion.[25] For my purposes here, I will focus primarily on the more general sense of religiousness and leave aside a more nuanced discussion of Kierkegaard's concept of Christianity.[26] This will allow me to highlight how Kierkegaard links religion and emotion.

Kierkegaard's primary articulation of religion occurs in a series of works he wrote parallel to his more philosophical and aesthetic texts. He calls them "edifying discourses" (*Opbyggelige Taler*). These writings, which fill thousands of pages, are still marginalized in the scholarship on Kierkegaard.[27] This is unfortunate, for they contain some of Kierkegaard's most striking and original thinking.

The problematic of religion in Kierkegaard is inseparable from that of overcoming bad faith concerning one's temporality and finitude. Like Schleiermacher before him, and in sharp contrast to Hegel, Kierkegaard links religion to the task of aligning self-consciousness and its representations of the real with reality "itself." Religion is a work of unlearning the desire to be infinite and penetrating into one's finitude. Schleiermacher links religion to a "feeling of absolute dependence." Hegel, by contrast, understands religion as a preparatory mode for what he called "absolute knowledge"—a knowledge, achieved through philosophical thinking, in which self-consciousness knows itself to be "all of reality," that is, infinite. Thus Kierkegaard stands firmly in the Schleiermachian line of religion. Nevertheless, as will become evident, religion for Kierkegaard is neither thinking nor feeling. Though the affective life of human beings is the center of his thinking, religion is for him fundamentally an act, a posture, an attitude whose basic sense, I shall argue, is captured in the phrase "being-today." It is a joy in existence itself, a joy inseparable from suffering.

In order to elicit Kierkegaard's conception of the religious and to link it to his account of emotions I will focus on just a few fundamental texts. Nothing will substitute for a full analysis of the strange world that opens up in the *Opbyggelige Taler*, but at least one may glimpse the main contours of this world through the discourses on concern, expectancy, patience, and joy.

Concern

Religion is for Kierkegaard a matter of "interiority." This does *not* mean, however, that it is merely private or individualistic matter. It means that religion is a matter of engaging *fundamental concerns* of human beings. In a discourse entitled "Strengthening in the Inner Being,"[28] Kierkegaard develops the notion of a fundamental concern (*Bekymring*). A concern is a kind of transcendental affect, that is, an affective tonality that puts one in touch with the enigmatic fact of existence itself. The awakening of concern, a complex notion that is inseparable from anxiety, signals for Kierkegaard the opening of an "inner life." Religion is a way of letting oneself undergo concern. Kierkegaard writes:

> Not until the moment when there awakens in his soul a concern about what meaning the world has for him and he for the world, about what meaning everything within him by which he himself belongs to the world has for him and he therein for the world—only then does the inner being announce its presence in the *concern*.[29]

Concern arises, and with it the possibility of a religious comportment toward existence, when one's place in the world becomes questionable. Concern refers to those moments where guiding coordinates—whether social, cultural, philosophical, religious, and so on—lose their power to orient one in the world. Concern coincides with the experience of a loss of one's foundations.

As an example of concern, Kierkegaard draws the picture of a prosperous business person. Prosperity might well lead, via cultural or theological norms, to a sense of confidence and stability concerning one's being-in-the-world—for example, to regarding oneself as "blessed." Yet, where concern awakens, the stable sense of self gets dirempted between contradictory estimates: "How indeed, would a person through this knowledge be sure that his prosperity is God's grace, so that he dares to rejoice in it and safely devote himself to it, or that it is God's wrath and is only deceitfully hiding the abyss of perdition from him so that his downfall might be all the more terrible?"[30] Is prosperity a sign of blessing or curse? Who in the midst of concern could say?

It is this kind of radical existential uncertainty concerning one's self-understanding that religion relates to. Religion is not a quelling of concern via some propositional content, but just the opposite: it is the risk of letting go of the need for existential security. Religion lets itself "sink deeper and deeper into concern," it lets itself be strengthened by concern, because it learns that concern "prevents [one] from being mistaken about life."[31] Life holds no certainties, and the affect of concern, if one lets it speak, allows the opportunity to become inwardly convinced of this. This, at least, is how the religious attitude uses concern—namely, as an opportunity to disabuse itself of stubborn illusions in its self-knowledge. To allow concern to guide one into a more sober knowledge of one's being-in-the-world, Kierkegaard thinks, leads one to seeing one's own existence—the sheer fact of being—as "a good and perfect gift."[32] One's own existence becomes the "witness" of an affirmation that resides at the heart of ambiguity.

Expectancy

As we have seen, the basic "structure" of the self is for Kierkegaard its ambiguity, its inability either to be or not to be. The self is beyond being and nonbeing—hence, its anguish. In the *Opbyggelige Taler*, though, this double bind appears as the self's anguish over its *temporality*. The present neither is nor is not; it is always already "underway." Yet for modern self-consciousness, which understands itself in terms of its power to project itself toward the future and to realize itself in realizing ends, the always "underway" character of the present produces an essential instability. The self finds itself caught in a double bind between two temporalities: on the one hand, it understands itself temporally in terms of being on the way toward ends it has projected for itself; on the other hand, there is the suddenness of reality itself that comes as an interruption to the temporality of self-consciousness. Thus there arises an essential problem: how existentially to deal with the future—not the future we are able to represent to ourselves, the future that stands continuously in relation to the present, but the future *as* what we cannot determine, the future that comes as the *unforeseeable* to interrupt the present.

The abyss of the future as the unrepresentable and the incalculable again manifests that excess of possibility that for Kierkegaard is central. In the discourse "The Expectancy of Faith" from 1843,[33] Kierkegaard presents religion as a certain posture—one of "expectancy"—toward the future. It gives a very clear sense as to how religion navigates what for Kierkegaard are the fundamental emotions.

The future, Kierkegaard suggests, is something that both does and does not have its origin in the projective power of self-consciousness. He writes: "The future is not; it borrows its power from [the person] himself, and when it has tricked him out of that it presents itself externally as the enemy he has to conquer."[34] Without consciousness aware of itself there could be no future. The future only *is* on condition that someone is *conscious of* it—that is to say, in terms of some intentionality toward the future. On the other hand, the future cannot be reduced to the intentionality of self-consciousness; it withholds itself. Thus consciousness of the future becomes irreparably split, a split legible in the "trick" that consciousness, through its awareness of temporality, becomes an enemy to itself. Kierkegaard writes: "When a person struggles with the future, he learns that however strong he is otherwise, there is one enemy that is stronger—himself; there is one enemy he cannot conquer by himself, and that is himself."[35] Through its relation to the future, then, self-consciousness is prevented from achieving a stable sense of presence to itself. Consciousness is estranged from itself.

"Faith" for Kierkegaard is, in the first instance, a readiness to shoulder this estrangement and so a capacity to stay within the double bind of temporality. It does not flee its temporality, but enters into it. But how does it do so? This is where Kierkegaard's discourse presents the possibility for cultivating an attitude of expectation: the attitude of faith expects "victory"—not victory concerning this or that but victory simply as such (without any representable content). The expectation of victory, which Kierkegaard carefully distinguishes from wish-fulfillment,[36] is emblematic of the kind of affection he links to religion. It is not an emotion, however, that is simply had. Inseparable from a "virtue," it is an emotion that must be won through a difficult praxis of learning to affirm the future as the incalculable, the unforeseeable. To affirm *what is coming*, in the absence of any knowledge of it, is for Kierkegaard to conquer oneself; it is to go beyond estrangement—to go "beyond" it not by putting it behind one, but rather by wearing it lightly, so to speak.

If one is capable of affirming the future—which is to say, capable, in the now, of affirming the totality of what one's life *will have been*—then for Kierkegaard one will have dealt radically with the future and its double bind. "The believer," Kierkegaard writes, "is finished with the future *before* he begins with the present."[37] The affirmation of the future as the incalculable is identical to the affirmation of the present in its basic character as always already "under way." Kierkegaard's discourse thus suggests the possibility of living wholly in the present *by way of* an embrace of the excess of possibility. Expectancy turns to a kind of groundless joy in the present. It is a kind of joy in existence as such, a joy unmediated by the successes or failures of projects. As to how one does this, Kierkegaard offers no road map. In a discourse titled "To Gain One's Soul in Patience," however, he does present patience as a crucial religious "virtue."

Patience

The discourse "To Gain One's Soul in Patience" addresses the question of what it means to discover the reality of the self as distinct from its representations of itself. To "gain one's soul" is to come to knowledge of oneself. Religion is for Kierkegaard always self-knowledge. Yet "knowledge" is here not perhaps the best word, for what is at issue is to allow the fundamental affectivity of the self to "speak." For Kierkegaard, there is a direct opposition between the *affection* the soul has of itself and its capability to *represent* itself to itself through intentional, reflective acts. Autoaffection opposes autorepresentation (and, as in the more radical case of Fichte, autogenesis). The reality of the self is disclosed in *feeling*, not knowledge (in particular, as has been said, in the feelings wherein the self feels its double bind).

To the extent, then, that religion involves the disclosure of the reality of the self, it is fundamentally a feeling. To this extent, Kierkegaard is similar to Schleiermacher. Yet, as "To Gain One's Soul in Patience" makes clear, *religious* feeling is not simply given or immediate; rather, it emerges as a "later immediacy" through an intentional process. Religious sentiments are gained or *acquired* in exactly the same way that one speaks of an "acquired taste." The feelings do not precede but arise in the midst of the doing. To this extent, "religious" affections, like expectancy and joy, as opposed to "transcendental-existential" affections, like anxiety and boredom, are always mediated by intentional acts (and, implicitly, by cultural practices).[38] They are the outcome of a way of posturing oneself in the world.

Patience, I suggest, is for Kierkegaard the intentional praxis par excellence through which a self discovers its reality and so experiences the joy of being simply. It is how one "gains one's soul." What, then, is patience? In his discourse, he makes a sharp distinction between patience as it is normally understood—namely, as the *deferral* of a pleasure in the name of some further object—and the patience whereby one gains one's soul. The fisherman has patience toward the end of catching fish. Once the end is achieved, patience gives way to enjoyment. In this sense, patience is a *means*. Religious patience, by contrast, is no mere means, but rather both means and end, condition and conditioned—both the *way* of gaining and *that which is gained*. What one gains in patience is nothing other than patience. At issue, then, is a kind of self-augmentation of patience, what Kierkegaard calls "a coming into existence within its own presupposition."[39] In this sense, patience refers to a deferral that is absolute, that is, not toward or in the name of some other end.

What sense is one to make of an *absolute* deferral? And in what way does one "gain one's soul" in the midst of it? We get a sense of this from Kierkegaard's reflections on what it means to "gain." Recalling the paradox of the acquisition of knowledge from Plato's dialogue *Meno*, Kierkegaard points to a "contradiction" found at the heart of this gaining: to gain implies not having, but where the *soul* is to be gained, it would seem that the soul could not gain itself unless it already possessed itself (for who would gain it?); and yet if the soul already possessed itself, it could not *gain* itself. Kierkegaard writes: "But if a person possesses his soul, he certainly does not need to gain it, and if he does not possess it, how then can he gain it, since the soul itself is the ultimate condition that is presupposed in every acquiring, consequently also in gaining the soul."[40] How is this knot to be loosed?

This knot points to the reality of self-consciousness as "a contradiction and a self-contradiction." Kierkegaard continues: "If [the soul] were not in contradiction, it would be lost in the life of the world; if it were not self-contradiction, movement [i.e., that of gaining] would be impossible."[41] That the self is a contradiction and self-contradiction means, once again, that it neither is nor is not (or both is and is not). That the soul is beyond being and nonbeing marks out its fundamental difference from "objects," which always either are or are not, and for which Aristotle's law of noncontradiction holds unimpeachable sway. Because the soul is beyond being and nonbeing, it both possesses and does not possess itself. It can be gained. But to gain the soul requires patience.

Now we can see what patience means: it means allowing one's irreducibility to being/nonbeing to come more and more freely to the fore. It means letting go the will and desire for what can only be had at the incipience of one's life, and even then not completely: namely, the oceanic sense of well-being. More plainly, the absolute deferral of patience signifies the willingness to let go the desire for absolute security. In patience one gains the soul in its nonabsoluteness—that is, the soul in its distinction from conceptions of itself. Patience, then, is not a means for dealing with temporality when it won't "cooperate" with one's projects, but rather a way of entering into temporality in its underway-ness. What this finally means is the achieved sense of "being today." To this I turn.

Joy: Being Today

Religion refers to an existential attitude toward nonbeing or indeterminate possibility. Reality overflows what can be anticipated of it, yet self-consciousness makes itself the origin of a temporality through its very act of existence. Hence, we have seen, the self remains ever caught in a double bind between two temporalities: one it controls, the other it does not. In truth, though, Kierkegaard's texts imply, the temporality it does not control, the one that arrives suddenly, "from nowhere," will have the last word (that is to say, we are mortal). Coming to grips with this temporality is the work through which the religious self emerges. As an *accomplished* movement, though, religion is for Kierkegaard a breakthrough to joy, to "being today" (*at være idag*). It is an existential attitude that knows nothing of tomorrow, only today.

Such religious joy is the theme of a number of Kierkegaard's discourses. The most striking of these is a discourse upon Matthew 6:26, a text he often returned to: "Behold the birds of the air: they sown not, neither do they reap."[42] In this discourse, the lilies of the field and the birds of the air are taken as instructors in joy. Joy signifies "being present to oneself." "Joy," he writes, "is the present tense, with the whole emphasis upon the *present*."[43] It is, then, the opposite of the *estrangement* from oneself that is so fundamental for Kierkegaard's understanding of self-consciousness. However, one should not conclude that religious joy is either a simple experience or the negation of estrangement. As with all the religious emotions in Kierkegaard, joy is an "*acquired* originality," that is, an emotion that arises only in the enactment of a certain stance toward existence itself. Moreover, such enactment is never simply accomplished—it remains a task. Thus, Kierkegaard's discourse on joy takes shape more as a discourse on the *possibility* of joy than as a description of its actuality. It will be necessary to say that joy lives within estrangement.

According to Kierkegaard, the lilies of the field and the birds of the air are appropriate teachers in joy because they are "unconditionally joyful." That is, they are not joyful over this or that condition, joyful vis-à-vis some realized purpose, but "joy itself." Once again one should particularly underscore the fact that joy is not *about* this or that, it does not refer to some state of affairs or gauge itself in terms of ends and purposes. Unconditional or absolute joy is rather about "nothing." It is not therefore a determinate judgment.

The lilies of the field and the birds of the air communicate a joy that has no referent by their very being. Yet, Kierkegaard asks, if they communicate, would it not be the case that they communicate *something*? Doesn't their instruction address itself to thinking? Should it not have propositional content? Indeed it should. Kierkegaard writes:

> But might it not be possible to state quite briefly how it is that joy is the content of this instruction of the lilies and the birds, or what is the content of this instruction of theirs on the subject of joy, that is to say, might it not be possible to define very briefly the thought-content of this instruction of theirs? ... But their instruction in joy (which their lives in turn express) is quite simply as follows. There is a today [*det er et Idag*]. Upon the word *is* there falls an infinite emphasis [*uendelig Eftertryk*].[44]

The content of joy is that "there is a today," with an *infinite* emphasis on "is." But given the infinite emphasis on "is," what seems to come most to the fore is simply the "there is." The lilies of the field and the birds of the air say simply: "There is." In other words, they disclose being itself in its nakedness, being without reasons, being apart from projects and ends. Their joy—a preeminently religious joy—is an affection of the astonishing, groundless fact that "there is" at all. But to remain in this affection is to remain entirely "today."

The lilies and the birds are entirely "today." Human beings, we have seen, are always already other to themselves owing to their temporality. The instant, the "now," on which the lilies and the birds put an infinite emphasis is for human beings a mere nothing, a mere point of division between the future that impends and the past that has been. Self-consciousness seems able to catch up with reality only once it has been; or, if not that, then through an anticipation of when it will have been. Meaning occurs either in the past perfect or future perfect tense, never in the present. Yet joy is being today, an infinite concentration on the present. Thus an essential gap opens up between self-consciousness and the absolute joy manifest in the lilies and the birds. This is why they are essentially *instructors* in joy.

Yet, we may ask, is absolute joy *possible* for human beings? The answer must be yes and no. In speaking of it, Kierkegaard is not referring to an experience he or anyone else may have had. Joy is—though it is paradoxical to say—not an experience but a task. I do not mean, however, that joy comes as a result of achieving a goal. Rather, for Kierkegaard, the joy comes in learning joy. Learning joy means un-learning overlooking the ever-uncertain present in favor of the recollected past or anticipated future. It means to allow the lilies and the birds to teach one that "tomorrow"—that is, what one can anticipate or project concerning tomorrow—is an ontological illusion.

This will be a difficult labor, insofar as it is the very function of self-consciousness to project itself toward the future. In fact, there is a certain "contradiction" embedded in such a praxis: if unlearning overlooking the present becomes itself a new project, a "goal" to be achieved, then one will land straight back in the same place—only worse. According to Kierkegaard, unlearning in the requisite way requires a "marvelous dexterity." Learning to put an infinite emphasis on "is" means, in the language Kierkegaard cites from the New Testament, to "cast all one's cares upon God." Yet he writes:

> The word "cast" suggests an expenditure of force, as if one had to collect all one's forces and with an immense expenditure of force... cast care away by sheer strength; and yet "strength" is exactly the thing which is not to be employed. What is to be employed is releasement [*Eftergivenhed*]—and yet one is to cast care away.[45]

Learning joy—an infinite task—means *letting go* of tomorrow, taking no thought for it. This will not mean, of course, failing to plan and so forth. It will not signify a simple drifting. Rather, it will mean giving one's attention to tasks of today in the absence of knowing what they will have meant.

One final comment. It is tempting to see Kierkegaard's discussion of joy as entirely classical, in that he would seem to reinscribe an essential dualism between nature and human self-consciousness: whereas nature is absolute present to itself and so exists in a timeless now, human beings are cultural and historical beings who must undergo the agony of having to determine themselves in the face of the double bind of temporality. History, temporality, and cultural endeavor become the insignia of a "fallen" condition that stands in contrast to the perfections of nature. Yet Kierkegaard does more than reinscribe this classical ontology. He is aware of the Pauline notion that nature itself is "subjected to corruption."[46] Though the lilies and the birds are unconditionally joyful, it is a joy that coincides with an "infinitely deep sorrow." What makes the joy of the lilies and the birds absolute is not that it is beyond suffering, but rather that it arises in the midst of suffering. In a certain way, it is even inseparable from suffering: insofar, namely, as "to be"—on which infinite emphasis falls—is always to suffer being.

Conclusion

I have explored a finite number of themes concerning Kierkegaard's way of relating religion and emotion. Kierkegaard links the two in a profound way, especially where the link concerns affects that are about "nothing." This is true for his well-known discussions of anxiety, despair, and boredom but also for his lesser known discussions of concern, expectancy, patience, and joy. The very spirituality of human beings, for Kierkegaard, rests in ambiguity of being able neither to be nor not to be. Our irreducibility to the polarity of being and nonbeing, something that strikes in the everyday phenomena of boredom and anxiety, is simultaneously a promise of "being today" beyond, and within, the torments of self-consciousness.

NOTES

1. Contemporary theorizing on emotion has produced a very sophisticated discussion on the appropriate method for the study of emotions. A crucial issue concerns whether emotions are "natural" objects, thus simply given, or more culturally inflected objects. See, for example, Paul Griffith, "Is Emotion a Natural Kind?" in *Thinking about Feeling*, edited by Robert Solomon (Oxford: Oxford University Press, 2004), 233–49. In this context, where the intention is to clarify Kierkegaard's contribution, I cannot weigh in on this methodological debate in any satisfying way. I will simply state my approach. In several important articles, Amélie Oksenberg Rorty has argued that the effort to study the emotions as natural objects is inherently contradictory. While emotions are seductively immediate, apparently always simply "given," and therefore not susceptible to any radical kind of historical analysis, she argues that it is a fundamental mistake to bypass historical genealogy. Though Rorty's approach is therefore broadly "constructivist," what distinguishes it—and what I shall pick up on here—is the demand that the analysis of emotion be accompanied by close attention to the *metaphysical horizons* in which emotions acquire significance as emotions. Emotions are not natural, but rather encode and manifest certain fundamental organizing principles, that is, the fundamental metaphors and distinctions, or fundamental ontologies, that inform a culture's engagement with the world. Emotions are not "natural" objects, then, but rather "metaphysical" objects. The analysis of emotions thus becomes inseparable from the task of excavating the metaphysical horizons in which particular "theories of emotions," whether Aristotelian, Stoic, Cartesian, Kantian, and so on, are embedded. I shall do something like this with respect to Kierkegaard's relation to the philosophies of German idealism. See Amélie Oksenberg Rorty, "Aristotle on the Metaphysical Status of Pathe," *Review of Metaphysics* 38 (March 1984): 521–46, and "Enough Already with the 'Theory of Emotions,'" in Solomon, *Thinking about Feeling*, 269–78.

2. *Introductions to the Wissenschaftslehre and Other Writings*, translated by Daniel Breazeale (Indianapolis: Hackett, 1994), 112.

3. *The Vocation of Man*, translated by Peter Preuss (Indianapolis: Hackett, 1987), 73 (my italics).

4. *Sickness unto Death*, translated by Howard and Edna Hong (Princeton, N.J.: Princeton University Press, 1980), 13.

5. Ibid., 13.

6. Ibid., 17.

7. Not only in Kierkegaard, then, but also in Hegel, Feuerbach, Marx, and Nietzsche, this estrangement (or alienation) becomes *the* philosophical-existential-political-economic problem. The modern tragedy, of which for Kierkegaard Hamlet would be the paradigmatic instance, is one in which the hero is undone *through his own autonomy*. He is undone, namely, precisely through his freedom to reflect, through the fact that his relation to the world is not already given and constituted, but rather awaits his involvement. Free reflection has no inherent measure; nothing is settled concerning the human place in the cosmos. Facing the world afresh, without the shackles of "miracle, mystery and authority," the modern subject thus faces an abyss of indetermination, an excess of possibility. Jean-Paul Sartre captured the ironic tragedy of modernity as well as anyone in proclaiming we are paradoxically "*condemned* to be free."

8. There is an important distinction in the contemporary literature on emotion between emotions and moods. Roughly, the distinction is this: emotions, as modes of

judgment or evaluation, are always "about" some definite object. They have intentionality, even if only dimly or not at all explicitly recognized by the subject of them. Moods, by contrast, are "objectless," they are a kind of background coloring to our experience. As both Martha Nussbaum and Robert Roberts concede, however, the distinction between emotions and moods is not always easy to draw. The more general and unfocused the object of the emotion is, for example, the harder it is to distinguish from a mood. In the concrete, no clean line can be drawn. See Robert Roberts's discussion of the relation between emotions and moods in his *Emotions: An Essay in Aid of Moral Psychology* (New York: Cambridge University Press, 2003), 112–15. Martha Nussbaum discusses the distinction in her *Upheavals of Thought* (New York: Cambridge University Press, 2001), 132–35. Like contemporary theory, Kierkegaard, too, thematizes a rough-and-ready distinction between emotions and moods. In his *Concept of Anxiety*, he argues that moods like anxiety, for example, differ from emotions like fear insofar as the former lack an object. Where Kierkegaard differs from the neo-Stoic account (as much as from the Stoic one) is that he reverses the order of priority. The human encounter, through distinctive moods like boredom, melancholy, anxiety, and despair, with the objectless, the indeterminate, the measureless—in short, with everything associated with "nonbeing"—takes precedence over the experience of harmony and limit. Rather than a "theory of emotion" one must speak, as does Vincent McCarthy, of a "phenomenology of moods." Central to this phenomenology is the metaphysical presupposition of the priority of the indeterminate to the determinate, the possible to the actual, nonbeing to being.

9. Martha Nussbaum rather breezily avoids the profound danger that hides in objectless moods for her whole account of emotion. Moods become "mere moods" whose revelatory power pales in comparison with the determinate, referentially centered emotions. See *Upheavals in Thought*, 133. Robert Roberts's account gives a much richer picture of the relation between the two: emotions have moods, but moods can also "detach" from emotions and stand free-floating. Generally, however, Roberts suggests that moods add intensity to emotions. Thus, emotions are again prioritized. See his *Emotion*, 114–15.

10. See his article "Existence, Emotion and Virtue: Classical Themes in Kierkegaard," in *The Cambridge Companion to Kierkegaard*, edited by Gordon Marino and Alastair Hannay (New York: Cambridge University Press, 1998), 177–206.

11. *Stages on Life's Way*, translated by Howard and Edna Hong (Princeton, N.J.: Princeton University Press, 1988), 276–88.

12. Ibid., 284.

13. Ibid.

14. It is interesting to note, as Patricia Meyer Spacks has, that the word "boredom" only first occurs in the English language in the nineteenth century. See her *Boredom: The Literary History of a State of Mind* (Chicago: University of Chicago Press, 1995), 116.

15. *Either/Or I*, translated by Edna and Howard Hong (Princeton, N.J.: Princeton University Press, 1987), 285.

16. Kierkegaard's pseudonymous author, an aesthete named "A," discovers boredom at the root, for example, of the quintessentially modern craving for amusement and spectacle. Tongue-in-cheek, he suggests that to cure boredom the state of Denmark should borrow—with no intention to pay back, that is—15 million rix dollars for the sole purpose of public entertainment: "Borrow fifteen million; use it not to pay off our debts but for public entertainment.... Everything would be free: the theater would be free, prostitutes would be free, rides to Deer Park would be free, funerals would be free." In case the bounty of free entertainment becomes wearisome, he suggests a second idea: kidnap the emperor of Persia and stage a coup d'état for the amusement of the citizenry. Kierkegaard's author

similarly discovers boredom at the root of the desire, characteristic of modernity, always to be *busy*: "There are people who have an extraordinary talent for transforming everything into a business operation, whose whole life is a business operation, who fall in love and are married, hear a joke, and admire a work of art with the same businesslike zeal with which they work at the office." Ibid., 289.

17. Ibid., 291. Here Kierkegaard's analyses anticipate the existentialisms of Heidegger and Sartre by regarding the nothing, or nonbeing, as no mere lack or privation—not simply "nothing"—but rather as a positive, uncanny power that has always already contaminated the purity of the autonomous subject.

18. *Emotions*, 248.

19. Roberts no doubt would not agree that a construal is the same as a judgment. The main difference he draws, however, seems to be that construals are less like acts of intellection than acts of perception. He writes: "My basic paradigm is that emotions are a kind of perception, and perceptions in the relevant sense may, but need not, be propositional"; ibid., 132. A construal is a kind of rough interpretation of a context of meaning that happens with a degree of immediacy. Nevertheless, the basic teleological and referential orientation of emotions remains the same both for Roberts and for Nussbaum, who regards emotions explicitly as forms of judgment.

20. Beyond that, one can also identify an aporia in the strategy of interpreting a state of disinterestedness as another modality of interest. Boredom for Roberts would be an interest in interest. But is an interest in interest the same as an interest? The essential difference between boredom (an interest in interest) and other interests is that the question of the possibility of fulfillment of the emotion's intentionality cannot properly be put. It is not that boredom is a vague interest but that it is an interest *without* an object. It is an illusion, then, to homologize boredom with other states of being interested.

21. *The Concept of Anxiety*, translated by Reidar Thomte (Princeton, N.J.: Princeton University Press, 1980), 42.

22. Ibid., 112.

23. Ibid., 44.

24. Ibid., 42.

25. See *The Concluding Unscientific Postscript*, translated by Howard and Edna Hong, 2 vols. (Princeton, N.J.: Princeton University Press, 1992), vol. 1, 555.

26. It should be said, however, that the distinction between religion A and B is not always clear-cut. In fact, for many of Kierkegaard's texts, particularly the *Opbyggelige Taler*, the distinction does little or no work. No doubt this is because Kierkegaard was not only a "religious" but also a "Christian" author from beginning to end. Even his discussions of a more general religiousness can easily be shown to have Christian roots. Thus it would be anachronistic to think of Kierkegaard as a "theorist of religion" in any contemporary sense.

27. One of the few full-length studies of the *Opbyggelige Taler* is George Pattison's recent *Kierkegaard's Upbuilding Discourses: Philosophy, Theology and Literature* (London: Routledge, 2002). The only exception to this rule is the extensive literature on Kierkegaard's *Works of Love*. An excellent recent commentary on the latter is Jamie Ferreira, *Love's Grateful Striving: A Commentary on Kierkegaard's "Works of Love"* (Oxford: Oxford University Press, 2001).

28. See *Eighteen Upbuilding Discourses*, translated by Howard and Edna Hong (Princeton, N.J.: Princeton University Press, 1990), 80–101.

29. Ibid., 86.

30. Ibid., 86.

31. Ibid., 95.

32. Ibid., 98–99.
33. See ibid., 8–29.
34. Ibid., 18.
35. Ibid., 18.
36. The distinction is simply that the victory expected has no representable content. It is an expectation inseparable from an expectation of "nothing." A wish, however, is always about something definite (even if only vaguely conceived).
37. Ibid., 19.
38. I do not mean to say that boredom and anxiety are not culturally mediated. As I have suggested, they are affects that arise specifically on the ground of modern self-consciousness. However, boredom and anxiety put the structure of intentionality under extreme pressure. One can will oneself neither into nor out of boredom, for example.
39. Ibid., 169.
40. Ibid., 162–63.
41. Ibid., 166.
42. *The Lilies of the Field and the Birds of the Air: Three Godly Discourses*, in *Christian Discourses*, translated by Walter Lowrie (Princeton, N.J.: Princeton University Press, 1971), 311–56. The third of these discourses focuses explicitly on joy.
43. Ibid., 349.
44. Ibid., 349.
45. Ibid., 353. Translation slightly altered.
46. Ibid., 352.

BIBLIOGRAPHY

Kierkegaard, Søren. *Christian Discourses*, translated by Walter Lowrie. Princeton, N.J.: Princeton University Press, 1940.

———. *The Concept of Anxiety*. Translated by Reidar Thomte in collaboration with Albert B. Anderson. In Hong and Hong, *Kierkegaard's Writings*, vol. 8. Princeton, N.J.: Princeton University Press, 1980.

———. *Eighteen Upbuilding Discourses*. Translated by Howard V. Hong and Edna H. Hong. In Hong and Hong, *Kierkegaard's Writings*, vol. 5. Princeton, N.J.: Princeton University Press, 1990.

———. *Either/Or I*. Translated by Howard V. Hong and Edna H. Hong. In Hong and Hong, *Kierkegaard's Writings*, vol. 3. Princeton, N.J.: Princeton University Press, 1987.

———. *Sickness unto Death*. Translated by Howard V. Hong and Edna H. Hong. In Hong and Hong, *Kierkegaard's Writings*, vol. 19. Princeton, N.J.: Princeton University Press, 1980.

———. *Stages on Life's Way*. Translated by Howard V. Hong and Edna H. Hong. In Hong and Hong, *Kierkegaard's Writings*, vol. 11. Princeton, N.J.: Princeton University Press, 1988.

McCarthy, Vincent A. *The Phenomenology of Moods in Kierkegaard*. Boston: Nijhoff, 1978.

Nussbaum, Martha. *Upheavals of Thought*. Cambridge: Cambridge University Press, 2001.

Roberts, Robert C. *Emotions: An Essay in Aid of Moral Psychology*. Cambridge: Cambridge University Press, 2003.

———. "Existence, Emotion and Virtue: Classical Themes in Kierkegaard." In *The Cambridge Companion to Kierkegaard*, edited by Alastair Hannay and Gordon Marino. Cambridge: Cambridge University Press, 1998, 177–206.

Solomon, Robert C., ed. *Thinking about Feeling: Contemporary Philosophers on Emotions*. Oxford: Oxford University Press, 2004.

CHAPTER 22

JONATHAN EDWARDS

MICHAEL McCLYMOND

JONATHAN Edwards (1703–1758)—pastor, philosopher, theologian, and Calvinist saint—was a man of deep piety and a meticulous observer of others' spiritual experiences. He devoted much of his life to the analysis and interpretation of religious emotions, which he called "affections." His writings on the religious revivals of his era, *Faithful Narrative* (1737), *The Distinguishing Marks of the Work of the Spirit of God* (1741), *Some Thoughts Concerning the Present Revival of Religion* (1742), and, above all, *A Treatise Concerning Religious Affections* (1746), are replete with reflections on emotional states and sensibilities. Other relevant texts include *Charity and Its Fruits* (1738), *The Life of David Brainerd* (1749), and the brief but telling autobiography or "Personal Narrative." Today most scholars regard Edwards as the greatest theologian in American history, and his writings have had vast influence in both church and academy. Currently there are well over a million Web sites that mention him, and interest in Edwards is mushrooming in Brazil, Korea, Nigeria, and other regions where Christianity has been rapidly expanding. Edwards might be dubbed the patron saint of religious revival and revivalism.

Like his Puritan predecessors, Edwards saw a dichotomy between true, God-given, and grace-filled religion on the one hand and false, counterfeit, hypocritical, and non-gracious religion on the other. His standards were exacting. What many imagined to be true religion was, for him, nothing of the kind. His desire to sift the wheat from the chaff of spiritual experience provoked him to lifelong inquiry. He devoured seventeenth- and eighteenth-century religious authors and scrutinized biblical texts that might provide a basis for judging spiritual experiences. As well as being a textual prodigy, Edwards was a kind of anthropologist or ethnographer *avant la lettre*, whose "thick description" of his informants' experiences—mostly his own congregants—is telling and textured. One side of Edwards links him to the later evangelical and revivalist tradition in America. Another side anticipates the late nineteenth-century psychologists and empirical investigators of religion, such as William James and Edwin Starbuck. Without exaggeration, Edwards's works offer a veritable cosmos of religious experience, and an attentive reader can delve into them for years and still discover unsuspected subtleties. An essay like this can only provide, as it were, a map of major constellations in the galaxy. Those who wish to explore the topic more fully should consult the twenty-five volume Yale University Press edition of *The Works of Jonathan Edwards* (cited here by volume and page number).

Basic Concepts: Understanding, Inclination, Affection, Passion, and Love

Near the beginning of *Religious Affections*, Edwards portrays the affections as "springs of action" for all forms of human activity:

> Such is man's nature, that he is very inactive, any otherwise than he is influenced by some affection, either love or hatred, desire, hope, fear, or some other. These affections we see to be the springs that set men agoing... take away all love and hatred, all hope and fear, all anger, zeal and affectionate desire, and the world would be, in a great measure, motionless and dead; there would be no such thing as activity amongst mankind, or any earnest pursuit whatsoever. 'Tis affection that engages the covetous man... 'tis the affections also that actuate the voluptuous man... so in religious matters, the spring of their actions are very much religious affections: he that has doctrinal knowledge and speculation only, without affection, never is engaged in the business of religion. (2:101)

Several things are noteworthy here. Human society is a bustling place, brimming with aspiration and endeavor. As on the floor of the New York Stock Exchange, everyone is going somewhere. Yet just below the surface are the affections that motivate these movements. Affections vary in kind as well as in intensity, and though Edwards never tallies up the possible human affections, the total number is sizeable. Religious affections are not qualitatively different from everyday affections such as the desire for wealth or for sensual pleasure. Instead religious affections are simply affections directed toward a religious object (i.e., God or spiritual things).

On inspection, Edwards's affections are not synonymous with emotions. A major difference is that Edwards always links affections to an object, while emotions may or may not have an object. In current English usage, the statement "I am emotional" need not imply an object of emotion. Yet the assertion "I am affectionate," raises the question "Toward what or whom?" Unlike "emote," which is an intransitive verb, "affect" is transitive—A "affects" B in some fashion—and thus "affections" denote the ways objects "affect" human subjects. *Webster's Third New*

International Dictionary (1986) defines "emotion" as "a state of feeling," and "feeling" as "the undifferentiated background of one's awareness considered apart from any identifiable sensation, perception, or thought." Feeling, in this sense, is not of interest to Edwards, and he has nothing to say regarding an "undifferentiated background" of awareness. Such a notion is more characteristic of Friedrich Schleiermacher in his analysis of religion as a "sense of the infinite" or "feeling of absolute dependence." In accordance with his empirical bent, Edwards is concerned with affections that center on concrete objects, cases, and situations.

To explain Edwards's position on the affections more fully, one must consider his theory of human nature. In *Religious Affections* he distinguishes two "faculties." One he calls "mind" or "understanding" and is "capable of perception and speculation." The other, which he calls "the inclination," is that whereby "the soul does not merely perceive and view things, but is some way inclined with respect to the things it views or considers." If one considers the inclination with respect to the actions that follow from it, one may use the term "the will." With respect to the mind's orientation, one may use the term "the heart." With respect to "more vigorous and sensible exercises of this faculty," one may use the term "affections" (2:96–97). Though there are many shades and nuances in the affections, a basic contrast exists between attraction and aversion, or inclination and disinclination. The term "passion" refers to "more violent" effects in which the mind is "less in its own command" (2:98) Affections are to some extent chosen, while passions are largely involuntary. Edwards hints at, but does not elaborate, a biological basis for human emotion. In a state of affection, "the motion of the blood and animal spirits begins to be sensibly altered; whence oftentimes arises some bodily sensation" (2:96–97). Edwards says little on the metaphysical issue of how soul and body interact, though he seems to imply that changes in either the soul or the body may affect the other. In discussing temptation, he suggests that Satan cannot directly implant ideas into the human mind, as God can, but must stir up the "animal spirits" and so excite the "imagination or phantasy" (2:288–89). This is one reason that Edwards was skeptical toward those claiming to have had visions of God. Diabolical influence or emotional arousal could counterfeit divine inspiration.

Certain consequences follow immediately from Edwards's definition of terms in *Religious Affections*. Though he mentions "mind" or "understanding" as the first of the faculties, he says little regarding its nature or function. This could be because he thought its status was less problematic than that of the other faculties. Yet his preoccupation with the will, inclination, and affections—indeed, his authorship of volumes like *Freedom of the Will, Religious Affections*, and *Original Sin*—situates him in an Augustinian tradition that characterized the human self more in terms of its desires and choices than its thoughts and concepts. This is not to say that Edwards was anti-intellectual but that will, desire, and inclination were the keys to his interpretation of human life. Furthermore, Edwards did not adhere to the threefold distinction of mind, will, and emotions that is common in nineteenth- and twentieth-century discussions and that, in outline, goes back to Plato. He declares that the will and affections "are not two faculties." In linking the inclination to the will, heart, affections, and passions, Edwards gives the inclination a large—and possibly problematic—role. For the choices of the will and the affections of the heart seem sometimes to be opposed to one another—though Edwards assigns both choices and affections to the faculty of inclination. A celibate monk might feel desire for a beautiful temptress and yet choose not to touch her. How does one explain this? Critics have proposed a threefold distinction of mind, will, and emotion (or feeling, passion), with the will as the intermediary between mind and emotion. Edwards might respond by saying that such a mediating will is a self-determining power that is logically incoherent and self-contradictory, as argued in *Freedom of the Will*. The will, he notes, cannot determine itself. A person has a will, but one's will itself does not have a will. Ultimately all faculties cohere with one another within the unity of the human self.

Even the twofold distinction of understanding and inclination tends to break down in the course of Edwards's discussion in *Religious Affections*. What one calls mind or understanding is the human self in one mode of operation, while inclination is another mode. Because both understanding and inclination are operations of the total human self, the distinction between them is more analytical than actual. They are not "parts" of the soul or self, as is commonly imagined. Furthermore, the inclination's affections include an intellectual dimension, while the mind's thoughts include an affective dimension, and thus the two faculties are interlocking in their operations. It is a basic error, therefore, to interpret Edwards in terms of any dichotomy of intellect versus affect, or head versus heart, although some interpreters have sought to claim him for one side or the other.

The eighteenth-century debates over the Great Awakening often set mind against heart. Opponents, like Charles Chauncy, argued that the revival preachers had merely stirred up "passions" and that true religion brought the self under the control of reason rather than emotion. Radical revivalists, like James Davenport, reveled in intense emotions and derogated the intellect. Indeed, a Connecticut judiciary charged Davenport, because of his erratic behavior, with being "disturbed in the rational faculties of his mind." Edwards differed from both Chauncy and Davenport. His mediating position in the revival debates rested on a unitary conception of the human self as intellectual and affective. For antirevivalists, an idea was a measure of intellectual content divorced from emotion, feeling, and affection. For Edwards, by contrast, an idea was a unit of affective response as well as intellectual content. Say the word "fire," and one person might be reminded of a delightful fireside encounter with a lover, while another might think of a catastrophic conflagration that destroyed a home and family. Even a simple idea like fire carries affective associations. Edwards asserted that affections focused on ideas: "The heart cannot be set upon an object of which there is no idea in the understanding" (22:88). Religious affections required religious ideas. Yet the revival debates brought oversimplification. Many prorevivalists assumed that religion was all about affections and had nothing to do with intellect. "Old Lights" were proreason, antiemotion, and antirevival, while "New Lights" were antireason, proemotion, and prorevival. Few grasped the subtlety of Edwards's position.

The affections singled out for discussion in *Religious Affections* include fear, hope, love, hatred, desire, joy, sorrow, gratitude, compassion, and zeal (2:102–8). Yet the affection that overshadows the rest is love, also called charity (in its eighteenth-century sense). In *Charity and Its Fruits*, Edwards demonstrates that love is "the sum of all virtue" (8:129–48) and is opposed to envy, pride, selfishness, and censoriousness (8:218–92). Love is not only the root of the virtues; for Edwards it is, in some sense, the root of all affections and all actions whatsoever. One recalls Augustine's statement in *City of God* that each person's love is the "gravity" that determines whether he rises or falls. For Edwards, the opposite of love is not hatred but indifference. A "hard heart," he writes, is an "unaffected heart" (2:117). He interprets the affections in their diversity as modifications of love, arising from the diverse circumstances in which love is expressed:

> From love arises hatred of those things which are contrary to what we love, or which oppose and thwart us in those things that we delight in: and from the various exercises of love and hatred, according to the circumstances of the objects of these affections, as present or absent, certain or uncertain, probable or improbable, arise all those other affections of desire, hope, fear, joy, grief, gratitude, anger, etc. (2:108)

Edwards speaks of a "counterfeit love" from which flow "other false affections" (2:150)—an idea reminiscent of Augustine's concupiscence in distinction from charity. Compared with other Protestant authors, Edwards says relatively much about love and little about faith.

The "New Sense"

A crucial yet elusive feature in Edwards's thought is his treatment of the "new sense," also referred to as the "spiritual sense," or "sense of the heart." With this phrase, he uses the language of the senses to capture something that transcends the senses. He describes his own conversion experience in his "Personal Narrative":

> The first instance that I remember of that sort of inward, sweet delight in God and divine things that I have lived much in since, was on reading those words, 1 Tim. 1:17. *Now unto the King eternal, immortal, invisible, the only wise God, be honour and glory for ever and ever, Amen.* As I read the words, there came into my soul, and was as it were diffused through it, a sense of the glory of the Divine Being; a new sense, quite different from any thing I ever experienced before. Never any words of scripture seemed to me as these words did. I thought with myself, how excellent a Being that was, and how happy I should be, if I might enjoy that God, and be rapt up to him in heaven, and be as it were swallowed up in him for ever! (16:792).

Edwards understood the "new sense" as discontinuous with all earlier life experiences. Previously he had "affections" for God, but these in time proved feeble, transient, and lacking in what he called an "inward, pure, soul animating and refreshing nature." In contrast to such feeble affections, the "new sense" was a delight in God for God's own sake. Edwards often used the word "sweetness" to describe it, and compared it to tasting honey. Varying his metaphor, he wrote elsewhere that it was as difficult to describe the "new sense" to someone who had not experienced it was to convey the taste of a pineapple to someone who had never eaten one. This "new sense" was not an awareness of being in God's favor but a response to God's own incomparable beauty or "excellency." Earlier Puritan writers recommended introspection and self-examination for individuals to discern whether or not God had saved them. Edwards, by contrast, spoke of a spiritual delight in God that brought self-forgetfulness. The true saint was like someone enraptured by the beauties of the Sistine Chapel, so focused on looking up that she loses track of time and forgets where she is. Aesthetic experience provided Edwards with a model or metaphor for gracious affections. No one could see God's beauty without feeling delight.

Scholars have debated Edwards's "new sense" and its relationship to everyday perception. On one side are those, like Paul Helm, who highlight the discontinuity between the "new sense" and all other human experiences. Since Edwards compares the "new sense" to Locke's "new simple idea" (2:205)—that is, an idea, like heat or wetness, that cannot be understood without a corresponding experience—these scholars maintain that the "new sense" has no connection to ordinary sense perception and implies a kind of sixth sense. On the other side are those, like Perry Miller, who note that Edwards denied that the "new sense" set aside the functioning of the natural senses. They interpret the "new sense" not as a sixth sense or vision of another world but as a *deeper vision* of the present world. For Miller, Edwards had much in common with Emerson. Both thinkers viewed nature as a vehicle for communion with God. My own position is that Edwards's "new sense" involved an interplay of natural and gracious experience. *Pace* Miller, the experience of conversion is foundational to Edwards's religious epistemology. Believers are able to perceive a holiness or beauty in God that is invisible to nonbelievers, and in this sense believers and nonbelievers live in two different universes. Subsequent to regeneration, the believer comes to appreciate even the beauties of the natural world in new ways. While Emerson and Schleiermacher held that a deeper vision was accessible to all human beings, Edwards made this vision dependent on a prior operation of divine grace. *Pace* Helm, however, the mental breakthrough of grace, or "divine light," operates *in and through* the natural sense faculties, and so grace does not destroy nature but perfects it. The "new sense" is not an epistemological quirk, detached from the rest of human life. Those who undergo regeneration find that this one experience unlocks the meaning of all human experience and sheds light on all of life. In conclusion, Edwards's "new sense" is a creative synthesis of Puritan and Enlightenment ideas, melding the discontinuities of grace with the continuities of human nature. Moreover the "new sense" became a basis for Edwards to judge between gracious and natural experiences in the midst of the eighteenth-century religious awakenings.

Edwards on Religious Revival

Edwards first became widely known as an author through a letter of 1736 that he later expanded into his book *Faithful Narrative* (1737), which described the events of the religious awakening in Northampton, Massachusetts, of 1734–1735. He could hardly have imagined that this short work was to provide the model for an entire genre of religious literature—the revival narrative—that would include thousands of works. When the Great Awakening arrived, in 1740–1741, *Faithful Narrative* of became the template for interpreting the larger and even more dramatic events that took place in Boston, New York, Philadelphia, Savannah, and throughout the colonies.

In *Faithful Narrative*, Edwards asserts that firsthand observation is needed for judging religious revivals. He offers his text as a second-best alternative to being present in the revival. As an ethnographer of sorts, he begins with a physical description of the town of Northampton, and grounds his analysis in space and place. The "mirth and jollity" of Northampton's youth, he notes, ended suddenly in 1734 with the unexpected death of a young man and a younger married woman (4:146–48). Over several months, almost the entire population of the town became preoccupied with spiritual matters:

> There was scarcely a single person in the town, either old or young, that was left unconcerned about the great things of the eternal world... in the spring and summer following, *anno* 1735, the town seemed to be full of the presence of God: it was never so full of love, nor so full of joy; and yet so full of distress, as it was then. (4:150–51)

Edwards mentions both joy and distress—the joy of those who experienced reconciliation and peace with God, and the distress of those who were unable to achieve such a breakthrough. The inhabitants of neighboring towns experienced almost the same thing at the same time, though they were unaware of the happenings elsewhere (4:154). In some cases, reports from Northampton sparked further revivals (4:155). The awakening was a sort of spiritual contagion that spread when the news of it was communicated.

In *Faithful Narrative*, Edwards noted that fear, vexation, or despondency preceded joy and assurance of salvation for most people: "People are first awakened with a sense of their miserable condition by nature, the danger they are in of perishing eternally" (4:160). On the other hand, there was tremendous variation in terms of the "fear and trouble" that came before "comfortable evidences of pardon" with God, and some had "ten times" more trouble than others—a fact Edwards noted but did not try to explain. "Persons are sometimes brought to the borders of despair, and it looks as black as midnight to them a little before the day dawns in their souls." Conversion liberated many from temptations they had long been subjected to (4:162). A sudden experience of grace brought some to the verge of laughter, and others to weeping. Certain persons continued for a long time in what Edwards took to be a state of grace and yet did not think that they were converted, and so had to be instructed that they were (4:174–75). Some in Northampton had visionary experiences, though Edwards adds that they were wise enough not to trust in such experiences as necessarily God-given. On hearing of hell, some vividly imagined a "dreadful furnace," while others were captivated by "a lively idea of Christ hanging upon the cross" (4:188).

Edward judged that Satan, during the distress induced by the revival, used "the distemper of melancholy" to cause some to give up hope (4:162). The most glaring instance was the suicide of Joseph Hawley—Edwards's uncle—who fell into despondency and cut his throat with a knife. Hawley came from a family prone to melancholy, and Edwards attributed the suicide both to Hawley's medical condition and to Satan's machinations. This shocking event had a chilling effect on the revival, and subsequently, Edwards writes, many people felt strange promptings to imitate Hawley and cut their own throats (4:206–7). Edwards caps off his description of the Northampton revival with the stories of two notable converts, both female. The more unusual case was Phebe Bartlet, a four-year-old child who felt sorrow for her sins during the revival, and prayed for forgiveness before undergoing conversion and release from guilt.

Edwards inherited from his Puritan forebears in England and New England a method for discriminating between spurious and gracious experience. Later scholars called it the "morphology of conversion." The essential idea was that conversions followed distinct, sequential steps and that an individual could chart his or her spiritual condition by using the steps as a guide. While some writers proposed as many as ten stages in the process of conversion, almost all Puritan authors agreed that "humiliation" or even "terror" had to come before "consolation," "conversion," or "grace." The method could be as wrenching to the psyche as the rack to the body. By ruthless introspection, individuals sought to strip away the onionskin layers of empty and self-flattering hopes, and find a reliable core of sincere faith. Though Edwards was well acquainted with the Puritan theory of conversion, he found that it did not match his own experiences or those of others. In his "Personal Narrative," humiliation or terror was not a prelude to the "new sense." In fact, his deeper experiences of compunction for sin came long after his conversion. When theory violated experience, Edwards altered theory. He jettisoned the "morphology of conversion." The "Diary" indicates that Edwards had likely abandoned it by the early 1720s. "Nothing can certainly be determined concerning the nature of the affections by this," he writes, "that comforts and joys seem to follow awakenings and convictions of conscience, in a certain order" (2:151). In *Faithful Narrative*, Edwards observed that some individuals experienced joy and spiritual confidence without first passing through a phase of fear or vexation, and he accepted them as genuinely converted. This does not mean he thought fear had no place in religious life. His famous sermon "Sinners in the Hands of an Angry God" appealed to fear as a motive for conversion. When criticized for preaching terror, Edwards said it was as reasonable to frighten people away from hell as to scare them out of a burning building. Yet Edwards's major theological innovation was to insist that terror and humiliation were not intrinsic to the process of conversion. Ironically, he became known as a purveyor of fear, when in fact he may have done more than anyone else to remove fear from the pastoral practice of the American church. Today it is hard to imagine that Christians once regarded fear as an essential ingredient in religious conversion.

Once Edwards gave up the "morphology of conversion," he was still left with the problem of discriminating true religion from hypocrisy and self-deception. This was a difficult task, even for a pastor obligated to make decisions regarding other peoples' spiritual condition. Only God, said Edwards, can fathom a human soul. Thus he writes that "it was never God's design to give us any rules by which we may certainly know, who of our fellow professors are his, and to make a full and clear separation between sheep and goats" (2:193). A recently published text, "Directions for Judging of Persons' Experiences," shows Edwards searching for principles to evaluate the members of his flock: "See to it: That the operation be much upon the will or heart, not on the imagination.... That the trouble of mind be reasonable.... That they have not only pretended convictions of sin; but a proper mourning for sin" (21:522–24). During his later years, Edwards became more skeptical about definitive judgments on one's own or others' spiritual condition. Hypocrites mimicked saints, and saints resembled hypocrites. The heart was deceptive, both to others and to itself.

In his *Religious Affections*, the overriding sign of genuine religion is "holy practice," which lies in the realm of actions rather than affections. If there is any affection that demonstrates divine grace, it is the "new sense," the delight in God for God's own sake, that plays such a conspicuous a role in Edwards's own experience. The argument of *Religious Affections* implies that individuals can introspect to see whether or not they delight in God for God's own sake. It may be a hard test, yet for Edwards it yielded decisive evidence of grace. *Religious Affections* says much about phenomena that are unreliable as signs of grace. Some persons become convinced of God's favor because verses of scripture, or words not contained in the Bible, come suddenly into their minds (2:142–45, 220). What some call "conversion" is only a feeling of terror followed by comfort (2:221). Affections are not gracious because they do not seem to arise from the individuals themselves (2:138–42) or because some people believe them to be so (2:167–81). Zeal in external acts of worship is no proof of gracious experience (2:163–65). Fluency in speaking of religious things is not a sign of grace (2:135–37). Bodily effects prove nothing (2:131–35). Some had visions of Jesus hanging on the cross, with blood streaming from his wounds, yet this is no proof of being in a gracious state (2:310). Such experiences are common among hypocrites, who also exhibit excessive confidence in themselves, a prideful and superior spirit, censorious or judgmental attitudes toward others, and a tendency toward self-satisfaction.

Enthusiasm, Visions, and the Ambiguous Status of Imagination

In the century prior to Edwards's birth, religious wars devastated Europe. The English Civil War of the 1640s brought social and religious turmoil, with streetcorner prophets announcing the end of the world and the overthrow of the social order. Many claimed to be God's messengers, and their intemperate words and actions stirred a reaction. By 1700, most Western intellectuals rejected modern claims to divine inspiration and stigmatized those groups asserting such with the derogatory term "enthusiasm." Eighteenth-century authors generally favored a religion that was calm, cool, and collected, and free from emotionalism, weeping, shouting, laughing, fainting, and other bodily manifestations. In defending religious affections, and suggesting that even intense emotions and bodily manifestations could play a role in true religion, Edwards confronted and challenged a contemporary prejudice against enthusiasm. In effect he narrowed the definition of the term, and spurned only a part of what others rejected. He separated religious affections—as essential to religion—from the idea of private inspiration or revelation from God—as nonessential, dubious, or even mischievous. In presenting such an argument, one of Edwards's conundrums related to the imagination, which played a role in all religious awakenings yet contributed to extreme or fanatical behavior.

Like his contemporaries, Edwards used "enthusiasm" as a pejorative term. He says that "nothing so puffs men up, as enthusiasm, with a high conceit of their own wisdom, holiness, eminency and sufficiency, and makes them so bold, forward, assuming, and arrogant" (7:93). *Religious Affections* characterizes "enthusiasm" as including

> all imaginary sights of God and Christ in heaven, all supposed witnessing of the Spirit, and testimonies of the love of God by immediate inward suggestion; and all impressions of future events, and immediate revelations of any secret facts whatsoever ... and applications of words of Scripture, as though they were words now immediately spoken by God to a particular person, in a new meaning. (2:285)

Such experiences often gave rise to false religion (2:285–8). What Romans 8:16 calls the "witness" of the Holy Spirit is a sense of divine love in one's heart or conscience and not a voice or vision from God (2:239). By the time he wrote

Religious Affections, Edwards had observed the decline of the religious awakenings in New England, and he noted that some who claimed to have had the most extravagant spiritual experiences later abandoned their faith. Consequently, he became increasingly suspicious of visionary experiences. His writings from five to ten years earlier, such as *Faithful Narrative* and *Distinguishing Marks*, were generally more open-ended.

Distinguishing Marks—a Yale commencement address in 1741—argues that visions are not antithetical to true religion: "That persons have many impressions on their imaginations, don't prove that they have nothing else." At this stage, Edwards wanted to differentiate true from false religion in such a way as to allow for visions among those who were genuinely converted. When the Holy Spirit stirred the human mind and heart, the imagination was liable to be influenced, and "such is our nature that we can't think of things invisible, without a degree of imagination." He stressed the positive functions of imagination: "It appears to me manifest in many instances I have been acquainted with, that God has really made use of this faculty [of imagination] to truly divine purposes; especially in some that are more ignorant." The difficulty noted in *Distinguishing Marks* was that "many persons," and especially those of "less understanding," are "apt to lay too much weight on the imaginary part" and regard their imaginings "as though they were prophetical visions" (2:235–37). A letter of 1744 addressed the question of whether Edwards regarded persons claiming visions as spiritual pretenders, and he denied this, saying that he neither accepted nor rejected such persons on that basis alone (4:560). On the whole, *Distinguishing Marks* was cautious yet not condemning of visions. Some visions resulted from a stirring of the imaginative faculty by the Holy Spirit, such experiences could be spiritually beneficial, and the problem arose when someone became firmly attached to these experiences and interpreted them as "prophetical" or authoritative. By the time he wrote *Religious Affections*, Edwards had shifted his position, and no longer suggested that visions played a positive role in the spiritual life.

The issue of enthusiasm arose in connection with David Brainerd, the zealous young missionary to the Pennsylvania Indians, who died of tuberculosis in Edwards's home, tended by Edwards's daughter Jerusha (who also contracted the disease and died). Edwards judged that Brainerd's diary might be edifying to devout readers, so he edited and brought it to press. *The Life of David Brainerd* became a bestseller among Edwards's works, and probably the single most influential missionary biography ever published. Yet Brainerd's brief but meteoric life showed telltale signs of enthusiasm. Yale College had expelled him for making the comment, uttered in youthful zeal during the fervor of the Great Awakening, that his tutor had "no more grace than a chair." In his preface, Edwards acknowledged that Brainerd was briefly caught up in enthusiasm, but assigned blame to the people he associated with. Enthusiasm, he suggested, spread by contact and communication. Recent notions of mass hysteria or collective insanity spring to mind, yet Edwards did not develop his point. Brainerd's diary included accounts of visions, which Edwards downplayed in his preface, and, in one case, edited out of the published work (7:81–82, 134–36). But the greatest issue in presenting Brainerd as an edifying example to others was his tendency to "melancholy and dejection of spirit." Edwards argued that Brainerd's melancholia—which Brainerd himself identified as such—did not mean that his religion was nothing more than "the fruit of a warm imagination." Edwards noted that persons of "a very gay and sanguine natural temper" are "much more exposed to enthusiasm" than others. Edwards thus regarded enthusiasm, at least partially, as determined by mental temperament. Brainerd gradually acquired ability "in discerning what within himself was to be laid to the score of melancholy." In his earlier period, "he imputed much of that kind of gloominess of mind and those dark thoughts, to spiritual desertion, which in the latter part of his life, he was abundantly sensible, were owing to the disease of melancholy" (7:91–94). Though Edwards's comments are sketchy and incomplete, he said enough to indicate that he regarded social and psychological factors as codeterminants of religious experience.

Edwards's Legacy Concerning Religion and Emotion

Religious revivalism, especially in its Pentecostal-charismatic forms, mushroomed during the twentieth century. In the mid- to late 1990s, spiritual awakenings erupted in Toronto and in Pensacola, Florida; more than two million visitors showed up at the Brownville Church in Pensacola over a three-year period, and perhaps a comparable number at the Toronto revival. Proponents and opponents of these revivals, in print and internet debates, both appealed to the same author to bolster their arguments: Jonathan Edwards. Proponents noted, correctly, that Edwards allowed for intense emotions and physical manifestations as a part of genuine religious experience. Therefore, they argued that the "holy laughter" in Toronto and "carpet time" (i.e., people in trance on the floor) as well as the more somber events in Pensacola met the tests for true revival set by Edwards. Opponents responded, just as correctly, that Edwards criticized the radical revivalists of the 1740s for reveling in emotion, for prideful and judgmental attitudes, and for relying on visionary experiences as signs of God's favor. Therefore, they argued, neither Toronto nor Pensacola matched Edwards's tests for revival.

Who was right? In a sense, both sides were both right and wrong in invoking Edwards. Each laid hold of one emphasis in Edwards's teaching, which was remarkable for its combination of openness and cautiousness. On the one hand, Edwards did not believe that anyone could dictate in advance how God might move in the midst of a religious revival. If novelty were a mark of heresy, he noted, then Jesus and his apostles would be judged heretical for their religious innovations. His foundational idea was not to judge spiritual phenomena through a priori assumptions. On the other hand, he warned that spiritual phenomena could not be taken at face value, that hypocrites deceive the righteous, and that the devil counterfeits true religion. In reading Edwards on the religious affections, one may feel as though lost in a hall of mirrors. Shapes shift and dissolve. Nothing is as it seems. A friendly face appears in the glass and transmogrifies into a ghoul. The dangers of spiritual deception are acute. In summary, then, Edwards's openness to new experiences and his caution in interpreting them balance one another like two sides of a scale. His writings make it hard to draw facile conclusions. From Edwards's standpoint, it is simple-minded to argue that *some extraordinary religious experiences are valid; therefore the extraordinary religious experiences of this group (to which I belong) are valid.* Equally fallacious would be the claim that *some extraordinary religious experiences are fanatical or diabolical; therefore the extraordinary religious experiences of this group (that I oppose) are fanatical or diabolical.* Neither statement is logically sound, though the prorevival and antirevival arguments of the last 250 years often boil down to little more than this.

A problem—if one chooses to call it that—springs from Edwards's intellectual profundity. Few readers can follow the nuances, caveats, and qualifications of his arguments. Mark Noll has commented that American evangelicalism is a tradition whose first major intellectual—Edwards—is its leading intellectual. This has had the striking effect of enlarging Edwards's shadow across history to unwieldly proportions—like a silhouette at sunset that fills the landscape behind it. Another issue relates to the publication history of Edwards's works. Although *Religious Affections* and some well-known works have been available since the 1740s, other texts pertaining to spiritual experience have only become available in the last decade or two, and a some have only appeared in print during the last few years. We have only now arrived at a point where it is possible to glimpse the panorama of Edwards's thought. Given the present global diffusion of evangelical and revivalist Christianity, and the recent completion of *The Works of Jonathan Edwards*, it is possible that the twenty-first century will become the greatest era yet for Edwards's intellectual and spiritual influence.

Emotions or affections mattered to Edwards in a profound way, and this set him apart from the enlightened thinkers of the eighteenth century, who generally attached little significance to what they termed "passions." They thought it beneath their dignity to philosophize concerning the emotions. Even less would they have considered it their life's work to observe, tabulate, categorize, and analyze subjective states of feeling. Edwards's gift to modern intellectual history is the way he made it possible, for religious and secular investigators, to view human emotions as phenomena worth considering. The book in hand may be a part of that legacy.

BIBLIOGRAPHY

Conforti, Joseph A. *Jonathan Edwards, Religious Tradition, and American Culture.* Chapel Hill: University of North Carolina Press, 1995.

Edwards, Jonathan. *The Works of Jonathan Edwards.* 25 vols. New Haven, Conn.: Yale University Press, 1957–2006.

Goen, C. C. *The Works of Jonathan Edwards*, vol. 4, *The Great Awakening*. Editor's introduction. New Haven, Conn.: Yale University Press, 1972.

Howe, Daniel Walker. *Making the American Self: Jonathan Edwards to Abraham Lincoln*. Cambridge, Mass.: Harvard University Press, 1997.

Marsden, George M. *Jonathan Edwards: A Life*. New Haven, Conn.: Yale University Press, 2003.

McClymond, Michael J. "Spiritual Perception in Jonathan Edwards." *Journal of Religion* 77 (1997): 195–216.

Miller, Perry. "From Edwards to Emerson." *New England Quarterly* 13 (1940): 589–617.

Noll, Mark A. *America's God: From Jonathan Edwards to Abraham Lincoln*. New York: Oxford University Press, 2002.

Smith, John E. *The Works of Jonathan Edwards*, vol. 2, *Religious Affections*. Editor's introduction. New Haven, Conn.: Yale University Press, 1959), 1–83.

Stein, Stephen J., ed. *The Writings of Jonathan Edwards: Text, Context, Interpretation*. Bloomington: Indiana University Press, 1996.

CHAPTER 23

WILLIAM JAMES

JEREMY CARRETTE

> There is no ground for assuming a simple abstract "religious emotion" to exist as a distinct elementary mental affection by itself, present in every religious experience without exception.
>
> —William James, *The Varieties of Religious Experience*

WILLIAM James's 1884 theory of emotion is perhaps the most well known of all his psychological ideas, particularly as it forms a key historical landmark in the history of the concept; and his notion of "religious emotion" in his seminal work *The Varieties of Religious Experience* (1902) is perhaps one of the most important in shaping the subject in the twentieth century. While James's work on emotion is remarkable for its seminal and defining nature, it is also one of the misrepresented and disputed in the secondary literature. "There are," as Gerald Myers believes, "major discrepancies between what James said he meant and what critical readers think he meant."[1] Confirming this situation in James scholarship, the sociologist Jack Barbalet has argued "that the conventional readings of James's theory of emotion are incomplete and inadequate."[2] The richness and complexity of James's thinking about emotion is a challenge to the textbook definitions and clichés that have hidden the detail of his thinking and his careful qualifications of the subject. In addition, those discussing the subject of emotion in James often ignore the later work on "religious emotion" and, likewise, those exploring "religious emotion" forget the early foundational studies.[3] The growing contemporary interest in emotion has brought about what Barbalet calls a "return to James,"[4] and there is a new appreciation of James's work for supporting physical, cognitive, and social models of emotion.[5] James offers a plurality of perspectives for the myriad of theoretical debates about emotion, and each interpretation seeks to find new arguments that can appeal to James. These readings of James illuminate as much about the brilliance and sophistication of James as a thinker as they do about the complexity of emotion and the theoretical allegiances of current discussions. In order to appreciate this situation and James's theory of "religious emotion," we have to turn to the multilayered nature of his work and the different strands of his thinking after 1884.

The complex history of James's theory of emotion, as opposed to his later theory of "religious emotion," begins when he and the Danish physician Karl Georg Lange (1834–1900)—who simultaneously developed a similar idea—established a post-Darwinian, organic theory of emotions, in what became known as the James-Lange theory.[6] Darwin's 1872 work *The Expression of Emotions* created the possibility of thinking about emotion inside the instinctual body and provided the link between physiology and the emerging "science" of psychology. James carried forward and refined a number of Darwin's ideas and saw the emotions as arising from the instinctual body. This view of emotion went against the grain of contemporary theories of emotion in the new psychology, particularly that put forward by Wilhelm Wundt in Germany, who argued for a theory of "apperception"—the process by which a state of mind (the affect or emotion) produces bodily effects. The key question in the debate between James and Wundt was whether the emotion was a primary or secondary effect. James, along with Lange, argued that the emotion was "a secondary feeling, indirectly aroused, the primary effect being the organic changes in question, which are immediate reflexes following upon the presence of the object."[7] While these early debates about emotion may appear to offer a clear sense of James's model of emotion, his understanding of religious emotion is far more complex and not easily reduced to a physiological dimension. James also recognized in his later work on emotion that there is no such thing as "religious emotion" as such, only emotions directed to religious objects. Here we see how James's writing holds an appreciation of both a physical understanding of emotion and an understanding of emotion as grounded in the "social environment."[8] The contemporary debt to James in the study of emotion becomes apparent in this appreciation of the different dimensions of emotion.

James's Work on Emotion

The complexity of James's theory of "religious emotion" results from his early overlapping of statements, his interweaving of related ideas, the strategic focus of his thinking, and the refinements of this thinking over time, particularly in relation to "religion" and emotion. While James's first "classical" statement on emotion arose in his 1884 article "What Is an Emotion?" (for *Mind*) it was elaborated with further material and responses to critics in chapter 25 of his seminal work *The*

Principles of Psychology, originally published in 1890. He then provided a summary of his position in chapter 24 of his 1892 work *Psychology: A Briefer Course*, and he offered some further comments in response to critics in his 1894 essay "The Physical Basis of Emotion." While some scholars appear to conclude their thinking on the topic at this point in James's writing and argue for a simple organic theory of emotion and others appreciate the range and subtlety of James's writing for a more complex reading of the early work, few refer to the later work on "religious emotion," which adds important material to his developing theory.

When there is an appreciation of James's work as a whole and the detail of his thinking, it is possible to detect, even between the first two pieces he wrote on emotion, a refinement in his understanding, even evidence of a developing set of qualifications and amendments. James was a dynamic thinker, and it is wrong to assume that all he said on the topic of the emotions is captured in the early work or that the early work is one-dimensional. The philosopher Richard Gale underlines this point: "James is too profound, subtle, and suggestive a philosopher for any interpretation to lay claim to being *the* correct one. Any account that makes this claim thereby shows itself to be a wrong interpretation."[9]

We have to appreciate James as a thinker in order to understand the way he unfolds his model of emotion. He first of all is putting forward a "hypothesis," which he seeks to demonstrate through a set of arguments and in a way that provides the "most fruitful way of conceiving of the emotions."[10] The elegance of his style and manner hold the quality of exploration and the desire for understanding, which takes his work in different directions. He is also careful to raise objections and provide counter-arguments, particularly in later revisions of the theory. He also holds a number of complex strands of argument, while focusing on one aspect of what he calls the "total situation" of the emotion.[11] He develops one strand or position while noting other dimensions or aspects, which are left unexamined because of the particular focus or concern.

In this essay, I want to argue that we can find a three-stage picture of James's theory of emotion. This three-stage picture reflects the priority he gives to his discussion of emotion at any one point but also acknowledges that features of each can be seen at the margins of his thinking at *every* stage of his thought. As James indicates, "Every way of classifying a thing is but a way of handling it for some particular purpose."[12]

As James expands his discussion of emotion in different contexts, he develops an emphasis that is different from the base of his key organic theory, and what emerges is a more complex picture of emotion than might originally be supposed from his work on the subject. This is not to say that James is without his own confusions and theoretical lacunae, but that there is a dynamic process in his thinking about emotion. We can, therefore, only understand his later theory of "religious emotion" in the context of his developing thinking on the subject.

In this essay, I will therefore outline three aspects of James's work on emotion, which has so far not been fully appreciated because of the reduction of his model to his early work and the failure to consider carefully the fragments in *The Varieties of Religious Experience*. The three stages of his work can be seen as follows: first, the theory of the "coarser" or "standard" emotions in his early model on the physical basis of emotion; second, the theory of the "subtler" or "complex" emotions, according to a cognitive-social picture of emotion—this relates to what he called the "spiritual" (mental) or "intellectual" emotions; and, finally, the theory of the "religious" and "metaphysical" emotions, which supports his wider social theory of emotion and opens complex questions about the object of "religious emotion."

It is also possible to see in the complex folds of James's early work on emotion important links to his later 1902 theory of emotion and religion. I see this as the silencing of the religious subtext of his theory of emotion, and only by recovering this wider picture of emotion in James can we appreciate the full range of his understanding of emotion. It is in this final stage of his work that we see the influence of Théodule Ribot (1839–1916). Ribot's 1896 study *The Psychology of the Emotions* had an important influence on James's later work and helped him incorporate some important qualifications, particularly with regard to his understanding of the social dimension of emotions in religion. In my view, the multiple picture of James's theory of emotion can only be appreciated when all the strands of his work are brought together. His later theory of "religious emotion" reflects the complex unfolding and interlocking of all aspects of his work on the subject. It is precisely this multiplicity of his thinking on emotion that makes his work amenable to the different schools of thinking about emotion found in contemporary debates.[13]

The "Coarser" or "Standard" Emotions: An Organic Theory

> The labors of Darwin and his successors are only just beginning to reveal the universal parasitism of each special creature upon other special things, and the way in which each creature brings the signature of its special relations stamped on its nervous system with it upon the scene.... But not even a Darwin has exhaustively enumerated *all* the bodily affections characteristic of any one of the standard emotions.[14]

In examining the main strands of James's work on emotions, there is no doubt that the central basis of his theory is grounded in the body. He makes it clear that instinct and emotion "shade imperceptibly into each other," but that while instinct results in some external response in relation to the stimulating object, emotion remains something located in the body.[15] In considering emotion, James therefore focuses on those emotions that show an obvious correlation to the instinctual body, such as rage, love, grief, and fear. As he says clearly in 1884: "I should say first of all that the only emotions I propose expressly to consider are those that have a distinct bodily expression."[16] These emotions he sees as the "coarser" or "standard" emotions, and from this the "classical' construction of James's theory is built, but this limited reading has allowed later commentators to qualify the restricted presentation.

James's central thesis is stated quite simply in 1884 and 1890, respectively, as follows: "My thesis... is that *the bodily changes follow directly the PERCEPTION of the exciting fact, and that our feeling of the same changes as they occur IS the emotion.*" He gives the basic example of the sighting of a bear, which causes the body to instinctively tremble, and subsequently produces the emotion of fear. Emotion is here the perception of a primary bodily sensation. The key feature of this hypothesis is that the body is the primary source of the emotion. The emotions are locked into the movements of the body from each nerve, the rhythms of the bowels and bladder, to the movement of the breath and the pace of the heartbeat. For example, in depression the body is tense and the breath slow, in elation the heart quickens, in worry the eyes and brows tense, and in anger the blood flow increases. The body is here a complex and subtle "sounding-board" to the external object, which produces a change in consciousness. As James makes clear: "no shade of emotion, however... slight should be without a bodily reverberation as unique, when taken in its totality, as is the mental mood itself."[17] The complexity of the interrelation of the body, the nervous system, and the sophisticated reflex system means that the number of emotions has "no limit" and also explains why emotions vary in different individuals.[18]

The next key feature James notes about emotion is that the bodily changes are *felt* "the moment it occurs." Thus, every change in the body results in a change of emotion. What James is trying to show is that there is no preexisting "mind-stuff" from which the emotion is (primarily) constituted. As he argues: "Every passion in turns tells the same story. A purely disembodied human emotion is a nonentity."[19] James gives great emphasis to the fact that "emotion dissociated from all bodily feeling is inconceivable," but to root emotion in the body does not necessarily, as we shall see, reduce emotion *only* to the body.

We must also note that James is aware that it is very difficult to test, "with certainty," his theory experimentally, particularly in distinguishing between the "spiritual" (mental) and corporeal emotions. The only possible proof would be an anaesthetic patient who would be able to exhibit the external emotion but not have any subjective sense of the feeling.[20] Such cases are difficult to find and previous studies of such patients were not concerned about James's question of emotion. The evidence James does provide is that of the change of the body when listening to music or poetry, which then produces a feeling. James provides much anecdotal and introspective evidence, but it remains at the level of a "hypothesis" and his presentation here contains the quality of an exploration, which is contextualized and refined.[21] Nowhere is this seen more clearly than in the question of the relation of the so-called spiritual (mental) emotions or intellectual emotions.

Mind, Body and Emotion

According to James, if we wish to change an emotional state of being we have to change the "outward motions" of our body.[22] Although not explored by James in the early work, such a view can find supporting evidence in yogic practices, and it raises important questions about the body in religious emotion and how ritual changes emotion through bodily acts.[23] This issue raises important questions for thinking about James's later theory of emotion, insofar as religious experience is rooted in the body. Emotion is always rooted in bodily sensation, but, as we shall see, this does not negate religious emotions, because as James makes clear in the *Varieties*, all religious experiences have a physical root.[24] He therefore locates all emotion in the body, as he writes:

> But our emotions must always be inwardly what they are, whatever be the physiological ground of their apparition. If they are deep, pure, worthy, spiritual facts on any conceivable theory of their physiological source, they remain no less deep, pure, spiritual, and worthy of regard on this present sensational theory.[25]

While James's understanding of the "spiritual" is a reference to the "mental," the physiological grounding of "religious emotion" is a position articulated more clearly in what I have called the third stage of his model, which is unfolded in the *Varieties*. He does not negate religion inside the physiological but grounds all human thought and action in a physical correlate. His hypothesis is that "our mental life is knit up with our corporeal frame, in the strictest sense of the term."[26] James does not regard his model of emotion as "materialistic"—that is, reducing everything to the physical process—but he rather notes that our emotions are "conditioned by nervous processes."[27] Emotions in this sense are a "reflex effect of the exciting object."[28]

The Reflex Circuit of Emotion

In his early work, James effectively offers a scheme representing the process of emotion according to a model of brain physiology. The process of emotion is here seen as part of the "ordinary reflex circuit." We can break up James's sequence of the physiological scheme of the emotion as follows:[29] first, "an object falls on a sense-organ," second, "it is apperceived by the appropriate cortical centre or in some way gives rise to an idea of the same object," third, "the reflex currents pass down through their pre-ordained channels, [and] alter the condition of muscle, skin and viscus," and fourth, "these alterations, apperceived like the original object in as many specific portions of the cortex[,]combine with it in consciousness," which results in, fifth, a transformation of the "object-simply-apprehended" into an "object-emotionally-felt."

Adding a number of corollaries to his study, James rejects the idea of a specific center of the brain related to emotion, but rather sees the reflex circuits combining sense-organ and parts of the cortex, which is then perceived in consciousness as an emotion. The existing reflex circuits provide all that is needed for a physiological grounding of the emotion,[30] but already we see that James is working with an "idea of the emotion and the emotion itself,"[31] and this brings us, as Barbalet has pointed out,[32] directly to related questions of consciousness, the self, and cognition in James's thinking. While James makes attempts to locate everything in a Darwinist evolutionary model of emotion,[33] in terms of a residue of former physical reactions or the weakening of previous physical registers, he accepts the complexity of how emotions emerge, and he acknowledges that there may be "accidental" reasons for some emotions emerging: "in an organism as complex as the nervous system, there *must* be many such reactions, incidental to others evolved for utility's sake, but which would never themselves have been evolved independently, for any utility they might possess."[34]

While James struggles to find a consistent position for a strict Darwinian model, there is evidence that in the 1890s he is still trying to maintain a strict physical basis for the coarser emotions, but this does not extend to all emotion. This leads us to the second stage of his theory of emotion.

The "Subtler" or "Complex" Emotions: A Cognitive Theory

In his 1884 discussion of emotion, James makes the important distinction between emotions that can be clearly located in the body, such as rapture, love, ambition, indignation, and pride, and "those inward sensibilities that appeared devoid at first sight of bodily results."[35] The latter he "left out of account," but he did add a few words on the matter, and in his 1890 work he included an extended section on, as he called them, the "subtler" emotions. These emotions are related to moral, intellectual, spiritual (mental), and aesthetic areas of life, which appear to be "genuinely *cerebral* forms of pleasure and displeasure."[36] In this respect, James acknowledges a "*cognitive* act," but seeks to ground this in the body, arguing that the "intellectual feeling *hardly ever* does exist thus unaccompanied."[37] He argues that there are "secondary emotions" in experiences of such things as the appreciation of beauty, music, and art that hold a "bodily reverberation."[38] Nonetheless, he goes even further and acknowledges an "intellectual emotion," as in the example he gives of the English couple in the Academy at Venice appreciating the "Assumption" by Titian. Their "intellectual emotions" in appreciating the picture separate them from their bodily awareness of the winter cold of February. While James is reluctant to completely separate bodily processes from "intellectual emotions," he does hold to this possibility in his very early work on the subject. "If there *be* such a thing as a purely spiritual emotion, I should be inclined to restrict it to this cerebral sense of abundance and ease... of unimpeded and not overstrained activity of thought."[39] It is clear that James recognizes a number of factors making up the emotion, but for him the "visceral ones seem by far the most essential."[40]

While James is keen in 1894 to emphasize the physiology of emotion in response to critics, he never rules out other dimensions. In 1894 he talks of his theory of "emotional consciousness" to show that there is a secondary process after the instinctual reflex in the body. He wants to locate emotion within another order of consideration than the body. However, he is also careful to avoid locating emotion simply in consciousness and denying the body.[41] He was particularly keen to avoid the criticism that his discussing the idea of "subtle" emotions somehow undermined his entire theory.[42] He nonetheless allows for emotions outside the body.

> I allow them hypothetically to exist, however, in the form of the "subtler" emotions, and in the mere intrinsic agreeableness and disagreeableness of particular sensations, images, and thought-processes, where no obvious organic excitement is aroused.[43]

James argues that his theory of emotions is always a theory of "emotional consciousness," and, as Barbalet has argued, it was only a "part" of his theory of emotion—something that has been "always missed" by those reading James.[44] The cognitive theory of emotion is given added significance in his later work "The Sentiment of Rationality" (1879), where he tries to appreciate the passion of philosophy and the "strong feeling" of desiring to know and understand the world.[45] According to Barbalet, this essay is important in securing the sense in which emotion can be a state of mind, which acts as an important bridge to a sociological reading of James.[46]

The debate gets more complex when James talks of the "emotional interests" of faith and recognizes the important connection between feeling and rationality,[47] something that had preoccupied contemporary neuroscience.[48] The idea of the "feelings of rationality" opens space for a cognitive theory of emotion in James more strongly, and when he talks of an "ontological emotion," he is trying to reconcile the emotional quality of religion and faith.[49] The full significance of these reflections on emotion, both in their cognitive and social framing, can only be appreciated by considering the *Varieties*, something ignored in the "secular" bias of later scholarship on James.

Despite this lack of appreciation for the later work on "religious emotion," commentators such as Fraser Watts and Barbalet have rescued the cognitive-social framing of emotion in James. Watts emphasizes the cognitive dimension of emotion, but links this to the social.[50] He appreciates the way James develops a "two-stage model" according to which religious feelings arise out of bodily states. While James holds a cognitive framing of the primary physical base of emotion, Watts is suspicious of the model of the exclusive genesis of emotion in the physical, rather than the recognition of the cognitive formation of emotion. Where Watts emphasizes the cognitive in James's cognitive-social framing, Barbalet emphasizes the social in James's understanding of the cognitive. Barbalet seeks to rescue James's appreciation of the "total 'situations,'" the "relational circumstances," and the importance of "history" in the understanding of emotion.[51] He also goes on to show the importance of emotion for self-knowledge and decision-making in James's wider work.[52] Barbalet also wants to emphasize the way James clarifies his position in response to critics in his 1894 essay "The Physical Basis of Emotion."[53] What Barbalet in effect does is pick up the scattered qualifications and modifications dotted throughout James's work on emotion, and this in turn allows for a more open-ended understanding of emotion. While I am indebted to the work of Watts and Barbalet (cited in the bibliography) and others for rescuing James's cognitive-social framing of emotion, they never sufficiently articulate the central ideas of such thinking that are found in the final stage of his writing on emotion in the *Varieties*.

The "Religious" and "Metaphysical" Emotions: A Social Theory

Throughout James's discussion of emotion that I have presented so far, he touches on a number of wider issues beyond the immediate reach of his central physical model of emotion. In 1884, he does not deny the influence of convention and the social environment,[54] and in 1890 he also acknowledges race and language in ordering the emotions.[55] Here, as already noted, he even shows awareness of a distinction between "the idea of the emotion and the emotion itself."[56] This returns James's theory to a theory of consciousness, because it is the awareness of the physical reflex that creates an emotion, and this demands a different order of statement to distinguish the way emotions are theorized in consciousness. Emotions for James are never simply reduced to the physical origin or bodily reflex but are framed by other factors. The question of "religious emotion" brings together all aspects of James's theory and exposes the tensions in his thinking. His discussion of emotion in the *Varieties* is framed by his understanding of religion, and this illustrates the contextual nature of his thinking. While writers such as Gerald Myers are surprised that the earlier model of emotion is not discussed in the *Varieties*,[57] others, like Watts,[58] believe that James would have "no difficulty in recasting" the work on "religious emotion" in the *Varieties* in terms of the earlier physical-cognitive position. Watts is right to see how the central issues supporting the theory of emotion are still evident in the *Varieties*, but there is much more in James's study of "religious experience" that helps in the theoretical understanding of emotion. While David Lamberth correctly suggests that the *Varieties* does not hold a coherent theory of emotion because the emphasis is on a concept of "experience," not "emotion,"[59] there are sufficient strands of thinking to supplement and extend James's early theory of emotion. The positioning of emotion in terms of "religion" also allows us to see the very specific social dimensions involved in James's construction of "religious emotion."

Religious Emotion

The idea of a "religious emotion" creates a problem for James in terms of the early somatic framing of emotion, because "religion" is an arbitrary and abstract category.[60] Long before contemporary theorists of religion started to question the category of religion,[61] James recognized that the object of religion could not "stand for any single principle or essence, but is rather a collective name."[62] He therefore used the term "religion" carefully and with qualification "for the purpose of these lectures."[63] James's "arbitrary" meaning, established from "the many meanings of the term," is important not only in understanding James's concept of "religious emotion" but also in understanding his idea of religion. Thus, according to James: "Religion, therefore, as I now ask you arbitrarily to take it, shall mean for us *the feelings, acts, and experiences of individual men in their solitude, so far as they apprehend themselves to stand in relation to whatever they may consider the divine.*"[64] The arbitrary nature of the category religion means that emotions are "religious" only in the context of the taxonomy of religion. There are no "religious" emotions as such for James—only "feelings" with reference to the cognitive category "religion."

> There is religious fear, religious love, religious awe, religious joy, and so forth. But religious love is only man's natural emotion of love directed to a religious object; religious fear is only the ordinary fear of commerce, so to speak, the common quaking of the human breast, in so far as the *notion* of divine retribution may arouse it; religious awe is the same *organic* thrill which we feel in a forest at twilight, or in a mountain gorge; only this time it comes over us at the *thought* of our supernatural relations; and similarly of all the various sentiments which may be called into play in the lives of religious persons.[65]

The cognitive and physical structures of emotion are clear from this passage from the *Varieties*, and it shows the continuity in James's thinking. The continuing importance of the somatic structure of religious emotion is also seen in his response to the medical materialists, those who wish to reduce religion to "'nothing but' expressions of organic dispositions."[66] James, in line with his physiological grounding of psychology, is happy to acknowledge the physical symptoms of religious mystics and gurus, because this in no way reduces the value of their insights. Saint Paul could have been having an epileptic seizure on the road to Damascus, but this does not invalidate the religious experience. As James makes clear: "there is not a single one of our states of mind, high or low, healthy or morbid, that has not some organic process as its condition. Scientific theories are organically conditioned just as much as religious emotions."[67]

Consistent with his 1884 position, religious emotion in the *Varieties* has an organic basis (stage 1) and a cognitive structure (stage 2), as the more complex emotions are organized, but it also has a social dimension (stage 3), insofar as the religious object is shaped in the religious context. Here we see how the *Varieties* embraces the different strands of James's work and in this sense consistently reflects his position, as well as developing his thinking on the subject with its particular emphasis. Religious emotion is not reduced to the body but is grounded in the body and determined by a cognitive-social dimension.

Once we recognize these interactive aspects of the religious emotion, it is possible to see how it is formed. Much of this becomes clear in recognizing the distinction between emotion and feeling, which is often confused in James's work. "If," according to Myers,[68] "James had worked out more clearly the link between emotion and feeling, he might have avoided the unfortunate confusion not only in his elaboration of the James-Lange theory, but in his very formulation of it."[69] Feeling in the *Varieties* seems to be linked to the experiential dimension of religion, which would explain why the term "feeling," as opposed to "emotion," appears in the arbitrary definition of religion; and confirms Lamberth's[70] sense of why the *Varieties* is focused on "experience" rather than emotion as such. Feeling, according to the register of experience, is a kind of "record of inner experience," which creates the basis of James's descriptive survey of personal accounts of religion.[71] James is concerned with "the immediate content of the religious consciousness,"[72] which is the "feeling" of a reality, a somatic emotion shaped by a cognitive register of the object. The tensions between feeling and emotion are useful points of reference in understanding how the theory of emotion is embedded in the *Varieties* and how these carry forward the earlier models.

The central question in considering this third stage of James's theory and how it elaborates the social dimension can be seen in relation to the question of how the religious "feeling" (the experiential aspect of emotion) is molded by the cognitive-social dimension. While, as we have seen, the organic structure of religious emotion is central, this does not displace the fact that religious emotion is the same as any other emotion, albeit "directed to a religious object."[73]

As concrete states of mind, made up of a feeling *plus* a specific sort of object, religious emotions of course are psychic entities distinguishable from other concrete emotions; but there is no ground for assuming a simple abstract "religious emotion" to exist as a distinct elementary mental affection by itself, present in every religious experience without exception.[74]

Religious emotions arise from the "common storehouse of emotions,"[75] but there is an additional quality created by the distinctive social aspect of religion—a paradoxical point, given the individualistic nature of James's study of religious experience in the *Varieties*. The cognitive component is marked out clearly in James's sense that "there is a state of mind, known to religious men, but to no others,"[76] and it is "an absolute addition" or "added dimension."[77] Religious consciousness is formed through an imaginative power, which feels something, a presence, or as if something were true.[78] The religious feeling is therefore more accurately seen as an "attitude."[79] The "attitude," or mental outlook, shapes the emotional response, resulting in the religious feeling. It is both a physical and mental process, but the "attitude" is also determined by a set of social processes and, in a move beyond conventional theory of emotion, the sense of something "More," or "an unseen order."[80] Here James moves between a social modeling of the religious feeling in tradition and a "metaphysical" understanding of emotion, although it is also the case that the social order of the community shapes the "metaphysical" belief. These aspects of James theory of religious emotion are some of the most unexplored and the neglected. They reflect his reliance on Ribot's 1896 work *Psychologie des Sentiments* (The psychology of the emotions) and the influence of such thinkers as Frederick Myers (1843–1901), not to mention James's own religious background.[81] However, in my view, Ribot is the key to James's social theory of religious emotion.[82] Once religious feelings are shaped by an "attitude," then the social traditions are central in the development of the emotion. As Ribot outlined: "Except the intellectual feelings themselves, no emotional manifestation depends more on the intellectual development than the religious sentiment, because every religion implies some conception of the universe—a cosmology and a system of metaphysic."[83]

In line with Ribot's analysis, James acknowledges that "conceptions and constructions are thus a necessary part of our religion."[84] Feelings depend on reason to give "public status," and he even acknowledges that "we construe our feelings intellectually."[85] James regards these interpretative frames as "over-beliefs," that is, "buildings-out performed by the intellect into directions of which feeling originally supplied the hint."[86] This return to a philosophical understanding of religious emotion at the end of the *Varieties* illustrates the way James is able to qualify ideas, even as he wants to give priority to feeling in his study.[87]

Mystical Emotions

The full complexity and multi-faceted nature of James's thinking about emotion becomes evident when he moves from discussing the "secondary accretions" of religion in dogmatic theology and philosophy[88]—the "over-beliefs"—to an acknowledgment of something beyond awareness and indicates the reality of some sort of "mystical emotion."[89] James's construction of "mysticism" has rightly been critiqued as a Western psychologized model of the "mystical," determining much thinking about mysticism in philosophy since,[90] and, although much of his definition of mysticism was "for the purpose of the present lecture," we can see the ways he wishes to frame the "mystical" inside a "state of feeling."[91] It is not my aim to recall the debates about James and mysticism,[92] but rather to identify the theoretical issues this opens for his model of emotion.

The abstract nature of "mysticism" puts James's model of emotion under some stress, especially with the allusion to the idea of "mystical emotion." The first problem is that he never fully theorizes the link between "states of consciousness" and "states of feeling." In support of Barbalet's argument that James's theory of emotion cannot be separated from his theory of consciousness,[93] it is important to recognize that the idea of a "mystical emotion" is always linked to an "experience" of the self, which, according to the "introspective" method, also seeks a classification.[94] The emphasis James gives to the "experience" or personal account means that he not only necessitates the mystical but also brings a whole series of emotions under this single category. This is related to a second problem of "mystical emotion." James has already made it clear that there is no such thing as a religious emotion as such, only "a common storehouse of emotions," and this means that "mystical" emotions are themselves powerful emotions directed to a religious object, such as feelings of "union," "safety," "rest," and "love." James seems to support this position, insofar as he sees "religious mysticism as only one half of mysticism,"[95] which allows such emotions to be directed to, so-called, "non-religious" objects (i.e., those not marked out as "religious" in the taxonomical system of a society). Somewhat surprisingly, we find added support for James's social theory of emotion at this point. He argues that religious mysticism derives from the "accumulated traditions" (a cognitive-social model of religious emotion) and that other forms of experience (without the religious tradition organizing the experience) result in a different kind of "mystical" experience.[96] James attributes all these states to the "great subliminal or transmarginal region of which science is beginning to admit the existence, but which so little is really known."[97] The third problem connected to James's idea of mystical emotion is the relation of thought to sensation, which brings us back to James's earlier work on complex emotions (stage 2). James believes that the "immediate feeling" in the mystical state does not have language but is known through the level of sensation. He argues that "mystical" truth "resembles the knowledge given to us in sensations more than that given by conceptual thought."[98] The understanding of mysticism at this point remains problematic and caught in the confused question of thought and feeling in the history of mysticism, such as can be seen in the contrast between a Jamesian "psychological" mysticism and the intellectual tradition of, for example, Pseudo-Dionysius. Nonetheless, it raises the question of the relation between somatic and cognitive features of emotion. James, both in the *Varieties* and in his 1902 Summer School lectures entitled "Intellect and Feeling in Religion,"[99] does establish some link between thought and emotion, especially with the idea of "over-beliefs," but his desire for an ideal "mystical" state outside the Kantian limits of knowledge leaves him with a number of unresolved issues in relation to a "mystical emotion."[100]

This can be seen from the fact that James believes that all states of mind, those classified as religious or not, have a root in the body but "mystics" claim that their experience is outside the senses.[101] The possibility of a physical root of mystical emotions does find support in James's acknowledgment that a mystical state can be experienced by means of intoxicants and anesthetics, such as alcohol and nitrous oxide.[102] However, the link between soma and cognition is found in the idea that the mystical state "add[s] a supersensuous meaning to the ordinary outward data of consciousness"—thus is a combination of body and mind forming a new perspective.[103] The reading of James's theory of emotion through the notion of mystical emotion shows how easily commentators overlook the detail of his naturalistic understanding of "mystical states" as related to the body and the subliminal. According to James, such an understanding did not reduce the value of the experience but rather demonstrated that we are physical beings, even in the face of the "More." Emotion for James was always a complex interaction among our bodies, our minds, and the social traditions that have provided the "over-beliefs" for our experience.[104] If the aim of the *Varieties* had been to clarify his theory of emotions rather than to unfold accounts of religious experience, James might have resolved the tensions that abound in the text, but as it stands, his 1902 text provides only fragments, albeit important ones, for thinking through the earlier questions about emotion.

Conclusion: Pluralism and Religious Emotion

> What is fair to say, given these different viewpoints, is that emotion is a complex, *multidimensional, multifaceted human compound,* including *irreducible* biological and cultural components, which arise or emerge in various socio-relational contexts.[105]

In the contemporary debates about emotion, those arguing for a neurophysiological model, a cognitive model, or a sociocultural model all have a debt to James. What is remarkable in James's thinking is his ability to hold together the different dimensions of emotion, even if he gives emphasis and priority to certain features at different points in his work and retains numerous confusions among the lines of his analysis. To think about "religious emotion" with James takes us back to the body, but does not reduce emotion to the body; it also frames "religious" emotion in the mental attitude and sees such emotion as ordinary emotion in the context of a religious tradition and community. We also find that despite the individualistic tones of his thinking, there is an extraordinary acknowledgment of the social conditions of religious emotion. James brings the study of "religious emotion" back into a qualified intellectual space that challenges scholars—and practitioners—to revaluate the importance of our embodied emotional consciousness, but he also shows how to hold tensions within any thinking about emotion. While there is room for reading James in many different ways, the detail of his texts reflects a more sophisticated James than those with allegiances to particular theories of emotion have perceived. James is a complex thinker and above all a pluralistic one. As he argued in the *Varieties*: "We must frankly recognise the fact that we live in partial systems, and that parts are not interchangeable in the spiritual life."[106] Thinking about religion and emotion "returns us" to James and gives us a new appreciation of the complex interaction among the body, the mind, and the social world. James also takes us to the limits of knowledge and the metaphysics of experience in his quest to understand the nature of religious emotion, especially in his appreciation of the "More." While he does not resolve every issue, he does provide the foundation for our contemporary pluralist understanding of the subject.

NOTES

1. G. E. Myers, *William James: His Life and Thought* (New Haven, Conn.: Yale University Press, 1986), 215.
2. J. M. Barbalet, "William James' Theory of Emotions: Filling in the Picture," *Journal for the Theory of Social Behaviour* 29, 3 (1999): 251–66.
3. See J. Carrette, "Passionate Belief: William James, Emotion, and Religious Experience," in *William James and "The Varieties of Religious Experience,"* edited by J. Carrette (London: Routledge, 2005), 79–93.
4. Barbalet, "William James' Theory of Emotions," 251.
5. F. Watts, "Psychological and Religious Perspectives on Emotion," *Zygon* 32, 2 (1997): 243–60.
6. Collected together in 1922 by Knight Dunlap: C. G. Lange and W. James, *The Emotions*, edited by Knight Dunlap (New York: Hafner, 1967).
7. "The Physical Basis of Emotion" (1894), in James, *Essays in Psychology* (Cambridge, Mass.: Harvard University Press, 1983), 299. In this essay, James responds to Wundt's critique of his own model of emotion.
8. James, "What Is an Emotion?" (1884), in James, *Essays in Psychology*, 175.
9. R. Gale, "The Ecumenicalism of James," in Carrette, *William James and "The Varieties of Religious Experience,"* 171 n. 2.
10. James, *Principles of Psychology*, vol. 2 (1890) (London: Macmillan, 1901), 454.
11. James, "The Physical Basis of Emotion," 301.
12. James, *The Will to Believe and Other Essays in Popular Philosophy* (1897) (New York: Longmans, Green, 1903), 70.
13. The ideas in this essay develop aspects of my original discussion on the topic of James and emotion in the *Varieties*: see "Passionate Belief: William James, Emotion and Religious Experience," in Carrette, *William James and "The Varieties of Religious Experience,"* 79–93.
14. James, "What Is an Emotion?" 171.

15. James, *Principles of Psychology*, vol. 2, 442.
16. James, "What Is an Emotion," 169.
17. Ibid., 170, 172. Emphasis in original.
18. James, *Principles of Psychology*, vol. 2, 454.
19. James, "What Is an Emotion," 174.
20. Ibid., 175; James, *Principles of Psychology*, vol. 2, 455–56; James, "The Physical Basis of Emotion," 310–14.
21. Ibid., "The Physical Basis of Emotion," 308.
22. James, "What Is an Emotion," 178.
23. See James, *The Varieties of Religious Experience* (1902) (Glasgow: Collins, 1960), 386; see also R. King, "Asian Religions and Mysticism: The Legacy of William James in the Study of Religions," in Carrette, *William James and "The Varieties of Religious Experience,"* 106–23.
24. James, *The Varieties*, 36.
25. James, *Principles of Psychology*, vol. 2, 453.
26. James, "What Is an Emotion," 181.
27. James, *Principles of Psychology*, vol. 2, 452.
28. Ibid., 453.
29. James, "What Is an Emotion," 184.
30. James, *Principles of Psychology*, vol. 2, 474.
31. James, "What Is an Emotion," 175.
32. Barbalet, "William James' Theory of Emotions," 259–61.
33. James, *Principles of Psychology*, vol. 2, 477.
34. Ibid., 484.
35. James, "What Is an Emotion," 181.
36. Ibid., 182.
37. Ibid.
38. James, *Principles of Psychology*, vol. 2, 470.
39. Ibid., 477.
40. James, "The Physical Basis of Emotion," 302.
41. Ibid., 304–5.
42. Ibid., 308 n. 10.
43. Ibid., 308.
44. Barbalet, "William James' Theory of Emotions," 256.
45. James, "The Sentiment of Rationality" (1879/1880), in James, *The Will to Believe*, 63.
46. Ibid.
47. Ibid., 73.
48. A. R. Damasio, *Descartes' Error: Emotion, Reason, and the Human Brain* (Oxford: Papermac, 1994).
49. James, "The Sentiment of Rationality," 74–75.
50. Watts, "Psychological and Religious Perspectives on Emotion," 249.
51. Barbalet, "William James' Theory of Emotions," 257–58.
52. Ibid., 259–60.
53. Ibid., 257.
54. James, "What Is an Emotion," 175.
55. James, *Principles of Psychology*, vol. 2, 485.
56. James, "What Is an Emotion," 175.
57. Myers, *William James*, 608.
58. Watts, "Psychological and Religious Perspectives on Emotion," 249.

59. D. C. Lamberth, "Experience and the Value of Religion: Overview and Analysis," in Carrette, *William James and "The Varieties of Religious Experience,"* 239.
60. James, *The Varieties*, 50.
61. See R. McCutcheon, *Manufacturing Religion: The Discourse on Sui Generis Religion and the Politics of Nostalgia* (Oxford: Oxford University Press, 1997); R. King, *Orientalism and Religion* (London: Routledge, 1999); T. Fitzgerald, *The Ideology of Religious Studies* (Oxford: Oxford University Press, 2000).
62. James, *The Varieties*, 46.
63. Ibid., 48.
64. Ibid., 50.
65. Ibid., 47; emphasis added.
66. Ibid., 35.
67. Ibid., 36.
68. Myers, *William James*, 240.
69. Myers's supposition is, however, strongly overwritten by the fact that James's entire theory of emotion is characterized by supplementary qualifications and fragmentary interventions.
70. Lamberth, "Experience and the Value of Religion," 239.
71. James, *The Varieties*, 28.
72. Ibid., 34.
73. Ibid., 47.
74. Ibid.
75. Ibid.
76. Ibid., 64.
77. Ibid., 64–65.
78. Ibid., 66–67.
79. Ibid., 67, 69.
80. Ibid., 69.
81. See E. Taylor, *William James on Consciousness beyond the Margin* (Princeton, N.J.: Princeton University Press, 1996).
82. For a more developed discussion of this point see Carrette, "Passionate Belief," 79–93.
83. T. Ribot, *The Psychology of the Emotions* (London: Walter Scott, 1911), 311.
84. James, *The Varieties*, 416.
85. Ibid., 415–16.
86. Ibid., 415.
87. See D. C. Lamberth, *William James and the Metaphysics of Experience* (Cambridge: Cambridge University Press, 1999).
88. James, *The Varieties*, 429.
89. Ibid., 415.
90. G. Janzten, *Power, Gender, and Christian Mysticism* (Cambridge: Cambridge University Press, 1998); King, *Orientalism and Religion*.
91. James, *The Varieties*, 367.
92. For contemporary discussion on the subject see Carrette, "Passionate Belief," 97–145.
93. Barbalet, "William James' Theory of Emotions," 256, 259.
94. Myers, *William James*, 66.
95. James, *The Varieties*, 410.
96. Ibid.

97. Ibid., 411.
98. Ibid., 391.
99. James, *Manuscript Lectures* (Cambridge, Mass.: Harvard University Press, 1988).
100. On the Kantian root of James's thinking about mysticism, see G. Jantzen, "Mysticism and Experience," *Religious Studies* 25 (September 1989): 295–315.
101. James, *The Varieties*, 36, 391.
102. Ibid., 373.
103. Ibid., 411.
104. Ibid., 486–87.
105. S. Williams, *Emotion and Social Theory* (London: Sage, 2001), 132.
106. James, *The Varieties*, 466.

BIBLIOGRAPHY

Barbalet, J. M. "William James' Theory of Emotions: Filling in the Picture." *Journal for the Theory of Social Behaviour* 29, 3 (1999): 251–66.
Carrette, J., ed. *William James and "The Varieties of Religious Experience."* London: Routledge, 2005.
Damasio, A. R. *Descartes' Error: Emotion, Reason and the Human Brain.* Oxford: Papermac, 1994.
Fitzgerald, T. *The Ideology of Religious Studies.* Oxford: Oxford University Press, 2000.
Gale, R. "The Ecumenicalism of James." In *William James and "The Varieties of Religious Experience,"* edited by J. Carrette. London: Routledge, 2005, 161–71.
James, W. "Answers to Pratt's Questionnaire" (1904). In *Psychology and Religion*, edited by L. B. Brown. London: Penguin, 1973, 123–25.
———. *Essays in Psychology.* Cambridge, Mass.: Harvard University Press, 1983.
———. *Manuscript Lectures.* Cambridge, Mass.: Harvard University Press, 1988.
———. "Notes for Philosophy 20b: Psychological Seminary—The Feelings" (1895–96). In James, *Manuscript Lectures.* Cambridge, Mass.: Harvard University Press, 1988, 212–30.
———. "The Physical Basis of Emotion" (1894). In James, *Essays in Psychology.* Cambridge, Mass.: Harvard University Press, 1983, 299–314.
———. *Principles of Psychology* (1890). Vol. 2. London: Macmillan, 1901.
———. *Psychology: A Briefer Course.* London: Macmillan, 1892.
———. "The Sentiment of Rationality" (1879/1880). In James, *The Will to Believe and Other Essays in Popular Philosophy* (1897). New York: Longmans, Green, 1903, 63–110.
———. "Summer School of Theology Lectures on 'Intellect and Feeling in Religion'" (1902). In James, *Manuscript Lectures.* Cambridge, Mass.: Harvard University Press, 1988, 83–100.
———. *The Varieties of Religious Experience* (1902). Glasgow: Collins, 1960.
———. "What Is an Emotion?" (1884). In James, *Essays in Psychology.* Cambridge, Mass.: Harvard University Press, 1983, 168–87.
———. *The Will to Believe and Other Essays in Popular Philosophy* (1897). New York: Longmans, Green, 1903.
James, W., and Lange, C. G. *The Emotions* (1922). New York: Hafner, 1967.
Jantzen, G. "Mysticism and Experience." *Religious Studies* 25 (September 1989): 295–315.

———. *Power, Gender, and Christian Mysticism*. Cambridge: Cambridge University Press, 1998.
King, R. "Asian Religions and Mysticism: The Legacy of William James in the Study of Religions." In *William James and "The Varieties of Religious Experience,"* edited by J. Carrette. London: Routledge, 2005, 106–23.
———. *Orientalism and Religion*. London: Routledge, 1999.
Lamberth, D. C. "Experience and the Value of Religion: Overview and Analysis." In *William James and "The Varieties of Religious Experience,"* edited by J. Carrette. London: Routledge, 2005, 235–46.
———. *William James and the Metaphysics of Experience*. Cambridge: Cambridge University Press, 1999.
McCutheon, R. T. *Manufacturing Religion: The Discourse on Sui Generis Religion and the Politics of Nostalgia*. Oxford: Oxford University Press, 1997.
Myers, G. E. *William James: His Life and Thought*. New Haven, Conn.: Yale University Press, 1986.
Ribot, T. *The Psychology of the Emotions* (1896). London: Walter Scott, 1911.
Taylor, E. *William James on Consciousness beyond the Margin*. Princeton, N.J.: Princeton University Press, 1996.
———. *William James on Exceptional Mental States*. New York: Scribner's, 1982.
Watts, F. "Psychological and Religious Perspectives on Emotion." *Zygon* 32, 2 (1997): 243–60.
Williams, S. *Emotion and Social Theory*. London: Sage, 2001.

CHAPTER 24

EMILE DURKHEIM

W. S. F. PICKERING

It would be short-sighted to try to expound the place of emotion in the religious thought of Emile Durkheim without first examining the role of emotion in his writings as a whole. This task, which here must of necessity be brief, becomes complicated by the fact that this founder of sociology in France seldom used the word *émotion*, except on the occasions when he referred to *émotion collective* (collective emotion).

Of the meanings put forward in the *Oxford English Dictionary*, the most pertinent calls emotion "any vehement or excited mental state," and with regard to psychology it refers to "a mental feeling or affection (e.g., of pain, desire, hope, etc.) as distinct from cognitions or volitions." One can deduce from this meaning that the emotional comes within the category of the nonrational, that is, human experience that stands outside the rational.

This last point is particularly apposite in looking at Durkheim's thought, because a cursory knowledge of it leads one to assume that the concept of emotion is an angular bedfellow in his analysis of the social. Emotion appears to have a reluctant place in what is essentially a thoroughgoing, rational understanding of society based on essentially cognitive and historical factors. Durkheim founded his sociology enterprise on the equation that in order to understand social phenomena, the social must be explained in terms of the social. This becomes practically explicit in his study of suicide, where the tendency to suicide among particular groups is "explained" by other social facts, by reference to those who are unmarried, widowed, of a particular religious persuasion, and so on. Further, statistics about those who are not married compared with those who are present observations that are hardly shot through with emotion![1] Social facts can never be explained by psychological facts. Such reductionism is against scientific explanation within sociology.

But there is another way of looking at Durkheim's position. The discomfiture in according a significant place to psychology within sociology is derived from his acclaimed standpoint of being first and foremost a Cartesian. In rather crude terms, this implied that he adopted as the foundation of his thought a cerebral approach to knowledge and action. The human being is primarily a thinking animal whose thought is determined by logic. The head rather than the heart rules, and should rule men and women.

Furthermore, Durkheim, trained in philosophy, was also steeped in the thought of Immanuel Kant. Kantianism was popular in the late nineteenth century, especially through the neo-Kantianism of Renouvier, which influenced Durkheim.[2] No matter what form of Kantianism is adopted, prior place is given to the rational, with the consequence that the emotional takes a back seat.

Durkheim held that all knowledge of experience is mentally mediated and is derived through the notion of representation.[3] For Durkheim, collective representations "originate only when they are embodied in material objects, things or beings of every sort—figures, movements, sounds, words and so on—that symbolize and delineate in some outward appearance."[4] This would *at first sight* suggest that in themselves, in their operation, they are not based on human emotion, although they may represent it. They mediate emotion and are therefore techniques operating on emotion.

There arises, however, another problem. Durkheim, like so many of his contemporaries, when he focuses on the rational wants to separate it clearly from the nonrational. But the nonrational is viewed as a residual category. It contains all that is not rational, and this makes it a difficult term to handle in any situation that might be seen in dichotomous terms—rational/irrational or nonrational. Clearly within the nonrational there exist elements that are cognitive and factual, which have no emotional content at all, as well as those that are emotional.[5] Facts about the nature of the cosmos, such as the evolution of the human species, *physical* facts about the human body, in themselves contain no emotional overtones. On the other hand, within social events, together with other social phenomena, there do indeed exist emotional components, for example, in the violation of a sacred command taboo or in the breakup of a marriage. Durkheim unquestionably assumes such components, but they are seen as following on, accompanying, or secondary to the primary analysis of such phenomena, which is rational or, better, "scientific." What is significant is that he does not start with the emotional as the raw material for understanding the social. Not surprisingly, as we shall see, Durkheim runs into difficulties when he deals with these "secondary factors." Throughout this chapter, I shall use the word "irrational" in the sense that it means all that is not rational and/or scientific, that is, it is a residual term.

More on the Nearness of Psychology to Sociology

In the development of the social and human sciences in the nineteenth century, psychology became the recognized discipline whose subject matter embraced the emotions. Durkheim, the Christopher Columbus of sociology, as one Frenchman once called him, readily accepted psychology as a science in its own right and at the same time, quite correctly, he saw the need to draw the boundaries between psychology and sociology. However, his position meant that the emotions could play only a limited part in the development of sociology.[6] Sociology started "out there" in the social, not with the emotional drives or outbursts of the individual.

One issue relating to the scientific study of emotion turns on the fact that emotion itself is subject to variable intensity. A person experiences levels of emotion that affect behavior. By contrast, in the sociology of Durkheim, there is no room for *degrees* of phenomena, for example, degrees of family life, of institutions, of totemism, of representations, and so forth. Social phenomena are seen to exist or not to exist. There may be, and indeed are, different forms of such phenomena, but there are no degrees of intensity. Durkheim openly admitted the difficulty of handling the concept of emotion. In his essay on primitive classification of 1903, he wrote, "Now emotion is naturally refractory to analysis, or at least, lends itself uneasily to it because it is too complex."[7] Having written these words, however, he went on to refer to emotion as a way out of a problem he had set himself in the matter of epistemology. Earlier, in this article, which he wrote in conjunction with Mauss, he set himself the task of showing how categories such as time and space have a distinct relation to social phenomena. At the end of what is a structural exercise of the social being explained by the social, he suddenly interjects a powerful emotional chord. In attempting to understand how notions of classes have been born, he admits he does not know what forces encourage people to divide things and to create classes. And he continues: "It is thus states of collective being [*âme*] which gave birth to the groupings, and these states are moreover manifestly affective. These are sentimental affinities between things as between individuals, and they are classed according to these affinities."[8] Rodney Needham has argued that this unexpected intrusion into his argument considerably weakens it.[9] It means that the nonlogical in the form of emotion has been inserted into the logical. Michio Nakayima does not find this a difficulty. He sees in Durkheim's epistemology an introduction of the emotional, but it does not, he argues, conflict with the logical.[10] I have argued elsewhere that while the subject of classification in the 1903 essay makes no reference to religion, this is not the case in *Les Formes élémentaires*, wherein Durkheim makes religion a key factor in the emergence of categories.[11] As I shall very shortly show, Durkheim assumes that religion has a high emotional component. Therefore, it could be argued that categories emerge through emotional factors. This raises large issues that cannot be pursued here. It is to be noted, nonetheless, that Durkheim never spoke of the emergence of categories in these terms.

In general, the apparently antiemotional approach of Durkheim is only partially justified. Whether they applaud it or not, scholars today see that emotional factors enter into Durkheim's work, in ways interpreters have overlooked in the past. The problem is not so much in admitting the place of the emotions in sociology but precisely the way they can be admitted and studied.

Emotion in Religion in General

Bearing in mind these preliminary remarks, we are now in a position to look at the area of religion where, in Durkheim's thought, references to the emotional are assuredly to be found. The largest written source is without doubt his classical study *Les Formes élémentaires de la vie religieuse* (1912).[12] His conclusions about the nature of religion and its role in society were based on ethnographic material from the earliest preliterate societies then known to scholars. Among the strongest criticisms leveled against the book was the one that challenged his assumption that the study of the Australian tribes could offer a reliable understanding of the religion of advanced societies, especially that found in twentieth-century Europe. Durkheim implied such a connection, but the leap he made, his critics have argued, is not warrantable.

Durkheim has been much praised for his employment and interpretation, as an armchair anthropologist, of ethnographic data reported by those working in the field. He plausibly argued that so-called primitive societies were much more complex than most people thought at the time. Nevertheless he was convinced that in them could be found fundamental or elemental (preferable to elementary) forms, which had universal application. On the other hand, he was convinced, along with others, that such societies were much more moved and motivated by nonrational forces than were modern Western societies. Here he meant emotional forces. Whether the change from preliterate to modern societies was sudden or gradual was a point that brought him into conflict with the philosopher Lévy-Bruhl. Durkheim stood opposed to a sudden break and was thus an evolutionist in a general sense of the word. One feature of this gradual process was that societies were moving toward a social way of life that was increasingly rational and, by inference, less irrational: also, therefore, less emotional. As he wrote in 1899 in connection with changes in attitude toward the individual over a long period of time:

> sensation is the origin [*le fait primitif*] from which superior intellectual functions develop by means of combinations, that the mind of a cultured adult consists, especially today, only of sensations. On the contrary, the importance of their role decreases to the degree to which intelligence develops.[13]

As for the individual, so for society. Evolution means for Durkheim the growth of the rational at the expense of the nonrational, that is, in Durkheim's word, "sensations." And if this can be said of society in general, it can also be said of religion, which stands at the very heart of society. Indeed, when he speaks of the religion destined for the future, which is partially present in contemporary society, namely, the cult of the individual, the element of sensation involving corporate ritual is minimal.

Allied Terms

I have already noted that Durkheim rarely uses the word *émotion* by itself. Yet it is clear that he does refer to phenomena within the nonrational, which in general parlance come clearly within the category of the emotional. One is, therefore, forced to search for allied words such as "sensation," "excitation" (*excitation*), "excitement" (*surexcitation*), "delirium," "ferment," and "force." He certainly employs "force" in abundance. These and other similar terms usually accompany his descriptions of certain social and religious actions and refer to phenomena that may accompany such actions, for example, ritual. In brief, these terms are indicators of the presence of emotion: little else, perhaps, can be said about them.

The Dynamogenetic Force of Religion

As noted, when Durkheim speaks of emotion per se he tends to couple it with the collective. As such, it is the emotion of the group, not that of the individual, that he refers to. One of the clearest examples of what he meant by his concept of *émotion collective* comes out in an impromptu speech he made at a conference in 1914. He said:

> above and beyond all the dogmas and all the denominations, there exists a source of religious life as old as humanity and which can never run dry; it is the one which results from the fusion of *consciences*, of their communion in a common set of ideas, of their co-operation in one work, of the morally invigorating and stimulating influence that every community of men imposes on us.... There exists in us, outside us, religious forces that depend on us for their release, need us to call them into being: forces that we cannot but engender by the mere fact of coming together, thinking together, feeling together, acting together.[14]

Here stands Durkheim's general thesis about emotional components that arise in socioreligious situations that occur within the gathering of those who have a common religious bond. Given the right circumstances, the gathering itself gives rise to irrational forces.

Durkheim's conception of such forces encouraged him to assert that religion was a reality—that is, a social reality, not a spiritual reality. It made people behave in ways they would not otherwise consider, for example, take part in rituals, believe in deities for which there was no empirical evidence, even perform ascetical acts that involved pain. Thus, religion is not an illusion. The very reality of religious behavior in these terms made Durkheim critical of old-fashioned rationalists who saw in religion nothing more than an evil phenomenon that had to be eliminated. The religious skepticism of Durkheim was not of that sort! Free Believers, a group of intellectual Liberal Protestants, were delighted that he spoke so positively about religion at the conference that he addressed. To participate in religious practices meant that people are able to rise above the ordinary and the mundane—to feel they are stronger, better people, they are capable of doing more. Durkheim referred to this as the dynamogenic (*dynamongénique*) function of religion.[15] In his division of religion into the two components of ritual and belief, he saw that in some fashion the same kind of forces are at work in both. However, religious belief does not provide "scientific" knowledge about the world, because religious knowledge is erroneous in the matter of truth. In previous times it was prudent to accept it, for it was all that was available in a given society and was necessary for the solidarity of that society. What is important is that religion provides the believer with greater energy and strength through taking part in ritual. In this way, emotional energy is released.

But surely this force, this bubbling forth of energy, is essentially psychological, since it comes from persons involved in a particular social situation. The religious situation stimulates basic human sensations, which would not be aroused were the situation different. Once again, one faces the ever-hovering discipline of psychology. To clarify the boundary of his discipline, and in simplistic terms, Durkheim appears to argue that the sociologist analyzes the social component—the catalyst—that causes the irrational forces to emerge, but it is the psychologist who then studies the nature of those forces.

To underline his distance from the psychologist, Durkheim held that the emotions involved in group behavior were different from those of the individual. He wrote: "Everyone knows how emotions and passions may break out in a crowd or meeting, often altogether different from those that the individuals thus brought together would have expressed had each of them been exposed to the same experiences individually rather than collectively."[16]

One axiom crucial to Durkheim's concept of *émotion collective* is that from time to time society—groups, clans, nations—needs to meet and to transcend monotony or dreariness of living. This need in societies, preliterate and modern, is met by large social gatherings, mainly of a religious kind.

The Concept of Force

Peppered throughout much of Durkheim's study of religion are the terms force (*force*) and power (*pouvoir*). These words were popular in contemporary physics, Durkheim found them appropriate in analyzing the nature of religion. One can speak of religion having a direct effect on peoples' lives, in giving rise to psychic energy. Where does this energy arise? Surely, nowhere else than from the emotions of individuals caught up in the many components of religion, as we see below.

When the notion of force is used within the physical sciences, it is usually quantifiable. This is not possible in the way Durkheim uses it. He can only refer to it as more or less, in a common-sense yet nonscientific way.

But, one may well ask, does Durkheim introduce the concept of force to "prove" the "reality" of religion, or does he hold that force is the best way to characterize religion? And is it not the case that he alone among his disciples, resorts to the concept of force? Perhaps they saw that the disadvantages of using the term outweighed its advantages?

Delirium

In *The Elementary Forms*, Durkheim refers to delirium. He speaks of an intense religious situation, involving individuals, that is associated with psychic exaltation. He writes:

> It is for this reason that prophets, founders of religions, great saints, in short, the men whose religious consciousness is exceptionally sensitive, very often show signs of an excessive nervous instability, which is even pathological. These physiological defects preordain them to pay great religious roles.[17]

He goes on to state that the ritual use of drinks that have an intoxicating effect can be explained in the same way. It causes him to suggest that religion "has its full share of delirium."[18] Durkheim then comes up with this rather astonishing statement:

> If we are going to call delirium every state in which the mind adds to data immediately perceived by the senses, and projects its sentiments and impressions onto things, there is perhaps no collective representation that is not delirious in some sense or other. Religious beliefs are only a specific instance of a very general law. The whole social environment appears to us to be populated with forces which, in reality, only exist in our minds.[19]

This would seem to contradict what I noted earlier on, namely, that Durkheim's concept of collective representations appears to be "rational," as a structural means of representing "facts" or phenomena that are by their nature social. Now, in this statement Durkheim holds that all collective representations possess some emotional content.[20] At least one question arises: how is this apparently ambiguous situation to be resolved? Very briefly, we might answer as follows: (1) Durkheim's ideas here about emotion are very general and are not developed or analyzed, and (2) he seems to have been obsessed with the notion of force. Since force in his eyes is not directly associated with social phenomena, it can only be located in the emotional.

Religious Experience

One would have thought that with Durkheim openly declaring that sensations are released when people are gathered together for a particular, usually religious, occasion, he would have referred to religious experience as a valid way of dealing with the outcome of such a gathering. But on no occasion does he speak in such terms. The person with whom one associates religious experience is William James, whose book *The Varieties of Religious Experience* was published in 1902 and translated into French by the freethinker Frank Abauzit in 1906. It is profitable to compare these two contemporary writers on the question of religion, as Stedman Jones has done.[21] Though Durkheim was critical of James—he gave lectures on James's concept of pragmatism—he nonetheless admired him.[22] Writing as a psychologist, James based his analysis of religion on a large area of mental life, including memory, the will, and the emotions. His definition, so unlike Durkheim's, involved feelings, acts, and the experiences of individual people in their solitude in encountering the divine. In assessing James's work on religion, Durkheim wrote:

> Along with a recent apologist for the faith [William James] we admit that religious beliefs are based on a specific experience whose demonstrative value is in a sense no way inferior to that of scientific experiments.... From the fact that there exists, if you like, a "religious experience" which can to some extent be justified—is there any case of an experience which cannot?—it does not follow that the reality justifying it conforms objectively to their believers' concept of it.[23]

Here again one sees Durkheim's mistrust of the raw experience of individuals as the basis of scientific analysis of the social, though he is satisfied in utilizing the concept of *émotion collective*. He admits that the experience is not imaginary, but its reality may not be what the "experiencer" experiences. It is the scientist who knows the reality behind the experience. Thus, collective representations very often attribute properties to the things they refer to that do not exist in any form or to any degree.[24] Collective representations (and any "raw material") have to be analyzed by scientific representations. In general, a religiously inclined person would not welcome a scientific interpretation that differed radically from that of the mind (or heart) of the believer.

Having examined the way Durkheim viewed the place of emotion within religion in somewhat general terms, it is now necessary to apply it to a particular area of religious life that engaged his attention.

EFFERVESCENCE

Rightly or wrongly, Durkheimian sociology has been attacked on the grounds that it does not give any significant place to social change. One early critic was Marc Boegner. In responding to Durkheim's impromptu speech in 1914, he criticized him because he offered no explanation of how new religions came into existence in the face of commonly held beliefs within a society.[25] In other words, how can change take place in the face of a uniformity of belief?

Some might parry these criticisms by turning to what Durkheim called collective effervescence. Here within religion is a glaring example of what he called dynamogenic force. It is in fact the *locus classicus* of *émotion collective*. Many scholars today would hold it to be one of the major—if not the major—contribution by Durkheim to the study of religion. Little explored by traditional Durkheimians in the middle of the twentieth century, it is now viewed as having great potentiality for certain types of sociological and anthropological discourse. However, before one becomes excited about effervescence, a note or two of warning should be sounded.

First while the concept was raised and criticized at the time of the publication of *Les Formes élémentaires* in 1912, and again in the 1920s, when Durkheim's ideas were subject to severe criticism at the time of the Affaire Lapie, the concept was all too readily passed over, save in the writing of Gaston Richard.[26] Some interest was rekindled with the publication of Steven Lukes's intellectual biography *Emile Durkheim* in 1973, and with other books on Durkheim.[27] Interestingly enough, in Lukes's book, the indexer thought it necessary to put inverted commas around the word "effervescence." The early critics of Durkheim's exploration of effervescence focused on a methodological issue—how far he had relied on the work of the psychologist Gustave Le Bon, who had written on crowd behavior.[28] The criticism of Durkheim abandoning sociology and following a psychological path is quite unjustifiable, as Talcott Parsons and others have shown.[29] Parsons comments: "Durkheim's theory of ritual [and effervescence therefore] is not anti-intellectual crowd psychology—in fact it is not psychology in any sense."[30] Durkheim in referring such occasions of collective effervescence did not imply an ad hoc crowd (*foule*) but rather a ritually or socially organized gathering of people. For this reason, I prefer the term "effervescent assembly" to "collective effervescence," and indeed Durkheim in some places refers to *rassemblement*.[31]

Second, recent scholars have tended to consider the concept of effervescence to be a vital key in accounting for social and religious changes. So be it. But the danger is that if this position is too enthusiastically adopted, the breadth of all Durkheim's contributions to the study of religion may be reduced to this one concept. Other contributions he made—his grand theories of religion, his study of ritual, the nature of belief, and so on—can be readily overlooked. Raymond Boudon has also made such a point in his recent book *Ya-t-il encore une sociologie?*[32]

Effervescence Described and Expounded

Durkheim describes how effervescence can be located and how it arises as follows:

> We indeed know from experience that when men are gathered together, when they live in a communal life, the very fact of their coming together causes exceptionally intense forces to arise which dominate them, exalt them, give them a quality of life to a degree unknown to them as individuals. Under the influence of collective enthusiasm they are sometimes by a positive delirium which compels them to actions in which they do not recognize themselves.[33]

It seems that his early interest in effervescence was aroused, or became all the more strong, as he came face to face with certain ethnographic studies where tribes assembled together for certain periods of the year after they had spent times of dispersal. Notable examples, where the data were brought to his attention by his nephew, Marcel Mauss, were the Eskimo and tribes in central Australia, for example, the Arunta. It was on regular occasions of reunion that collective effervescence burst forth. Prompted by such tribal rhythmical movements, Durkheim then pointed to a modern example, the events that surrounded the French Revolution—and by extension any occasions where social gatherings exhibited intense excitement. He wrote, in now famous words that bear repetition,

> There are periods in history when, under the influence of some collective upheaval, social interaction becomes much more frequent and more active. Individuals seek each other out and assemble more often. As a result there is a general effervescence characteristic of revolutionary and creative periods.[34]

And for further examples, Durkheim points to what occurred at the time of the Crusades and Joan of Arc and, more recently, the French Revolution and the Dreyfus Affair. Of such intensity of excitement Durkheim further wrote:

> When it attains a certain degree of intensity, the collective life excites religious thought because it gives rise to a state of effervescence, which changes the conditions of psychic activity. Vital energies are overstimulated [*surexcitées*], passions become more animated, sensations are strong: there are even some which are only produced at that moment. Man no longer recognizes himself; he feels transformed.[35]

One can point to collective effervescence as a technique for the production of some given end, but it also contains its own techniques, which involve, among other things, rhythmic music, acceleration of movement, repetitious chanting of words and slogans, and the use of drugs and intoxicating liquids.

Effervescence: Its Two Functions

As early as 1893, in *De la Division du travail social*, Durkheim was firmly convinced that the process of effervescence can take place within assemblies. He wrote: "Identical states of consciousness, as they interchange with one another, reinforce each other."[36] He then went on to observe one particular outcome: "From this fusion emerges a new idea which absorbs the previous ones and which, as a result, is more vivid than each of them taken in isolation. That is why, in large assemblies the emotion turns to violence."[37] Thus, it is possible to argue that as a result of such a gathering, a sacred object can become a profane one and vice versa. This type of effervescence Durkheim actually calls *effervescence créatrice*. He wrote, in well-known words, "So it is in the midst of these effervescent social environments and out of effervescence itself that the religious idea seems to be born."[38] One thing is certain: such gatherings can give rise to uncertainty of outcome, in terms of ideas, ideals, and beliefs. This type of effervescence is closely associated with *surexcitation*. In applying Durkheim's ideas, one of the most obvious and clearest examples of collective effervescence of a creative kind in very recent times has been the assemblies held in connection with the Second Vatican Council. Here the great excitement of the gathering of large numbers of bishops and their advisors gave rise to radical changes in certain beliefs and practices within the Catholic Church.

Durkheim, however, also points to collective assemblies that produce effervescence and where people dissipate considerable energy and feel, if Durkheim's words are accepted, psychically stronger for it. But in contrast with the first type just mentioned, no new ideas or changes in practice result. Sometimes they recall the creation of the world. The annual celebration of Pentecost, for example, among Christians is one example, and the same can be said for Christmas and Easter. These are similar to the annual gatherings of the Arunta, who, after a period of separation, realize in collective assembly the events that commemorate the great mythical foundations of their society. It is the reenactment of the past that is the focus of the assemblies, not the seeking of new ideals and ideas. The rituals are surrounded by the sacred, that which by definition does not change, cannot change, as a result of the ritual.

Durkheim himself implied these two types or, in a loose sense, these two functions when he referred in 1911 to "periods of creation *and* renewal" (emphasis added) at communal gatherings.[39]

From what Durkheim has written, it is surely legitimate to relate these two modes of effervescent assembly to the two necessary components of religion. The creative type of effervescence, emphasizing ideas and values, is clearly in line with religious belief; whereas the relatively less intense type of effervescence, that is, of a confirming and strengthening form, relates to ritual. People become involved in well-established ritual. Emotions may be seen to be strong, but nothing radical occurs by way of changes to belief or religious action. Some evidence for this assertion is evident when Durkheim in the conclusion of *The Elementary Forms* refers to intense collective effervescence. He also does so in the section that deals not with ritual but with religious belief.

The connection we have made between creative effervescence and belief on the one hand and the affirming form of effervescence with ritual on the other raises the issue of the relation between belief or representation and ritual. Which is the more significant in Durkheim's thought? Which is prior? On some occasions, it would seem that ritual is more important, especially if one considers the influence Robertson Smith is said to have had on Durkheim's analysis of religion. There are other occasions when Durkheim, the critical rationalist and follower of Descartes, regards belief as the starting point for understanding social life, not least in religion. The evidence shows that Durkheim did not settle for one or the other: they would appear to be on a par and thus form a true dichotomy.[40] What is more important is that he sees the two dimensions mutually supporting each other—the ritual acting out the myth and the myth giving a *raison d'être* for the ritual.

Effervescence: Criticisms and Assessment

From the way Durkheim approached collective effervescence, it is obvious that he never intended it to be restricted to religious occasions, although these form the best examples. Indeed, the effects and structure of such occasions can be located in any social gathering where there exists an intense emotional interaction among those present. Precisely here is located one of the reasons why Gaston Richard objected to Durkheim's loose use of the concept. Richard, once a colleague of Durkheim in Bordeaux and a collaborator with him on *Année sociologique*, agreed that every society sees the need of gathering together from time to time to maintain and strengthen collective sentiments. However, he went on to say that Durkheim's broad approach meant that "this [collective effervescence] is no less true of a group of drinkers, gastronomes, race-goers, sportsmen, enthusiasts and gamblers, of an association of patriots or a community of believers. Everywhere, the act of gathering reinforces collective states without drawing a distinction between them."[41] The deliberate reason for the occasion—in other words, the context—is, in Durkheim's view, of no importance. It is a technique, we might say, just as applicable to a football crowd as to Pentecost. The latter is a classic example of a well-annotated effervescent assembly, central to the emergence of the Christian church. The common technique reduces religious life to nothing more than social life, to *émotion collective*. Further, *émotion collective* in the form of crowd assembly can on occasions give rise to all forms of triviality and may leave cruelty and violence in its wake, as we see in the hooliganism emanating from many football matches in Europe today.[42] Thus, evil and good emerge from the same source. Where religion is concerned, Richard argued, refined sentiments and moral concerns stem from it—and here, of course, he implied the Christian religion.[43] Apart from any personal religious bias, Richard does have a point, in that Durkheim's approach is too naïve or simplistic and one needs to go beyond description. To be sure, Durkheim became aware of such criticism. Shortly after the publication of *The Elementary Forms*, he said:

> Every communion of consciousness does not produce what is religious. It must, moreover, fulfil [sic] certain specific conditions. Notably it must possess a degree of unity, of intimacy, and the forces which it releases must be sufficiently intense to take the individual outside himself and to raise him to a superior life. Also, the sentiments so roused must be fixed on an object or concrete objects which symbolize them.[44]

That is to say, in searching for an explanation or an adequate understanding of an occasion of collective effervescence, one must look beyond the concept of effervescence per se and take into account "rational" factors relating to the "object" of the effervescent assembly, and indeed with an eye to a "superior life," some kind of moral judgment. Collective effervescence, crudely used, can become a *deus ex machina* in accounting for social change. The problem, however, is to get behind its dynamics, and that Durkheim did not undertake.

It would be fruitful, in trying to unravel the dynamics of effervescent assembly, to take an example, such as that given earlier on—to analyze the Second Vatican Council. It would mean doing so not only in terms of effervescence but in conjunction with the knowledge that is available from records and observations—from the available historical and "ethnographical material." From what is known already, it is crystal clear that academic theologians had worked out the ideas for reform by some time before. What was required to achieve reform was the acceptance of their ideas by the Church as a whole. And it was precisely at this point, we may assume, that collective effervescence played a crucial role. The point is that a technique came into play that was the catalyst of transformation. If the assemblies at Second Vatican Council were valid examples of what Durkheim meant by collective effervescence in its creative mode, then here is no occasion of the withdrawal of reason. Reason plays as much a part as other factors.

One might also point to the great rallies organized by Hitler in the 1930s. Clearly it was these effervescent assemblies, highly organized in a Germanic fashion, that created an enormous amount of collective emotion. They were entirely nation- and Hitler-affirming events that contained no creative impulse or outcome. Their achievement came by way of emotional outburst. Nonetheless, so far as is known, they have not been analyzed or categorized in a Durkheimian mode.

Other Points Should Be Raised

Is it true that every social group, from a cycling club to a modern Western state, needs to have periodic occasions where collective emotions are raised above those of everyday life? Some would deny or have doubts about this, because certain societies appear to assemble more frequently than others and for longer periods of time. Compare, for example, the many Christian festivals once held in medieval Europe, and contrast them to the few that now take place in modern Europe. Why should there be this difference? And since wide cultural variations exist between society and society, zero must logically be a possibility. Note, this is not a question of personal or social holidays, since they contain no ideological component.

Another point has to do with the utter unpredictability of the outcome of an occasion of creative effervescence. The so-called hard sciences reach their goal when they are able to predict an outcome from the fusion or juxtaposition of prior events or elements. This is not the case for collective effervescence. The explanation or even description is ex post facto.

With regard to the two types or modes of effervescent assembly, both of them, of course, generate religious energy or force of one kind or another. How, then, can one say which function—the one focused on ritual gathering or the one focused on the emergence of change and creativity—is occurring at any given gathering?[45]

Collective effervescence as a theory of change can be acceptable only if the one function is selected, namely, that of creativity. Collective effervescence *in itself* is hardly a theory: it is more like a mystery—it is inexplicable and insoluble.

Durkheim lumped together all kinds of effervescent activity on the assumption that they had common characteristics. That is acceptable, but he moves from one form to another, for example, from the regular assembling of Eskimo groups, to the French Revolution, to the Dreyfus Affair.

This leads to the need for some kind of internal classification of types of collective effervescence, perhaps going beyond the two major types we have given. Further, such classification will call also for the introduction of "rational factors"—historical and ethnographical material. I repeat: the study of emotions in themselves will not do the trick!

A Pioneering Concept That Has Not Been Developed

In exploring the phenomenon of effervescent assembly within the framework of sociology and anthropology, Durkheim undertook pioneering work. No one prior to him had employed the concept in the way he did. On the other hand, no subsequent scholar has developed the idea in detail. There have been those who have discovered further examples rather than developing and analyzing the concept. Scholars seem content to hide behind the socioemotional cloud that hangs over effervescent assemblies, without trying to explain its inner dynamics and paradoxes.[46]

Curbing the Emotions

One thing one can say with conviction about Durkheim's thought is that it is not straightforward or unambiguous, despite what initially seems straightforward and "scientific." In the past, there have been those who would label him as some kind of idealist, realist, functionalist, and so on. The result is often the emergence of a vulgar or simplistic Durkheimianism, where the subtleties of his thought can all too easily be overlooked.[47]

Further, the way he employed concepts was frequently ambiguous and complex, as in the case of the sacred and profane. Durkheim deals in unresolved dualisms or ambiguities—individual/society, soul/body, rational/irrational, mechanical/organic, and so on.

Such ambiguity emerges in examining the role of emotion in religion. Attention has been drawn to the presence and effectiveness of emotion in collective situations, such as ritual, and on occasions of *superexcitation*, as in collective effervescence. Religion has dynamogenic powers that cause people to rise above themselves and feel themselves stronger, and may give rise to new beliefs and ideas.

There is another side to the coin, however. Religion, in Durkheim's eyes, not only encourages the release of emotional power but also curbs it. It prevents people from being dominated by passion and limits free expression, which is often associated with emotional outbursts. Moreover, religion makes the individual act in ways that can be personally unpleasant and involve suffering, as in ascetism and self-denial and, I would add, in the extreme cases of persecution and martyrdom. It restrains egoism and is therefore a, perhaps the, foundation of a society in which people can live together harmoniously. Social solidarity or social order can only be established by this means.

To put it crudely, Durkheim considers self-control and self-discipline to be as important as, if not more important than, *émotion collective* in understanding the role of religion in society. He had a sentimental attachment to medieval Roman Catholicism, in part because of its ascetical element and its control over the lives of individuals.[48] In considering suicide he held, rightly or wrongly, that the higher rate of suicide among Protestants than among Catholics was due to the emphasis Protestants placed on individual freedom, with a corresponding weakening of social controls, which in turn prevent people from turning to suicide in the face of stressful or emotionally disturbing events. Again, on social and moral grounds, Durkheim attacked modern art, insofar as he held that it disregarded social and moral restraints and expressed what he saw as decadent—with, might we say, overtones of uncontrolled emotion?

Durkheim firmly held that all down the ages in Christian Europe the authority for morality has been based on religion. Take away religion, and the foundation for morality crumbles. Without an authoritative trumpet call, people will disregard moral directives. Thus, in the light of modern secularization—laicization, in French terms—with its rejection of the truth value of religion, the only possible solution to the problem of moral authority has been to turn to society itself. The sacred of religion has had to be replaced by the sacredness of society. Such an alternative brings with it problems beyond the scope of this chapter.

Durkheim, that puritan of sociologists, had a fear of uncontrolled emotional exuberance, which Calvin also had. Social security or social order, which is absolutely essential for the individual, can only be achieved when people accept the norms dictated by society—norms that contain and control emotional impulses.

Conclusion

The path has turned full circle. The alleged structural analysis of social phenomena devoid of all reference to the emotional is, as I showed at the beginning, a distortion of Durkheim's thought. The presence of the emotional is observable even within social facts, although Durkheim does not consider its nature in detail. While it is true that religion is a social area in which the emotional is most explicit, as in ritual and collective effervescence, it is also true that religion is instrumental in checking the emotions and preventing egoistical tendencies, which is a sine qua non of social life.

Notes

1. Emile Durkheim, *Le Suicide* (Paris: Alcan, 1897).
2. Susan Stedman Jones, "Representation in Durkheim's Masters: Kant and Renouvier," in *Durkheim and Representations*, edited by W. S. F. Pickering (London: Taylor and Francis, 2000), 38–40.
3. Pickering, *Durkheim and Representations*, chaps. 1 and 6.
4. Emile Durkheim, "The Dualism of Human Nature and Its Social Conditions," in *Emile Durkheim, 1858–1917*, edited by Kurt H. Wolff (Columbus: Ohio State University Press, 1960), 335–36.
5. Philip A. Mellor, "Sacred Contagion and Sacred Vitality: Collective Effervescence," *Durkheimian Studies* 4 (1998): 73–114.
6. Durkheim's guide for studying the social—his handbook of 1895, *Les Règles de la méthode sociologique*—contains little or no reference to emotion at all. In the book we find him expounding the first canon of sociology, namely, the social must be explained by the social. Surely, if the emotions were in any way central to the concerns of sociology, they would have received such a recognition. The point is that Durkheim would establish knowledge about the social by basing it on history and ethnography, not on an understanding of the emotions.

Jonathan Fish has argued for a greater recognition of the place of the emotional in interpreting the writings of Durkheim. See, for example, Jonathan Fish, "Religion and the Changing Intensity of Emotional Solidarities in Durkheim's *The Division of Labour in Society* (1893)," *Journal of Classical Sociology* 2, 2 (2002): 203–23.

7. Emile Durkheim and Marcel Mauss, *Primitive Classification*, translated by Rodney Needham (London: Cohen and West, 1963), 88.
8. Ibid., 85.
9. Rodney Needham, introduction to ibid., xxii.
10. Michio Nakayima, "Emotion and the Sociology of Knowledge in Durkheimian Thought," *Durkheimian Studies* 7 (2001): 34.
11. W. S. F. Pickering, "The Origins of Conceptual Thinking in Durkheim," in *Emile Durkheim: Sociologist and Moralist*, edited by S. P. Turner (London: Routledge, 1993), 57.
12. Emile Durkheim, *Les Formes élémentaires de la vie religieuse* (Paris: Alcan, 1912).

13. Emile Durkheim, preface to vol. 2 of *L'Année sociologique*, in Wolff, *Emile Durkheim 1858–1917*, 353.

14. Emile Durkheim, "Contribution to Discussion 'Religious Sentiment at the Present Time,'" in *Durkheim on Religion*, edited by W. S. F. Pickering (London: Routledge and Kegan Paul, 1975), 185.

15. Emile Durkheim and Marcel Mauss, "Review of Frazer, *Totemism and Exogamy*, and Durkheim, *Les Formes élémentaires*," in Pickering, *Durkheim on Religion*, 180.

16. Emile Durkheim, *Moral Education*, translated by Everett K. Wilson and Herman Schnurer (New York: Free Press of Glencoe, 1961), 62.

17. Emile Durkheim, *The Elementary Forms of the Religious Life*, translated by J. R. Redding and W. S. F. Pickering, in Pickering, *Durkheim and Religion*, 136.

18. Ibid.

19. Ibid.

20. See comments of J. Alexander in W. S. F. Pickering, "Representations as Understood by Durkheim: An Introductory Sketch," in Pickering, *Durkheim and Representations* (London: Taylor and Francis, 2000), 19.

21. Susan Stedman Jones, "From *Varieties* to *Elementary Forms*," *Journal of Classical Sociology* 3, 2 (2003): 99–121.

22. See Emile Durkheim, *Pragmatisme et sociologie* (Paris: Vrin, 1955).

23. Durkheim, *The Elementary Forms of the Religious Life*, 146.

24. See ibid., 137.

25. In the 1914 conference already referred to, Marc Boegner attacked Durkheim precisely at this point when he responded to the impromptu speech of Durkheim. Durkheim, Boegner argued, had offered no explanation of how new religions came into being in the face of a common collectivity holding presumably common beliefs; nor did he account for the influence of great religious leaders, such as Jeremiah and Jesus. Durkheim, "Contribution to Discussion 'Religious Sentiment at the Present Time,'" 189.

26. In 1920, Paul Lapie, director of Teachers Training Colleges in France (Ecoles Normales Primaires) and sympathetic to Durkheim, attempted to include texts by Durkheim in the compulsory syllabus (the texts related in the main to morals). This aroused a great deal of opposition. The Affaire Lapie rumbled on, bringing with it strong anti-Durkheim sentiments. In the end, Lapie was made vice-rector of the Academy in Paris in 1925. See Roger Geiger, "Durkheimian Sociology Under Attack," in *The Sociological Domain*, edited by Philippe Besnard (Cambridge: Cambridge University Press, 1983).

27. Steven Lukes, *Emile Durkheim: His Intellectual Life and Work* (London: Penguin Books, 1973).

28. See W. S. F. Pickering, *Durkheim's Sociology of Religion: Themes and Theories* (London: Routledge and Kegan Paul, 1984), 395–403.

29. Talcott Parsons, *The Structure of Social Action* (New York: Free Press of Glencoe, 1937), 437. And see Pickering, *Durkheim's Sociology of Religion*.

30. Parsons, *The Structure of Social Action*, 437.

31. Pickering, *Durkheim's Sociology of Religion*, 399–403.

32. Raymond Boudon, with Robert Leroux, *Ya-t-il encore une sociologie?* (Paris: Odile Jacob, 2003), 111.

33. Durkheim, "Contribution to Discussion 'Religious Sentiment at the Present Time,'" 183.

34. Durkheim, *The Elementary Forms of the Religious Life*, translated by J. R. Redding and W. S. F. Pickering, in Pickering, *Durkheim and Religion*, 129.

35. Ibid., 151.

36. Emile Durkheim, *The Division of Labor in Society*, translated by G. Simpson (New York: Macmillan), 99.

37. Ibid.

38. Emile Durkheim, *The Elementary Forms of the Religious Life*, translated by Joseph Ward Swain (London: Allen and Unwin, 1915), 218–19.

39. Emile Durkheim, *Sociology and Philosophy*, translated by D. F. Pocock (London: Cohen and West, 1953), 134.

40. For a full discussion of these issues, see Pickering, *Durkheim's Sociology of Religion*, chap. 20.

41. Gaston Richard, "Dogmatic Atheism in the Sociology of Religion," translated by J. R. Redding and W. S. F. Pickering and edited by W. S. F. Pickering, in Pickering, *Durkheim on Religion*, 247.

42. In his earlier days, Durkheim used the term "morbid" (*maladive*) effervescence, which obviously involves some kind of moral judgment. It appears in his book *Le Suicide* (1897), where he refers to what is happening in contemporary society alongside progress (422). Nowhere else does he appear to have used the term. It bears out my point that he did not develop the concept or technique of effervescence in any systematic way.

43. Ibid., 248.

44. Emile Durkheim, "The Problem of Religion and the Duality of Human Nature," translated by Robert Alun Jones and W. Paul Vogt, in *Knowledge and Society*, 5 (1984): 18 (translation modified). This important item involving Durkheim and other scholars is all too infrequently overlooked by students of Durkheim, especially in connection with the subject of this chapter.

45. Pickering, *Durkheim's Sociology of Religion*, 410–11, 414–17.

46. Henri Delacroix, in debating with Durkheim, said that what Durkheim had written about collective effervescence was only the beginnings of a study, and "that study would have to be extremely detailed and strict as one attributed more importance to this phenomenon." From Durkheim's 1913 contribution to the discussion of "Le problème religieux et la dualité de la nature humaine," in *Bulletin de la Société française de philosophie* 10:59–63, 65–67, 69–70; see Durkheim, "The Problem of Religion and the Duality of Human Nature," translated by Robert Alun Jones and W. Paul Vogt, in *Knowledge and Society*, 5 (1984): 13.

47. See Susan Stedman Jones, *Durkheim Reconsidered* (Cambridge: Polity Press, 2001), especially chap. 1.

48. See Pickering, *Durkheim's Sociology of Religion*, 427–28.

BIBLIOGRAPHY

Durkheim, Emile. *The Elementary Forms of the Religious Life*. Translated by Joseph Ward Swain. London: Allen and Unwin, 1915.

———. *Moral Education*. Translated by Everett K. Wilson and Herman Schnurer. New York: Free Press of Glencoe, 1961.

———. *Le Suicide*. Paris: Alcan, 1897.

Durkheim, Emile, and Marcel Mauss. *Primitive Classification*. Translated by Rodney Needham. London: Cohen and West, 1963.

Fish, Jonathan. "Religion and the Changing Intensity of Emotional Solidarities in Durkheim's *The Division of Labour in Society* (1893)." *Journal of Classical Sociology* 2, 2 (2002): 203–23.

Jones, Susan Stedman. *Durkheim Reconsidered*. Cambridge: Polity Press, 2001.

———. "From *Varieties* to *Elementary Forms*." *Journal of Classical Sociology* 3, 2 (2003): 99–121.

———. "Representation in Durkheim's Masters: Kant and Renouvier." In *Durkheim and Representations*, edited by W. S. F. Pickering. New York: Taylor and Francis, 2000, 37–79.

Mellor, Philip A. "Sacred Contagion and Sacred Vitality: Collective Effervescence." *Durkheimian Studies* 4 (1998): 73–114.

Nakayima, Michio. "Emotion and the Sociology of Knowledge in Durkheimian Thought." *Durkheimian Studies* 7 (2001): 34.

Pickering, W. S. F. *Durkheim and Representations*. New York: Taylor and Francis, 2000.

———. "The Origins of Conceptual Thinking in Durkheim." In *Emile Durkheim: Sociologist and Moralist*, edited by S. P. Turner. London: Routledge, 1993, 52–70.

CHAPTER 25

FRIEDRICH SCHLEIERMACHER AND RUDOLF OTTO

JACQUELINE MARIÑA

Two names often grouped together in the study of religion are Friedrich Schleiermacher (1768–1884) and Rudolf Otto (1869–1937). Central to their understanding of religion is the idea that religious experience, characterized in terms of feeling, lies at the heart of all genuine religion. In his book *On Religion*, Schleiermacher speaks of religion as a "sense and taste for the Infinite."[1] It is "the immediate consciousness of the universal existence of all finite things, in and through the infinite" and is "to know and to have life in immediate feeling" (*OR* 36). In *The Christian Faith*, Schleiermacher grounds religion in the immediate self-consciousness and the "feeling of absolute dependence."[2] Influenced by Schleiermacher, Otto, too, grounds religion in an original experience of what he calls "the numinous," which "completely eludes apprehension in terms of concepts" and is as such "ineffable"; it can only be grasped through states of feeling.[3] In this chapter I critically examine their views on religion as feeling. The first part of the chapter is devoted to a general understanding of how both men conceived of feeling, the reasons they believed religion had to be understood in its terms, and the common threads linking their perspectives. In the second and third parts, I develop the views of each thinker individually, contrast them with one another, and discuss the peculiar problems that arise in relation to the thought of each.

Common Elements in Schleiermacher and Otto

Both Schleiermacher and Otto insist that religion cannot be reduced to ethics, aesthetics, or metaphysics. Schleiermacher notes it cannot be "an instinct craving for a mess of metaphysical and ethical crumbs" (*OR* 31) and indeed insists that religious feeling is grounded in an original unity of consciousness from which both theoretical and practical reason proceed. Otto famously notes that both rational and irrational elements in the holy are "*sui generis* and irreducible to any other"(*IH* 7); for this reason, the holy "is a category of interpretation and valuation peculiar to the sphere of religion" (*IH* 5). Hence religion cannot be explained through categories that lie outside of it, but can properly be understood only "from within." In order for it to be properly understood, religious feeling either must be presupposed or evoked. To think that one can understand religion by reducing it to concepts derived from the natural or social sciences is to completely miss the mark.

There are several reasons why Schleiermacher, and Otto following him, believed that the category of feeling was the most appropriate for understanding religion. First is the influence of Immanuel Kant (1724–1804). In the *Critique of Pure Reason,* Kant had argued that the concepts of the understanding could find application only insofar as they were schematized by the forms of intuition, namely space and time. As such, the categories of the understanding were applicable only to finite empirical objects given through sense perception; we therefore could not have knowledge of things in themselves. The object of religion, however, is not an object alongside other objects in the spatio-temporal continuum. It is not a thing limited in its being by other things. As such, it cannot be known through the schematized concepts of the understanding. Second, if the object of religion is indeed infinite, then it cannot be an object that stands over against a subject, for then it would be limited by that subject. For Schleiermacher, a grasp of the Infinite is possible only through an original unity of consciousness that precedes the subject–object dichotomy. In the *Speeches* Schleiermacher notes:

> How now are you in the Whole? By your senses. And how are you for yourselves? By the unity of your self-consciousness, which is given chiefly in the possibility of comparing the varying degrees of sensation. How both can only rise together, if both together fashion every act of life, is easy to see. You become sense and the Whole becomes object. Sense and object mingle and unite, then each returns to its place, and the object rent from sense is a perception, and you rent from the object are for yourselves, a feeling. It is this earlier moment I mean, which you always experience yet never experience. The phenomenon of your life is just the result of its constant departure and return. It is scarcely in time at all, so swiftly it passes; it can scarcely be described, so little does it properly exist. (*OR* 43)

This consciousness of the Infinite, in which both self and world are united, is given in a moment of immediate awareness that precedes the subject's awareness of itself *as* a subject over against a world of objects. The use of concepts, however, presupposes self-consciousness, that is, consciousness of the self as accompanying each of its representations, as well as an awareness of a representation as *distinct* from that which it represents. Since consciousness of the Infinite can be given only through such a moment of *immediate* awareness that precedes self-consciousness, the Infinite cannot be apprehended through concepts. It is rather, given directly in an intuition and is apprehended through feeling; no concept can ever be adequate to it.

The feeling of which Schleiermacher speaks is not an *empirical* feeling aroused by an object given to the senses. In the *Speeches*, he notes that since this moment of unity precedes the moment in which the self is conscious of itself as over against the world, knowledge of the Infinite can only be had through *anamnesis* or recollection, a movement toward the inmost depths of the self (*OR* 44). In *The Christian Faith*, Schleiermacher argues that the God-consciousness—the feeling of absolute dependence—can only be given in the immediate self-consciousness:

> any possibility of God being in any way given is entirely excluded because anything that is outwardly given must be given as an object exposed to our counter-influence, however slight this may be.... The transference of the idea of God to any perceptible object, unless one is all the time conscious that it is a piece of purely arbitrary symbolism, is always a corruption, whether it be a temporary transference, i.e., a theophany, or a constitutive transference, in which God is represented as permanently a particular perceptible existence. (*CF* 4.4, 18)

If the God-consciousness is to be experienced as a feeling of *absolute* dependence, then it cannot have anything in the world as its object, for anything in the world is "exposed to our counter-influence." As such, the self could not experience itself as *absolutely* dependent on it. Rather, what is experienced in the feeling of absolute dependence is the "*Whence* of our receptive and active existence," which is "not the world, in the sense of the totality of temporal existence, and still less is it any single part of the world" (*CF* 4.4, 16). Hence there is an important sense in which the feeling of absolute dependence is logically *prior* to experience of the world, since it does not arise from it.

In *The Idea of the Holy* Otto also speaks of both the rational and irrational aspects of the Holy as being a priori. He notes that in accounting for the concepts through which we think of God (such as absoluteness, completion, and goodness), we are "referred away from all sense-experience back to an original capacity of the mind implanted in the 'purest reason' independently of all sense perception" (*IH* 112). More important, the *irrational* aspect of the holy, the numinous, is apprehended through a faculty in the deepest recesses of the self, what mysticism calls the *fundus animae*, that is, the ground of the soul. In explaining how this faculty relates to the experience of the numinous, Otto makes reference to the first lines of the B edition introduction to Kant's first *Critique*, where Kant notes that "though all our knowledge begins *with* experience, it by no means follows that all arises *out of* experience" (*IH* 113). If religion functions in such a manner, there can be no development of religion outside of historically conditioned experience, that is, the experience of the holy begins *with* experience. As such, there can be no such thing as "religion in general" but only the historically conditioned expressions of the numinous and the feelings that correspond to them. On the other hand, Otto's point in referring to the holy as an a priori category is that experience of the numinous is not something we can just *acquire* through our ability to be receptive of stimulus from without. The numinous is not something that can be simply encountered in the world. As Otto notes, "it issues from the deepest foundation of cognitive apprehension that the soul possesses..." (*IH* 113). The experience of the numinous is already present within the self and merely requires certain occasions for it to be brought to consciousness. As such, things in the world experienced as "holy" are not holy in themselves; they are, rather mere occasions for the experience to be brought to consciousness. Beliefs and feelings about such objects are not evoked by natural sense perception, since it is not the objects themselves that are the source of the experience. Otto's next points are worth quoting at length:

> They are themselves not perceptions at all, but peculiar interpretations and valuations, at first of perceptual data, and then–at a higher level–of posited objects and entities, which themselves no longer belong to the perceptual world, but are thought of as supplementing and transcending it. And as they are not themselves sense-perceptions, so neither are they any sort of "transmutation" of sense-perceptions.... The facts of the numinous consciousness point therefore— as likewise do also the "pure concepts of the understanding" of Kant and the ideas and value-judgments of ethics and aesthetics—to a hidden substantive source, from which the religious ideas and feelings are formed, which lies in the mind independently of sense-experience; a "pure reason" in the profoundest sense, which, because of the "surpassingness" of its content, must be distinguished from both the pure theoretical and the pure practical reason of Kant, as something yet higher or deeper than they. (*IH* 13–14)

On several of these points, Otto is in agreement with Schleiermacher. The beliefs and feelings at play in the experience of the numinous come from a "hidden substantive source" already present *inside* the self. Otto can agree with Schleiermacher that the religious experience is ultimately a kind of recollection, since it springs from the very depths of human consciousness. Moreover, these depths are such that they are themselves the ground of both theoretical and practical reason. Nevertheless, despite these real similarities, it is important to keep in mind that at several important junctures Otto sought to distance himself from Schleiermacher. For instance, what Schleiermacher called the intuition and feeling of the Infinite Otto dubbed "the faculty of divination." He criticized Schleiermacher for thinking that this faculty of divination was active in everyone; his own position is that it is a universal *potentiality* (*IH* 149). Only certain persons possessed of "divinatory natures" actualize this consciousness; it is through them that others are awakened to it. For a large part of humanity, the predisposition to religion consists only in "receptivity" and a "principle of judgment and acknowledgement" (*IH* 177). Further, Otto criticized Schleiermacher for not having recognized that not only are there persons capable of divining the holy, there are also persons—for instance, Christ—that are holy themselves (*IH* 155).

Schleiermacher: Religious Feeling as Transcendental Experience

Key to Schleiermacher's "Copernican revolution in theology" is the idea that the basic datum of theology is not dogma, the letter of Scripture, or the rational understanding, but feeling. Prior to Schleiermacher it was thought that religious feelings were occasioned by the content of what was confessed in Scripture and the Christian creeds and confessions. For instance, classical Lutheran theology has the believer reacting with gratitude to the promises of God as revealed and fulfilled in Jesus Christ; this religious emotion is evoked by the content of what is believed. Schleiermacher's theology turned this scheme on its head: religious feeling is the basis of doctrine. The heading of section 15 in *The Christian Faith* reads, "Christian doctrines are accounts of the Christian religious affections set forth in speech" (*CF* 15, 76). And at the end of that section, Schleiermacher remarks that "the doctrines in all their forms have their ultimate ground so exclusively in the emotions of the religious self-consciousness, that where these do not exist the doctrines cannot arise" (*CF* 15, 78). As such, revelation does not operate on us simply as cognitive beings but rather operates at a much deeper level—that of the immediate self-consciousness itself. Revelation, and the doctrines arising from it, are not a set of theoretical propositions about the nature of God as God is in God-self and God's relation to the world. We have access only to God as God stands in relation to us, as the whence of our active and receptive existence.[4] Hence we know God only as God is *experienced*, through the God-consciousness.[5] The original expressions of piety are the poetic and rhetorical, out of which arise symbols pointing past themselves to the ground of all that is (*CF* 15–16,). Christian doctrines are second order statements reflecting and systematizing these original expressions (*CF* 16.1, 79). Insofar as it is *immediate*, the fundamental religious experience has not been worked through by consciousness and is not yet, at this stage, understood in terms of historically conditioned thought forms and categories. However, the expression of this fundamental religious datum in poetry and rhetoric, and their subsequent systematizations, are thus historically conditioned, since they have been mediated by consciousness.

While he understood the immediate self-consciousness universally present in all to be a condition of genuine religion, Schleiermacher did not believe that there was such a thing as religion in general. Religion is always positive religion. It can only make its appearance in a historically conditioned moment as an expression of such a moment. Important in this regard is Schleiermacher's distinction between three grades of consciousness: the confused, animal grade of consciousness, the sensible self-consciousness through which the individual becomes conscious of the distinction between self and world, and the higher consciousness. In the animal grade of consciousness, there is no clear distinction between the self—as that which feels and is receptive—and the object it intuits (*CF* 5.1, 18). Only at the level of the sensible self-consciousness is there a clear distinction between self and world; such a distinction, however, implies self-consciousness, since in order to distinguish between self and world, consciousness must be able to make itself its own object. By the time he writes *The Christian Faith*, Schleiermacher has refined the position initially developed in *On Religion*: the higher consciousness only develops once there is self-consciousness and a clear distinction between self and world. Only insofar as the two are clearly distinguished can the individual become aware of the unitary ground of both. This awareness is *immediate,* insofar as it cannot become a thematized object *for* consciousness; paradoxically, however, it can only make its appearance once the self is clearly aware of the distinction between self and world and is therefore self-conscious. This is why the feeling of absolute dependence is a product of the immediate *self*-consciousness. Since the immediate self-consciousness is never thematized, it is always in the background, remaining self-identical throughout the changing states of an individual's sensible self-consciousness. The "consciousness of absolute dependence... is quite simple, and remains self-identical while all other states are changing" (*CF* 5.3, 21). Decisive for the historically conditioned character of religion, however, is the relation of the higher self-consciousness to the sensible self-consciousness, which always approaches the world from a particular historically conditioned point of view, hence through historically conditioned categories. In a key passage, Schleiermacher notes:

> It is impossible for anyone to be in some moments exclusively conscious of his relations within the realm of the antithesis, and in other moments of this absolute dependence in itself and in a general way; for it is as a person determined for this moment in a particular manner within the realm of the antithesis that he is conscious of his absolute dependence. This relatedness of the sensibly determined to the higher consciousness in the unity of the moment is the consummating point of self-consciousness. (*CF* 5.3, 22)

The genesis of positive religion lies at this consummating point of self-consciousness. At the level of immediate self-consciousness, the God-consciousness is always present and remains the same, but at the level of the antithesis, it can express itself in varying degrees. The God-consciousness is transcendental; it is like a light that casts its rays on all the objects of consciousness affecting how they are understood, valued, and felt. Schleiermacher tells us that it "accompanies our whole existence" and "is never at zero" (*CF* 4.3, 16). As such, the higher consciousness stands in relation to every moment of the sensible self-consciousness. It can, however, be obscured and overshadowed through inattention to the influence of the higher (transcendental) consciousness on moments of the sensible self-consciousness. The "evil condition" from which humans need redemption is precisely such an "obstruction or arrest of the vitality of the higher-consciousness, so that there comes to be little or no union of it with the various determinations of the sensible self-consciousness..." (*CF* 11.2, 55). In its most extreme form, it is "God-forgetfulness." Nevertheless, even when "painted in its darkest colors," the opposition between God-forgetfulness and redemption is always a relative one, that is, a matter of degree, since the feeling of absolute dependence is never at zero. Schleiermacher's characterization of the evil condition is an important one:

> Given an activity of the sensible self-consciousness to occupy a moment of time and to connect it with another: its "exponent" or "index" will be greater than that of the higher self-consciousness for uniting itself therewith; and given an activity of the higher self-consciousness, to occupy a moment of time through union with a determination of the sensible, its "exponent" or "index" will be less than that of the activity of the sensible for completing the moment for itself alone. (*CF* 11.2, 55)

How the moments of the sensible self-consciousness are *connected* is the key to the antithesis. In the evil condition, any given moment of the sensible self-consciousness is given more power to determine the next moment of consciousness than the transcendental consciousness itself. Since the moments of the sensible self-consciousness are made up of the opposition between self and world, the evil condition amounts to the belief (itself having determinative power) that what determines states of the self are intraworldly causes. Each state of the self is understood as determined by prior states of the self and its interaction with the world in accordance with natural laws. As such, the grounds for each state can eventually be traced to events preexisting the agent. This way of understanding one's situation amounts to a state of "captivity or constraint" (*CF* 11.2, 54), since one views oneself and one's actions as ultimately completely determined by outside forces. Moreover, this frame of mind promotes identification of the self with the body. Schleiermacher defines sin as "an arrestment of the determinative power of spirit, due to the independence of the sensuous functions"; it is a "turning away from the creator" (*CF* 66.2, 273). To value what is given through the senses independently of what grounds them promotes fear, for what is given through the senses is finite and corruptible. Schleiermacher remarks that if

> the predominant factor is not the God-consciousness but the flesh, every impression made by the world upon us and invoking an obstruction of our bodily and temporal life must be reckoned as an evil, and the more so, the more definitely the moment of experience terminates solely in the flesh apart from the higher consciousness. (*CF* 75.1, 316)

The body, too, can be threatened, and to identify oneself with it also brings fear.

In redemption, on the other hand, the person understands his or her states as determined principally by the *whence* of his or her active and receptive existence. Central to Schleiermacher's understanding of the Christian faith is that redemption "has been universally and completely accomplished by Jesus of Nazareth" (*CF* 11.3, 56), whose own God-consciousness was perfectly and fully developed. In virtue of this fact, Jesus is able to awaken the God-consciousness in all human beings and so redeem them. Insofar as the God-consciousness is awakened, the person understands herself as *free* in relation to the world, that is, not determined by intraworldly causes. So Schleiermacher: "no one can doubt that the results of free activity take place in virtue of absolute dependence" (*CF* 49.1, 190). He further notes that "the God-consciousness surely... has a content which relates exclusively to human freedom and presupposes it" (*CF* 62.2, 260).[6] Awakening of the God-consciousness empowers the individual to work for the establishment of the kingdom of God on earth. As such, the strength of the God-consciousness makes possible certain kinds of behavior, explored by Schleiermacher in his *Christian Ethics*. There he remarks that "the Kingdom of God on Earth, however, is nothing other than the manner and way of being a Christian, which must always be understood through action."[7] The Christian religious emotions are such that "all pain and all joy are religious only in so far as they are related to activity in the Kingdom of God" (*CF* 9.2, 43). The "will for the Kingdom of God" is "at once love to men and love to Christ and love to God," which is at the same time "Christ's love working in and through us" (*CF* 112.3, 520). Hence the feeling of absolute dependence expresses itself in the activity of the kingdom of God; this activity has as its basis love for God and neighbor springing from the God-consciousness itself. While sin and God-forgetfulness result in fear, in a contraction of the self (insofar as the self is viewed as merely passive and only suffering what happens to it), awakening of the God-consciousness spurs the self to the activity of loving through the love of Christ. Identification of the self with this activity expands the self, insofar as the self no longer identifies itself with the limited and changeable body but with spirit.

For Schleiermacher, the way that an individual *represents* the world ("knowing") and the spring of action ("doing") are the two prongs of human *activity* or spontaneity. This activity stands in contrast with receptivity, that is, how the person is affected from without. Both knowing and doing are integral components of how the God-consciousness *expresses* itself in its relation to the sensible self-consciousness. While both knowing and doing are elements of piety, "they only pertain to it inasmuch as the stirred up Feeling sometimes comes to rest in a thinking which fixes it, sometimes discharges itself in an action which expresses it" (*CF* 3.4, 10). Hence it must be stressed that the feeling of absolute dependence lying at the ground of Christian piety is *transcendental*, that is, it does not merely accompany the way something is represented *as a result* of its having been represented in a particular way. It is, rather, the ground of the manner in which representations at the level of the sensible self-consciousness occur. Piety (the God-consciousness) does not consist of "having certain representations." Rather "representations as such are thereby always merely secondary."[8] Both knowing and doing, the way something is represented and the motive impulses for action, are related to one another in virtue of the fact that the immediate self-consciousness lies at the ground of both. Hence Schleiermacher notes that "A 'Doing' can arise from a 'Knowing'" only "as mediated by a determination of self-consciousness" (*CF* 4.5, 12).[9] Moreover, Schleiermacher recognizes that in all knowledge there is a connection between one representation and the next, and that this movement is due to the *activity* of consciousness; hence knowing, too, is a species of doing mediated by a determination of the immediate self-consciousness. He tells us that the "thinking activity... is also an endeavor to connect the apprehended truth with other truths or to seek out cases for its application, and thus there is always present simultaneously the commencement of a Doing..." (*CF* 3.5, 11). The immediate self-consciousness ultimately grounds the transition from one representation to the next, the movement from representation to desire (as the spring of action) and vice versa, and the incentives to action themselves.

The problem of how to understand the relation of what is represented (what is known) to desire (the impulse to action) preoccupied Schleiermacher in many of his writings on ethics. His mature solution to the problem, found here in *The Christian Faith* and the *Christian Ethics*, is quite different from those proposed in his much earlier *Dialogues on Freedom* (1789) and in *On Freedom* (1790–1792).[10] In the *Dialogues on Freedom*, Schleiermacher argued that *desire* influences what is represented and how long it is dwelt upon.[11] For instance, the individual who is madly in love may choose to ignore the signs that he or she is being cheated on by his or her lover. In such cases, desire can influence what one chooses to dwell upon as well as the inferences that might be made from bits and pieces of information that are put out of mind. In *On Freedom*, on the other hand, Schleiermacher argued the opposite: how something is represented influences whether and how it is desired. There he notes that "even if in some particular case the preponderance of one impulse over others is based in such accidental determinations of the faculty of desire as having been produced through its preceding activities, these in turn have their first ground in the faculty of representation."[12] Here *how* one understands the world is key to desire, the spring of action. Hence if I tell myself that a coworker is not doing his or her fair share of the work, I will have a different attitude to that person, and hence behave in different ways to him or her, than if I thought that he or she was doing more than required. By the time that Schleiermacher writes the *Christian Faith*, he concludes that what makes possible the transition from representation to desire (as the spring of action) and vice versa is something much deeper than both and lying at their ground, namely, the immediate self-consciousness. As such, the immediate self-consciousness lies at the ground of both theoretical and practical reason.

Because the immediate self-consciousness is foundational for both representation and desire, "the world will be a different thing to a man according as he apprehends it from the standpoint of a God-consciousness completely paralyzed or of one absolutely paramount" (*CF* 64.2, 267). In other words, how one understands the world will depend on the relation of the God-consciousness to the sensible self-consciousness. Schleiermacher continues:

> it will accordingly be possible to distinguish in the Christian life itself between what in our conception of the world is to be placed to the account of sin, and what to the account of grace. The like holds good also of the results of man's action upon the world as far as these are realities to himself and come within his consciousness. (*CF* 64.2, 276)

There are ways of looking at the world that are the result of grace, and others that are the result of sin. Whether or not the God-consciousness is operative has an effect on the way the whole world is perceived, understood, and felt. Consequently, the world of the individual receptive of grace is a different one from the world of the individual whose mind has been darkened by sin. The whole Gestalt is different. Schleiermacher understood well before Wittgenstein that *how* the world is perceived has an effect on *what* is perceived.

Rudolf Otto

While Otto was influenced by Schleiermacher, he sought to distance himself from him. In 1904, he was converted to the views of the neo-Kantian Jakob Freidrich Fries (1773–1843). While acknowledging his debt to Schleiermacher, Otto was often critical of him, preferring a Friesian analysis of feeling in religion. In 1909, he published *The Philosophy of Religion Based on Kant and Fries*, where he criticized Schleiermacher for never quite emerging from "that lack of precision" in the *Speeches*; Fries, on the other hand, is commended for his "exact anthropology."[13] Influenced by Fries, Otto speaks of *Ahnung*, an "utterly confused feeling which defies any symbolic expression," of the "depth and mystery of existence." This feeling of the mystery behind all existence persists, despite the understanding of the universe in terms of natural law. It "can surge up in the guise of a disconcerting force, from the deepest places of a man's consciousness, and can make him quiver in every nerve."[14] The Friesian neo-Kantian philosophy helped Otto consolidate his view that what can be known and conceptualized in terms of natural laws are mere phenomena, that is, appearances that are given to the senses. This knowledge, however, does not penetrate to what things are in themselves. This, as well as their ground, remains as mysterious as ever. Religion should not be used to fill in gaps in scientific knowledge. Science concerns itself with mere phenomena; religion, however, is grounded in the feeling for the mystery behind the phenomena themselves.[15]

Despite some of the similarities between Schleiermacher's and Otto's analyses of religious feeling, there are also marked differences between the two. While Schleiermacher's analysis of religious feeling concentrates on the *transcendental* nature of the God consciousness, Otto explores how this feeling becomes manifest in elements given *to consciousness*.[16] It is not that Otto denies the transcendental basis for the genesis of religious feeling, but his focus is on the phenomenology of the religious experience as it develops historically. Shortly into *The Idea of the Holy*, he takes issue with Schleiermacher's analysis of the feeling of absolute dependence, on two counts. First he faults Schleiermacher for making the distinction between the feeling of absolute dependence and the *relative* feeling of dependence on things in the world one of mere *degree* (IH 9). Second, he argues that the religious category Schleiermacher discovered was merely a category of "self-valuation, in the sense of self-depreciation." As such, the religious feeling is "directly and primarily a sort of *self*-consciousness, a feeling concerning oneself in a special determined relation, viz., one's dependence" (*IH* 10). One is first conscious of *the self* as absolutely dependent, and only of God secondarily, as the result of an inference. Putting aside the issue of whether Otto truly grasped the transcendental character of Schleiermacher's analysis of religious feeling, Otto's point is that a phenomenological analysis of religious feeling reveals that its primary datum is not the dependent self. According to Otto, "the 'creature-feeling' is itself a first subjective concomitant and effect of another feeling-element, which casts it like a shadow, but which in itself indubitably has immediate and primary reference to an object outside the self" (*IH* 10–11). This object Otto identifies as "the numinous," which is the irrational element in the Holy. The creature feeling, the feeling of being but "dust and ashes," is the result of another feeling that is prior to it, namely, the feeling of coming into contact with the *tremenda majestas,* the "awful majesty" of God, which cannot be apprehended through concepts but only directly intuited through feeling. The numinous is felt directly as an object *outside* the self. While Otto's analysis is of the feeling states of the individual that comes into contact with the numinous, the numinous should not be confused with these feeling states themselves, nor is the numinous the mere result of an inference from a subjective state; it is apprehended directly as *mysterium tremendum et fascinans*.

Much of Otto's most famous work, *The Idea of the Holy,* is concerned with providing a phenomenological analysis of the feeling elements through which the numinous is apprehended. While the Holy also comprises rational elements (e.g., spirit, selfhood, reason, purpose, and good will), it is with the category of the numinous that Otto is principally concerned. Because the numinous cannot be thought, only felt, Otto calls it *irrational*. The numinous is apprehended as mystery (*mysterium*), as an overwhelming force and overpowering might (*tremendum*), and as fascinating (*fascinans*).

Otto first provides an analysis of the *mysterium*. The numinous is apprehended as something that "strikes us dumb" and brings with it "amazement absolute" (*IH* 26). As such, the numinous is apprehended as "wholly other" (*ganz Anderes*), since it is immediately grasped as something that is of a completely different nature from anything that can be known by the "natural" individual. The *mysterium* is "that which is quite beyond the sphere of the usual, the intelligible, and the familiar, which therefore falls quite outside the limits of the 'canny' and is contrasted with it, filling the mind with blank wonder and astonishment" (*IH* 26). As such, the numinous completely transcends the categories of the mundane. Concepts that are applied to things in this world are only analogically applicable to it, for it is of a radically different order than the world or anything in it. While we can have a positive *experience* of it through feeling, it eludes all apprehension through concepts.[17] Here lies the genesis of negative or apophatic theology that stresses the fact that all our concepts are inadequate to it. The concepts we use to refer to it, such as *mysterium,* are mere ideograms "for the unique content of feeling." In order to understand these ideograms, the person "must already have had the experience himself."[18] What the numinous is "cannot, strictly speaking, be taught, it can only be evoked, awakened in the mind; as everything that comes 'of the spirit' must be awakened" (*IH* 7). All of this carries with it the implication that the category of the numinous is *sui generis*, that is, it cannot be reduced to other categories such as those of psychology or the social sciences, which strive to understand the human being in merely naturalistic terms.

The numinous, according to Otto, is also experienced as *tremendum* and as *fascinans*. The element of the *tremendum* can be further analyzed into three distinct moments. These are (1) that of awfulness, (2) that of overpoweringness, and (3) that of energy or urgency. The three moments are intrinsically related and can easily pass over into one another. Otto describes the element of awfulness as the sense of the absolute unapproachability of the numinous. This sense of its unapproachability brings with it a peculiar dread of a completely different nature from the fear that can be experienced of objects in the natural world. Hence to mark something off as hallowed is to mark it off by this feeling of peculiar dread, which recognizes its numinous character. Otto notes that this feeling of dread is the starting point in the evolution of religion. It first begins as the experience of something "uncanny" or "weird." The feeling can take "wild and demonic forms and can sink to an almost grisly horror and shuddering" (*IH* 13). Examples from the Bible include the *emah* of Yahweh (fear of God), which Yahweh can pour forth to paralyzing effect. In the New Testament, we find the strange idea of the wrath (*orge*) of God, which Otto finds analogous to the *ira deorum* of the Indian pantheon. As Otto notes, this *orge* "is nothing but the *tremendum* itself, apprehended and expressed by the aid of a naïve analogy" (*IH* 18). The naïveté of the analogy consists in thinking of God as wrathful, thereby attributing to God human purpose and emotion. The element of awfulness has two other features worthy of note. First, the divine *orge* is devoid of moral qualities. Second, the way it is "kindled and manifested" is quite strange: "'it is like a hidden force of nature,' like stored-up electricity, discharging itself upon anyone that comes too near. It is 'incalculable' and 'arbitrary'" (*IH* 18). That the *tremendum* is experienced as such a force of nature is further evidence of the insufficiency of the analogy with the idea of "wrath," which has as its basis the idea of personal purposiveness.

Associated with the experience of awfulness is the experience of the *tremendum* as an overpowering might. Its concomitant is the feeling of the self as impotent, as a mere nullity, as something that is not entirely real. Only the numen is felt to be absolutely real. This apprehension of the numen has both ontological and valuational components; the numen is not only that which is absolutely real, it is also felt as that which has absolute worth. This experience is at the heart of mysticism, which witnesses that the I is not essentially real, and which rejects the delusion of selfhood as manifested in the ego. Lastly, partially implied by the experience of the *tremendum* as an overpowering might, but containing other elements as well, is the experience of the energy and urgency of the numen. This is the experience of the living God, of "a force that knows not stint nor stay, which is urgent, active, compelling and alive" (*IH* 24). In love mysticism, it is experienced as the fire of divine love that the mystic can hardly endure.

Despite its daunting character, the numen is also experienced as fascinating. It is an object of search, desire, and longing. Augustine's famous words well express this fascination: "You have made us for yourself, and our hearts are restless until they rest in Thee." As such, the numinous ultimately must be sought out, for only it will quench the deepest desires of the soul. Otto notes: "... above and beyond our rational being lies hidden the ultimate and highest part of our nature, which can find no satisfaction in the mere allaying of the needs of our sensuous, psychical, or intellectual impulses and cravings. The mystics call it the basis or ground of the soul." (*IH* 36).

Further, the numen can be ultimately experienced as the source of unspeakable bliss; this bliss is of a completely different order from natural happiness. Otto speaks of the "*wonderfulness* and rapture which lies in the mysterious beatific experience of the deity" (*IH* 32), an experience that is beyond comparison with any earthly joys. This element of wonderfulness is vaguely apprehended at the very beginning of the religious quest, and is at the heart of the fascinating element of the numen.

For Otto the rational aspect of the Holy, its attributes of reason, goodness, and purpose, are also a priori. Later parts of *The Idea of the Holy* are concerned with a discussion of the relationship between rational and irrational aspects of the Holy. At the very beginning of the book, Otto notes that the rational attributes of the deity do not exhaust the idea of deity, but rather "imply a non-rational or supra-rational Subject of which they are predicates. They are 'essential' (and not merely 'accidental') attributes of that subject, but it is important to notice, *synthetic* essential attributes" (*IH* 2). In other words, the rational elements of the Holy cannot be derived from our concepts of the experience of the irrational elements, and that is why they are *synthetic*. The rational aspects of the Holy somehow schematize the irrational aspects (*IH* 140–41). Critics of Otto rightly point out that how this process of schematization occurs is not clear.[19] This is important, since Otto clearly holds that the experience of the irrational aspect of the numen is foundational to religion; only later does it become schematized. Hence it is not clear what relation the personal aspects of deity—and with these, conceptions of God's goodness and purposes for creation—have to the experience of the irrational numen.[20] The relation of ethics to religion is a problem for Otto.

Both Schleiermacher and Otto make religious experience foundational to religion. The ways they conceive of this experience, while initially grounded in similar assumptions, turn out to be rather different. Schleiermacher develops a sophisticated transcendental analysis of the conditions of the possibility of religious experience. While Otto was highly influenced by Schleiermacher's thought, it is not clear that he grasped the transcendental character of Schleiermacher's analysis. Otto, on the other hand, developed a very powerful phenomenological analysis of the religious experience. Through certain minor revisions, it can be made compatible with Schleiermacher's analysis, that is, through stipulating that the transcendental experience grounds the possibility of the phenomenological experience of the numinous. Moreover, some of the problems I have noted with Otto's analysis of religion—for instance, how to relate rational to nonrational elements—may have the genesis of a solution in Schleiermacher. For Schleiermacher, it will be recalled, the immediate self-consciousness is the ground of both theoretical and practical reason. As such, rational concepts about the deity, as well as precepts regarding the ethical life of the believer, proceed from it as well. Hence the God-consciousness ultimately expresses itself in symbols and concepts having direct ethical implications.

NOTES

1. Friedrich Schleiermacher, *On Religion: Speeches to Its Cultured Despisers*, translated by John Oman (New York: Harper and Rowe, 1958), 103. This is a translation of the third edition of Schleiermacher's *Speeches*. All subsequent citations of the *Speeches* are to this translation and are indicated in the text by *OR*, with page numbers following. The first edition has been introduced, translated, and annotated by Richard Crouter (New York: Cambridge University Press, 1996).

2. Friedrich Schleiermacher, *The Christian Faith*, translated by H. R. MacKintosh and J. S. Stewart (Edinburgh: T & T Clark, 1986), sec. 4, 12–18. Subsequent references to *The Christian Faith* are to this translation and are shown parenthetically in the text as *CF*, followed by the paragraph and section numbers and then page numbers.

3. Rudolf Otto, *The Idea of the Holy*, translated by John W. Harvey (Oxford: Oxford University Press, 1950), 5. Subsequent references to this work are to this translation and are shown parenthetically in the text as *IH*, with followed by the page numbers following.

4. Kant's argument that we cannot have knowledge of things in themselves but only of phenomena given to the senses no doubt played a role in Schleiermacher's turn to the grounding of dogmatics in religious *experience*. In the first edition of the *Speeches* (1799), Schleiermacher notes: "All intuition proceeds from the influence of the intuited on one who intuits.... What you thus intuit and perceive is not the nature of things, but their action upon us. What you know or believe about the nature of things is far beyond the realm of intuition"; Crouter, *On Religion*, 104–5. This passage was slightly altered in later editions, where the word "intuition" is often replaced by "feeling." On the nature of intuition, Schleiermacher follows Kant, for whom intuition is that through which a cognition "relates immediately" to objects. Immanuel Kant, *Critique of Pure Reason*, translated and edited by Paul Guyer and Allen W. Wood (Cambridge: Cambridge University Press, 1998), A19/B33, 172. In the *Speeches*, Schleiermacher defines intuition as an "immediate perception" (Crouter, *On Religion*, 105).

5. For a discussion of how Schleiermacher's basing of religion in religious experience offers a coherent basis for religious pluralism, see my "Schleiermacher on the outpourings of the Inner Fire: Experiential Expressivism and Religious Pluralism," *Religious Studies* 40 (June 2004): 125–43.

6. My own understanding of Schleiermacher is quite different from that presented by Julia Lamm in her book *The Living God: Schleiermacher's Theological Appropriation of Spinoza* (University Park: Pennsylvania State University Press, 1996). As the title of her book suggests, she reads Schleiermacher as heavily influenced by Spinoza. My own reading of Schleiermacher finds him much more indebted to Kant. While Schleiermacher was certainly critical of Kant, he ultimately he came to agree with him that the human being is not determined by intraworldly causes, that is, the person is transcendentally free. While

some of the early essays espouse determinism, by the time he writes *The Christian Faith* (1821–1822) Schleiermacher provides a transcendental analysis of consciousness that is able not only to deal with many of the riddles he struggled with in his early essays but also to account for genuine human freedom in relation to the world.

7. The standard edition of Schleiermacher's *Christian Ethics* still remains *Die christliche Sitte nach den Grundsätzen der evangelischen Kirche im Zusammenhange dargestellt, aus Schleiermacher's handschriftlichen Nachlasse und nachgeschriebenen Vorlesungen*, edited by Ludwig Jonas (Berlin: 1843), in *Friedrich Schleiermacher's sämmtliche Werke*, part I vol. 12. All translations of the *Christian Ethics* are my own.

8. Ibid., 21.

9. Cf. sections 3.4, 8, of *The Christian Faith*: "... the immediate self-consciousness is always the mediating link in the transition between moments in which Knowing predominates and those in which Doing predominates so that a different Doing may proceed from the same knowing according as a different determination of self-consciousness enters in."

10. For an in-depth discussion of the development of Schleiermacher's early ethics, see my "Schleiermacher on the Philosopher's Stone: the Shaping of Schleiermacher's Early Ethics by the Kantian Legacy," *Journal of Religion* 79, 2 (1999): 193–215.

11. The *Dialogues on Freedom* (*Freiheitsgespräch*) can be found in *Schleiermacher Kritische Gesamtausgabe, Jugendschriften, 1787–1796*, edited by Günter Meckenstock (Berlin: de Gruyter, 1984), 139–64.

12. Friedrich Schleiermacher, *On Freedom*, translated by Albert L. Blackwell (Lewiston, N.Y.: Edwin Mellen Press, 1992), 22. The German can be found in Meckenstock, *Schleiermacher Kritische Gesamtausgabe, Jugendshcriften, 1787–1796*, 237.

13. Rudolf Otto, *The Philosophy of Religion Based on Kant and Fries*, translated by E. B. Dicker (London: Williams and Norgate, 1931), 174.

14. Ibid., 137.

15. In *The Philosophy of Religion*, Otto notes: "Instead of crude Dualism, the conviction now begins to gain ground that Nature and Nature's happenings, and obedience to her laws, are rather to be regarded as inadequate, mere phenomena, an image of real things conditioned by limited comprehension, and therefore insufficient as an image of the real world, which is a world free from laws of Nature, free from mathematics and mechanics, a world of spirit and intelligence, a "realm of grace," a world of God." Ibid., 42.

16. Critics of Otto believe that his theory is problematic precisely insofar as it weaves together an empirical, phenomenological analysis of the religious consciousness with philosophical considerations borrowed from Kant and Schleiermacher. Philip Almond, for instance, notes that "it is exactly in the attempt to interweave his empirico-psychological account of religion with his theoretical assumptions as to how it ought to be that the fabric of Otto's analysis unravels. The empirical analysis of religious states of consciousness does imply a *variety* of religious experiences, whereas, by contrast, the presuppositions of Otto's philosophical analysis of the Holy entail a *unity* of religious experience." Philip Almond, *Rudolf Otto* (Chapel Hill: University of North Carolina Press, 1984), 63. Cf. David Bastow, "Otto and Numinous Experience," *Religious Studies* 12, no. 2 (1976): 159–76.

17. Otto notes: "The divine transcends not only time and place, not only measure and number, but all categories of the reason as well. It leaves subsisting only that transcendent basic relationship which is not amenable to any category"; *Religious Essays* (London: Oxford University Press, 1931), 87.

18. Ibid., 39.

19. See for instance Almond, who quotes Bernard Häring's assessment: Otto's "theory of the 'schematization of the numinous by the rational-moral' has met with almost universal criticism;" *Rudolf Otto*, 98. These criticisms are developed by Almond in subsequent pages.

20. On this point, see Melissa Raphael's excellent study *Rudolf Otto and the Concept of Holiness* (Oxford: Clarendon Press, 1997), chapters 4 and 5.

BIBLIOGRAPHY

Almond, Philip. *Rudolf Otto*. Chapel Hill: University of North Carolina Press, 1984.
Bastow, David. "Otto and Numinous Experience." *Religious Studies* 12, no. 2 (1976):159–76.
Frank, Manfred. *Selbstgefühl: Eine Historisch-Systematische Erkundung*. Frankfurt: Suhrkamp, 2002.
Kant, Immanuel. *Critique of Pure Reason*. Translated and edited by Paul Guyer and Allen W. Wood. Cambridge: Cambridge University Press, 1998.
Lamm, Julia A. "The Early Philosophical Roots of Schleiermacher's Notion of Gefühl, 1788–1794." *Harvard Theological Review* 87 (1994): 67–105.
———. *The Living God: Schleiermacher's Theological Appropriation of Spinoza*. University Park: Pennsylvania State University Press, 1996.
Mariña, Jacqueline, ed. *The Cambridge Companion to Friedrich Schleiermacher*. Cambridge: Cambridge University Press, 2005.
———. "A Critical-Interpretive Analysis of Some Early Writings by Schleiermacher on Kant's Views on Human Nature and Freedom (1789–1799) with Translated Texts." *New Athanaeum/Neues Athanaeum* 5 (1998): 11–31.
———. "Schleiermacher on the Outpourings of the Inner Fire: Experiential Expressivism and Religious Pluralism." *Religious Studies* 40, no. 2 (2004): 125–43.
———. "Schleiermacher on the Philosopher's Stone: The Shaping of Schleiermacher's Early Ethics by the Kantian Legacy." *Journal of Religion* 79, no. 2 (1999): 193–215.
———. *Transformation of the Self in the Thought of Friedrich Schleiermacher*. Oxford: Oxford University Press, forthcoming.
Otto, Rudolf. *The Idea of the Holy*. Translated by John W. Harvey. Oxford: Oxford University Press, 1950.
———. *The Philosophy of Religion Based on Kant and Fries*. Translated by E. B. Dicker. London: Williams and Norgate, 1931.
———. *Religious Essays*. London: Oxford University Press, 1931.
Raphael, Melissa. *Rudolf Otto and the Concept of Holiness*. Oxford: Clarendon Press, 1997.
Schleiermacher, Friedrich. *The Christian Faith*. Translated by H. R. Mackintosh and James Stuart Stewart. Edinburgh: T. and T. Clark, 1928. Reprint, with a foreword by B. A. Gerrish, 1999.
———. *Die Christliche Sitte Nach Den Grundsätzen Der Evangelischen Kirche Im Zusammenhange Dargestellt, Aus Schleiermacher's Handschriftlichen Nachlasse Und Nachgeschriebenen Vorlesungen*. Edited by Ludwig Jonas. In *Friedrich Schleiermacher's sämmtliche Werke*, pt. 1, vol. 12. Berlin, 1843.
———. *Kritische Gesamtausgabe*. Edited by H. J. Birkner, G. Ebeling, H. Fischer, H. Kimmerle, and K. V. Selge. Berlin: de Gruyter, 1980–.

———. *On Freedom*. Translated by Albert L. Blackwell. Lewiston, N.Y.: Edwin Mellen Press, 1992.

———. *On Religion: Speeches to Its Cultured Despisers* (1799). Translated by Richard Crouter [from the first German edition]. Cambridge Texts in the History of Philosophy. New York: Cambridge University Press, second edition, 1996.

———. *On Religion: Speeches to Its Cultured Despisers* (1799). Translated by John Oman [from the third German edition], with an introduction by Rudolf Otto. New York: Harper, 1958.

CHAPTER 26

CONSTRUCTIONISM AND ITS CRITICS

JOHN KLOOS

THE notion that emotions are largely physiological broke down some thirty years ago. Since the 1970s, social scientists increasingly have cast human emotions in the arenas of culturally or linguistically constructed expression. Although a wide spectrum of theoretical terminology has been employed, ranging from "constructionism" to "constructivist," I will use the terms "constructionist" and "constructionism," because the language of "constructivism" and its variants appear to be primary catalog terms claimed largely by the disciplines of art and architecture.[1] This essay reviews constructionist theories that bear on the study of religion and emotion. Constructionist theories will be critiqued as both determinist and relativist. Finally, a new road will be suggested by following the recent historical ethnographic work of an important anthropologist of emotion, William M. Reddy.

When one thinks of emotion and religion, the tent revival, like the one described in *I Know Why the Caged Bird Sings*, by Maya Angelou, comes to mind.[2] So (while it is tempting to ask, why does a caged bird sing?) for our purposes, it is the nature of the cage—its structure, its make, its relation to the singing—that is of interest. Timothy Nelson, a sociologist of religion, found "feeling rules" even in the apparently spontaneous emotional outbursts of the African Methodist Episcopal (AME) Church that he studied. Such cues guided the shouting and the mutual encouragement that seemed to bubble over in worship.[3]

How do religious emotions get constructed? What forms serve to give them expression? Generally, religious ritual is a form that can function in such a way so that the emotional lows of loss and grief are made less low. Conversely, ritual can heighten the feelings of joy and happiness at times of celebration. The construction of ritual form reflects specific religious traditions, yet cultures also share more broadly emotional forms for handling death, birth, marriage, and personal formation. Theories of the construction of emotion have been helpful in the study of human societies at times of loss and at times of celebration. We will look at the articulation of such constructs.

The current wave of interest in constructionism crested in the 1970s, and the social scientific research generated by the idea has been significant and wide-reaching. "Constructionist" theories hold that cultures are constructed realities that distinctively shape the personal lives of their members. Indeed, some have held that personal lives are so thoroughly and deeply constructed by such powerful social forces that one's thoughts and feelings are not really one's own. The most influential scholar is the anthropologist Michelle Z. Rosaldo, who pioneered the constructionist approach; she did her fieldwork in the mid-1970s on headhunting societies in the Philippines. More recently, some social theorists have departed from the term "culture" in order to ground the work of construction in language, more specifically in "discourse." We will return to Rosaldo's work, as well as to the turn toward an interest in language.

The back-story is complex enough to require treatment of its own. At present, we can single out a few significant historical influences. By pedigree and lineage, constructionism goes back to the rise of the social scientific disciplines (especially the basic frame and governing assumptions of Emile Durkheim, though a case could be made that the attention to "personality" of Ruth Benedict and Margaret Mead in the early twentieth century played an important role); constructionism owes its contemporary incarnation to seminal work by Peter Berger and Thomas Luckmann. In *The Social Construction of Reality: A Treatise in the Sociology of Knowledge*, they developed a sociology in order to show how social orders went about the process of internalizing reality through highly charged human emotions.[4] This work continues to be a cornerstone of current interest in constructionism.

Berger and Luckmann's forerunners in the "sociology of knowledge" were Max Scheler, Karl Mannheim, Robert Merton, Alfred Schutz, and George Herbert Mead. In 1920s Germany, Scheler coined the term "sociology of knowledge" (*Wissenssoziologie*).[5] First and foremost a philosopher, Scheler made sure to keep ideas and society distinct. No direct link, or one-to-one correspondence, was seen between "real" and "ideal factors," and so ideas were kept apart from any direct social shaping. Karl Mannheim was bolder. Society determined not only the form but also the content of ideas. Ideology, which may not raise nonrational forces to the level of consciousness and may even conceal them, may nevertheless employ emotions in order to persuade. It was the "utopian mentality" that was capable of integrating emotions.[6]

Constructionist theory has made inroads into anthropology as well as sociology. Before turning to anthropology, however, I will briefly consider constructionism in the discipline of psychology. James R. Averill employed the constructionist theory in works on anger and on love. In *Anger and Aggression: An Essay on Emotion*, he reviewed a long tradition, including Plato, Aristotle, Seneca, Lactantius,

Aquinas, and Descartes, interpreting their ideas in biological, psychological, and sociocultural terms.[7] In "The Social Construction of Emotion: With Special Reference to Love," Averill studied romantic love and viewed "falling in love" as an "emotional syndrome," or a set of socially organized and constructed responses. Love's components from this standpoint lifted up the idealization of the beloved, suddenness of onset, physiological arousal, and long-term commitment.[8] The kind of psychology best suited to constructionist studies of emotion is social psychology. As will be apparent, such study may help overcome a major weakness in constructionist theory, namely, the difficulty in getting at inwardness or subjective experience.

Michelle Rosaldo set the terms for the study of the cultural construction of emotions. In her early and influential study of the Ilongot in the Philippines, *Knowledge and Passion: Ilongot Notions of Self and Social Life*, Rosaldo examined the ways emotions shaped the relationship between the self and the local culture.[9] She found emotions to be physiological but also cognitive in the way they link to moral and ideological attitudes. The Ilongot hunters and farmers practiced headhunting for a long time. In recent years—in fact, it was during Rosaldo's fieldwork—they were forced to abandon the tribal ritual, and many Ilongot subsequently took up Christianity.

In her study of these people, Rosaldo found that their emotions were deeply felt and expressed in and through the tribal lexicon of *liget*, an emotion word denoting anger, along with numerous other, related emotions such as jealousy and envy, as well as states like energy and heat. For instance, grief over the death of a loved one or a friend could intensify *liget* and thereby drive the mourner out of control. Confusion, dangerous behavior, irrationality could only be quelled by a great celebration led by the tribe's elders following the headhunting raid. At this time, the group would burst into celebrations that finally brought closure to the heightened feelings of grief and the out-of-control expressions of loss and mourning. Rosaldo concluded from this that the emotions surrounding *liget* motivated the Ilongot to participate in the practice of religious ritual in order to bring about a balance in their feelings.

Interestingly, on her return to the Philippines, Rosaldo found that the headhunting ritual had been banned, so she was able to check the conditions of the emotional life of the Ilongot and to determine the levers for action. At this time, after many had become Christian, an anthropological comparison, before and after, was possible. It began when the Ilongot asked the anthropologist to play her tape-recording of their headhunting ritual party. The sounds of their joy proved too much to bear, and so they demanded that she stop the playback. So attractive was the system for handling *liget* that they could no longer bear the memory of it! Christianity had provided a model and means for dealing with death, but it did so in blander, more superficial ways. From this observation, Rosaldo adduced that the depth of emotion among the Ilongot was deeper than she and others had seen. Appreciation for the depth of feeling provoked by the handling of *liget* indicated that symbol systems capable of steering group emotions could not be easily substituted. They had been constructed in a particular and a powerful way. The social terms of emotions within this local ritual order had an incomparable authority that could not be abridged.

This local reality, and how it was constructed, became supremely important to Rosaldo's beliefs and subsequent claims about culture. Locally constituted perspectives, including religious perspectives, shape thought and everyday life. To know how, the scholar must study the language and the social cues in each specific culture, because language is more than a system of classifications. Common discourse, habits of conversation, communication patterns, and daily expressions are worthy of close examination, since meaning is "bound up with use." Emotions link person, act, and social environs.

In her reflective essay "Toward an Anthropology of Self and Feeling," Rosaldo argues that there is no human psychic unity, no genetic mind. Persons are social first and individuals second. Each culture—each religious culture, one might add—must be viewed on its own terms. As a caveat, she reminds scholars that their own mental ties to their own cultures will limit their abilities to understand others. Because emotions cannot be classed in universal terms, the only recourse is to study the terms and frames and languages of the cultures that shape personalities.[10] Rosaldo's attention to local Ilongot ways and her claims about the value of particular societies have been criticized for their apparent relativity. We will examine this critique shortly.

First we consider the work of Lila Abu-Lughod and Catherine Lutz, who, in the 1980s, shifted the methodological emphasis. Rosaldo had followed the Geertzian concept of "culture," but Abu-Lughod and Lutz preferred the term "discourse." Their nuances show that discourses within a culture can stand in opposition to the culture in which they develop. Through this refinement, both constructionists became critical of the dominant Western cultures in which emotions, and theories about emotions, were shaped. Lila Abu-Lughod published *Veiled Sentiments: Honor and Poetry in a Bedouin Society* in 1986.[11] Her study of Bedouin love poetry and the cultural constraints on love and marriage was done within a society that severely limited the work of a female anthropologist. She simply could not conduct her own work in public, and, as a result, she had to accommodate herself to the private home of one of the Bedouin families. There, as adoptive daughter, she was able to unveil private sentiments, and in so doing, she found that oral poetry was the vehicle through which women and men express feelings that violate the moral code. Indeed, within this world, she found a construction of emotion that ran counter to external male perceptions. Such meanings can betray social constructions.

In 1988, Catherine Lutz published *Unnatural Emotion: Everyday Sentiments on a Micronesian Atoll and Their Challenge to Western Theory*.[12] On Ifaluk, thought and emotion were not distinguished, and, in particular, women were not looked down on for expressing emotion. Rather, men and women shared the emotion of *song*, which Lutz called "righteous anger." Each gender was capable of its expression, as well as the emotion of fear or anxiety (*metagu*), which accompanied one's submission to the authority of one filled with righteous anger. Lutz's discovery among the Ifaluk led to a sustained critique of Western attitudes regarding emotion, especially the assigning of irrational emotion to women's role. The perception that the female was less capable of reason than the male, and therefore, in the West, she was weaker, is, for Lutz, pure nonsense.

Constructionist assumptions and theory aided Abu-Lughod and Lutz in their studies of emotions and women, yet at the same time, these anthropologists were critical of the dominant culture and its biased assumptions regarding male priority. Significantly, both studies used the term "discourse" instead of "culture," perhaps as a way of limiting the domain of control for the construction of emotion. That is, for Geertz, cultural examples inform or shape practice and do not open the door for much self-critique. However, the notion that discourse shapes emotion allows societies to change their discourse, or even adopt new discourses for informing emotions. It is noteworthy that the new discourses uncovered do not always agree with the larger cultural meanings. Indeed, emotions shaped by new discourses could effectively critique present cultural values.

Although theories of constructionism have generated serious scholarly discovery, the fundamental framework is open to important criticism. Constructionism can be overly deterministic, not leaving room for subjectivity, or inwardness. How does one account for those members who depart from the larger social code? Can the theory allow for expression of unique personal feeling apart from the collective? A second criticism is that constructionist theory is relativist; one society and its values provide a particular knowledge not open to comparison. Each society must be studied and appreciated on its own terms, its own plane of reference, so comparative judgments are difficult. This is especially true of any attempts to say which values are better or worse. A third critique is that constructionism describes static social systems, rather than accounting for historical change. If societies are constructed, it ought to be easy to narrate a social development showing how the construction process takes place.

Clifford Geertz, in his essay "Religion as a Cultural System," notes that the term "perspective" has an advantage over the more common term "attitude," which seems less scientific. He admits that he "avoided" the term "attitude"

> because of its strong subjectivist connotations, its tendency to place the stress upon a supposed inner state of an actor rather than on a certain sort of relation—a symbolically mediated one—between an actor and a situation. This is not to say, of course, that a phenomenological analysis of religious experience, if cast in intersubjective, nontranscendental, genuinely scientific terms... is not essential to a full understanding of religious belief, but merely that that is not the focus of my concern.[13]

Of course, the study of the construction of society, especially the structuring of religious emotions or the shaping of ritual action by the emotions, is open to criticism from the vantage point of subjectivity, if only one could get to it. How one bridges this divide is a mark of fidelity, depth of insight, and openness. Such attention is especially important for the study of religion and emotion.

Look, for instance, at "attachment theory," which could be employed in a psychological constructionist analysis. The caregiver, in protecting the little one, forms the mode for the expression of love that lasts throughout a lifetime. A frontal smiley face above the crib opens the door to infant happiness, readies the child to play the game of love, and, ultimately, to begin to construct an image of, and a relationship with, the divine.[14] As much as attachment theory can explain of intimate emotion and behavior, the subjective view somehow trumps this construction of emotions and social interaction. Say what you will about objective relations of infant to caregiver—analyze the constructed lifelong attachment all you want—it is *my mother lying on her deathbed in the intensive care unit!*

In "Missing Emotion: The Limitations of Cultural Constructionism in the Study of Emotion," Margot Lyon sees a real flaw in that the theory cannot account for subjective differences. She claims that one "must go beyond constructionism if one aims, for example, to understand the role of contemporary institutional contexts in the generation and development of cultural difference."[15] Because private meanings and public symbols, including religious activities, are not the same thing, subjective experience must be studied carefully. For Lyon, the constructionist account of emotion cannot get at the inner life of the private individual, no matter how much it is argued to the contrary.[16] Innerness—emotion—is not merely culturally constructed code. There is no one-to-one correspondence between a culture's symbolic field and a person's heart. For Lyon, "emotion is more than a domain of cultural conception, more than a mere construction," and to spell out personal emotions in a coded way that is based on cultural codes found within self and society is "chasing one's own tail."[17]

Differences exist within a single culture. There is not true accounting without clarity at that most crucial point where public and private meet. This is precisely the value of psychological analysis: to help mark out that area between outside and inside. The sociologist Edward Shils worked out a similar project in describing "tradition" as having "intrinsic value." He noted how differences happen at the same time—how, even within the same tradition, individuals of different generations find different meanings in the same event. This is Karl Mannheim's idea that "things of different ages" can exist "at the same time."[18] For Shils, to be "in the Grip of the Past" shows how different people living in the same present hold varied recollections. The key to the intrinsic value is that persons experience their worlds in distinctive, subjective ways. The limitation for the constructionist framework is that it does not often acknowledge such latitude. In fact, it often appears flat and two-dimensional. This problem is not new. C. Wright Mills tried to get at subjectivity from a sociological perspective in 1959 when he wrote of "the sociological imagination."[19]

Not far off, William Wordsworth's idea of poetry as "emotion recollected in tranquility" suggests a level of personal meaning beyond the empirical, beyond the common. Can scientists get at poetic recollection? T. S. Eliot believed that a marker was necessary:

> The only way of expressing emotion in the form of art is by finding an "objective correlative"; in other words, a set of objects, a situation, a chain of events which shall be the formula of that *particular* emotion; such that when the external facts, which must terminate in sensory experience, are given, the emotion is immediately evoked.[20]

Can aesthetic roads lead to competent understandings of emotion, ones that might pave the way to future thinking about religion? Not if one follows in lockstep Peter Berger. For this conservative sociologist, reality is properly legitimated by religion in orderly fashion. But what about when life happens otherwise? Furthermore, how does one account for the great political breakthroughs? For Berger, religion sponsors the order of society, and it relates disorder

> to that yawning abyss of chaos that is the oldest antagonist of the sacred. To go against the order of society is always to risk plunging into anomy. To go against the order of society as religiously legitimated, however, is to make a compact with the primeval forces of darkness. To deny reality as it has been socially defined is to risk falling into irreality.[21]

Is not this exactly what the Prophet Mohammed did? Is not this just why he and his followers fled to Yathrib? More recently, President F. W. de Klerk let Nelson Mandela out of prison thinking the old warrior was all used up and, should he try out the prophetic voice, he would become a laughingstock! The construction of religious knowledge and reality cannot account very well for the existence of extraordinary beings, for the phenomenon of historic breakthroughs. It must also be said that the constructivist approach to emotion cannot account for extraordinary religious feelings. This is so for two reasons: first, they emerge out of the same descriptive system sharing the same assumptions, the same frame (Berger admits as much when he says, "the ecstasy of marginal situations is a phenomenon of individual experience");[22] second, the power of religious feeling cannot be contained in thought about it. Perhaps Geertz was right. There is a subjective way of knowing religion and emotion, but it is simply not the way of social science.

Specialists like the mystic, the poet, the prophet, the seer, and the shaman care nothing for constructionist schemes. They would break the mold, would break through the formed world, like Neo in the film *The Matrix*.[23] Do all but a few have the same feelings? Are most if not all cultures the same in this regard? Are there no ways to evaluate them in terms of the quality of their ideals and values? Inquiry into the existence of universal emotions has become one way to think about subjectivity. Some address the issue by identifying "basic emotions."[24] Particularists will have none of it. For them, local culture is the only template for the construction of emotions. Is there to be no comparison? No possibility of judgment or of the evaluation of cultures or discourses?

The term "relativism" denotes the view that particular social orders are so entirely unique that they cannot possibly be compared for the purposes of ranking. Each local system has merit; to learn what it is, one must be immersed in its study, learn the culture's language, and examine each social ordering on its own plane of reference. The relativist denies the presence of universal emotions.

Melford Spiro, an elder statesman in the discipline of anthropology, has described constructionism as deterministic, and he decries the constructionist perspective as a form of intellectual relativism. In his essay "Some Reflections on Cultural Determinism and Relativism with Special Reference to Emotion and Reason," Spiro writes that when scholars press for the uniqueness of the objects of their study, cross-cultural comparison becomes impaired.[25] What if, he asked, the Ilongot philosophers deemed headhunting to be more valuable than feeding the starving Ifugao? Given such a choice, Spiro would stand with the ideals represented in the cultures that have been the heirs of Buddha, Christ, Isaiah, Lao-tzu, Gandhi, and Socrates. Spiro might ask: has the Christian turn in this culture benefited the poor by breaking the economic system of headhunting? And, he goes on, the problem identified in current constructionism, that only the enculturated can understand the local system, challenges and undermines any possibility of history. Indeed, if it were true that only the local culture mattered, he wonders, how could historians ever do their work? Without being able to walk around, observing and interviewing participants, how might we ever hope to achieve confidence in our understanding of, say, the French Revolution? Further, such relativist theories, specializing in synchronic snapshots of culture, cannot aid in explaining changes over time, cannot evaluate development or innovation in terms of improvement or degradation of cultural values.

In his criticism, Spiro asks how anyone is ever to sort out the array of cultural values and rank them if one can never get beyond the horizons of the local, beyond the contemporary. Spiro's historical test, asking how anyone could study, with any degree of understanding, the French Revolution, sets the stage, by coincidence, for me to introduce here William M. Reddy, the recent and important critic of constructionism. A Duke University anthropologist trained in ethnographic history, Reddy uses the French Revolution as a case study for his theory of "emotives," which he defines as follows:

> a type of speech act different from both performative and constative utterances, which both describes (like constative utterances) and changes (like performatives) the world, because emotional expression has an exploratory and a self-altering effect on the activated thought material of emotion.[26]

Emotives can be the subject for understanding more fully how societies exert control over their members, how they offer desired liberty of expression, or how central values change over time. Strict emotional regimes manipulate emotives in order to achieve their political goals. Persons in relatively open societies use their "emotional liberty" to navigate through important social interactions. The scholar with an eye for history can record more precisely how emotives are used in the navigation of feeling. The dual character of emotives, their curious ambiguity, is especially worth noting, as it directly speaks to the determinist limitations of constructionist theory.

No one has critiqued constructionism while employing its many useful aspects more than Reddy. Most valuable, Reddy's approach offers a means to evaluate just how responsive a social order can be to the emotional lives of its members. His *Navigation of Feeling* (2001) assumes that there are social scientific ways to assess emotion in different cultures and seeks to gauge how adequately different cultures provide the means to help members resolve conflict. At the center of such a judgment is the phenomenon of "emotional suffering." Historically considered, it is the intensification or alleviation of this experience that is the key to evaluating cultural constructions. Further, the idea of "emotional suffering" speaks directly to the problem of relativism, because it offers a means of comparison.

Cultures construct contexts for the experience of feelings. In time, conflicts in the primary goals of individuals emerge. This is Reddy's definition of suffering. "Emotional suffering" is the conflict between primary life goals. His chief illustration is torture. The primary goals brought into conflict by the torturer are patriotism and personal well-being. Because one does not want to give up loyalty to country, one is faced with painful sacrifices to body and mind. Or, by preserving self, one comes to suffer feelings of remorse for having betrayed one's comrades. Unrequited love is another form of emotional suffering, in that the beloved does not wish to be in the company of the lover, who then has the painful choice of disobeying the loved one or denying his or her own feelings.[27]

Strict emotional regimes manipulate individuals and their insides in order to shape social behavior and influence social norms. Victor Turner, in his study of Ndembu ritual, found that opposite meanings become switched in religious ritual. The "oretic" pole he named for the Latin *orexis*: desire, appetite. For Turner, religious symbols have two poles of meaning: one is physiological and oretic, that is, what one longs for, grasps after, relating to desire or appetite; the other pole is related to moral norms, those basic principles that govern society. At its core, the drama of ritual causes a powerful exchange between the oretic and normative poles. Biology thus becomes ennobled, while morality takes on emotional significance. In the process, what is necessary is rendered desirable; duty becomes what one wants to do.[28] Strict emotional regimes navigate emotions in similar ways.

Schools, country clubs, secret societies, monasteries, military orders can be refuges from conflict, or they can employ emotives in order to achieve the organization's mission. How well does a culture over time address and alleviate suffering among its own? This is a moral question. It is a social-historical one too. In the course of studying how various individuals translate emotives, the scholar can place a culture on a spectrum from the rigidity of a strict emotion regime to the flexibility of a society where emotional liberty is enjoyed. One gauges how a culture does by seeing how high or low a level of emotional suffering is present.

Due to the indeterminacy of translation, emotives work in very different ways. Interpreting social cues, where the emotion statement itself can become a self-altering expression, helps Reddy speak to the problems of subjectivity. The space where cultural translation takes place is internal and indeterminate.

> Here "emotions" come to life, to vex, enlighten, guide, encumber, to reveal goal conflicts we have overlooked.... When we speak of such matters, we inevitably alter their configuration. When we "describe" this space through which we are obliged to navigate, we change its map. This is a frustrating, paradoxical sea... a certain conception of emotional liberty can help us to evaluate the emotional

styles that communities and states attempt to impose.... These emotional "regimes" may make navigation easier or more difficult; minimizing human suffering inevitably entails that we seek to make navigation... as easy as we can.[29]

The bridge between culture and self that constructionist accounts try to describe is handled by the notion of "translation." Not only can the course of navigation change in the expression of emotives, so can the destination! Again, the dual character of emotives can lead to an ambiguity in how they are to be translated. Reddy's way does not lead to full prediction or comprehension, because emotives can change in the feeling of them, but his call for historical study is made stronger by his appreciation of nuance and how change takes place by way of the translation of cultural meanings. These ideas soften the overly deterministic character of theories of social construction; they also counter the problems of relativism. Various cultural regimes can be judged on how poorly they exploit their members' feelings or how well they support the possibility of emotional liberty among their people. Over time, the level of emotional suffering can be measured.

Reddy's case study of revolutionary France shows how an emotional regime shifted over time and, curiously, how even emotional liberty could be used to clamp down on individuals. This is precisely what happened in France at the time of the reign of terror. Liberty became translated into a style of expression known as "sentimentalism," which was then used to judge the loyalty of French men and women to the ideals of the revolution. Initially, the more open expression of feelings seemed to be an improvement over the culture of the *ancien régime* in France. But with the beheading of Robespierre, on July 28, 1794, the emotional regime of sentiment quickly came to an end. It was seen for what it was, an overly strict, manipulative style of expression that generated as great emotional suffering as had the newly overthrown monarchy of Louis XIV. History is reviewed to make a comparative point: over time, cultures can be evaluated, so that the mere claim of emotional liberty can be seen for what it was.

Reddy brings to the construction discussion a means of cultural assessment. The historical shifts in society can show its capacity to address the suffering of members by alleviating emotional conflicts. It is this dimension of Reddy's anthropology that stands to help correct the relativist approaches that resist any such comparison and assessment. Convinced that cultural understanding is supremely local, some constructionists will not and cannot judge one regime by outside criteria. Yet critics wonder what the conditions for the poorest members of Philippine society would be if the headhunting cult had redirected its resources. Reddy does not answer this question, but his theory of emotives and his ideas of how cultures can be navigated emotionally to relieve suffering provide a model for future work. For example, Ilongot headhunters have become Christian. This shift was imposed on them. Yet a history of the region in accord with Reddy's principles might offer scholars an opportunity to gauge how well or how badly the elite treats the poor of this society. It is not merely Western bias that goes into such a judgment. Reddy has developed the tools for such analysis in any historical context. Recognize emotional suffering, the conflict between primary life goals, and then judge how well or how poorly a society reforms.

The problem of human suffering is of special interest to scholars of religion. Max Weber once claimed that explanations for suffering help the privileged to legitimate their own happiness and good fortune.[30] Reddy is one of those theorists who claim that cultures can be judged by how well or how poorly they attend to the emotional suffering of their members. If justice and the prophetic outcries against mistreatment are central to religious authority, then concerns over emotional suffering must bear directly on the study of religion.

A brief look at African American religious history shows a use for Reddy's theory. Southern slavery with its dehumanizing sanctions was a "strict emotion regime." The conflict producing suffering was to live enslaved as property in a land built on the Declaration of Independence. Even after Emancipation, blacks were not free. In fact, Africans celebrated American freedom on July 5, suggesting that they were not yet independent and equal.[31] The separate black church became a refuge after the Civil War, a place where African Americans did not have to wait.

In Reddy's idea of emotional navigation, persons and groups experience conflicts between prime life goals; this produces "emotional suffering." Social orders shape emotions to control members and impose navigation routes by exploiting conflict. Or societies alleviate the conflict that causes suffering by allowing persons to navigate their own feelings. On the way to greater liberty, an emotional refuge can be a "haven in a heartless world," or it can be the arm of a "strict emotional regime." The military and the monastery enforce rules so as to prioritize life goals for members and resolve possible conflicts by downplaying self-interest. The liberating affects of a refuge can be gauged: "emotional liberty" marks how much freedom is given to persons for navigating their own way.

Black churches were the great emotional refuge for those who were no longer slaves but still subject to the exclusionary pressures of white society. Of the needs these churches met—social, economic, spiritual—none was more vital than the emotional. This refuge became the place where emotional liberty was expressed. The ring dance ("the shout") elevated worshipers to an ecstatic level where time and history were abolished and where any distance between past oppression and the freedom of the present collapsed.[32] In the heights of worship, the conflict that made for "emotional suffering" was transcended. In "call and response," in dance, in joyous celebration (as portrayed in the film *Say Amen, Somebody*),[33] freedom was experienced firsthand, and blacks knew immediately the dignity of their existence.

Church ritual mirrored the mythic adoption of the Exodus narrative in songs, sermons, and in politics. Reinterpretation in which the old Hebrew story became an account of the plight of Africans creatively offered grounds for critiquing the slaveowners while at the same time holding out hope that one day God's people would be free. The warrant behind African American Christianity's use of the Exodus story was simple and clear: blacks were not supposed to be slaves.

The civil rights struggle was costly. Southerners did not want to ease the way for blacks even after one hundred years. It took the prophetic voice (and perhaps the martyrdom) of Martin Luther King to call for freedom and justice. No coincidence, he used Exodus language coupled with republican ideals of freedom. American society, though it remains troubled by racism, has changed. It has come far from the deaths of four black girls in a church bombing on September 15, 1963, in Birmingham, Alabama—the catalyst for the civil rights movement. One mark of progress is that in October 2004, the debates between Barack Obama and Alan Keyes, two black candidates for the U.S. Senate, took place in Representative Hall of the Old State Capitol in Springfield, Illinois—the same chamber where Abraham Lincoln delivered his speech "House Divided." Senator Barack Obama returned to this same site on February 10, 2007, to announce his candidacy for president of the United States.

Reddy's theory calls for a close eye on the ambiguous ways that emotives can be used and translated. That enslaved Africans would see in Exodus a warrant and hope for future freedom led to a redrawing of the navigational map: they embraced the religious tradition of their slave-masters. Dr. King used the same biblical language combined with the ideals of the republic to persuade the dominant society to reframe its values, both biblical and republican.

The suffering endured has shaped feelings, making a bridge for expressions of hope. Sorrow songs, old Negro spirituals, and gospel music have given rise to secular feelings in rhythm and blues and in jazz. These creative, improvisational, emotion-filled works have been accepted internationally as great American art. As such, these distinctive achievements, arising out of the separate black church, expose to criticism that strict regime that tried to tightly govern emotions and force the labor of America's Africans.

Caveats regarding translation, what emotional utterances really mean, require ongoing careful study. In the end, full understanding may remain beyond the grasp of the social scientist. That feelings are constructed within human societies cannot be denied. The sociologist Georg Simmel showed that feelings of gratitude rise as the social division of labor increases.[34] Another arena in which constructed emotions can be found is the theatre, where the standing ovation has become de rigueur.[35] How emotions are recollected continues to puzzle. For Wordsworth, lounging on a couch remembering in tranquility a field of daffodils brought joy. Social scientists may "translate" some of that, especially if they keep an eye on how interpretations shift through time. In the end, nonetheless, a good portion of human emotion and the understanding of it remains the dominion of poets, shamans, and mystics.

NOTES

1. The World Catalog, an online database, cites constructions of race, gender, nation, grammar, manhood, pottery, houses, and memory (http://worldcat.org). "Dingo discourse" appears as a subtitle under the construction of language. I focus here primarily on

social constructions within the field of cultural anthropology, though psychology plays an important role, as will be noted.

2. Maya Angelou, *I Know Why the Caged Bird Sings* (New York: Random House, 1970).

3. Timothy J. Nelson, "Sacrifice of Praise: Emotion and Collective Participation in an African-American Worship Service," *Sociology of Religion* 57 (1996): 379–96.

4. Peter L. Berger and Thomas Luckmann, *The Social Construction of Reality: A Treatise in the Sociology of Knowledge* (Garden City, N.Y.: Doubleday, 1966).

5. Max Scheler, *Die Wissensformen und die Gesellschaft* (Bern: Francke, 1960).

6. Karl Mannheim, *Ideology and Utopia: An Introduction to the Sociology of Knowledge*, translated by Louis Wirth and Edward Shils (New York: Harcourt, Brace and World, 1936), 97–97 n., 116, 122–23, 128 n., 251; see Alfred Schutz, "On Multiple Realities," in *Collected Papers*, vol. 1 (The Hague: Nijhoff, 1962), especially his notion of "paramount realities."

7. James R. Averill, *Anger and Aggression: An Essay on Emotion* (New York: Springer-Verlag, 1982).

8. James R. Averill, "The Social Construction of Emotion: With Special Reference to Love," in *The Social Construction of the Person*, edited by Kenneth J. Gergen and Keith E. Davis (New York: Springer-Verlag, 1985), 89–109; for an example of Averill's social-construction model in the study of guilt and religion, see Donna Ann Attivissimo, "A Constructivist Analysis of the Experience of Guilt: Sex, Religion, and Psychopathology Correlates," Ph.D. diss., Hofstra University, 1995.

9. Michelle Z. Rosaldo, *Knowledge and Passion: Ilongot Notions of Self and Social Life* (Cambridge: Cambridge University Press, 1980).

10. Michelle Z. Rosaldo, "Toward an Anthropology of Self and Feeling," in *Culture Theory: Essays on Mind, Self, and Emotion*, edited by Richard A. Shweder and Robert A. LeVine (Cambridge: Cambridge University Press, 1984), 137–57.

11. Lila Abu-Lughod, *Veiled Sentiments: Honor and Poetry in a Bedouin Society* (Berkeley: University of California Press, 1986).

12. Catherine Lutz, *Unnatural Emotion: Everyday Sentiments on a Micronesian Atoll and Their Challenge to Western Theory* (Chicago: University of Chicago Press, 1988).

13. Clifford Geertz, "Religion as a Cultural System," in *The Interpretation of Cultures: Selected Essays by Clifford Geertz* (New York: Basic Books, 1973), 87–125; Geertz, 110 n. 35, credits Edmund Husserl with developing the term "perspective" as the meaning and usage is described by Alfred Schutz in *The Problem of Social Reality*, vol. 1 of *Collected Papers*.

14. Lee A. Kirkpatrick, "Attachment Theory and Religious Experience," in *Handbook of Religious Experience*, edited by Ralph W. Hood, Jr. (Birmingham, Ala.: Religious Education Press, 1995), 446–75.

15. Margot L. Lyon, "Missing Emotion: The Limitations of Cultural Constructionism in the Study of Emotion," *Cultural Anthropology* 10 (1995): 246.

16. Ibid., 247.

17. Ibid.

18. Edward Shils, *Tradition* (Chicago: University of Chicago Press, 1981), 38–39.

19. C. Wright Mills, *The Sociological Imagination* (New York: Grove Press, 1959), 5.

20. T. S. Eliot, "Hamlet and His Problems," in *Selected Essays* (London: Faber and Faber, 1951), 144–45.

21. Peter Berger, *The Sacred Canopy: Elements of a Sociological Theory of Religion* (Garden City, N.Y.: Doubleday, 1967), 39.

22. Berger, *Sacred Canopy*, 44.

23. No sooner is the idea out when a new one arrives: Hollywood "constructed" that upside-down world, and its parameters were laid bare in two dismal sequels.

24. Andrew Ortony and Terence J. Turner, "What's Basic about Basic Emotions?" *Psychological Review* 97 (1990): 315–31.

25. Melford E. Spiro, "Some Reflections on Cultural Determinism and Relativism with Special Reference to Emotion and Reason," in *Culture Theory: Essays on Mind, Self, and Emotion*, edited by Richard A. Shweder and Robert A. LeVine (Cambridge: Cambridge University Press, 1984), 323–46.

26. William M. Reddy, *The Navigation of Feeling: A Framework for the History of Emotions* (Cambridge: Cambridge University Press, 2001), 128–29.

27. Ibid., 123–24.

28. Victor Turner, *The Forest of Symbols: Aspects of Ndembu Ritual* (Ithaca, N. Y.: Cornell University Press, 1967).

29. Reddy, *The Navigation of Feeling*, 332.

30. Max Weber, "The Social Psychology of the World Religions," in *From Max Weber: Essays in Sociology*, translated by H. H. Gerth and C. Wright Mills (New York: Oxford University Press, 1946), 267–301.

31. William B. Gravely, "The Dialectic of Double-Consciousness in Black American Freedom Celebrations, 1808–1863," *Journal of Negro History* 67 (1982): 302–17.

32. Albert J. Raboteau, "African Americans, Exodus, and the American Israel," in *African American Christianity: Essays in History*, edited by Paul E. Johnson (Berkeley: University of California Press, 1994), 1–17.

33. *Say Amen, Somebody* (1982) features Willie Mae Ford Smith, Thomas A. Dorsey, and other gospel music stars; on the jacket of the video, the critic Roger Ebert is quoted as having called it a "happy" movie: "Terrific, joyous, funny, unabashedly emotional."

34. Georg Simmel, "Faithfulness and Gratitude," in *The Sociology of Georg Simmel*, edited by Kurt Wolff (New York: Free Press, 1950), 379–95.

35. Liz Smith, quoted in Jesse McKinley, "The Tyranny of the Standing Ovation: How the Highest Compliment Became the Standard Response," *New York Times*, December 21, 2003, sec. 2, 4.

BIBLIOGRAPHY

Abu-Lughod, Lila. *Veiled Sentiments: Honor and Poetry in a Bedouin Society*. Berkeley: University of California Press, 1986.

———. "Shifting Politics in Bedouin Love Poetry." In *Language and the Politics of Emotion*, edited by Catherine A. Lutz and Lila Abu-Lughod. Cambridge: Cambridge University Press, 1990, 24–45

Appadurai, Arjun. "Topographies of the Self: Praise and Emotion in Hindu India." In *Language and the Politics of Emotion*, edited by Catherine A. Lutz and Lila Abu-Lughod. Cambridge: Cambridge University Press, 1990, 92–112.

Attivissimo, Donna Ann. "A Constructivist Analysis of the Experience of Guilt: Sex, Religion, and Psychopathology Correlates." Ph.D. diss., Hofstra University, 1995.

Averill, James R. "Historical Teachings on Anger." In *Anger and Aggression: An Essay on Emotion*. New York: Springer-Verlag, 1982.

———. "The Social Construction of Emotion: With Special Reference to Love." In *The Social Construction of the Person*, edited by Kenneth J. Gergen and Keith E. Davis. New York: Springer-Verlag, 1985, 89–109.

Basu, Helen. "Hierarchy and Emotion: Love, Joy, and Sorrow in a Cult of Black Saints in Gujarat, India." In *Embodying Charisma: Modernity, Locality, and the Performance of Emotion in Sufi Cults*, edited by Pina Werbner and Helen Basu. London: Routledge, 1998, 117–39.

Berger, Peter. *The Sacred Canopy: Elements of a Sociological Theory of Religion*. Garden City, N.Y.: Doubleday, 1967.

Berger, Peter L., and Thomas Luckmann. *The Social Construction of Reality: A Treatise in the Sociology of Knowledge*. Garden City, New York: Doubleday, 1966.

Fisher, Gene A., and Kyum Koo Chon. "Durkheim and the Social Construction of Emotions." *Social Psychology Quarterly* 52 (1989): 1–9.

Francis, David. "The Golden Dreams of the Social Constructionist." *Journal of Anthropological Research* 50 (1994): 97–108.

Geertz, Clifford. *The Interpretation of Culture*. New York: Basic Books, 1973.

Gorringe, Timothy. *God's Just Vengeance: Crime, Violence, and the Rhetoric of Salvation*. Cambridge: Cambridge University Press, 1996.

Grima, Benedicte. *The Performance of Emotion among Paxtun Women*. Austin, Tex.: University of Texas Press, 1992.

Harré, Rom, ed. *The Social Construction of Emotions*. Oxford: Blackwell, 1986.

Harré, Rom, and W. Gerrod Parrott, eds. *The Emotions: Social, Cultural, and Biological Dimensions*. London: Sage, 1996.

Harris, Scott R. "Studying Equality/Inequality: Naturalist and Constructionist Approaches to Equality in Marriage." *Journal of Contemporary Ethnography* 32 (2003): 200–232.

Levy, Robert I. "Emotion, Knowing and Culture." In *Culture Theory: Essays on Mind, Self, and Emotion*, edited by Richard A. Shweder and Robert A. LeVine. Cambridge: Cambridge University Press, 1984, 214–37.

Lewis, Jan. "'Mother's Love': The Construction of an Emotion in Nineteenth-Century America." In *Social History and Issues in Human Consciousness: Some Interdisciplinary Connections*. New York: New York University Press, 1989, 209–29.

Lutz, Catherine A. "The Domain of Emotion Words on Ifaluk." *American Ethnologist* 9 (1982): 113–28.

———. *Unnatural Emotion: Everyday Sentiments on a Micronesian Atoll and Their Challenge to Western Theory*. Chicago: University of Chicago Press, 1988.

Lutz, Catherine A., and Lila Abu-Lughod, eds. *Language and the Politics of Emotion*. Cambridge: Cambridge University Press, 1990.

Lutz, Catherine, and Geoffrey M. White. "The Anthropology of Emotions." *Annual Review of Anthropology* 15 (1986): 405–36.

Lynch, Owen, ed. *Divine Passions: The Social Construction of Emotions in India*. Berkeley: University of California Press, 1990.

Lyon, Margot L. "Missing Emotion: The Limitations of Cultural Constructionism in the Study of Emotion." *Cultural Anthropology* 10 (1995): 244–63.

Mannheim, Karl. *Ideology and Utopia: An Introduction to the Sociology of Knowledge*. Translated by Louis Wirth and Edward Shils. New York: Harcourt, Brace and World, 1936.

Marcus, George E., and Michael M. J. Fisher. *Anthropology as Cultural Critique: An Experimental Moment in the Human Sciences*. Chicago: University of Chicago Press, 1986.

Mazzaroni, Christina. *Saint Hysteria: Neurosis, Mysticism, and Gender in European Culture.* Ithaca, N.Y.: Cornell University Press, 1996.

Merlan, Francesca. "The Limits of Cultural Constructionism: The Case of Coronation Hill." *Oceania* 61 (1991): 340–52.

Nussbaum, Martha. "Narrative Emotions: Beckett's Genealogy of Love." *Ethics* 98 (1988): 225–54.

Peletz, Michael G. *Reason and Passion: Representations of Gender in a Malay Society.* Berkeley: University of California Press, 1996.

Ratner, Carl. "A Social Constructionist Critique of the Naturalistic Theory of Emotion." *Journal of Mind and Behavior* 10 (1989): 211–30.

Reddy, William M. "Against Constructionism: The Historical Ethnography of Emotions." *Current Anthropology* 38 (1997): 327–51.

———. "Emotional Liberty: History and Politics in the Anthropology of Emotions." *Cultural Anthropology* 14 (1999): 256–88.

———. *The Navigation of Feeling: A Framework for the History of Emotions.* Cambridge: Cambridge University Press, 2001.

Rosaldo, Michelle Z. *Knowledge and Passion: Ilongot Notions of Self and Social Life.* Cambridge: Cambridge University Press, 1980.

———. "Toward an Anthropology of Self and Feeling." In *Culture Theory: Essays on Mind, Self, and Emotion*, edited by Richard A. Shweder and Robert A. LeVine. Cambridge: Cambridge University Press, 1984, 137–57.

Rosaldo, Renato I. "Grief and a Headhunter's Rage: On the Cultural Force of Emotions." In *Text, Play, and Story: The Construction and Reconstruction of Self and Society*, edited by Stuart Plattner and Edward Bruner. Washington, D.C.: American Ethnological Society, 1984, 178–95.

Sant-Cassia, Paul. "Absences and Losses: Psychoanalysis, Anthropology and the Cultural Construction of Emotions." *Anthropological Journal on European Cultures* 10 (2001): 143–62.

Sayer, Andrew. "Essentialism, Social Constructionism, and Beyond." *Sociological Review* 45 (1997): 453–87.

Spiro, Melford E. "Some Reflections on Cultural Determinism and Relativism with Special Reference to Emotion and Reason." In *Culture Theory: Essays on Mind, Self, and Emotion*, edited by Richard A. Shweder and Robert A. LeVine. Cambridge: Cambridge University Press, 1984, 323–46.

Stewart, Charles. "Fields in Dreams: Anxiety, Experience, and the Limits of Social Constructionism in Modern Greek Dream Narratives." *American Ethnologist* 24 (1997): 877–94.

CHAPTER 27

EMOTIONS RESEARCH AND RELIGIOUS EXPERIENCE

ROBERT C. ROBERTS

INQUIRY aims at information, understanding, and insight. Research is inquiry that is methodologically self-conscious, systematic, and sustained, and focused on particular well-formulated questions. As such, research strategies are highly specific to subject matter.

I shall attempt to clarify the concept of research into religious emotions. I shall not summarize that research or adjudicate its questions.[1] The examples I exploit should be construed as illustrating the ways religious emotions can be investigated. I shall develop a conception of research in this field and say something about the value and limits of the various kinds of research and their relations to one another.

EMOTIONS AS OBJECTS OF RESEARCH

Human emotions are many-sided phenomena and have multiple connections to other aspects of our life. They have several *physical* dimensions. Emotions are crucially determined by events and processes in the brain involving both the newer cortical parts and older parts that have strong analogues in other animals, even such animals as birds and reptiles. These events and processes have consequences in other parts of the body, some of which are subbehavioral, such as pulse rate, skin conductance, and blood pressure, while others are behavioral, such as facial and postural expressions and other kinds of muscular tension and relaxation. These bodily phenomena can "feed back" into the central nervous system to reinforce, sustain, and even create emotions or emotion-like states. Emotions are an important part of the human *motivational* repertoire, so that not only behavioral and subbehavioral changes but also full-fledged actions are among their expressions (and such actions also feed back into emotions). Paradigmatically, emotions are *responses to situations* of determinate types—for example, situations of threat, of offense, of good fortune, of aid, of rivalry, of loss, of good prospects, and so on.

But the situations that human emotions are "about" are not usually simple stimuli, as are, perhaps, the situations that "trigger" emotions in some of our fellow animals. Instead, we vary widely in our *readings* of the situations of our lives; we respond to situations via one or another interpretive grid, so it is possible for a person who is in a situation of good fortune, say, to respond emotionally as though the situation were one of bad fortune, and vice versa. Often the interpretive grid with which we view a situation emotionally is a narrative or incipient narrative— our awareness of a situation's historical background. Emotions in response to fiction and other literary representations also illustrate the power of narrative to affect emotions. Thus a person's conceptual framework or worldview or self-understanding also affects his or her emotions. This means that many human emotional dispositions are highly susceptible to education, and thus to *culture* and *historical traditions*. Furthermore, an individual's or society's patterns of emotional response may be more or less healthy, more or less *constitutive of a good human life*; differences between two individuals' emotional response patterns can be differences of character and thus of human excellence, and also of what psychologists call "subjective well-being." And no small part of such differential excellence is due to the way emotional response patterns determine the quality of an individual's *personal relationships* with other human beings and with God. Emotion response dispositions seem to come bundled with others in some systematic way; thus there may be positive systematic correlation between a disposition to feel grateful and a disposition to feel empathy with others and not to feel envious or bear grudges. Furthermore, emotions are often, but not always, felt; and the process of emotional maturation involves, among other things, bringing to greater *consciousness* emotions that are partly or wholly submerged. Such a reflective process is an occasion for the extrusion of our emotions through yet another interpretive grid—now applied not to the situation the emotion is about but to the emotion itself as a state of the subject.

Even this quick survey of the ways emotions are woven into the fabric of human life—tangled inextricably with our brains and other body parts, our evolutionary history, our behavior and actions, our consciousness, our cultures and reading and philosophies and outlooks, our character and thus our excellence as individuals, and our personal relationships and happiness—suggests the multiplicity of avenues by which, and angles from which, emotions may be investigated. Neuroscientists investigate the anatomy and chemistry of the brain and other parts of the nervous system as they give rise to emotional states. Psychologists often study emotions by looking at facial expressions and other behavioral and subbehavioral expressions, as well as actions, and the self-report of subjects of conscious emotions is often an important element of their research; psychologists also study the correlations between one emotion disposition and another. Biologists and evolutionary psychologists speculate about the paleohistory of the human emotion-repertoire. Historians and anthropologists study the effects of cultures and worldviews on the emotional life of peoples. Clinical and personality psychologists, ethicists, and theologians attempt to apply one or another norm of human nature and human excellence to determine what ideal emotional formation would be and how emotions are related to virtues and vices, good and bad relationships, and happiness or well-being. Philosophers of emotion attempt to see the connections of all these things to one another and thus to clarify the concept of emotion itself, as well as the concepts of the various emotion-types (for example, love, anger, envy, hope). If religious emotions have, potentially, all the kinds of dimensions and connections that human emotions in general have, then any and all of these disciplinary approaches should be applicable, in principle, to the study of religious emotions.

What Makes an Emotion Religious?

"Religion" and "religious" are rather indeterminate terms, and in what follows I hope to avoid trading on an artificially narrow conception. However, it seems wrong to treat all emotions as religious—even all the emotions of religious people—unless we have something like an Augustinian conception of human life, according to which people have constant reference to God in their experience even though they disbelieve in God and are unconscious of having any relation to God. I will not take an Augustinian viewpoint in this chapter, but will assume that only some emotions are religious. God is central to some religions, but not all. Not everything religious has reference to God, but it seems to me that the paradigm cases, at least, have fairly explicit reference to something big, important, and encompassing that is beyond the familiar objects that constitute the empirically accessible world; that is, religion has reference to "the transcendent." For example, the emotion Schleiermacher calls the feeling of absolute dependence does not, I think, have any reference to God (though Schleiermacher himself seems to think it does);[2] but for present purposes it counts as a religious emotion because it has reference to the Void that is beyond all things that exist. Zen emotions will be another example of nontheistic religious emotions.[3] Some thinkers include ghosts as religious objects;[4] perhaps we can stretch the concept of the transcendent to take them in, even though they are a lot "smaller" than God, or the Void, or Being as a Whole, or Nature. One author proposes that the mark of religious objects is that they are counterintuitive agents;[5] but the vacant Beyond is not an agent and does not strike me as especially counterintuitive; and whether God is counterintuitive depends on how an individual's dispositions of intuition have been formed. Of course, emotions that refer to God count as religious on my proposal, because the various conceptions of God in the religions are conceptions of a superimportant being that transcends ordinary everyday objects. The Void or the Whole or Nature is, as it were, an analogue of God, and ghosts are at least uncanny.

Religious emotions, as I will understand them here, come in most of the standard emotion-types: joy, sorrow, fear, gratitude, hope, anger, awe, reverence, compassion, contrition, hatred.[6] An emotion becomes religious by referring to God or something else transcendent: thus joy in the Lord, fear of the Lord, awe before Being, reverence for Life, and so on.

What is it for an emotion to "refer" to God or to something else transcendent? On the conception of emotion that I prefer, emotions are about situations (conceptually or narratively ordered configurations of objects). For example, the emotion of gratitude is a "perception" or "construal" of a situation composed of three main kinds of elements: a benefice, a benefactor, and a beneficiary. The beneficiary construes himself or herself as having received a benefice from a benefactor.[7] The grateful person need not be focusing, particularly, on himself or herself as the beneficiary, and in many instances of gratitude, the focus will be on either the gift or the giver. Furthermore, it would be odd to say that the beneficiary is the "object" of his or her own gratitude; so an emotion can essentially refer to something without that something being the "object" of the emotion; the emotion refers to an object in virtue of the object's playing an essential role in the situation to which an emotion of this type is directed. It is in this sense that I take reference to God or something else transcendent as essential to religious emotions. An instance of the emotion of gratitude will thus be religious if the construed benefactor is God, but not if the only construed benefactor is an ordinary human being.

The transcendent term in a religious emotion can occupy various roles in the construed situation. Thus Mother Teresa's love for a sick indigent counts as a religious emotion even though the "object" of her love is the indigent, since she loves that person *for the sake of* Christ.[8] A devout terrorist's hatred of the infidel counts as a religious emotion inasmuch as he hates the infidel *out of devotion to* Allah. The excited joy or penitence of the Pentecostal worshiper counts as a religious emotion if she or he is, for example, delighted *in God* or sorrowful *about his or her offenses against God*. Further, he or she construes the emotion as *an effect of* God's spirit in the congregation. Christian hope is a religious emotion because it is *God's* kingdom that is hoped for, and God is the *basis for* this hope (the one who is trusted to effect it). On this conception of religious emotions, it is possible that the emotions of some church- or synagogue- or mosque-goers would not be religious emotions at all, if the reference to the transcendent had dropped out of their mental life, despite the continued use of religious language and other trappings of religion.

Figuring out the criteria for distinguishing such simulacra from genuinely religious emotions might be one of the tasks of normative emotions research.

Physiological Research

Physiological emotions research consists in correlating emotions of one type or another with concomitant or causal physiological processes. For example, a psychologist might monitor blood pressure, pulse rate, skin conductance, or configuration of facial muscular tension in persons in states of joy, sadness, anxiety, anger, and amusement (at jokes, say) to see whether any regularities of concomitance can be discerned.[9] Someone researching religious emotions might conduct this kind of investigation using subjects in worship situations where they experience such emotions as contrition (during confession, say) or joy or gratitude (at absolution, or at proclamation of the gospel). The researcher might look for ways the physiology of religious gratitude, say, differs from that of nonreligious gratitude.

Another important kind of physiological research on emotions focuses on the central neurological processes underlying them. All mental states depend on electrochemical activities that typically (though not always) start in peripheral parts of the nervous system (eyes, ears, etc.), travel to specific regions of the brain, and are relayed from one region to another and then back, often, to the periphery of the body; information from the periphery is then sent back to the brain. Neurological research is an attempt to specify the parts of the brain that are involved in some given mental, behavioral, or physiological process and to specify how each of the involved parts contributes to the overall process.

Deficit studies use people or animals who have suffered damage to some particular part of the brain and proceed by carefully analyzing the functional deficits that result. Antonio Damasio's studies of emotion used patients who had suffered damage to the prefrontal cortex, the amygdala, and other parts of the brain and found that deficits of emotional responsiveness were associated with such damage.[10] The use of animals such as rats, cats, and monkeys allows deficit research to be much more precise, since the scientist can systematically and precisely damage various parts of the animals' brains as he or she observes loss of function, whereas with human subjects the researcher has to be "lucky" enough to find patients with the kind of damage he or she is interested in and must work with whatever configuration of damage the patients happen to have. Another research technique is to inject an animal with a dye that will be carried by the synaptic action along the neural pathways, leaving a stain-trace, induce the emotion in the animal, and then kill the animal and examine cross-sections of the stained brain. By using these techniques, Joseph LeDoux was able to develop a quite precise account of the neurology of a kind of conditioned fright that animals like rats are capable of.[11] For purposes of understanding the neurological mechanisms underlying human emotions, the value of animal research is limited by the fact that many emotions, including distinctively human fear, fright, and anxiety, and religious emotions, involve brain parts (notably the prefrontal cortex and the verbal/conceptual area located at the junction of the temporal, parietal, and occipital lobes) that are absent or only virtual in experimental animals.

For these reasons, deficit studies have not been prominent in neurological research on religious emotions. Instead, the studies seem to use *activation techniques*. In activation studies, the neurologist attempts to catch the subject in the midst of the mental or behavioral process he or she wishes to study, and then uses a detection device to locate and measure brain activity. Some such devices are positron emission tomography (PET), single photon emission computed tomography (SPECT), and functional magnetic resonance imaging (fMRI). The older electroencephalograph (EEG) is another example. In one investigation, the neuroscientists studied subjects engaged in Tibetan Buddhist meditation. When the subject indicated that he was at the peak of his meditative experience, he was injected with a radioactive dye that locks into brain cells, thus leaving a radioactive trace of blood flow to the brain at the time of the meditative peak. A SPECT camera then scanned inside the subject's head for the radioactive traces, thus producing a crude picture of differential brain activity at the time of the religious experience. The resulting picture showed significantly reduced activity in the posterior section of the parietal lobe, a part of the brain that is responsible for our sense of orientation in space and of the boundary between the self and its surrounding world. The investigators speculate that at the high point of this kind of meditation, this orientation area of the brain is receiving significantly reduced sensory information, with the result that the normal boundary between self and world is breached in consciousness, and the subject has a sense of his or her self expanding infinitely into the whole of being.[12] The experience would be something like the oceanic feeling Freud discusses in the first chapter of *Civilization and Its Discontents*.

Activation studies can also be conducted in the other direction, so to speak, by artificially stimulating selected parts of the brain and noting what kind of behavior or experience the subject undergoes. The transcranial magnetic stimulator is a helmet-like device that shoots a fluctuating magnetic field onto a selected patch of brain tissue. Under the condition of this specific stimulation, the experimenter observes function, either overt behavior or reported subjective experience, and thus gets an idea of the division of labor within the brain. Michael Persinger has used the device to implicate the temporal lobe in experiences of God.[13]

Behavioral Research

Earlier I distinguished behavior from action, but here I will include action as a type of behavior. Emotions are connected with behavior and action on both ends, so to speak. That is, emotions are expressed by (that is, they cause, in some broad sense) behaviors and actions; and a subject's behaviors and actions can contribute causally to his or her emotions. An example of the first connection is a person smiling (behavior) from joy (emotion). An example of the second is a person feeling gratitude to God (emotion) as a result of praying a prayer of thanksgiving (action). But I might have used the same example for both cases, since a person can often enhance his feeling of joy by smiling and can express prior gratitude to God by giving thanks in prayer. These connections suggest research strategies.

Researchers at the Institute of HeartMath and Quantum Intech in Boulder Creek, California, have developed a behavioral technique for inducing a positive emotion that they call "appreciation." The technique consists in consciously disengaging from unpleasant emotions by shifting attention to one's physical heart, which they think most people associate with positive emotions, and focusing on feeling appreciation toward someone, appreciation being an active emotional state in which one dwells on or contemplates the goodness of someone. Rollin McCarty and Doc Childre have found that heart rhythm patterns associated with "appreciation" differ markedly from those associated with relaxation (neutral emotion) and anger (negative emotion). This finding provides a criterion for the presence of "appreciation" that may be more reliable than self-report. They admit that they have not been able to discriminate "between specific positive ... emotions on the basis of heart rhythm patterns alone," suggesting that "appreciation" might function as a summary term for such widely different positive emotions as hope, gratitude, joy, admiration, contentment, relief, pride, and gloating. Thus heart rhythm patterns currently discriminate emotion types only roughly, but McCarty and Childre voice optimism that "future developments in pattern analysis technologies will enable a more refined discrimination of emotions than is currently possible."[14]

If they eventually manage to identify physiological marks that are distinctive of the kind of gratitude or contrition that is canonical in Christian spirituality, this would facilitate behavioral research into these religious emotions. The experimenter could vary gratitude- or contrition-behavior while monitoring subjects' physiological markers, to see which behavior is most conducive to the emotion. For example, the experimenter might have subjects say strongly rhetorical prayers of thanksgiving or confession, comparing the emotion-output of such behavior with that of saying matter-of-fact, rhetorically weak prayers. Or the researcher might compare praying standing with praying kneeling, or praying in a congregation with praying in single confession with a priest. The subtler "mental" side of such actions could also be investigated. For example, the subject could be trained to associate clauses in such prayers with carefully selected events and persons of his or her past which he or she counts as blessings (thus "counting one's blessings") but carefully referring each such blessing to God the Father of Jesus Christ as the Giver. This might be compared with merely appreciating the blessings without referring them to any giver. Such research could provide information about the role of religious behavior—both bodily and mental—in the formation of religious emotions. And of course, the measurement of physiological markers could be supplemented by the subjects' self-reports.

HISTORICAL AND CULTURAL RESEARCH

Historical and anthropological studies address a variety of cultural questions about emotions. Anthropologists of emotion tend to address the following questions. How does a given culture conceive of emotions in general (if it does)? For example, does it conceive them as occurring in the body, and if so, where (the stomach, the chest, the neck)? Or are they understood to occur outside the individual body—in the community, in animals or physical objects, or in the whole environment? How do particular emotion-types in the culture differ from their closest analogues in another culture (how does Ifaluk *song* differ from Euro-American anger)?[15] How do members of the culture under investigation evaluate a particular emotion-type (how do the Ilongots evaluate the emotion they call *liget*)?[16] What is the range of objects that evoke an emotion of a certain type in the culture? (For example, not sharing game acquired during a hunt is an occasion for the analogue of anger among the Ilongots, but not, generally, for anger among North Americans.) What associations does the emotion have, in virtue of diverse usage of the word for the emotion type, in the culture in question? For example, Ilongot *liget* sometimes refers to an emotion that is about the same as North American anger, but it also refers to the intensity with which a farmer works her field and the boldness with which a young man approaches a potential mate, thus creating very different associations from those of North American anger—even in the particular usage that is like that of our "anger." Such differential associations may color the experience of the emotion. It is rare that anthropologists of emotion clearly distinguish these different questions that are addressed in their work; in this way they could profit from greater conceptual (philosophical) clarity about their enterprise.[17]

The typical and most basic approach for anthropology is fieldwork. The investigator lives among the people whose emotions she is investigating and learns their language, if she does not already know it. She asks them questions that are formulated to reveal their emotion-types and how they think about them, and she observes the practices and other situations in which these emotions arise and have significance for the people. As in historical research, anecdote is fundamental to both the development and the scholarly transmission of anthropological understanding. The investigator is particularly attentive to the vocabulary of emotion in the culture and its usage in practice, often making lists of quasi synonyms and collections of instances of usage *in situ*. From the resulting field notes and memory, the anthropologist then attempts to formulate generalizations about the emotions and their significance in the culture. Comparison is crucial to the anthropologist's heuristic; nearly always she has explicitly in mind a comparison culture's emotion vocabulary, emotion-types, and understanding of emotions, with which to highlight the important features of the target culture.

Consider Gananath Obeyesekere's account of the analogue of Euro-American depression among Buddhists in Sri Lanka. Obeyesekere compares an emotion-like state cultivated by serious Buddhists with a certain kind of Western depression as conceptualized by typical members of the psychiatric profession. This depression is despair—a hopelessness not about this or that life prospect but about the whole of human life. In both cultures, such hopelessness is often triggered by a particular loss, but the generalization of the state is essential to its diagnosis as depression by Western psychiatrists, and to its being the sought outcome of the kind of Buddhist meditation called "meditation on revulsion" (*pilikul bhāvanā*). The Western psychiatric tradition construes such generalized hopelessness as illness and treats it with various therapeutic practices—say, a cognitive therapy designed to induce the patient to see the world in a more hopeful light, and chemical antidepressants to elevate mood. In Sri Lanka, by contrast, serious Buddhists use the meditation on revulsion to deepen, confirm, and generalize this hopelessness, which they take to be a proper grasp of the real nature of the world and of human life. In the monastic tradition in Sri Lanka, "meditation on foulness pertained to the actual contemplation of the corpse in ten separate stages of decay, each stage associated with special techniques of meditation and goals of realization of the nature of life." Lay virtuosi practice a milder but more difficult version of this meditation in which "one conjures in one's own mind the putrescence of the body and the world."[18] Feces is a major theme of this meditation. The meditator dwells on the fact that his or her body, and the bodies of everyone else, are full of stinking shit. The aim is to drive home into consciousness that there is not much of a future here.

The stress on cultural difference, sometimes carried to an extreme in my opinion, is characteristic of much anthropological emotions research, in contrast with more biological kinds of investigations, which stress human universals. Obeyesekere begins the concluding section of his article by expressing his "disquiet" that Sri Lankan despair may after all share a common physiology and a universal sociocultural matrix with its Western psychiatric counterpart. This seems likely; and he himself begins his paper by observing the commonality of a generalized despair. But he ends by reasserting the stark cultural differences in the way this emotion is conceptualized and the practices in which it is embedded; and these differences make for a rather striking divergence of emotional experience, even if there is some identifiable commonality between the Buddhist emotion and its psychiatric counterpart.

Historical work on emotions addresses a variety of questions. One study attempts to chart change in the incidence of "positive" emotions among the ancient Hebrews over a twelve-century period.[19] Another chronicles the supposed rise of a new emotion-type—boredom—and its vicissitudes in Europe in the eighteenth and nineteenth centuries.[20] One study investigates the mobility of emotions among subjects as this mobility was understood by British writers in the eighteenth and early nineteenth centuries—that is, emotions' potential to float free of any subject, to migrate from subject to subject, to take on a kind of personal identity of their own, to be picked up through reading, to be concocted as a work of the imagination, to be in a subject without really belonging to that subject, as well as to be a subject's own in the "ordinary" sense.[21] Historical emotions research differs from anthropological investigations in that fieldwork is absent from it (due to the current unavailability of time-machines). Apart from very recent history, all historical research on emotions must be conducted on the basis of documents. From documents, the investigator can get an idea how subjects used emotion vocabulary and what they said about emotions, and can often get narrative reports of the types of behavior and actions that were associated with emotion episodes, the circumstances in which the emotions arose, and the practices subjects used to promote, shape, or control them.

In *Business of the Heart*, John Corrigan investigates Protestant Bostonians' understanding of emotions during the Businessmen's Revival of 1858.[22] Looking at diaries, letters, newspapers, magazines, sermons, and literature in 1850s Boston in which emotions are discussed in connection with religion and other matters, Corrigan finds that the Bostonians thought of religious emotions (presumably penitence, joy in the Lord, gratitude, longing for God, peace with God—though Corrigan focuses little on particular emotion types) as a tradable commodity. One pays emotions to God and gets favors in return; one should be a good steward of one's emotions, and not squander them on unworthy objects. The Bostonians also thought of the emotions circulating in a communal religious setting as analogous to money in a stock market: if a market is too "excited" through an inflow of too much money, trading can get out of control, and a crash will follow. Thus they thought of religious emotions as at once a necessary good and dangerous—in need of proper control. They also thought (or half-thought) of emotions as "performances" in prayer that might be well- or ill-performed by the standards of the above-mentioned rules. And socially, emotions so performed functioned as markers of one's membership in the white Protestant majority, a way of distinguishing oneself as different from and superior to one's black Protestant and Irish Catholic neighbors.

Normative Research

Since the time of Socrates, Plato, and Aristotle, human virtues have been thought to be, in significant part, dispositions of proper emotional responsiveness, while vices are dispositions of defective emotional responsiveness. As Aristotle comments, "to feel [anger and pity, for example] at the right times, with reference to the right objects, toward the right people, with the right motive, and in the right way, is what is both intermediate and best, and this is characteristic of virtue" (*Nicomachean Ethics* 1106b13–15).[23] Aristotle's statement is thus one of the earliest products of normative research into emotions. His formula is vague, but the project is clear enough: to try to specify the standards for appropriate emotional responsiveness. In Aristotle's understanding of virtues, they are dispositions to live well and thus to be a properly functioning, happy, socially well-adjusted specimen of humanity.

Though our contemporary psychotherapists sometimes assert that emotions are neither good nor bad, but "just are," their therapies are largely efforts to modify dysfunctional emotional responsiveness and to replace it with something better. Thus, whether or not they admit it, psychotherapists agree with Aristotle that norms apply to emotions as much as they do to actions, and their therapies embody such norms, at least implicitly.

Religions are normative systems of ideas that bear on the conduct and the fulfillment of their adherents. Thus, for the Buddhists of Sri Lanka, depressive affect is a feature of advanced human maturity and well-being (though it is not the highest state; ideally it leads on to the experience of selflessness [nirvāna] which in some versions is not an emotion at all);[24] the practitioners of the meditation on revulsion aim to foster this despair in themselves and are considered "virtuosi" if they are good at accomplishing this result. Each religion has its own emotional norms, which may overlap with those of some other religions, but may also contrast starkly with some of them. In the Christian tradition, for example, despair—generalized hopelessness—is sin,[25] and hope (which is surely, among other things, a disposition to feel hopeful) is one of the cardinal theological virtues. Similarly, Christianity has been suspicious of mental states in which one loses the sense of one's own identity or comes to feel oneself continuous with the divine. Thus in Christian hope the believer, as a distinct subject, looks forward to the excellent things that God, a distinct agent, will do, and trusts God to do them.[26]

Because psychological, ethical, and spiritual well-being of human beings depend essentially on proper emotional functioning, and because improper emotional functioning is so ubiquitous in human life, theologians and other leading adherents of religions, and people in charge of forming and preserving ethical outlooks, have often undertaken to specify the standards governing human emotional life. As representatives of traditions, they attempt to go beyond merely reporting—as, say, a historian of some tradition might do—how some members of the tradition have actually been formed emotionally, and to say how members of that tradition *ought* to be formed, or *would* be formed were they *ideal* representatives of the tradition. Thus normative emotion researchers appeal to standards that are implicit, if not explicit, in their tradition; and the research consists in the effort to draw out, clarify, formulate, and give access to these standards. Aristotle, for example, appeals to a notion of *eudaimonia* that was arguably vaguely current among Greeks in the city-states that he most admired, but was at the same time quite confused, some people thinking that *eudaimonia* was honor, others that it was pleasure, and so on. Aristotle's own contribution was to sort out these various opinions by "dialectic" and to propose and articulate the view he took to be best.

In religious traditions, the standards for proper emotional functioning are often closely tied to scripture. Scriptures in turn may be canonical because they were written by some extraordinarily wise or otherwise authoritative person (for example, the apostle Paul) or because they narrate the actions and passions of a paradigm individual (Jesus of Nazareth, the Buddha). Normative emotions research often takes the form of pointed scriptural exposition. All the texts of Kierkegaard cited earlier have this character. An example in a more "scholarly" style is Benjamin B. Warfield's article "The Emotional Life of Our Lord,"[27] in which he explores four major kinds of emotions explicitly attributed to Jesus in the Gospels—compassion, anger, joy, and anguish—and correlates them with the kinds of occasions on which Jesus had these emotions. The effect is to provide some guidance, or at least a basis for some guidance, for Christian attempts to form church members emotionally.

A much more concerted and explicitly criteriological example of normative religious emotions research is Jonathan Edwards's work *A Treatise Concerning Religious Affections*.[28] The treatise is the most mature of several that Edwards wrote in response to the dual errors of an emotionless Christianity and a revivalistic "enthusiasm" that mistakes emotional intensity for the work of the Holy Spirit. After an introduction on the nature and importance of the affections in the Christian life, the book consists of a discussion of twenty-four supposed "signs" or criteria for the genuineness of Christian emotions. Edwards develops his account of these signs by a combination of biblical scholarship and careful conceptual (philosophical) thinking. The first twelve signs (part 2 of the *Treatise*) Edwards determines to be not genuine criteria: that is, a person's emotions might have the feature in question if his or her emotion is a genuine work of the Spirit, but then again, also if it is not. For example, the emotions a person experiences in the course of a revival might be very *intense*, or attended by a lot of *physiological perturbations*, or accompanied by a disposition to *talk volubly* about religious matters, but these marks of emotion show nothing one way or the other about whether the affection is genuine.

The heart of the treatise (part 3) is a discussion of the twelve positive signs, the ones that do indicate the gracious work of the Holy Spirit in the believer's life. The twelfth sign is Christian practice: affections that dissipate themselves in excitement and feelings without eventuating in Christian action are spurious; genuine spiritual affections motivate characteristic Christian behavior. The seventh sign is that such behavior is persistent: genuine spiritual affections signal a lasting change of character. The fifth sign is that the emotions are characterized by an immediate conviction of the truth of the great things of the gospel, and the sixth sign is what Edwards calls "evangelical humiliation," a strong disinclination to judge oneself to be better than others or to think that one's own spiritual attainments entitle one to any claim on God. A sense of superiority to others or of entitlement before God is a sign that one's religious affections are bogus. Accordingly, Edwards commends the signs not as criteria by which to discern how well one's neighbor measures up in the kingdom of God, but as criteria to be used in self-examination and self-discipline. Yet Edwards's exposition of the signs is pointed, and it points at actual abuses in the revivalism of his time.

And, it seems, not only of his own time. By Edwards's biblical criteria, a tremendous percentage of the emotions manifest a century later in Boston must have been not religious affections at all. If Corrigan's generalizations are correct, the generality of Protestants who participated in the Businessmen's Revival of 1858 thought of their joy, their penitence, their longing for God as a tradable commodity that could buy them God's favors. They seem to have evaluated them by a quantitative criterion—it being important to have just the right amount of emotion, neither too little nor too much—rather than by the qualitative criteria laid down in Edwards's *Treatise*. And they thought of their admirable success in satisfying this quantitative criterion as making them superior to their black Protestant and Irish Catholic neighbors!

Final Comments

Human emotions are multidimensional phenomena that are central to human life. Their importance strongly motivates the study of them, and their complexity dictates that they be studied from widely divergent angles—by physiologists, behavioral psychologists, social psychologists, sociologists, anthropologists, historians, ethicists, philosophers of mind, and theologians. The activities of these different kinds of investigators overlap to some extent. For example, when anthropologists study a culture-specific emotion-type, they engage in conceptual analysis that is very much like what a philosopher or theologian might practice. When ethicists or theologians evaluate emotions by reference to some particular standard of proper human functioning, they will be interested in the kind of health benefits that physiologists of emotion sometimes investigate. But still, each kind of practitioner has his or her own legitimate place in the emotional sun. Neuroscientists can instruct us in aspects of emotion that would not be discovered in ten thousand years by a large team of the most brilliant philosophers, sitting around their seminar table, or historians poring over diaries and old sermons. And philosophers, anthropologists, and historians can tell us things about emotions that no amount of neurological mapping and chemistry would ever bring to light; it seems likely, for example, that physiology will never be able to provide the kind of fine-grained account of differences among emotion-types that philosophers are especially good at providing, nor can it place emotions in their contexts of public life, as history and anthropology do. Soaring thinkers sometimes forget the importance of plain old information; and plodding fact-finders often forget the place that concepts always play—and sometimes play rather detrimentally—in their investigations. Both do their work poorly unless they consult at least a little bit with one another. The reductionism that we see in some accounts of emotions is almost always a result of disciplinary chauvinism and the resulting ignorance.

If we make our paradigm of emotion the kind of fright-response that can be conditioned into rats, or the quasi emotion we call "startle," a purely physiological account may seem adequate to tell us "what emotions really are"; but in that case, in the words of Wittgenstein, we "feed on too narrow a diet of examples." Religious emotions in particular call for the fullest range of investigative strategies. They vary widely across cultures and are highly sensitive to disciplined formation; they are strongly associated with sets of beliefs about the nature of the universe and human nature and are often a response to verbal communication. They are associated with ritual and in many traditions are subject to rather strict criteria of legitimacy. Yet, despite the salience of these cultural conditions, religious emotions are no less physiological than other kinds.

NOTES

1. For a summary and extensive bibliography, see John Corrigan, Eric Crump, and John Kloos, *Emotion and Religion: A Critical Assessment and Annotated Bibliography* (Westport, Conn.: Greenwood Press, 2000). For adjudication of the questions, see other chapters in this volume.

2. See Friedrich Schleiermacher, *The Christian Faith*, edited and translated by H. R. Macintosh and J. S. Stewart (New York: Harper and Row, 1963), proposition 4.3, and Robert Roberts, *Emotions: An Essay in Aid of Moral Psychology* (Cambridge: Cambridge University Press, 2003), 271.

3. James Austin, *Zen and the Brain* (Cambridge, Mass.: MIT Press), 1998.

4. Pascal Boyer, *The Naturalness of Religious Ideas: A Cognitive Theory of Religion* (Berkeley: University of California Press, 1994), chap. 4.

5. Illka Pyysiäinen, *How Religion Works: Towards a New Cognitive Science of Religion* (Leiden: Brill, 2001).

6. See William James, *The Varieties of Religious Experience* (Garden City, N.Y.: Doubleday, 1978), xx.

7. Robert Roberts, "The Blessings of Gratitude: A Conceptual Analysis," in *The Psychology of Gratitude,* edited by Robert Emmons and Michael McCullough (New York: Oxford University Press, 2004), 58–78.

8. See Malcolm Muggeridge, *Something Beautiful for God* (Garden City, N.Y.: Doubleday, 1977).

9. See Nico Frijda, *The Emotions* (Cambridge: Cambridge University Press, 1986), chap. 3, for a review of the findings.

10. Antonio Damasio, *Descartes' Error: Emotion, Reason, and the Human Brain* (New York: Avon Books, 1994).

11. Joseph LeDoux, *The Emotional Brain: The Mysterious Underpinnings of Emotional Life* (New York: Touchstone, 1996).

12. Andrew Newberg and Eugene D'Aquili, *Why God Won't Go Away* (New York: Ballantine Books, 2001).

13. V. S. Ramachandran and Sandra Blakeslee, *Phantoms in the Brain: Probing the Mysteries of the Human Mind* (New York: Quill, 1998), chap. 9.

14. Rollin McCarty and Doc Childre, "The Grateful Heart: The Psychophysiology of Appreciation," in Emmons and McCullough, *The Psychology of Gratitude,* 230–55; quotations from 250.

15. See Catherine Lutz, *Unnatural Emotions: Everyday Sentiments on a Micronesian Atoll and Their Challenge to Western Theory* (Chicago: University of Chicago Press, 1988), chap. 6.

16. See Michelle Rosaldo, *Knowledge and Passion: Ilongot Notions of Self and Social Life* (Cambridge: Cambridge University Press, 1980).

17. For further discussion see Roberts, *Emotions*, 180–227.

18. Gananath Obeyesekere, "Depression, Buddhism, and the Work of Culture in Sri Lanka," in *Culture and Depression,* edited by Arthur Kleinman and Byron Good (Berkeley: University of California Press, 1985), 134–52; quotations from 141.

19. John Mayer, "Emotion over Time within a Religious Culture: A Lexical Analysis of the Old Testament," *Journal of Psychohistory* 22 (1994): 235–48.

20. Patricia Meyer Spacks, *Boredom: The Literary History of a State of Mind* (Chicago: University of Chicago Press, 1995).

21. Adela Pinch, *Strange Fits of Passion: Epistemologies of Emotion, Hume to Austen* (Stanford, Calif.: Stanford University Press, 1996).

22. John Corrigan, *Business of the Heart: Religion and Emotion in the Nineteenth Century* (Berkeley: University of California Press, 2002).

23. Aristotle, *Nicomachean Ethics,* translated by W. D. Ross and revised by J. L. Akrill and J. O. Urmson (Oxford: Oxford University Press, 1980), 38.

24. See Paul J. Griffiths, *On Being Mindless: Buddhist Meditation and the Mind-Body Problem* (LaSalle, Ill.: Open Court, 1986), chap. 1.

25. See Søren Kierkegaard, *The Sickness unto Death,* translated by Howard Hong and Reidar Thomte (Princeton, N.J.: Princeton University Press, 1980).

26. For normative investigations of religious hope, see Kierkegaard, *Eighteen Upbuilding Discourses,* translated by Howard V. Hong and Edna H. Hong (Princeton, N.J.: Princeton University Press, 1990), 7–30, 205–26, 253–73, and *Works of Love,* translated by Howard V. Hong and Edna H. Hong (Princeton, N.J.: Princeton University Press, 1995), 246–63, and Robert Roberts, "The Virtue of Hope in *Eighteen Upbuilding Discourses,* in *International Kierkegaard Commentary: Eighteen Upbuilding Discourses,* edited by Robert B. Perkins (Macon, Ga.: Mercer University Press, 2003), 181–203.

27. In *The Person and Work of Christ* (Philadelphia: Presbyterian and Reformed, 1950), 93–145.

28. Jonathan Edwards, *A Treatise Concerning Religious Affections,* edited by John E. Smith (New Haven, Conn.: Yale University Press, 1959).

BIBLIOGRAPHY

Aristotle. *Nicomachean Ethics.* Translated by W. D. Ross. Revised by J. L. Akrill and J. O. Urmson. Oxford: Oxford University Press, 1980.

Austin, James. *Zen and the Brain.* Cambridge, Mass.: MIT Press, 1998.

Boyer, Pascal. *The Naturalness of Religious Ideas: A Cognitive Theory of Religion.* Berkeley: University of California Press, 1994.

Corrigan, John. *Business of the Heart: Religion and Emotion in the Nineteenth Century.* Berkeley: University of California Press, 2002.

Corrigan, John, Eric Crump, and John Kloos. *Emotion and Religion: A Critical Assessment and Annotated Bibliography.* Westport, Conn.: Greenwood Press, 2000.

Damasio, Antonio. *Descartes' Error: Emotion, Reason, and the Human Brain.* New York: Avon Books, 1994.

Edwards, Jonathan. *Treatise Concerning Religious Affections*. Edited by John E. Smith (1746). New Haven, Conn.: Yale University Press, 1959.
Emmons, Robert, and Michael McCullough, eds. *The Psychology of Gratitude*. New York: Oxford University Press, 2004.
Freud, Sigmund. *Civilization and Its Discontents*. Translated by James Strachey. New York: Norton, 1961.
Frijda, Nico. *The Emotions*. Cambridge: Cambridge University Press, 1986.
Griffiths, Paul J. *On Being Mindless: Buddhist Meditation and the Mind-Body Problem*. LaSalle, Ill.: Open Court, 1986.
James, William. *The Varieties of Religious Experience*. Garden City, N.Y.: Doubleday, 1978.
Kierkegaard, Søren. *Eighteen Upbuilding Discourses* (1843/1844). Translated by Howard V. Hong and Edna H. Hong. Princeton, N.J.: Princeton University Press, 1990.
———. *The Sickness unto Death* (1849). Translated by Howard Hong and Reidar Thomte. Princeton, N.J.: Princeton University Press, 1980.
———. *Works of Love* (1847). Translated by Howard V. Hong and Edna H. Hong. Princeton, N.J.: Princeton University Press, 1995.
LeDoux, Joseph. *The Emotional Brain: The Mysterious Underpinnings of Emotional Life*. New York: Touchstone, 1996.
Lutz, Catherine. *Unnatural Emotions: Everyday Sentiments on a Micronesian Atoll and Their Challenge to Western Theory*. Chicago: University of Chicago Press, 1988.
Mayer, John. "Emotion over Time within a Religious Culture: A Lexical Analysis of the Old Testament." *Journal of Psychohistory* 22 (1994): 235–48.
McCarty, Rollin, and Doc Childre. "The Grateful Heart: The Psychophysiology of Appreciation." In *The Psychology of Gratitude*, edited by Robert Emmons and Michael McCullough. New York: Oxford University Press, 2004, 230–55.
Muggeridge, Malcolm. *Something Beautiful for God*. Garden City, N.Y.: Doubleday, 1977.
Newberg, Andrew, and Eugene D'Aquili. *Why God Won't Go Away*. New York: Ballantine Books, 2001.
Obeyesekere, Gananath. "Depression, Buddhism, and the Work of Culture in Sri Lanka." In *Culture and Depression*, edited by Arthur Kleinman and Byron Good. Berkeley: University of California Press, 1985, 134–52.
Pinch, Adela. *Strange Fits of Passion: Epistemologies of Emotion, Hume to Austen*. Stanford, Calif.: Stanford University Press, 1996.
Pyysiäinen, Ilkka. *How Religion Works: Towards a New Cognitive Science of Religion*. Leiden: Brill, 2001.
Ramachandran, V. S., and Sandra Blakeslee. *Phantoms in the Brain: Probing the Mysteries of the Human Mind*. New York: Quill, 1998.
Roberts, Robert. "The Blessings of Gratitude: A Conceptual Analysis." In *The Psychology of Gratitude*, edited by Robert Emmons and Michael McCullough. New York: Oxford University Press, 2004, 58–78.
———. *Emotions: An Essay in Aid of Moral Psychology*. Cambridge: Cambridge University Press, 2003.
———. "The Virtue of Hope in *Eighteen Upbuilding Discourses*." In *International Kierkegaard Commentary: Eighteen Upbuilding Discourses*, edited by Robert B. Perkins. Macon, Ga.: Mercer University Press, 2003, 181–203.
Rosaldo, Michelle. *Knowledge and Passion: Ilongot Notions of Self and Social Life*. Cambridge: Cambridge University Press, 1980.

Schleiermacher, Friedrich. *The Christian Faith*. Edited and translated by H. R. Macintosh and J. S. Stewart. New York: Harper and Row, 1963.

Spacks, Patricia Meyer. *Boredom: The Literary History of a State of Mind*. Chicago: University of Chicago Press, 1995.

Warfield, Benjamin B. "On the Emotional Life of Our Lord." In *The Person and Work of Christ*. Philadelphia: Presbyterian and Reformed, 1950, 93–145.

Index

Abauzit, Frank, 445
Abdul Quadir Jilani, 253
abeg, 53, 55
Abhidhamma, 20–24, 30–31
Abhinavagupta, 203
Aboriginal totemism, 270, 271
Abot de Rabbi Natan, 99, 101
absolute dependence, 391, 406, 459, 463, 466, 467, 492
Abulafia, Abraham, 299
Abu-Lughod, Lila, 45, 477, 478
action, 491, 492, 495–96
activation techniques, 495
adab, 39, 40
Adam (biblical figure), 165, 173, 355, 356, 357, 360
al-'Adawiyyah, Rabi'a, 41, 302, 320
Advaita Vedanta, 52
aesthetics
  of hope, 284–87
  in Islam, 43–45
  in Sanskrit literary tradition, 55
affect
  in Abhidhamma, 21
  analysis of, 131–32
  and confirmation of religious belief, 132–33
  and disaffiliation, 134–35
  in global systems, 46–47
  in Islam, 35, 46–47
  lack of, 4
  in new religious movements, 127–35
  patterns in Japan, 88
  performance of, 131
  and postaffiliation, 135
  and religious practice, 130–32
  Tomkins's theory of, 120
affections, 18, 404–9, 412, 501
affective bonding, 129–30
affective coercion, 128–29
affective enticement, 127–28
affective expression, 44
affective mysticism, 372–73
affective resonance, 28
affectivity, 380
Africa, 262
African Americans, 484–85
agape, 317–18, 327, 366

Ahmed Rifa'i, 252–53
ai jen, 327
aisthesis, 369
Akiba, Rabbi, 315
Alankara, 55–56, 57
Albert the Great, 370, 371
Alcher of Clairvaux, 370
Allport, Gordon W., 340
Almond, Philip, 471n.16
altered states of consciousness, 242
alternative self, 59–60
Ānanda, 29–30
ananda, 61, 62
Anatomy of Melancholy, The (Burton), 295
Anderson, Gary A., 99–100
Angela of Foligno, 374
anger, 22, 25, 65, 341, 475, 496
animal research, 494–95
anomie, 278
Anselm of Canterbury, 374
Antal, 65
Anthony, Saint, 374
anthropology, 33n.33, 112, 475, 497–98
anubhava, 53, 55, 70n.16
anxiety, 389–90, 402n.38
apatheia, 4, 353–54, 360, 362n.7, 365
Apollo (god), 113–14, 201
apophaticism, 298, 373
apperception, 420
appreciation, 496
Aquinas, Thomas, 4, 115, 116, 117, 247
architecture, 228–29, 231
Argo (ship), 202
Aristotle, 102, 114, 116, 117, 214, 380
  eudaimonia, 500
  on hatred, 341
  on music, 204, 205
  theory of emotion, 3, 4, 98
  on virtue, 499
Arnold, Patrick, 193
artifacts, 224–25
Arunta, 447, 448
Asad, Talal, 149, 152
āsavas, 134
asceticism, 102, 170, 292–93, 297, 373, 452
asobi, 85–86
attachment theory, 479

Attic Nights (Gellius), 352
attitude, 478
Augustine of Hippo, Saint, 115, 116, 349–63, 469, 492
 on body, 350, 362n.10
 City of God, 349, 351–54, 356, 357, 408
 Confessions, 206, 349, 351, 358, 361, 367
 on creation narrative, 356–57, 360
 on emotions, 4, 350
 on God, 317, 349, 351, 356, 359
 on love, 351, 408
 on music, 206, 207
 three degrees of disaffection, 358–59
Averill, James, 100, 475–76
Avvakum, 335
aware, 86
awareness, 216
awfulness, 468

Bach, Johann Sebastian, 208, 212
Bainbridge, William Sims, 129
Bandyopadhyaya, Jayanarayana, 68
banka, 78
Barbalet, Jack, 419, 425–27, 431
baroque music, 208–9
Bartholomew's Day Massacre, 334
Bartlet, Phebe, 411
Baruck, Rebbe, 300
Bashō, Matsuo, 84
al Basri, Hasan, 301
Basvanna, 67
Bataille, Georges, 168, 170
Bauman, Zygmunt, 155
Baxter, Richard, 293
Beatrijs of Nazareth, 374
Bedouins, 45, 477
Beethoven, Ludwig van, 209
Begbie, Jeremy, 217
behavioral research, 495–96
Bellah, Robert, 7
Benedict, Ruth, 475
Bengali language, 53, 54
Bengali Vaishnavism, 53, 57–60, 63, 64, 170
bereavement. *See* grief
Bereavement and Consolation: Testimonies from Tokugawa Japan (Bolitho), 74
Berger, Peter, 475, 480
Berkeley, George, 117
Bernard of Clairvaux, 318, 322, 328, 366, 370, 372–74
Besht (Rabbi Ba'al Shem Tov), 300
Bhagavad Gita, 322, 340
Bhagwan Shree Rajneesh, 131, 134
bhakta, 58, 323, 324, 328
bhakti Hinduism, 53, 63, 67, 191, 249, 250, 314, 323–25
bhakti rasa, 58
Bhakti-rasamritasindhu, 58

bhakti yoga, 58, 322
Bharata, 56
bhava, 53–54, 55, 56–57, 67, 250
Bhavaprakashana (Saradatanaya), 56
Bhupala, Singa, 56
Bible, 96, 100, 112, 188, 203, 226, 317, 373
Biblical Myth and Rabbinic Mythmaking (Fishbane), 98
Birth of Tragedy, The (Nietzsche), 114
bisexuality, 166, 173
al-Bistami, Abu Yazid, 41, 302
Blackwell, Albert, 217
bliss. *See ananda*
Bloch, Ernst, 278
Bloch, Maurice, 262, 263, 267
Bly, Robert, 192
bodhisattva, 84–85, 86, 326
body
 Augustine on, 350, 362n.10
 Bloch on, 264
 Damasio on, 215–16
 Durkheim on, 263
 in emotional religion, 119
 and emotions, 491
 James on, 422–23
 and joy, 23
 Mauss on, 157
 and ritual, 157, 424
 and soul, 362n.10, 406
 in study of religion and emotion, 9
Boegner, Marc, 446, 454n.25
Boethius, Anicius, 207
Bolitho, Harold, 74
Bonaventure, 370, 371
Bonhoeffer, Dietrich, 207
Book of Margery Kempe, 364
boredom, 388–89, 400n.16, 401n.20, 402n.38, 498
Borowitz, Eugene, 105
Bosnia, 335, 336, 341
Boston (Mass.), 499
Boudon, Raymond, 447
Bourdieu, Pierre, 74, 154
Boyarin, Daniel, 97, 98, 99, 100, 101, 105, 191
Boyer, Pascal, 153–54, 264–65, 270
Brahman, 314
brain, 121, 123n.18, 154, 215–16, 424–25, 494–95
Brainerd, David, 414–15
brainwashing, 126, 128, 129
Bright, Timothie, 295
Brill, Alan, 104
Bringing Ritual to Mind (McCauley and Lawson), 155
Bromley, David G., 126, 137n.9
Brothers, Leslie, 120
Brown, Norman, 164
Browne, Sir Thomas, 208
Buber, Martin, 96, 191
Budd, Malcolm, 215

Buddha, 17, 24, 27, 29–30, 82, 192, 228, 232, 325
Buddhism, 17–34
   Abhidhamma, 20–24, 30–31
   cultivation of affective life, 24–26
   grief in literature of, 26–29
   in Japan, 78, 82, 84, 86, 87, 90
   love in, 314, 325–26
   male emotion in, 191–92
   meditation in, 24–25, 31, 143–44, 157, 230, 249, 495, 498
   orgasm in, 186
   prayer beads of, 233
   relics of, 228, 230–31
   religious hatred of, 335
   reponses to death, 78
   sensibilities of friendship in, 29–30
   in Sri Lanka, 497–98, 500
   sublimation in, 171
   in Thai monastery, 143–44, 157
Bunyan, John, 293
Burke, Peter, 154–55
Burton, Robert, 295
Businessmen's Revival (1858), 499, 501
Business of the Heart (Corrigan), 499

Caitanya Mahaprabhu of Navadvipa, 58, 70n.19, 250, 251
Call Me Crazy (Heche), 174
Calvin, Jean, 294
Calvin, John, 206
Camus, Albert, 281, 282, 285, 286
Cartesian model, 183
Cassian, John, 293, 298
Cathars, 335
cathedrals, 118
Catherine of Siena, 299, 374
Catholic Church
   choral singing in, 207
   conflict with Cathars, 335
   Day of the Dead ritual, 131
   distancing by Protestant reformers, 119
   doctrine of dyadic soul, 117
   mystical union in, 299
   in Northern Ireland, 339
   Roman Ritual, 114
   women in, 157, 184
celibacy, 168, 170, 173
Chandidasa, 63
character formation, 102–3, 105
charismatics, 130
charity, 408
Charity and Its Fruits (Edwards), 408
Chauncy, Charles, 407
Chiang Mai (Thailand), 143–44
child abuse, 136
Childre, Doc, 496
Children of God (The Family), 128, 134

Childs, Margaret, 86
China, 203, 230, 335
Christ. *See* Jesus
Christian Faith, The (Schleiermacher), 457, 459, 461, 462
Christian History, The (Prince), 296
Christianity
   as ascetic, 102
   celibacy in, 173
   emotion in, 5–6, 111–24
   female saints, 187
   historical underpinnings of, 112–19
   love in, 314, 317–20
   male religious emotion in, 192–93
   music of, 118–19, 203–4, 206–7
   persecution of, 334
   relics of, 228
   rites of passage in, 184
   and science, 120–22
   sin of despair in, 500
   women in, 183–84
Christmas, 148
Chrysippus, 350
Church of Jesus Christ of Latter-day Saints, 127, 129–30, 132–33, 137n.9, 229, 335, 338
Church of Scientology, 128, 131, 134
Cicero, 350, 353–55
citta-vrittis, 60, 61
City of God (Augustine), 349, 351–54, 356, 357
classification, 21
clothing, 229, 230
Cloud of Unknowing, The, 373
coalitions, 264–65
cognition, 4, 18
   and culture, 156, 157
   and emotion, 3, 32n.4, 55, 113, 120, 121, 123n.21, 214, 215, 476
   James on, 5, 425–27
   and ritual, 153–57
cognitive science, 122n.6
Cohen, Hermann, 191
Cohen, Jonathan, 105
Cole, Jennifer, 342
collective effervescence, 270, 278, 446, 447, 449–51, 455n.46
collective memory, 342
collective representation, 146, 445
colonialism, 335
Commentary on the Dream of Scipio (Macrobius), 205
compassion, 19, 25, 26, 84–85, 311, 325–26
Concept of Anxiety, The (Kierkegaard), 389, 400n.8
concern, 392–93
Concluding Unscientific Postscript (Kierkegaard), 391
confabulatio, 367, 371
Conferences, The (Cassian), 293

Confessions (Augustine), 206, 349, 351, 358, 361, 367
conflict, 262
Confucianism, 6, 311, 312, 326
Confucius, 203
consciousness
 altered states of, 242
 effect of emotions on, 55, 69n.9, 491
 feeling in, 20
 of Infinite, 458–59
 James on, 424–25, 427, 431
 Kierkegaard on, 382, 387, 393
 in *raja* yoga, 60–61
 Schleiermacher's three grades of, 461–62
 of self, 459
 and sexuality, 170
 triad, 123n.18
 unity of, 458, 459
 See also self-consciousness
construals, 401n.19
constructionism, 474–89
contemplation, 367, 369, 370, 371
conversion, 129–30, 132, 137n.9, 170, 409, 411, 412
Cooke, Deryck, 211
Corbin, Henry, 302
Cordovero, Moses, 316
Corrigan, John, 95, 106, 150, 291, 499, 501
Council of Trent, 207
courtly love, 319
Crapanzano, V., 243
craving for existence, 22
crime, 265, 358–59
Critique of Pure Reason (Kant), 458, 459
Crump, Eric, 95
Crusades, 334
Csikszentmihalyi, Mihalyi, 233
cults. See new religious movements
cultural psychology, 163, 164
cultural relativism, 163
cultural research, 497–99
culture(s)
 and cognition, 156, 157
 as constructed reality, 475
 differences in, 6
 place of emotion in, 8, 476, 491, 497
 and ritual, 153–57
 Rosaldo on, 476–77
 suffering in, 482, 483–84

Dalai Lama, 325, 337
Daly, Mary, 194
Damasio, Antonio, 121, 215–16, 494
Dan, Joseph, 103, 104
Darwin, Charles, 5, 420
dasya bhava, 65
Davenport, James, 407
David of Augsburg, 368, 369, 370

Dawson, Lorne, 125
death, 28, 78–82
Deeley, Peter, 150, 156, 157
deficit studies, 494–95
de Klerk, F.W., 480
Delacroix, Henri, 455n.46
de Leon, Moshe, 299
delirium, 444–45
Delumeau, Jean, 9
delusion, 22
dependence, 391, 406, 459, 463, 466, 467, 492
depression, 498, 500
Descartes, René, 4–5, 115, 116, 117
Desert Fathers, 293, 298
desire, 5, 167–68, 194, 278, 365
despair, 384, 411, 498, 500
Desroche, Henri, 278
determination, 381
de Vidas, Elijah Moses, 103
Dewey, John, 214
dharmic Hinduism, 52–53
dhikr, 46, 47, 302–3
Diamond, Eliezer, 100, 102
Dionysius the Pseudo-Areopagite, 370, 373
Dionysus (god), 113–14, 201
disaffection, 358–59
Discalced Carmelites, 298
discourse, 475, 477, 478
disobedience, 356–57
Distinguishing Marks (Edwards), 414
Division of Labor, The (Durkheim), 278–79, 282
Dixon, Thomas, 96, 98
Donne, John, 294
drama, 285
Dreyfus Affair, 447
drive models, 170
dualism, 115, 116, 117
Durkheim, Emile, 7, 438–56, 475
 boundaries between psychology and sociology, 440–41
 collective representations, 146, 445
 on delirium, 444–45
 Division of Labor, 278–79
 dramatic representations, 284–85
 and dynamogenetic force of religion, 442–43
 Elemental Forms, 278, 280, 282, 284, 286, 440–41, 444, 446
 and emotion in religion, 441–42
 insights into rites of terror, 261
 notion of effervescence, 150, 270, 278, 446–51, 455n.42, 455n.46
 sacred/profane dichotomy, 263
Dvaita Vedanta, 52
dvesha-bhakti, 257n.23
dyadic soul, 117
dynamogenetic force, 442–43

Ebersole, Gary, 152
Ebner, Christine, 374
Ebner, Marguerite, 374
Ecstasy (drug), 245–46
ecstasy (emotional state), 241–58
ecstatic utterance, 41
Edwards, Jonathan, 404–17
　affections, 404–9, 412
　Distinguishing Marks, 414
　on enthusiasm, 413–15
　Faithful Narrative, 296, 410, 411, 414
　Freedom of the Will, 406, 407
　on God, 412
　legacy concerning religion and emotion, 415–16
　Life of David Brainerd, 414
　Northampton revival, 296–97, 410–11
　"Pesonal Narrative," 408, 411
　Religious Affections, 405–8, 412, 413, 416
　on religious revival, 410–13
　Treatise Concerning Religious Affections, 501, 502
　treatment of "new sense," 408–10
EEG. *See* electroencephalograph
effervescence, 150, 270, 278, 446–51, 455n.42
egoism, 278
Eguchi (Zeami), 85, 86
Eightfold Path, 18
Eilberg-Schwartz, Howard, 191
Ekman, Paul, 5
election, 294, 351
electroencephalograph (EEG), 495
Elemental Forms, The (Durkheim), 278, 280, 282, 284, 286, 440–41, 444, 446
Eliade, Mircea, 61, 245, 257n.22
Elimeloch, Rebbe, 300
Eliot, T.S., 479
Elisabeth of Schönau, 374
embarrassment, 74–75
Emerson, Ralph Waldo, 409
Emile Durkheim (Luke), 446
emotional intelligence, 193
"Emotional Life of Our Lord, The" (Warfield), 501
emotional suffering, 482–84
emotion(s)
　Augustine on, 4, 350
　in Bengali Vaishnavism, 57–60
　in Buddhism, 17–34
　in Christianity, 5–6, 111–24
　and cognition, 3, 32n.4, 55, 113, 120, 121, 123n.21, 214, 215, 476
　definitions of, 8, 18, 32n.4, 406, 438
　discourses of, 150–51
　Durkheim on, 438–55
　as existential disclosures, 386–88
　in Hinduism, 51–72
　in Islam, 35–50
　James's theory of, 5, 419–33
　in Japanese religions, 73–94
　in Judaism, 95–110
　in Kierkegaard, 380–91
　linguistic expression of, 8
　in Medieval mysticism, 364–79
　and music, 211–17
　as natural objects, 399n.1
　in new religious movements, 125–40
　and objects, 223–34
　passion of Christ and history of, 373–74
　place in culture, 8, 476, 491, 497
　in *raja* yoga, 60–62
　religious, 492–94
　research, 490–506
　ritualized, 143–61
　social aspects of, 29
　and spiritual sensation, 369–72
　and study of religion, 3–10
　vis à vis moods, 399–400nn.8–9
　women and, 181–99
　See also specific emotional states
emotives, 481–83
Empedocles, 3
English Civil War, 413
engrams, 131
Enlightenment, 409
enthusiasm, 413–15
Epictetus, 352, 353
episodic memories, 268
equanimity, 25, 26
eros, 317–18, 366
eroticism, 168–70
ethics
　Hume on, 5
　Judaic, 96, 97, 105
　of music, 204–5, 208
　Solomon on, 31
　virtue, 97, 102, 105
Etkes, Immanuel, 104
eudaimonia, 500
Euripides, 113
Eurydice (mythological figure), 201
evangelicalism, 416
evangelical pietism, 294, 296
Eve (biblical figure), 165, 173, 183–84, 196n.22, 355, 357, 360
evil, 462–63
existentialism, 380
expectancy, 393–94
experience
　in Abhidhamma, 20, 21–22
　Buddhist shaping of, 19
　Durkheim on, 439
　Kant on, 459
　and mystical emotion, 431
　religious, 445–46, 460, 469, 470n.4, 471n.16, 490–506
Expression of Emotions, The (Darwin), 420
eyes, of icons, 227

facial expression, 31n.2
faith, 394
Faithful Narrative, A (Edwards), 296, 410, 411, 414
fear, 9, 65, 259, 353, 355, 410, 412
fearful reverence, 75
feeling(s)
  definition of, 20
  in Islam, 37, 43–45
  James on, 428–31
  love as, 122
  and rationality, 426
  in religion, 457–58, 461–67
  See also emotion(s)
feminism. *See* women
Fichte, J.G., 382
Finney, Charles G., 297
First Nations rituals, 153
Fishbane, Michael, 97–98, 99, 100, 102, 104
flagellation, 119, 374
flashbulb memories, 268
Flowing Light of the Godhead (Mechthild of Magdeburg), 367
fMRI. *See* functional magnetic resonance imaging
Fonrobert, Charlotte Elisheva, 187
food, 9, 128
force, 444
forgiveness, 103
Forgy, Howell, 283
Foucault, Michel, 168, 281
Four Noble Truths, 17
Francis, Saint, 371, 374
Franciscans, 371, 374
Frank, Daniel, 102
Franzmann, Majella, 185
Free Believers, 443
Freedberg, Daniel, 227
freedom, 390, 485
Freedom of the Will (Edwards), 406, 407
Freeman, Susan, 105
free reflection, 399n.7
French Revolution, 447, 481, 483
Freud, Sigmund, 7, 169, 170, 191, 495
Friedman, Maurice, 316
friendship, 29–30
Fries, Jakob Friedrich, 466
Frijda, Nico, 5
From Passions to Emotions (Dixon), 96
Fujiwara no Shunzei, 84, 87
functional magnetic resonance imaging (fMRI), 495
funeral laments, 78–82

Gale, Richard, 421
Galen, 291
Gallus, Thomas, 372–73
gangs, 265

Gaudiya Vaishnavism. *See* Bengali Vaishnavism
Geertz, Clifford, 7, 75, 150, 290, 292, 477, 478, 480
Gellius, Aulus, 352, 353
gender, 165–67, 172, 181–99
Genesis According to the Letter (Augustine), 356
genitals, 163
German idealism, 382, 383
German Jews, 105
Gertrude the Great, 374
Gesualdo, Carlo, 208
al–Ghazzali, Abu Hamid, 43, 44
Gibbon, Edward, 334
Girard, René, 338–39
Gluckman, Max, 262, 269
Gnosticism, 112
God
  Augustine on, 349, 351, 356, 359
  Edwards on, 412
  God-consciousness of Schleiermacher, 459, 461–66, 470
  of Hindus, 322–23
  of Islam, 37, 320–22
  of Judaism, 191, 314–16
  love of, 4, 313–20
  and Medieval mysticism, 364–69, 372–74
  and religious emotions, 492–93
  and soul, 319, 364, 367–69
  wrath of, 468
goddess feminism, 194–95
Goldstein, Niles, 103, 104
Goodman, George, 293
Goodman, Lenn, 102
Go-Shirakawa, 87
Gosvamin, Rupa, 58
Govinda-dasa, 64
gratitude, 89, 493, 496
Graver, Margaret, 361n.2
Great Awakening, 296, 407, 410, 414
Great Britain, 192, 413
Greece, ancient, 112–14, 203–4, 205
greed, 22
Green, Arthur, 104
Greenfield, Susan, 121
Greenham, Richard, 294
Gregory of Nyssa, 4, 365, 366, 369, 372
Gregory the Great, 366
grief
  Anderson on, 99
  in Buddhist literature, 26–29, 30
  Cicero on, 355
  in Japan, 74
  of women, 188–89
Gruber, Meyer, 100
Guide of the Perplexed, The (Maimonides), 299
guilt, 100

Gujarat (India), 252, 253
Guyon, Madame, 298

Habad movement, 301
Hadewijch of Antwerp, 373, 374
hadith, 38, 44, 320
Hadot, Pierre, 101
Hajj, 38, 46
hal, 254
halakhot, 105
Halflants, M. Corneille, 318
Hall, Timothy D., 296
al-Hallaj, 41, 320
Hallisey, Charles, 28
Hamlet, 384, 399n.7
Handel, Georg Friedrich, 207, 208
Hansen, Anne, 28
Hanslick, Eduard, 211
happiness, 22–23, 98, 352–53
Happiness in Premodern Judaism (Tirosh-Samuelson), 98
Hardacre, Helen, 88–89
Hardman, Charlotte, 9–10
Hare Krishna. *See* International Society for Krishna Consciousness
Hartman, David, 105
Harvey, Warren Zev, 102
Hasan of Basra, 40–41
Hasidim, 96–97, 100, 104, 190, 191, 299, 300, 315–16
hatred, 22, 257n.23, 333–45
Hawley, Joseph, 411
heart, 8, 54, 406, 407, 496
Heche, Anne, 173, 174–75
Hegel, Georg, 209, 391
Heike monogatari, 90
Helm, Paul, 409
heresy, 115, 116
Herp, Hendrik, 373
Heschel, Abraham Joshua, 100, 105, 191
Heyward, Carter, 194
Hinduism, 51–72
  Caitanya tradition, 250–52
  deities of, 53
  emotion in, 53–62
  folk tradition, 51–52
  literary tradition, 63–69
  love in, 314, 322–25
  Muslim conflict, 335, 341
  ritual in weddings, 151
  Sufi Rifa'i brotherhood, 252–54
  tantric tradition, 53
  types of, 51–53
Hippocrates, 3
historical research, 497–99
historical tradition, 491
Holy Seer of Lublin. *See* Horowitz, Yaakov Yitzhak

Holy Sonnets (Donne), 294
homo sapiens, 112
homosexuality, 173, 185, 251, 321
hope, 276–89
Hopkins, Jeffrey, 171, 185, 186
Horowitz, Yaakov Yitzhak (Holy Seer of Lublin), 300
hostages, 264, 265
household goods, 233
hridaya, 54
Hubbard, L. Ron, 131, 134
Hugh of Balma, 373
Hugh of Saint Victor, 369, 370, 372–73
al-Hujwiri, 41
Hume, David, 5, 115, 117, 195n.4
Humphrey, Caroline, 266
Husayn, Imam, 46
Husserl, Edmund, 115, 117
hylomorphism, 116, 117
hysteria, 242

Ibn Adhan, Ibrahim, 301
Ibn al-'Arabi, 302
Ibn al-Farid, 'Umar, 45
Ibn Taimiyyah, 40
icons, 227, 230
idealism, 382, 383
ideal type, 291, 292–93
Idea of the Holy, The (Otto), 226, 459, 466, 467, 469
Idel, Moshe, 103, 104
identity, 183, 280, 337–38, 339
ideology, 475
Ifaluk (Micronesia), 477–78
ignorance, 22
Ilongot, 476, 477, 481, 483, 497
images, 226–27, 232, 233, 263
imagination, 414
imayō, 87
impulse, 101
inclination, 406–7
indetermination, 381, 384, 399n.7
India, 53, 69n.4, 209, 252, 324, 335, 341
Indonesia, 46, 47
Infinite, 458–59
information theory, 214
Ingall, Carol, 105
initiation rites, 264, 265
Innocent III (pope), 334
instinct, 422–23
Institute of HeartMath and Quantum Intech, 496
institutions, 263, 281
International Society for Krishna Consciousness (ISKCON), 128, 131, 134
intuition, 116, 458, 460, 470n.4
ISKCON. *See* International Society for Krishna Consciousness

Islam, 35–50
  aesthetics in, 43–45
  affect and performance in global systems, 46–47
  cultivation and expression of sentiment in, 39–43
  good and beautiful in, 43
  Hindu conflict, 335, 341
  love in, 313–14, 320–22
  music of, 203–4
  Muslims in Bosnian conflict, 335, 336, 341
  Qur'an, 35–40, 44, 47
  Sufism, 39–45, 252–54, 299, 301–3, 320–22
  weeping during prayer, 152
  women in, 183, 185, 229
Islam, Kazi Nazrul, 67
Isma'ili Shi'a, 43

Jackson, Stanley, 293
Jagannatha (god), 251, 252
Jakuren, 83
James, William, 7, 405
  on "coarser" or "standard" emotions, 422–23
  on mystical emotions, 430–32
  objects in work of, 225
  scheme of reflex circuit of emotion, 424–25
  social theory of "metaphysical" emotions, 427–28
  on "subtler" or "complex" emotions, 425–27
  theory of emotion, 5, 419–33
  Varieties of Religious Experience, 5, 225, 419, 421–22, 424, 426–33, 445
  work on religious emotion, 419, 420, 421, 427–30, 432–33
Japanese religions, 73–94
  ancient, 75–82
  emotion in new, 88–89
  medieval, 82–88, 90
jealousy, 76, 87
Jean of Fécamp, 374
Jehovah's Witnesses, 127
jen, 311, 312, 326–27
Jesuits, 118
Jesus
  in *Book of Margery Kempe*, 364, 369
  call to love, 313
  expression of emotion, 192
  on hatred, 340
  as inherently holy, 460
  in Lutheranism, 461
  paintings of, 233
  redemption of, 463
  suffering of, 111, 373–74, 411, 412
Jews. *See* Judaism
al-Jilani, 41
Jnana-dasa, 63
John of the Cross, Saint, 298, 311, 319
Jospe, Raphael, 102

joy, 23, 99, 104, 396–98, 410
"Joy and Jewish Spirituality" (Fishbane), 97–98
Juan de Avila, 227
Judaism
  emotions in, 95–110
  Hasidim, 96–97, 100, 104, 190, 191, 299, 300, 315–16
  love in, 313, 314–17
  men in, 191
  music of, 203–4
  mysticism, 299–300, 301
  religious hatred of, 333, 334
  women in, 183–84, 186, 187, 188, 196n.20
judgment, 214, 385, 401n.19
Juergensmeyer, Mark, 337, 339
Julian of Norwich, 372
al-Junayd, 41

kabbalism, 299, 313, 315, 316
kabuki theater, 86
Kafka, Franz, 285–86
Kakar, Sudhir, 335, 339, 341
al-Kalabadhi, 41
Kalika, 68
kama, 55, 63, 170
kanashiki, 77
kanashimo, 77
Kant, Immanuel, 115, 117, 439, 458–60, 470n.4, 470n.6, 471n.16
Kapferer, Bruce, 33n.33
Kaplan, Lawrence, 102
Kapoor, O.B.L., 58
kari no yado, 85
katami, 77, 78
Kaufman, Peter Iver, 294
Kempe, Margery, 187, 364, 372
Kenkō, 82
Keyes, Alan, 485
Khmer Rouge, 28
Kierkegaard, Søren, 380–403
  articulation of religion, 391–98, 401n.26
  Concept of Anxiety, 389, 400n.8
  emotions in, 380–91, 500
  Opbyggelige Taler, 391, 392, 393, 401n.26
  "Possibility," 386–87
  self in context, 382–85
  Sickness Unto Death, 383, 384
  views on anxiety, 389–90
  views on boredom, 388–89, 400n.16
  views on concern, 392–93
  views on expectancy, 393–94
  views on joy, 396–98
  views on patience, 394–96
King, Martin Luther, 485
Ki no Tsurayuki, 76
Kisāgotamī, 27–28, 29
Kivy, Peter, 212, 214
kleshas, 60–61

Kloos, John, 95
knowledge, 183, 356, 358, 366, 391, 394, 470n.4
Kojiki texts, 75–76, 86
kokoro, 89
Konjaku monogatari-shū, 84, 87
Korea, 6
Kravitz, Leonard S., 103
Kress, Jeffrey S., 105
Krishna (god), 58–60, 63–64, 70n.16, 70n.18, 170, 250, 251, 314, 323, 324
Kroner, Richard, 382
Kruger, Paul, 100
Kuhn, Thomas, 123n.21
kundalini yoga, 69n.5

LaFleur, William, 90, 327
Laidlaw, James, 266
Lamberth, David, 428, 429
laments, 78–82, 188
Lamm, Julia, 470n.6
Lamm, Norman, 104
Lange, Karl Georg, 5, 420
Langer, Susanne, 211, 212
language
 of Buddhism, 18, 23–24
 metaphor, 23–24
 of mystics, 243
 of poetry, 45
 of prayer, 8
 in Qur'an, 37
 Sufi, 42–43
Lapie, Paul, 454n.26
latent tendencies, 22
Lawson, E. Thomas, 155–56
Layla and Majnun (Nizami), 45
Le Bon, Gustave, 446
LeDoux, Joseph, 494
Lee, Mother Ann, 173–75
Levinas, Emmanuel, 117, 191
Levi-Yithak, Rebbe, 300
Lévy-Bruhl, Lucien, 441
Lewis, C.S., 318
Lewis, Ioan M., 188, 243
li, 311
libido, 170
Life of David Brainerd, The (Edwards), 414
liget, 476, 497
Lincoln, Abraham, 485
Lindfield, Olive, 129
Lipner, Julius, 317
Lloyd, Genevieve, 183
Locke, John, 117, 409
Lofland, John, 129
Lohorung Rai, 9, 10
loneliness, 83–84
Lonergan, Bernard, 313
Lorde, Audre, 194
L'Orfeo (Monteverdi), 201

loss, 28
love, 310–32
 as attribute of transcendent, 313–14
 Augustine on, 351, 408
 to conquer grief, 30
 Edwards on, 408
 as feeling, 122
 in Hindu lore, 58–60, 250–52
 in Hindu poetry, 63–66
 and Medieval mysticism, 366, 367, 372, 373
 Muffs on, 99
 nature of, 311–13
 parental, 26
 as response to transcendent, 314–27
 romantic, 311–12, 321, 476
 salvation of, 112
 Solomon on, 311–12
 in Sufi Rifa'i brotherhood, 253, 255
 as transformation of self, 327–28
 varieties of, 25
 vis à vis hatred, 257n.23, 340
loving-kindness, 25, 26
luck, 283–84, 286
Luckmann, Thomas, 475
Ludolf of Saxony, 374
Luke, Steven, 446
Luria, Isaac ben Solomon, 316
lust, 278
Luther, Martin, 206, 294, 301
Lutheranism, 461
Lutz, Catherine, 477–78
Lyon, Margot, 156, 479

Madagascar, 342
Madell, Geoffrey, 215
Maffesoli, Michel, 281, 282
mahabhava, 64
Mahadeviyakka, 65–66
Mahayana Buddhism, 82, 311, 325–26
Mahler, Gustav, 215
Mahmood, Saba, 152, 153
Maimonides, Moses, 102, 103, 191, 299, 315
mana, 54
Mandel, Scott, 105
Mandela, Nelson, 480
Manichaeism, 115
Manikkavacakar, 66, 67
Mannheim, Karl, 475, 479
Man of Light in Iranian Sufism, The (Corbin), 302
Man of Reason, The (Lloyd), 183
mantras, 249, 251
Man'yōshū, 76, 77, 78, 87
Mao Zedong, 231
Marcel, Gabriel, 276–80, 286
martyrdom, 373–74, 452
masculine religious emotion, 181, 190–93
Mason, Steven S., 103
Material Christianity (McDannel), 233

material culture, 223–37
  emotions attributed to objects, 231–32
  everyday objects and ordinary feelings, 232–33
  manipulation of emotions through, 229–31
  objects as triggers for emotions, 226–29
  and study of religion, 224–26
mathematics, 204, 208
Mathnawi (Rumi), 322
Matson, Gladys, 130
Mauss, Marcel, 149, 157, 440, 447
McCarty, Rollin, 496
McCauley, Robert N., 5, 155–56
McDaniel, June, 324
McDannel, Colleen, 233
McGinn, Bernard, 373
Mead, Margaret, 475
Mechthild of Hackeborn, 374
Mechthild of Magdeburg, 367, 373, 374
Medieval mysticism, 364–79
meditation
  Buddhist, 24–25, 31, 143–44, 157, 230, 249, 495, 498
  kundalini yoga, 69n.5
  on revulsion, 498, 500
  shikan, 87
  silent ecstasy of, 247–49
Meier, Fritz, 302
melancholy, 290–309
memory, 147, 268, 366–69
Mendelssohn, Felix, 209
Meno (Plato), 395
men's crisis, 192
menstrual cycle, 185
metaphor, 21, 23–24, 31
Methodism, 297
Meyer, Leonard, 214
midot, 102, 105
Milgrom, Jacob, 100
Miller, Perry, 409
Mills, C. Wright, 479
mimetic rite, 284
mind
  cultivation of, 24
  Edwards on, 406, 407
  James on, 424
  theory of, 266–69
  tripartite division of, 18–19, 31n.3
Mirabai, 191, 311, 324
Mirror of Simple Souls (Porete), 367
Missa Solemnis (Beethoven), 209
Mithen, Steven, 260
Mo'ed Katan, 188
Mohammed (prophet). *See* Muhammad
monastic asceticism, 373
mono no aware, 77, 82, 84, 86
Monteverdi, Claudio, 201, 208
mood, 386, 399–400nn.8–9

Moore, Barrington, 337
moral states
  in Abhidhamma, 21
  in cultures, 482
  in Judaism, 97, 102
  See also ethics
morbid effervescence, 455n.42
Mormons. *See* Church of Jesus Christ of Latter-day Saints
morphology of conversion, 411, 412
Moses (biblical figure), 37, 299
mosque movement, 152
Muffs, Yochanan, 99, 100
Muhammad (prophet), 35, 36, 38, 43, 45, 336, 480
al-Muhasibi, 42
multiple personality disorder, 59, 71n.21
Murdoch, Iris, 23–24
Musar movement, 104
music, 118–19, 200–222
  ancient, 203–4
  Christian, 118–19, 203–4, 206–7
  and emotion, 211–17
  ethics of, 204–5, 208
  expression and form, 207–10
  metaphysics of, 205, 208
musical instruments, 206
Muslims. *See* Islam
Muster, Nori, 134
Myers, Frederick, 430
Myers, Gerald, 419, 427, 429
mysticism, 297–303, 320, 321, 364–79, 430–32, 468
Myth of Sisyphus, The (Camus), 281, 285
mythology, 284–85

Nahman, R., 104
Nakayima, Michio, 440
nama-sankirtana, 257n.24
Nammalvar, 323
Napier, Richard, 295
narrative, 280
Native Americans, 153, 336
Nature, 471n.15
Natyashastra (Bharata), 56, 70n.10, 203
Ndembu ritual, 482
Needham, Rodney, 440
negative theology, 372–73
Nelson, Benjamin, 290
Nelson, Timothy, 474
Nenets, 230
neoorthodox theology, 380
Neoplatonism, 205, 208
neo-Stoicism, 385–86
Nepal, 6, 9
neurobiology, 215
neurology, 156, 494–95
Neusner, Jacob, 100–101

Newar, 6
New Guinea, 264
New Lights, 407
new religious movements (NRMs)
  affect and confirmation of religious belief, 132–33
  affect and religious practice, 130–32
  affective bonding in, 129–30
  affective coercion in, 128–29
  affective enticement in, 127–28
  Bromley model, 126, 127, 134
  definition of, 126
  disaffiliation from, 134–35
  emotional abuse in, 133–34
  emotion and, 125–40
  issues for future research, 136
  postaffiliation, 135
  recruitment and affiliation, 127
New Testament, 115, 317
Nietzsche, Friedrich, 114
nirvāna, 17
Noll, Mark, 416
nondualism, 82
nō plays, 85, 86, 87
Norbeck, Edward, 262, 269
Norman, Donald, 121
normative research, 499–502
Northampton (Mass.), 296, 410–11
Northern Ireland, 339
Nozick, Robert, 310, 312
NRMs. *See* new religious movements
nuga, 6
numinous, 182, 457, 459–60, 467–69
Nussbaum, Martha, 5, 32n.4, 183, 215, 385, 400nn.8–9
Nygren, Anders, 317–18, 327

Obama, Barack, 485
Obeyesekere, Gananath, 497–98
objectivity, 114
objects, 223–33, 439, 497
occasionalism, 154–55
Old Lights, 407
Olitzky, Kerry M., 103, 105
On Ends (Cicero), 353
On Free Choice (Augustine), 350
Ōno no Komachi, 87
On Religion (Schleiermacher), 457, 462
Opbyggelige Taler (Kierkegaard), 391, 392, 393, 401n.26
orgasm, 170, 171, 186
Origen (church father), 365, 369, 372
Original Sin (Edwards), 406
Orissa (India), 251
Orpheus (mythological figure), 201–2
Orthodox Church, 335

Other Worlds (Hardman), 9
Ōtomo Tabito, 78, 81
Otto, Rudolf, 7, 75, 471nn.16–17
  commonalities with Schleiermacher, 457–60, 469–70
  Idea of the Holy, 226, 459, 466, 467, 469
  mysterium tremendum et fascinans, 172–73
  numinous, 182, 457, 459–60, 467–69
  Philosophy of Religion Based on Kant and Fries, 466, 471n.15
overalertness, 242, 246
Oxford Movement, 296

Paganism, 133
pain, 5, 28
Paisley, Ian, 339
Pakistan, 335
paleontology, 112
Palmer, Phoebe, 297
Papua New Guinea, 148
parental love, 26
Parsons, Jonathan, 296
Parsons, Talcott, 446
passions, 4, 5, 18, 352, 354, 355, 365, 366, 369, 372, 406, 407
Patācārā, 26–27, 28, 29
Patanjali, 52, 60, 61, 248
paternity, 167
patience, 394–96
patriotism, 67
Péguy, Charles, 282, 286
Pentecostals, 131
Perkins, William, 294
Persian language, 45
Persinger, Michael, 495
"Personal Narrative" (Edwards), 408, 411
personal relationships, 491
perspective, 478
perturbatio, 354–55, 361n.2
PET. *See* positron emission tomography
Peter of Ailly, 370
Philippi, Donald, 75
Philippines, 476, 483
Philo, 99
Philosophy of Religion Based on Kant and Fries, The (Otto), 466, 471n.15
physiological research, 494–95
pietism, 294, 296, 380
pilgrims, 9
pineal gland, 5
Pinker, Steven, 166
Plague, The (Camus), 281, 285
Plater, Felix, 295
Plato, 3, 114–17, 204–6, 395, 406
pleasure, 5, 23
Plotinus, 3, 205
pluralism, 432–33

poetry
    Bedouin, 45, 477
    Hindu, 63–69
    Islamic, 44–45
    Japanese, 76–85, 87
Politics (Aristotle), 205
Porete, Marguerite, 319, 320, 367, 373
positron emission tomography (PET), 495
possession, 242–45, 297
"Possibility, A" (Kierkegaard), 386–87
postmodernism, 380
power, 444
Prabhupada, A.C. Bhaktivedanta, 134
prayer, 8, 131, 152, 208, 284, 366–69, 370, 371, 496
Prayers for Forgiveness (al Basri), 301
prema, 55, 63, 170
pride, 357–58
primitive societies, 441
Prince, Thomas, 296
Principles of Psychology, The (James), 420–21
property dualism, 116
prophets, 100
Protestantism, 117, 119, 184, 225, 226, 452, 499, 501
Psalms, 203, 206, 207
psychedelic states, 178n.30
psychic entropy, 233
psychoanalytic hermeneutics, 169
psychology
    Buddhist, 19, 21, 22
    constructionism in, 475–76
    cultural, 163, 164
    Jewish, 104
    and physiology, 420
    and sociology, 440–41
Psychology: A Briefer Course (James), 420
Psychology of the Emotions, The (Ribot), 422, 430
Puri (India), 251
Puritans, 226, 293, 295, 409, 411
Pythagoras, 204
Pyysiäinen, Ilkka, 5

Qur'an, 35–40, 44, 47, 203, 303, 314, 320
qur'an, as term, 44
al-Qushayri, 41

Radden, Jennifer, 291
Radha (goddess), 58–59, 63–65, 70n.16, 70nn.18–19, 170, 250, 251
Raëlian movement, 131
raga, 53, 54, 69n.6, 203, 209
raganuga bhakti sadhana, 58
rage, 194
Rahner, Karl, 369
raja yoga, 53, 60–62

Rameau, Jean-Philippe, 208
rasa, 56–57, 58, 65, 70nn.13–14, 203, 251
rasabhasa, 56
Rasarnavasudhakar (Bhupala), 56
rationalism, 191, 195n.4
rationality. *See* reason
reason, 171, 182–83, 191, 195n.4, 426
Rebel, The (Camus), 281
rebounding violence, 262, 264
Reddy, William M., 474, 481–85
redemption, 462, 463
reflex circuit of emotion, 424–25
reflexivity, 24
regicide, 262
relativism, 163, 480–81, 482, 483
relaxation, 496
relics, 228, 230–31
Religion and Emotion (Corrigan), 95, 106
religion(s)
    ecstatic practices, 241–58
    feeling in, 457–58, 461–67
    Geertz's definition of, 290, 292
    of head and heart, 111, 113
    Japanese, 73–94
    Kierkegaard on, 391–98, 401n.26
    and material culture, 224–26
    new religious movements, 125–40
    revivals, 410–13, 415
    ritual ordeals that inspire terror, 259–75
    and sexuality, 162–63, 165, 170, 175
    study of emotion and, 3–10
    women's role in, 181–90, 193–95
    See also specific religions
Religious Affections (Edwards), 405–8, 412, 413, 416
religious experience, 445–46, 460, 469, 470n.4, 471n.16, 490–506
religious hatred, 333–45
Renaissance, 208
representation, 284, 439, 445
Republic, The (Plato), 204–5
research, 490–506
    behavioral, 495–96
    emotions as objects of, 490–92
    historical and cultural, 497–99
    normative, 499–502
    physiological, 494–95
Reshit Chochmah (de Vidas), 103
revelation, 461
revival narrative, 410
revivals, religious, 410–13, 415
Revivification of the Religious Sciences (al-Ghazzali), 43, 44
Ribot, Théodule, 422, 430
Richard, Gaston, 446, 449
Ridley, Aaron, 215
Rifa'i brotherhood, 252–54
Rig Veda, 52
Rinzai school, 131

rites of passage, 145, 184
rites of terror, 260–70
ritual(s), 143–61
　African, 262
　authenticity of emotion in, 151–53
　cognition and culture in, 153–57
　cognitive theory of, 147
　construction of, 474–75
　definitions of, 145–50
　doctrinal, 147–48, 149, 156
　First Nations, 153
　food, 9
　Hindu, 53
　imagistic, 147–49, 155, 156
　that inspire terror, 259–75
　Islamic, 46
　Japanese, 87
　Ndembu, 482
　symbols of, 146–47, 149
Robbins, Joel, 148
Roberts, Robert, 385, 386, 389, 400n.8,
　401nn.19–20
robots, 121
Rogers, Richard, 294
Roman Catholic Church. *See* Catholic Church
Roman empire, 334
Roman Ritual, 114
romanticism/Romanticism, 182, 195n.4, 209, 213
Rorty, Amélie Oksenberg, 399n.1
Rorty, Richard, 283
Rosaldo, Michelle, 146, 475, 476–77
"Rotation of Crops, The" (Kierkegaard), 388
Rousseau, Jean Jacques, 337
Rubenstein, Jeffrey, 100, 101–2
Rudolf of Biberach, 370, 371
Ruether, Rosemary Radford, 195n.4
Rumi (Jalal al-Din Rumi), 45, 302, 311, 313,
　321–22
Russia, 335
Ruusbroec, 372
Ryōzan, 83

Sabath, Rachel T., 105
sabi, 82
sacramental mimesis, 375n.13
Sacred in Music, The (Blackwell), 217
sacred/profane dichotomy, 263
sacrifice, 262, 338–39
sadness, 77
Safed, 103
Saigyō, 83, 86
St. Trudperter Hohelied, 367, 370
Salanter, R. Israel, 104
salvation, 294, 295, 297, 303
sama', 44
samadhi, 257n.22
Samuelson, Norbert, 102
Sanchez, Andres, 132

Sankashū, 83
Sanskrit language, 53, 54
Sāntideva, 25
Saradatanaya, 56
Satan, 38, 295, 298, 406, 411
sattvika bhavas, 70n.20
saya, 9
scapegoating, 338–39
Schatz-Uffenheimer, Rivka, 104
Scheler, Max, 117, 475
Schichinin no bikuni, 86
Schimmel, Annemarie, 321
Schimmel, Solomon, 103
Schleiermacher, Friedrich, 7, 394, 409, 471n.16
　on absolute dependence, 391, 406, 459, 463,
　　466, 467, 492
　Christian Faith, 457, 459, 461, 462
　commonalities with Otto, 457–60, 469–70
　on devotional aids, 225
　On Religion, 457, 462
　religious feeling as transcendental experience,
　　461–66, 467
　Speeches, 458, 459, 466, 470n.4
Schofer, Jonathan, 100, 101, 103
Scholem, Gershom, 96, 104
Schopenhauer, Arthur, 209, 211
Schwartz, Regina, 337, 339, 342
science, 120–22
Seeman, Don, 104
Sefer Ma'alot HaMidot, 103
self, 382–85, 388–90, 393–95, 406–7, 459, 462, 463,
　467, 468
self-assessment, 20
self-consciousness, 381–82, 384, 387–89, 393,
　395–98, 402n.38, 459, 461–65, 467
Sells, Michael A., 336, 341
Semnani, Alaoddawleh, 302
Sen, Ramprasad, 54, 68
sensual meditation, 131
sensuous desire, 22
Septem gradus orationis (David of Augsburg),
　368, 370
Serbs, 336, 341
Sered, Susan Starr, 189
serpent symbolism, 171
sexual abuse, 174
sexual intercourse, 173, 174
sexuality, 162–80
　eroticism, 168–69
　female, 185
　and gender, 165–67
　and religion, 162–63, 165, 170, 175
　trauma of, 172–73, 174
sexual orientation, 166, 167
al-Shaf'i, 38
shaikh, 42
Shakers, 173
Shakespeare, William, 208
Shakti (goddess), 68

Shaktism, 67
shamanism, 203, 230, 242, 244–46
shame, 20–21, 74–75, 76, 86
Shamsuddin, 322
Shatz, David, 105
Shemonah Peraqim (Maimonides), 103
Sherwin, Byron, 103
Shi'i Ashura, 46
Shi'ite Muslims, 185
shikan, 87
Shils, Edward, 479
al-Shirazi, Hafiz, 45
Shiva (god), 65
Shweder, Richard, 163, 164
Sickness unto Death (Kierkegaard), 383, 384
siddha, 170
siddhis, 249
simile, 23, 31
Simmel, Georg, 485
sin, 9, 196n.22, 301, 356–58, 390, 463, 500
Sin and Fear (Delumeau), 9
single photon emission computed tomography (SPECT), 495
slavery, 484
smasana, 69n.4
Smith, Jonathan Z., 145–46, 147, 150, 152
Smith, Margaret, 301
Social Construction of Reality, The (Berger and Luckmann), 475
social psychology, 476
society, 475
sociology, 440–41, 453n.2, 475
Socrates, 3, 205
Soliloquies (Augustine), 349
Solomon, Robert C., 5, 31, 100, 311–12, 385
Soloveitchik, Joseph Dov, 105
Somalia, 189
Song of Songs, 4, 315, 318, 365–67, 370, 372–73
Sorabji, Richard, 352, 353
Sotoba no Komachi, 87
Soto Zen, 131
soul
  activity of, 4
  Augustine on, 349, 354–55
  and body, 362n.10, 406
  Cartesian, 4–5
  dyadic, 117
  and God, 319, 364, 367–69
  Kierkegaard on, 394–95
  and love, 319
  Otto on, 469
  sensory within, 370, 372
  triadic, 117
space, 458
SPECT. *See* single photon emission computed tomography
Speeches (Schleiermacher), 458, 459, 466, 470n.4
Spinoza, Benedict, 4, 5
spirit manifestation, 189

spirituality movement, 192
spiritual sensation, 369–72
spiritual sense, 408–10
Spiro, Melford, 481
split personality, 59
Sri Lanka, 497–98, 500
Stagel, Elisabeth, 374
Starbuck, Edwin, 405
Stark, Rodney, 7, 129
state, Sufi, 42
station, Sufi, 42
Stearns, Carol Z., 10
Stearns, Peter N., 10
Stoicism, 3, 4, 350–58, 360, 365, 380, 385–86
Stravinsky, Igor, 212
Strelley, Kate, 134
stress, 268
stribhava, 251
Structure of Scientific Revolutions (Kuhn), 123n.21
subjective well-being, 491
subjectivity, 114, 482
sublimation, 169, 171
substance dualism, 115, 116, 117
suffering, 17–18, 19, 28, 111, 482–85
Sufism, 39–45, 252–54, 299, 301–3, 320–22
suggestive absorption, 242
suicide, 279, 411, 452
sunnah, 38, 40, 43, 47
Sunni jurisprudence, 35, 38
superconscious, 61
Surdas, 323
Suso, Henry, 374
Swazi royal rituals, 262
symbols, 146–47, 149
sympathetic joy, 25, 26

Takechi Furuhito, 76
Tang dynasty, 335
tantric traditions, 53, 170, 171, 172, 326
Tanya, 301
Taoism, 169, 171
tariqah, 42
tasawwuf, 39, 40, 41, 42, 47
Taves, Ann, 150
"Techniques of the Body" (Mauss), 149
Tennent, Gilbert, 9, 296
Teresa of Avila, 226–27, 298, 319, 320
terma, 177n.16
terror, 259–75
terrorism, 264, 265, 337
Theology, Music, and Time (Begbie), 217
theory of mind (TOM), 266–69
Theravada Buddhism, 82, 143
Thirty Years' War, 334
Thomas à Kempis, 370
Timaeus (Plato), 205
time, 458

Tirosh-Samuelson, Hava, 97, 98–99, 100, 102, 103
Tishby, Isaiah, 104
Tokugawa period, 74
TOM. *See* theory of mind
Tomkins, Silvan, 120
Toomey, Paul M., 9, 128
Torah, 196n.20, 313, 315
torture, 264, 268
Touching Our Strength (Heyward), 194
tradition, 479, 491
trance, 242
transcendent, 313–27, 461–66, 467, 492–93
transcranial magnetic stimulator, 495
transvestism, 262
trauma, 172–73, 174
Treatise Concerning Religious Affections, A (Edwards), 501, 502
Treatise of Melancholie (Bright), 295
tremendum, 172–73, 467, 468
triadic soul, 117
Tristan und Isolde (Wagner), 209
truth, 368
Tsurezuregusa (Kenkō), 82
Tuc D'Audoubert (France), 260
Turner, Victor, 146–47, 150, 482
Tuzin, Donald, 264, 270

Ujjvala-Nilamani (Gosvamin), 58
ummah, 47
Underhill, Evelyn, 298
understanding, 116, 406, 407, 458
Unheroic Conduct (Boyarin), 105
Unification Church, 128, 129
unmada, 251
Unnatural Emotion (Lutz), 477
Upanishads, 52, 314, 322

Vaishnavism, 53, 57–60, 63, 64, 170
Vajrayana Buddhism, 171
Vanacari, Danavir dasa, 128, 131
van Gennep, Arnold, 145, 146, 261
Varieties of Religious Experience, The (James), 5, 225, 419, 421–22, 424, 426–33, 445
vedana, 53
Vedantic Hinduism, 52
Vedic Hinduism, 52
Veiled Sentiments (Abu-Lughod), 477
vices, 499
victory, 394, 402n.36
Vidyapati, 63, 64, 65
Vines, Jerry, 336
violence, 262–65, 333, 337, 338, 340, 341, 342
Vipassana ritual, 144
Virgil, 201
Virgin Mary, 232, 374
virtue ethics, 97, 102, 105
virtues, 101, 103, 105, 499
visions, 414
Visvanatha, 55, 69n.8
Vita Jesu Christi (Ludolf of Saxony), 374
Vocation of Man, The (Fichte), 382
volition, 4, 18, 99, 112, 120, 350, 360, 406–7
von Hildebrand, Dietrich, 117
von Hügel, F., 113

al-Wahid, Abd, 301
waka, 76, 83, 87
Wakefield, Margery, 134
Warfield, Benjamin B., 501
War Requiem (Britten), 213
Watts, Fraser, 426–27
Way to Holiness, The (Palmer), 297
Weber, Max, 127, 290–91, 292–93, 297, 484
weddings, 148, 151–52, 254, 262
weeping, 40, 103, 151–53, 192, 232, 301, 302
Weiss, Raymond L., 102
Wen (emperor), 230
Wesley, Charles, 209, 296
Wesley, John, 207, 296
Whitefield, George, 296
Whitehouse, Harvey, 5, 147–48, 149, 155, 156
Wiccan, 133
Wiesel, Elie, 300
Wile, Douglas, 171
will. *See* volition
William of Saint Thierry, 366, 367, 370, 372, 373, 374
Williams, Miriam, 134
Winn, Kenneth H., 335
Wolfson, Elliot, 103, 175
women
    Catholic, 157, 184
    feminist criticism and gendering of religious emotion, 182–84
    feminist reclamation of religious emotion, 193–95
    grief of, 86, 188–89
    in Hindu tradition, 251, 252
    Islamic, 183, 185, 229
    in Japanese literature, 86
    under Judaism, 183–84, 186, 187, 188, 196n.20
    Micronesian, 477–78
    sexualization of religious emotion, 185–87
    in Sidi community, 254
    subversion, power, and religious emotion, 187–90
Wordsworth, William, 479
wrong views, 22
Wujud, 302, 303
Wundt, William, 420

Wurzburger, Walter, 105
Wyschogrod, Michael, 191

yeser, 98, 101
yoga, 52, 60–62, 171, 177n.16, 248–49
Yogasutra (Patanjali), 61, 248

Zalman, Shneur, 301, 316
zangemono, 86, 89
Zeami, 85
Zen emotions, 492
Zhou Enlai, 231
Zohar, 103
Zoroastrianism, 336

CPSIA information can be obtained
at www.ICGtesting.com
Printed in the USA
BVHW011551091218
534878BV00011B/15/P